3 1526 05729869 4

THE MOST
TRUSTED NAME
IN TRAVEL

Frommer's

IRELAND

29th Edition

By Yvonne Gordon

D0912022

FrommerMedia LLC

Published by:
Frommer Media LLC

Copyright © 2022 by Frommer Media LLC. All rights reserved. No part of this publication may be reproduced, stored in a retrieval system, or transmitted in any form or by any means, electronic, mechanical, photocopying, recording, scanning or otherwise, except as permitted under Sections 107 or 108 of the 1976 United States Copyright Act, without the prior written permission of the Publisher. Requests to the Publisher for permission should be addressed to the support@ frommermedia.com.

Frommer's is a registered trademark of Arthur Frommer. Frommer Media LLC is not associated with any product or vendor mentioned in this book.

Frommer's Ireland, 29th Edition
ISBN 978-1-62887-509-6 (paper), 978-1-62887-510-2 (e-book)

Editorial Director: Pauline Frommer
Editor: Alexis Lipsitz Flippin
Production Editor: Heather Wilcox
Cartographer: Roberta Stockwell
Photo Editor: Meghan Lamb
Cover Design: Dave Riedy

Front cover photo: © mikemike10/shutterstock.com
Back cover photo: © stifos/shutterstock.com

For information on our other products or services, see www.frommers.com.

Frommer Media LLC also publishes its books in a variety of electronic formats. Some content that appears in print may not be available in electronic formats.

Manufactured in Malaysia

5 4 3 2 1

FROMMER'S STAR RATINGS SYSTEM

Every hotel, restaurant and attraction listed in this guide has been ranked for quality and value. Here's what the stars mean:

★ Recommended
★★ Highly Recommended
★★★ A must! Don't miss!

AN IMPORTANT NOTE

The world is a dynamic place. Hotels change ownership, restaurants hike their prices, museums alter their opening hours, and buses and trains change their routings. And all of this can occur in the several months after our authors have visited, inspected, and written about these hotels, restaurants, museums, and transportation services. Though we have made valiant efforts to keep all our information fresh and up-to-date, some few changes can inevitably occur in the periods before a revised edition of this guidebook is published. So please bear with us if a tiny number of the details in this book have changed. Please also note that we have no responsibility or liability for any inaccuracy or errors or omissions, or for inconvenience, loss, damage, or expenses suffered by anyone as a result of assertions in this guide.

CONTENTS

LIST OF MAPS

ABOUT THE AUTHOR

Yvonne Gordon is an award-winning travel writer who writes about Ireland for publications around the globe, including the *Washington Post, AFAR.com, BBC Travel,* the *Guardian, Cara* magazine, and *Hemispheres* magazine. Her awards include Irish Travel Writer of the Year. She is from Dublin and spends as much time as possible exploring Ireland north and south, hiking coastal and mountain trails, learning about traditions, hearing local stories, and finding atmospheric places to stay.

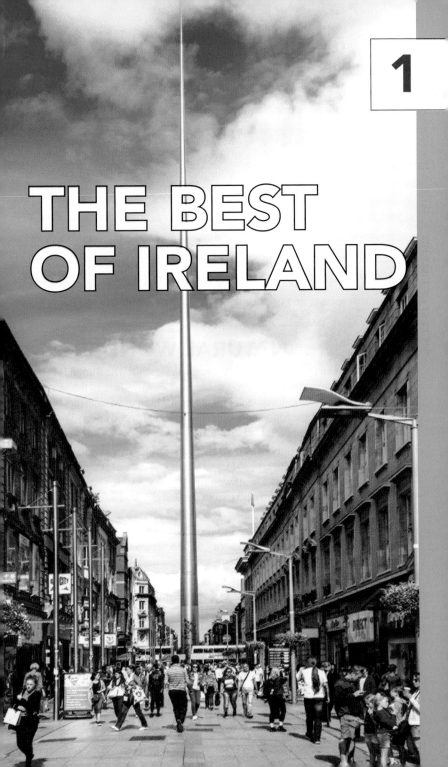

THE BEST OF IRELAND

reland is a captivating place to explore. Within a few miles, you can travel from plunging cliffs and flat pastureland to towering mountains and gloomy peat bogs. You can spend the night in an ancient castle or state-of-the-art spa hotel, dine on fine Irish cuisine or snack on crispy fish and chips served in a paper bag. Ireland is tiny, but its scenery is ever-changing, and the sheer number of sights, little villages, charming pubs, and adorable restaurants and shops can be overwhelming—you always feel that you might be missing something. So, it's nice to have someone to help you focus, and that's why we've put together this list of some of our favorite places and things to do in Ireland. We hope that while you're exploring this magical country, you'll discover a few favorites of your own.

THE best NATURAL WONDERS

o **The Burren** (County Clare): We can guarantee this: The Burren is one of the strangest landscapes you're likely to see anywhere in the world. Its stark limestone grassland is spread with a quilt of wildflowers from as far afield as the Alps, and its inhabitants include nearly every species of butterfly found in Ireland. See p. 348.

o **Mizen Head** (County Cork): While most travelers flock to the better-known Cliffs of Moher (p. 351), you won't find crowds at these majestic sea cliffs at Ireland's southwest tip. Watch the waves crash against the 210m-high (689-ft.) cliffs from the excellent visitor center. See p. 282.

o **Malin Head** (County Donegal): From one extreme to the other—literally! The Malin Head promontory, in the remotest part of Ireland's remotest country, looks out over a seemingly unending sea. Next stop: Iceland. See p. 485.

o **The Twelve Bens** (County Galway): Amid Connemara's central mountains, bogs, and lakes, the rugged Twelve Bens range crowns a spectacular landscape. The loftiest, Benbaun, in Connemara National Park, reaches a height of 729m (2,392 ft.). See p. 401.

o **Sliabh Liag** (County Donegal): As the Sliabh Liag (or Slieve League) coastline stretches along Donegal Bay, its pigmented bluffs rise to

Rock climbing at Malin Head.

600m-high (1,968-ft.) sea cliffs. You can walk along them, if you dare. See p. 473.

o **MacGillycuddy's Reeks** (County Kerry): Cresting grandly over the Iveragh Peninsula, MacGillycuddy's Reeks not only has the best name of any mountain range in Ireland, it also has the highest peak on the island, Carrantuohill (1,041m/3,414 ft.). See p. 299.

o **Giant's Causeway** (County Antrim): At the foot of a cliff by the sea, this mysterious mass of tightly packed, naturally occurring hexagonal basalt columns is nothing short of astonishing. Formed 60 million years ago, this volcanic wonder looks even better when negotiated (cautiously) on foot. See p. 527.

THE best MUSEUMS

o **Chester Beatty Library** (Dublin, County Dublin): Not just a library, this is one of Ireland's best museums, with a wealth of books, illuminated texts, and small art objects. Its collection of rare religious manuscripts is among the most unique in the world. See p. 93.

o **National Museum of Ireland: Archaeology** (Dublin, County Dublin): Ireland's National Museum is split into four separate sites, of which this is far and away the best. The collection dates back to the earliest settlers, but it's the relics from the Viking invasion and the early Christian period that dazzle the most. See p. 101.

o **Irish National Famine Museum** (Strokestown Park, County Roscommon): This reflective museum, part of a grand historic estate, does a

Titanic Belfast.

brilliant job of making the darkest period in Irish history seem immediate and real, including a collection of heartbreaking letters from destitute tenants to their callous landlords. See p. 424.

o **Titanic Belfast** (Belfast, County Antrim): Belfast is incredibly proud of having built the most famous ocean liner in history, despite its ultimate fate—though, as they're fond of saying, "She was alright when she left here." This gleaming, high-tech museum is the best of several *Titanic*-related attractions in Belfast. See p. 500.

o **Ulster Folk & Transport Museum** (Cultra, County Antrim): Ireland has several so-called living history museums, where stories of people and times past are told through reconstructions of everyday life. This one, just outside Belfast, is one of the liveliest and most engaging. See p. 507.

THE best CASTLES & HISTORIC HOUSES

o **King John's Castle** (Limerick): This impressive castle was built for King John around 1200. It's fun to explore the towers and courtyard, and a fantastic exhibition in the castle interior will take you right through Irish history. See p. 362.

o **Kilkenny Castle** (County Kilkenny): Although parts of this stout, towered castle date from the 13th century, the existing structure looks more like a 19th-century palace. Beautifully restored, it also has extensive gardens; the old stables now hold art galleries and shops. See p. 235.

o **Powerscourt Estate** (County Wicklow): The exquisite setting and gardens make it worthwhile to visit the magnificent Powerscourt estate in County Wicklow, with the formerly grand Palladian house as a backdrop. See p. 198.

o **Castletown House** (County Kildare): This grand whitewashed mansion was built in the early 18th century and soon became one of Ireland's most imitated buildings. The grounds house the most delightfully named barn in Ireland: the Wonderful Barn. See p. 187.

o **Bunratty Castle & Folk Park** (County Clare): This grand old castle has been well restored and filled with a curious assortment of medieval furnishings, offering a glimpse into the life of its past inhabitants. It's the first stop for many arrivals from Shannon, so expect crowds. See p. 350.

o **Carrickfergus Castle** (County Antrim): This huge Norman fortress on the bank of Belfast Lough is surprisingly intact and well-preserved, complete with an imposing tower house and a high wall punctuated by corner towers. See p. 506.

Kilkenny Castle.

o **Dunluce Castle** (County Antrim): Set atop a razor-sharp promontory jutting into the sea, these castle ruins are picturesque and evocative. Unlike many other castles, it wasn't demolished by human enemies, but it had to be abandoned after a large section collapsed and fell into the breakers below. See p. 526.

THE most beautiful PICTURE-POSTCARD TOWNS

o **Adare** (County Limerick): Literally a picture-postcard town, Adare is hardly a secret, but if you manage to visit when the roads aren't clogged with tour buses, you'll leave with a memory card full of photos. See p. 361.

o **Athlone** (County Westmeath): Sitting at the edge of the River Shannon, its streets curving around a fortresslike castle, Athlone is a charmer with a real spirit of fun. Houses are painted in bright hues, and streets are lined with funky boutiques, good restaurants, and lively pubs. See p. 415.

o **Dalkey** (County Dublin): The cutest of a string of upscale seaside towns unfurling south from Dublin, Dalkey is both a short drive and a million miles away from the busy city. With a castle, two tiny harbors and some fine restaurants, it tempts you into its affluent embrace. See p. 124.

o **Kinsale** (County Cork): Kinsale's narrow streets all lead to the sea, dropping steeply from the hills around the harbor. The walk from

Martello fort on Dalkey Island.

Kinsale through Scilly to Charles Fort and Frower Point is breathtaking. ***Bonus:*** It's a gourmet hotspot, full of good restaurants. See p. 268.

o **Kenmare** (County Kerry): It's easy to fall in love with Kenmare, with its stone cottages, colorful gardens, and flowers overflowing from window boxes. Home to several elegant hotels, it makes an enchanting base when exploring the Ring of Kerry. See p. 309.

o **Dingle (An Daingean)** (County Kerry): In this charming and vibrant town, stone buildings ramble up and down hills, and the small population is relaxed about visitors. You'll find lots of little diners and picturesque pubs, plus a lovely historic church. See p. 330.

o **Ardara** (County Donegal): On the southwest coast of Donegal, tiny Ardara looks as if it were carved out of a solid block of granite. Its hilly streets are lined with boutiques and charming arts shops, many selling clothes crafted from the famed Donegal wool. See p. 478.

THE best FOR LOVERS OF LITERATURE

o **MoLI, Museum of Literature Ireland** (Dublin, County Dublin): Newman House is filled with exciting exhibits about the world of Irish writing, including film, sound and books, with rare items from the James Joyce archive. See p. 117.

o **Seamus Heaney Homeplace** (Bellaghy, County Derry): Even as his literary fame took him around the world, the poetry of Seamus Heaney (1939–2013) remained rooted in the boglands, fields, and farms of the land here where he grew up. This literary center is dedicated to the Nobel Prize–winning poet. See p. 566.

o **Dublin Writers Museum** (Dublin, County Dublin): Filled with letters, manuscripts, personal possessions, and other eclectic ephemera, this great museum in Dublin is a mecca for lovers of Irish literature. Naturally, it has a good bookshop. See p. 98.

o **Davy Byrnes pub** (Dublin, County Dublin): After a stop at the **James Joyce Centre** (p. 116), make a pilgrimage to this venerable pub, which crops up in Joyce's masterpiece *Ulysses:* The hero, Leopold Bloom, famously orders a lunch of burgundy and a Gorgonzola sandwich. The pub is acutely aware of its heritage but knows better than to ruin the appeal by being too touristy. See p. 169.

o **County Sligo:** With its many connections to the beloved poet W. B. Yeats, this county is a pilgrimage destination for poetry fans. The landscape shaped the poet's writing, and many of its landmarks—Lough Gill, Glencar Lake, Ben Bulben Mountain, Maeve's tomb—appear in his verse. Be sure to visit Yeats's somber grave in Drumcliffe. See p. 449.

The Hill of Tara, ancient seat of Irish kings, offers amazing views on a clear day.

o **The Aran Islands:** Though playwright John Millington Synge was born in County Dublin, as a leading figure in the Irish literary revival of the late 19th century, he became passionately interested in these brooding islands off the Galway coast—the setting for his most famous play, *The Playboy of the Western World.* See p. 384.

THE best PREHISTORIC SITES

o **Newgrange** (County Meath): One of the archaeological wonders of Western Europe, Newgrange is the centerpiece of a megalithic cemetery dating back 5,000 years. Its massive mound and passage tomb are amazing feats of engineering. Still, the question remains: What was it all for? See p. 177.

o **Hill of Tara** (County Meath): Of ritual significance from the Stone Age to the early Christian period, Tara has seen it all and kept it a secret. This mostly unexcavated site was the traditional center and seat of Ireland's high kings; it's a place to be walked slowly. Although the hill is only 154m (512 ft.) above sea level, on a clear day, you can see each of Ireland's four Celtic provinces from here. See p. 179.

o **Knowth** (County Meath): Another impressive passage tomb, Knowth's awesome presence is matched only by its inscrutability. Hundreds of prehistoric carvings were discovered here when the site was first excavated in the 1960s, and yet nobody seems to quite understand it to this day. See p. 178.

o **Dún Aengus** (Aran Islands, County Galway): The eminent archaeologist George Petrie called Dún Aengus "the most magnificent barbaric monument in Europe." No one knows who built this massive stone fort or what year it was constructed. Facing the sea, where its three stone rings meet steep 90m (295-ft.) cliffs, Dún Aengus still stands guard today over the southern coast of Inishmore, the largest of the Aran Islands. See p. 384.

- **Carrowmore & Carrowkeel** (County Sligo): These two megalithic cities of the dead (Europe's largest) may have once contained more than 200 passage tombs. The two together—one in the valley and the other atop a nearby mountain—convey an unequaled sense of the ancient peoples' reverence for the departed. Carrowmore is well presented and interpreted, while Carrowkeel quietly awaits those who seek it out. See pp. 453–454.

- **Corlea Trackway** (County Longford): The amazing thing about this simple wooden trackway in a remote bog is just how unbelievably old it is—people were walking its well-preserved planks well over 2,000 years ago. See p. 420.

THE best EARLY CHRISTIAN RUINS

- **Glendalough** (County Wicklow): Nestled in "the glen of the two lakes," this remote monastic settlement was founded by St. Kevin in the 6th century. Today its atmospheric ruins preside over an endlessly scenic setting with lakes and forests surrounding it. It's quite simply one of the loveliest spots in Ireland. See p. 196.

- **Jerpoint Abbey** (County Kilkenny): Jerpoint is the finest of many Cistercian abbeys whose ruins dot the Irish landscape. Somehow, hundreds of years of rain and wind have failed to completely wipe away its medieval carvings, leaving us a rare chance to glimpse how magnificent these abbeys once were. Don't miss the splendid richly carved cloister. See p. 239.

- **Skellig Michael** (County Kerry): Early Irish monks built this hermitage dedicated to the archangel Michael on a remote, rocky crag rising sharply 214m (702 ft.) out of the Atlantic, some 13km (8 miles) offshore of the Iveragh Peninsula. Both the journey to Skellig across choppy seas and the arduous climb to its summit are challenging—and equally unforgettable. See p. 320.

- **The Rock of Cashel** (County Tipperary): In name and appearance, "the Rock" suggests a citadel, a place designed more for power than prayer. In fact, Cashel (or *Caiseal*) means "fortress." The rock is a huge outcropping—or an *up*cropping—of limestone topped with beautiful ruins, including what was once Ireland's finest Romanesque chapel. The seat of clerics and kings, it was a power center to rival the Hill of Tara; now the two sites vie for the attention of tourists. See p. 371.

o **Clonmacnoise** (County Offaly): The old Irish high kings came to this place to find spiritual solace, and it's still a profound and thought-provoking place to visit. Don't leave without checking out the monumental ancient slabs, inscribed with personal messages in Celtic script. See p. 420.

o **Inishmurray** (County Sligo): This uninhabited island off the Sligo coast holds another striking monastic ruin, this one surrounded by what appears to be the walls of an even more ancient stone fort. Vikings sought out this remote outpost of peace-seeking monks and destroyed it in A.D. 807. Today its circular walls and the surrounding sea create a stunning view, well worth the effort required to reach it. See p. 456.

THE best FAMILY ACTIVITIES

o **Dublin Zoo in Phoenix Park** (Dublin, County Dublin): Kids love this sympathetically designed zoo featuring wild creatures, animal-petting corners, and a train ride. The surrounding park has room to run, picnic, and explore. See p. 121.

o **Irish National Heritage Park** (Ferrycarrig, County Wexford): Millennia of history are made painlessly educational for children and adults at this engaging "living history" museum. It's a fascinating, informative way to while away a couple of hours or more. See p. 223.

o **Fota Island & Wildlife Park** (Carrigtwohill, County Cork): In this wildlife park, rare and endangered animals roam freely. You'll see everything from giraffes and zebras to kangaroos, flamingos, penguins, and monkeys wandering the grassland. Add in a tour train, picnic tables, a playground, and a gift shop, and you have the makings of a wonderful family outing. See p. 264.

o **Muckross House & Gardens** (Killarney, County Kerry): Today the gateway to Killarney National Park, this impressive mansion has been preserved in all its Victorian splendor. Nearby, at Muckross Traditional Farms, workers engage

Galway Atlantaquaria.

in traditional farm activities while dressed in authentic period clothing. See p. 297.

o **Dingle Boat Tours** (Dingle, County Kerry): While Fungie the dolphin is no longer in the bay, you might still see wild dolphins, whales, seals and lots of other wildlife (depending on the season) on a sea safari or harbor cruise from Dingle. The kid-friendly **Dingle Oceanworld Aquarium** is right by the harbor as well. See p. 330.

o **Bunratty Castle & Folk Park** (Bunratty, County Clare): Kids love Bunratty, which looks every bit as satisfyingly medieval as an old castle should. The grounds have been turned over to a replica 19th-century village, complete with actors playing Victorian residents going about their daily lives. It's great fun to wander through. See p. 350.

o **Galway Atlantaquaria** (Galway, County Galway): Formally known as the National Aquarium of Ireland, this is the place your kids will remember long after they've forgotten the hundredth dolmen you passed by the roadside. Highlights include a shark tank and touch pools full of curious rays. See p. 397.

THE best DRIVING TOURS

o **The Wild Atlantic Way** (County Cork to County Donegal): Stretching 2,500km (1,553 miles) along Ireland's West Coast, between Kinsale in County Cork and Inishowen in Donegal, this drive takes in some of Ireland's wildest and most beautiful coastal scenery. While it's better to do a small section of the drive on one trip (don't even attempt the entire drive in one visit), you will see lots of Wild Atlantic Way road signs and various "discovery points" along the way. See p. 477.

o **The Ring of Kerry** (County Kerry): It's by far the most well-traveled of Ireland's great routes, but there's no denying the Ring of Kerry's appeal—a seductive combination of stunning countryside, charming villages, and inspiring historical sites. The road gets quite busy in summer, but come in the spring or autumn and it's a much more peaceful experience. See p. 292.

o **Slea Head Drive** (County Kerry): This drive, starting from Dingle Town and heading down the Ventry road, follows the sparkling sea past a series of ancient sites such as the Dunbeg Fort and the beehive-shaped Gallarus Oratory. At Dunquin, you can embark on boats to the mysterious abandoned Blasket Islands. See p. 336.

o **Horn Head** (County Donegal): Drive pretty much anywhere in County Donegal, and before long you'll be in beautiful, wild, unspoiled countryside—that's one reason why we never mind getting lost here. One of the best drives is around Horn Head, near Dunfanaghy, where quartzite sea cliffs glisten like glass when the sun hits them just right. See p. 479.

○ **Inishowen Peninsula** (County Donegal): This far-flung promontory in Ireland's northern end stretches out from Lough Foyle to the east and Lough Swilly to the west toward Malin Head, its farthest point. Driving the perimeter, you'll pass ancient sites, pretty villages, and fine sandy beaches in fierce rocky coves. If you are looking to get lost, this is a great place to do it. See p. 483.

○ **Causeway Coastal Route** (County Antrim): Sweeping views of midnight-blue sea against gray, unforgiving cliffs and deep-green hillsides make this 97km-long (60-mile) coastal route unforgettable. Start in gorgeous Glenarm with its castle walls and barbican gate, then head north along the coast past Bushmills and the Giant's Causeway to Portrush. Best of all, you often have the road quite to yourself. See p. 524.

○ **The Sky Road** (County Galway): Perhaps the least-known on this list, but certainly the best-named, the Sky Road is the loop around the Kingstown Peninsula on the tip of Connemara. Just a glimpse of those soul-stirring Atlantic Ocean vistas is enough to tell you why. See p. 404.

THE best HOTELS

○ **Ashford Castle** (Cong, County Mayo): Live like royalty with a stay at this fairy-tale castle in County Mayo. The great and the good have been coming here for decades to see what the fuss is about. The fuss, it turns out, is justified. See p. 443.

○ **Adare Manor** (Adare, County Limerick): A haven for the sporty and non-sporty alike, Adare Manor has vast grounds, including a championship golf course, if that's your thing. If not, well, you only have the run of a beautiful Victorian Gothic manor and three outstanding restaurants as compensation. Bummer! See p. 363.

○ **The Shelbourne** (Dublin, County Dublin): Certainly one of the best hotels in Ireland's capital city, the Shelbourne also holds a unique place in Irish history as the site where Michael Collins led the drafting of the country's first Constitution. See p. 128.

○ **The Westbury** (Dublin, County Dublin): What the Shelbourne is to old Dublin, so this place is to new: a top-class hotel for fashionistas and sophisticates to rest their well-heeled feet. See p. 129.

○ **Mount Juliet** (County Kilkenny): Both the historic Manor House here and nearby Hunter's Yard (set in a converted stable yard) make relaxing and luxurious hideaways. There are plenty of grounds to roam, and the Manor House has a Michelin-starred restaurant to boot. See p. 241.

○ **Inchydoney Lodge & Spa** (Clonakilty, County Cork): Almost leaping distance from the sparkling sea, this wonderfully relaxing hotel has one of the best spas in the west. Unusually for a top-tier place, it's also great for kids. See p. 284.

- **Cliff House Hotel** (Ardmore, County Waterford): This luxury boutique hotel is known as much for its amazing views as for the awards with which it has been bestowed—including a Michelin star for its restaurant. See p. 218.

- **Monart Spa** (Enniscorthy, County Wexford): A sumptuous countryside retreat, this pampering paradise is consistently rated among the top spas in Ireland. It's a serene, adults-only zone in a lovely setting. See p. 231.

- **Aghadoe Heights** (Killarney, County Kerry): Another of Ireland's top spas, this one overlooks the Lakes of Killarney from a high vantage point just north of the town. See p. 300.

- **Ard na Sidhe Country House** (Killorglin, County Kerry): When a house is named for an Irish phrase meaning "king of the fairies," you kind of expect something magical—and that's exactly what you'll find. See p. 322.

- **The Europe** (Killarney, County Kerry): Lake views, sumptuous beds, a wonderful spa . . . what's not to like? Well, very little apparently: The Europe is widely seen as one of the best hotels in Ireland. See p. 302.

- **Park Hotel Kenmare** (County Kerry): An Irish newspaper described this place as "as close as you'll get to Downton Abbey without going on set." The Park Hotel also has one of the very best spas in Ireland. See p. 311.

- **The Bervie** (Keel, County Mayo): Overlooking the Atlantic Ocean on an island off the Mayo coast, the Bervie is a haven of magnificent views and gourmet food. See p. 445.

Lakeside views at the Europe Hotel in Killarney.

o **The Ice House** (Ballina, County Mayo): Tranquility, peace, and relaxation await at this charming boutique hotel overlooking the River Moy. Relax in the spa, fall in love with the restaurant, and contemplate whether you should come back every year. See p. 445.

o **Temple House** (Ballymote, County Sligo): Proving that not all the top accolades go to five-star luxury hotels, Temple House is a historic countryside B&B that seems in a world of its own. This might just be our favorite place to stay in all of Ireland. See p. 458.

Welcoming staff at the gracious Park Hotel Kenmare.

o **Titanic Hotel** (Belfast, County Antrim): Located in what was once the offices of the Harland & Wolff shipping company, this wonderful hotel just outside Belfast's historic quarter melds Victorian and modern with spectacular aplomb. Fantastic restaurant, too. See p. 510.

o **Galgorm Spa & Golf Resort** (Ballymena, County Antrim): One of the best hotels in the north, this riverside resort delivers the wow factor from the moment you pull up outside. See p. 530.

o **Newforge House** (Magheralin, County Armagh): A supremely relaxing manor house in the middle of the Armagh countryside, Newforge House has sensational food to boot. Come, stay, adore. See p. 550.

o **Castle Leslie** (Glaslough, County Monaghan): This luxurious northern retreat has been a jet-set hideaway for decades. Care to join the fan club? See p. 571.

o **Grand Central** (Belfast, County Antrim): The tallest hotel in Belfast is a relative newcomer to the city, but boy, has it made its mark. Effortlessly chic with exceptional service, this one, we hope, is here to stay. See p. 508.

THE best RESTAURANTS

o **Aimsir** (County Kildare): The food here showcases the best from Ireland's land and sea in creative and sometimes surprising ways. It's one of Ireland's best restaurants (it has two Michelin stars), so book well in advance. See p. 193.

- **Chapter One** (Dublin, County Dublin): In the vaulted basement of the Dublin Writers Museum, this is one of Dublin's very best restaurants. It's quite a splurge, but come at lunchtime and you can enjoy the same wonderful food at almost half the price. See p. 146.

- **The Oak Room** (Adare, County Limerick): This fine-dining restaurant at the opulent Adare Manor hotel is a real treat. It's formal and old-school, but in these sorts of surroundings we'd expect nothing less. See p. 367.

- **The Greenhouse** (Dublin, County Dublin): The food at this two-Michelin-starred restaurant resembles miniature works of art. But is it too good to eat? Absolutely not. See p. 149.

- **Everett's** (Waterford City, County Waterford): Located in a 15th-century house, this wonderful modern Irish restaurant burst onto the scene in 2019 and has been wowing the critics ever since. See p. 220.

- **Richmond House** (Cappoquin, County Waterford): A converted 18th-century mansion, Richmond House serves exquisite seasonal meals, with ingredients sourced from its own grounds. See p. 221.

- **The Black Pig** (Kinsale, County Cork): Think every place on this list is fancy fine dining? This simple wine bar with heaps of atmosphere is one of our favorite spots in Ireland's "foodie capital," Kinsale. See p. 274.

- **Ichigo Ichie** (Cork, County Cork): Probably one of the best Japanese restaurants in Europe, Ichigo Ichie is a master class in simple elegance. You'll be lucky to snag one of the 25 seats, but if you do, prepare to be wowed. See p. 258.

- **Fishy Fishy Café** (Kinsale, County Cork): The seafood is so local that the menu tells you who caught it—and we're talking dish by dish, name by name. See p. 274.

- **Restaurant Chestnut** (Ballydehob, County Cork): A tiny pub in a darling village is the setting for one of the most respected restaurants in Ireland. Playful, experimental, unpredictable. See p. 286.

- **The Lake Room** (Killarney, County Kerry): Special-occasion views to go with the special-occasion food: The in-house restaurant at the fabulous Aghadoe Heights hotel manages to combine flawless cooking with some of the warmest service we've encountered. See p. 305.

Dessert at Aniar in Galway.

Inis Meáin restaurant.

o **Wild Honey Inn** (Lisdoonvarna, County Clare): Another unique dining experience in the surroundings of a historic inn, the Wild Honey brings in diners from all over the world. See p. 358.

o **Aniar** (Galway, County Galway): Galway City's most sought-after table has a tiny but perfectly judged menu of innovative modern Irish cuisine—enough to earn a Michelin star, a rarity in Ireland. See p. 388.

o **Gallagher's Boxty House** (Dublin, County Dublin): A local man keen on preserving the fading culinary traditions of his childhood started this captivating Temple Bar restaurant. See p. 138.

o **Inis Meáin** (Inis Meáin, County Galway): Now this is what we call a destination restaurant! Pretty much the main reason for visiting the rather overlooked Aran island for which it is named, it's a place to stay and savor for days, not just a meal. See p. 386.

o **Eala Bhan** (Sligo, County Sligo): With the sort of cooking more readily associated with big cities, Eala Bhan has been named the best restaurant in Ireland at the Irish Restaurant Awards . . . five times in under 10 years. See p. 461.

o **Wilde's at the Lodge at Ashford** (Cong, County Mayo): On the grounds of Ashford Castle, this joyous restaurant is run by a real star of the Irish culinary scene. The dining room has an amazing view of Lough Corrib. See p. 448.

o **The Cook & Gardener** (Rathmullan, County Donegal): Ingredients don't get much fresher, picked straight from the garden. The results are simply sensational. See p. 482.

o **Ox** (Belfast, County Antrim): Cool and contemporary, this Michelin-starred restaurant is one of Belfast's most sought-after dining hotspots. See p. 514.

- **Harry's Shack** (Portstewart, County Derry): Not an actual shack, but a casual, rustic, inexpensive dining room on the beach, serving legendary seafood. See p. 532.

IRELAND'S best SHOPPING

- **Brown Thomas** (Grafton St., Dublin): Among the most quintessential of Dublin's grand old department stores, Brown Thomas has the works, from top-hatted doormen to the latest in designer fashions. See p. 157.

- **Claddagh Records** (Temple Bar, Dublin): One of the best music stores in a country that takes its music very seriously, Claddagh Records is a must for lovers of traditional Irish music. In addition to instruments and sheet music, it sells some great (and tuneful) souvenirs. See p. 155.

- **Avoca** (Moll's Gap, County Kerry): One of the most Irish of Irish brands, Avoca sells beautiful blankets, clothes, household items, food and gifts. The flagship store is in Kilmacanogue, County Wicklow, but our favorite is the little branch clinging to a bend in the road near the Ring of Kerry. See p. 155.

- **Lorge Chocolatier** (Kenmare, County Kerry): French chocolatier Benoit Lorge makes exquisite creations from his workshop just south of Kenmare. The wrapped gift boxes are little works of art in themselves. See p. 315.

- **Belleek China** (Belleek, County Fermanagh): The world-famous brand of fine china has been furnishing the tables of the upper crust since 1864. The visitor center, near Donegal, has a magnificent collection for sale—and will ship internationally if you're worried about getting your delicate selection home in one piece. See p. 569.

- **Steensons** (County Antrim): This long-established jewelry design firm has recently gained a whole new kind of fame, thanks to its specially commissioned work for *Game of Thrones*. The pieces are as elegant as they are collectible. See p. 518.

> ## What's the Score?
>
> In this book, we award listings up to three stars based on the overall experience of a place. Just because a hotel has all the best facilities, or a restaurant is super-trendy, doesn't necessarily mean it'll score a full house from us. But please remember, our view is subjective! Your own favorites will be based on *your* experience of Ireland, and that may be different from anyone else's. That's one of the joys of travel. So, if you have a favorite Ireland discovery that we've left out, please write and tell us. We can't wait to discover it too. *Also:* We thoroughly update this guide every year, checking on any closures, but it's always a good idea to call ahead to confirm that an establishment is open before you go.

Ireland

SCOTLAND
ATLANTIC OCEAN
North Channel
To Troon
Stranraer
To Douglas, Heysham, Liverpool
To Heysham, Douglas
Malin Head
Ballygorman
Culdaff Bay
Rathlin I.
Giant's Causeway
Fair Head
Ballyliffin
Tory I.
Rosguill
Tory Sound
Inishowen
Fanad
Portrush
Portstewart
Bushmills
Ballycastle
Coleraine
Cushendun
Red Bay
Cushendall
Bloody Foreland
Gola I.
Owey I.
Donegal
Arranmore I.
Ballintra
Milford
Buncrana
Lough Foyle
Limavady
Ballymoney
Antrim Mts.
Carnlough
Glenveagh National Park
Derryveagh Mts.
Letterkenny
Derry (Londonderry)
Bann
DONEGAL
Lifford
Strabane
Sion Mills
Newtownstewart
Sperrin Mts.
Maghera
Magherafelt
Randalstown
Ballymena
Larne
Island Magee
Belfast Lough
Carrickfergus
Antrim
Belfast Int'l
Newtownabbey
Bangor
City
Newtownards
Gweebarra Bay
Loughros More Bay
Glenties
Finn
Blue Stack Mts.
Glencolumbkille
Mountcharles
Donegal
Derg
Ballintra
Inver Bay
Donegal Bay
Omagh
Cookstown
NORTHERN IRELAND
Lough Neagh
BELFAST
Lisburn
Comber
Ards Peninsula
Strangford Lough
Dromore
Sixmilecross
Ballygawley
Craigavon
Portadown
Armagh
Banbridge
Portaferry
Strangford
Downpatrick
Ardglass
Inishmurray
Cliffoney
Lough Melvin
Lower Lough Erne
ULSTER
Enniskillen
Ennis Head
Mullet Peninsula
Belmullet
Killala Bay
Sligo Bay
Ballycastle
Killala
Sligo
L. Macnean
Dromahair
L. Gill
Upper Lough Erne
Monaghan
Newry
Mourne Mts.
Dundrum Bay
Newcastle
Annalong
Bangor Erris
Ballina
Slieve Gamph (Ox Mts.)
SLIGO
Lough Allen
Newtownbutler
MONAGHAN
Belturbet
Ballybay
Warrenpoint
Carlingford
Ballycroy National Park
Blacksod Bay
Ballymote
Lough Arrow
Iron Mts.
Lough Oughter
Croaghaun
Achill Head
Achill Island
Nephin Beg Ra.
Lough Conn
Foxford
Curlew Mts.
Lough Key
LEITRIM
Cavan
Inniskeen
Dundalk
Lough Gara
Charlestown
Carrick-on-Shannon
Drumsna
CAVAN
Louth
Dundalk Bay
Newport
MAYO
Arva
Clew Bay
Castlebar
Frenchpark
Lough Sheelin
Virginia
LOUTH
Dunany Point
Clare I.
Knock
ROSCOMMON
Lough Gowna
LONGFORD
L. Ramor
Kells (Ceanannus Mór)
Clogherhead
Westport
Louisburgh
Partry Mts.
Castlerea
Longford
Drogheda
Inishturk
Sheffrey Hills
CONNACHT
Shannon
Edgeworthstown
Boyne
Newgrange
Lough Mask
Ballinrobe
Lough Derravaragh
Navan
Inishbofin
Roscommon
MEATH
Skerries
L. Owel
Inishark
Maamturk Mts.
Ballymahon
Trim
Rush
Connemara National Park
Cong
Mullingar
Lambay I.
Tuam
Ballygar
Lough Ree
Royal Canal
Connemara
Lough Corrib
Mountbellew
WESTMEATH
Dublin Int'l
Malahide

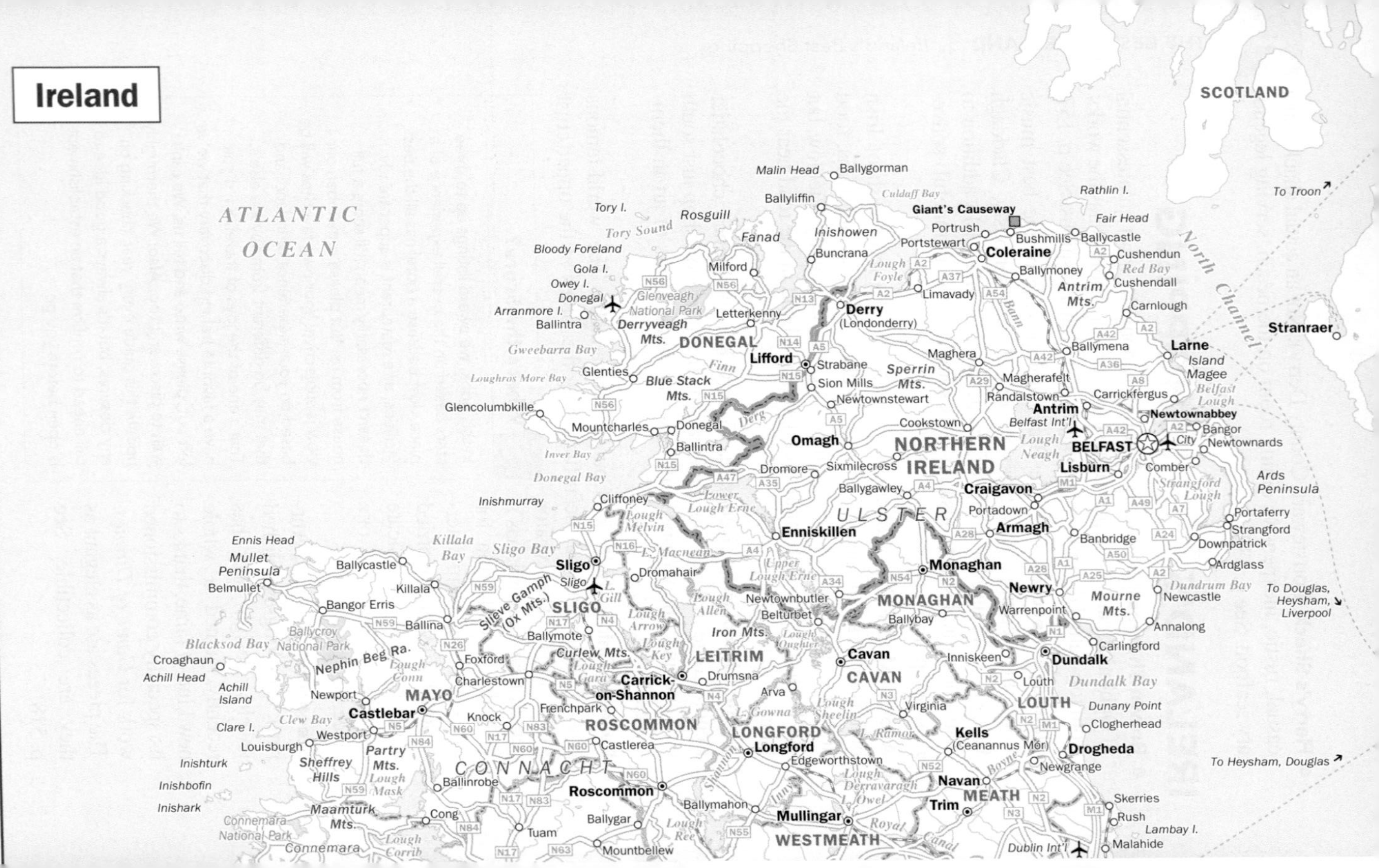

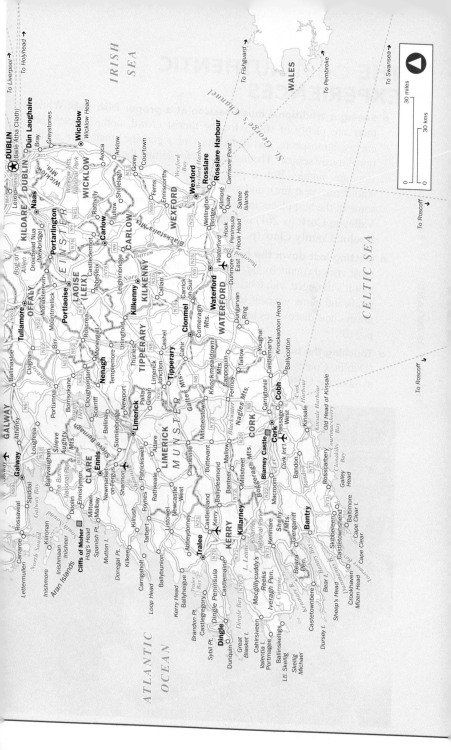

THE best AUTHENTIC EXPERIENCES

- **Seeing a traditional music session at a proper Irish pub:** While there are plenty of shows for the tourist crowd, nothing beats the energy, atmosphere, and authenticity of a genuine small-town traditional music session. The instructions for getting the most out of a session are simple: Buy a pint, grab a seat (preferably one near a smoldering peat fire), and wait for the action to begin. We've listed some of the best places in this book, including pubs such as the **Long Valley** in **Cork** (p. 261) or **Gus O'Connor's** and **McGann's** in little **Doolin, County Clare** (p. 353).

- **Getting lost down the back roads of County Kerry:** It's Ireland's most visited county by far, and if you stick to the beaten path, in summer it's thronged with tourists. Instead, veer off onto the winding back roads and allow yourself to get gloriously, hopelessly lost. There are always new discoveries to be made along its breathtaking byways. See p. 310.

- **Touching the bullet holes in the walls of the General Post Office** (Dublin, County Dublin): It's hard to overstate what a potent national symbol the G.P.O. is. Yes, it's still a working post office, but Patrick

Enjoying a music session in a Galway pub.

Pearse read his independence proclamation from its front steps in 1916 (the original document is displayed inside), and in 1922, it was the scene of fierce civil war fighting. Bullet scars still pock the facade. Touch them and you touch history. See p. 112.

o **Walking down the long stone passage at Newgrange** (County Meath): Sacred to the ancients, this passage tomb is more than 5,000 years old—that's older than the Egyptian pyramids or Stonehenge. Wander down the atmospheric central tunnel and try to visualize how many generations have passed since it was built—it's a mind-blowing exercise. See p. 177.

o **Browsing the Old English Market in Cork** (County Cork): Cork is a county made for foodies. In addition to Kinsale (see p. 268), a coastal village that's become a hub for top restaurants, the eponymous main city is home to one of the country's finest (and oldest) food markets. A walk through here is a feast for the senses. See p. 250.

o **Driving through the Burren** (County Clare): Ireland is full of memorable landscapes, but this is the most unique. For miles, this exposed coastal countryside has a haunting, alien feel, although it's strikingly beautiful, too. Try to be here as the sun goes down, when the craggy limestone planes turn an evening shade of red. See p. 348.

o **Hiking the path down to the Giant's Causeway** (County Antrim): Taking the half-mile walk down to this extraordinary natural wonder—37,000 columns of basalt sitting at the base of cliffs along the Antrim Coast—is like passing through a fantasy landscape. Geologists claim these rocks were formed millions of years ago by cooling volcanoes. But don't you prefer to believe they were really made by giants, as the ancients imagined? See p. 527.

SUGGESTED
IRELAND
ITINERARIES

reland is such a small island that you can cover a lot of ground in a week and feel quite at home within two. But even with the best of intentions and all the energy in the world, you'll never see it all on a short visit. So pace yourself and choose your wish list early.

The suggested itineraries in this chapter will help you get the most out of this extraordinary and varied country—no matter how long you have to see it. If you've only got a week to spend here, the southern regions probably have more to offer. They're generally easier to get around, and the major sights are closer together. If you're traveling with kids, Dublin and County Kerry have particularly rich troves of kid-friendly attractions. However, those in search of the road less traveled will be drawn northward, especially to places such as Mayo, Sligo, and the beautiful Antrim Coast.

All of these tours (except one) assume that you have a week to see the country. Where there's potential for a longer trip, we've given some alternatives for an extended version. Pick and choose the parts that appeal to you, add in your own favorite shopping or scenic drives, and turn it all into a custom-made holiday for yourself.

THE REGIONS IN BRIEF

The island of Ireland is divided into two political units: the **Republic of Ireland,** which makes up the vast majority of the country, and **Northern Ireland,** which along with England, Scotland, and Wales is part of the United Kingdom. Of Ireland's 32 counties, all but 6 are in the Republic.

The island is also divided into four provinces: Ulster is north, Munster is south, Leinster is east, and Connacht is west. Each region is divided into counties:

In Ulster (to the north)   Cavan, Donegal, and Monaghan in the Republic; Antrim, Armagh, Derry, Down, Fermanagh, and Tyrone in Northern Ireland.

In Munster (to the south)   Clare, Cork, Kerry, Limerick, Tipperary, and Waterford.

In Leinster (to the east)   Dublin, Carlow, Kildare, Kilkenny, Laois, Longford, Louth, Meath, Offaly, Westmeath, Wexford, and Wicklow.

In Connacht (to the west)   Sligo, Mayo, Galway, Roscommon, and Leitrim.

DUBLIN & ENVIRONS With 40% of the Republic's population living within 97km (60 miles) of Dublin, the capital is the center of the profound changes that have transformed Ireland into a prosperous European country. Within an hour's drive of Dublin are Dalkey, Dún Laoghaire, Howth, and many more engaging coastal towns, as well as the rural beauty of the Wicklow Mountains and the neolithic ruins in County Meath.

THE SOUTHEAST The southeast offers sandy beaches, **Wexford**'s lush and mountainous countryside, **Waterford** city and its famous Crystal Factory, Kilkenny's and Cahir's ancient castles, and the Irish National Heritage Park at Ferrycarrig.

CORK & ENVIRONS **Cork,** Ireland's second-largest city, is a buzzy university town and a congenial gateway to the south and west of the island. Within arm's reach are Blarney Castle (and its famous stone), the culinary and scenic delights of Kinsale, the historic emigration port of Cobh, and the dazzling landscape of West Cork.

THE SOUTHWEST The once-remote splendor of **County Kerry** has long ceased to be a secret, at least during the high season. The Ring of Kerry (less glamorously known as roads N70 and N71) encircling the Iveragh Peninsula is one of Ireland's most visited attractions. That's both a recommendation and a warning. While Killarney National Park provides a stunning haven from buses, the town of Killarney is filled with souvenir shops and tour groups. Marginally less visited highlights include the rugged Dingle Peninsula and two sets of islands with rich histories: the Skelligs and the Blaskets.

Surfing at Garretstown Beach, near Kinsale, County Cork.

THE WEST   The west of Ireland offers a first taste of Ireland's wild beauty and striking diversity, especially handy for those who fly into Shannon Airport. **County Clare**'s natural offerings—particularly the unique landscapes of the Burren—are unforgettable, and the county also has an array of impressive castles: Knappogue, Bunratty, and (just over the county line in Galway) Dunguaire.

GALWAY & ENVIRONS   **Galway City** is busy, colorful, and funky—a youthful port and university town and the self-proclaimed arts capital of Ireland with lots of theater, music, and dance. County Galway is the gateway to **Connemara**'s moody, magical mountains and boglands. Offshore lie the atmospheric, mysterious Aran Islands.

THE MIDLANDS   The lush center of Ireland, bisected by the lazy River Shannon, is a land of pastures, rivers, lakes, woods, and gentle mountain slopes. It's a retreat, in high season, from the throngs of tourists who crowd the coasts. The Midlands also hold remarkable sites—Birr Castle and its splendid gardens, for example, and Clonmacnoise, the evocative ruins of a famous Irish monastic center.

MAYO AND SLIGO   Farther up the coast to the north, past Galway, **County Mayo** offers the sweet town of Westport on Clew Bay and Achill Island (accessible by car), with its beaches and stunning cliff views. **County Sligo** inspired the poetry of W. B. Yeats, and offers a dense collection of stone circles, passage tombs, and cairns at such sites as Carrowmore, Knocknarea, and Carrowkeel, plus surfing beaches.

THE NORTHWEST   In Ireland it's easy to become convinced that isolated austerity is beautiful. Nowhere is this more evident than in **County Donegal,** with its jagged, desolate coastline. (If you don't mind the cold, it offers some fine surfing.) Inland, Glenveagh National Park has as much wilderness as you could want.

NORTHERN IRELAND   Across the border, Northern Ireland's six counties boast such attractions as the stunning **Causeway Coast,** the extraordinary basalt columns of the Giant's Causeway, and the Glens of Antrim. The old city walls of **Derry,** the past glory of Carrickfergus Castle, and **Belfast**'s elaborate political murals and thriving food scene make a trip across the border worthwhile.

How to See Ireland

Let's get one thing straight: You don't *have* to rent a car to see Ireland. Millions of people don't. Ireland has a decent public transportation network, and you're spoiled for choice when it comes to tour bus excursions. And that's a fine way to do it. This is *your* trip, after all.

However, if your ideal Ireland involves wandering through the countryside, visiting small villages, climbing castle walls, hailing history from a ruined abbey, or finding yourself alone on a rocky beach—you cannot do those things independently without a car.

Short of hiring private guides, or taking some very expensive taxi rides, there just aren't many other options. Out of the main towns, public transportation exists, but it's slow and limiting. Most major sites in the countryside are doable on organized bus tours, but there's only so far that can take you. Fortunately, every major town has car-rental agencies, if you decide to explore by car.

Just remember to drive on the *left*.

The next step is deciding **where to start.** That decision can be made for you by where your flight arrives. If you're flying into **Shannon Airport** or **Cork Airport,** then it makes geographic sense to start out on the west coast. If you're flying into **Dublin,** you might as well explore that city first, then either head up to the North and the ruggedly beautiful Antrim Coast, or south down to the Wicklow Mountains, Kilkenny, Wexford, and Waterford.

Still, if you fly into Dublin but your heart is in Galway, no worries. You can traverse the width of the country in a couple of hours, thanks to motorways out of Dublin. Just bear in mind that rural roads are not well lit or well signposted, so driving at night should be avoided. Being lost in unfamiliar territory (where it can be many miles between villages) is no fun at all.

THE BEST OF IRELAND IN 1 WEEK

There's something terribly romantic about flying into Dublin. The compact, laidback city awaits a few miles down the road, packed with old-fashioned pubs, modern restaurants, and absorbing sights all laid out for walking. If you've never been here, a couple of days in Dublin make for a quick primer on Ireland. It's just enough time to do some shopping on **Grafton Street,** head up O'Connell Street to the **General Post Office,** and discover the Georgian beauty of **St. Stephen's Green** and **Merrion Square.** You can give the surface of the city a good brush in a couple of days, and then head south to **Kilkenny** and **Wicklow,** on to **Waterford, Cork,** and **Kerry,** and up to **Clare** for a quick glance before the clock runs out. You'll only be hitting the high points but, as high points go, they're hard to beat.

DAYS 1 & 2: ARRIVE IN DUBLIN

If it happens that you're arriving from North America, you start with an advantage: Most flights arrive early in the morning, which effectively gives you an extra day's sightseeing. Check into your hotel (or drop off your bags if check-in is not until the afternoon), say yes to any tea and scones offered, take a minute to relax, get a map from your concierge, and then head out on foot.

The Best of Ireland Itineraries

ATLANTIC OCEAN

Malin Head

Rathmullan • • Bucrana
• Derry

DONEGAL

NORTHERN IRELAND (U.K.)

North Channel

Glencolumbkille •

Donegal Bay

Ballyshannon •

Sligo Town •

SLIGO

Achill Island

M A Y O

Westport •

Clifden

G A L W A Y

Galway City

Galway Bay

THE BURREN

Cliffs of Moher

CLARE

Bunratty •

Mouth of the Shannon

Limerick •

REPUBLIC OF IRELAND

Irish Sea

Dublin

WICKLOW

Wicklow

Kilkenny •

WATERFORD

Waterford •

K E R R Y

Killarney •

KILLARNEY NATIONAL PARK

C O R K

Cork •

CELTIC SEA

0   50 mi
0   50 km

WEEK 1
- **1-2** Dublin
- **3** Wicklow & Kilkenny
- **4** Waterford & Cork
- **5-6** Ring of Kerry
- **7** Cliffs of Moher/ The Burren

WEEK 2
- **8** The Burren
- **9-10** County Galway
- **11** County Mayo
- **12** County Sligo
- **13** County Donegal
- **14** Dublin

Stay south of the River Liffey and head down Dame Street to **Dublin Castle** (p. 111), home of the magical **Chester Beatty Library** (p. 93) with its vast collection of gorgeous illuminated manuscripts. Later, take in **St. Patrick's Cathedral** (p. 103) and the vibrant green quadrangles of **Trinity College** (p. 105) before heading over to Merrion Square, with its handsome granite architecture and two of the main sites of Ireland's **National Museum** (a third is on the west side of the city). The **Archaeology** museum has an extraordinary hoard of ancient gold, while the **Natural History** building contains a fascinating zoological collection from the past. It's a short stroll from here up to **St. Stephen's Green.** Rest your weary toes and soak up the floral view here, before strolling down **Grafton Street** for some shopping before collapsing in your hotel.

On **DAY 2,** have a hearty breakfast in your hotel before striking out for the trendy cultural hub of **Temple Bar.** Stroll north to the river, then take a right and walk along the noisy, vibrant waterfront to the landmark **Ha'penny Bridge.** Walk across and head east on **O'Connell Street,** where you pass its many statues to reach the bullet-ridden columns of the **General Post Office** (p. 112), site of the 1916 Easter Rising. After exploring its displays, head farther up O'Connell Street to the **Dublin Writers Museum** (p. 98), which bookish types love for its extensive display of memorabilia. Let someone else do the work in the evening, either on a walking tour—such as the **Irish Music Pub**

Strolling through Library Square at Trinity College in Dublin.

IS NORTHERN IRELAND safe to visit?

In short, **yes.** Do not be put off visiting this wonderful part of Ireland because of its troubled past. It's been at peace for nearly a quarter of a century. Belfast and Derry are safer for visitors than almost any comparable American city, and the Ulster countryside is idyllic and serene. So we really wouldn't worry.

That said, you do need to be aware of a few issues—particularly after Brexit. Be sensitive to the fact that there are still deep divisions here, and follow these basic rules:

- **Do not** discuss politics with anyone you don't know well.

- **Never** get involved in political or religious arguments relating to Northern Ireland.

- **Avoid** traditional Catholic or Protestant marches and parades, such as those by the Orange Order especially around July 12. They may look like local color, but they can get unpleasant quickly. People do get hurt.

- **Remain** informed. Follow the news to keep abreast of current events and any areas of tension.

Crawl, perhaps (p. 101)—or some good-natured scares aboard the **Dublin Ghost Bus** (p. 122). Those in search of less organized fun may prefer the simple, atmospheric pleasure of **An Evening of Food, Folklore & Fairies** (p. 171).

DAY 3: SOUTH TO WICKLOW & KILKENNY

It takes less than 2 hours to drive from the hustle and traffic of Dublin to the peace and quiet of the **Wicklow Mountains** (p. 201). Drive through the village of Enniskerry to the great estate of **Powerscourt** (p. 198) just past the village. After lunching in its Avoca Café, head on to **Glendalough** (p. 196) and feel your soul relax in the pastoral mountain and lake setting of this ancient monastic retreat. From there drive south to the colorful town of **Kilkenny,** where you can spend the rest of the day shopping in its pottery and crafts shops and exploring noble **Kilkenny Castle** (p. 235). This is a good place to spend your first night outside of Dublin.

DAY 4: WEST TO WATERFORD & CORK

Waterford, Ireland's oldest city, is less than an hour south of Kilkenny—you'll get there with plenty of time left for sightseeing. Have a quick look around some or all of the **Waterford Treasures** museums (p. 211) before dropping in for a tour of the **House of Waterford Crystal.** After lunch, you have a choice—either head to **Cork** (p. 246), Ireland's busy second city, or **Kinsale** (p. 268), a quieter harbor town near Cork that has lately become a foodie destination. Each has plenty to keep you busy for the rest of the day and good hotels in which to spend the night.

DAYS 5 & 6: THE RING OF KERRY

If you're not allergic to touristy things, you could stop at **Blarney Castle** (p. 253) on your way out of Cork in the morning; otherwise, on to County Kerry at the southwest tip of the island. Here the most popular place to explore—and one of the busiest tourist spots in Ireland—is the **Ring of Kerry** (p. 292). It is a beautiful drive, filled with historic sites and tiny villages, but you will have to brave the masses. If you have the stamina, the entire Ring is doable at a reasonable pace over 2 days, although you'd have to skip pretty much everything else around it to make that goal.

Alternatively, you could just explore the short section of the Ring that runs from lovely **Kenmare** (p. 309) to the bucolic peace of **Killarney National Park** (p. 294). Here you can indulge in a buggy ride around the lakes and drink in beautiful landscapes.

DAY 7: COUNTY CLARE

Time is short now, so as you drive through County Clare, promise yourself to come back someday and do it justice. For now, head for the perilously tall **Cliffs of Moher** (p. 351), where the view seems to stretch all the way to America (although the price to park will make you shiver). Then you've another choice: Spend the rest of the day exploring **Bunratty Castle** (p. 350)—where medieval fortress meets historical theme park—or marveling at the otherworldly limestone landscape of the **Burren** (p. 348). Either would be a perfect, quintessentially Irish end to your all-too-short trip.

THE BEST OF IRELAND IN 2 WEEKS

With 2 weeks, your visit to Ireland will be much more relaxed. You can stretch out a bit more in your travels, heading to less crowded counties with more time to meet the locals. In your second week, head along the Wild Atlantic Way to Galway, Mayo, and Donegal, taking time to smell the heather along the way.

DAYS 1–7

Follow "The Best of Ireland in 1 Week" itinerary, as outlined above.

DAY 8: THE BURREN

After spending **DAY 7** exploring County Clare, you'll discover that you need more time to explore this region. If you didn't make it to the **Burren,** spend most of your day here. Otherwise, you could visit another of the county's great medieval buildings such as the exquisite ruins of **Corcomroe Abbey** (p. 349). Lovers of live music will want to spend the evening in the pubs of **Doolin** (p. 353), one of the very best places in Ireland for proper traditional music.

DAYS 9 & 10: COUNTY GALWAY

Start the day with a drive up to Galway City (it will take around an hour), your base for **DAY 9.** You could spend a relaxing day walking the delightful streets of this artsy, vibrant town or cruising out to the misty **Aran Islands** (see p. 384). If you've got kids to keep amused, take them to the fabulous **Galway Atlantaquaria** (p. 397). On the following day, head either east or west. Go west to explore **Connemara National Park** (p. 401), where it's time to get out from behind the wheel and maybe even see this lovely park by horseback if you're feeling brave. If you head east, you'll be traveling inland for a whistle-stop tour of the Irish Midlands (chapter 11). Either return to your Galway City hotel or spend the night in a countryside B&B.

DAY 11: COUNTY MAYO

Drive up from Galway through spectacular scenery, where the rocky shoreline plunges into the cobalt sea in glorious fashion. The south Mayo town of **Westport,** sitting at the edge of a picturesque river, is a delightful place to wander. Probably depending on whether or not you're traveling with youngsters, you could either spend a couple of hours at **Westport House and Pirate Adventure Park** (p. 437) or visit the **National Museum of Ireland: Country Life** (p. 436) near Castlebar. Ancient-history buffs may want to press on to a hotel in County Sligo (see below), but if it's a quiet retreat you're after, drive across the strangely empty flatlands to **Achill Island** (p. 440). The

Sunset at the towering sea cliffs of Slieve League, in County Donegal.

route along the coast and out across the bridge to the island is slow and winding, but the views are fantastic. If you do make it out to Achill, consider an overnight stay at the **Bervie** (p. 445), where the sea is right outside the door.

DAY 12: COUNTY SLIGO

Depending on where you spent the night, you may be in for a long drive, so start early. **Sligo Town** (p. 450) has a few worthwhile attractions, but it's mostly useful as a lunch stop. The real reason to come this far lies in the surrounding countryside. The area has an astonishing concentration of ancient burial sites, including **Carrowkeel** and **Carrowmore,** some of the world's oldest pieces of freestanding architecture. Our favorite place to stay the night in these parts is the extraordinary **Temple House** (p. 458).

DAY 13: NORTH TO DONEGAL

You're really entering the wilds of Ireland now. Head up the coast past Donegal Town, then follow the N15 road around the breathtaking coastline to the busy hill town of **Ballyshannon** (p. 469), an excellent spot for crafts shops and glorious hilltop views. The adventurous can explore the **Catsby Cave** (p. 470), a picturesque grotto at the edge of the Abbey River. But here the drive is really the thing, so head on to the darling town of **Glencolumbkille** (p. 472). The excellent folk park here is well worth an hour of your time before you head on to the stone-cut town of **Ardara** at the foot of a steep hill—it's wall-to-wall arts-and-crafts shops and a pleasure to explore. Art lovers won't want to miss the revelatory gallery at **Glebe House** (p. 480). You've spent a lot of time in the car today, but if you can face another 40 minutes or so, head for the wonderful **Rathmullen House** (p. 481), an elegant retreat on Lough Swilly waiting for you on your last night.

DAY 14: HEADING HOME

If your flight leaves late, you could rise early and spend the morning driving up to **Malin Head** (p. 485), the northernmost tip of Ireland. It's a wild and wooly place just a couple of hours' drive from Rathmullan. From there, expect the journey to the airport to take at least 4 hours, but allow plenty of time in case of traffic backups around Dublin—they're virtually constant.

IRELAND FOR FREE OR DIRT CHEAP

Ireland is no longer a cheap country to visit—and hasn't been for some time. The economic crash of the late 2000s and early 2010s drove prices down a bit, but the economy has since recovered and hotels and restaurants can be pricey. Here's the good news: You can visit a lot of great sites

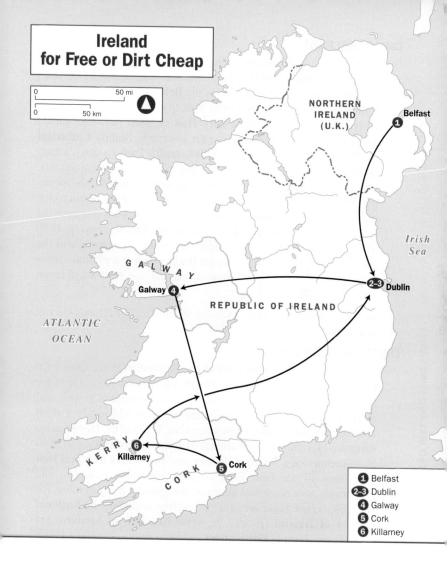

Ireland
for Free or Dirt Cheap

NORTHERN
IRELAND
(U.K.)

Belfast ❶

Irish
Sea

G A L W A Y

Galway ❹

REPUBLIC OF IRELAND

❷-❸ Dublin

ATLANTIC
OCEAN

K E R R Y

Killarney ❻

C O R K

❺ Cork

❶ Belfast
❷-❸ Dublin
❹ Galway
❺ Cork
❻ Killarney

for free in Ireland, including some of the biggest tourist attractions in the country. You can also save a lot of money by sticking mainly to places that can be reached by public transport, thus eliminating the need to rent a car (every place we list is easily accessible by train or bus). You'd be surprised by how much of Ireland you can see without blowing the budget. We're starting this tour in Northern Ireland (maybe you got a great deal on a flight to Belfast!), because it's one of the more budget-friendly regions. For more information on train and bus timetables, see **www.irishrail.ie** and **www.buseireann.ie**.

DAY 1: BELFAST

Belfast is rich with free attractions—here are just a few. The excellent **Ulster Museum** (p. 502) displays artifacts from across 9,000 years of Irish history. Right next door is the **Belfast Botanic Gardens & Palm House** (p. 496), only a short walk from the campus of **Queen's University** (p. 505). **Belfast City Hall** (p. 498) runs free guided tours. Another exceptional Victorian landmark, **Belfast Cathedral** (p. 504), is also free, as is **Cave Hill Country Park** (p. 504), a tranquil place with good walking trails and incredible views of the city. Last but not least, because Belfast is still most famous for the sectarian strife of the mid– to late 20th century, a highlight of your visit may be to view the political murals remaining in what was once the epicenter of the conflict, the **Falls and Shankill roads areas** (p. 497). These neighborhoods are now safe for visitors to explore, and the street art is utterly free to see. To get the most out of the murals, however, you may want to spend some of that cash you've saved so far on a **Black Taxi Tour** (p. 496).

Catch a train from Belfast to Dublin (Connolly Station). Time: 2 hr. 10 min. Fares start at about €22 for adults.

DAYS 2 & 3: DUBLIN

Ireland's capital is also the number-one destination in the country for free sites. We think the **Chester Beatty Library** (p. 93) is one of the best museums in Europe. The collection of illuminated gospels and early copies of the Bible, Torah, and Koran would justify a steep entrance fee, but it doesn't cost you a cent. Three of the four separate museums constituting the **National Museum of Ireland** are in Dublin—**Archaeology, Natural History,** and **Decorative Arts and History**—and all are free. Each contains incredible treasures, and collectively have enough to keep you occupied for a day or more. All of Dublin's best major art galleries are free, including the **National Gallery of Ireland** (p. 99), the **Irish Museum of Modern Art** (p. 107), the **Temple Bar Gallery** (p. 107), and the excellent **Hugh Lane Gallery** (p. 98). Many of Dublin's most historic public buildings, such as the **Bank of Ireland/Parliament House** (p. 110) and the **Four Courts** (p. 111), don't charge admission. You can walk right into the **General Post Office** (still a working post office; p. 112) on O'Connell Street to see exhibits devoted to the Easter Rising, including the original Declaration of Independence. There's no charge to visit the **President's House** (Áras an Uachtaráin; p. 110) in Phoenix Park, accessible only by tour (alas, just Sat). Add to this the great public spaces such as **Phoenix Park** (p. 119), **St. Stephen's Green** (p. 120), and **Trinity College** (p. 105), and you'll see that it's possible to spend a full 2 days here without spending a penny on sightseeing.

SAVING MONEY ON trains & buses

The cost of rail travel can quickly mount up, but there are ways to save money. Whenever you can, buy your tickets online in advance. The sample fares listed in this itinerary are all prebooked; walk-up fares can be higher. The downside for booking that way is that you have to specify times of travel—but Irish Rail has a handy policy of letting you upgrade a prebooked ticket into something more flexible for just €10.

If you're going to be spending a lot of time on public transportation, you should also strongly consider buying a money-saving pass. **Eurail Pass** is good for travel on trains, and also offers discounts on Stena Line ferries and Irish Ferries routes between England, Scotland, Wales or France and Ireland. You can select particular countries, or go for a Global Pass, which covers 28 European nations. If you choose to buy a pass for 3 days of unlimited travel in Ireland within 1 month, a second-class pass starts at €161. First-class passes are also available. The passes are valid throughout Ireland (including Northern Ireland). For

details or for purchase, visit **www.eurail. com**. You can also buy Eurail passes from **Railpass** (www.railpass.com; ✆ **877/375-7245** in the U.S.) and other travel agents.

While the pass can save you money, first check out route prices on **www. irishrail.ie**. It may work out cheaper just to book tickets for each journey. If you do buy a Eurail pass, it's still advisable to make seat reservations to guarantee a space—this may cost a few extra euro each time in booking fees. Note that if you're already a resident of the European Union, you can travel with the Europeans-only equivalent of the Eurail Pass: the **Interrail Pass**. See **www.interrail.eu** for details.

Catch a train from Dublin (Heuston Station) to Galway. Time: 2 hr. 40 min. Fares start at about €33 for adults.

DAY 4: GALWAY

Ireland's artsy, seductive west-coast city offers plenty of free pursuits. The **Galway Arts Centre** (p. 380) usually has good exhibitions, and you can often score cheap tickets for performances. The **Galway City Museum** (p. 381) makes for a stellar introduction to the region, with its fine collection of artifacts from the medieval period onward. **St. Nicholas' Collegiate Church** (p. 383), the oldest church in the city, contains a 12th-century crusader's tomb and other extraordinary historic pieces. Make sure you also devote some time to just wandering the streets of this eminently walkable town; its central medieval district is a tiny, twisty area with lots of cafes, shops, and photogenic corners.

Catch a bus from Galway Bus Station to Cork (Parnell Place Bus Station). Time: 3½ hr. with one change or 4 hr. 20 min. direct. Fares start at about €27 for adults.

DAY 5: GALWAY TO CORK

Busy, youthful Cork City doesn't have a great deal of free historic attractions, but if you're up for a large dose of culture, you'll find

Ross Castle, Killarney National Park.

plenty to do without paying a cent. Start with a trip to the **Old English Market** (p. 250) for a browse and a cheap lunch. Afterward, head to the **Crawford Art Gallery** (p. 250)—it's one of the very best in Ireland and completely free. More excellent free art is to be found at the **Lewis Glucksman Gallery** (p. 253) on the campus of **University College Cork.** In the evening, check out a few of Cork's exceptional pubs, among the best in the country for traditional music (see "A Tuneful Pint," on p. 262).

Catch a train from Cork to Killarney. Most change at Mallow. Time: 1 hr. 20 min. direct, or 2 hr. with change. Fares start at about €29 for adults.

DAY 6: CORK TO KILLARNEY

It's not exactly difficult to reach **Killarney National Park** (p. 294) from Killarney Town; you just walk toward the cathedral and turn left. This 65-sq.-km (25-sq.-mile) expanse of forest, lakes, and mountains is crisscrossed with several well-conceived nature trails, plus more challenging routes for serious hikers. Formerly the grounds of a great mansion, the **Knockreer Estate** (p. 300) still has lovely gardens and beautiful views. Free sites in Killarney Town itself include the rather grand neo-Gothic **St. Mary's Cathedral** (p. 300). For dinner, the frugal traveler will be drawn to the **Laurels** (p. 307)—a lively pub in the center of Killarney town serving steaks, seafood, and stone-baked pizzas, with live music on the side.

Catch a train from Killarney to Dublin—again, nearly all change at Mallow. Time: 3½ hr. Fares start at about €44 for adults.

DAY 7: HOMEWARD BOUND . . .

Assuming your airline will let you fly out of Dublin, an early-ish train back to the capital should give you some time to pick up any of the free sites you may have missed earlier in the tour. Otherwise, you'll have to catch a train straight to Belfast for your flight home (about 7½ hr. with up to three changes; fares from Killarney start at about €38 adults). And that's it! You've done a fair bit of Ireland without breaking the bank. Pick your accommodations early and wisely to save the most—plenty of inexpensive B&Bs are listed in this book for each of these cities. Your other main expense on this itinerary will be rail fares, but you can save money on those too (see "Saving Money on Trains & Buses," p. 35).

THE BEST OF IRELAND FOR FAMILIES

Traveling with children is always a bit of an adventure, and you'll want all the help you can get. Luckily, Ireland—with its vast open countryside, farm hotels, and castles—is like a fairy-tale playground for kids. You may have trouble finding babysitters outside major towns, so just take the kids with you wherever you go—most restaurants, sights, and even pubs (during the day) welcome children. The best part of the country for those traveling with kids is arguably Cork and Kerry, where everything seems to be set up for families. Here's a sample itinerary for a kid-friendly trip.

DAYS 1 & 2: DUBLIN

The extensive greens of **Phoenix Park** (p. 119) are a great place for little ones to let off steam (it's the best place in the city for a picnic, too, if the weather's good). Within the park, **Dublin Zoo** (p. 121) is designed to appeal to the younger ones (you can take a train ride around the zoo, for instance). Inquisitive young minds will be inspired by the cabinets of curiosity and zoological treasures at the **National Museum of Ireland: Natural History** (p. 102). The guides at another museum, the **Little Museum of Dublin** (p. 117), do a great job putting into context the ordinary lives of Dubliners in the last hundred years for younger visitors. The interactive exhibits at **EPIC, the Irish Emigration Museum** (p. 113), are a big kid magnet, and even younger kids (the braver ones anyway) are all but guaranteed to love an evening aboard the **Dublin Ghost Bus** (p. 122).

DAY 3: COUNTY CORK

Okay, so it's not exactly untouched by the tourism fairy, but kids find plenty to love about **Blarney Castle** (p. 253), just outside Cork City. They can kiss the famous stone if they don't mind an attendant holding them upside-down. A few miles away, the **Fota Wildlife Park** (p. 264) is a well-designed zoo where docile animals (those that don't bite, kick, or stomp) roam among the visitors.

DAYS 4 & 5: COUNTY KERRY

Kerry is probably Ireland's most kid-friendly county, with enough to keep you busy for at least a couple of days. On the Dingle Peninsula, they might spot seals, dolphins or basking sharks on a **Dingle boat tour** (p. 330). On the Iveragh Peninsula, Kenmare's **Seafari** cruises and seal-watching trips (p. 310) teach kids about conservation issues by putting them in touch with the underwater residents of Kenmare Bay. **Blueberry Hill Farm** (p. 319), in Sneem, is a working old-fashioned farmstead where kids can help milk cows, make butter, and take part in a treasure hunt. Meanwhile, an underground tour of the atmospheric **Crag Cave** (p. 328) is a surefire winner—as is a stop for high-energy playtime at the **Crazy Cave** (p. 328) adventure playground. And don't overlook what **Killarney National Park** (p. 294) has to offer little ones—what could be better than a ride around the mountains and lakes in an old-fashioned horse-drawn "jarvey"?

DAY 6: BUNRATTY FOLK PARK

You could spend most of the day at **Bunratty Castle & Folk Park** (p. 350), an attraction that combines one of Ireland's best medieval castles with a living-history museum. It's a brilliant re-creation of a 19th-century village, complete with costumed actors strolling down the street, chatting to passers-by, and even working in the shops. Bunratty is also the setting for the lively (and hugely popular) **Medieval Banquet.** It's raucous but surprisingly good fun; book an early-evening sitting to suit young bedtimes.

DAY 7: HEADING HOME

If you have time before the drive back to the airport, head into the otherworldly landscape of the **Burren** (see p. 348), where young imaginations will be fired up by dolmens and other ancient sites. It's also where you'll find the **Burren Birds of Prey Centre** at Aill-wee Cave (p. 346), a working aviary full of buzzards, falcons, eagles, and owls in flight.

Learning about blacksmithing at the Bunratty Castle & Folk Park.

The Best of Ireland for Families

1-2 Dublin

REPUBLIC OF IRELAND

Irish Sea

Galway Bay

THE BURREN
Cliffs of Moher
7 CLARE
Bunratty
6
Limerick

Mouth of the Shannon

K E R R Y
Killarney
4-5
KILLARNEY NATIONAL PARK

3 Cork

C O R K

CELTIC SEA

1-2 Dublin
3 County Cork
4-5 County Kerry
6 Bunratty Folk Park
7 The Burren

BEYOND A WEEK . . .

If your trip extends beyond a week, your family will find plenty of standout attractions for kids farther north.

The **Atlantaquaria** (p. 397), just outside Galway City, is a state-of-the-art aquarium, while pony trekking across **Connemara National Park** (p. 401) is a unique way to see this beautiful, wind-swept landscape.

In Mayo, **Westport House and Pirate Adventure Park** (p. 437) has all the ingredients for high-activity fun; young girls in particular will enjoy learning about the region's real-life pirate hero, **Grace O'Malley** (p. 438).

If you're going as far as Belfast, the attractions around the Titanic Quarter hold plenty of youthful appeal. Try the hands-on science center, **W5** (p. 506), and the state-of-the-art **Titanic Belfast** museum (p. 500).

Finally, the **Causeway Coast Drive** (see p. 524) has two key highlights that children will adore: the perilous (but fun) **Carrick-a-Rede Rope Bridge** (p. 523) and the awe-inspiring alien shapes of the **Giant's Causeway** (p. 527).

EXPLORING ANCIENT IRELAND

Ireland treasures its ancestral past, with mysterious stone circles, cairns, and huge stone tables known as dolmens, standing perfectly preserved in pastures and on hillsides all over the island. Some of the oldest tombs predate the Egyptian pyramids by centuries, and in many cases, the meaning and purpose of several preserved sites remain intriguing riddles. To delve into this misty past, you'll need to be intrepid and cover a lot of ground in the car, but it'll be worth it—exploring these rocky symbols can be the most memorable part of any trip to Ireland.

DAY 1: KNOWTH & THE BOYNE VALLEY

After an early breakfast, head north to the rich, rolling Boyne Valley (about an hour's drive north of Dublin off the N2) to the **Brú na Bóinne Visitor Centre** (p. 176) and this extensive Neolithic burial ground. The huge necropolis holds numerous sites to visit, such as **Newgrange** (p. 177), **Knowth** (p. 178), and **Dowth.** Register at the center to tour Newgrange first. A tour here, early in the day before it gets crowded, is spectacular. You can also view the outside of Knowth. In the afternoon, head down the N3 to the **Hill of Tara** (p. 179), where mounds and passage graves date from the Bronze Age.

DAY 2: CÉIDE FIELDS

It takes a couple of hours to drive from Dublin to this remote location in north County Mayo, but your efforts will be rewarded. This

Giant's Causeway on the Antrim Coast.

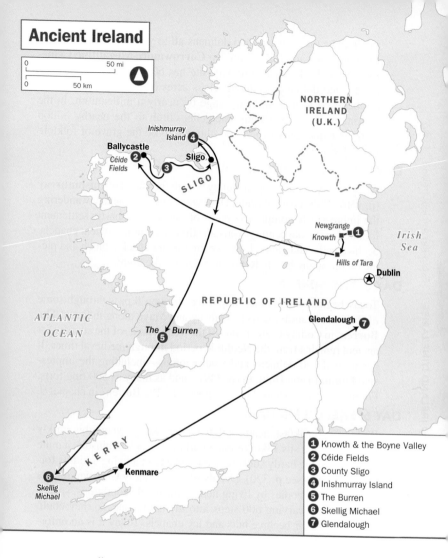

Ancient Ireland

0 _____ 50 mi

0 _____ 50 km

NORTHERN IRELAND (U.K.)

Inishmurray Island ④

Ballycastle ②

Céide Fields

③ Sligo

S L I G O

Newgrange

Knowth ■ ①

Irish Sea

Hills of Tara

★ Dublin

REPUBLIC OF IRELAND

ATLANTIC OCEAN

The ⑤ Burren

Glendalough ⑦

K E R R Y

⑥

Skellig Michael

Kenmare

① Knowth & the Boyne Valley
② Céide Fields
③ County Sligo
④ Inishmurray Island
⑤ The Burren
⑥ Skellig Michael
⑦ Glendalough

extraordinary ancient site (p. 439) holds the stony remains of an entire prehistoric farming village on top of a cliff, with a bonus of breathtaking views of the sea and surrounding countryside. Spend an hour exploring the 5,000-year-old site, and lunch in the excellent visitor center.

DAY 3: COUNTY SLIGO

In the morning, drive east to County Sligo. On the N4, south of Sligo Town, visit the **Carrowkeel Passage Tomb Cemetery** (p. 453), which is perched on a hilltop with wide, sweeping views overlooking Lough Arrow. It's often very quiet early in the day—with luck you might have the 14 cairns and dolmens all to yourself. Then head on to Sligo Town and follow signs to **Carrowmore Megalithic Cemetery** (p. 454). This extraordinary site has 60 stone circles, passage tombs, and dolmens scattered across acres of green pastures. They are believed to predate Newgrange by nearly a millennium. In the afternoon, if you're feeling energetic, climb to the nearby hilltop cairn of **Knocknarea** (p. 457)—thought to be the grave of folklore fairy Queen Maeve.

DAY 4: INISHMURRAY ISLAND

After a relaxing morning, travel by boat to the island of **Inishmurray** (p. 456) off the coast of Sligo. Here you can spend the day wandering the impressively complete remains of the early monastic settlement founded in the 6th century. You can still make out its ancient chapels, beehive cells, and altars. If the weather is fine, pack a lunch and picnic on the sunny beach. Return to Sligo for the night.

DAY 5: THE BURREN

Today begins with another long drive, but you'll pass through some of the most beautiful parts of Galway and Mayo along the way. **The Burren,** in County Clare, is one of the richest areas of the country for ancient remains from the Neolithic period through medieval times. It has around 120 dolmens and wedge tombs—including the impressive **Poulnabrone Dolmen** (p. 349)—and as many as 500 ring forts. For more on this extraordinary region, see "The Burren" in chapter 9.

DAY 6: SKELLIG MICHAEL

Right after breakfast, head south to County Kerry, where this starkly beautiful island sits 13km (8 miles) off the Iveragh Peninsula, a mute memorial to the hardy souls who once eked out a living amid its formidable cliffs (see p. 320). Deeply observant early Christian monks punished their bodies by living here in miserable conditions, spending their days carving 600 steps into the hard stone, so they could climb up to their beehive huts and icy chapels. Today it is an unforgettable landscape, and the ruins of the monks' homes are profoundly moving. A trip out here by boat and an afternoon's exploration will take up much of the day. Once you return to the mainland, reward yourself with a relaxing evening in Kenmare.

DAY 7: GLENDALOUGH

Drive east today to County Wicklow, where the evocative ruins of the monastery at **Glendalough** (p. 196) are sprawled around two serene lakes nestled in a peaceful valley. Get a map from the visitor center before beginning your exploration of the round towers, chapels, and huts dotted around the wooded site. Don't miss the ancient church ruin known as **St. Kevin's Kitchen.** If the weather is warm, bring your lunch and picnic by the lake. You can easily spend a day here.

IRELAND OFF THE BEATEN PATH

We start this tour in Belfast, a city that has undergone an immense transformation since the 1998 Good Friday Agreement, which finally established a detente in Northern Ireland. Tourism has steadily increased in this region over the last decade, thanks in part to the many locations here used in the popular HBO series *Game of Thrones*. If the best sites of the Antrim Coast were in County Cork or Kerry, they'd be overrun with tourists; as it is, you can still visit a spectacular setting such as the Giant's Causeway and find yourself alone with nature. This tour then heads west to take in a couple of Sligo's prehistoric sites and continues south for a visit to Achill Island, a peaceful retreat off the coast of County Mayo.

DAYS 1 & 2: BELFAST

Northern Ireland's capital—and second-largest city on the island of Ireland—is a historic, vibrant town. Start with a visit to the **Ulster Museum** (p. 502) and experience some of the city's more recent past firsthand with a **Black Taxi Tour** (p. 496). The museums in the Titanic Quarter, such as the immense **Titanic Belfast** (p. 500), provide a more high-tech dose of history; alternatively, you could immerse yourself in the city's present by exploring its busy shopping districts. The **Belfast Botanic Gardens & Palm House** (p. 496) and **Queen's University** (p. 505) are also worth a look. Round off the day with a pint at one of Belfast's extraordinarily pretty pubs, like the **Crown Liquor Saloon** (p. 499), and a meal at one of the small but growing number of world-class restaurants.

DAY 3: COUNTY ANTRIM

One of the North's loveliest counties, Antrim is home to two gorgeous parks: **Castlewellan Forest Park** (p. 538), with formal gardens and gorgeous woodland walks, and the **Silent Valley Mountain Park** (p. 541), with beautiful walks and even more incredible views. Alternatively, the Causeway Coastal Route is one of Ireland's great coastal drives—and one of the least spoiled. Those who do this drive will reap spectacular rewards. Start in **Carrickfergus,** with a brief stop to look around its medieval castle (p. 506), before heading north along the coast road. For the best views, take the **Torr Head Scenic Road** (p. 529), located just after the village of **Cushendun** (p. 526). It's an alternative signposted road running parallel to the main route, best for those with a good head for heights. From up here on a clear day, you can see all the way to the Mull of Kintyre in Scotland. The Causeway Coast's most remarkable attraction is the **Giant's Causeway** (p. 527), an uncanny natural rock formation comprised of thousands of tightly packed basalt columns. You could do the drive in about 2 hours, but you'll want to allow considerably longer than that to give yourself time to stop along the way. There are places along the coast to spend the night, or you could go straight on into **Derry** (p. 553), another hour farther from the Giant's Causeway.

DAY 4: DERRY TO SLIGO

Straddling the border between Northern Ireland and the Republic, this vibrant city for years was synonymous with political strife. Though it's peaceful these days, it's still a divided place—the residents can't even agree on its name. Road signs from the Republic point to Derry; those in the North point to Londonderry. How can a place like that *not* be full of character and history? Check out the award-winning **Tower Museum** (p. 560) and the Gothic 17th-century **St. Columb's Cathedral** (p. 558) before recharging for the long drive to County Sligo in the afternoon.

DAY 5: COUNTY SLIGO

Nestled within the gentle, verdant hills of this underrated county are some dramatic archaeological sites. Within a short drive from Sligo Town are two of the most incredible: **Carrowkeel Passage Tomb Cemetery** (p. 453), packed with 14 cairns, dolmens, and stone circles, and the impossibly ancient **Carrowmore Megalithic Cemetery** (p. 454). Here's something to ponder while clambering around the latter: The innocuously named tomb 52A is thought to be 7,400 years old, making it the earliest known piece of freestanding stone architecture in the world.

Keel Beach on Achill Island.

DAY 6: SLIGO TO ACHILL ISLAND

Just off the coast of County Mayo, this is a wild and beautiful place of unspoiled beaches and spectacular scenery. But you'll also find a handful of excellent little hotels and B&Bs, mostly in the vicinity of **Keel,** the island's most attractive village. This is major outdoor sports territory as well, as the constant wind off the Atlantic Ocean is ideal for windsurfing, kitesurfing, hang gliding, and any other sport that depends on a breeze. One of the best (and least-known) discoveries on Achill Island is a deserted village on the slopes of **Mount Slievemore** (p. 440). Not too many people venture up there, making it an even more extraordinary and moving place to visit.

DAY 7: ACHILL ISLAND TO SHANNON

It's a long drive to whichever airport you're flying home from, but a flight out of Shannon will give you the most spectacular route. If you can extend your trip a little, a ferry ride over to Mayo's **Clare Island** (p. 435) is a lovely way to spend a day. Clare is even more peaceful and isolated than its near neighbor, Achill, with a permanent population that amounts to just 150 people. You can go a long way without bumping into any of them.

IRELAND IN CONTEXT

3

The past few decades have been a time of great change for Ireland, first with the Celtic Tiger economy boom from 1995 to 2007, and then the property crash and economic slump that followed. In recent years the Republic of Ireland's economy has bounced back, although the Covid-19 pandemic has brought a new set of economic challenges. Meanwhile, Northern Ireland and the rest of the U.K. are working through the after-effects of Brexit, Britain's departure from the EU. As ever, it's a fascinating time to visit and see Ireland. A complex, small country with a tumultuous history, this is a land immensely rich with tradition, beauty, culture, and life.

IRELAND TODAY

The story of Ireland in the 21st century so far has been one of enormous change. The ups and downs of a turbulent economy took the country from dizzying boom at the turn of the new millennium to crushing bust after 2008, then most of the way back again.

But there are much more significant ways in which Ireland today is a very different place to what it was a generation ago. In 2015, same-sex marriage was legalized, making Ireland the first country in the world to do so as the result of a referendum. Then, in 2018, after an even more extensive public debate, abortion was finally made legal too.

The previous year, Leo Varadker had become Taoiseach (prime minister, or head of the government), the first openly gay man to hold the post. For a country that had always been deeply conservative on social issues, these were all monumental sea changes—virtually inconceivable just a generation ago.

As the 2020s rolled around, it was as if Ireland had left behind one kind of identity, and moved instead towards a more modern, liberal, European version of itself. In short, Ireland today is a *really* interesting place to visit.

In 2020 and 2021, the Covid-19 pandemic roiled the nation. Festivals were canceled or postponed, and many attractions, restaurants, and pubs moved to restrict opening hours and visitor numbers. Check the latest public health measures at **www.gov.ie**.

For details on pandemic protocols in Ireland, see p. 578.

FACING PAGE: **Admiring a lake in County Wicklow.**

THE MAKING OF IRELAND
The First Settlers

With some degree of confidence, we can place the date of the first human habitation of the island somewhere after the end of the last ice age, around the late 8000s B.C. Ireland's first colonizers, Mesolithic *Homo sapiens,* walked, waded, or floated across the narrow strait from what is now Britain in search of flint and, of course, food.

The next momentous prehistoric event was the arrival of Neolithic farmers and herders, sometime around 3500 B.C. Unlike Ireland's Mesolithic hunters, who barely left a trace, this second wave of colonizers began to transform the island at once. They came with stone axes that could fell a good-size elm in less than an hour. Ireland's hardwood forests receded to make room for tilled fields and pastureland. Villages sprang up, and more permanent homes, planked with split oak, appeared at this time.

Far more striking, though, was the appearance of massive megalithic monuments, including court cairns, dolmens (stone tables), round subterranean passage tombs, and wedge tombs. Thousands of these tombs are scattered around Ireland, and to this day only a small percentage of them have been excavated. These megalithic monuments speak volumes about the early Irish. To visit **Newgrange ★★★** (see p. 177) and **Knowth ★★★** (see p. 178) in the Boyne Valley and

Some of Ireland's megalithic monuments date from as far back as 3500 B.C.

Carrowmore ★★★ (see p. 454) in County Sligo is to marvel at the mystical practices of the early Irish. Even today little is known about the meaning or purpose of these mysterious stone relics. Later Celtic inhabitants assumed that the tremendous stones and mounds were raised by giants, a race they called the people of the *sí*—a name that eventually became the *Tuatha Dé Danann,* and, finally, *fairies.* Over many generations, oral tradition downsized the mythical people into "little people," who were believed to have led a magical underground life in thousands of *raths* (earthwork structures) coursing the island like giant mole tunnels. All of these sites were believed to be protected by fairies. Tampering with them was thought to bring bad luck, so nobody ever touched them. Thus, they have lasted to this day—ungraffitied, undamaged, unprotected by any visible fences or wires, but utterly safe.

The Celts

Of all the successive waves of outsiders who have, over the years, shaped, cajoled, and pockmarked the timeline of Irish history, none have made quite such an impact as the Celts. They came, originally from Central Europe, in waves, the first perhaps as early as the 6th century B.C. and continuing until the end of the first millennium. They fled from the Roman invasion and clung to the edge of Europe—Ireland being, at the time, about as far as you could go to elude a Roman force. In time, they controlled the island and absorbed into their culture everyone they found there.

Despite their cultural potency, however, the Celts developed little in the way of centralized government, existing instead in a near-perpetual state of conflict with one another. The island was divided among as many as 150 tribes, grouped in alliances under five provincial kings. The provinces of **Munster, Leinster, Ulster,** and **Connaught** date from this period. They fought fiercely among themselves over cattle (their "currency" and standard of wealth), land, and women. No one tribe ever ruled the entire island, though not for lack of trying. One of the most impressive monuments from the era of the warring Celts is the stone fortress of **Dún Aengus,** on the windswept hills of the Aran Islands (see p. 384).

The Coming of Christianity

The Celtic chiefs neither warmly welcomed nor violently resisted the Christians who came ashore beginning in the A.D. 5th century. Although threatened, the pagan Celts settled for a bloodless rivalry with this new religion. In retrospect, this may have been a mistake.

Not the first, but eventually the most famous, of these Christian newcomers was a man called Maewyn Succat, a young Roman citizen torn from his Welsh homeland in a Celtic raid and brought to Ireland as a slave, where he was forced to work in a place called the Forest of Foclut (thought to be around modern County Antrim). He escaped on a ship bound for

Early Christian monks lived in seclusion on Skellig Michael.

France, where he spent several years as a priest before returning to Ireland as a missionary. He began preaching at sacred Celtic festivals, a tactic that frequently led to confrontations with religious and political leaders, but eventually he became such a popular figure that after his death in 461, a dozen clan chiefs fought over the right to bury him. His lasting legacy was, of course, the establishment in Ireland of one of the strongest Christian orthodoxies in Europe—an achievement for which he was later beatified as **St. Patrick.**

Ireland's conversion to Christianity was a somewhat negotiated process. The church at the time of St. Patrick was, like the man who brought it, Roman. For Ireland, an island still without a single proper town, the Roman system of dioceses and archdioceses simply didn't make sense. So the Irish adapted the church to their own situation. They built isolated monasteries with extended monastic "families," each more or less autonomous.

For several centuries, Ireland flourished in this fashion, becoming a center of monastic learning. Monks and scholars were drawn here in droves, and they were sent out in great numbers as well, to Britain and the Continent, as emissaries for the island's way of thinking and praying.

Like their megalithic ancestors, these monks left traces of their lives behind, enduring monuments to their spirituality. Early monastic sites such as gorgeous **Glendalough ★★★** in County Wicklow (p. 196), windswept **Clonmacnoise ★★★** in County Offaly (p. 420), and isolated **Skellig Michael** off the Kerry coast (p. 320) give you an idea of how they lived, while striking examples of their work can be seen at **Trinity**

College ★★ (p. 105), which houses the Book of Kells, and at the **Chester Beatty Library** ★★★ (p. 93) at Dublin Castle.

The Viking Invasions

The monastic city-states of early medieval Ireland might have continued to lead the world's intellectual development—but then the **Vikings** came along and ruined everything.

After centuries of relative peace, the first wave of Viking invaders arrived in Ireland in A.D. 795, making their base in the Southeast, in what is now **Waterford City** (see p. 211). The wealthy Irish monasteries were among their first targets. Unprepared and unprotected, the monasteries, which had amassed collections of gold, jewels, and art from followers around the world, were decimated. The round towers to which the nonviolent monks retreated for safety were neither high enough nor strong enough to protect them and their treasures from the onslaught.

Once word spread of the wealth to be had on the small island, the Scandinavian invaders just kept on coming. Though they were experts in the arts of pillage and plunder, they had no knowledge of or interest in literature. In fact, most didn't know how to read. Therefore, they paid scant attention to the magnificent books they came across, passing them over for more obvious riches. This fortunate quirk of history allowed the monks to preserve their dying culture—and their immeasurably valuable work—for the benefit of future generations.

The monastery cemetery at Glendalough.

monk-y BUSINESS

The Iliad and the Odyssey may have taken place on the turquoise depths of the Aegean, but it was on the dark waters of the Irish Sea that many classics of Roman and Greek literature survived the sack of Rome and the ensuing Dark Ages. But how did it happen? How did—in the words of bestselling author and historian Thomas Cahill—the Irish save civilization?

The year is A.D. 464. The mighty Roman Empire is on its knees. The Eternal City is under eternal siege, and its great libraries and universities are about to be looted and burned. The world order is quite literally falling apart. Meanwhile, the far-flung backwater of Ireland is undergoing a spiritual revolution. The pagan Gaels are being converted to Christianity by an escaped Roman slave from Wales with a good line in stubbornness. They call him Patricio—known today as St. Patrick.

The Irish wholeheartedly embrace monastic life. Centers of Christian learning pop up across the island, including the remote **Skellig Islands** (p. 320), where monks copy the Bible and other works. Masters of calligraphic arts, they produce beautiful illuminated texts such as the **Book of Kells** (p. 92). Gaeilge becomes the first vernacular language (slang, effectively) in Europe to have been written down. Some of Europe's finest minds flee the continental anarchy for Ireland, bringing books and learning with them. Knowledge-hungry monks duplicate great Latin and Greek works of literature.

After St. Patrick, Irish missionaries such as **Columcille** and **Columbanus** began to look abroad. With the end of the Roman Empire, Europe had become a fragmented patchwork of fiefdoms. The hardy Celtic monks set up new monasteries in France, Germany, Switzerland, and Italy—and they took their skills with them. Beautifully decorated Irish manuscripts from this period have been found as far away as Russia, where the monks continued to advance the art of bookmaking.

After the Vikings left, Ireland enjoyed something of a renewal in the 11th and 12th centuries. Its towns grew, its regional kings continued to try (unsuccessfully) to unite the country under a single high kingship, and its church came under increased pressure to conform to the Vatican's rules. All of these factors ripened a prosperous and factionalized Ireland for the next invasion.

It was, tragically, an Irish king who opened the door to the next predator. **Diarmait Mac Murchada,** king of Leinster, whose ambition was to be king of all of Ireland, decided he could do it, with a little help. So he called on **Henry II,** the Norman king of England. Diarmait offered Henry a series of incentives in return for military aid: Not only did he bequeath his eldest daughter to whoever led the army; he also offered overlordship of the Kingdom of Leinster. To put it bluntly, he made Henry an offer he couldn't refuse. So it was that an English expeditionary force, led by the Earl of Pembroke, Richard de Clare—better known as **Strongbow**—was sent to Diarmait's aid. After a successful invasion, victorious Strongbow remained in Ireland as governor, and thus gave the English their first foothold in Ireland. What Diarmait did not realize, of course, was that they would never leave.

The Norman Invasion

In successive expeditions from 1167 to 1169, the **Normans,** who had already conquered England, crossed the Irish Sea with crushing force. While Dublin Castle was for years the Norman seat of power, over the next century the Norman-English continued to consolidate their power in new towns and cities.

Many of these settlers, however, grew attached to the island and began to integrate with the local culture; marriages between the native Irish and the invaders became commonplace. Inevitably, as time passed the Anglo-Normans became more Irish and less English in their loyalties.

Meanwhile, independent Gaelic lords in the North and West maintained their territories. By the late 1400s, English control of the island was effectively limited to **the Pale,** a walled and fortified cordon around what is now greater Dublin. (The phrase "beyond the pale" comes from this—meaning anything that is uncontrollable or unacceptable.)

English Power & the Flight of the Earls

The Tudor dynasty in England, which ruled from 1485 to 1603, changed all that, setting in motion the brutal reconquest of Ireland. In 1542, **Henry VIII** boldly proclaimed himself king of all Ireland—something even his warlike ancestors had stopped short of doing—and later that century his daughter, **Elizabeth I,** declared that all Gaelic lords in Ireland must surrender their lands to her, with the dubious promise that she would immediately grant them all back again.

Unsurprisingly, the proposition was hardly welcomed in Ireland, and a rebel army was raised by Hugh O'Neill and "Red" Hugh O'Donnell, two Irish chieftains. They scored some significant victories early on in their decade-long campaign, most notably over a force led by the Earl of Essex, whom Elizabeth had personally sent to subdue them. Still, by 1603 O'Neill was left with few allies and no option but to surrender, which he did on March 23rd, the day before Elizabeth died. In 1607, after failing to win back much of their power and prestige, around 90 of O'Neill's allies fled to mainland Europe, hoping Spain would try to invade again. This never happened. The **Flight of the Earls,** as it became known, marked a crucial turning point in Irish history—the point at which the old Gaelic aristocracy effectively came to an end.

The Coming of Cromwell

By the 1640s, Ireland was effectively an English plantation. Family estates had been seized, and foreign (Scottish) labor brought in to work them. A systematic persecution of Catholics, which began with Henry VIII's split from Rome but did not die with him, barred Catholics from practicing their faith. Resentment against the English and their punitive laws led to fierce uprisings in Ulster and Leinster in 1641, and by early 1642 most of Ireland was again under Irish control. Unfortunately for the rebels, any hope of extending the victories was undermined by internal disunion, and then by a fatal decision to support the Royalist side in the Civil War that had just broken out in England. After King Charles I of England was beheaded in 1648, **Oliver Cromwell,** the commander of the parliamentary forces, was installed as England's ruler. It wasn't long before Cromwell's supporters took on his enemies in Ireland. A year later, the Royalists' stand collapsed in defeat at Rathmines, just south of Dublin.

Defeat for the Royalist cause did not, however, mean the end of war. Cromwell became paranoid that Ireland would be used to launch a French-backed insurgency; he also detested the country's Catholic beliefs. So it was that as the hot, sticky summer of 1649 drew to a close, Cromwell set sail for Dublin with an army of 12,000 men, and a battle plan so ruthless that it remains notorious to this day.

In the town of **Drogheda** (see p. 178), more than 3,552 Irish soldiers were slaughtered in a single night. When a group of men sought sanctuary in the local church, Cromwell ordered the church burned down with them locked inside—an act of such monstrosity that some of his own men risked a charge of mutiny and refused the order. On another day, in **Wexford,** more than 2,000 were murdered, many of them civilians. The trail of destruction rolled on, devastating counties **Galway** and **Waterford.** When asked where the Irish citizens could go to be safe from him, Cromwell famously suggested they could go "to hell or Connaught"—the latter being the most far-flung, rocky, and unfarmable part of Ireland.

After a rampage that lasted 7 months, killing thousands and leaving churches, monasteries, and castles in ruins, Cromwell finally left Ireland in the care of his lieutenants and returned to England. Hundreds of years later, the memory of his infamous violence lingers painfully in Ireland. In certain parts of the country, people still spit at the mention of his name.

The Anti-Catholic Laws

Cromwell died in 1658, and 2 years later the English monarchy was restored. Still, anti-Catholic oppression continued in Ireland. Then in 1685 something remarkable happened: The new Stuart king, **James II,** refused to relinquish his Catholic faith after ascending to the throne. It looked for a while as if Catholic Ireland had found a royal ally at last. However, such hopes were dashed 3 years later, when James was ousted from power, and the Protestant **William of Orange** installed in his place.

James fled to France to raise support for a rebellion and then sailed to Ireland to launch his attack. He struck first at **Derry** (see p. 553), laying siege for 15 weeks, before finally being defeated by William's forces at the **Battle of the Boyne.** The battle effectively ended James's cause, and with it, the hopes of Catholic Ireland for the best part of a century.

After James's defeat, English power was once more consolidated across Ireland. Protestant landowners were granted full political power, while laws were enacted to tamp down the Catholic population. Being a Catholic in late-17th-century Ireland was not exactly illegal per se, but in practice life was all but impossible for those who refused to convert to Protestantism. Catholics could not purchase land, and existing landholdings were split up unless the families who owned them converted to Protestantism. Catholic

Canoeing by Trim Castle on the banks of the Boyne River.

schools were banned, as were priests and all forms of public Catholic worship. Catholics were barred from holding government office, practicing law, or joining the army. Those who refused to relinquish their faith were forced to pay a tax to the Anglican Church. And, because only landowners were allowed to vote, Catholics whose land had been taken away also lost the right to vote.

The new British landlords settled in, planted crops, made laws, and sowed their own seeds. Inevitably, over time, the "Anglos" became the **Anglo-Irish.** Hyphenated or not, they were Irish, and their loyalties were increasingly unpredictable. After all, an immigrant is only an immigrant for a generation; whatever the birthright of the colonists, their children would be Irish-born and bred. And so an uncomfortable sort of stability set in for a generation or three, albeit of a kind that was very much separate and unequal. There were the haves, the wealthy Protestants, and the have-nots, the deprived and disenfranchised Catholics.

This unhappy peace held for some time. But by the end of the 18th century, the appetite for rebellion was whetted again—in the coffee shops and lecture halls of Europe's newest boomtown: **Dublin.**

The United Irishmen & the 1798 Rebellion

By the 1770s, Dublin was thriving as never before. As a center for culture and learning, it was rivaled only by Paris and London; thanks to the work of such architects as Henry Gratton (who designed the **Custom House ★** [p. 111] and the **Four Courts ★** [p. 111]), its very streets were being remodeled in a grand, neoclassical style that was more akin to the great cities of southern Italy than of southern Ireland.

The Custom House dates from the late 18th century.

While the urban classes reveled in their newfound wealth, the stringent **Penal Laws** that had effectively cut off Catholic workers from their own countryside drove many of them to pour into the city, looking for work. Alongside Dublin's buzzing intellectual scene, political dissent soon brewed. Even after a campaign by Irish politicians succeeded in getting many of the Penal Laws repealed in 1783, Dublin was a breeding ground for radicals and political activists. The results were explosive.

When war broke out between Britain and France in the 1790s, the **United Irishmen**—a nonviolent society formed to lobby for Catholic Irishmen to be admitted to the Irish Parliament—sent a secret delegation to persuade the French to intervene on Ireland's behalf against the British. Their emissary in this venture was a Dublin lawyer named **Wolfe Tone.** In 1796 Tone sailed with a French force bound for Ireland, determined to defeat forces loyal to the English crown. As luck would have it, though, they were turned back by storms.

In 1798, full-scale insurrection led by the United Irishmen spread across much of Ireland, particularly the southwestern counties of **Kilkenny** and **Wexford,** where a tiny republic was briefly declared in June in Wexford's Bull Ring square (see p. 223). But it was soon crushed by Loyalist forces, which then went on a murderous spree, killing tens of thousands of men, women, and children and burning towns to the ground. The nadir of the rebellion came when Wolfe Tone, having raised another French invasion force, sailed into Lough Swilly in Donegal and was promptly captured by the British. At his trial, Tone wore the uniform of a French soldier; he slit his own throat while in prison waiting to be hung.

The rebellion was over. In the space of 3 weeks, more than 30,000 Irish had been killed. As a final indignity in what became known as **The Year of the French,** the British tricked the Irish Parliament into dissolving itself, and Ireland reverted to strict British rule.

A Conflict of Conflicts

In 1828, a Catholic lawyer named **Daniel O'Connell**—who had earlier formed the Catholic Association to represent the interests of tenant farmers—was elected to the British Parliament as Member of Parliament for Dublin. (His home, in Caherdaniel, County Kerry, can be visited today—see p. 318.) Public opinion was so solidly behind O'Connell, he was able to persuade the British prime minister that the only way to avoid civil war in Ireland was to force a **Catholic Emancipation Act** through Parliament. O'Connell remained an MP until 1841, when he was elected Lord Mayor of Dublin, a platform he used to push for repeal of the direct rule imposed from London after the 1798 rebellion.

O'Connell organized enormous rallies—nicknamed "monster meetings"—attended by hundreds of thousands and provoked the conservative government to such an extent that it eventually arrested him on charges of seditious conspiracy. The charges were dropped, but the incident—coupled with growing impatience toward his nonviolent approach of protest and reform—led to the breakdown of his power base. "The Liberator," as he had been known, faded, his health failed, and he died on a trip to Rome.

The Great Famine

Even after anti-Catholic legislation began to recede, the vast majority of farmland available to Ireland's poor, mostly Catholic rural population was unfertile and hard to cultivate. One of the few crops that could be grown reliably was the potato, which therefore became the staple diet of the rural poor. So when, in 1845, a fungus destroyed much of the potato crop of Ireland, widespread devastation followed. (In Country Kerry's Dingle Peninsula, the **Irish Famine Cottage**—see p. 338—stands as stark evidence of this desolation.)

To label the **Great Irish Famine** of the 1840s and '50s as merely a "tragedy" would be inadequate. It was, of course, tragic—but at the same time, the word implies a randomness to the whole sorry, sickening affair that fails to capture its true awfulness. The fact is that what started out as crop failure was turned into a disaster by the callous response of the British establishment.

As the potato blight worsened, it became apparent to many landlords that their farm tenants would be unable to pay rent. Instead of helping to feed their now-starving tenants, these landlords shipped their grain overseas, determined to recoup what they were losing in rent. The British Parliament, meanwhile, was reluctant to send aid, putting the reports of a

reading LIST

If you want to know about Ireland and the Irish, plenty of talented writers in and out of the country are willing to tell you.

Jonathan Bardon's *A History of Ireland in 250 Episodes* is a good general introduction to Irish history. The book is broken up into 250 short chapters—learned without being too dense, and a very useful primer.

To understand more about the Famine, try the British author **Cecil Woodham-Smith**'s *The Great Hunger*. Written in 1962, it's still viewed as the definitive dispassionate examination of this dark period in Irish history.

The author **Tim Pat Coogan,** son of an IRA volunteer, has written two excellent books, *The Irish Civil War* (2001) and *The Troubles: Ireland's Ordeal 1966–1996* (1997), both of which are essential reading for anyone wanting to understand the complexities of 21st-century Ireland. He also wrote a controversial biography, *Eamon de Valera*, criticizing the former Irish president's actions and legacy.

For a look at Ireland in recent history, try **John Ardagh**'s *Ireland and the Irish* (1995) or **F. S. Lyons**'s *Ireland Since the Famine* (1973). Or for something original (and slightly irreverent), check out *Ireland's Forgotten Past: A History of the Overlooked and Disremembered* (2020) by **Turtle Bunbury.**

In terms of fiction, *The Spinning Heart,* by **Donal Ryan** (2012), gives an accurate and absorbing account of rural Ireland after the crash of 2008. *The Gathering*, by **Anne Enright** (2007), tells the tale of an Irish family through the medium of a funeral. The Irish writer **Sally Rooney** won the Booker Prize in 2018 for her novel *Normal People*, a love story that speaks on universal themes as well as some specific to Irish life and went on to become a hit TV series. Other recent hits include *Oh My God, What a Complete Aisling*, by **Emer McLysaght** and **Sarah Breen** (2018), a light and irreverent look at the life of young, single women in modern Ireland that is hilarious and delightfully refreshing and has spurred three hit follow-ups, including *Aisling and the City* (2021).

crisis down to, in the words of Prime Minister Robert Peel, "the Irish tendency to exaggerate."

People started to die by the thousands.

Eventually it became clear to the government that something had to be done. Emergency relief was sent to Ireland in the form of cheap, imported Indian cornmeal. However, this contained virtually no nutrients. Ultimately, it was malnutrition that spread such diseases as typhus and cholera, which claimed more victims than starvation itself.

To make matters worse, the cornmeal was not simply given to those in need of it. Fearful that handouts would encourage laziness among the "shiftless poor," the British government forced people to work for their food. Entirely pointless make-work projects were initiated, just to give the starving men something to do for their cornmeal; roads were built that led nowhere, and elaborate follies constructed that served no discernible purpose. Some of these still litter the countryside today, memorials to cruelty and ignorance.

One of the most difficult things to comprehend, more than a century and a half later, is the sheer futility of it all. For behind the statistics, the memorials, and the endless personal anguish lies perhaps the most painful truth of all: that the Famine was easily preventable. Enormous cargoes of imported corn sat in Irish ports for months, until the British government felt that releasing them to the people would not adversely affect market rates. Meanwhile, huge quantities of meat and grain were exported from Ireland. (Indeed, in 1847, cattle exports went up 33% from the previous year.)

Given the circumstances, it is easy to understand why so many chose to leave Ireland. More than a million emigrated over the next decade, about three-quarters of them to America, the rest to Britain or Europe. (In Dublin, both **EPIC, the Irish Emigration Museum** [see p. 113] and the *Jeanie Johnston* **Tall Ship** [see p. 116], and in County Wexford, the **SS *Dunbrody* Famine Ship Experience** [see p. 229] movingly depict this emigration and the grueling journeys involved.) It drained the country. In 1841, Ireland's population was 8 million; by 1851 it was 6.5 million.

The Struggle for Home Rule

As the Famine waned and life returned to something like normality, the Irish independence movement gained new momentum. New fronts, both violent and nonviolent, opened up in the struggle for what was called **Home Rule.** Significantly, the Republicans now drew considerable support from overseas—particularly from America. There, groups such as the **Fenians** fundraised and published newspapers in support of the Irish cause, while more audacious schemes—such as an 1866 "invasion" of Canada with fewer than 100 men—generated awareness, if little else.

Back home in Ireland, partial concessions were won in Parliament. By the 1880s, nationalists such as **Charles Stewart Parnell,** the MP for Meath, were able to unite various factions of Irish nationalists (including the Fenian Brotherhood in America) to fight for Home Rule. In a tumultuous decade of legislation, Parnell came close to winning Home Rule—until revelations about his long affair with Kitty O'Shea, the wife of a supporter, brought about his downfall as a politician.

By 1912, a bill to give Ireland Home Rule was passed through the British House of Commons but was defeated in the House of Lords. Many felt that the political process was all but unstoppable, that it was only a matter of time before the bill passed fully into law. Then World War I broke out in 1914, forcing the issue onto the back burner once again. Many in the Home Rule movement began to grow tired of pursuing their goal through legal political channels.

The Easter Rising

On Easter Monday 1916, a group of nationalists occupied the **General Post Office ★** (p. 112) in the heart of Dublin, from which they proclaimed the foundation of an Irish Republic. Inside were 1,500 fighters, led by schoolteacher and Gaelic League member **Patrick Pearse** and Socialist leader **James Connolly.**

The British government, panicking over an armed uprising on its doorstep while it fought a massive war in Europe, responded with overwhelming force. Soldiers were sent in, and a battle raged in the streets of Dublin for 6 days before the leaders of the rebellion were captured and imprisoned. (The walls of the post office and other buildings and statues up and down O'Connell St. still have bullet holes in them.) Pearse, Connolly, and 12 other leaders were imprisoned, secretly tried, and speedily executed.

Ultimately, though, the harsh British reaction was counterproductive. The ruthlessness with which the rebellion's ringleaders were pursued and dispatched acted as a lightning rod for many who were still on the fence about how best to gain Home Rule. It's a fact that has become somewhat lost in the ensuing hundred or so years: On that cold Monday morning when Patrick Pearse stood on the post office steps to read a treatise on Irish independence, a great many Irish didn't support the rebellion. Many believed that the best course of action was to lay low until the war had ended, when, they felt, concessions would finally be won. Others felt that the uprising was simply the wrong thing to do, as long as sons of Ireland were sacrificing their lives in the trenches of Europe.

The aftermath of 1916 all but guaranteed, for better or for worse, that Ireland's future would be decided by the gun.

Rebellion & the Anglo-Irish Compromise

A power vacuum was left at the heart of the nationalist movement after the Easter Rising, and it was filled by two men: **Michael Collins** (see p. 282) and **Eamon de Valera.** On the surface, the two men had much in common; Collins was a Cork man who had returned from Britain in order to join the Irish Volunteers (later to become the **Irish Republican Army,** or IRA), while de Valera was an Irish-American math teacher who came back to Ireland to set up a new political party, **Sinn Féin.**

When de Valera's party won a landslide victory in the general election of 1918, its MPs took the provocative step of refusing to take their seats in London. Instead, they proclaimed the first **Dáil,** or independent parliament, in Dublin. De Valera went to rally support for the cause in America, while Collins stayed in Ireland to concentrate on his work as head of the Irish Volunteers. Tensions escalated into violence, and for the next 2 years, Irish nationalists fought a tit-for-tat military campaign against the British in Ireland. The low point of the struggle came in 1920, when Collins ordered 14 British operatives to be murdered in their beds. In response, British troops opened fire on the audience at a football game at **Croke Park** in Dublin (see p. 113), randomly killing 12 innocent people.

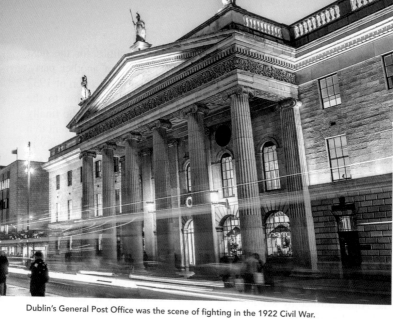
Dublin's General Post Office was the scene of fighting in the 1922 Civil War.

A truce was eventually declared on July 9, 1921. Six months later, the Anglo-Irish treaty was signed in London, granting legislative independence to 26 Irish counties (known collectively as the **Irish Free State**). The compromise through which that freedom was won, though, was that six counties in the north would remain part of the United Kingdom. Sent to negotiate the treaty, Collins knew that that compromise—which he felt was the best deal he could get at the time—would not be accepted by the more strident members of his rebel group. He also knew they would blame him for agreeing to it in the first place. When he signed the treaty he told the people present, "I am signing my own death warrant."

As he feared, nationalists were split between those who accepted the treaty as a platform on which to build, and those, led by the nationalist de Valera, who saw it as a betrayal. The latter group would accept nothing less than immediate and full independence at any cost. Even the withdrawal of British troops from Dublin for the first time in nearly 800 years did not quell their anger. The result was an inexorable slide into civil war. The flashpoint came in April 1922, when violence erupted around the streets of the capital, raging on for 8 days until de Valera's supporters were forced to surrender.

The government of the fledgling free state ordered that Republicans be shot on sight, leading to the deaths of 77 people. And Collins had been right about his own fate: Four months later, he was assassinated while on a visit to his childhood home.

A Republic at Last

The fallout from the Civil War dominated Irish politics for the next decade. De Valera split from the Republicans to form another party, **Fianna Fáil** ("the Warriors of Ireland"), which won the election of 1932 and governed for 17 years. Despite his continuing dedication to the Republican ideal, however, de Valera was not to be the one who finally declared Ireland a republic, in 1948. Ironically, that distinction went to a coalition led by de Valera's opponent, **Douglas Hyde.** Hyde's victory in the 1947 election was attributed to the fact that de Valera had become too obsessed with abstract Republican ideals to govern effectively.

One of the more controversial decisions that Eamon de Valera made while in office was to stay neutral during World War II. His reasons for this decision included Ireland's relatively small size and economic weakness, as well as a protest against the British presence in Northern Ireland. Although that may have made sense to some extent, it left Ireland in the peculiar position of tacitly favoring one side in the war but refusing to help it. After the death of Adolf Hitler in April 1945, de Valera alienated the Allies further by sending his personal sympathies to the German ambassador. His stance didn't find much favor among the Irish population, either. During the war, as many as 300,000 Irish men still found ways to enlist, in the British or U.S. armies. In the end, more than 50,000 Irish soldiers perished in a war their country had refused to join.

Trouble on the Way

After the war, 2 decades passed without violence in Ireland. Then, in the late 1960s, sectarian conflict erupted in the North. What started out as a civil rights movement, demanding greater equality for Catholics within Northern Ireland, soon escalated into a cycle of violence that lasted for 30 years.

It would be a terrible oversimplification to say that the **Troubles** were a clear-cut struggle between those who wanted complete Irish unification and those who wanted to remain part of the United Kingdom. That was, of course, the crux of the conflict. However, many other factors, such as organized crime and terrorism, together with centuries-old conflicts over religious, land, and social issues, make the conflict even harder for outsiders to understand.

The worst of the Troubles came in the 1970s. In 1972, on a day forever remembered as "Bloody Sunday," British troops inexplicably opened fire on a peaceful demonstration in **Derry** (see p. 553), killing 12 people—many of whom were shot while they tended to the wounds of the first people injured. The IRA took advantage of the mood of public outrage to begin a civilian bombing campaign on the British mainland. The cycle of violence continued for 20 years, inexorably and depressingly. All the while, none of the myriad sides in the conflict would talk to each other.

EVERYONE,
REPUBLICAN
& OTHERWISE
IS THEIR OWN
PARTICULAR
ROLE TO PLAY

...OUR
REVENGE
WILL BE THE
LAUGHTER
OF OUR
CHILDREN

Bobby Sands MP
POET, GAEILGEOIR, REVOLUTIONARY, IRA VOLUNTEER

Belfast street mural depicting IRA hunger striker Bobby Sands.

Finally, in the early 1990s, secret talks were opened between the British and the IRA, leading to an IRA cease-fire in 1994 (although the cease-fire held only shakily—an IRA bomb in Omagh 4 years later killed 29, the most to die on any single day of the Troubles).

The peace process continued throughout the 1990s, helped significantly by the mediation efforts of U.S. President Bill Clinton, who became more involved in Irish affairs than any president before him. Eventually, on **Good Friday 1998,** a peace accord was finally signed in Belfast. The agreement committed all sides to a peaceful resolution of the conflict in Northern Ireland and reinstated self-government for the region in a power-sharing administration. However, it stopped short of resolving the territorial issue once and for all. In other words, Northern Ireland is still part of the U.K., and will be for the foreseeable future.

To some extent, the conflicts rage more bitterly and more divisively than ever before. The difference is that, with notable exceptions, nowadays they are fought through the ballot box, rather than the barrel of a gun. In 2005 the IRA fully decommissioned its weapons, and officially dissolved itself as a paramilitary unit. Since then, there have been wobbles—including the occasional act of violence by splinter groups who don't want to accept peace—but these have been very few and far between. Queen Elizabeth's visit to Ireland in 2011, and the 2016 decision by the

(Protestant and staunchly pro-British) First Minister of Northern Ireland to attend the centenary celebrations of the Easter Rising in Dublin, have proved hugely symbolic events.

Rebirth

While Northern Ireland struggled to find peace, the Republic of Ireland flourished. The 1990s brought unprecedented wealth and prosperity to the country, thanks in part to European Union subsidies, and partly to a thriving economy, which was nicknamed the **Celtic Tiger** for its new global strength. Ireland became a rich country, increasingly seen as one of the best places in the world to live and work.

However, that boom came crashing down after the banking crisis of 2008. The Irish government was forced to seek financial aid from the European Union, a package worth more than 50% of the whole economy, to save the country from bankruptcy. The op-ed pages of Irish newspapers expressed real feelings of betrayal and a sense of opportunity lost. Things have improved a lot since then, but the crash changed Ireland for good, as much in terms of its character as mere economics.

The past decade has been one in which Ireland has addressed serious questions about its own identity. Certain things that once seemed indelible to Irish society are now evolving, and the country is becoming more socially liberal. The legalization of abortion, once considered anathema here, became a reality in 2018. The influence of the church, while still profound, is less keenly felt than it once was—particularly among the younger generation. One of the most powerful emblems of this change came in 2015, when a referendum to allow **same-sex marriage** passed by a landslide—making this the first country in the world to pass such a law through a popular vote.

IRELAND IN CULTURE

Literature

Ireland holds a place in literature disproportionate to its small size and modest population. Four writers from this tiny country have won the Nobel Prize for literature. Inspired by the country's unique beauty, the inequities of its political system, and its cruel legacy of poverty and struggle, Ireland's authors, poets, and playwrights wrote about the Irish for the Irish, and to raise awareness in the rest of the world. No matter where you live, you've probably been reading about Ireland all your life.

One of the country's best-known early writers was satirist **Jonathan Swift** (see p. 102), who was born in Dublin in 1667. Educated at Trinity College, he left Ireland for England in 1688 to avoid the Glorious Revolution. Though he spent much of his adult life in London, he returned to Ireland when he was over 50 years old, at which point he began to write his most famous works. Greatly moved by the suffering of the poor in

A statue of Irish writer Oscar Wilde in Merrion Square, Dublin.

Ireland, he translated his anger into dark, vicious humor. His tract *A Modest Proposal* is widely credited with inventing satire as we now know it. Swift's best-known works have political undertones—even *Gulliver's Travels* is a political allegory.

Best known for his novel *Dracula,* the novelist and theater promoter **Bram Stoker** was born in Clontarf, a coastal suburb of Dublin, in 1847. As a young man fresh out of Trinity College, he began reviewing theater productions for local newspapers, which is how he met the actor Henry Irving. He spent much of his time promoting and working for Irving, writing novels on the side for extra money. He lived most of his life in England, which largely inspired his work, although it is said that **St. Michan's Church ★★** in Dublin (p. 107), with its ghostly crypt, and **St. Mary's Cathedral ★** in Killarney (p. 300) contributed to *Dracula*'s creepy feel.

Born in Dublin in 1854, **Oscar Wilde** was a successful student at Trinity College, winning a scholarship to continue his studies in England at Oxford. After a flamboyant time there, he graduated with top honors and returned to Ireland, only to lose his girlfriend to Bram Stoker in 1878, after which he left Ireland forever. His writing—including the novel *The Picture of Dorian Gray,* plays including *The Importance of Being Earnest,* and books of poetry—were often overshadowed by his scandalous personal life. Although a statue of him stands in Dublin in **St. Stephen's Green ★** (p. 120), his works were largely inspired by British and French writers, and he spent the majority of his life abroad.

George Bernard Shaw was born in Dublin in 1856 and attended school in the city, but never went to college. He developed a self-taught literary style. He moved to England as a young man, giving many of his works a distinctly English feel. His plays are known both for their sharp wit and for their sense of outrage over unfairness in society and the absurdity of the British class system. He is the only person ever to have won both the Nobel Prize and an Oscar (for *Pygmalion*).

Born in Sandy Mount outside Dublin in 1865, **William Butler Yeats** attended the Metropolitan School of Art in Dublin, but his poetry and prose were heavily inspired by County Sligo, where he spent much of his time (and where he is buried, in **Drumcliffe** churchyard; p. 455). One of the leading figures of the Irish literary revival in the early 20th century, he won the Nobel Prize in 1923.

James Joyce was born in the Dublin suburb of Rathgar in 1882 and educated at Jesuit boarding schools, and later at Trinity College. He wrote vividly—and sometimes impenetrably—about Dublin, despite spending much of his life as an expat living nomadically in Europe. His controversial and hugely complex novels *Ulysses* and *Finnegans Wake* are his most celebrated (and least understood) works. They and his collection of short stories, *Dubliners,* touch deeply on the character of the people of Dublin. The **James Joyce Centre** ★ (p. 116) is a mecca for Joyce fans.

The poet and playwright **Samuel Beckett** was born in 1906 in the Dublin suburb of Foxrock and educated at Trinity College. His work, however, was heavily influenced by German and French postmodernists, and he spent much of his life abroad, even serving with the Resistance in France during World War II. Best known for his complex absurdist play *Waiting for Godot,* he won the Nobel Prize in 1969.

The controversial writer, erstwhile terrorist, and all-round bon vivant **Brendan Behan** was born in Dublin in 1923. Behan came by his revolutionary fervor honestly: His father fought in the Easter Rising, and his mother was a close friend of Michael Collins. When he was 14, Behan joined Fianna Éireann, the youth organization of the IRA. An incompetent terrorist, he was arrested on his first solo mission to blow up England's Liverpool Docks when he was 16 years old. His autobiographical book, *Borstal Boy,* describes this period in his life in exquisite detail. His play *The Quare Fellow* made him an international literary star, but he would spend the rest of his life as a jolly, hopeless alcoholic, drinking his way through London, Dublin, and New York, better known for his quick wit and bons mots than for his plays.

Among modern Irish writers, the Nobel Prize–winning poet **Seamus Heaney** may be the best known. Born in 1939 near a small town called Castledawson in Northern Ireland, as a child he won scholarships to boarding school in Derry and later to Queen's University in Belfast. His years studying classic ancient Greek and Latin literature and Anglo-Saxon writing heavily influenced his poetry, but all of his writing is marked by his life in the troubled region where he grew up. His works, including *The Cure at Troy* (based on the works of Sophocles), *The Haw Lantern, The*

Government of the Tongue, and a modern translation of *Beowulf,* earned him the Nobel Prize in 1995. Heaney's death in the summer of 2013 brought an outpouring of affection from fans across the world.

Other contemporary Irish writers include the award-winning novelist and memoirist **Edna O'Brien** (*The Country Girls, House of Splendid Isolation*); **Marian Keyes** (whose hugely popular novels include *Lucy Sullivan Is Getting Married* and *This Charming Man*); **Roddy Doyle** (*The Commitments, Paddy Clarke Ha Ha Ha*); and the late **Maeve Binchy** (*A Week in Winter, Circle of Friends*). Writers making waves lately include **Sally Rooney,** who won the Booker Prize in 2018 for her novel *Normal People.* The novels of **Anne Enright** (*The Gathering*) look at Ireland with sympathy and tremendous beauty. Younger writers on the rise include **Louise O'Neill** (*Only Ever Yours*), whose award-winning young-adult novels offer a bleak look at youth in Ireland, and **Emer McLysaght** and **Sarah Breen** (*Oh My God, What a Complete Aisling*), whose hilarious novels take the exact opposite approach, finding humor in all aspects of young Irish life.

Film & Television

Many controversial, complex, and difficult Irish subjects have been tackled by an international array of directors and actors. Here are some of the better-known ones—and a few obscure gems worth seeking out.

Man of Aran (directed by Robert Flaherty, 1934) is a "docufiction" about life on the Aran Islands. Long respected as a documentary, it's now known that much of it was staged by its American director. Still, it's an interesting view on what the islands looked like in the early 20th century.

Virtually unknown today, *Maeve* (directed by John Davis/Pat Murphy, 1982) is a fascinating piece of Irish independent film from the early 1980s, following an Irish expat in England who decides to return to strife-torn Northern Ireland.

The Commitments (directed by Alan Parker, 1991) may be the most famous Irish musical ever made. With its cast of young, largely inexperienced Irish actors playing musicians dedicated to American soul music, it's a delightful piece of filmmaking.

Michael Collins (directed by Neil Jordan, 1996) is a fine biopic about the Irish rebel, filmed largely on location and starring Irish actor Liam Neeson.

Veronica Guerin (directed by Joel Schumacher, 2003) is a dark, fact-based film (with Australian actress Cate Blanchett doing an excellent Irish accent) about a troubled Irish investigative reporter on the trail of a drug boss.

Intermission (directed by Jim Crowley, 2003) is a lively urban romance filmed on location in Dublin, featuring Irish actor Colin Farrell (talking in his real accent for a change). A great look at Dublin right in the middle of its economic boom.

The Wind That Shakes the Barley (directed by Ken Loach, 2006), with a mostly Irish cast and English director, won the Palme d'Or at Cannes for its depiction of Ireland's early-20th-century fight for independence.

Once (directed by John Carney, 2007) is a touching, Oscar-nominated portrait of two struggling young musicians: an Irish singer (played by actor/musician Glen Hansard) and a Czech piano player trying to make it big in Dublin. The film was subsequently turned into a hit stage musical.

Silence (directed by Pat Collins, 2012) is a meditative, dreamlike art film about a sound recordist who travels deep into the Irish countryside in search of places completely free of manmade sound (spoiler alert: He has a hard time finding any).

Shadow Dancer (directed by James Marsh, 2012) is an exciting spy thriller set in early 1990s Belfast. A hit at the Sundance Film Festival, the film pulls off the rare trick of being about the Troubles without getting bogged down in politics.

71 (directed by Yann Demange, 2014) has been acclaimed as one of the best films about the Troubles in recent years.

The flipside to Northern Ireland in the '70s is beautifully portrayed in ***Good Vibrations*** (directed by Lisa Barros D'Sa and Glenn Layburn, 2013). The film tells the story of Terri Hooley, who opened a record store in the most bombed street in Belfast—the name reflected his optimistic hope that music could bring warring communities together. The store, which is still open on Winetavern Street in Belfast, went on to spawn a successful record label.

Calvary (directed by John Michael McDonagh, 2014) is a controversial drama about a small-town priest who receives a death threat from one of his parishioners, which leads him to discover dark truths about the community he lives in.

Based on a popular TV sitcom, ***Mrs. Brown's Boys D'Movie*** (directed by Ben Kellett, 2014) is a broad, slapstick comedy about a no-nonsense Dublin matriarch. The film became one of the most successful Irish films of the decade at the box office, despite being almost universally derided as terrible by critics (spoiler alert: They're right).

Brooklyn (directed by John Crowley, 2015) is an incredibly touching drama about a young Irish woman who emigrates to New York in the 1950s. The film, adapted from a novel by Colm Tóibín, was nominated for Best Picture at the Oscars in 2016.

Ordinary Love (directed by Lisa Barros D'Sa, 2019) is a searing romantic drama about a married couple faced with an uncertain future after one of them is diagnosed with cancer. Many critics hailed it as one of the best Irish films of the decade.

Although it's set in Scandinavia and England, the rip-roaringly good History Channel drama series ***Vikings*** was almost entirely shot in Ireland.

The stunning scenery is a great way to whet your appetite for exploring the Irish countryside.

Music

Music is inescapable in Ireland, and if you hear a band play in a bar and you like them, we strongly advise you to buy a CD from them.

In the days of Internet radio, the best way to discover new sounds is to tune in to Irish radio stations online. An excellent list of stations that stream live (including links) can be found at **www.radiofeeds.co.uk/ irish.asp**. Good places to start are the stations run by **RTÉ,** the national broadcaster, particularly the music and entertainment-oriented **2FM** (www.rte.ie/2fm); **Today FM** (www.todayfm.com), a national station that's extremely popular with a young demographic; and **TXFM** (www. txfm.ie), a Dublin-based station that specializes in the latest indie and alternative sounds.

Some cool, quintessentially Irish names to check out, both in and out of the mainstream: **Damien Rice,** who has risen to huge chart success over the past decade; **Lisa Hannigan,** a singer-songwriter with a line in infectiously romantic indie-pop; **Hozier,** a singer-songwriter from County Wicklow who has been making waves globally since 2014; **Burnt Out,** an angsty, artsy pair of indie-punk-influenced artists whose work is deeply

Traditional music session in a pub in Donegal.

rooted in Dublin's working-class culture; rapper **Jafaris,** part of an interesting new wave of Irish hip-hop artists; **Lyra,** a Cork native whose music draws comparisons to Enya and Kate Bush; **Soak,** an absurdly talented young Derry native who's been wowing the music world with her simple but enchantingly beautiful ballads; and **Eden,** an electronic music producer and songwriter who burst onto the international scene in 2016 and has been selling out venues across the world.

At the same time, traditional music is alive and well in Ireland, particularly in close association with Irish step dancing. The folk culture is primarily found outside of Dublin, although some pubs in the city do still showcase traditional music. Good places to catch live music are the coastal village of **Doolin,** in County Clare (p. 353), the lively pubs of **Cork City** (p. 261), and the town of **Ballyshannon** in County Donegal (p. 469). Local pubs in small towns almost always can be counted on to host Irish music and sometimes dancing, too.

Social Media

Users of social media, particularly Twitter, can absorb a sense of what modern-day Ireland is really like through the tweets of journalists, thinkers, and just ordinary folk with something to say. Good Irish accounts include **Hozier** (@Hozier), the delightful Wicklow-born singer-songwriter; the constantly laugh-out-loud funny author **Marian Keyes** (@MarianKeyes); **Colm Tóibín** (@colmtobin), a writer with bone-dry wit who just happens to share the name of a famous author (a frequent cause of misadventure); **Panti Bliss** (@Pantibliss), a Dublin drag queen and activist; radio host **Louise McSharry** (@louisemcsharry), known for discovering some of the hottest talents in Irish music; **Sharon Horgan** (@SharonHorgan), an Irish comedian, mostly based in London, known for her hilarious sketches and hit sitcom *Catastrophe;* **Aisling Bea** (@WeeMissBea), another big name in the new wave of Irish stand-up comics; and **Amy Huberman** (@amyhuberman), an actress who describes herself as "10% exhausted, 10% feared, and 80% chocolate."

EATING & DRINKING IN IRELAND
Restaurants

Restaurants in Ireland are surprisingly expensive. The cost of eating out here is still well above the European average. On the plus side, Ireland's restaurants are varied and interesting—settings range from old-world hotel dining rooms, country mansions, and castles to sky-lit terraces, shopfront bistros, riverside cottages, thatched-roof pubs, and converted houses. Lately, appreciation has grown for creative cooking with an emphasis on locally grown produce and meat.

Before you book a table, here are a few things you should know.

- If you want to try a top-rated restaurant but can't afford dinner, have your main meal there in the middle of the day by trying the **set-lunch menu.** You'll experience the same great cuisine at half the price.

- Try **pub food.** Pub menus usually include a mix of sandwiches and traditional Irish food, including stews and meat pies. In recent years, many pubs have converted or expanded into restaurants, serving excellent, unpretentious meals at (somewhat) reasonable prices. Check the menu before you sit down at a table (most places post them by their doors).

- Supermarkets and grocery stores in Ireland sell good **premade sandwiches** (much better than supermarket sandwiches in the U.S.) for a few euro. These can make a good, cheap lunch or dinner.

RESERVATIONS   Except for self-service eateries, informal cafes, and some popular seafood spots, most restaurants encourage reservations; most expensive restaurants require them. In the most popular places, Friday and Saturday nights are often booked up a week in advance, so have a few options in mind if you're booking at the last minute.

PRICES   Meal prices at restaurants include national sales taxes (universally referred to as VAT, or Value Added Tax), at the rate of 13.5% in the Republic of Ireland and 20% in Northern Ireland. Many restaurants include the tip as a service charge added automatically to the bill (usually listed at the bottom, just before the bill's total); it generally ranges from 10% to 15%. When no service charge is added, tip around 12% or so, depending on the quality of the service. But do check your bill—some unscrupulous restaurants do not make it clear that you have already tipped, thus causing you to inadvertently tip twice.

The price categories used in this book are based on the price of a complete dinner (or lunch, if dinner is not served) for one person, including tax and tip, but not wine or alcoholic beverages.

DINING TIPS   Don't be surprised if you are not ushered to your table as soon as you arrive at some upscale restaurants. This is not a delaying tactic—many of the better dining rooms carry on the old custom of seating you in a lounge while you sip an aperitif and peruse the menu. Your waiter then comes to discuss the choices and to take your order. You are not called to the table until the first course is about to be served. You are not under an obligation to have a cocktail, of course. It's perfectly fine to order a soft drink or just a glass of water.

Pubs

The pub is a mainstay of Irish social life—every city, town, and hamlet have a pub. Most people have a "local"—a favorite pub near home—where they go for a drink and conversation with neighbors, family, and friends. Pubs are more about socializing than drinking, and many people you see are just having a soft drink (lime cordial and soda water is a favorite, or orange juice and lemon soda). So even if you don't drink alcohol, feel free to go to the pub. It's a good way to meet the locals.

PUB HOURS   Pubs in the Republic set their own hours, although closing times are bound by the type of alcohol license they have. Those with a regular license must shut by 11:30pm from Sunday to Thursday, and 12:30am on Friday and Saturday. Those with late licenses can stay open until 2:30am Monday to Saturday and until 2am on Sunday. In Northern Ireland (which is governed by different laws), hours are slightly more restrictive, although this is currently the subject of debate. On Friday and Saturday nights, many pubs stay open until midnight or 1am, and a few even later than that, particularly in large towns and cities. It should also be noted that legal closing times can be hard to police in rural areas.

You'll notice that when "closing time" comes around, nobody clears out of the pub. "Closing time" is simply the time when the barmen must stop serving alcohol—often indicated by pub lights flickering briefly or a bartender shouting out "Last orders!" Anyone wanting to order one last drink does so then. You'll have about 20 to 30 minutes to finish before the pub closes. Eventually, bartenders shout "Time please!," lights are turned up brightly, and patrons head to the exit.

A seafood tower pairs well with a pint of stout in a Dublin pub.

TIPS ON ACCOMMODATIONS

Foreign visitors to Ireland should always have at least their first night's room booked, since you will be required to give an address at Immigration when you arrive at the airport. If you need help finding accommodations for subsequent nights once you're in Ireland, contact the local tourism office as soon as possible.

Booking in advance is your best strategy anyway, especially in the summer, when prices can spike up and fall within the course of a week. If you book a month or two in advance, you can often get a better rate at a 4-star hotel than at a 2-star guesthouse—the most expensive hotels often offer in-advance discounts of up to 50%. So before you book that cheap hotel with no services, just have a peek at your dream hotel's prices and see if it's not as cheap, or maybe even cheaper.

Accommodations in Ireland range widely in quality and cost. Often these variations are due to location: A wonderful budget B&B in an isolated area of countryside may be dirt-cheap, while a mediocre guesthouse in Dublin or Cork may cost much more. Even in the same lodging, the size and quality of the rooms can vary, especially in older hotels and houses converted to B&Bs. Don't be discouraged by this, but do a little research so you know what you're booking.

Among your various options, **B&Bs** are often hard to beat. These smaller lodgings, usually in residential areas, can be charming and homey—we list several of the best in this book. Breakfast is included in the rate, and it's often hearty. Note that while most B&Bs are regulated and inspected by Ireland's Tourism Quality Services (look for the shamrock seal of approval), many perfectly fine establishments choose not to pay the annual fee that the stamp of approval requires—so don't assume that a place without the shamrock is subpar. **Hidden Ireland** (www.hiddenireland.com; ℂ 098/66650) is a collection of particularly elegant and unique B&Bs on the higher end of the price spectrum. Another interesting option if you're traveling in the countryside, especially if you're with children, is a stay in a **farmhouse B&B** on a family-run farm. Contact **B&B Ireland** (www.irishfarmholidays.com) for an annual guide to farmhouse accommodations. For something more high end, **Ireland's Blue Book** (www.irelands-blue-book.ie; ℂ 01/676-9914) has a great list of Irish country-house hotels, manors, and castles.

If you want to stay awhile and establish a base, consider renting a **self-catering** apartment, townhouse, or cottage. Self-catering is a huge business in Ireland. The minimum rental period is usually 1 week, although shorter periods are negotiable in the off-season. Families especially appreciate the convenience of having more room to spread out and a kitchen for preparing meals. **Rent an Irish Cottage** (www.rentacottage.ie; ℂ 061/411-109) offers a selection of traditional cottages all over Ireland, fully modernized. The not-for-profit **Irish Landmark Trust** (www.

irishlandmark.com; © **01/670-4733**) offers historic properties, refurbished in period style, at prices lower than you might expect. On the more opulent end of the scale, **Elegant Ireland** (www.elegant.ie; © **01/473-2505**) has anything from a chic seaside bungalow to a medieval castle with room for you and 20 of your BFFs.

Nowadays, Ireland's **hostels** are redesigning to attract travelers of all ages, including families. Many have private rooms and may cost a fraction of even a modest bed-and-breakfast. Contact **An Óige**, the Irish Youth Hostel Association (www.anoige.ie), or, in the North, **HINI** (Hostelling International Northern Ireland; www.hini.org.uk), for listings.

WHEN TO GO

A visit to Ireland in the summer is very different from a trip in the winter. Generally speaking, in summer, airfares, car-rental rates, and hotel prices are highest and crowds are at their most intense. But the days are long (6am sunrises and 10pm sunsets), the weather is warm, and every sightseeing attraction and B&B is open. In winter, you may get rock-bottom prices on airfare and hotels, but it will rain, and the wind will blow, and many rural sights and a fair proportion of rural B&Bs and restaurants will be closed.

All things considered, we think the best time to visit is in spring and fall when the weather falls in between seasons, but prices are lower than in high season and the crowds have yet to descend.

Weather

Rain is the one constant in Irish weather, although a bit of sunshine is usually just around the corner. The best of times and the worst of times are often only hours, or even minutes, apart. It can be chilly in Ireland at any time of year, so think *layers* when you pack.

Winters can be brutal, as the wind blows in off the Atlantic with numbing constancy, and strong gales are common. But deep snow is rare, and temperatures rarely drop much below freezing. In fact, Ireland is a fairly temperate place: January and February bring frosts but seldom snow, and July and August are very warm but rarely hot. The Irish consider any temperature over 68°F (20°C) to be "roasting" and below 34°F (1°C) bone-chilling.

Average Monthly Temperatures in Dublin

	JAN	FEB	MAR	APR	MAY	JUNE	JULY	AUG	SEPT	OCT	NOV	DEC
TEMP (°F)	36–46	37–48	37–49	38–52	42–57	46–62	51–66	50–65	48–62	44–56	39–49	38–47
TEMP (°C)	2–8	3–9	3–9	3–11	6–14	8–17	11–19	10–18	9–17	7–13	4–9	3–8

Holidays

The Republic observes the following national holidays, also known as Bank Holidays: New Year's Day (Jan 1); St. Patrick's Day (Mar 17); Easter Monday (variable); May Day (May 1); first Mondays in June and August (summer Bank Holidays); last Monday in October (autumn Bank Holiday); Christmas (Dec 25); and St. Stephen's Day (Dec 26). Good Friday (the Fri before Easter) is also observed. In the North, the schedule of holidays is the same as in the Republic, with some exceptions: The North's summer Bank Holidays fall on the last Monday of May and August; the Battle of the Boyne is celebrated on Orangeman's Day (July 12); and Boxing Day (Dec 26) follows Christmas.

In both Ireland and Northern Ireland, holidays that fall on weekends are celebrated the following Monday.

Ireland Calendar of Events

For the most up-to-date listings of events, check out **www.discoverireland.ie** and **www.entertainment.ie**. Note that some festivals may be temporarily suspended or postponed depending on current Covid-19 protocols and restrictions—always check in advance.

JANUARY

First Fortnight. Nationwide. This innovative festival challenges mental-health stigmas through art and culture. Events include plenty of comedy, music, and theater. (www.firstfortnight.ie; ✆ **01/598-6263**). Early January.

Funderland. Royal Dublin Society, Ballsbridge, Dublin. An annual indoor fun fair, with white-knuckle rides, carnival stalls, and family entertainment (www.funderland.com; ✆ **01/485-3045**). Smaller events in Cork, Limerick, and Belfast later in the year; check website for details.

Tradfest. Temple Bar, Dublin. Ireland's largest traditional music festival features exhibitions, film screenings, master classes—and, of course, a lot of concerts. Most events take place in Temple Bar, but some are held farther afield. Late January.

FEBRUARY

Virgin Media Dublin International Film Festival. Irish Film Centre, Temple Bar, and various cinemas in Dublin. Ten days of screenings of more than 100 films, from both Ireland and abroad, plus seminars and lectures on filmmaking (www.

diff.ie; ✆ **01/662-4260**). Late February and early March.

MARCH

St. Patrick's Dublin Festival. This massive 4-day festival is open, free, and accessible to all. Street theater, carnival acts, sports, music, fireworks, and other festivities culminate in Ireland's grandest parade, with marching bands, drill teams, floats, and delegations from around the world (www.stpatricksday.ie; ✆ **01/604-0090**). On and around March 17.

St. Patrick's Day Parades. Held all over Ireland and Northern Ireland, celebrating Ireland's patron saint. March 17.

APRIL

Cúirt International Festival of Literature. Galway City. One of Ireland's most established literary festivals, Cúirt takes place over a week in Galway. The packed lineup includes panels, talks, spoken-word events, and theater (www.cuirt.ie). Mid- to late April.

Pan Celtic Festival. For 5 days, the wider Celtic family (including Cornwall, Isle of Man, Scotland, Wales, and Brittany) unites for culture, song, dance, sports, and parades with marching bands and pipers. The festival moves to a different part of a Celtic nation or region every year—but Ireland is a frequent host (www.panceltic.ie). April.

World Irish Dancing Championships. Belfast. The premier international competition in Irish dancing features more than 4,000 contenders from as far away as New Zealand (www.clrg.ie). April.

Dublin Dance Festival. Very much an international event, the DDF hosts dancers from around the globe as part of its innovative program, which has the self-proclaimed intention to "unlock new perspectives on our changing world" (www.dublindancefestival.ie; ☎ **028/679-8658**). Late May/November.

Belfast City Marathon. This 42km (26-mile) race of 17,000 international runners through the city starts at City Hall and finishes at the Maysfield Recreation Centre (www.belfastcitymarathon.com; ☎ **028/9060-5933**). Early May.

International Literature Festival Dublin. One of the biggest events in the Irish arts calendar, this 9-day festival draws high-profile authors from around the world. Events take place at venues across the city, including Dublin Castle (www.ilfdublin.com; ☎ **01/415-1295**). Mid-May.

The Cat Laughs Comedy Festival. Various venues, Kilkenny Town. Past performers at this international festival of stand-up comedy include American comics Bill Murray, George Wendt, and Emo Phillips, and Ireland's Dara O'Briain (www.thecatlaughs.com). Late May/early June.

Carlow Arts Festival. This eclectic 10-day festival includes something for everyone, from visual arts, theater, and music to virtual reality and circus performances. Many events are family-friendly, and almost everything is completely free (www.carlowartsfestival.com; ☎ **083/400-6112**). Early June.

Taste of Dublin. Iveagh Gardens, Dublin. One of Ireland's biggest and most high-profile food festivals, where for 4 days visitors can sample dishes prepared by some of the country's top chefs and over 100 artisan producers. The event is usually a sellout, so booking is advisable (dublin.tastefestivals.com). Mid-June.

Bloomsday Festival. Various Dublin venues. This unique daylong fest celebrates Leopold Bloom, the central character of James Joyce's *Ulysses*, by replicating the aromas, sights, sounds, and tastes of Dublin on June 16, 1904, the day when *Ulysses* takes place. Ceremonies are held at the James Joyce Tower and Museum; guided walks visit Joycean sights (www.bloomsdayfestival.ie). June 11–16.

Cork Midsummer Arts Festival. Emmet Place, Cork City. The program includes musical performances and traditional Irish *céilí* bands, and always has a strong literary content. Bonfire nights are particularly popular (www.corkmidsummer.com; ☎ **021/421-5131**). Mid-June.

Hinterland Festival. Kells, County Meath. Devoted to literature and the arts, Hinterland draws an increasingly high-profile guest list, including famous Irish writers (www.hinterland.ie; ☎ **089/436-9868**). Late June.

Irish Derby. The Curragh, County Kildare. Ireland's version of the Kentucky Derby or Royal Ascot is a fashionable gathering (**Hint:** jackets for men, posh hats for women) of racing fans from all over the world. It's one of the richest middle-distance horse races in Europe. Booking recommended (www.curragh.ie; ☎ **045/441-205**). Late June.

West Cork Chamber Music Festival. Bantry, County Cork. One of the biggest classical music festivals in Ireland, this presents a huge program of concerts, including work from the best up-and-coming new classical artists (www.westcorkmusic.ie; ☎ **027/52788**). Late June.

Galway International Arts Festival. Galway City. This 2-week fest features international theater, concerts, literary evenings, street shows, arts, parades, and music (www.giaf.ie; ☎ **091/509700**). Mid-July.

Tread Softly. Sligo Town, County Sligo. The mythical landscape of Sligo is the inspiration for this 2-week festival celebrating the region's folklore and arts. Highlights include storytelling, guided walks, and art exhibitions (www.tread softly.ie). Late July or early August.

AUGUST

Fleadh Cheoil na hÉireann. Ireland's premier summer festival of traditional music since 1951 changes its host city every year. Competitions are held to select all-Ireland champions in all categories of instruments and singing. Visit **https:// fleadhcheoil.ie** to find out this year's location. Early to mid-August.

Lughnasa Fair. Carrickfergus Castle, County Antrim. On the grounds of this 12th-century Norman castle, this event features people in period costumes, medieval games, traditional food, entertainment, and crafts. Early August.

Kilkenny Arts Festival. Kilkenny Town. Weeklong event has classical and traditional music, plays, readings, films, poetry, and art exhibitions (www.kilkenny arts.ie). Early to mid-August.

Puck Fair. Killorglin, County Kerry. In one of Ireland's oldest festivals, the residents of this tiny Ring of Kerry town (see p. 292) capture a wild goat and enthrone it as "king" over 3 days of merrymaking—open-air concerts, horse fairs, parades, and fireworks (www.puckfair.ie; ✆ **066/976-2366**). August 10–12.

Rose of Tralee International Festival. Tralee, County Kerry. A gala atmosphere prevails at this 5-day event (see p. 327), with a full program of concerts, street entertainment, horse races, and a beauty-and-talent pageant leading up to the televised selection of the "Rose of Tralee" (www.roseoftralee.ie). Late August.

National Heritage Week. More than 400 events are held throughout the country—including walks, lectures, exhibitions, music recitals, and open-house days at historic buildings (www.heritageweek.ie; ✆ **185/020-0878**). Mid- to late August.

Electric Picnic. Stradbally, County Laois. This midsize music festival, held on the grounds of Stradbally Hall, is known for its eclectic lineup. Recent acts have included Sonic Youth, St. Vincent, and Rage Against the Machine. Book early—tickets for the 2020 fest sold out within 3 hours of going on sale the previous December (www.electricpicnic.ie). Early September.

Irish Antique & Fine Art Fair. The Royal Dublin Society, Ballsbridge, Dublin. Ireland's premier annual antiques fair, with hundreds of dealers from all over the island (www.iada.ie; ✆ **087/693-3602**). Usually in September.

Dublin Fringe Festival. "Art is a power tool—start digging" proclaimed the website of the 2020 edition of this super-cool fringe festival. Pretty much sums up the vibe. Expect cutting-edge theater and other live performances over 2 weeks (www.fringefest.com; ✆ **01/670-6106**). Mid-September.

Galway International Oyster and Seafood Festival. The highlights of this festival include the World Oyster Opening Championship, a grand opening parade, a yacht race, an art exhibition, a gala banquet, traditional music, and, of course, lots of oyster eating (www. galwayoysterfest.com; ✆ **091/394637**). Late September.

Dublin Theatre Festival. Showcases for new plays by every major Irish company, plus productions from abroad (https:// dublintheatrefestival.ie; ✆ **01/677-8439**). Late September/mid-October.

OCTOBER

Kinsale Gourmet Festival. Kinsale, County Cork. The foodie capital of Ireland hosts this well-respected annual fest, featuring special menus in all the restaurants and plenty of visiting star chefs (www.kinsalerestaurants.com; ✆ **087/167-1004**). Mid-October.

Baboró International Arts Festival for Children. Galway. A fun-filled, educational festival geared to kids 3 to 12 years of age, with theater, music, dance, museum exhibitions, and literary events (www.baboro.ie; ℂ 091/562-667). Mid-October.

Guinness Cork Jazz Festival. Cork City. Ireland's second city stages a first-rate festival of jazz, with an international lineup of live acts playing in hotels, concert halls, and pubs (www.guinness jazzfestival.com). Late October.

Bram Stoker Festival. Dublin. Bigger than you might expect, this 4-day celebration of the author of *Dracula* includes giant art installations, open-air film screenings, parades, and other Gothic fun (www.bramstokerfestival.com). Late October.

Wexford Festival Opera. Wexford, County Wexford. Famous as much for its jubilant, informal atmosphere as for acclaimed productions of lesser-known 18th- and 19th-century operatic masterpieces, this festival also has classical-music concerts and more (www.wexfordopera.com; ℂ 053/912-2144). Late October/early November.

NOVEMBER

Cork International Film Festival. Cinemas throughout Cork. Now in its 76th year, Ireland's oldest film festival offers a plethora of international features, documentaries, short films, and special programs (www.corkfilmfest.org; ℂ 021/427-1711). Early to mid-November.

DECEMBER

Christmas Markets. You'll find Christmas fairs all over Ireland from late November through December. A handful of the best: **Killarney, Cork, Galway City, Waterford City,** and **Belfast.** Expect quality local crafts, food, and general festive magic and sparkle. December.

DUBLIN

4

Dublin is an ancient city with a young soul. Its grand old buildings line the banks of the River Liffey and the streets beyond. It has cathedrals, universities, pubs and museums that are hundreds of years old. But the Irish capital is also one of Europe's most youthful cities, with a large population of university students and young workers. In fact, Dublin is the island's most cosmopolitan city by far. This vibrant, modern, European capital wears that status on its sleeve. Busy bars and snazzy restaurants buzz alongside traditional pubs that have stood their ground for centuries. Chic boutiques and cafes fill medieval streets and historic buildings. Glass-and-steel offices holding the European headquarters of the world's biggest tech companies shine in the newly regenerated docklands. This captivating city is yours to discover—and even if you think you know what to expect, you'll always be surprised by what you find.

ESSENTIALS

Arriving

BY PLANE   Aer Lingus (www.aerlingus.com; ✆ **0818/365-000**), Ireland's national airline, operates regular, direct scheduled flights between Dublin Airport and numerous cities worldwide. From the United States, direct routes include Boston, Chicago, Hartford, Los Angeles, Miami, Minneapolis-St. Paul, New York (JFK and Newark), Philadelphia, Seattle, San Francisco, and Washington, D.C. (Not all of these routes operate in winter.) On the return journey, passengers bound for the U.S. may pre-clear customs and immigration at Dublin airport (meaning you get to skip passport control on the American side). **American Airlines** (www.aa.com; ✆ **800/433-7300**), **Delta** (www.delta.com; ✆ **800/241-4141**), and **United** (www.united.com; ✆ **800/864-8331**) all fly direct to Dublin from at least one of those same cities. From Canada, direct flights are operated by **Air Canada** (www.aircanada.com; ✆ **888/247-2262**). From Australia and New Zealand, **Quantas** (www.qantas.com; ✆ **13-13-13**) and **Air New Zealand** (www.airnewzealand.co.nz; ✆ **080/0737-000**) both fly to Dublin, with at least one change. Virtually all of the major European airlines have direct flights to Dublin.

PREVIOUS PAGE: **St. Ann's Church on South Anne Street.**

TRAVEL disruptions IN DUBLIN

As the country's capital city, Dublin has been hit relatively hard by the coronavirus pandemic, but a comprehensive and timely public health response has resulted in high levels of citizen compliance. Still, virtually any travel guidance for Dublin should appear with the suffix "but call ahead or check the website for the most current information." The situation with pandemic-related closures and operational changes remains fluid. We've always encouraged readers to buy tickets in advance for the attractions they really want to see; that advice is even more pertinent now. Most museums and attractions require advance booking, so venues can control numbers and avoid long lines; a maximum of six people from a family or social unit is allowed per booking. Attendance is limited at theaters and sports arenas.

Currently, an **EU Digital COVID Certificate (COVID pass)** vaccine or recovery certificate (or non-EU proof-of-vaccine equivalent) is required for entry into hotel bars and restaurants, indoor events, cinemas and theaters, and gyms. You are required to wear face coverings in all public transport and in shops, libraries, theaters, museums, concert halls, banks, airports, and government buildings; exemptions include children under 9. Currently, the Irish government has instigated an 8pm curfew for restaurants, pubs, and organized indoor events. Look for businesses bearing the white and green logo of the Safety Charter, which indicates that the staff adheres to strict hygiene measures. See p. 578 for more on Ireland protocols. Before you go, check the updated Covid pages at **www.gov.ie**.

Dublin Airport (www.dublinairport.com; ☏ **01/814-1111**) is 11km (6¾ miles) north of the city center. A travel information desk in the arrivals concourse provides information on public bus and rail services throughout the country. All major international and local car-rental companies operate desks at Dublin Airport. There is no rail service from Dublin airport.

For speed and ease—especially if you have a lot of luggage—a **taxi** is the best way to get directly to your hotel or guesthouse from the airport. It is the most expensive, however. Depending on your destination, taxi fares to the city center average between €25 and €35, plus €1 for each additional passenger (but they shouldn't charge you extra for luggage). Fares are more expensive from 8pm to 8am. A tip of a couple of euro is standard. Cabs are lined up at a first-come, first-served taxi stand directly outside the arrivals terminal (turn right as you walk out the door—you can't miss it).

The **Dublin Express** (www.dublinexpress.ie; ☏ **01/903-9508**) runs express coach services from the airport to 10 different stops in the city center. Services from the airport run every 30 minutes between 4:05am and 11:05pm. It takes about 30 minutes (in light traffic) to travel from the airport to the city. A one-way fare from the airport is €8 for an adult and €3 for a child; a return is even better value at €9 for an adult and €4 for a

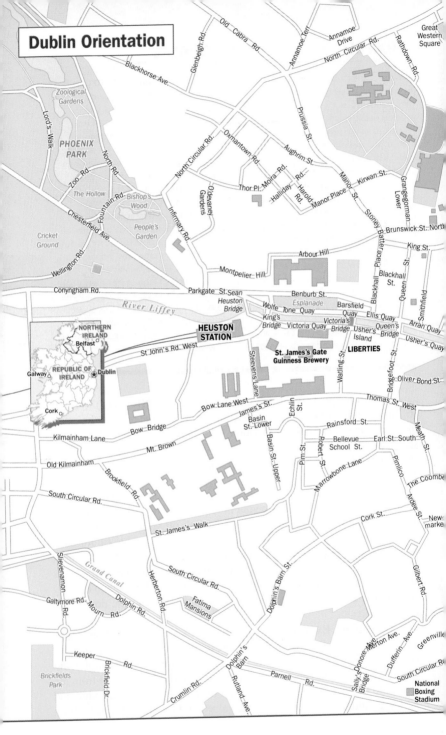

Dublin Orientation

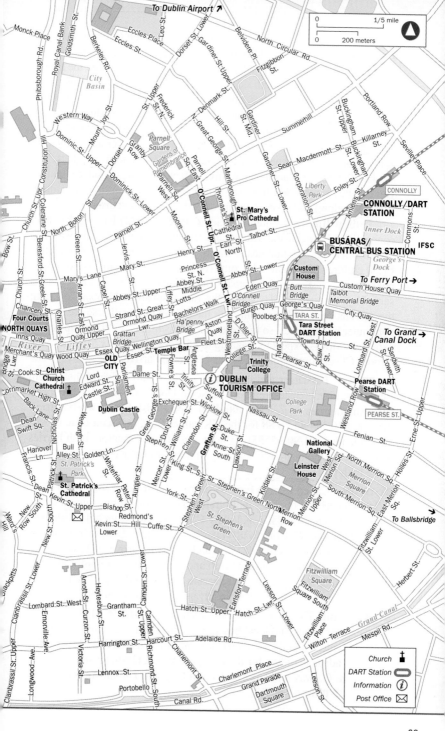

child. Another excellent shuttle bus service **AirCoach** (www.aircoach.ie; ℘ **01/844-7118**) operates 24 hours a day, making runs every 15 minutes (hours can vary, so check in advance). Its buses go direct from the airport to Dublin's city center, south side, and Greystones. Not all the major stops are covered on every service, so do check that you've got the right one before you board. City-center fares are €8 one-way, depending on where you are going; fares to Ballsbridge, Leopardstown, or Killiney/Dalkey are up to €11 (€2.50–€4 children 5–12; children 13 and over are counted as adults), and return tickets are better value than two one-way tickets. You can buy tickets in advance on the AirCoach website to guarantee a seat, or you can buy your ticket from the driver. AirCoach is faster than Dublin Bus (see below) and takes travelers directly to the hotel districts.

Dublin Bus (www.dublinbus.ie; ℘ **01/873-4222**) has regular daily connections between the airport and the city center. The one-way trip takes from around 50 minutes upwards, with fares starting at €3.30 adults, €1.30 children. Payment is in coins (not notes), and change is not given, but fares are cheaper with a prepaid **Leap Card** (p. 90). The city center is served by routes 16 and 41. The 16 bus runs from around 5:30am to 11pm; the 41 runs every half-hour through the day and night. These are normal commuter bus services, so luggage capacity is limited, and the trip can be extremely slow—expect to make up to 35 stops on the way to or from the airport. Check routes and timetables before you arrive.

BY FERRY Passenger and car ferries from Britain arrive at the Dublin Ferryport, on the eastern end of the North Docks. Contact **Irish Ferries** (www.irishferries.ie; ℘ **0818/300-400**), **P&O Irish Sea** (www.poferries. com; ℘ **44/1304 44 88 88** for the UK call center), or **Stena Line** (www. stenaline.ie; ℘ **01/907-5555**) for bookings and information. Irish Ferries also sails to Dublin from Cherbourg in northern France. Buses and taxis serve both ports.

BY TRAIN Called Iarnród Éireann in Irish, **Irish Rail** (www.irishrail.ie; ℘ **1890/77-88-99**) operates daily train services to Dublin from all major cities and towns in Ireland including Cork, Galway, Limerick, Killarney, Sligo, Westport, Wexford, and Waterford and from Belfast in Northern Ireland. Trains from the south, west, and southwest arrive at **Heuston Station,** St. John's Road; from the north and northwest at **Connolly Station,** Amiens Street; and from the southeast at **Pearse Station,** Westland Row. For the lowest fares, buy tickets in advance from the Irish Rail website.

BY BUS Bus **Éireann** (www.buseireann.ie; ℘ **01/836-6111**) operates daily express coach and local bus service from all major cities and towns in Ireland into Dublin's central bus station, **Busáras,** on Store Street. Buy tickets in advance online for the cheapest prices. **GoBus** runs coach services from Galway and Cork to Dublin City and Dublin Airport (www. gobus.ie; ℘ **091/564-600**).

BY CAR If you are arriving by car from other parts of Ireland or on a car ferry from Britain, all main roads lead into the heart of Dublin and are well-signposted to the City Centre. The quickest way into Dublin from the airport is to take the Dublin Tunnel. The toll for cars is €3 (€10 during peak time, Mon–Fri 6–10am). You can pay using cash (euro or British pounds) or card. To bypass the city center, follow signs to the East Link toll bridge (€1.40) or the M50 highway toll (€3.10). The M50 circuits the city on three sides. From Wexford, Galway, or Belfast the drive takes around 2 hours; from Limerick 2½ hours and from Cork 2½ to 3 hours. Your car-rental agency should inform you of all anticipated tolls.

Spherical sculpture at Trinity College.

Visitor Information

Visit Dublin (www.visitdublin.com; ℃ **1890/324-583**) operates two Discover Ireland tourist offices in Dublin city, at 25 Suffolk St. and 14 Upper O'Connell St. Both are open Monday to Saturday 9am to 5pm.

For guides to what's on in Dublin, see **Lovin Dublin** (www.lovin dublin.com/whats-on), **Dublin Live** (www.dublinlive.ie/whats-on), **Totally Dublin** (www.totallydublin.ie), **Visit Dublin** (www.visitdublin. com/whats-on), and **Dublin.ie** (www.dublin.ie/whats-on).

City Layout

Dublin is divided by the curves of the River Liffey, which flows into the sea at the city's eastern edge. To the north and south, canals encircle the city center: The Royal Canal arcs across the north and the Grand Canal through the south. Traditionally, the area south of the river has been Dublin's buzzing, prosperous hub. It still holds many of the best hotels, restaurants, shops, and sights, but the Northside is on the upswing, and hip new bars and hotels give it a trendy edge.

Dublin is compact and easily walked in an hour. In fact, a 45-minute walk from peaceful St. Stephen's Green, down bustling Grafton Street, and across the Liffey to the top of O'Connell Street offers a good overview of the city's prosperous present and storied past.

The Liffey Boardwalk follows the river's north bank in Central Dublin.

MAIN STREETS & SQUARES   In the town center just south of the river, the main east-west artery is **Dame Street,** which merges with College Green at one end, and Lord Edward Street and on to High Street at the other, as it connects **Trinity College** with **Dublin Castle** and **Christ Church Cathedral.** Just off Dame Street, you'll find the winding medieval lanes of the **Temple Bar** area, Dublin's party central, packed with noisy late-night bars and cheap, cheerful restaurants.

At its eastern end, where Dame Street becomes College Green, the sturdy gray stone walls of **Trinity College** make an excellent landmark to get your bearings. At the southwest corner of the campus is the bottom of **Grafton Street,** a lively pedestrianized thoroughfare lined with clothing boutiques, and side streets with restaurants and pubs. It leads, eventually, to the bucolic park of **St. Stephen's Green.** From there, head back down Kildare Street for museums, or along Merrion Row and down Merrion Street, passing Leinster House (seat of the Irish Parliament) to reach **Merrion Square,** another of Dublin's extraordinarily well-preserved Georgian squares.

To cross the River Liffey and get to the Northside, take the photogenic arch of the **Ha'penny Bridge** (p. 112), or for a bridge wider than it is long, cross at **O'Connell Bridge** nearby. You can be different and cross via the Ha'penny's sleekly modern neighbor, the **Millennium Bridge,** which is beautifully illuminated after dark. O'Connell Bridge leads directly onto broad **O'Connell Street,** the Northside's main thoroughfare. O'Connell Street runs north to **Parnell Square,** which holds a couple of marvelous museums and marks the top edge of central Dublin. The street running along the Liffey's embankment is called the **North Quays** by everyone, though its name changes on virtually every block, reflecting the long-gone docks that once lined it; today a pedestrian boardwalk runs along the riverfront here.

Dublin Neighborhoods in Brief

TRINITY COLLEGE AREA   On the south side of the River Liffey, Trinity College stands at virtually the dead center of the city. Its shady quadrangles and atmospheric stone buildings are surrounded by bookstores, shops, and noisy traffic.

TEMPLE BAR   There are really two Temple Bars, depending on when you visit. During the day, Temple Bar is an artsy, cultured district full of trendy shops and modern art galleries. But such refinement gives way to an altogether more raucous atmosphere at night. With its myriad selection of pubs, bars, and hip clubs, this is definitely where it's at in Dublin after dark.

THE LIBERTIES   The Liberties district takes its name from the fact that it was once just outside the city walls and, therefore, exempt from Dublin's jurisdiction. Although it prospered in its early days, the Liberties fell on hard times in the 17th and 18th centuries and stayed that way for centuries. Today it is undergoing regeneration with the opening of new hotels and distilleries. For visitors, its main attraction is the Guinness Brewery.

ST. STEPHEN'S GREEN/GRAFTON STREET AREA   One of the main tourist areas of the city, this district is home to Dublin's finest hotels, restaurants, and shops. Filled with impressive Georgian architecture, today it is primarily a business and shopping zone.

KILDARE STREET & MERRION SQUARE   Between Trinity College and St. Stephen's Green, this area is where you'll find the National Gallery, National Library, and two national museums. Leafy Merrion Square and its neighbor Fitzwilliam Square are surrounded by grand Georgian town

Murky Origins

For most visitors, the very word "Dublin" may conjure up a heady, romantic mix of history, but the name actually has a more prosaic origin. It comes from the Irish words *dubh linn*, meaning "the black pool." Specifically, it refers to a natural inlet where the River Liffey met the River Poddle, and the waters were dark and murky. Long since buried, the inlet is thought to be somewhere around Dublin Castle.

An allusion to these watery origins still survives in the city's Irish name, *Baile Átha Cliath*, which means "the town of the hurdled ford"—a ford being a point where a stream or river crosses a road. When fords were "hurdled" in medieval times, it meant that they were covered at low tide with woven sheets of willow, making them easier to cross.

houses, where some of Dublin's most famous citizens once lived; today they house offices for doctors, lawyers, and government agencies.

O'CONNELL STREET (NORTH OF THE LIFFEY)   Lined with statues from bottom to top, O'Connell Street was the epicenter of the 1916 Easter Rising and the 1922 Civil War (bullet holes still pock the statue of its namesake, politician Daniel O'Connell). The surrounding area was fashionable in the 19th century but lost much of its charm as it declined in the 20th century. The wide street has experienced some revitalization in recent years, with many great pubs, restaurants, and theaters within walking distance.

SMITHFIELD   Urban renewal in the 21st century has transformed this formerly seedy market area into a trendy district east of Phoenix Park, with such attractions as the Old Jameson Distillery.

BALLSBRIDGE/EMBASSY ROW   Immediately south of the Grand Canal, this upscale suburb is just barely within walking distance of the city center. Primarily a prestigious residential area, it is also home to hotels, restaurants, and embassies.

THE DOCKLANDS AND THE IFSC   The north and south quays of the River Liffey are home to the gleaming glass-and-steel office and apartment blocks around the International Financial Services Centre (IFSC) on the northside, and Grand Canal Dock on the southside. The new builds include a number of hotels and restaurants. The area is also home to the 3Arena (northside) and Bord Gáis Energy Theatre (southside).

St. Stephen's Green is a serene respite from the Grafton Street shopping crowds.

North Americans may be baffled by this phrase, which you'll see a lot on lists of opening times. It simply means a public holiday, often on a Monday. Many shops (and banks!) are closed or run on reduced hours on Bank Holidays.

Ireland has nine regular Bank Holidays: New Year's Day (Jan 1); St. Patrick's Day (Mar 17); Easter Monday; the first Mondays in every month from May to August, except July; the final Monday in October; Christmas Day (Dec 25); and St. Stephen's Day (Dec 26).

GETTING AROUND

If your stay in Dublin is short, geography is on your side. The vast majority of the capital's top sights are concentrated in the city center, which is small and very walkable. This leads to your first, most important (and quite frankly, easiest) decision: If you have a car, leave it behind at your hotel. Dublin's streets are choked with traffic, with baffling one-way streets and inadequate signage. If your feet get tired, there's a good tram and bus system, and taxis are everywhere.

By Bus

After walking, buses are the most convenient and practical way to get around the city center sights. **Dublin Bus** (www.dublinbus.ie; ℭ **01/873-4222**) operates a fleet of double-deckers and single-deckers. Most originate on or near O'Connell Street, Abbey Street, and Eden Quay on the Northside, and at Aston Quay, College Street, and Fleet Street on the south side. Look for bus-stop markers resembling big yellow lollipops—they're every few blocks on main thoroughfares. To tell where a bus is going, look at the destination street and bus number displayed above its front window.

Bus service runs daily throughout the city, starting at 6am (10am on Sun), with the last bus at about 11:30pm. On Friday and Saturday nights, **Nitelink** service runs from the city center to the suburbs from midnight to 4am. Buses operate every hour for most night runs. Bus schedules are posted on revolving notice boards at bus stops, on www.dublinbus.ie, and on the Dublin Bus app—both the website and app give live updates on the arrival time of the next bus.

Inner-city fares are based on distances traveled. Daytime journeys that take place entirely within the designated "City Centre Zone" cost €0.50. This zone stretches from Parnell Square in the north to Connolly Station and Merrion Square in the east, St. Stephen's Green in the south, and Ormond Quay in the west. Longer journeys cost anywhere up to €4 if you're going as far as the outer suburbs.

4

DUBLIN | Getting Around

Leap Cards

If you're likely to use public transport a lot while in Dublin (which we highly recommend), do as the locals do: Get a **Leap Card,** a prepaid smart card for reduced-cost travel on all Dublin buses (including Nitelink), DART, Luas, and commuter trains. You can buy Leap Cards at some 400 shops in and around the city—look for the distinctive green logo depicting a somewhat over-excited frog in mid-leap. (In Dublin Airport, you can pick one up at the **Easons, Kiosk,** and **Spar** shops.) Ticket machines in some city center DART and railway stations also dispense Leap Cards. Or you can order them online at **www.leapcard. ie**. Unless you're here for more than a week, the best option is to ask for a Leap **Visitor Card,** which allows for unlimited travel on the network—including to and from the airport. It costs €10 for 24 hours, €19.50 for 3 days, and €40 for 7 days. It's valid at any time and the clock doesn't start until you first use it.

You pay on board the bus, using an automatic fare machine located in front of the driver. You can pay with exact change (coins only) or with a smart card known as a **Leap Card** (see below). **No Dublin bus accepts notes or gives change.**

By DART

An acronym for Dublin Area Rapid Transit, the electric DART trains travel above ground, linking the city center stations including **Connolly Station, Tara Street,** and **Pearse** with suburbs and seaside communities. Check a map to see if it serves your area. Service operates roughly every 10 to 20 minutes Monday to Saturday from around 6am to 11:30pm and Sunday 9:30am to 11pm. For further information, check the DART website (www.dart.ie; ☏ **0818/366-222**).

By Tram

The sleek, modern (and wheelchair-accessible) light-rail tram system known as **Luas** (www.luas.ie; ☏ **1850/300-604**) runs from around 5:30am to midnight Monday to Friday, 6:30am to midnight Saturday, and 7am to 11pm on Sunday. (The last trams to certain stations are earlier, so be sure to check the timetable.) There are two lines, Red and Green (see map on p. 82). Ticket prices depend on the length of your journey and how many city zones it crosses. A single peak-travel journey within the city center (zone 1) costs €2.10, rising to €3.20 for rides to zones 5 to 8. Ticket vending machines are located at every Luas stop. Purchase your ticket in advance using coins, paper money, or a credit card. Leap Cards are also accepted on Luas and include a small discount. For more information, contact Luas.

On Foot

Marvelously compact, Dublin is ideal for walking. Just remember to look right and then left (and in the direction opposite your instincts if you're from North America) before crossing the street. Cross the road at the pedestrian crossings which usually have pedestrian traffic lights (or sometimes a zebra-striped crossing).

By Taxi

Taxis are everywhere in Dublin, and they are a cheap and handy way to get around. You can either hail a cab on the street (if the light on top of the car is lit, it's available) or find one at the many taxi stands (called "ranks") throughout the city—located outside hotels, at bus and train stations, and on prime thoroughfares such as Upper O'Connell Street, College Green, and the north side of St. Stephen's Green. The taxi apps are **Free Now** and **Lynk.** If you use Uber, you will get a regular taxi, not a private car, thanks to the city's taxi regulations. You can also phone for a taxi (see "Fast Facts," below).

By Car

We'll say it again: You do *not* want to drive around Dublin if you can possibly avoid it. However, if Dublin is your first stop on a wider tour of Ireland, you may want to rent a car to leave town and see the rest of the country. If that's the case, try **Hertz** (www.hertz.ie) at Dublin Airport (✆ **01/844-5466;** or 2 Haddington Rd., Dublin 4 (✆ **01/668-7566).** **Europcar** (www.europcar.com) also has branches at Dublin Airport (✆ **01/812-2800),** Spencer Dock off the North Quays (✆ **01/648-5900),** and Ballsbridge (✆ **01/8122800).**

[Fast FACTS] DUBLIN

ATMs/Banks   Nearly all banks are open Monday to Friday 10am to 4pm. Convenient locations include the **Bank of Ireland,** at 2 College Green, 88 Camden St. Lower, and at Trinity College; and the **Allied Irish Bank (AIB),** at 100 Grafton St. and 37 O'Connell St.

Currency Exchange   Currency-exchange services, signposted as **Bureau de Change,** are in most Dublin banks and at many branches of the Irish post office system, known as **An Post.** A bureau de change

operates daily during flight arrival and departure times at Dublin Airport. (It's handily situated in the baggage reclaim hall, just opposite carousels 6 to 10—the first ones you come to.) Some hotels and travel agencies offer currency exchange. *Tip:* The best rate of exchange is almost always when you use your bank card at an ATM.

Dentists   For dental emergencies, your hotel will usually contact a dentist for you; otherwise, try **Smiles Dental Spa,** 28 O'Connell St. (✆ **01/872-8335),** or

Molesworth Dental Clinic, 2 Molesworth Place (✆ **01/661-5544).**

Doctors & Hospitals   For emergencies, dial ✆ **999.** If you need a doctor, have your hotel contact one for you. Otherwise you could try **Dame Street Medical Center,** 16 Dame St. (✆ **01/679-0754),** or the **Suffolk Street Surgery,** 107 Grafton St. (✆ **01/679-8181).**

Emergencies   For police, fire, or other emergencies, dial ✆ **999.**

Luggage Storage   If you arrive at your hotel too

91

early to check in, or if checkout isn't until the morning and your flight isn't until the evening, many hotels will happily look after your baggage. Alternatively, the **Dublin Visitor Centre** (www.dublinvisitorcentre.ie; ℂ 01/898-0700), at 17 Lower O'Connell St., 16A Upper O'Connell St., or 118 Grafton St., can store bags securely for €7 each per 24 hours. There are also luggage facilities at Terminal 1 Arrivals at Dublin Airport, or check out luggage storage services like **Nannybag** (www.nannybag.com) and **Stasher** (www.stasher.com).

Mail   The **General Post Office** on O'Connell Street (ℂ 01/705-7600) is open Monday through Saturday 8:30am to 6pm. **An Post** (www.anpost.com), the Irish postal service, has numerous smaller offices throughout the city.

Pharmacies   Dublin does not have 24-hour pharmacies. **City Pharmacy,** 14 Dame St. (ℂ 01/670-4523), stays open until 9pm weekdays, 7pm Saturday, and 6pm Sunday; **Boots the Chemist,** 20 Henry St. (ℂ 01/873-0209), is open until 7pm Monday to Saturday and 6pm on Sundays. Other branches of Boots are at 12 Grafton St. (ℂ 01/677-3000) and in the St. Stephen's Green Centre (ℂ 01/478-4368).

Taxis   Taxi ranks are outside major hotels, at bus and train stations, and on Upper O'Connell Street, College Green, and St. Stephen's Green. To call a cab, try **VIP Taxis** (ℂ 01/478-3333), **Xpert taxis** (ℂ 01/677-0777), or **Trinity Taxis** (ℂ 01/708-2222) or use the **FreeNow** or **Lynk** apps (you can also use Uber to hire a ride).

EXPLORING DUBLIN

Wandering Dublin—just walking along its streets, resorting to the map or your phone only if you get *really* lost—is one of the great pleasures of a visit here. The city center, where the vast majority of the sights are located, is small enough to traverse on foot. One minute you're walking along a quiet, leafy street and suddenly a beautiful row of Georgian houses or a Georgian square like Merrion Square appears before you. Then you find yourself facing the granite buildings of Trinity College, before stumbling upon some amazing old pub or tiny cafe you just have to stop at—and on and on. So pack a sturdy pair of shoes, have your umbrella at the ready, and head out to discover how rewarding this wonderful old city can be.

Top Attractions

Book of Kells and Old Library ★★ LIBRARY   It's definitely one of Ireland's national treasures, this magnificent hand-drawn manuscript of the four gospels, dating to the year 800, with elaborate calligraphy and colorful illumination drawn by Irish monks. It's an astonishing work of art—but whether it really warrants all the fuss is debatable, especially given the effort involved in seeing it. In high season you may face a lengthy queue, only to find it hard to peer past the hordes of onlookers into the dim glass box where the book is kept—and you're handsomely charged for the privilege. You can secure a more comfortable viewing experience by taking a Trinity College tour (p. 104) or by booking fast-track tickets online for an extra €3—these have smaller groups, and more

dublin PASS

If you're planning a lot of sightseeing in Dublin, the tourism board would like you to consider purchasing its **Dublin Pass,** which offers free admission to most of the city's major sights, as well as free travel from the airport on the AirCoach shuttle, and discounts at a number of shops, bars, and restaurants.

Unfortunately, the pass is a bit pricey, given that so many of Dublin's sights are free. So our advice is this: If you're going heavy on the sightseeing, buy the pass, but plan carefully how best to use it. For example, consider buying a pass good for 1 or 2 days, and then see all of the city's most expensive sights (the Guinness Storehouse, EPIC, the Irish Emigration Museum, Big Bus Dublin tours, and so forth) on those days. On the other days of your trip, you can devote your time to the museums, parks, and galleries that charge no entrance fee. But do add up the admission costs of all your planned sights first, to make sure the pass is right for you.

An adult pass costs €70 for 1 day, €86 for 2 days, €100 for 3 days, €106 for 4 days, and €110 for 5 days. A child's pass is a little over half the adult price. The pass is digital and can be purchased online at **www.dublinpass.ie**. Simply download it to your phone or print it out at home.

An alternative is the **DoDublin Days Out card,** which includes admission to six different attractions (within a generous time limit). Cost is adults €39, children €23, students and seniors €33, and families €124. You can buy the pass at **www.dodublin.ie**, and a voucher is sent by email.

time with the display. Either way, factor in a little extra time to check out the library's impressive **Long Room,** which is included in the price. The grand chained library holds many rare works on Irish history and presents frequently changing displays of classic works. The Book of Kells is located in the Old Library building, on the south side of Library Square, inside Trinity College's main campus.

The Old Library Building, Trinity College, College Green, Dublin 2. www.tcd.ie/visitors/book-of-kells. (C) **01/896-2320.** Admission €12–€16 adults; €13 seniors, students, and children 12 and above; €32 families. May–Sept Mon–Sat 9:30am–5pm, Sun 9:30am–5pm; Oct–April Mon–Sat 9:30am–5pm, Sun noon–4:30pm. Last admission 30 min. before closing. DART: Pearse., Tara St., Connolly. Luas: Dawson, Trinity. Bus: Nassau St. entrance: 4, 7, 7a, 11, 25, 26, 37, 38, 39, 46a, 66, 67, 70, 145, 155 College Green entrance: 13, 27, 40, 49, 54a, 56a, 65, 77a, 151

Chester Beatty Library ★★★ LIBRARY   If there's a better small museum in Ireland, we have yet to find it. This dazzling collection of early religious texts and other priceless artifacts in Dublin Castle is named in honor of Sir Alfred Chester Beatty, an Anglo-American industrialist who bequeathed his unique private collection to the Irish nation when he died in 1968. And what a collection it is! Beatty was one of the great 20th-century adventurer-collectors, of the kind that simply could not exist

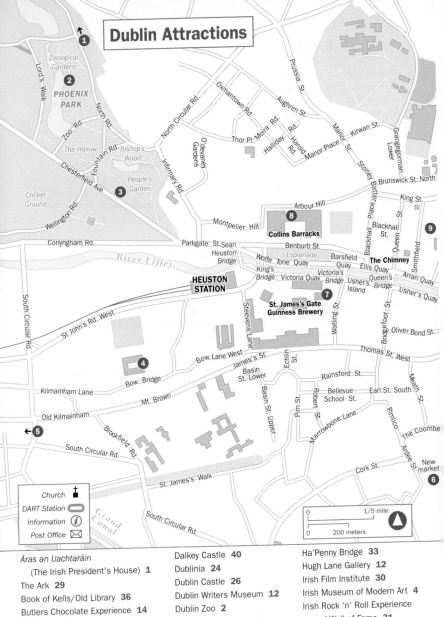

Dublin Attractions

Map labels:
- Zoological Gardens
- PHOENIX PARK
- Lord's Walk
- North Rd
- Zoo Rd
- The Hollow
- Fountain Rd
- Bishop's Wood
- Chesterfield Ave.
- People's Garden
- Cricket Ground
- Wellington Rd
- Conyngham Rd.
- Infirmary Rd.
- O'Devaney Gardens
- North Circular Rd.
- Oxmantown Rd.
- Aughrim St.
- Prussia St.
- Thor Pl.
- Mora Rd.
- Halliday Rd.
- Harold Rd.
- Manor Place
- Manor St.
- Kirwan St.
- Stoney Batter
- Grangegorman Lower
- Brunswick St. North
- King St.
- Montpelier Hill
- Arbour Hill
- Collins Barracks
- Blackhall Place
- Blackhall St.
- Queen St.
- Smithfield
- The Chimney
- Parkgate St.
- Benburb St.
- Esplanade
- Barsfield Quay
- Ellis Quay
- Arran Quay
- Sean Heuston Bridge
- Wolfe Tone Quay
- King's Bridge
- Victoria Quay
- Victoria's Bridge
- Queen's Bridge
- Usher's Quay
- Usher's Island
- River Liffey
- HEUSTON STATION
- St. James's Gate Guinness Brewery
- Watling St.
- Bridgefoot St.
- Oliver Bond St.
- St John's Rd. West
- Steevens Lane
- Bow Lane West
- James's St.
- Thomas St. West
- Meath St.
- South Circular Rd.
- Bow Bridge
- Basin St. Lower
- Rainsford St.
- Kilmainham Lane
- Mt. Brown
- Echlin St.
- Basin St. Upper
- Bellevue
- School St.
- Earl St. South
- Old Kilmainham
- Brookfield Rd.
- Robert St.
- Pim St.
- Marrowbone Lane
- Pimlico
- The Coombe
- South Circular Rd.
- St. James's Walk
- Cork St.
- Ardee St.
- New-market
- Grand Canal
- South Circular Rd.

Legend:
- Church ✝
- DART Station
- Information (i)
- Post Office ✉

Scale: 0 — 1/5 mile; 0 — 200 meters

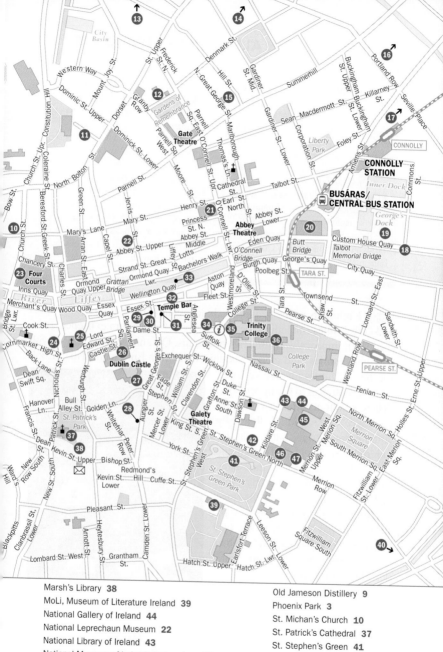

Few people embody the term "citizen of the world" as much as Sir Alfred Chester Beatty. Born in New York in 1875, Beatty launched an American mining business that earned him the nickname "the King of Copper"—and a multimillion-dollar fortune to boot. This fabulous wealth gave him the means to pursue his passion for ancient manuscripts and works of art, and by the time he was an old man, his collection rivaled that of some of the world's greatest museums.

Beatty became a British citizen in the 1930s and was knighted by Queen Elizabeth in 1954, after he made a generous bequest to the British Museum. However, he left the vast majority of his collection to Ireland—his ancestral home and a place dear to his heart. In return Beatty was made an honorary Irish citizen in 1957. He died 11 years later in Monaco but was brought back to Dublin for a state funeral.

Despite all this, Beatty is a surprisingly little-known figure in his adoptive home today. Some Dublin guides don't list the Chester Beatty Museum among the city's top attractions, and some Dubliners have never heard of the collection, or the man himself.

today. Highlights of the bequest include breathtaking illuminated gospels and early Bibles (including the oldest known fragment in existence, from A.D. 150); impeccable 15th-century Qurans; Quranic scrolls from the 8th and 9th centuries; and sacred Buddhist texts from Burma and Tibet. Look for the ancient Egyptian love letter, near the entrance to the upper floor. (There's no translation—a museum employee once told us that they commissioned one, but it was far too rude to display.) Though the core collection remains the same, exhibits are constantly changing, and you're unlikely to see the same manuscripts on every visit. Why queue and pay a tenner to see two pages from the Book of Kells when you can lose yourself in this wonderful place for free?

On the grounds of Dublin Castle, Dame St., Dublin 2. www.chesterbeatty.ie. ✆ **01/407-0750.** Free admission (suggested donation of €5). Mon–Fri 9:45am–5:30pm (Nov–Feb closed Mon); Wed 9:45–8pm; Sun noon–5:30pm. Luas: Jervis, Trinity, St. Stephen's Green. DART: Tara St. Bus: 27, 49, 54a, 56a, 77a, 123, 150, 151.

Viewing bibliophile treasures at the Chester Beatty Library.

Christ Church Cathedral ★★ CATHEDRAL This magnificent cathedral was designed to be seen from the river, so walk to it from the riverside in order to truly appreciate the size. It dates from 1038, when Sitric, Danish king of Dublin, built the first wooden Christ Church here. In 1171, the original foundation was extended into a cruciform layout and rebuilt in stone under the leadership of the Norman warrior Strongbow. The present structure dates mainly from 1871 to 1878, when a huge restoration took place—work that remains controversial to this day, as much of the building's old detail was destroyed in the process. Still, magnificent stonework and graceful pointed arches survive. (There's also a statue of Strongbow inside, and some believe his tomb is here as well, although historians are not convinced.) The best way to get a glimpse of what the original building must have been like is to visit the 12th-century crypt, which has been kept untouched.

Christchurch Place, Dublin 8. www.christchurchcathedral.ie. © **01/677-8099.** Admission €8 adults; €6.50 seniors and students; €3.50 children under 12; €20 families. Free entry for prayer or services. Tours are guided or self-guided (check online for details). Apr–Sept Mon–Sat 9:30am–7pm, Sun 12:30–3:15pm and 4:30–7pm; Mar and Oct Mon–Sat 9:30am–6pm, Sun 12:30–3:15pm and 4:30–6pm; Nov–Feb Mon–Sat 10am–5pm, Sun 12:30–3:15pm. Last entry 45 min. before closing (Mon–Sat). Bus: 13, 27, 40, 49, 77a, 77x, 123.

4

DUBLIN | Exploring Dublin

Christ Church Cathedral.

Dublin Writers Museum ★★ MUSEUM Manuscripts, early editions, personal possessions, and other pieces of ephemera relating to Ireland's most famous writers are on display at this fascinating museum in Parnell Square. The exhibits are laid out across two rooms, tracing the development of Irish literature up to the present day. Lovers of Behan, Joyce, Shaw, Stoker, Wilde, Yeats, and other greats of the canon will find plenty to savor here—from the trivial (Brendan Behan's postcard from Los Angeles extolling its virtues as a place to get drunk) to the profound (a first edition of Patrick Kavanagh's *The Great Hunger*, complete with a handwritten extra section that his publisher refused to publish, fearing it too controversial). You can take a self-guided audio tour, and there's an excellent bookshop—of course. Talks, readings, and other special events are occasionally held here; call or check the website for details.

Letters and mementoes of Ireland's greatest writers are displayed in the Dublin Writers Museum.

18 Parnell Sq., Dublin 1. ℭ **01/872-2077.** Admission €8 adults; €7.50 seniors and students; €5 children; €20 families. Mon–Sat 10am–5pm; Sun 11am–5pm. Last admission 45 min. before closing. Bus: 1, 4, 7, 9, 11, 13, 16, 38, 38a, 38b, 40d, 40e, 44, 46a, 46e, 118, 120, 122, 140, 155.

Hugh Lane Gallery ★★ ART MUSEUM This small art gallery, housed in the glorious classical Charlemont House, punches well above its weight. The strong collection of Impressionist works includes Degas's *Sur la Plage,* Manet's *La Musique aux Tuileries,* and Daumier's *In the Omnibus* (stolen from the gallery in 1992 but recovered in 2014). There are also sculptures by Rodin; a stunning collection of Arts and Crafts stained glass by Dublin-born artist Harry Clarke (don't miss his masterpiece, *The Eve of St. Agnes*); and numerous works by modern Irish artists. One room holds the maddeningly cluttered studio of the Irish painter Francis Bacon, moved here from London and reconstructed behind glass. They moved everything—right down to the dust.

Parnell Sq. North, Dublin 1. www.hughlane.ie. ℭ **01/222-5550.** Free admission. Tues–Thurs 9:45am–6pm; Fri 9:45am–5pm; Sat 10am–5pm; Sun 11am–5pm. Closed Mon. Bus: 7, 11, 13, 16, 38, 40, 46A, 123.

GRAVE robbing

Twice in the last decade, Dublin has found itself rocked by high-profile cases of theft and desecration at some of its most famous churches.

It all started on Saturday, March 3, 2012, when thieves staged an audacious raid on Christ Church Cathedral (p. 97). But they were not after money, or priceless treasure: They had come instead for the preserved heart of St. Laurence O'Toole (1128–80), patron saint of Dublin.

The thieves hid in the Cathedral overnight, then stole the relic, which was encased in a heart-shaped cage. Before leaving, they paused to light two candles on the altar. Nothing else was taken, leading the police to believe that the heart may have been stolen on the orders of a macabre collector.

All leads drew a blank, until 6 years later when—plot twist!—the heart was discovered, abandoned, in Phoenix Park.

The relic was subsequently returned to its rightful place in the Cathedral in 2018.

Rather more disturbing was an incident that took place at St. Michan's Church in 2019. A local man broke into the crypt, where he not only desecrated some of the mummified bodies laid to rest there, but also ripped the head off a centuries-old corpse and stole it as a memento.

In this case, police were able to track down the thief, who ultimately sent to jail. The head, meanwhile, was restored to the body with the help of a local undertaker. The St. Michan's crypt has since reopened and remains one of the city's most unique and unsettling attractions—see p. 107 for more information.

Kilmainham Gaol ★★ HISTORIC SITE   Anyone interested in Ireland's struggle for independence from British rule should not miss visiting this former prison. Within these walls, political prisoners were incarcerated, tortured, and killed from 1796 until 1924. The leaders of the 1916 Easter Uprising were executed here, along with many others. Future president Eamon de Valera was its final prisoner. To walk along these corridors through the grim exercise yard, or to venture into the walled compound, is a moving (at times even overwhelming) experience that will linger in your memory. An exhibition illuminates the brutal history of the Irish penal system; there's also a well-presented historical film. An art gallery on the top floor houses thought-provoking exhibitions. Only a limited number of tickets are sold each day, and visits are by guided tour only. The tours get completely booked up surprisingly far ahead, so do reserve your tickets online, especially if you're visiting in the summer.

Inchicore Rd., Kilmainham, Dublin 8. www.kilmainhamgaolmuseum.ie. ℰ **01/453-5984.** Admission €8 adults; €6 seniors; €4 students and children 12–17; €20 families. Apr–May and Sept 9am–6pm; June–Aug daily 9am–7pm; Oct–Mar daily 9:30am–5:30pm. Last admission 1 hr. 15 min. before closing. Luas: Suir Rd. Bus: 13, 40, 69, 79.

National Gallery of Ireland ★★ ART MUSEUM   The playwright George Bernard Shaw loved this place so much that he left it one-third of his royalties in perpetuity after he died. He saw it as paying a debt, so

Small and compact, Dublin was made for walking. And you could hardly be in better or more learned hands than with the **Historical Walking Tours of Dublin** (www.historicaltours.ie; ☎ **087/688-9412**), whose guides are all history graduates from Trinity College, Dublin, and National University of Ireland. Established for more than 30 years, these engaging tours offer peerless historical insight. Tours leave from the front gates of Trinity College on College Green daily at 11am and 3pm May to September; daily at 11am April and October; and Friday to Sunday at 11am November to March. Tickets cost €14 adults, €12 students and seniors (accompanied kids under 14 are free), and you can just pay the guide on the day. An intriguing variety of private tours are also available—subjects include Medieval Dublin, Revolutionary Dublin, and Dublin's architecture. These need to be booked in advance, with a minimum of four people, and cost €190.

If you prefer a livelier pace, try the **Literary Pub Crawl** (www.dublin pubcrawl.com; ☎ **01/670-5602**). Walking in the footsteps of Joyce, Behan, Beckett, Shaw, and other Irish literary greats, this tour visits Dublin's most famous pubs and explores their deep literary connections. Actors provide humorous performances and commentary between stops. Tours start upstairs at the **Duke Pub,** 9 Duke St. (☎ **01/679-9553**), nightly at 7:30pm April to October; and Thursday to Sunday at 7:30pm November to March. Tickets are €15 adults, €13 students. A limited number of tickets are sold on the night (cash only; doors open 7pm), but it's best to book online. The walking distance is around 1km (0.6 mile). No children are allowed for obvious reasons, but the tour organizers are keen to stress that the tour is safe and enjoyable for women traveling alone.

important was the gallery to his education. It is still a place to wander, wonder, and just be in thrall to so much beautiful art. Highlights of the permanent collection include paintings by Caravaggio, Gainsborough, Rubens, Goya, Rembrandt, Monet, and Picasso. The Irish national portrait collection is housed in one wing, while another area is devoted to the career of Jack B. Yeats (brother of W. B. Yeats), an Irish painter of some note. A 6-year €30-million renovation that was completed in 2017 reopened two wings and added a glass-covered courtyard. (Check out the gravity-defying, 7m/22-ft. freeform sculpture by Cork artist Joseph Walsh, which stands sentinel over the light-filled space.) Major exhibitions change regularly, and the subjects are often more imaginative than just the usual run of retrospectives and national landscapes. In keeping with the "art for all" ethos that so enamored Bernard Shaw, entry to the permanent collection and many of the temporary shows is free.

Merrion Sq. West, Dublin 2. www.nationalgallery.ie. ☎ **01/661-5133.** Free admission. Mon 11am–5pm; Tues–Sat 9:45am–5:30pm; Sun 11:30am–5:30pm. DART: Pearse. Luas: Dawson. Bus: 4, 7, 8, 39a, 46a.

More sightseeing for the thirsty can be enjoyed on the **Traditional Irish Music Pub Crawl** (www.musical pubcrawl.com; ☎ **01/475-8345**). Tours are led by two professional musicians, who describe the experience as a "moving concert," as you make your way from one famous musical pub to another in Temple Bar. Tours meet upstairs at The **Oliver St. John Gogarty** pub, Fleet and Anglesea streets (☎ **01/671-1822**). Tours run daily at 7:30pm April to October; and Thursday to Saturday at 7:30pm November to March. The cost is €16 adults, €14 students. Another higher-priced option also includes a show and a meal at **Flanagans Bar & Restaurant** on O'Connell Street. You can book in advance or buy on the night; again, no kids. However, the same company has recently started doing an early-evening version that ends with dinner and a live show—and children are allowed. It starts at 6pm, also at the Oliver St. John Gogarty, and dinner is served at 7:15pm in **Flanagans** on O'Connell Street (☎ **01/873-1388**). The price is €49.50 adults, €47.50 students, €25 children (minimum age 6), and €140 families. There's also an adult-show-only ticket costing €18.

If you're looking for less booze and more history, the **1916 Rebellion Walking Tour** (www.1916rising.com; ☎ **086/858-3847**) takes you into the heat of the action at the General Post Office, explaining how the anger rose until the rebellion exploded on Easter Sunday in 1916. The 2-hour tour is well thought-out and run by local historians who authored a book on the events of that year. Tours are at 11:30am Monday to Saturday and 1pm Sunday. Tickets cost €15 per adult and €9 per child. Booking is advisable. Meet at the **International Bar,** 23 Wicklow St., Dublin 2. (☎ **086/858-3847**).

National Museum of Ireland: Archaeology ★★★ MUSEUM

The most impressive of the four sites that collectively make up the National Museum of Ireland, this excellent museum is devoted to the ancient history of Ireland and beyond, from the Stone Age up to the Early Modern period. Highlights include a stunning collection of Viking artifacts from the archaeological digs that took place in Dublin from the 1960s to the early 1980s—a haul so important that in one fell swoop the history of Viking settlement in Ireland was rewritten. There is also an enormous range of Bronze Age gold and metalwork, as well as iconic Christian treasures from the Dark Ages, including the Ardagh Chalice, the Moylough Belt Shrine, and the Tara Brooch. It's not just the relics of ancient Irish people that can be seen here—there are also four "bog bodies," human beings whose remains were naturally preserved in bogs, sometime between 400 and 200 B.C. Other notable artifacts include Ralaghan Man, a carved wooden Bronze Age statue from County Cavan; 2nd-century Roman figurines and homewares; and an extraordinary granite table made in Egypt circa 1870 B.C.

Kildare St., Dublin 2. www.museum.ie. ☎ **01/677-7444.** Free admission. Tues–Sat 10am–5pm; Sun–Mon 1–5pm. Luas: Dawson. Bus: 25, 33, 41, 51, 66, 67, 84.

hard to love: **JONATHAN SWIFT**

The acerbic 18th-century wit Jonathan Swift, author of *Gulliver's Travels*, was born in Dublin, and except for a decade or so in England lived in Ireland most of his life. After trying (and failing) to win a position at the English court, he became a Church of Ireland clergyman. Yet he continued to write and publish essays and poetry—in fact, he wrote his most controversial works while acting as dean of St. Patrick's Cathedral.

Many nations might have banned Swift for his scandalous writing. He certainly could not live in England—his works were considered too shocking. But the Irish always forgave him, and the church protected him, even after he published his most infamous essay, "A Modest Proposal," in 1729. In that essay, still read in English classes around the world, he advocated (ironically) that the Irish sell their children to be eaten as food in order to solve the problem of Irish poverty. He assured the reader that Irish babies would be delicious "whether stewed, roasted, baked or boiled. . . ."

Satire was relatively unknown at the time, and many readers at first believed he was seriously recommending cannibalism. The essay caused public outrage and calls for him to be punished. But the church stood by him, as did the town, allowing him to continue to push the limits of 18th-century patience.

Swift believed passionately in humane treatment for the mentally ill, which in his time was unheard of. When he died, he bequeathed much of his estate to found St. Patrick's Hospital for the mentally ill. Typically, though, he couldn't just leave it at that. He wrote one last caustic verse about himself, and the country he loved:

"He left the little wealth he had
To build a house for fools and mad;
Showing in one satiric touch
No nation needed it so much."

National Museum of Ireland: Decorative Arts & History, Collins Barracks ★★ MUSEUM This branch of the National Museum of Ireland tells the story of Irish (and world) history through fashion, jewelry, furniture, and other decorative arts, with the bulk of the collection spanning the 1760s to the 1960s. One gallery is devoted to the work of Eileen Gray (1878–1976), an Irish designer who became one of the most important figures of the Modernist movement; another showcases an extraordinary collection of Asian art bequeathed to the nation in the 1930s. Set in a converted 18th-century army building, the museum isn't entirely devoted to the arts; eight galleries cover Irish military history from the 16th century to the present, including a fascinating section on the Easter Rising of 1916.

Collins Barracks, Benburb St., Dublin 7. www.museum.ie. ℗ **01/677-7444.** Free admission. Tues–Sat 10am–5pm; Sun–Mon 1–5pm. Luas: Museum. Rail: Heuston. Bus: 25a, 39, 39a, 79a, 145.

National Museum of Ireland: Natural History ★★ MUSEUM The core collection at this museum has changed little since the museum was founded in the mid–19th century, and that's part of the attraction. Its display cases are filled with native Irish animals, from stuffed birds and mice to the skeletons of enormous sea creatures. While there are recent additions—including the Discovery Zone, in which visitors can open a series of drawers to discover unusual specimens within—it feels quaintly old-fashioned. Upstairs you'll find the most unique parts of the collection, such as the avian galleries and the "crystal jellies" collection—beautiful oversize glass models of microscopic sea creatures, made in the 19th century by the eccentric and brilliant Blaschka brothers of Dresden. There's no doubt that this is a strange place—the locals call it "the dead zoo." Still, kids find it fascinating, and it is, in many ways, a trip into the past.

Merrion St., Dublin 2. www.museum.ie. © **01/677-7444.** Free admission. Tues–Sat 10am–5pm; Sun–Mon 1–5pm. Luas: St. Stephen's Green. Bus: 4, 7, 8, 39a, 46a.

St. Patrick's Cathedral ★★ CATHEDRAL   The largest—and most famous—church in Ireland, St. Patrick's is one of the most beloved places of worship in the world. The original church was built between 1220 and 1260 in honor of Ireland's patron saint, on a site where Patrick was said to have baptized converts; most of what you see now dates from the 14th century, along with some 19th-century renovations. The building is mainly Early English in style, with a square medieval tower that houses the largest ringing peal bells in Ireland; its spire, nearly 150 feet tall, soars above the city's low skyline. The main body of the church has a cavernous nave, glorious high ceiling, and historic displays. Tucked away at the back of the

St. Patrick's Cathedral is the largest church in Ireland.

A TOUR OF trinity college

A beautiful, grand, romantic place to wander around, the Trinity campus is open free of charge to the public year-round. No trip to Dublin is complete without spending a little while on the college grounds. Here are a few highlights (see map on p. 105).

Trinity's most striking and famous monument, the white **Campanile,** or bell tower, grabs your attention as soon as you enter through the main archway. Dating from the mid–19th century, it stands on the site of the college's original foundations, from 300 years earlier.

Built in the 18th century to a design by Thomas Burgh, the neoclassical **Old Library Building** is the only building on campus you have to pay to see. It's where you'll find the **Book of Kells** (p. 92) and the library's magnificent **Long Room**—both of which are unmissable.

Home to the geography and geology departments, the **Museum Building** is one of Trinity's hidden gems. Built in the mid–19th century, it has Byzantine and Moorish influences. Walk through and look up to the glorious domed ceiling and the green marbled banisters.

Set between these two architectural masterpieces, the stark 1967 **Berkeley Library Building** sharply divides opinion with its austere modernism. Designer Paul Koralek's library honors Bishop George Berkeley, famed for his philosophical theory of "immaterialism" (things that can't be proven cannot exist),

which went against the theories of both Isaac Newton and the Catholic Church. The gleaming sculpture outside the library is *Sphere with Sphere* by Arnaldo Pomodoro (1983).

Also facing the Old Library across Fellows Square, the 1970s **Arts Building** includes the **Douglas Hyde Gallery,** with a regularly changing program of modern art. Exhibitions switch out about every 3 months, and admission is always free.

Tucked away in the far northeastern corner of the campus, the excellent **Science Gallery** is a combination art space, science museum, and debating forum, with fun and thought-provoking exhibitions, workshops, public lectures, and even shows. Entry is free, except to certain special events. See **www.science gallery.com** for details.

One of the more benign remnants of English rule, the **College Park Cricket Pitch** is a small park where you'll often find a cricket match in progress on summer weekends. The sport is notoriously arcane for the uninitiated—but everyone can enjoy the picturesque sight of the players in their white uniforms.

nave is a moving collection of war memorials, including a low-key tribute to the Irish dead of World War II. (Ireland was neutral in that war, but still around 300,000 men volunteered to fight with the Allies.) You can also see the tomb of the satirical 18th-century writer Jonathan Swift, once a dean at this cathedral. Free guided tours are offered regularly throughout the day— no set times, but the front desk will tell you when the next one is leaving. There's also an irregular program of lunchtime classical-music recitals. St. Patrick's Close, Dublin 8. www.stpatrickscathedral.ie. © **01/453-9472.** Admission €8 adults; €7 seniors and students; €18 families. Mar–Oct Mon–Fri 9:30am–5pm; Sat 9am–6pm; Sun 9–10:30am, 12:45–2:30pm, and 4:30–6pm. Nov–Feb Mon–Fri 9:30am–5pm; Sat 9am–5pm; Sun 9am–10:30am and 12:45–2:30pm. Last admission 30 min. before closing. Bus: 49, 54a, 56a, 77a, 151.

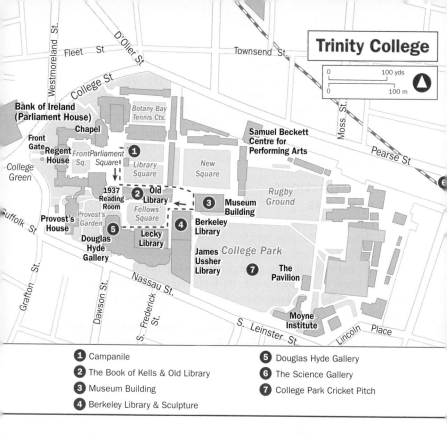

0   100 yds

0   100 m

Westmoreland St.

Fleet St

D'Olier St

College St

Townsend St.

Moss St.

Pearse St

Bank of Ireland
(Parliament House)

Botany Bay
Tennis Cts.

Chapel

Samuel Beckett
Centre for
Performing Arts

Front
Gate

Regent
House

Front
Sq.

Parliament
Square

①

Library
Square

New
Square

College
Green

Rugby
Ground

Suffolk St.

1937
Reading
Room

② Old
Library

Fellows'
Square

③ Museum
Building

Provost's
Garden

Provost's
House

⑤

Lecky
Library

④

Berkeley
Library

Douglas
Hyde
Gallery

James
Ussher
Library

College Park

⑦

The
Pavilion

Grafton St.

Dawson St.

S. Frederick St.

Nassau St.

Moyne
Institute

S. Leinster St.

Lincoln Place

① Campanile

② The Book of Kells & Old Library

③ Museum Building

④ Berkeley Library & Sculpture

⑤ Douglas Hyde Gallery

⑥ The Science Gallery

⑦ College Park Cricket Pitch

Trinity College ★★ UNIVERSITY   The oldest extant university in Ireland, Trinity was founded in 1592 by Queen Elizabeth I to offer an education to the children of the upper classes and protect them from the "malign" Catholic influences elsewhere in Europe. Now it is one of the most respected universities on the continent. Among its alumni are Bram Stoker, Jonathan Swift, Oscar Wilde, and Samuel Beckett, as well as an array of rebels and revolutionaries. Step through the portico off College Green, into the historic gray stone courtyard, and it wouldn't take much more than a lick of fog and a top hat or two to make you think you'd stepped back in time a century or more. The campus spreads across central Dublin just south of the River Liffey, with charming cobbled squares, lush gardens, and picturesque quadrangles. Most of the architecture dates from the 17th to the 19th century. You can wander the campus for free (see map above); alternatively, take either a guided or self-guided tour of all the main sights before you visit the Old Library and the Book of Kells (p. 92). The 45-minute self-guided tour is delivered via an app and includes 14 points of interest, plus virtual tours and audio recordings from experts. Guided tours are also 45 minutes and give an engaging view of the main attractions as well as some insider access around the 42-acre campus. All tours depart from the front gate.

College Green, Dublin 2. www.tcd.ie/visitors. ☏ **01/896-1000.** Guided campus tours €15; €45 families. Self-guided tours €3. Tours leave regularly throughout the day, subject to restrictions during term time and must be booked online. Call or check online for daily schedule. DART: Pearse., Tara St., Connolly St. Luas: Lower Abbey St., St. Stephen's Green. Bus: College Green entrance: 7N, 15N, 15X, 44N, 46N, 48N, 49N, 51D, 51X, 54N, 56A, 70B, 70X, 77A, 77N, 92. Nassau St. entrance: 25X, 32X, 33X, 41X, 51D, 51X, 58X, 67X, 84X, 92.

More Attractions
ART MUSEUMS

Irish Film Institute ★ ARTS CENTER This arthouse film institute is a hip Temple Bar hangout for Dublin cinephiles. It houses three cinemas, the Irish Film Archive, a library, a small but comprehensive bookshop, a busy bar, and a cafe that's a good place for a cup of coffee on a cold afternoon. Although the emphasis is on Irish cinema, groundbreaking films from all over the world are shown here, with a good mixture of new and older titles.

6 Eustace St., Temple Bar, Dublin 2. www.ifi.ie. ☏ **01/679-3477.** Free admission. Cinema tickets €10–€12.50. Mon–Sun 12:30pm–10pm. Bus: 27, 40, 49, 54A, 56A, 65, 65B, 68, 68A, 69, 69X, 77A, 77X, 79, 79A.

Attendees at the Dublin Web Fest.

Monumental Wit

Few cities have such a love-hate relationship with their statues as Dublin. Locals have an acerbic rhyming nickname for each one, many of them unprintable. The very buxom statue of Molly Malone (heroine of the Irish folk song, who sold "cockles and mussels, alive alive, oh . . .") on Suffolk Street is variously known as "the Tart with the Cart," "the Trollop with the Scallop," or "the Flirt in the Skirt." In the same vein, the James Joyce statue on O'Connell Street is "the Prick with a Stick"; the statue of Anna Livia (a character in Joyce's *Finnegans Wake* who symbolized the Liffey), rising from an ornamental pond in Croppies Park, is "the Floozie in the Jacuzzi"; and, depending on whom you talk to, the Spire of Dublin on O'Connell Street is either "the Stiletto in the Ghetto," "the Skewer in the Sewer," "the Stiffy by the Liffey," or "the Nail in the Pale."

Irish Museum of Modern Art (IMMA) ★ ART MUSEUM   Set in the Royal Hospital Kilmainham, a beautiful 17th-century classical building with a striking facade and courtyard, IMMA has a small but strong collection of modern art dating from the 1940s to the present day. Highlights include a striking series of mid-1970s photographs by Serbian conceptual artist Marina Abramovic; etchings and lithographs by Alice Maher, Louis le Brocquy, and Marcel Duchamp; and the Madden Arnholz Collection with around 2,000 old master prints, including works by Rembrandt. The beautifully restored grounds are also used as an exhibition space and worth a stroll, and there's also a courtyard café.

Royal Hospital Kilmainham, Military Rd., Kilmainham, Dublin 8. www.imma.ie. ✆ **01/612-9900.** Free admission. Tues–Fri 11:30am–5:30pm, Sat 10am–5:30pm, Sun and bank holidays noon–5:30pm. Last admission 45 min. before closing. Closed Mon. Luas: Heuston. Bus: 13, 40, 79, 79A, 123, 145.

Temple Bar Gallery + Studios ★★ ART GALLERY/STUDIOS This big, rambling art gallery sums up all that is good about Temple Bar. Founded in 1983, it's one of the largest studio and gallery complexes of its kind in Europe. It's filled with innovative work by contemporary Irish artists—more than 30 of them, in a variety of disciplines, including sculpture, painting, printing, and photography. The level of creativity is dazzling, and it's run by helpful, friendly people. Only the gallery section is open to the public, but you can make an appointment in advance to view individual artists at work. The Studios host free talks and discussion panels, featuring the great and the good of the Irish arts scene. Call or go online for details.

5–9 Temple Bar, Dublin 2. www.templebargallery.com. ✆ **01/671-0073.** Free admission. Tues–Sat 11am–6pm. Bus: 26, 37, 39, 39A, 39B, 39C, 49X, 50X, 65X, 66, 66A, 66B, 66D, 67, 67A, 69X, 70, 70A, 77X.

CHURCHES & CATHEDRALS

St. Michan's Church ★★ CHURCH   Built on the site of an earlier, Danish chapel dating from 1095, this plain-looking 17th-century church is almost puritan in its simplicity. The humble, whitewashed interior is pleasant, though not much to write home about in a city full of beautiful churches. Handel is said to have played his *Messiah* on the organ, which dates from 1724, but otherwise you'd be forgiven for wondering what the fuss is about. Well, unsuspecting visitor, prepare yourself for what lies beneath. There's something about the atmospheric conditions in the church's underground vaults that drastically slows decomposition, and the mummified remains of several people have lain here for centuries, in extraordinary states of preservation. A few still have their hair and fingernails on them. The tallest mummy is known as "the Crusader"; his legs were broken in order to fit him into the coffin. Others include "the Nun" and "the Thief"; their true identities were lost when the church records were destroyed during the Civil War in 1922. (The bodies have only recently been restored to public display after a shocking act of vandalism in 2019; see p. 99). It's creepy and definitely not for the easily unnerved. It is said that Bram Stoker was inspired to write *Dracula* in part by having visited as a child. *Note:* The church is wheelchair-accessible, but the vaults are not.

Church St., Dublin 7. ✆**01/872-4154.** Admission €5 adults; €4 seniors and students; €4 children; €15 families. Crypt: Mid-Mar to Oct Mon–Fri 10am–12:45pm and 2–4:30pm; Sat 10am–12:45pm. Nov to mid-Mar Mon–Fri 12:30–3:30pm; Sat 10am–12:45pm. No crypt tours Sun. Luas: Four Courts, Smithfield. Bus: 51D, 51X.

Whitefriar Street Carmelite Church ★ CHURCH   This 19th-century Byzantine-style church is unexpectedly (perhaps dubiously) one of the city's most romantic spots, as it holds the relics of St. Valentine. The pieces of bone are believed to be authentic; they were given to the church by Pope Gregory XVI in 1836. They're kept in a casket on an altar to the right of the main altar, but once a year (on St. Valentine's Day), they are carried out in procession for a special Mass. The church also holds an icon known as **Our Lady of Dublin,** a 15th-century woodcarving that, in 1824, was rescued from a nearby farm where it had been used as a pig trough.

56 Aungier St., Dublin 2. www.whitefriarstreetchurch.ie. ✆ **01/475-8821.** Free admission. Mon, Wed–Fri 7:30am–6pm; Tues 7:30am–9pm; Sat 7:30am–7pm; Sun 7:30am–8pm. Bus: 16, 16A, 19, 19A, 83, 122, 155.

DISTILLERIES & BREWERIES

Guinness Storehouse ★ MUSEUM   Opened in 1759, the Guinness Storehouse is one of the world's most famous breweries, producing the distinctive dark stout that is known and loved the world over. You can explore the Guinness Hopstore, tour a converted 19th-century building housing the World of Guinness Exhibition, and view a film showing how the stout is made; then move on to the Gilroy Gallery, dedicated to the graphic design work of John Gilroy (whose work you will have seen if you've ever been in an Irish pub); and last but not least, stop in at the breathtaking **Gravity Bar.** Here you can sample a glass of the famous brew

Entrance to the Guinness Storehouse brewery.

in the glass-enclosed bar 61m (200 ft.) above the ground, complete with 360-degree views of the city. Ticket prices vary based on the time of day. St. James's Gate, Dublin 8. www.guinness-storehouse.com. ℂ **01/408-4800.** Admission €18–€26 adults; €14.50–€22 seniors and students over 18; €10 children 5–17; free for children 4 and under. Sept–June daily 9:30am–7pm (last tour 5pm). July–Aug daily 9:30am–9pm (last admission 7pm). Luas: St. James's Hospital. Bus: 123.

The Old Jameson Distillery ★ MUSEUM   Easy to spot from nearly a mile away by its chimney-shaped glass viewing tower, this distillery visitor center is a good place to come if you want to learn about one of Ireland's most famous whiskeys. After seeing how it is made, you get to sip a little of the old firewater yourself (or do a full tasting of four premium whiskeys for a few euro extra). Tours run throughout the day, about every 30 minutes, and last 40 minutes. Check opening times, as these can change.
Bow St., Smithfield Village, Dublin 7. www.jamesonwhiskey.com. ℂ **01/807-2355.** Tours from €25 adults; €19 seniors and students; €11 children under 18 (€5 discount for morning tours). Sept–May Mon, Thurs–Fri 10am–6pm (last tour); Tues–Wed and Sun 10am–5:30pm (last tour). June–Aug Mon–Thurs 10am–6pm (last tour 5:30pm); Fri–Sat 10am–7:30pm (last tour 7pm); Sun 10am–6pm (last tour 5:30pm). Luas: Smithfield. Bus: 67, 67A, 68, 69, 79, 90.

Teeling Whiskey Distillery ★★ DISTILLERY TOUR   If you want to soak up the inner machinations of a real working whiskey distillery, this is a great option. Your visit starts with an overview on the history of Irish whiskey and the highs and lows of Dublin distilleries over the years. Guides then take you through the whiskey-making process, with a walk through the live production area and past the three whiskey stills, finishing with a whiskey tasting in a small barrel room. Tours last 45 minutes.

Tickets are based on three different tasting options and all include Teeling small-batch or a soft drink (soda) for under-18s. There's a cafe and gift shop on-site for all things whiskey.

13-17 Newmarket, Dublin 8. www.teelingdistillery.com. © **01/531-0888.** Tours €17–€30 adults; €10 children 10–18; children under 10 free. Tours Sun–Fri noon–6pm; Sat 11am–7pm. Gift shop noon–7pm; cafe Mon–Fri 8am–4pm; Sat–Sun 10am–6pm

HISTORIC ARCHITECTURE & BUILDINGS

Áras an Uachtaráin (The President's House) ★★ HISTORIC HOUSE   Set in Phoenix Park, Áras an Uachtaráin was once the Viceregal Lodge, the summer retreat of the British viceroy, whose main digs were in Dublin Castle. From what were never humble beginnings, the original 1751 country house was expanded several times, gradually becoming the splendid neoclassical white mansion you see today, which now serves as the official residence of Ireland's president. Guided tours leave from the Phoenix Park Visitor Centre every Saturday. After an introductory historical film, a bus brings visitors to and from the house for a 1-hour tour of the state reception rooms (tours run a little longer in summer, when the gardens are included on the itinerary, weather permitting). Since the building is still the official home of the Irish president, a strictly limited number of tickets are given out, on a first-come, first-served basis. The house may occasionally be closed for state events, so call ahead. *Note:* For security reasons, no backpacks, travel bags, strollers, cameras, or mobile phones are allowed on the tour.

Tour departs from Phoenix Park Visitor Centre, Dublin 8. www.president.ie. © **01/677-0095** (Phoenix Park Visitor Centre). Free admission. Sat 10am and 11:15am, 12:30, 1:45, and 3pm. Closed Dec 24 to 26 and for occasional state business. Bus: 37.

College Green ★ ARCHITECTURAL SITE   The grand colonnaded facade of this building was allegedly the model for the Capitol building in Washington, D.C., with one key difference: It's completely devoid of windows. When Parliament House was built in the 1730s, it had windows, but they were bricked up in the early 1800s for security reasons. The Irish Parliament met here until 1801, when, by an extraordinary quirk of history, it was tricked into voting for its own abolition. (William Pitt the Younger, then Prime Minister of Britain, had promised sweeping reform of the anti-Catholic laws if Ireland agreed to a formal union with Britain. They did so, but then Pitt was deposed by King George III, the reforms never happened, and the Irish lost what little self-government they had.) Today the building is a branch of the **Bank of Ireland,** but you can see parts of the magnificent interior featuring oak woodwork, 18th-century tapestries, and a sparkling crystal chandelier. Friendly porters are on hand to fill you in on the history. In our experience, they may also give informal tours of rooms you can't normally see, if you ask nicely.

2 College Green, Dublin 2. © **01/661-5933.** Free admission. Mon–Fri 10am–4pm. DART: Tara St. Luas: Trinity. Bus: 9, 13, 16, 27, 40, 54a, 65, 65b, 68, 77a, 83, 150.

The Custom House ★ ARCHITECTURAL SITE   Completed in 1791, this beautifully proportioned Georgian building has a long classical facade of graceful pavilions, arcades, and a central dome topped by a statue of Commerce. The 14 keystones over the doors and windows are known as the Riverine Heads, because they represent the Atlantic Ocean and the 13 principal rivers of Ireland. Although it burned to a shell in 1921, the building has been masterfully restored. The exterior is the main attraction here, and most of the interior is closed to the public; those with a real interest in finding out more about the building can drop by the visitor center, which has exhibits telling the story of the building, burning and reconstruction.

Custom House Quay, Dublin 1. www.heritageireland.ie ✆ **046/940-7140.** Self-guided tour €6 adults, €5 seniors, €3 children and students; €15 families. Guided tours €8 adults; €6 seniors, €4 children and students; €20 families. Two tours per day; check online for times. Visitor center: daily 10am–4:45pm. Luas: Busáras. DART: Connolly. Bus: 27C, 41X, 53A, 90, 90A, 92, 151, 747, 748.

Dublin Castle ★ CASTLE   The center of British power in Ireland for more than 700 years, this 13th-century castle was finally taken over by the new Irish government in 1922 following Ireland's independence. You can wander the grounds for free, but they're somewhat plain—the Gardaí (police) and government agencies use a significant section of the castle as office space. You'll need to take a guided tour to see the impressive State Apartments, Viking Excavation, and the Gothic-style Chapel Royal, with its fine plaster decoration and carved-oak gallery. The castle's only extant tower is a 13th-century structure once used to imprison suspected traitors. There's a small museum dedicated to An Garda Síochána (the Irish police) in the Treasury Building. In 1583 the castle's Upper Yard was the scene of Ireland's last trial by mortal combat; today it is dominated by an impressive Georgian structure called the Bedford Tower. The Irish crown jewels were kept in the tower until they were stolen in 1907 (they have never been recovered). If it's open, check out the Medieval Undercroft, an excavated site on the grounds where an early Viking fortress once stood. *Note:* This is a government building, so some areas may be closed for state events.

Dame St., Dublin 2. www.dublincastle.ie. ✆ **01/645-8813.** Castle grounds free. Guided tour of State Apartments €12 adults; €10 seniors; €10 students; €6 children 6–17; €30 families. Daily 9:45am–5:45pm (last admission 5:15pm). Luas: Trinity. Bus: 13, 27, 40, 49, 54A, 56A, 77A, 123, 150, 747.

The Four Courts ★ ARCHITECTURAL SITE   Home to the Irish legal courts since 1796, this fine 18th-century building was designed by James Gandon (who also designed the Custom House; see above). It is distinguished by its graceful Corinthian columns, massive dome, and exterior statues of Justice, Mercy, Wisdom, and Moses. Badly damaged by the fighting during the Civil War of 1922, this building was later artfully restored, although some details, such as the statues of famous Irish lawyers that once adorned the niches of the Round Hall, were lost. No public tours are offered, but if you want to see the interior, slip in to watch a trial.

Inns Quay, Dublin 8. www.courts.ie. ✆ **01/888-6000.** Luas: Four Courts. Bus: 25, 25A, 51D, 51X, 68, 69, 78, 79, 79A, 83, 151, 172.

General Post Office (GPO) ★ HISTORIC SITE   Don't be fooled by the nondescript name: With a facade of Ionic columns and Greco-Roman pilasters 60m long (197 ft.) and 17m high (56 ft.), the GPO is more than a post office—it is the symbol of Irish freedom. Built between 1815 and 1818, it was the main stronghold of the Irish Volunteers during the Easter Rising. On Easter Sunday, 1916, Patrick Pearse stood on its steps and read a proclamation declaring a free Irish Republic. It began, "In every generation the Irish people have asserted their right to national freedom and sovereignty." Then he and an army of supporters barricaded themselves inside. A siege ensued that ultimately involved much of the north of the city. Before it was over, the building was all but destroyed. It had barely been restored before civil war broke out in 1922, and it was heavily damaged again. It's still a working post office today, but you can learn all about the building's past at the excellent **GPO Museum** (p. 114) and even touch the bullet holes in the walls out front.

O'Connell St., Dublin 1. www.anpost.ie. ✆ **01/705-7000.** Free admission. Post Office building: Mon–Sat 8:30am–6pm. Closed Sun and public holidays. Museum: Wed–Sat 10am–5pm. Luas: Abbey St. Bus: 10, 10A, 32X, 33X, 39X, 40A, 40C, 41X, 46A, 46B, 46C, 46D, 46E, 116, 123, 145, 747.

Ha'penny Bridge ★ LOCAL LANDMARK   Built in 1816, and one of the earliest cast-iron bridges in Europe, the graceful pedestrian-only Ha'penny Bridge (pronounced *Hay*-penny) is the still the most attractive of Dublin's bridges. Officially named the Liffey Bridge, it's universally known by the toll once charged to cross it: half a penny. The turnstiles were removed in 1919 when passage was made free. The bridge is at its prettiest after sundown, when the old lamps atop its three filigreed arches are lit, and the underside at each end is illuminated in green.

Connects Wellington Quay and Lower Ormond Quay, Dublin 2. Luas: Jervis. Bus: 39B, 51, 51B, 51C, 51D, 51X, 68, 69, 69X, 78, 78A, 79, 79A, 90, 92, 206.

Leinster House ★ ARCHITECTURAL SITE   The home of the Dáil (Irish House of Representatives) and Seanad (Irish Senate), this is the modern center of Irish government. Dating from 1745, it was originally known as Kildare House and was the seat of the Dukes of Leinster. Like the former Parliament House building at College Green (see below), it is said to have been a major influence on the architects of Washington, D.C.; the resemblance to Irish-born James Hoban's design for the White House, built 78 years later, is certainly clear enough. When the Dáil is not in session, tickets are available for guided tours, twice a day, on Mondays and Fridays. You don't have to book in advance, but tour numbers are strictly limited; and be sure to check online to see if they are running at all. To reserve tickets, the events desk prefers an e-mail (event.desk@oireachtas.ie; include your full name, address, and telephone number), or you can call (© **01/618-3781**). *Note:* You need to bring photo I.D. (such as a driver's license or passport) to gain admission and leave large or bulky bags at home. Because this is a government building, you should arrive a few minutes early to allow for security checks before your tour.

Kildare St. and Merrion Sq., Dublin 2. www.oireachtas.ie. © **01/618-3186** or 01/618-3781. Free admission. Entry by guided tour only, Mon and Fri 10:30am and 2:30pm. DART: Pearse. Luas: St. Stephen's Green. Bus: 4, 7, 11, 14, 15, 15A, 15B, 25A, 25B, 38, 38A, 39, 39A, 46A, 66, 66A, 66B, 67, 120, 128, 145.

MUSEUMS & LIBRARIES

Croke Park Stadium & GAA Museum ★ SPORTS MUSEUM

Croke Park is the headquarters, and main sports ground, of the Gaelic Athletic Association (GAA), which oversees most of the traditional Irish sports—including hurling, camogie and Gaelic football. The museum does a good job of setting out the history of Gaelic games and putting them into a wider historical context regarding the importance of sport to the Irish way of life. There are interactive exhibits, and you can take a tour of the stadium or hit the rooftop walkway on a thrilling Skyline tour for views down into the stadium and right across the city. The most excitement, of course, happens on match days—check the website if you want to come and hear the roar of the crowd for real.

Jones Rd., Dublin 3. www.crokepark.ie. © **01/819-2323.** Tour and museum: €10 adults; €8 seniors and students; €7 children; €30–€32 families. Museum only: €8 adults; €7 seniors and students; €6 children; €20–€21 families. Skyline tour: €21 adults; €19 seniors and students; €13 children; €54–€62 families. Museum open Mon–Sat 9am–5pm; Sun and public holidays 10am–5pm. Stadium tours: Jan–July Sun–Fri hourly 11am–3pm; Sat hourly 10am–3pm; Aug Mon–Sun 10:30am–3pm; no tours Dec. Skyline tour times vary, check website. On match days, call to confirm hours. Bus: 3, 11, 11a, 16, 16a, 41.

EPIC: The Irish Emigration Museum ★★★ MUSEUM

This completely digital museum tells the fascinating stories of how and why millions of people emigrated from Irish shores in search of a better life—and the impact they made on other countries when they got there in all fields from sport and music to science. The exhibits have a fun interactive element, with plenty of high-tech storytelling. While not aimed specifically at children, the museum will keep younger visitors entertained as well as informed. You've given a "passport" with your ticket, which you can get stamped in each of the 20 galleries. There's also a genealogy center onsite. For help tracing your own Irish roots, you can book a consultation with a genealogist either in person or online.

CHQ, Custom House Quay, Dublin 1. www.epicchq.com. © **01/906-0861.** Admission €16.50 adults; €10.50 ages 13–17, €15 seniors and students; €8 children 6–15; free for children 5 and under; €36–€42 families. Combined ticket with The Jeanie

Johnston (p. 116) €24.50 adults; €22 seniors and students; €17 children 13–17; €12 children 6–12, children under 5 free. Genealogy consultation: €55–135. Daily 10am–6:45pm (last admission 5pm). Luas: George's Dock. DART: Connolly, Tara St.

14 Henrietta Street ★★ MUSEUM

A tour of this townhouse on Henrietta Street takes you through 300 years of its history, from its construction as an elegant single-family home in the 1740s and Georgian heyday as a social hub for the wealthy class, through some of the city's social and economic decline and its later years as a tenement house—in 1911 it housed more than 100 people. The last residents left in the 1970s. The restoration of the house took more than 10 years, and 14 Henrietta opened as a museum in 2018. Some rooms are simply decorated (but not furnished) as they would have been in Georgian times, while others look as they would have in tenement times. A local guide brings the tour to life with personal stories and anecdotes. Tours take 75 minutes (note that the tours include stairs).

14 Henrietta St., Dublin 1. www.14henriettastreet.ie. ✆ **01/524-0383.** €10 adults; €8 seniors, students; €6 children 5–18; children under 5 free. Wed–Sun 10am–4pm. Closed Mon–Tues. Tours on the hour from 10am. Luas: Dominick St. or Broadstone. DART: Connolly. Bus: 1, 4, 9, 11, 13, 16, 38, 38A, 40, 46A, 83, 122, 140.

Glasnevin Cemetery & Visitor Centre ★ CEMETERY

North of the city center, the Irish national cemetery was founded in 1832 and covers more than 50 hectares (124 acres). Most people buried here were ordinary citizens, but there are also many famous names on the headstones, ranging from revolutionary commander Taoiseach (prime minister) and President Eamon de Valera to other political heroes and rebels including Michael Collins (p. 282), Daniel O'Connell, Countess Constance Markievicz (p. 454), and Charles Stewart Parnell. Literary figures also have their place here—including writers Christy Brown (immortalized in the film *My Left Foot*) and Brendan Behan. Guided tours allow you access to the beautiful O'Connell Crypt, resting place of "The Liberator" Daniel O'Connell (1775–1847). The visitor center, **Experience Glasnevin,** is devoted to the cemetery and its famous occupants. Guided tours run 5 days a week, or you can take a self-guided-tour with an audioguide and map. Printed maps showing who's buried where are sold in the visitor center. *Tip:* At 2:30pm every Friday to Sunday during the summer months, there is a reenactment of a famous speech that the 1916 revolutionary Pádraig Pearse made at the graveside of Fenian leader Jeremiah O'Donovan-Rossa (1831–1915).

Finglas Rd., Glasnevin, Dublin 11. www.glasnevintrust.ie. ✆ **01/882-6550.** Visitor center and tour €13 adults; €11 seniors, students, and children; €35 families. Visitor center only €6 adults; €5 seniors, students, and children. Visitor Centre: Wed–Sun 10am–5pm (including public holidays). Tours daily 11:30am and 2:30pm. Bus: 4, 9, 40, 83, 140.

GPO Museum ★★ MUSEUM

For years the General Post Office seemed to struggle with how best to preserve and present its historical credentials while also fulfilling the continuing needs of a working post office. Now, at last, it has the balance right with this informative little museum, which mainly focuses on the Easter Rebellion of 1916, during which the post office was a key player. Highlights include one of the few remaining original copies of the independence proclamation. Exhibits related to Irish history and the struggle for independence are told through thoughtfully presented interactive content. The cafe and gift shop are located in the building's beautiful courtyard. Informative guided tours of the museum cost an extra €2 over general admission; these run daily at 11am and 2:30pm (no morning tour on Sun).

O'Connell St., Dublin 1. www.gpowitnesshistory.ie. ℂ **01/872-3101.** Admission €15 adults; €12 seniors and students; €7.50 children 5 and over. Tues–Sat 10am–5pm (last admission 4pm). Luas: Abbey St. Bus: 10, 32, 40, 46, 116, 123, 145, 747.

Irish Rock 'n' Roll Museum Experience and Wall of Fame ★

MUSEUM   Not so much a museum as a tour of a demo studio with a few exhibits thrown in, the Rock 'n' Roll Museum opened to some fanfare in 2015. The tour culminates with the chance to form a "band" with your fellow visitors and lay down a track in the studio. Exhibits on display include vintage instruments and assorted memorabilia, such as a blank check signed by Bono for an autograph hunter. Outside, on Curved Street, is the **Irish Music Wall of Fame,** where giant photographic portraits of

The Irish Music Wall of Fame adorns an outside sidewall of the Irish Rock 'n' Roll Museum Experience in Temple Bar.

Ireland's top music stars, including Van Morrison, U2, and the Cranberries, adorn one side of the building.

Curved St., off Temple Bar, Dublin 2. www.irishrocknrollmuseum.com. © **01/635-1993.** Tours (must be prebooked) €16.50 adults; €14.50 senior and students; €45 families. Mon–Fri 11:30am–5:30pm (last tour); Sat–Sun 11am–5:30pm (last tour). DART: Tara St. Luas: Trinity. Bus: 9, 13, 16, 27, 40, 54a, 65, 65b, 68, 77a, 83, 150.

James Joyce Centre ★ MUSEUM   This idiosyncratic museum is set in a grand Georgian house that once belonged to the Earl of Kenmare. Joyce himself never lived here; however, he was rather taken with a former owner of the house named Denis Maginni—an eccentric Irishman, who added an "i" to his name to give himself an air of Italian sophistication. (Maginni appears as a character in Joyce's masterpiece *Ulysses.*) Today the center functions as both a small museum and a cultural center devoted to Joyce and his work. Actual exhibits are a little thin on the ground, but they hold interesting (at least for Joyce fans) lectures and special events, and also organize a Joyce-themed walking tour of Dublin. Unsurprisingly, this place becomes an explosion of activity around Bloomsday (June 16), the date upon which *Ulysses*'s fictional events take place. Unlike the rest of Dublin, which makes do with a single day of celebrating its most famous 20th-century literary hero, the James Joyce Centre turns it into a week-long festival.

35 North Great George's St., Dublin 1. www.jamesjoyce.ie. © **01/878-8547.** Admission €5 adults; €4 seniors, students, and children. Apr–Sept Mon–Sat 10am–5pm, Sun noon–5pm; Oct–Mar Tues–Sat 10am–5pm, Sun noon–5pm. Last admission 30 min. before closing. Luas: Parnell. Bus: 1, 4, 7, 7b, 7d, 8, 9, 11, 13, 16, 38, 38a, 38b, 40, 44, 122, 123, 140, 747.

The Jeanie Johnston ★★★ MUSEUM   The beautiful tall ship tied up on the north quays in Dublin city is actually the *Jeanie Johnston*, a replica of a so-called "famine ship." It tells the story of the terrible humanitarian disaster and the 2 million people who fled Irish shores on ships like this for a better life in North America between 1845 and 1855. The 50-minute tour is an extremely moving experience. You stroll the breezy upper decks, then head below deck, where you can sense how grueling and cramped the voyages were—with passengers suffering from disease, seasickness, and starvation and having to endure crowded conditions and bad weather. Remarkably, no lives were ever lost on the 16 Atlantic crossings of the original *Jeanie Johnston*, which later became a cargo ship before it sank in 1858. This replica was built in 2002, and it's a must-do if you want more insight into this tragic period in Irish history.

Custom House Quay, Dublin 1. www.jeaniejohnston.ie. © **01/473-0111.** €12 adults; €10 seniors and students; €9 children 13–17; €7 children 6–12; children under 5 free; €26 families. Combined ticket with Epic (p. 113) €24.50 adults; €22 seniors and students; €17 children 13–17; €12 children 6–12, children under 5 free. Tours Wed–Sun 10am, 11am, noon, 2pm, and 3pm. DART: Connolly. Luas: St. George's Dock.

The Little Museum of Dublin ★★★ MUSEUM   Stuffed full of ephemera relating to the lives of ordinary Dubliners—art, toys, photographs, newspapers, prints, and other artifacts of the everyday—this delightful museum chronicles what it was like to live in the city throughout the 20th century. Thoughtfully laid out inside a Georgian town house, the vast majority of the items on display were donated by the people of Dublin, and the collection is growing all the time. Among the curios are genuine documents of social history, including items relating to the First World War, the struggle for independence, and the suffrage movement. Several objects have charming anecdotes connected—such as the music stand that, in June 1963, was hurriedly borrowed from the home of a local antiques dealer by visiting U.S. President John F. Kennedy, when he realized he had nowhere to put his papers during a speech. Entry is by guided tour (on the hour, every hour); tours are lively and informative, and guides are great with children. Book tickets online in advance during the high season. *Note:* **DoDublin** bus tour tickets (p. 122) include free entry to the museum.

15 St. Stephen's Green, Dublin 2. www.littlemuseum.ie. ℂ **01/661-1000.** Admission €10 adults; €8 seniors and students; €20 families. Daily 10am–5pm. Luas: St. Stephen's Green. Bus: 15X, 32X, 39X, 41X, 46X, 51X.

Marsh's Library ★★★ LIBRARY   Founded by the wonderfully named Narcissus Marsh, the Archbishop of Dublin, in 1701, this library is still much today as it was in the archbishop's time. Tall, long rows of books sit between paneled walls, and rolling ladders slant upward so readers can reach the high shelves. It is a magnificent example of a 17th-century scholar's library, its shelves filled with scholarly volumes, chiefly focused on theology, medicine, ancient history, and maps, along with Hebrew, Greek, Latin, and French literature. You can still see the wire cages where readers would be locked in with valuable tomes. It's still a working library, but readers are no longer imprisoned. The library has an excellent collection of books by and about Jonathan Swift (see box on p. 102), including volumes with his editing comments in the margins. Ironically, Swift himself said of Archbishop Marsh, "He is the first of human race, that with great advantages of learning, piety, and station ever escaped being a great man."

St Patrick's Close, Dublin 8. www.marshlibrary.ie. ℂ **01/454-3511.** Admission €5 adults; €3 seniors and students; 18 and under free. Tues–Fri 9:30am–5pm; Sat 10am–5pm. Closed public holidays and last week in Dec. Bus: 49, 49A, 50X, 54A, 56A, 77A, 77X, 150, 151.

MoLI, Museum of Literature Ireland ★★ MUSEUM   This museum dedicated to Ireland's rich literary tradition is in UCD Newman House, a historic Georgian townhouse on St. Stephen's Green where the original University College Dublin was founded (as the Catholic University of Ireland). A series of exhibits about Irish literature is spread across three floors, taking in everything from digital displays to a model of James Joyce's Dublin. There's also an interesting room with advice from writers, plus pen and paper if you feel inspired yourself. Look for rare items from the Joyce archive (he was a student in Newman House in 1902), including the first copy of *Ulysses*. You can't see a page because it's closed up in a glass case, but there are copies on display nearby. The shop is well worth a browse for books and literary-themed gifts, and the outdoor part of the Commons cafe is a gorgeous spot in nice weather.

UCD Newman House, 86 St. Stephen's Green, Dublin 2. www.moli.ie. ℰ **01/716-5900.** €10 adults; €8 (or free Wed until noon) seniors, students, and children; €23 families. Guided tour €12. Tues–Sun and bank holiday Mon 10:30am–6pm. Last admission 5pm. Closed Mon. Luas: St. Stephen's Green. DART: Pearse. Bus 7, 11, 15, 16, 39A, 44, 46A, 140, 145 and 155.

National Leprechaun Museum ★ MUSEUM/STORYTELLING

Not quite what it seems from the outside, this is really more of an experience than a conventional museum. You go from room to room, each decorated in weird and imaginative and often wacky style, where storytellers spin tales from Celtic mythology. One room is done like an oversized living room, where adults can feel pixie-sized while sitting on giant chairs and sofas. It's a bit strange—definitely a love-it-or-loathe-it experience. Although the emphasis is on fun and whimsy, the content is such that the experience isn't suitable for children under 7. If you prefer your folklore darker, come in the evening for an adults-only version.

Jervis St., Dublin 1. www.leprechaunmuseum.ie. ℰ **01/873-3899.** Day tours €10–16 adults; €14 seniors and students; €10 children 7–17; €44 families. Night tours €18 adults (18 and over) only. Day tours: Daily on the hour 11am–5pm. Night tours: Feb and Sept Fri–Sat 7:30 and 8:30pm; Mar–Aug 7, 7:30, 8, and 8:30pm. No night tour Oct–Jan. Arrive at least 10 minutes before tour. Luas: Jervis.

National Library of Ireland ★

LIBRARY If you're coming to Ireland to research your roots, one of your first stops should be this library, where thousands of volumes and records yield ancestral information. Open at this location since 1890, it's also the principal library of Irish studies, particularly noted for its collection of first

Founded in the 17th century, Marsh's Library is full of rare scholarly tomes.

HORSE-DRAWN carriage tours

Touristy it may be, but on a fine day there's something nice about the idea of clattering around Dublin's streets in a horse-drawn carriage, with a driver who will comment on the sights as you clop past. Drivers and their carriages congregate at the Grafton Street side of St. Stephen's Green. Simply walk up to one and arrange your tour—anything from a short swing around the green to a half-hour Georgian tour or an hour-long city tour.

Rides are available on a first-come, first-served basis from April to October (weather permitting) and cost about €30 to €60 for one to four passengers.

Alternatively, to book a tour in advance, **Bernard Fagan Horse Drawn Carriages** (www.horsedrawncarriages dublin.com; ✆ **086/874-8691**) is one recommended company. Tours are customized to what you're interested in seeing; prices vary, but expect to pay upwards of €25 per person for an hour-long tour.

editions and the papers of Irish writers and political figures, such as W. B. Yeats, Daniel O'Connell, and Patrick Pearse. Parts of the collection are always on display to the general public (the Yeats exhibition is particularly good). The library also has an unrivaled collection of maps of Ireland. A specialist **Genealogy Advisory Service** is open Monday to Friday 9:30am to 4:45pm, and Saturdays in June to September from 9:30am to 12:45pm. It's free of charge and you don't have to make an appointment. The library has two other sites: in Temple Bar, the **National Photographic Archive** (Meeting House Square; ✆ **01/603-0373**) always has some interesting photographic exhibitions and entry is free. It's open daily from 10am to 4:45pm (from noon on Sun). Free tours of the photographic archive can be prebooked at ✆ **01/603-0346.** The **Seamus Heaney Listen Now Again** exhibition (Bank of Ireland Cultural and Heritage Centre, College Green; entrance via Westmoreland St.) features archive material and manuscripts from the poet's life and work and is open Tuesday to Saturday 10am to 4pm. Entry is free.

2–3 Kildare St., Dublin 2. www.nli.ie. ✆ **01/603-0200.** Free admission. **Reading rooms:** Mon–Wed 9:30am–5pm (by appt.). **Kildare St. exhibitions:** Mon–Fri 9:30am–5pm (last admission 4pm). DART: Pearse. Luas: Dawson. Bus: 7B, 7D, 10, 10A, 11, 11A, 11B, 14, 14A, 15, 15A, 15B, 15C, 20B, 25X, 32X.

PARKS & GARDENS

Phoenix Park ★★ PARK   The vast green expanses of Phoenix Park are Dublin's playground, and it's easy to see why. This well-designed, user-friendly park is crisscrossed by a network of roads and quiet pedestrian walkways that make its 704 hectares (1,739 acres) easily accessible. It's a working park—livestock graze peacefully on pasturelands, deer roam the forested areas, and horses romp on polo fields. The home of the Irish president (p. 110) is in the park, as is the **Dublin Zoo** (p. 121). The visitor center is partly located inside **Ashtown Castle,** a tower house built in the 1430s that was only discovered in 1978, when a later building that had completely enveloped it was demolished. Free parking is adjacent to the center. Also next to the center, the quaint **Phoenix Park Tea Rooms** (✆ **01/677-0900**) serves snacks and light lunches; it also has toilets. The park is 3km (2 miles) west of the city center on the north bank of the River Liffey.

Phoenix Park, Dublin 8. www.phoenixpark.ie. ✆ **01/677-0095.** Free admission. Park open 24 hr.; visitor center 9:30am–6pm. Last admission 45 min. before closing. Tea Rooms: Apr–Oct 9:30am–5:30pm; Nov–Mar 9:30am–4:30pm. Luas: Heuston. Bus: Castleknock Rd. entrance: 37. Navan Rd. entrance: 37, 38, 39, 70. North Circular Rd. entrance: 46A.

St. Stephen's Green ★★ PARK   This lovely city-center park is filled with public art, and there always seems to be something new and imaginative hidden amid its leafy walkways. Among them is a beautiful statue commemorating the Irish rebel Wolfe Tone (beside an affecting monument to the Great Famine) and a garden of scented plants for blind visitors. This is a great place for a summer picnic.

Dublin 2. Luas: St. Stephen's Green. Bus: 20B, 32X, 33X, 39X, 40A, 40C, 41X, 46B, 46N, 46X, 51X, 58X, 70B, 70X, 84X, 92.

Especially for Kids

Sure, Dublin is rich in history and culture, but if you've got restless kids in tow, museums and historic buildings can get old fast. Luckily, the Irish capital also has a good complement of attractions that are tailor-made for families. Besides the attractions listed below, consider taking the **Dublin Ghost Bus** (see below), or, if you've got jaded teenagers, **Castle Dracula** (p. 123) or the **Irish Rock 'n' Roll Museum Experience** (p. 115). A seaside excursion to the heritage village of **Dalkey** (p. 124) or the **National Sea Life Centre** in **Bray** (p. 199) can also be a welcome antidote to city touring. And don't overlook **Butlers Chocolate Experience** (p. 123), a treat for any kid with a sweet tooth.

The Ark: A Cultural Centre for Children ★ ARTS CENTER   This is a great option for children who are makers, thinkers, doers, listeners, and watchers. Age-specific programs are geared to small groups of kids from 2 to 12 years old. Mini courses (1–2 hr. long) are designed around themes in music, visual arts, and theater; there are also workshops in photography, instrument making, and the art of architecture. The custom-designed arts center has three modern floors that house a theater, a gallery, and a workshop for hands-on learning sessions. Tickets include one child and one adult; prices vary, but expect to pay around €6 to €12 for most events. Check the current schedule on the Ark's website.

11a Eustace St., Dublin 2. www.ark.ie. ✆ **01/670-7788.** Ticket prices vary. Event times vary; call ahead. DART: Tara St. Luas: Trinity. Bus: 15E, 15F, 16, 16A, 16C, 19, 19A, 19C, 49, 49A, 50, 51, 51B, 51C, 54A, 56A, 65, 65B, 68, 69, 69X, 77, 77A, 77X, 78, 78A, 79, 79A, 83, 121, 122, 123, 150, 151.

Dublin Zoo ★★ ZOO   A perennial kid-pleaser, this modern, humane zoo in Phoenix Park provides a home for more than 235 species of wild animals and tropical birds. The animals live inside a series of realistically created habitats such as the African Savanna, home to giraffes, rhinos, and ostriches; the Gorilla Rainforest, a 12,000-sq.-m (7½-sq.-mile) enclosure that houses five lowland gorillas; Asian Forest, home to Sumatran tigers and lions; the South American House, with an eclectic range of almost unbearably cute species, including tiny pygmy marmosets and two-toed sloths; and the Pacific Coast, where you can watch sea lions swim underwater and view a flamingo aviary that's big enough for the gracious birds to take flight. Playgrounds and gift shops are scattered throughout. Feeding times and scheduled talks are posted on the zoo website (several times daily Mar–Sept; weekends only Oct–Feb). On-site is a restaurant, plenty of smaller cafes, and picnic areas for those who prefer to bring their own meals. There's a slight discount for booking online.

Phoenix Park, Dublin 8. www.dublinzoo.ie. ✆ **01/474-8900.** Admission €20 adults; €15 seniors and students; €14.50 children 3–15; €7.50 special-needs children; €11.50 special-needs adults; €56–€64 families. Book online for discounts. Mar–Sept daily 9:30am–6pm; Oct–Dec 9:30am–4pm; Jan 9:30am–4:30pm; Feb 9:30am–5pm. Last admission to zoo 1 hr. before closing; last admission to African Savanna 30 min. before closing. Luas: Heuston (15-min. walk). Bus: 25, 26, 46A, 66, 66A, 66B, 67, 69.

Pair of southern white rhinos at the Dublin Zoo, which participates in a European breeding program for the breed, under threat by poaching.

Convenient, comfortable, and—remember this when the heavens open in June—relatively immune to inclement weather, bus tours are a great way to pack a lot of sightseeing into a little time. And while Dublin has more than its fair share of standard tourist buses, some are more original.

Of the many "hop on, hop off" bus tours of the city, one of the best is the **DoDublin** tour (www.dodublin.ie; ✆ **01/873-4222**), thanks in part to the commentary of the witty driver-guides as you make your way among the sites. The 24-stop tour runs all around the city center, taking in sights such as **Trinity College** (p. 105), **Dublin Castle** (p. 111), and the **Guinness Storehouse** (p. 108). You can leave and rejoin the tour at any point, and as many times as you like within a 24- or 48-hour period, depending on which ticket you buy. The cost includes free entry into the **Little Museum of Dublin** (but you'll still need to book yourself on a tour; see p. 117) and the option of a free walking tour with a local guide. Buses run all day, every hour from 9am daily; the last tour starts its loop at 5pm. Every other bus is multilingual. Tickets cost €27 adults, €25 seniors and students, €10 children. One child under 15 travels free with every adult. The 48-hour tickets cost €32 adults, €30 seniors and students, €15 children. You can usually get a 10% discount by booking online. DoDublin also

runs full-day excursions to attractions such as **Glendalough** (p. 196) and **Powerscourt** (p. 198). See website for details.

A spooky evening tour in a bus decked out in, um . . . spooky wallpaper, the **Dublin Ghost Bus** (www.ghostbus.ie; ✆ **01/844-4265**) addresses Dublin's history of felons, fiends, and phantoms. You'll see haunted houses, learn of Dracula's Dublin origins, and even get a crash course in body snatching. It's all ghoulish fun, but not suitable for kids under 14. Tickets cost €28.

Likewise, the entertaining **Gravedigger Ghost Tour** (www.thegravedigger.ie; ✆ **01/709-3999**) takes you in pursuit of a few ghoulish and well-intentioned scares. Just when it all seems like too much for the faint-hearted, the bus stops at the Gravediggers Pub by Glasnevin Cemetery (p. 114) for a fortifying drink—included in the ticket price of €29. Tours depart from College Green every night at 7:45pm. Live actors and 4D technology help bring the whole spooky experience to life. Or should that be. . . .

Dublinia ★ HERITAGE SITE   Covering the history of Dublin from the Viking age through medieval times, this child-friendly history experience is presented as a series of interactive tableaux—complete with sound effects, smells, and audio "reconstructions" of *olde worlde* Dublin. Kids can try on clothes like the ones their ancestors may have worn, or even find themselves placed in the Dublin stocks. Check the website for details of special tours, with costumed guides, and other activities. Climb the 96 steps to the top of the viewing tower, which was once part of the (now vanished) medieval **Church of St. Michael the Archangel.**

St. Michael's Hill, Christ Church, Dublin 8. www.dublinia.ie. ✆**01/679-4611.** Admission €12 adults; €11 seniors and students; €7 children; €30 families. Mar–Sept daily 10am–6:30pm; Oct–Feb Thurs–Sun 10am–5:30pm. Last admission 1 hr. before closing. Luas: Four Courts. Bus: 49, 49A, 54A, 123.

Outlying Attractions

Butlers Chocolate Experience ★ FACTORY TOUR   The delectable confections produced at this factory in an industrial park on the road to Malahide are sold in shops all over Dublin. The tour takes you around the factory to see the chocolate makers in action, with tastings aplenty. Space is quite limited (there are three tours daily) so book in advance. No chocolates are made on Saturday, so the weekday tours are definitely the most fun.

Clonshagh Business and Technology Park, Oscar Traynor Rd., Dublin 17. www.butlers chocolates.com/chocolateexperience. ℭ **01/851-2151.** Admission €14.50 adults and children; €52.50 families. Booking essential. Bus: 27. From Dublin, take R105 to R107 toward Malahide; after about 3.5km (2½ miles), turn left onto Oscar Traynor Rd., take 5th right turn and look for sign on the left.

Castle Dracula ★ INTERACTIVE ENTERTAINMENT   Well, this is a novel way to spend Saturday night. Part live theater, part museum, this homage to Dublin-born author Bram Stoker is set up as a tour of "Castle Dracula," through a series of elaborately constructed sets and tunnels. Costumed actors try to scare you and make you laugh in almost equal measure, while you learn more about Bram Stoker and the Dracula phenomenon. (They have a real lock of Stoker's hair, taken from his corpse

Painting chocolate bears at Butlers Chocolate Experience.

by his wife.) The tour ends in an underground auditorium made to look like a spooky graveyard, where you watch a live show that includes comedy and two magicians. The emphasis overall is on laughs rather than scares (although there are a few of the latter, so no kids under 14 are allowed). You meet at the reception lobby of the Westwood Club, a modern gym. Tickets must be booked in advance. Clontarf DART station is right next door, or it's about a 15-minute cab ride from central Dublin.

Meet at Westwood Gym, Clontarf Rd. (next to Clontarf DART), Dublin. www.castle dracula.ie. ℂ **01/851-2151.** Admission €25 adults; €15 seniors, students, and children 15–18. Apr–Aug Sat only 7:45pm (arrive 7:30pm). May not run every week—check website for schedule. DART: Clontarf. Bus: 130. Or you can take a bat.

Dalkey Castle & Heritage Centre ★★ HERITAGE SITE   Housed in a 15th-century tower house, this center tells the history of venerable Dalkey town in a few sweet, if unsophisticated, displays. Don't leave without taking in the view from the battlements. Adjoining the center is a medieval graveyard and the **Church of St. Begnet** (Dalkey's patron saint), whose foundations date back to Ireland's early Christian period. Dalkey itself is worth a wander; a heritage town with plenty of historic buildings, it also has lots of charming pubs and restaurants. If you enjoy nature walks, climb **Killiney Hill** in Killiney Hill Park, just south of town, for great views of Killiney Bay, Bray Head, and the Wicklow Mountains. From Coliemore Harbour, a 10-minute walk from the train station, you can take a 5-minute ferry ride to clamber around rocky, abandoned **Dalkey Island,** with its ruined church and guard tower, wild goats, and adjacent seal colony.

Castle St., Dalkey (16km/10 miles SE of Dublin on R119). www.dalkeycastle.com. ℂ **01/285-8366.** Admission €14 adults; €13 seniors and students; €10.50 children 4–12; €38 families. Mon, Wed–Fri 10am–5pm; Sat–Sun 11am–5pm. Last tour 4:05pm. Closed Tues. DART: Dalkey. Bus: 7D, 59.

WHERE TO STAY IN DUBLIN

Lots of new hotels have opened up in Dublin in the past few years, many of them in areas such as the Docklands, the Liberties, and suburbs like Ranelagh. A number of the newcomers are bursting with personality, with uber-cool rooftop bars and retro design fittings. Dublin has many great classics too, ranging from Georgian townhouses with character to grand dames where you can treat yourself to afternoon tea beside the fire. We've listed our favorites here.

To get the best price, book your rooms as far in advance as possible and avoid times that coincide with the city's major concerts, festivals, and sports matches. And don't write off four-star hotels—there are great deals to be had if you book in advance, especially for off-peak times.

Note: Irish immigration authorities require visitors to have already arranged a place to stay at least for the first night.

South City Centre

The cobblestone streets of Temple Bar are the liveliest (and noisiest) section of the city, on the doorstep of all the action. The neighborhoods around St. Stephen's Green and Merrion Square are almost bucolic by comparison, even though they're only a few minutes' walk away. Head east along the River Liffey for the sparkling glass and steel of the Docklands, or a short jaunt south for the parks and tree-lined roads of Ballsbridge.

EXPENSIVE

The Alex ★★   This stylish hotel near Trinity College has been gaining attention for its modern approach and spacious, well-designed rooms. Located on the site of an old train station, the hotel is designed within an inch of its life, with Art Deco touches mixed with design elements that nod to its past as a station. Bedrooms are spacious and artfully designed with comfortable, king-size beds and soft throws made of Irish wool. Bathrooms are sizeable and up to date—some with freestanding tubs and separate showers. There's room to work in the bright lobby, and good coffee on offer. The hotel restaurant is popular with locals for its light sandwiches and salads at lunch, and tapas options for dinner.

41–47 Fenian St., Dublin 2. www.thealexhotel.ie. © **01/607-3700.** 103 units. €179–€377 double; €292–€484 suite. Lower rates do not include breakfast. Parking (in a nearby lot) €15 per day. **Amenities:** Restaurant; bar; room service; Wi-Fi (free). DART: Pearse. Luas: Dawson. Bus: 25, 25a, 25b, 26, 66, 66e, 67.

Conrad Dublin ★★★   Right beside St. Stephen's Green and opposite the National Concert Hall, this hotel is all about the luxury. Beds in the spacious, bright guest rooms are sumptuously comfortable. Earthy color schemes with soft green hues help convey an air of elegance—and bespoke desks with wooden bases are a lovely feature. It's blissfully quiet inside, where there's a stylish lounge for cocktails and afternoon tea and a fine-dining restaurant. A more informal bistro and small outdoor terrace are popular with locals.

Earlsfort Terrace, Dublin 2. www.conradhotels3.hilton.com. © **01/602-8900.** 192 units. €259–€500 double; €659–€900 suite. Parking €20 per day or valet parking €29 per day. Breakfast included. **Amenities:** Restaurant; bar; room service; gym; Wi-Fi. Bus: 126.

The Merrion Hotel ★★★   This luxurious, five-star hotel is set in a row of Georgian townhouses. The large, warm, and quiet rooms are all elegantly decorated in a traditional style, with king-size orthopedic beds. In the lobbies, fires crackle at the hearth, surrounded by button-backed chairs and velvet sofas. It's all lavish and peaceful. **Restaurant Patrick Guilbaud** has two Michelin stars and is one of the best restaurants in the city. There's also the publike **Cellar Bar,** the **No. 23** cocktail bar, and the **Garden Room,** another fine-dining alternative. The spa is a gloriously

4

DUBLIN | Where to Stay in Dublin

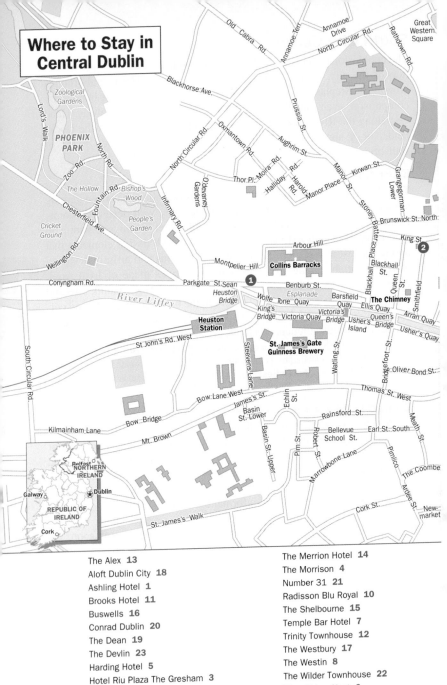

Where to Stay in Central Dublin

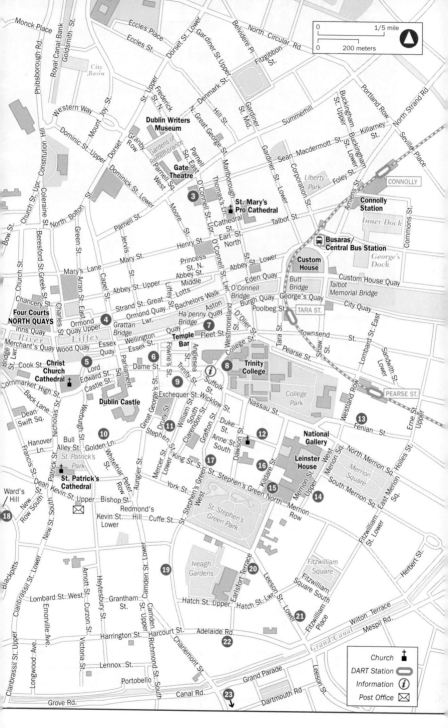

The Radisson Blu Royal's bar showcases elite whiskies and cognacs.

relaxing getaway, with a pool and thermal suite, but reserve your treatments in advance, as they do get booked up.

Upper Merrion St., Dublin 2. www.merrionhotel.com. ✆ **01/603-0600.** 142 units. €310–€470 double. €895–€1,650 suite. Parking €20. **Amenities:** 3 restaurants; 2 bars; room service; spa; pool; gym; Wi-Fi (free). Luas: St. Stephen's Green. DART: Pearse. Bus: 5, 38, 39, 51, 66, 70.

Radisson Blu Royal ★★   The exterior of this hotel may not look like much, but inside it's all about convenience and comfort. Guest rooms are spacious and modern, with comfortable beds. Large bathrooms are equipped with baths and walk-in showers. Soundproofing is excellent throughout, and service is friendly and helpful across the board. Here, you're a 3-minute walk from St. Patrick's Cathedral and 8 minutes from Dublin Castle. Guests have free access to the nearby Iveagh Club gym and swimming pool. This place may not be flashy, but it's got everything you need.

Golden Lane, Dublin 8. www.radissonblu.com. ✆ **01/898-2900.** 233 units. €198–€350 double. Parking €15. Breakfast included. **Amenities:** Restaurant; bar; spa; room service; Wi-Fi (free). Bus: 27, 49, 54a, 56a, 77a, 150, 151.

The Shelbourne ★★★   Dublin hotels simply don't come with a better historic pedigree than this. The Shelburne is nearly 200 years old, and the Irish Constitution was written in this very building. A sense of history and elegance pervades the lobby rooms, with high ceilings, crystal chandeliers, and a grand staircase. Guest rooms have a contemporary elegance, with luxurious beds and large bathrooms. There's also a spa, pool and gym. The hotel is a popular gathering spot for Dublin society—the **Horseshoe Bar** is a favorite of writers and politicians. Afternoon tea in the **Lord**

Mayor's Lounge is a Dublin institution. The **Saddle Room** restaurant is the fine-dining option and there is casual dining in the buzzing **No. 27 The Shelbourne Bar** or the outdoor terrace.

27 St. Stephen's Green, Dublin 2. www.theshelbourne.com. © **01/663-4500.** 265 units. €450–€980 double; €1,850–€5,000 suite. Valet parking €35 per day. Breakfast €22–€30. Dinner, bed-and-breakfast packages available. **Amenities:** 2 restaurants; 3 bars; gym; pool; spa; accessible rooms; Wi-Fi (free). Luas: St. Stephen's Green. DART: Pearse. Bus: 7B, 7D, 10, 10A, 11, 11A, 11B, 14, 14A, 15, 15A, 15B, 15C, 15X, 20B, 25X, 32X, 39X, 40A, 40C, 41X, 51X, 70B, 84X.

The Westbury ★★★   Basically conceived with well-heeled shopaholics in mind and popular with visiting celebrities, this top-end hotel just steps from busy Grafton Street is a stylish retreat. The first-floor lobby is vast, with lots of comfy sofas for post-shopping cocktails or an excellent afternoon tea with bubbles. Bedrooms are sizeable with large, comfortable beds, and are decorated in warm tones, while some suites have their own rooftop terraces with city views. **Wilde** restaurant also has a beautiful terrace looking towards Grafton Street, the buzzing **Balfes** bistro is on the lower level, and the 1930s-style **Sidecar Bar** has its own martini trolley.

Grafton St., Dublin 2. www.doylecollection.com/hotels/the-westbury-hotel. © **01/602-8900.** 205 units. €305–€470 double; €350–€2950 suite. Valet parking €25 per day. **Amenities:** 2 restaurants; bar; room service; gym; Wi-Fi (free). Bus: 11, 14, 15, 20, 27, 33, 39, 46.

The Westin ★★   With its grand, imposing facade (thanks to its former incarnation as a bank), this hotel has many handsome 19th-century features and a lovely inner courtyard with an atrium. Even those parts that feel more modern have an impeccably well-maintained elegance to them. Best of all, the location is hard to beat, right in the city center. The large guest rooms have a refined decor, with wide leather headboards and outrageously comfortable beds, and some overlook the inner courtyard. Located in the original bank vault, the **Mint Bar** has a creative cocktail menu, while the **Morelands Grill** steakhouse is popular with the local business set. The only thing missing is a spa, but you can book pampering treatments in your room.

Westmoreland St., Dublin 2. www.thewestinhoteldublin.com. © **01/645-1000.** 163 units. €374–€530 double, €520–€1220 suite. Breakfast included. Dinner, bed-and-breakfast packages available. Valet parking €30 per day. **Amenities:** Restaurant; bar; gym; room service; Wi-Fi (free). DART: Tara St. Luas: Trinity. Bus: 1, 7B, 7D, 9, 11, 13, 16, 16C, 33N, 39N, 44, 100, 133.

MODERATE

Aloft Dublin City ★★   This outpost of the Marriott hotel chain's uber-modern Aloft brand is well located in the historic Liberties neighborhood, which is undergoing a renaissance with a mix of old and new pubs and restaurants. It's around a 20-minute walk to a central point like Trinity College or a 10-minute cab ride. The hotel has big windows, artfully simple rooms with good beds, and a low-key vibe. The vividly decorated bar is located on the top floor, giving exceptional views all the way to the Wicklow Mountains on a sunny day. Even the reception desk is on the seventh floor, so this hotel is aptly named.

1 Mill St., Dublin 8. ww.marriott.co.uk/hotels/travel/dubal-aloft-dublin-city. ✆ **01/963-1800.** 202 units. €101–€296 double. **Amenities:** Restaurant; bar; Wi-Fi (free). Bus: 49, 54.

Brooks Hotel ★★★

Brooks Hotel isn't much to look at from the outside, but on the inside, where it counts, it's attractive, warm, and welcoming. Only minutes from bustling Grafton Street, Brooks is an oasis of calm. Inside, the attractive lounges have a muted color palette and traditional decor, with modern Irish art brightening the walls. The soundproofed rooms are compact but comfortable, with tasteful wallpaper and good desks. Beds have firm mattresses and soft linens, and a pillow menu lets you choose your firmness. Bathrooms are good-sized and modern. Despite the busy location, the street outside is quiet. The joy is in the clever touches, including a small cinema where guests can watch movies (popcorn available on request). Plus, the hotel gives guests an Irish "book of the month." **Francesca's** restaurant offers upscale Irish cuisine from an open kitchen. **Jasmine Bar** is a popular place for a whiskey or light meal. Everything has been given great thought here.

59 Drury St., Dublin 2. www.brookshotel.ie. ✆ **01/670-4000.** 98 units. €149–€375 double. **Amenities:** Restaurant; bar; Wi-Fi (free). Luas: Dawson. Bus: 9, 16, 65, 83.

Buswells ★★

An old-school air pervades this traditional hotel, a 5-minute walk from Grafton Street. The Georgian building's original features have been carefully maintained, from the intricate cornices of 19th-century plasterwork to the marble fireplaces, which warm the lobby on cold days. It can come as a surprise, therefore, to find that the guest rooms are modern and somewhat featureless. But even with its faults, this is a charming place on a peaceful street, with friendly staff and quiet rooms. Plus, you're in the very heart of the action. Guests with mobility problems should ask for a room on a lower floor; the old building has many staircases.

23–25 Molesworth St., Dublin 2. www.buswells.ie. ✆ **01/614-6500.** 67 units. €152–€302 double. Discount parking at nearby lot (€18/24 hr.). Lower rates do not include breakfast. **Amenities:** Restaurant; bar; room service; Wi-Fi (free). DART: Pearse. Luas: Dawson. Bus: 7B, 10, 10A, 11, 13, 14, 15, 20B, 25X, 33X, 39B, 40A, 92.

The Dean Hotel ★★

This trendy hotel is a decent option near St. Stephen's Green. Rooms are stylish and modern and most are medium-sized, with big windows, up-to-date bathrooms, and interesting Irish art. The top-floor restaurant **Sophie's** has an approachable menu and gorgeous city views. A tram stop is just a few steps away. Light sleepers beware, however—the basement nightclub is loud and runs very late (some guests have reported hearing the music from as far away as the fourth floor), and the street itself can be busy with late-night revelers. Bring earplugs or book a quieter hotel.

33 Harcourt St., Dublin 2. www.deandublin.ie. ✆ **01/607-8110.** 52 units. €150–€300 double. Some rates do not include breakfast. **Amenities:** Restaurant; bar; accessible rooms; Wi-Fi (free). Luas: Harcourt St. Bus: 15, 16, 19, 65, 83, 122.

Number 31 ★   Tucked away on a quiet street near St. Stephen's Green, this B&B is made up of two houses—one Georgian townhouse and one modern mews—connected by an attractive courtyard. Rooms vary, but some have original features including high ceilings, sash windows, and decorative fireplaces (not in use). All have modern bathrooms. Few rooms have air-conditioning, but each has a Dyson fan. Beds are mostly doubles, with orthopedic mattresses. Breakfast is epic here: fresh fruit compote, homemade cranberry and orange bread, and hot dishes made to order. *Note:* There are stairs but no elevator. This is an old house so quirks like creaky floors and minimal soundproofing between floors may not suit light sleepers.

31 Leeson Close, Dublin 2. www.number31.ie. ✆ **01/676-5011.** 22 units. €119–€450 double. Parking (limited) €10 or on-street (€3.20/hr.). Rates include breakfast. **Amenities:** Wi-Fi (free). BUS:133.

Temple Bar Hotel ★   This cheerful, well-run hotel certainly wins in the location stakes if you want to be in the center of the action and crowds—it's right in the middle of trendy (and noisy) Temple Bar. The pleasant guest rooms have a clean, modern style, with big, comfortable beds. Executive rooms offer extra space for a small premium. Teeny-tiny "Pod" rooms (14 sq. m/151 sq. ft.) provide the best value but absolutely no space. The downstairs **Buskers Bar** has live music nightly, which can make sleeping a challenge. But this is Temple Bar, so if you're up for a party, you're in the right place.

10 Fleet St., Dublin 2. www.templebarhotel.com. ✆ **01/612-9200.** 129 units. €149–€435 double. Lower rates do not include breakfast. No parking. **Amenities:** Bar; Wi-Fi (free). DART: Tara St. Luas: Trinity Bus: 100X, 133.

Trinity Townhouse ★★   Originally built as townhouses in the 1730s, this boutique hotel is set across three Georgian buildings on South Frederick Street. The location is fantastic, right in the heart of the fashionable south city area, steps from Grafton Street shops and Trinity College, not to mention pubs and restaurants. Some of the bedrooms retain a historic feel, with high ceilings and features like original fireplaces, while others are more modern. All have air-conditioning and up-to-date modern bathrooms. There's a small restaurant too. These old houses are full of character but not well-soundproofed, plus there's no elevator, so you'll have to take the stairs to reach the upper floors.

29 South Frederick St., Dublin 2. www.trinitytownhousehotel.com. ✆ **01/617-0900.** 31 units. €130–€310 double. Parking at nearby lot (€22.50/24 hr. or €12.50 5–10am with discount ticket). **Amenities:** Restaurant; Wi-Fi (free). Luas: Dawson. DART: Pearse. Bus: 7B, 10, 11, 14, 15, 20B, 25X, 27C, 32X, 33X, 84X, 92.

The Wilder Townhouse ★★ Just a short walk from St. Stephen's Green, this independent boutique hotel is quickly gaining fans, drawn by its character and charm. Behind an impressive Victorian facade, guest rooms come in a variety of sizes, from tiny "Shoebox" doubles to spacious suites. All have tasteful decor in neutral tones and original features such as fireplaces, sash windows, and plaster cornices. Beds are comfortable with good mattresses; bathrooms are small but modern. Still, it's the thoughtful touches that bring people back. Books are left on bedside tables. Guests arriving after long flights are offered cups of tea or a complimentary drink from the bar. Staff are thoughtful and helpful. The breakfast buffet is served in the sunny garden room, and the bar hits the spot for a pre-dinner beverage. This is a find.

22 Adelaide Rd., Dublin 2. www.thewilder.ie. ℰ **01/969-6958.** 42 units. €170–€369 double. Rates include breakfast. Limited free parking (or on-street parking per hour) **Amenities:** Bar; Wi-Fi (free). Luas: Harcourt St. BUS: 7, 39, 45, 56, 70.

Wren Urban Nest ★★ Tucked away on St. Andrew's Lane, just steps from Grafton Street and Temple Bar, this hotel makes no bones about its compact "urban nests." You have your choice of "snug nest" (10 sq. m/108 sq. ft.) or "cosy nest" (12 sq. m/129 sq. ft.) and what the rooms lack in space, they make up for in clever design and details, such as storage cubbies, a fold-down desk, smart TV, minibar, power/rainfall shower, and good soundproofing. What's great is that the hotel is passionate about the environment and is zero-carbon—it's not in your face about it, but you won't find single-use plastics here, energy is renewable, water comes in small cartons, and there's a machine in the corridor to fill your bottle. Even though you are surrounded by bars and restaurants, the food and cocktails at **ALT** bar and restaurant are superb; a large table is popular as a communal workspace.

St. Andrew's Lane, Dublin 2. www.wrenhotel.ie. ℰ **01/223-4555.** 137 units. €99–€179 double. Breakfast €8–€20. Discount parking at nearby lot (€20/24 hr.) **Amenities:** Restaurant; bar; Wi-Fi (free). Luas: Dawson. Dart: Tara St.

INEXPENSIVE

Harding Hotel ★ Just central enough not to require a long trek to the main tourist sites, but on a quieter street at the edge of the busy Temple Bar area, this is a reasonable option in the city center. The polished wood and floor-to-ceiling windows of the lobby give off a pleasantly traditional vibe. Guest rooms are comfortable if plain. Triple rooms typically cost just a little bit more than standard doubles, which makes them useful for families. It's not fancy, but it's pleasant and clean and has everything you need.

Copper Alley, Fishamble St., Dublin 2. www.hardinghotel.ie. ℰ **01/679-6500.** 52 units. €69–€129 double. No parking. Breakfast not included in lower rates. **Amenities:** Restaurant; bar; accessible rooms; Wi-Fi (free). Bus: 37, 39, 49, 50, 70.

Mespil Hotel ★ Just across the Grand Canal from all the sights, and a 10-minute walk from Merrion Square, this modern hotel has a lot to offer: sizeable contemporary rooms with orthopedic beds, up-to-date bathrooms with walk-in rainfall showers, and pleasant canal views. Triple rooms often clock in at the same price as doubles—handy for families. The trendy **Lock Four** restaurant has a good menu that draws local office workers at lunch. The **Lounge Bar** is an attractive place for a tipple. One negative: The street can be noisy—light sleepers should ask for an upper-floor room. *Tip:* A **gourmet food market** is held nearby on Thursdays from 11am to 2pm (www.irishvillagemarkets.com).

50–60 Mespil Rd., Dublin 4. www.mespilhotel.com. *C* **01/448-4600.** 255 units. €99–€189 double. Parking (limited). Breakfast €15. **Amenities:** Restaurant; bar; gym; room service; accessible rooms; Wi-Fi (free). Bus: 10, 15X, 49X, 50X, 66D, 92.

O'Connell Street Area Northside

The area north of the Liffey has some good offerings in the way of hotels. It's also within walking distance of all the major sights and shops, and hotel rates tend to be lower on this side of the river.

EXPENSIVE

The Morrison ★★   Rooms at this chic hotel owned by Doubletree Hilton verge on futuristic, with ultra-modern furniture, moody uplighting, and a host of flashy extras, such as 40-inch HDTVs. Bathrooms are sur-prisingly utilitarian, given how fancy everything else is. The art can be a bit of an acquired taste, but song lyrics painted onto the walls here and there add an edge of Irish literary romance. There's a good restaurant, the **Morrison Grill,** and a funky cocktail lounge, **Quay 14.** The afternoon tea here is dubbed "Fancy Pants Afternoon Tea" on the menu, so how can you resist? The staff is excellent, and regulars swear that the amazing service never falters.

Lower Ormond Quay, Dublin 1. www.morrisonhotel.ie. *C* **01/887-2400.** 145 units. €205–€371 double. Discount parking at nearby lot (€19/24 hr.). Lower rates do not include breakfast. **Amenities:** Restaurant; bar; room service; gym; Wi-Fi (free). Bus: 25, 25A, 25B, 25N, 25X, 26, 66, 66A, 66B, 66N, 66X, 67, 67N, 67X, 69N.

MODERATE

Hotel Riu Plaza The Gresham ★★   One of Dublin's most historic hotels, the Gresham first opened in 1817, though it was almost destroyed during the Easter Rising of 1916. The public areas have a glamorous Art Deco feel. Although the suites and deluxe rooms are opulent, the cheaper guest rooms are quite basic—but they're comfortable, quiet, and, most important, surprisingly affordable for a hotel with this kind of pedigree. The **Writer's Lounge,** a remnant of the hotel's Jazz Age heyday, is a popular spot for afternoon tea. The Luas, Aircoach airport bus and a taxi rank are directly outside, and it's about a 10-minute walk to Temple Bar.

23 Upper O'Connell St., Dublin 1. www.gresham-hotels-dublin.com. *C* **01/874-6881.** 323 units. €94–€250 double. Discount parking at nearby lot (€19/24 hr.). Lower rates do not include breakfast. **Amenities:** 2 restaurants; 2 bars; room service; Wi-Fi (free). Luas: O'Connell. Bus: 2, 3, 4, 5, 7, 8, 10, 11, 13.

The Docklands & IFSC

EXPENSIVE

The Marker ★★★   This sleek, ultra-modern hotel on Grand Canal Square overlooks the Grand Canal Quay waterfront in the south docklands. It's a short walk from the city center, but the pedestrianized location means it's away from noise and traffic. Guest rooms are spacious and extremely quiet with minimalist, unfussy decor and high-end amenities. There's a relaxing spa, a 23m (75-ft.) pool, jacuzzi, sauna, steam room, and sizable gym. The **Brasserie** is a bright space serving creative and contemporary Irish cuisine (wine buffs will love the well-researched selection), and the rooftop bar is great in summer, with 360-degree views over the city and to the Dublin mountains. *Tip:* The hotel has courtesy bikes and a courtesy car for short local journeys.

Grand Canal Square, Docklands, Dublin 2. www.anantara.com/en/the-marker-dublin. ✆ **01/687-5100.** 187 units. Doubles €275–€600; suites €1,500–€3,000. Valet parking (€24/day). Breakfast included. **Amenities:** Restaurant; 2 bars; bikes; gym; pool; spa; courtesy car; Wi-Fi (free). DART: Grand Canal Dock. Bus: 1, 15a, 15b, 55a, 77a.

MODERATE

The Mayson ★★   This trendy hotel on the north city quays is divided between a modern new building and a restored redbrick warehouse and townhouse with lots of choice for room types. The old part has the restored pub **Bottle Boy,** plus **Elephant & Castle** restaurant, a handful of individually designed suites, and even a barber shop, while rooms in the new building are ultra-modern with floor-to-ceiling windows. The smallest rooms are tiny indeed (just 12 sq. m/129 sq. ft.), but all units have a speaker, fridge, and a great selection of snacks and drinks (for purchase) and bathrooms with rainfall showers. The terrace of **Ryleigh's** steakhouse on the sixth floor has views over the River Liffey. There is a small relaxation pool plus a large gym, a spin studio, and a climbing studio, and guests can join classes for €15. It's not a quiet hotel but well-suited for guests craving some of the buzz and action of the city.

81/82 North Wall Quay, Dublin 1. www.themayson.ie. ✆ **01/223-4519.** 94 units. Doubles €125–€275; suites €425–€625. Rates do not include breakfast. Fitness classes €15. **Amenities:** 2 restaurants; bar; gym; relaxation pool; Wi-Fi (free). Luas: The Point.

Smithfield

MODERATE

Ashling Hotel ★★   Close to Heuston Station and Phoenix Park on the western end of the city, the Ashling is a modern six-story hotel. Basic double rooms have generic corporate-style decor, but deluxe rooms are more distinctive and spacious, with comfortable beds and large windows overlooking the city. The in-house restaurant is good, if nothing special. Central Dublin is a 10-minute tram ride or a 25-minute walk. *Tip:* Stroll through Coppies Memorial Park, opposite the hotel, to see the semi-nude bronze statue of Anna Livia, a character in James Joyce's *Finnegans Wake*. She appears to float in a pool of water—thus earning her the nickname "the Floozie in the Jacuzzi." For more on the acerbic wit of Dublin statues' nicknames, see p. 107.

Parkgate St., Dublin 8. www.ashlinghotel.ie. ℰ **01/677-2324.** 226 units. €145–€329 double. Parking €12.50/24 hr. Lower rates do not include breakfast. Dinner, bed-and-breakfast packages available. **Amenities:** Restaurant; bar; Wi-Fi (free). Luas: Museum. Bus: 25, 26, 66, 66A, 66B, 67, 69.

Maldron Hotel Smithfield ★ Part of a small Irish hotel chain, the Maldron Smithfield is a decent midpriced option, a stone's throw from the Old Jameson Distillery. The guest rooms are modern and comfortable, and windows are soundproofed. Go for an upper-floor room with a balcony; the view across the low-slung skyline of Dublin's north side is lovely, particularly at sunset. The on-site restaurant and bar have fairly limited offerings, but several bars and restaurants are right outside, around Smithfield Square. Alternatively, the front desk can order you a pizza from a local delivery company (there's a menu in your room; pay in cash). While you're here, you should definitely visit the **Cobblestone** (p. 169), probably the best pub in Dublin for live traditional music, and less than 30 seconds from the hotel front door.

Smithfield Terrace, Dublin 7. www.maldronhotelsmithfield.com. ℰ **01/485-0900.** 92 units. €118–€329 double. Parking €18/24 hr. at adjoining lot. Breakfast included. **Amenities:** Restaurant; bar; Wi-Fi (free). Luas: Smithfield. Bus: 37, 39, 39A, 70, 83, 83A, 747.

Ballsbridge & the Southern Suburbs

South of the canal, this pricey Dublin residential neighborhood is coveted for its leafy streets and historic buildings. Half the foreign embassies in Dublin are located out here. It's an upscale hotel quarter in part because of its beauty and peaceful streets. It's about a 10-minute cab or DART train ride or 30-min. walk from the center, but most hotels have parking, and it's handy for exploring south of Dublin and if you're driving to County Wicklow for the day. It's also on the Aircoach bus route from Dublin Airport.

EXPENSIVE

InterContinental Dublin ★★★ It looks modern from the outside, but this hotel has been outfitted in a traditional style with plush carpets, elegant lamps, and chandeliers more redolent of a historic hotel than you'd think from the brick-and-glass exterior. Guest rooms are spacious, peaceful and bright, some with views over to Dublin Bay, and bathrooms are large with deep bathtubs. There's a full-service spa, pool, a decent gym and a host of thoughtful touches. For dining, **Seasons** restaurant is the more formal option, there's also the **Garden Terrace** and **Lobby Lounge,** a lovely place for afternoon tea (often with live piano), plus a well-stocked **Whiskey Bar.** Ballsbridge is lovely and quiet—come here for the ultimate in five-star treatment and service in an area of tranquility and beauty.

Simmonscourt Rd., Ballsbridge, Dublin 4. www.intercontinental.com/dublin. ✆ **01/665-4000.** 207 units. €295–€625 double; €445–€775 suite. Breakfast not included in rates (€23/€29). Check website for special offers. Parking €18 per night, valet parking €25. **Amenities:** Restaurant; bar; spa; pool; gym; Wi-Fi (free). DART: Sandymount. Bus: 4, 7, 7N, 8.

MODERATE

Aberdeen Lodge ★★ Drive up to this elegant Regency building in the springtime, and its front is so covered in ivy, it looks like a vertical lawn. Inside, the decor is endearingly old-fashioned; neat-as-a-pin public spaces have heavy, antique-style furnishings and embroidered pillows scattered hither and thither. Guest rooms are comfortable and quiet, if a little plain, but have modern bathrooms. Some have views of the large garden, where guests can have tea—often in the company of the hotel's friendly cat. It's a short walk to the nearest DART station.

53–55 Park Ave., Ballsbridge, Dublin 4. www.aberdeen-lodge.com. ✆ **01/283-8155.** 16 units. €219–€299 double. Free parking. Rates include breakfast. **Amenities:** Restaurant; bar; use of nearby spa; Wi-Fi (free). DART: Sydney Parade, Sandymount. Bus: 2, 3, 18, 84N.

Ariel House ★★ This charming guesthouse in Ballsbridge has won legions of fans over the years. And rightly so—it's a smoothly run, value-for-the-money operation, on a quiet Victorian street. The most obvious landmark you can see is the Aviva Stadium, one of Ireland's major sports grounds, a block away. Inside, the vibe is decidedly old-school. Simple guest rooms are tastefully decorated. The lounge is a pleasant space with an honesty bar and piano; guests are free to tickle the ivories. Breakfasts are legendary, with good-size portions and plentiful options, and afternoon tea is served. The neighborhood is quiet enough to make you feel tucked away from the crowds, but with good links to central Dublin.

50–54 Lansdowne Rd., Ballsbridge, Dublin 4. www.ariel-house.net. ✆ **01/668-5512.** 37 units. €99–€179 double. Free parking. Breakfast not included in lower rates. **Amenities:** Honesty bar; room service; Wi-Fi (free). DART: Lansdowne Rd. Bus: 4, 7, 8, 84.

The Devlin ★★ This on-trend small hotel is worth making the commute to Ranelagh for. The quiet guest rooms are small but perfectly formed, with beds custom-made to fit the space, done up in crisp cotton sheets and firm mattresses. Everything is thought of—Smeg mini-fridges hold drinks and nibbles, and shelves are stocked with power cables, USB adaptors, Dyson hair dryers, pod coffeemakers, even guitars in some cases. Bathrooms are tiny but modern, and the showers are good. Throughout, the decor is soothing, smoky grays and blues, with exposed brick and reclaimed oak touches. On the top floor, trendy **Layla's** restaurant offers drinks and French-influenced food with views of the treetops. Or grab a

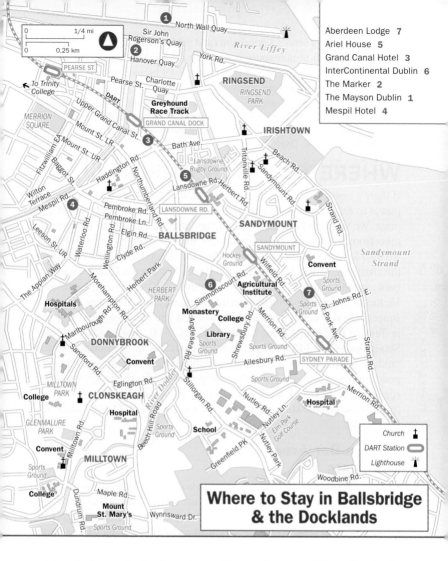

Church †
DART Station
Lighthouse

Where to Stay in Ballsbridge & the Docklands

pint and a burger in the **Americana Bar** on the ground floor. Or simply grab coffee and a muffin from the **DIME** coffee hatch downstairs. There's a handy Luas stop around the corner to sweep you to the city center in 10 minutes.

117–119 Ranelagh, Dublin 6. www.thedevlin.ie. ✆ **01/406-6550.** 40 units. €132–€241 double. **Amenities:** Restaurant; bar; coffee shop; Wi-Fi (free). Luas: Ranelagh.

Grand Canal Hotel ★   Right beside the Grand Canal, this large hotel is close to the Aviva Stadium and popular with sports fans. It's also a haven for business travelers and tourists looking for a pleasant, no-frills place to stay. Rooms are large by Dublin standards and plain. Downstairs, the **Gasworks** bar serves a good pint (and gets packed on game days). The city center is a 20-minute journey away by DART. You could even walk if you wanted to work off one of the hearty hotel breakfasts—Trinity College is about 25 minutes on foot.

Grand Canal St. Upper, Ballsbridge, Dublin 4. www.grandcanalhotel.ie. ℰ **01/646-1000.** 142 units. €139–€499 double. Theater and shopping packages available. Free parking. Breakfast not included in lower rates. **Amenities:** Restaurant; bar; accessible rooms; Wi-Fi (free). DART: Grand Canal Dock. Bus: 4, 5, 7, 8, 45, 63, 84.

WHERE TO EAT IN DUBLIN

If there's one thing we can say for certain, it's that there is no shortage of places to eat in Dublin. You can find any kind of cuisine, at just about any price. We've picked our favorites here and tried to include the best restaurants from all sections of the central city. In addition to those listed below, we also love the smaller places that line the streets here. We recommend the charming **Music Café** in Temple Bar (1 Wellington Quay; www.facebook.com/TheMusicCafebyCaffeMomento), a tiny, glass-enclosed Victorian coffee shop with wonderful cakes and excellent coffee. The cafe squeezes in jazz bands a few nights a week. If you're looking for breakfast in Temple Bar, **Stage Door Café** (11 Essex St. E.; www.facebook.com/Stage-Door-Café-148389536216) is the place. Sit in the sunshine at the outdoor tables and try the creamy scrambled eggs, savory omelets, and good coffee. Another great coffee shop near St. Stephen's Green is the super-trendy **Network Café** (39 Aungier St.; www.networkcafe.ie), and for the best organic sourdough and pastries, try **Bread 41** (41 Pearse St.; bread41.ie).

Temple Bar Area
MODERATE

Cleaver East ★★ ASIAN   A tasty mixed bag of Asian-influenced flavors is served up at this popular restaurant in the Clarence Hotel at the northern edge of Temple Bar. Start with the spiced Indian-style *bhaji* (fritter) or a plate of steamed gyoza, followed up by Barbary duck breast with pomegranate and cucumber salsa, or sticky pork belly with sesame and ginger. The "bottomless" brunches and suppers (Fri–Sun) can be upgraded to offer unlimited drinks for 2 hours (a "weekend brunch to remember," as they put it, perhaps not fully realizing the implications). Early-bird menus (Wed–Sun 5–6pm) are good value for money, at just €25 for two courses.

6–8 E. Essex St., Dublin 2. www.cleavereast.ie. ℰ **01/531-3500.** Entrees €22–€30. Wed–Fri 5–9:30pm; Sat–Sun 11am–4pm, 5–9:30pm. Luas: Westmoreland or Jervis. DART: Tara St. Bus: 22, 39B, 49X, 50X, 65X, 66, 66A, 66B, 66D, 67, 67A, 69X, 77X.

Gallagher's Boxty House ★★★ IRISH   There's a great story behind this small but delightful restaurant in Temple Bar. While living in Venezuela as a young man, the owner was struck by the pride his fellow workers took in simple, traditional home cooking. He came home and

BOXTY

"Boxty on the griddle, boxty on the pan. If you can't bake boxty, sure you'll never get a man."

—Traditional Irish rhyme

Boxty—which comes from an old Irish term meaning "poor bread"—is a traditional Irish food, with recipes handed down in families from parent to child through generations. It's basically a thin potato pancake, made with buttermilk and sometimes eggs, that's cooked, crepelike, on a griddle pan, and then stuffed with meat or vegetable filling and wrapped up like a tortilla.

Each region has its own distinctive spin on the boxty. Although boxty is usually fried, it can also be baked or served as a dumpling (similar to the Polish pierogi). More often than not, modern chefs will accompany their boxty with meat or fish, in various creative (and delicious) ways.

founded a restaurant to preserve and update some Irish traditions in his own style. Boxty—a paper-thin potato pancake (see above)—is the house signature dish, served with a variety of delicious meat and fish fillings. Also on the menu are thick steaks, seafood chowders, and Irish stews. The atmosphere buzzes as crowds form outside the door, waiting for their chance at one of the tables. Reservations are recommended on weekends, but even on busy nights they can usually squeeze you in (*squeeze* being the operative word, as tables are packed tightly together).

20–21 Temple Bar, Dublin 2. www.boxtyhouse.ie. © **01/677-2762.** Entrees €19–€26. Mon–Sun noon–9:30pm. Luas: Westmoreland or Jervis. DART: Tara St. Bus: 22, 39B, 49X, 50X, 65X, 66, 66A, 66B, 66D, 67, 67A, 69X, 77X.

The Old Storehouse ★★ IRISH/PUB

There isn't much in the way of innovation on the menu of hearty Irish classics at this popular pub in Temple Bar—and that's precisely why it's so popular. What you get is delicious traditional pub food mixed with just a hint of bistro style around the edges: dishes like Irish stew; West of Ireland seafood chowder; bangers and mash (sausages and mashed potato); and Guinness beef casserole. There's a small wine list, but the beer selection is better. As much of a draw as the food is the nightly live music, all traditional and all free, with up to 20 acts a week in the summer, either in the main bar or downstairs. The Old Storehouse doesn't accept reservations, so be prepared to wait for a table when it's busy.

Crown Alley, off Cope St., Dublin 2. www.theoldstorehouse.ie. © **01/607-4003.** Entrees €15–€25. Mon–Sun noon–9pm. DART: Tara St. Luas: Westmoreland or Jervis. Bus: 39B, 49X, 50X, 65X, 77X.

INEXPENSIVE

Bunsen ★★ BURGERS This is one of the best places in Dublin for classic, diner-style burgers. It's as stripped down as can be—choose from

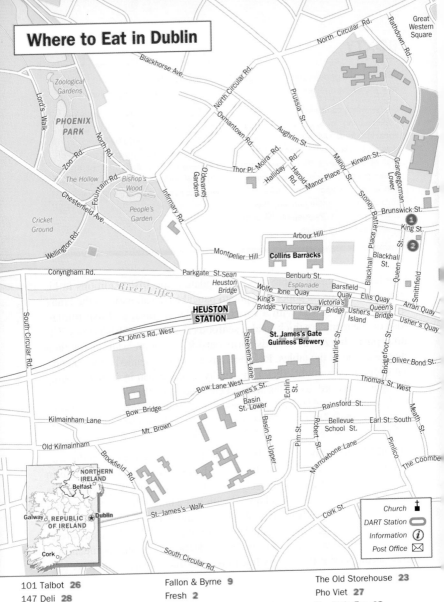

Where to Eat in Dublin

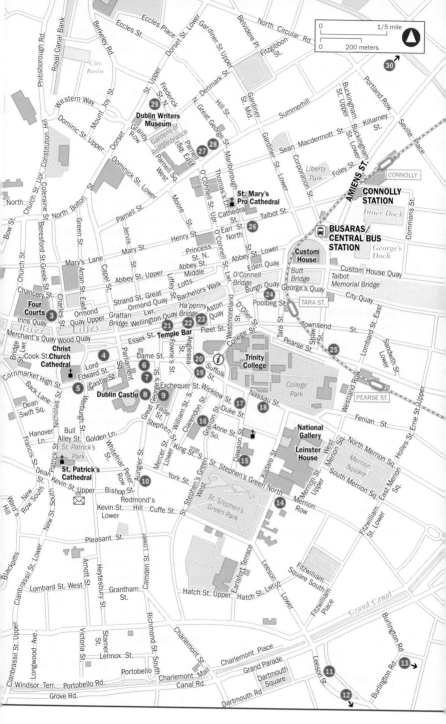

Eccles Place
Eccles St.
Berkeley Rd.
North Circular Rd.
Belvidere Pl.
Dorset St. Lower
Gardiner St. Upper
Fitzgibbon St.
0   1/5 mile
0   200 meters
Phibsborough Rd.
Royal Canal Bank
City Basin
Western Way
Mountjoy St.
Dominick St. Upper
Frederick St. Upper
Denmark St.
Gardiner St. Mid.
Summerhill
Buckingham St. Upper
Buckingham St. Lower
Portland Row
Killarney St.
Seville Place
30
Dublin Writers Museum
29
Granby Row
Parnell Sq. East
Gardens of Remembrance
N. Great George's St.
Hill St.
North
Constitution Hill
Church St. Upper
Coleraine St.
Dominic St. Lower
Dorset St.
27 **28**
Parnell Sq. West
O'Connell St. Upper
Marlborough St.
Gardiner St. Lower
Sean Macdermott St.
Corporation St.
Foley St.
Liberty Park
AMIENS ST.
CONNOLLY
CONNOLLY STATION
nner Dock
Commons St.
North Bolton
Parnell St.
Thomas's St. Upr.
Cathedral St.
St. Mary's Pro Cathedral
Talbot St.
26
BUSARAS/CENTRAL BUS STATION
George's Dock
Bow St.
Beresford St.
Greek St.
Green St.
Jervis St.
Mary St.
Henry St.
Earl St. North
Abbey St. Lower
Custom House
Custom House Quay
Talbot Memorial Bridge
City Quay
Church St.
Mary's Lane
Arran St. East
Capel St.
Abbey St. Upper
Princess St. N.
Abbey St. Middle
Liffey St. Lower
Lotts
Eden Quay
O'Connell Bridge
Butt Bridge
Burgh Quay
George's Quay
24
Poolbeg St.
TARA ST.
Chancery St.
Charles St.
Ormond Quay Upper
Strand St. Great
Ormond Quay Lwr.
Bachelors Walk
Grattan Bridge
Wellington Quay
Ha'penny Bridge
Aston Quay
D'Olier St.
Westmoreland St.
Townsend St.
Tara St.
Shaw St.
25
Lombard St. East
Sandwith St.
Four Courts
3
Inns Quay
Merchant's Quay
Cook St.
Wood Quay
River Liffey
Essex St. East
Temple Bar
Fleet St.
College St.
Pearse St.
PEARSE ST.
Lombard St. Lower
Westland Row
Christ Church Cathedral
4
Lord Edward St.
Dame St.
Parliament St.
Fownes's St.
Anglesea St.
20
6
7
Suffolk St.
19
Trinity College
College Park
Bridge St. Lwr.
Cornmarket
High St.
5
Castle St.
Dublin Castle
8
9
Exchequer St.
Wicklow St.
Nassau St.
17
18
Werburgh St.
Back Lane
St. Patrick's Park
Great George's St.
Fade St.
William St. South
King St. South
Clarendon St.
Duke St.
Dawson St.
National Gallery
Leinster House
Kildare St.
Dean Swift Sq.
Hanover Ln.
Bull Alley St.
Golden Ln.
Nicholas St.
Whitefriar St.
Peter Row
Mercer St. Lower
Anne St. So.
16
Grafton St.
15
Merrion Square
North Merrion Sq.
East Merrion Sq.
Francis St.
Dean St.
Patrick St.
St. Patrick's Cathedral
Kevin St. Upper
Bishop St.
York St.
St. Stephen's Green West
St. Stephen's Green North
South Merrion Sq.
Merrion St. Upper
Fitzwilliam St. Lower
New St. South
New Row South
Ward's Hill
Kevin St. Lower
Redmond's Hill
Cuffe St.
10
St. Stephen's Green Park
14
Merrion Row
Merrion St. Lower
Fitzwilliam St. Lower
Pleasant St.
Camden St. Lower
Arnott St.
Heytesbury St.
Grantham St.
Hatch St. Upper
Hatch St. Lwr.
Leeson St. Lower
Fenian St.
Fitzwilliam Square South
Fitzwilliam Place
Blackpitts
Clanbrassil St. Lower
Lombard St. West
Richmond St. South
Charlemont St.
Charlemont Place
Grand Canal
Burlington Rd.
Clanbrassil St. Upper
Longwood Ave.
Victoria St.
Stamer St.
Lennox St.
Portobello
Charlemont Mall
Grand Parade
Dartmouth Square
13
11
Windsor Terr.
Portobello Rd.
Grove Rd.
Charlemont Canal Rd.
Dartmouth Rd.
Dartmouth Road
Leeson St.
12

141

hamburger or cheeseburger, single or double, then pick a couple of toppings and what style of fries you want (hand-cut, shoestring, or sweet potato). And that's it. No veggie options are on the menu, though if you ask for a grilled cheese sandwich they'll happily fix you one. You can eat in the industrial-style dining room or get your slice of fast-food heaven to go. There are also branches at 36 Wexford St. (✆ **01/552-5408**), 3 S. Anne St. (✆ **01/652-1022**), and 53 Dame St. (✆ **01/561-3853**).

22 Essex St. E, Dublin 1. www.bunsen.ie. ✆ **01/559-9532.** Entrees €8–€11. Mon–Tues noon–9pm; Wed–Thurs noon–9:30pm; Fri noon–10:30pm; Sat noon–10pm; Sun 1–9:30pm. Luas: Westmoreland or Jervis. DART: Tara St. Bus: 22, 39B, 49X, 50X, 65X, 66, 66A, 66B, 66D, 67, 67A, 69X, 77X.

Gourmet Burger Kitchen ★ BURGERS   There's something for everyone at this upscale mini-chain—get your burger classic and simple or opt for one of the more imaginative creations (such as the chicken, Camembert, and cranberry version, or the spicy Rocket Man, with a habañero jam and paprika). Good veggie choices, too. Dessert options are a little limited, but the enormous shakes more than make up for that. Other Dublin branches are at 5 S. Anne St. (✆ **01/672-8559**) and 14 S. William St. (✆ **01/679-0537**).

Temple Bar Sq., Dublin 1. www.gbk.ie. ✆ **01/670-8343.** Entrees €9–€14. Sun–Wed 11am–10pm; Thurs–Sat 11am–11pm. DART: Tara St. Luas: Westmoreland or Jervis. Bus: 22, 39B, 49X, 50X, 65X, 66, 66A, 66B, 66D, 67, 67A, 69X, 77X.

Queen of Tarts ★★ CAFE   This cheerful little tearoom in the heart of Temple Bar is perfect for a pot of tea and a diet-busting snack. Cakes and tarts are the specialty; try the old-fashioned Victoria sponge cake (with a jam-and-cream filling and a dusting of sugar on top). It also serves generously proportioned breakfasts until 11:30am during the week, 1pm on Saturday, and a 2pm on Sunday. A second branch is just around the corner on Lord Edward Street, directly opposite the junction with Cork Hill.

Cow's Lane, Dame St., Dublin 2. www.queenoftarts.ie. ✆ **01/633-4681.** Breakfast €5–€13; lunch €6.50–€14. Wed–Sat 9am–4pm; Sun 10am–4pm. DART: Tara St. Luas: Westmoreland or Jervis. Bus: 37, 39, 39A, 39C, 70, 70A.

Roberta's ★★ INTERNATIONAL   The dining room at Roberta's is about as industrial chic as you can get, all exposed brick walls, bare bulbs, and leather booths. The warehouse-style windows have views of the Liffey and Temple Bar. The food pitches in at the level of an upmarket diner—pizzas, steaks, burgers, and salads, at just-above-budget prices. There's an extensive brunch menu too. This is a quintessentially Temple Bar kind of place.

1 Essex St. E, Dublin 2. www.robertas.ie. ✆ **01/616-9612.** Brunch €5–€16.50; main courses €14–€23. Sun–Wed 5–9pm; Thurs–Fri 5–9:30pm; Sat–Sun 11am–3:30pm. Luas: Westmoreland or Jervis. DART: Tara St. Bus: 22, 39B, 49X, 50X, 65X, 66, 66A, 66B, 66D, 67, 67A, 69X, 77X.

Trinity College Area

EXPENSIVE

The Pig's Ear ★★ MODERN IRISH   A deliciously inventive approach to traditional Irish tastes pervades at this super-cool restaurant overlooking Trinity College. But this isn't one of those trendy eateries where the menu is too concerned with being clever to be satisfying. Here, classic ingredients are offered with imagination: salmon cured with Earl Gray tea, or pork belly with spelt and smoked eel. Dishes on the constantly changing menu are light and beautifully presented in an atmosphere of modern elegance. This is one of the city's most interesting restaurants, and one of its trendiest, so make reservations as early as you can.

4 Nassau St., Dublin 2. www.thepigsear.ie. ✆ **01/670-3865.** Entrees €22–€29. Wed–Sat 5:30–9pm. Luas: Dawson. DART: Pearse. Bus: 25X, 32X, 33X, 41X, 51D, 51X, 58X, 67X, 84X, 92.

The Vintage Kitchen ★★★ IRISH   Vintage artworks line the dining room of this stripped-down, funky little restaurant. (Everything's for sale, but there are no fixed prices, so just make an offer if you like something.) It's a small place with a limited number of tables but you can see why people crowd in: The classic cooking is truly excellent, artfully presented in a contemporary style and generously proportioned. Start with the cod croquette, before tackling slow-roasted lamb shank with treacle gravy, or roast chicken with sweet corn and chili gratin. There's a small wine and beer list. Make reservations for dinner.

7 Poolbeg St., Dublin 2. www.thevintagekitchen.ie. ✆ **01/679-8705.** Lunch small plates €8, main courses €14; dinner fixed-price menus €35–€41. Tues–Sat noon–2:30pm, 5:30–10pm. Luas: Trinity. DART: Tara St. Bus: 65, 65B.

MODERATE

Avoca Café ★★ CAFE   So much better than just another department store cafe, this eatery on the top floor of the famous Avoca shop is a great place for breakfast, lunch, or a mid-shopping snack. The morning menu is more varied and interesting than at most hotels: roasted mushrooms with arugula and rosemary focaccia, avocado on toast with tomato and chutney. Lunches are healthful and delicious—try the famously good soups. Or just drop in for an afternoon sweet treat (including vegan options) and a restorative cup of tea.

11–13 Suffolk St., Dublin 2. www.avoca.ie. ✆ **01/677-4215.** Breakfast €7–€13.50; lunch €7–€18. Mon–Sat 9am–4pm; Sun 10am–4pm. Luas: Trinity. DART: Pearse. Bus: 15X, 32X, 33X, 39X, 41X, 51D, 51X, 58X, 70X, 84X.

The Bank on College Green ★★ PUB   Built as a bank in 1895, at the height of Victorian opulence, this has to be one of the most handsome interiors in all of Dublin. Several remnants of the original were preserved when it was converted into a pub (including the old-style safes that you can still see downstairs). In the hour after local offices close, you'd be lucky to walk in and snag a table right away, but waiting for a table at least gives you an opportunity to admire the beautiful architecture. Tucked away behind the bar are bronze busts of the seven signatories of the 1916 Proclamation of Independence. A small and fairly traditional lunch menu of burgers, fish and chips, sandwiches, and salads gives way to a more extensive selection in the evening. Come on Sundays for brunch or to sample a traditional roast.

20-22 College Green, Dublin 2. www.bankoncollegegreen.com. *C* **01/677-0677.** Entrees €16–€31. Mon–Wed 11am–12:30am; Thurs–Sat 11am–1:30am; Sun 11am–midnight (food served until about 9pm). Luas: Trinity. DART: Tara St. Bus: 15X, 32X, 33X, 39B, 39X, 41X, 49X, 50X, 51X, 58X, 65X, 70X, 77X, 84X.

INEXPENSIVE

Umi Falafal ★ MIDDLE EASTERN   The mostly vegetarian menu at this cheap and cheerful place has something for everyone . . . as long as you like falafels. The spiced chickpea patties are freshly made and flash-fried, served up with plenty of creamy hummus and piled with cabbage, cucumber, radish, and other fresh vegetables. Salads are generously sized and inventive; the fatoush is our favorite—it features tomatoes, cucumber, parsley, dry mint, scallions, and lettuce, topped with toasted bread and pomegranate molasses. They also do a mean halloumi sandwich. Takeout is available, or you can eat in the busy dining room. There's another branch in George's Street Arcade, Rathmines.

13 Dame St., Dublin 2. www.umifalafel.ie. *C* **01/670-6866.** Entrees €5–€7. Daily noon–9pm. Luas: Trinity. DART: Tara St. Bus: 54a, 56a, 150.

Near Dublin Castle

MODERATE

Brasserie Sixty6 ★★ IRISH/INTERNATIONAL   This cheerful, well-run bistro near Trinity College is a popular choice with locals for special occasions. Roast meats cooked rotisserie-style are a house specialty. Try the beef filet with fondant potatoes or dig into a plate of juicy prawns flavored with sea salt and jalapeño peppers, served with crab claws, lemongrass, and thick-cut fries. Vegetarians are catered to as well, with choices such as vegetable tagine. Service is topnotch and the portions generous. The early evening menu is €31.50 for three courses (served all night Sun–Wed and until 6:30pm Thurs–Sat). A popular Sunday brunch served until 3:30pm is accompanied by a jazz band.

66 South Great Georges St., Dublin 2. www.brasseriesixty6.com. *C* **01/400-5878.** Entrees €19.50–€38. Wed–Sat noon–9pm; Sun noon–6pm. Luas: Trinity. DART: Tara St. Bus: 15E, 15F, 16, 16A, 19, 19A, 65, 65B, 65X, 83, 122.

Fallon & Byrne ★★ MODERN EUROPEAN   A top-floor adjunct to the wonderful food and wine store **Fallon & Byrne Food Hall** (p. 159), this restaurant serves delicious seasonal Irish fare sourced from artisan producers. Nothing seems to have come very far: crab from the tiny port of Castletownbere, County Cork; lamb from Lough Erne; oysters from

Carlingford. The menu manages a nice balance between ambitious dishes and more down-to-earth options. It also has vegetarian and vegan menus. And if you prefer to fend for yourself, an enormous selection of deli items is downstairs, available to go. There's also a small bistro menu available to enjoy over wine at the **Lower Depths** (p. 166), in the basement.

11–17 Exchequer St., Dublin 2. www.fallonandbyrne.com. *©* **01/472-1010.** Entrees €22–€36. Mon–Sun noon–3pm; Sun–Tues 5:30–9pm; Wed–Thurs 5:30–10pm; Fri–Sat 5:30–11pm. Luas: Trinity. DART: Tara St. Bus: 15E, 15F, 16, 16A, 19, 19A, 65, 65B, 65X, 83, 122.

San Lorenzo's popular French toast, topped with a Coco Pops square.

San Lorenzo's ★★ BRUNCH/ITALIAN   This upscale Italian restaurant serves creative, modern Italian meals daily for lunch and dinner. But that's not what it's famous for in Dublin. San Lorenzo's is one of the most popular spots in town for brunch (the "brunch of champions," if you will), especially on weekends. Abandon your hotel buffet and come here for the heavenly French toast topped with caramelized bananas, Coco Pops, whipped cream, and thick chocolate sauce; or opt for the Belgian waffles with salted caramel ice cream. Many of the savory options have a Latin edge: huevos rancheros with polenta, or brunch tacos. Just be prepared to wait for a brunch-time table—and one you're required to vacate after 75 minutes.

South Great Georges St., Dublin 2. www.sanlorenzos.ie. *©* **01/478-9383.** Brunch €15.95–€18.95. Lunch fixed-price menus €23–€28. Dinner entrees €20–€27. Fri noon–2:30pm, 5–9pm; Sat 11am–3pm, 5–9pm; Sun 11am–4pm. Luas: Trinity. DART: Tara St. Bus: 15E, 15F, 16, 16A, 19, 19A, 65, 65B, 65X, 83, 122.

INEXPENSIVE

Leo Burdock's ★ FISH & CHIPS   Proof that not all good food experiences come with a hefty price tag, Leo Burdock's is probably the most famous fish and chip shop in Ireland. In fact, it's virtually *de rigueur* for passing celebrities to pop in; the photographic "wall of fame" includes Sandra Bullock, Russell Crowe, and Tom Cruise. But don't come expecting cutting-edge cuisine, because Leo Burdock's still trades on the same simple, winning formula it has used since 1913: battered fresh fish (cod, sole, ray, or scampi) and thick chips (like very fat steak fries), all cooked the old-fashioned way, in beef drippings.

2 Werburgh St., Dublin 8. www.leoburdock.com. *©* **01/454-0306.** All dishes €3.50–€14. Daily 11:30am–midnight (1am Fri–Sat). Luas: Trinity. DART: Tara St. Bus: 49X, 50X, 54A, 50X, 56A, 77, 77A, 77X, 78A, 150, 151.

O'Connell Street Area/North of the Liffey

EXPENSIVE

Chapter One ★★★ MODERN IRISH   The atmospheric vaulted basement of the excellent Dublin Writers Museum (p. 98) houses one of the city's most feted restaurants, with a fixed-price menu that uses innovative techniques and organic ingredients. Feast on gourmet dishes that fuse diverse parts, such as ravioli of Coolea cheese with pumpkin and black truffle, wild mallard with blackberry sauce, or game terrine with pickled cherry and brioche. Book the chef's table, located in the kitchen, if you want the full experience. The wine list is excellent; consider splurging on a Meerlust Rubicon 2013, an outstanding and little-seen South African vintage with a sublime, smoky flavor.
19 Parnell Sq. North, Dublin 1. www.chapteronerestaurant.com. ✆ **01/873-2266.** Three-course lunch menu €65. Four-course dinner menu €120. Tues–Sat 12:30–2pm, 6:30–9:30pm. Closed Sun and Mon. Luas: Abbey St. DART: Connolly. Bus: 1, 2, 14, 14A, 16, 16A, 19, 19A, 33X, 39X, 41X, 48A, 58X, 70B, 70X.

MODERATE

101 Talbot ★★ IRISH/INTERNATIONAL   This cheery and informal spot, a 3-minute walk from the General Post Office on O'Connell Street, is strong on delicious Irish cuisine with global influences and a healthy

Chapter One restaurant's elegant dining room.

twist. The bright, airy dining room is lined with modern art. Specials may include roast cod with parmesan herb crust, or game pie with champ (mashed potato with scallion) and red wine sauce. The early-bird menu (two courses €23; 5–7:15pm) is a particularly good deal and popular with pre-theater diners attending the Abbey Theatre just around the corner.

101–102 Talbot St., Dublin 1. www.101talbot.ie. *(C)* **01/874-5011.** Entrees €18.50–€28.50. Tues–Sat 5–11pm. Closed Sun and Mon. Luas: Abbey St. DART: Connolly. Bus: 20B, 32X, 33X, 41, 41A, 41B, 41C, 42, 42A, 42B, 43, 51A, 130, 142.

The Winding Stair ★★ MODERN IRISH   A sweet old bookstore downstairs and a chic restaurant upstairs, the Winding Stair is just a stone's throw from the Ha'penny Bridge. The views of the Liffey are romantic, but it's the inventive modern Irish cooking that pulls in the crowds for lunch and dinner. After a starter of bleu cheese fritters with grilled pear, you could opt for a tranche of local Dunmore cod with crumbed mussels, or sea trout with trout caviar and pickled cucumber. Desserts are seductive here—you won't want to resist. The enormous wine list, which is helpfully arranged by character rather than region, features several decently priced options. The fixed-price lunch (€25–€35) and the pre-theater menus (€29–€35) are great values for money.

The chic and inventive Winding Stair, located above a vintage bookstore.

40 Lower Ormond Quay, Dublin 1. www.winding-stair.com. *(C)* **01/872-7320.** Entrees €25–€32. Wed–Thurs 5pm–11:30pm; Fri–Sun noon–3:30pm, 5–11:30pm. Luas: Jervis. DART: Tara St. Bus: 39B, 51, 51B, 51C, 51D, 51X, 68, 69, 69X, 78, 78A, 79, 79A, 90, 92, 206.

INEXPENSIVE

147 Deli ★★ DELI   Widely viewed as among the best sandwich makers in the city, the team at 147 pride themselves on piling it high and making it fresh. This small place just off O'Connell Street might not look like much from the outside, but sandwich magic is happening behind that counter. It has a few tables at the back where you can sit down with your pulled pork and slaw on sourdough bread or New York–style Reuben, among many others. There are also plentiful vegetarian options and outstanding coffee. Whatever way you go, you're likely to be happy. In the morning you can also get poached eggs, fresh cinnamon buns, and breakfast sandwiches. If you're feeling run-down, try the mini-doughnuts—the sugar will save you.

147 Parnell St. Rotunda, Dublin 1. www.147delic.com. ©**01/872-8481.** Sandwiches €8. Mon–Fri 9am–3:30pm; Sat 10am–3pm. Closed Sun. Luas: Abbey St. DART: Connolly St. Bus: 1, 2, 14, 14A, 16, 16A, 19, 19A, 33X, 39X, 41X, 48A, 58X, 70B, 70X.

Pho Viet ★★ VIETNAMESE   This bright and cheerful eatery is very popular with Dubliners, and it's easy to see why. It packs in the flavor in every single dish. From the crispy spring rolls to the big, steaming bowls of titular *pho* (a spicy meat and noodle soup), everything is memorable. Try the *bun cha gio* (noodles with vegetables and spring roll)—piled high with bean sprouts, chiles, and fresh herbs, it's got just enough spice. Or stick to the traditional beef pho—the rich and luscious beef stock filled with finely slivered vegetables, noodles, and fresh herbs. The atmosphere is lively, and the service quick and efficient. *Tip:* The lemon iced tea is the most refreshing option on the drinks list.

162 Parnell St., Dublin 1. www.phokim.ie. ©**01/878-3165.** Entrees €13–€18. Sun–Thurs noon–10pm; Fri–Sat noon–11pm. DART: Connolly St. Luas: Abbey St., Parnell St. Bus: 40a, 40d, 120.

Smithfield Area
INEXPENSIVE

Fresh ★ INTERNATIONAL   No, you haven't come to the wrong place—this *is* a supermarket. But step inside and you'll be met with a row of fresh cooking stations serving up delicious street food from around the world. The Mexican stand is popular, but for us the real standout is the incredible pan-Asian station, where a delicious pad Thai or crispy chili chicken can be whipped up in minutes, completely from scratch. Delicious, quality fast food doesn't come much fresher than this. Portion sizes are generous, and you can get a full meal, with nibbles on the side, for well under €20. There are a few tables, or you can get it all to go. It's a great option for lunch or an early, no-fuss dinner—but be aware that the food stations usually wind down by around 7pm.

Smithfield Sq., Dublin 7. www.freshthegoodfoodmarket.ie. ©**01/485-0272.** Hot food €4–€13. Mon–Fri 8am–10pm; Sat–Sun 9am–10pm. Luas: Smithfield. Bus: 37, 39, 39A, 70, 83, 83A, 747.

Namaste India ★★ INDIAN   This exceptional takeout has served many a hungry late-night, post-pub customer in this part of Dublin over the years. And while it may look rough-and-ready, the cooking is some of the best Indian in the city. Everything is prepared in an open kitchen right in front of you—as tantalizing as it is hypnotic—and everything is to-go only. If, alas, your hotel doesn't allow takeout food in the guest rooms, our advice is this: Smuggle! Cheat! Every mouthful will be worth it. Try a classic jalfrezi or Madras, with your choice of meat, prawns, or vegetables, or perhaps a juicy, barbecued chicken tikka, with pilau rice (spiced with cumin and cardamom). Be sure to order a few poppadoms (large pieces of very thin, fried crispbread made from chickpeas) and a naan bread to mop up the thick, perfectly balanced sauces. No frills, no fuss, just deliciously authentic cooking.

88 North King St., Dublin 7. www.namasteindia.ie. ℰ **01/873-3013.** Entrees €9–€13. Mon–Fri 4pm–midnight; Sat–Sun 12:30pm–1am. Luas: Smithfield. Bus: 37, 39, 39A, 70, 83, 83A, 747.

St. Stephen's Green/Grafton Street Area
EXPENSIVE

Bang ★ MODERN IRISH   The presence of so many Irish place names on the menu indicates how much this spot has embraced the Slow Food ethos. Many ingredients are regionally sourced from specialist Irish producers, with local flavors prevailing throughout. You may find Wicklow venison with charred parsnips and blackberries, chicken with black pudding and buckwheat, or a tasty filet of roasted halibut with cauliflower, fennel, and mussels. The wine list is expertly chosen, and there's a delightful seasonal cocktail menu—if it's on the menu when you're there, try the beehive julep, with spiced whiskey, Manuka honey, and black-walnut bitters.

11 Merrion Row, Dublin 2. www.bangrestaurant.com. ℰ **01/400-4229.** Entrees €24–€36. Lunch Fri–Sat noon–3pm. Dinner Wed–Sat 5–11pm. Luas: St. Stephen's Green. DART: Pearse. Bus: 25X, 51D, 51X, 65X, 66X, 67X, 77X.

The Greenhouse ★★★ EUROPEAN   One of the top dining spots in Dublin, the Greenhouse gained its second Michelin star in 2020—only the fourth restaurant in Ireland ever to do so. Chef Mickael Viljanen creates dishes that qualify as miniature works of art in his exquisite four- and six-course tasting menus. And once you're done admiring how gorgeous it all looks, just wait until the flavors hit: Turbot with ginger and katsuobushi flakes; scallop with jalapeño, elderflower, horseradish, and caviar—whatever he's invented that night, it'll be memorable. Despite the trendiness of this place (and the, let's be frank, eye-watering cost), the dining room is a casual and relaxed place. So sit back and savor every mouthful.

Dawson St., Dublin 2. www.thegreenhouserestaurant.ie. ℰ **01/676-7015.** Fixed-price menus €130–€150. Lunch Thurs–Sat noon–2pm. Dinner Tues–Sat 5:30–9:30pm. Luas: Dawson. Bus: 7, 7B, 7D, 11, 37, 38, 38A, 38B, 38D, 39, 39A, 39X, 44,46A, 46E, 61, 70, 84X, 116, 118, 145, 155.

Dessert made of Amedei Chocolate at the Greenhouse.

INEXPENSIVE

Bewley's ★ CAFE   A Dublin landmark since 1927, Bewley's has a literary pedigree as well as a historic one: James Joyce was a regular (the cafe makes an appearance in his book *Dubliners*), and a host of subsequent literary greats made this their regular stop-off for a cup of tea and a bun or slice of cake. It's still hugely popular, and all of the breads and cakes are made fresh each day on-site. *Fun fact:* The ornate faux-Egyptian facade (incongruously framing its never-really-used full name, "Bewley's Oriental Café") is a relic of a European craze for all things Ancient Egyptian, following the discovery of Tutankhamen's tomb just 5 years before the cafe opened.

78–79 Grafton St., Dublin 2. www.bewleys.com. ℂ **01/672-7720.** Breakfast €2.50–€13; lunch and dinner entrees €8–€14. Mon–Fri and Sun 9am–6pm; Sat 8:30am–6:30pm. DART: Pearse. Luas: Dawson. Bus: 11, 11A, 11B, 14, 14A, 15A, 15C, 15X, 20B, 27C, 33X, 39B, 41X, 46B, 46C.

Lemon Crepe & Coffee Co. ★★ CAFE   This simple, straightforward eatery on South William Street serves fresh hot crepes, pancakes, eggs, and sandwiches, all made to order. Walk straight to the bar to order your Californian omelet, with guacamole and bacon, or the Power Crepe, filled with spinach, cheddar, and ham. The cafe serves both sweet crepes (with fillings like fruit, chocolate, and Nutella) and savory crepes (choose

Sweet and savory crepes headline the menu at Lemon Crepe & Coffee Co.

from cheese, meats, fish, or veggies), as well as a variety of sandwiches, waffles, and pancakes. If the weather's fine, sit out front and watch the world go by. It might not be the healthiest meal you have all day, but it will be delicious. The coffee is also excellent here, and the staff are friendly.

60 South William St., Dublin 2. www.lemonco.com. ℭ **01/672-8898.** Entrees €6–€7.50. Mon–Fri 8am–5pm; Sat 8:30am–5pm; Sun 9:30am–5pm. DART: Pearse. Luas: Dawson. Bus: 11, 11A, 11B, 14, 14A, 15A, 15C, 15X, 20B, 27C, 33X, 39B, 41X, 46B, 46C.

Fitzwilliam Square Area

EXPENSIVE

The Sussex ★★ IRISH   This gastropub, 10 minutes' walk south of St. Stephen's Green, takes classic pub fare and elevates it, in dishes like beer-battered fish and chips with pea and mint puree; linguine served with tiger prawns, clams, garlic, and chiles; and a delicious house burger topped with cheddar cheese from County Cork. For dessert, try the *posset* (a syllabub-like concoction containing cream and lemon) served with spiced shortbread. As you'd expect, all the ingredients are sourced as locally as possible, with plenty of attention to what's in season. The wine and ale lists are well curated, with lots of reasonably priced options.

9 Sussex Terrace (at junction of Sussex Rd., above M. O'Briens Pub), Dublin 4. www. thesussex.ie. ℭ **01/538-8100.** Entrees €17–€32. Wed–Sat from 5pm. Bus: 7B, 7D, 11, 11A, 11B, 27C, 39B, 39X, 46B, 46C, 46D, 46E, 58C, 58X, 70B, 70X, 116.

Ballsbridge & the Southern Suburbs

MODERATE

Roly's Bistro ★ BISTRO   This lovely, easygoing bistro, just across the street from the United States Embassy, is one of the best places to eat south of the city center. Local meats and fish predominate; start with some chestnut, mushroom, and rosemary soup with hazelnut cream, or perhaps a Dublin Bay prawn cocktail. For the main event, try the roast Clare Island salmon with wilted greens, or, for a dose of traditional comfort food, a Kerry lamb and vegetable pie. There's also an adjacent cafe. Reservations are recommended for the restaurant.

7 Ballsbridge Terrace, Dublin 4. www.rolysbistro.ie. ℭ **01/668-2611.** Entrees €14–€30. Lunch Sun noon–3pm. Dinner Wed–Sun 6–9:30pm. Bus: 4, 7, 8, 18.

North of Dublin

EXPENSIVE

Aqua ★★★ SEAFOOD   With a jaw-dropping view over the Irish Sea, this has to be one of the most romantic dining spots in the region. Service is excellent—attentive without being overbearing—and the seafood is delicious and fresh as can be. You might start with a half-dozen oysters from Connemara in County Galway, before moving on to Bere Island scallops with carrot puree, or a dish of pasta with salmon, smoked coley,

Waterside dining at Aqua Restaurant.

and mussels in a saffron cream sauce. It's not cheap, but it's reliably good. Howth is a seaside village, about 16km (10 miles) northeast of the city center. The restaurant is a 10-minute walk from the Howth DART station, while a cab here from the city should run you about €30. Definitely worth the splurge.

1 West Pier, Howth, Co. Dublin. www.aqua.ie. (*) **01/832-0690.** Entrees €19–€45. Lunch Wed–Sat 12:30–3:30pm, Sun noon–5pm. Dinner Wed–Sat 5:30–9:30pm, Sun 6–8:30pm. DART: Howth. Bus: 31.

South of Dublin
MODERATE
The Merry Ploughboy ★ IRISH/PUB   An exuberant live show of traditional music and dancing accompanies dinner at this hugely popular pub in Rathfarnham, one of Dublin's farther-flung southern suburbs. Admittedly it's all very touristy, but you certainly get your money's worth—the show runs for 2 hours, and the menu, while limited, is actually pretty good. Expect plates of beef braised in Guinness and served with roasted root vegetables, or scampi cooked in tempura batter, served with chips (thick fries). The only real drawback is the time it takes to get here (Rathfarnham is about 6km/3¾ miles from the city center), although a dedicated minibus will deliver you there and back to the city for a bargain round-trip price of €9.

Edmondstown Rd., Rockbrook, Rathfarnham, Dublin 16. www.mpbpub.com. (*) **01/493-1495.** Dinner and show €55. Bar menu €5–€23. Daily dinner arrive 6:30–7pm, show 8–10pm. Bar food: Mon–Sat 12:30–9:30pm, Sun 12:30–8pm. Special bus serves six locations in central Dublin (€9 per person; must be prebooked).

SHOPPING

There's no question, Dublin is a fantastic city for shopping. Independent shops and boutiques line up alongside their chain-store rivals, and you can often find excellent craftsmanship in the form of handwoven wool blankets and clothes, high-quality crafts and antiques, and chic fashions from the seemingly limitless line of Dublin designers.

The hub of mainstream shopping south of the Liffey is indisputably **Grafton Street,** with its mix of big chains, chi-chi department stores, and little shops on side streets. It's also a popular site for buskers and street performers, where you're almost guaranteed an impromptu show, rain or shine. Grafton Street is crowned by the city's most fashionable department store, Brown Thomas (known as BT's; see p. 157), and the jeweler Weir & Sons (p. 160), but much better shopping is on the smaller streets radiating out from Grafton Street, such as **Duke Street, Dawson Street, Nassau Street,** and **Wicklow Street,** where you'll find shops that specialize in books, handicrafts, jewelry, gifts, and clothing. For clothes, look out for tiny **Cow's Lane,** off Lord Edward Street in Temple Bar—it's popular with those in the know for its excellent boutiques selling the works of local designers. Also in Grafton's penumbra are **South William Street, Castle Market,** and **Drury Street,** all of which have smart boutiques and irresistible tiny shops. On South William Street, check out the **Powerscourt Townhouse Centre,** a small, elegant shopping center in a grand Georgian town house (see p. 156). Not far away, the **George's Street Arcade** is a marvelous clutter of bohemian jewelry, used books, vintage clothes, and other things appealing to the alternative crowd (it even has a resident fortune-teller).

HOURS Generally, Dublin shops are open from 9am to 6pm Monday to Saturday and until 9pm on Thursday. Most shops have Sunday hours, although these vary; some open at 9am, but most are open 11am to 6pm.

SHOPPING MALLS Dublin has several clusters of shops in **multistory malls** or ground-level **arcades,** ideal for indoor shopping on rainy days. On the south side,

Grafton Street bustles with shoppers and passersby.

there's the gleaming wrought-iron-and-glass **St. Stephen's Green Centre,** at the top of Grafton Street (www.stephensgreen.com; ✆ **01/478-0888**); and the **Powerscourt Townhouse Centre,** 59 William St. S. (www.powerscourtcentre.com; ✆ **01/679-4144**). On the Northside, these include the **ILAC Centre,** off Henry Street (www.ilac.ie; ✆ **01/828-8900**), and the **Jervis Shopping Centre** (www.jervis.ie; ✆ **01/878-1323**), at 125 Abbey St. In the southern suburbs, about 8km (5 miles) south of the city center, the large **Dundrum Town Centre** on Sandyford Road (www.dundrum.ie; ✆ **01/229-1700**) has several major fashion outlets and high street chains.

Art & Antiques

Caxton ★★   Antique prints from the 16th, 17th, and 18th centuries are a specialty of this wonderful art store. (In 2012, someone even identified a lost Renaissance masterpiece among the stock.) The prices can be astronomical, but even if you're not buying, for lovers of the antiquarian browsing here is like being a kid in a candy store. 63 Patrick St., Dublin 8. ✆ **01/453-0060.** Bus: 49, 54A.

Christy Bird ★   Variety is our specialty proclaims a sign at this appealing antique store, which has been in business since the 1940s. And it certainly lives up to the promise, stocked with a happy jumble of knick-knacks, collectibles, tat, and genuine antiques. The joy is that you never quite know what you're going to find. 32 S. Richmond St., Dublin 2. www.christybird.com. ✆ **01/475-4049.** Luas: Charlemont, Harcourt St. Bus: 14, 14A, 14B, 15, 15B, 65B, 74, 83, 128.

The Doorway Gallery ★★★   Both new and established Irish artists display their work at this cheerful art gallery. There's always something wonderful to discover, and many prices are affordable, too. 24 S. Frederick St., Dublin 2. www.thedoorwaygallery.com. ✆ **01/764-5895.** Bus: 4, 7, 8, 7B, 7D, 25, 25A, 25B, 25X, 26, 27X, 46A, 66, 66A, 66B, 66X, 67, 67X, 120, 145.

Green on Red ★★   Outstanding contemporary art can be found at this little gallery in the docklands, about a mile northwest of the city center. It holds a dozen or so exhibitions per year. Park Lane, Spencer Dock, Dublin 1. www.greenonredgallery.com. ✆ **087/245-4282.** Rail: Docklands. Luas: Spencer Dock. Bus: 151.

Books & Stationery

Eason ★   There are outlets of this popular book chain all over Ireland, but this multi-story shop on O'Connell Street is one of Ireland's oldest, having been in business since 1819. Pretty much everything you could want is here, from history and local-interest titles to the latest bestsellers. Dublin has 15 other Eason branches, including ones at Nassau Street and Heuston Station. 40 Lower O'Connell St. www.easons.com. ✆ **01/858-3800.** Luas: Abbey St. Bus: 1, 11, 38, 38A, 38B, 39N, 88N, 120, 122, 123, 747.

Hodges Figgis ★　Another enormous *grande dame* Dublin bookshop, this one's even older than Easons—they've been dealing in the printed page here since 1768. Now owned by the Waterstones chain, Hodges Figgis one of the go-to places in the city for books of all kinds. 56–58 Dawson St., Dublin 2. www.waterstones.com/bookshops/hodges-figgis. ℂ **01/677-4754.** Luas: Dawson. DART: Pearse. Bus: 15A, 15B, 44, 61, 140.

The Pen Corner ★★★　Keeping the flame alive for the dying art of letter writing, this place is an utter delight. The Pen Corner sells exquisite fountain pens, paper, and other writing implements, and also stocks beautiful notebooks and cards. 12 College Green, Dublin 2. ℂ **01/679-3641.** Luas: Trinity. DART: Tara St. Bus: 9, 13, 16, 16C, 19, 49N, 54A, 83, 83A, 122, 123, 150, 747, 869.

Ulysses Rare Books ★★　When lovers of Irish literature and antiquarian books die, if they've been good, they get to spend eternity in this shop. Formerly called Cathach Books, this is where to come for rare copies of Joyce, Yeats, Wilde, Behan, Stoker, and just about every luminary of the Irish canon you can think of. Prices range from the barely affordable (€375 for a rare 1927 *Dracula* on our last visit) to the stratospheric (€35,000 for a first-edition *Ulysses*), but it's simply heaven to browse. 10 Duke St. (off Grafton St.), Dublin 2. www.rarebooks.ie. ℂ **01/671-8676.** DART: Pearse. Luas: Dawson. Bus: 10, 11A, 11B, 13, 20B.

CDs & Music

Claddagh Records ★★★　Renowned among insiders in traditional Irish music circles, this is where to find "the genuine article" in traditional music and perhaps discover a new favorite. Not only is the staff knowledgeable and enthusiastic about new artists, but they're also able to tell you which venues and pubs are hosting the best music sessions that week. 2 Cecilia St., Dublin 2. www.claddaghrecords.com. ℂ **01/677-0262.** Luas: Jervis. Bus: All cross-city buses.

Crafts, Design & Housewares

Avoca ★★★　An Irish institution, Avoca is a wonderland of vivid colors, soft blankets, light woolen sweaters, food and gifts, all in a delightful shopping environment spread over three floors near Trinity College. Avoca fabrics are woven in the Vale of Avoca in the Wicklow Mountains (see p. 201). The store also sells pottery, jewelry, and adorable little things you really don't need, but can't live without. Hands down, this is one of the best stores in Dublin. The top-floor **cafe** is a great place for lunch (p. 143). 11–13 Suffolk St., Dublin 2. www.avoca.ie. ℂ **01/677-4215.** Bus: All cross-city buses.

The Design Tower ★★　A cutting-edge convocation of hot designers and craftspeople work at this former sugar refinery at the Grand Canal Quay on the eastern side of the city. Occupants include Seamus Gill, who makes extraordinary, almost organic-seeming silverware; conceptual artist and fashion designer Roisin Gartland; and jewelry designer Brenda

Haugh, whose work includes interesting modern interpretations of Celtic motifs. Some designers here have walk-in shops, but most prefer appointments, so call ahead if you want to see someone specific. The Design Tower is near the Grand Canal Dock DART station, or about a 20-minute walk from Grafton Street. Trinity Centre, Pearse, and Grand Canal Quay, Dublin 2. www.thedesigntower.com. ℰ **01/677-5655.** DART: Grand Canal Dock. Bus: 1, 2, 3, 50, 56A, 77A.

Kilkenny ★★★ This is the city's largest design and craft shop. It has been here since 1976, and at this stage it is an Irish institution. You'll find a super selection of Irish designers with everything from pottery sets and ranges of crystal to clothing, jewelry, art, and all sorts of unique finds. You could easily lose a couple of hours in here, and it's a fantastic place for gifts or some Irish memento of your trip. For a post-shopping treat, a cafe on the first floor serves home-style Irish cooking and great desserts. 6 Nassau St., Dublin 2. www.kilkennyshop.com. ℰ **01/677-7066.** DART: Pearse. Luas: Dawson. Bus: 7B, 7D, 25, 25A, 25B, 25X, 26, 46A, 66, 66A, 66B, 67, 67X, 145.

Powerscourt Townhouse Centre ★★ In a restored 1774 town house, this four-story complex consists of a central sky-lit courtyard and more than 60 boutiques, craft shops, art galleries, snack bars, wine bars, and restaurants. The wares include all kinds of crafts, antiques, paintings, prints, ceramics, leatherwork, jewelry, clothing, chocolates, and farmhouse cheeses. You can also book a behind-the-scenes tour to learn more about the house's history, where you'll poke around the old kitchen and cellars, the former Lord and Lady's bedrooms and dressing rooms, the music room, ballroom, and dining room. 59 S. William St., Dublin 2. www.powers courtcentre.ie. ℰ **01/679-4144.** DART: Pearse. Luas: St. Stephen's Green. Bus: 11, 11A, 11B, 14, 14A, 15A, 15C, 20B, 27C, 39B, 46B, 46C, 46N, 46, 51, 58, 65, 84.

Department Stores

Arnotts ★★ Ireland's original department store, Arnotts first opened its illustrious doors in 1843. Its selection of womenswear, menswear, gifts, and beauty products is enormous. Arnotts stays open for late shopping until 9pm on Thursdays and 8pm on Fridays. Henry St.,

Powerscourt Townhouse Centre is the place to shop for crafts, artworks, antiques, and more.

Dublin 1. www.arnotts.ie. ☏ **01/805-0400.** Luas: Abbey St. Bus: 1, 7, 7B, 7D, 8, 11, 38, 38A, 38B, 39N, 40, 88N, 120, 122, 123, 747.

Brown Thomas ★★★   The top-hatted doorman out front sets the tone for this great old Dublin institution filled with designer clothes and accessories. We've always found this a relaxed and friendly place, even if the credit card takes a bit of a beating. Stop by for most of the major fashion labels before getting your nails done, having a one-to-one at the cosmetics counters, or indulging at the bar and cafe or the elegant restaurant. 88–95 Grafton St., Dublin 2. www.brownthomas.com. ☏ **01/605-6666.** Luas: Dawson or St. Stephen's Green. Bus: 11, 11A, 11B, 14, 14A, 15A, 15C, 15X, 20B, 27C, 32X, 33X, 39B, 39X, 41X, 46B, 46C, 51X, 58X, 70X, 84X.

Fashion & Clothing

Alias Tom ★★   This has long been one of Dublin's top boutique clothing stores. Alias Tom made its name in menswear, but now sells designer fashions (mostly Italian) for women, too. Prices tend to be high, but so does the quality. Duke Lane, Grafton St., Dublin 2. www.aliastom.com. ☏ **01/671-5443** (menswear); ☏ **01/677-8842** (womenswear). Bus: 15A, 15B, 44, 61, 100X, 101X, 111, 133, 140.

China Blue ★   Shelves upon shelves of women's and men's footwear can be found at this trendy shoe store—including an enticing range of designer Doc Martens. It also carries a good selection of kids' shoes. Merchants Arch, Temple Bar, Dublin 2. www.chinablueshoes.com. ☏ **01/671-8785.** Bus: 25, 25A, 25B, 25N, 37, 39A, 51D, 67N, 69, 69X, 70, 70N, 79, 79A.

Costelloe & Costelloe ★   This sweet clothing and accessories store sells a great range of handbags, pashminas, shrugs, and—delightfully—colorful fascinators and headpieces. Best of all, prices are thoroughly reasonable. 14A Chatham St., Temple Bar, Dublin 2. www.costelloeandcostelloe.com. ☏ **01/671-4209.** DART: Tara St. Bus: 15A, 15B, 44, 61, 140.

Kevin & Howlin ★   There's nothing cutting-edge whatsoever about this place—and that's just why people like it. Dublin's go-to store for Donegal tweed, it's been selling handwoven jackets, coats, hats, and other traditional Irish countrywear since 1936. 31 Nassau St., Dublin 2. www.kevinandhowlin.com. ☏ **01/633-4576.** DART: Pearse. Bus: 7B, 7D, 25, 25A, 25B, 25X, 26, 46A, 66, 66A, 66B, 66X, 67, 67X, 145.

Louise Kennedy ★★★   Undoubtedly one of the biggest names in contemporary Irish fashion—so respected that she was put on a postage stamp a few years ago—Louise Kennedy has dressed everyone from heads of state to Hollywood superstars. Her boutique in Merrion Square showcases the best of her current collection. Among the items she's famous for is the gorgeous "Kennedy bag," a limited-edition handbag that is a must-have among the Irish *glitterati*—yours for a mere €1,500. 56 Merrion Sq., Dublin 2. www.louisekennedy.com. ☏ **01/662-0056.** DART: Pearse. Bus: 25, 25A, 25B, 26, 66, 66A, 66B, 67.

STEP away FROM THE LEPRECHAUN: THREE ALTERNATIVE DUBLIN SOUVENIRS

Sure, you can stop by any of the multitude of souvenir stores in Dublin for a keychain shaped like a shamrock, something with sheep on it, or a T-shirt with an "amusing" slogan. But unless your friends really *do* want slippers shaped like a pint of Guinness, you'll score better points back home with one of these more authentic mementos.

o **A pennywhistle.** At Waltons (Blanchardstown Centre, Dublin 15; www.waltons.ie; ℂ **01/960-3232**), which has been in the music business since the 1920s, you'll find instruments both traditional and modern, ranging from an authentic *bodhrán* (drum) starting around €30, to an "absolute beginners" Dublin tin whistle set, complete with DVD tutorial and songbook, for around €14. They also deliver.

o **Flapjacks.** If you ask for a flapjack in Ireland, you won't get a pancake, but a sweet biscuit (cookie to North Americans) made from rolled oats, butter, brown sugar, and honey, often with fruit, nuts, or yogurt added. These traditional treats can be bought

in boxes at food stores, or grab one in a coffee shop for a couple of euro. They stay fresh for a few days and are sturdy enough to survive the trip home.

o **Hedgerow jam.** Known for its soft-as-silk handwoven wool items, Avoca (see p. 155) offers more than just lovely clothing. You can also pick up a jar of their traditional Irish breakfast marmalade or the delightfully named hedgerow jam—each an Avoca specialty costing €5.15. (Meanwhile, buy yourself a luxurious Avoca blanket, dyed with traditional methods in vibrant shades of blue, green, or pink—a relative bargain, given their quality, starting at around €64.)

Om Diva ★★★ Proof that not every designer emporium has to be the kind of place where they check your credit rating at the door, Om Diva is a delightful, cheery shop, with a great selection of designer women's fashion, handmade jewelry, vintage clothes, and accessories. One of Dublin's real finds. 27 Drury St., Dublin 2. www.omdivaboutique.com. ℂ **01/679-1211.** Bus: 9, 16, 16A, 83.

Stable ★★ This small shop is filled with the best in contemporary Irish designs with luxurious wool and linen clothing, scarves, homewares, and accessories sourced from weavers, knitters, and other artisan producers around Ireland. 2 Westbury Mall, Balfe St., Dublin 2. www.stable.ie. No phone. DART: Pearse. Luas: Dawson or St. Stephen's Green.

Gourmet Food

Butlers Chocolate Café ★★ These chocolatiers now sell their delicious wares all over the world, but the business is still family-owned and run. Their **Chocolate Cafés** are all over Dublin, including Grafton Street,

Henry Street, and the airport, but the one on Wicklow Street is the flagship. In addition to an enormous selection of gourmet chocolates, it sells cakes, cookies, flapjacks—and a mean cup of joe. The hot chocolate is spectacular; try the white chocolate version for the purest hit of sweet choccy joy. True addicts can take a tour of the Butlers factory, just north of Dublin (see p. 123). 24 Wicklow St., Dublin 2. www.butlerschocolates.com. © **01/671-0591.** Bus: 9, 16, 49N, 54A, 65, 65B, 68, 68A, 83, 83A, 100X, 101X, 109, 111, 122, 133, 150.

Fallon & Byrne Food Hall ★★★
This exceptional artisan food and wine store is like a high-end deli crossed with an old-fashioned grocer's—albeit a posh modern version. Produce is laid out in open crates, and shelves are stocked with epicurean treats of all kinds, including cheese, charcuterie, and a great selection of wine. There's also an outstanding restaurant on the top floor (p. 144) and a wine bar in the basement (p. 166). 11–17 Exchequer St., Dublin 2. www.fallonandbyrne.com. © **01/472-1010.** Bus: 9, 16, 16C, 49N, 65, 65B, 68, 68A, 83, 83A, 122, 150.

Sheridans Cheesemongers ★★★
Serious cheese lovers need look no further than this wonderful cheesemonger on South Anne Street. The shop stocks around 100 different varieties of cheese—French, English, Italian, you name it—but traditional Irish varieties are a particular specialty. They also sell other deli items, such as wine and cold meats, and do sandwiches to go. 11 S. Anne St., Dublin 2. www.sheridanscheesemongers.com. © **01/679-3143.** Dart: Pearse. Luas: Dawson. Bus: 15A, 15B, 44, 61, 140.

Jewelry

DESIGNyard ★★★
Some of Ireland's leading designers of contemporary jewelry have creations for sale here. Prices tend to be quite high—the cheapest items are around €100 and rise to thousands—but you'll be walking away with something beautiful and unique. They carry an especially beautiful range of engagement rings. 25 S. Frederick St., Dublin 2. www.designyard.ie. © **01/474-1011.** DART: Pearse. Bus: 7B, 7D, 25, 25A, 25B, 25X, 26, 46A, 66, 66A, 66B, 66X, 67, 67X, 145.

Gollum's Precious ★
Come here for classic vintage and designer jewelry—especially French—with a particularly good collection of contemporary pearl earrings, bracelets, and necklaces. Ground floor, Powerscourt Townhouse, Dublin 2. www.gollumsprecious.ie. © **01/670-5400.** DART: Pearse. Luas: St. Stephen's Green. Bus: 11, 11A, 11B, 14, 14A, 15A, 15C, 15X, 20B, 27C, 32X, 33X, 39B, 39X, 41X, 46B, 46C, 46N, 46X, 51X, 58X, 65X, 70X, 84X.

Rhinestones ★
This small but delightful jewelry store specializes in costume jewelry, contemporary and vintage. The antique pieces go back to the early Victorian age, but the mid-20th-century collection has a particular air of glamour. 18 St. Andrews St., Dublin 2. © **01/679-0759.** Bus: 9, 13, 16, 16C, 49N, 54A, 83, 83A, 100X, 101X, 109, 111, 122, 123, 133, 150, 747, 869.

TEMPLE BAR street markets

On weekends, chic Temple Bar shopping isn't only indoors—it spills outside into three of Dublin's finest street markets.

The most glamorous of the three is the **Designer Mart,** a showcase for fashion designers and craftspeople from all over Ireland, which takes place in uber-trendy Cow's Lane every Saturday from 10:30am until 5pm. The more low-key **Book Market** takes up residence in Temple Bar Square all weekend, from 11am to 6pm; there's always some piece of printed treasure or other to be unearthed among its secondhand book stalls.

A must for foodies, the **Food Market** makes its presence felt most of all, as tempting aromas waft around Meeting House Square from 10:30am to 4pm on Saturday. Should the weather take a turn for the worse, a fancy retractable roof will keep you dry while you deliberate over which Irish farmhouse cheese to take away, before waiting in line for a freshly cooked snack.

For details on the Temple Bar street markets, check out **www.templebar markets.com**.

Weir & Sons ★★   Established in 1869, this is the granddaddy of Dublin's fine-jewelry shops. It sells new and antique jewelry, as well as silver, china, and crystal. The ground floor of the main branch on Grafton Street also has a section devoted to 17th-, 18th-, and 19th-century antique silver from Ireland and Britain. A second branch can be found in Dundrum, about 7km (4⅓ miles) south of the city center. 96–99 Grafton St. and 1–3 Wicklow St., Dublin 2. www.weirandsons.ie. ℰ **01/677-9678.** Bus: 15X, 32X, 33X, 39X, 41X, 51X, 58X, 70X, 84X.

Specialist

Forbidden Planet ★   Geeks, assemble! This treasure trove of comics, books, DVDs, and other assorted memorabilia celebrates everything cult. The range of comics and graphic novels is enormous. 5–6 Crampton Quay, Dublin 2. www.forbiddenplanet.co.uk. ℰ **01/671-0688.** Luas: Jervis. Bus: 25, 25A, 25B, 25N, 37, 39, 39A, 51D, 67N, 69, 69X, 70, 70N, 79, 79A.

The R.A.G.E. ★★   Imagine the kind of shop where 1980s teenagers hung out in John Hughes movies, and you've got this place about right. It stands for Record Art Game Emporium, and everything here is vintage—plenty of classic vinyl (all of which can be sampled first). You can even play some of the old video games on an original arcade machine. 16B Fade St., Dublin 2. www.therage.ie. ℰ **01/677-9594.** Bus: 9, 16, 49N, 65, 65B, 68, 68A, 83, 83A, 122.

SPORTS & OUTDOOR PURSUITS

BEACHES Plenty of fine beaches are accessible by city bus or DART, which follows the coast from Howth, north of the city, to Bray, south of the city in County Wicklow. Some popular beaches include **Dollymount,** 5km (3 miles) away; **Sutton,** 11km (6¾ miles) away; **Howth,** 15km (9⅓ miles) away; and **Portmarnock** and **Malahide,** each 11km (6¾ miles) away. The southern commuter town of **Dún Laoghaire** (pronounced Dun *Lear*-y), 11km (6¾ miles) away, makes a particularly good day trip. Not only does it offer a beach (at Sandycove) and water sports (there are four yacht clubs), but it also has cafes and restaurants, two long piers, and a bucolic park with a buzzing Sunday market. For more details, see www. visitdublin.com.

GOLF Dublin is one of the world's great golfing capitals, with a quarter of Ireland's courses—including 5 of the top 10—within an hour's drive of the city. Visitors are welcome, but phone ahead and make a reservation. The following four courses—two parkland and two links—are among the best 18-hole courses in the Dublin area.

    Elm Park Golf & Sports Club ★, Nutley Lane, Donnybrook, Dublin 4 (www.elmpark.ie; ✆ **01/269-3438**), is a beautifully manicured par-69 course in the mostly residential south side of Dublin, only 6km (3¾ miles) from the city center. Greens fees are €50.

Sailing at Dún Laoghaire.

    The respected links course at **Portmarnock Golf Club ★**, in Portmarnock (www.portmarnock golfclub.ie; ✆ **01/846-2968**), lies about 16km (10 miles) from the city center on Dublin's Northside, on a spit of land between the Irish Sea and a tidal inlet. Opened in 1894, this par-72 championship course has over the years hosted many leading tournaments, including the Dunlop Masters (1959, 1965), Canada Cup (1960), Alcan (1970), St. Andrews Trophy (1968), and many an Irish Open. You won't be surprised, then, to discover that fees are a bit pricey. Greens fees are €250 weekdays (€145 Nov–Mar), €275 weekends.

    Often compared to Scotland's St. Andrews, the century-old **Royal Dublin Golf Club ★**, Bull Island,

the birds of **BULL ISLAND**

With a wealth of estuaries, salt marshes, sandflats, and islands, Dublin Bay provides a varied habitat for a number of bird species, making it surprisingly rewarding for bird-watching expeditions. Your all-around best bet lies just north of Dublin city harbor, in the suburb of Clontarf: a bird sanctuary called **Bull Island,** also known as the North Bull Island.

Bull Island isn't an island at all, but a 3km (2-mile) spit of marshland and sand connected to the mainland by a bridge. It was inadvertently created early in the 19th century by Captain William Bligh, of *Mutiny on the Bounty* fame. As head of the Port and Docks Board, Bligh ordered the construction of a harbor wall at the mouth of the River Liffey, in an effort to stop the entrance to Dublin Port from silting up. In fairly short order the shifting sands created this small landmass, a unique beachscape of dunes, salt marsh, and extensive intertidal flats that attracts thousands of seabirds.

Hundreds of species have been recorded on Bull Island, and some 40,000 birds regularly shelter and nest. In winter, they are joined by tens of thousands of migrants from the Arctic Circle, along with North American spoonbills, little egrets, and sandpipers. Together, they all make a deafening racket. A visitor center is open daily 10am to 4:30pm; admission is free.

Dollymount, Dublin 3 (www.theroyaldublingolfclub.com; ✆ **01/833-6346**), is a par-73 championship seaside links on an island in Dublin Bay, 4.8km (3 miles) northeast of the city center. Like Portmarnock, it has been rated among the world's top courses and has played host to several Irish Opens. The home base of Ireland's legendary champion Christy O'Connor, Sr., the Royal Dublin is well known for its fine bunkers, close lies, and subtle trappings. Greens fees are €160 Monday to Thursday and €185 Friday to Saturday (€110–€125 Nov–March); a second round may be played at half-price if space is available. Before 8:20am or last-minute (booked 48 hr. in advance, subject to availability), green fees are €115 Monday to Thursday and €130 Friday to Saturday.

St. Margaret's Golf & Country Club ★, in St. Margaret's, North County Dublin (www.stmargaretsgolf.com; ✆ **01/864-0400**), is a stunning, par-72 parkland course 4.8km (3 miles) west of Dublin Airport. Greens fees are around €40 Monday to Thursday; €45 Friday and €50 Saturday to Sunday.

HORSEBACK RIDING   For trail riding through Phoenix Park, **Ashtown Riding Stables** (www.ashtownstables.com; ✆ **01/838-3807**) is ideal. It's in the village of Ashtown, adjoining the park and only 10 minutes by car or bus (no. 37, 38, 39, 70, or 120) from the city center. You can also get there by train from Dublin Connolly station in less than 15 minutes; Ashtown station is directly opposite the stables. One hour starts at €65.

WATERSPORTS   Instruction and equipment rental for watersports like paddleboarding, windsurfing, and wakeboarding are available at **Surfdock,** Grand Canal Dock Yard, Dublin 4 (www.surfdock.ie; ☎ **01/668-3945**). The center is beside 17 hectares (42 acres) of enclosed fresh water.

SPECTATOR SPORTS

GAELIC GAMES   If your schedule permits, try to get to a **Gaelic football** or **hurling** match—the only indigenously Irish games and two of the fastest-moving sports around. Gaelic football is vaguely a cross between soccer and American football; you can move the ball with either your hands or feet. **Hurling** is a lightning-speed game in which 30 men use heavy sticks to fling a hard leather ball called a *sliotar*—think field hockey meets lacrosse. The women's version is called *camogie*. These amateur sports are played every weekend throughout the summer. Every county has a team, and the games culminate in September with the **All-Ireland Finals,** like an Irish version of the Super Bowl. For schedules and admission fees, phone the **Gaelic Athletic Association,** Croke Park, Jones Road (www. gaa.ie; ☎ **01/836-3222**).

GREYHOUND RACING   Races are held throughout the year at **Shelbourne Park Greyhound Stadium,** South Lotts Road, and **Harold's Cross Stadium,** 151 Harold's Cross Road. Both can be contacted via the **Irish Greyhound Board** (www.igb.ie) or call ☎ **061/448023.**

HORSE RACING   The closest racecourse to the city center is the **Leopardstown Race Course,** off the Stillorgan road (N11), Foxrock (www. leopardstown.com; ☎ **01/289-0500**). This modern facility with all-weather, glass-enclosed spectator stands is 9.7km (6 miles) south of the city center. Racing meets—mainly steeplechases, but also a few flats—are scheduled throughout the year, two or three times a month.

RUGBY & SOCCER   The **Aviva Stadium,** 62 Lansdowne Rd. (www.aviva stadium.ie; ☎ **01/238-2300**), is, depending on your perspective, either a gleaming modern monument to Irish sports or one of Dublin's biggest eyesores. Either way, you really can't miss it. This is the official home of both the national rugby and football (soccer) teams.

DUBLIN AFTER DARK

Nightlife in Dublin is a mix of traditional old pubs, where the likes of Joyce and Behan once imbibed and where Irish music is often reeling away, and cool modern bars, where the hottest new international sounds fill the air, and the crowd knows more about Prada than the Pogues. There's little in the way of crossover, although you'll find a couple of quieter bars and a few with an alternative angle.

WHAT'S ON   Aside from the eternal "old" pubs, things change rapidly in the world of Dublin nightlife, so go online for the latest event listings.

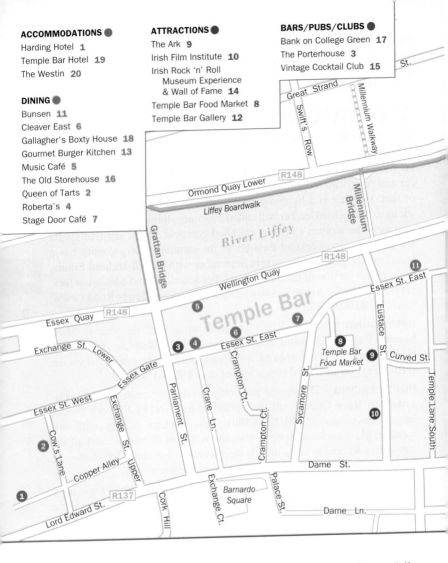

ACCOMMODATIONS ●
Harding Hotel **1**
Temple Bar Hotel **19**
The Westin **20**

DINING ●
Bunsen **11**
Cleaver East **6**
Gallagher's Boxty House **18**
Gourmet Burger Kitchen **13**
Music Café **5**
The Old Storehouse **16**
Queen of Tarts **2**
Roberta's **4**
Stage Door Café **7**

ATTRACTIONS ●
The Ark **9**
Irish Film Institute **10**
Irish Rock 'n' Roll
   Museum Experience
   & Wall of Fame **14**
Temple Bar Food Market **8**
Temple Bar Gallery **12**

BARS/PUBS/CLUBS ●
Bank on College Green **17**
The Porterhouse **3**
Vintage Cocktail Club **15**

Dublin's tourism website **www.visitdublin.com/whats-on** offers a daily guide to art, theater, music, sports, and whatever other entertainment you're up for. You can search by type of experience or view complete events listings by date. Other sites like **Dublin Events Guide,** at www.dublinevents.com or **www.entertainment.ie** also provide a comprehensive listing of the week's entertainment possibilities.

TICKETS   As with any big city, ticket prices for shows vary considerably, from around €10 to over €100. Advance bookings for most large concerts, major plays, and so forth can be booked directly on the event or venue

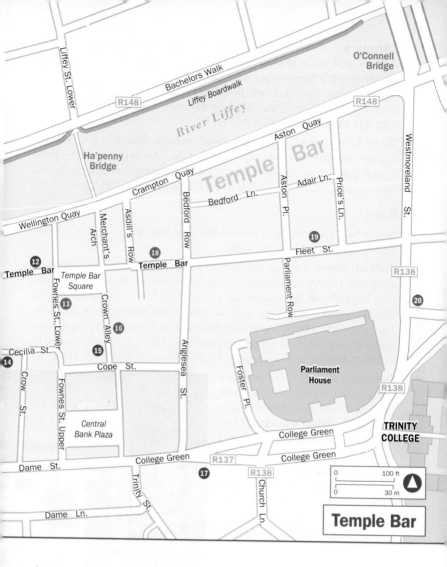

website, or through **Ticketmaster Ireland** (www.ticketmaster.ie; ☎ **81/871-9300** or 353/818-719-300 internationally).

Arenas & Concert Venues

National Concert Hall ★★   If classical music is more your thing, this is the place to be. The program also covers opera, world music, jazz, show tunes, and musicals. Something is on virtually every night; check the website for full listings. Earlsfort Terrace, Dublin 2. www.nch.ie. ☎ **01/417-0000.** Luas: Harcourt. Bus: 100X, 101, 101X, 109, 111, 126, 133.

3Arena ★ This enormous indoor arena (previously known as the **O2**) is the biggest venue in Dublin, and the fifth-best attended in the world at this writing. It's the go-to place for major international acts, standup comedy, and other big-ticket entertainment events—all top-of-the-bill stuff. North Wall Quay, Dublin 1. www.3arena.ie. Box office: 𝄐 **081/871-9300.** Inquiries: 𝄐 **01/819-8888.** Luas: The Point. Bus: 151.

Vicar Street ★★ This much-loved venue is definitely not Dublin's largest—its capacity is roughly ¹⁄₁₄th that of the 3Arena (see above)—but it attracts consistently big names in music and standup comedy. 58–59 Thomas St., Dublin 8. www.vicarstreet.ie. 𝄐 **01/775-5800.** Bus: 13, 25N, 40, 69N, 123.

Bars

Dublin bars generally open at noon and may stay open as late as 2:30am, depending on the day of the week.

Café en Seine ★★ At this elegant, 1920s-style cafe/bar, the interior is all terribly Gatsby, with hanging lamps, glass ceilings, faux-baroque furniture, and polished brass statuettes. The cocktail list is straight-up fun, the whiskey menu a page long, and the atmosphere appropriately decadent. They also serve a bistro menu until 9pm, and on Sundays there's a popular jazz brunch from noon to 5pm. 40 Dawson St., Dublin 2. www.cafeenseine.ie. 𝄐 **01/677-4567** for bookings. Luas: St. Stephen's Green. Bus: 15A, 15B, 44, 61, 140.

Dakota ★★ Small but perfectly curated, this stylish bar on South William Street has a hip clientele and an outstanding selection of bottled beers and cocktails. The crowd is young and the atmosphere raucously sophisticated. 9 S. William St., Dublin 2. www.dakotabar.ie. 𝄐 **01/672-7969.** Bus: 9, 16, 49N, 54A, 65, 65B, 68, 68A, 83, 83A, 122, 150.

Lower Depths ★★ In the basement at the wonderful Fallon & Byrne (p. 144) sits this equally wonderful wine bar. The concept is simple: Pick a bottle from the multitude on display in the candlelit cellar (with or without the advice of the waitstaff), pay a couple of euro corkage, and enjoy. There's also a small menu of nibbles and bistro-style food. 11–17 Exchequer St., Dublin 2. www.fallonand byrne.com. 𝄐 **01/472-1010.** Bus: 15E, 15F, 16, 16A, 19, 19A, 65, 65B, 65X, 83, 122.

The atmospheric Café en Seine.

37 Dawson Street ★★   This sumptuous cocktail bar is crammed with antiques and curios—everything from a stuffed bull's head on a polished wood wall to old anatomical drawings and ornate vases. Its cocktail list is as extensive and imaginative as the quirky surroundings would suggest, and at the back of the building is a proper, old-style whiskey bar. There's also a good restaurant. 37 Dawson St., Dublin 2. www.37dawsonstreet.ie. ✆ **01/902-2908.** Luas: Dawson. Bus: 15A, 15B, 44, 61, 140.

The Vintage Cocktail Club ★★★   There's a definite speakeasy vibe to this Temple Bar cocktail lounge., starting with the super-discreet black door marked only with the initials VCC. Brilliantly—perhaps uniquely?—the cocktail menu is divided into eras, starting with those invented in the 1400s (who knew?) and going up to the 1940s, before leaping forward to the VCC's own decadent creations. It really feels as if like you've joined a club, discovering this place—but sorry, kiddo, you have to be over 23. 15 Crown Alley, Dublin 2. www.vintagecocktailclub.com. ✆ **01/675-3547.** Luas: St. Stephen's Green. Bus: 27, 40, 49, 115, 120.

The Woolshed Baa and Grill ★   Looking for somewhere to watch a big game? This is the place. Enormous TV screens flank the bar, showing whatever's hot in the sporting world—football (the European kind), rugby, U.S. sports (including football, the American kind), and whatever else is on the schedule. They also serve crowd-pleasing bar food. Parnell St., Dublin 1. www.woolshedbaa.com. ✆ **01/872-4325.** Luas: Jervis. Bus: 13, 40, 40B, 40D, 140.

Comedy Clubs

The International Bar & Comedy Cellar ★★   Hosted by the International Bar, the Comedy Cellar is one of the country's top comedy clubs, showcasing the best young pretenders in the world of Irish standup every Wednesday night. Keep an eye on the website and the club's Facebook page to see who's on when you're in town. Tickets cost €10. The International, 23 Wicklow St., Dublin 2. www.theinternationalcomedyclub.com. ✆ **01/677-9250.** Wed 9:30pm (doors open 9pm). Bus: 16, 49N, 54A, 83, 83A, 100X, 101X, 109, 111, 133, 150.

Laughter Lines ★★   What is it about Dublin on a Wednesday that everybody needs cheering up? Another midweek pub takeover, this one happens at the Duke on Duke Street, every Wednesday night at 8:30pm (show starts 9pm). The talented company improvises sketches according to whatever the audience suggests. It's chaotic and great fun. Tickets are €5. The Duke, Duke St., Dublin 2. ✆ **085/829-2571.** Wed 8:30pm. €5. Bus: 11, 11A, 11B, 14, 14A, 15A, 15C, 15X, 20B, 27C, 33X, 39B, 41X, 46B, 46C.

Nightclubs

Admission to nightclubs varies, from free if you arrive early-ish, to around €20 for the very fanciest places. Prices are usually higher on Friday and

Saturday nights. Check club websites before going so you won't be surprised.

The Liquor Rooms ★★★   It's easy to get lost trying to navigate the two bars and numerous, artfully draped corner snugs that comprise this basement club underneath the Clarence Hotel, but that's all part of the charm. The cocktails are outstanding—seeing the nimble bartenders at work serves as a reminder that mixology is as much an art as anything. Check out the lively dance floor or grab a table in one of the many side rooms and watch the time melt away like the ice in an appletini. Reservations are a good idea on weekends. 5 Wellington Quay, Dublin 2. www.the liquorrooms.com. ✆ **087/339-3688.** Bus: 26, 66, 66A, 66B, 66D, 67, 67A.

Panti Bar ★★   One of Dublin's most famous gay bars and clubs, this place is hugely popular and riotously good fun. Saturday night is cabaret night, often hosted by drag queen Panti Bliss herself, and on Sundays there's a "gay ole' tea dance" from 3pm. Panti's tireless campaigning for LGBTQ+ rights has recently made her quite a public figure; to watch her here, in her natural habitat, in full fabulous flow, is a thing to behold. 7–8 Capel St., Dublin 1. www.pantibar.com. ✆ **01/874-0710.** Luas: Jervis, Four Courts. Bus: 25, 25A, 25B, 25N, 25X, 26, 66, 66A, 66B, 66N, 66X, 67, 67N, 67X, 69, 69N, 79, 79A.

Pubs

How could you go to Dublin and not stop by a pub or two? More than mere drinking dens, pubs are the secular temples of Ireland, a cultural export that has conquered the world. The Irish didn't invent the pub, exactly, but many would say they perfected it. In *Ulysses,* James Joyce referred to the puzzle of trying to cross Dublin without passing a pub; his characters quickly abandoned the quest as impossible and stopped to have a few pints instead. You may want to look upon that as a challenge.

Pub hours generally begin as early as 10 or 11am and end by 12:30am, after which you'll need to head to a nightclub if you crave more action.

The Bank on College Green ★★   This handsome place was built as a bank in 1892, at the height of Victorian opulence. While it's also an appealing place to eat (p. 143), you can enjoy its stunning interior just as well by simply grabbing a pint or a wee dram. 20 College Green, Dublin 2. www.bankoncollegegreen.com. ✆ **01/677-0677.** Bus: 15X, 32X, 33X, 39B, 39X, 41X, 49X, 50X, 51X, 58X, 65X, 70X, 77X, 84X.

The Brazen Head ★★★   This is a serious contender for the coveted title of "oldest pub in Ireland," having served the locals continually since at least 1661 (although an alehouse was reputedly on the same spot for hundreds of years before that—they claim 1198 as the foundation date, and who's to argue?). It was once a hangout for Irish revolutionaries, and Joyce mentioned the place in *Ulysses,* although today it's more famous for

Dublin's oldest pub, the Brazen Head.

lively traditional music sessions. Every night features a different act; worthies who've played here include Van Morrison, Tom Jones, and Garth Brooks. 20 Lower Bridge St., Dublin 8. www.brazenhead.com. ℂ **01/679-5186.** Luas: Smithfield. Bus: 25, 25A, 25B, 25X, 26, 37, 39, 39A, 51D, 51X, 66, 66A, 66B, 66X, 67.

The Cobblestone ★★★ We recently asked a Dublin taxi driver to recommend the best place for live music in Temple Bar. Answer: "Now why would you bother, when the Cobblestone is so close?" This is an authentic musician's place, as much a traditional music venue as a pub, such is the standard of the music. Free sessions are in the front bar nightly, with ticketed acts in the **Backroom,** a dedicated performance space. The pub is on the Northside, 5 minutes' walk from the Old Jameson Distillery (p. 109). 77 North King St., Smithfield, Dublin 7. www.cobblestonepub.ie. ℂ **01/872-1799.** Bus: 37, 39, 39A, 70, 70N.

Davy Byrnes ★★ "He entered Davy Byrnes," wrote Joyce of Leopold Bloom, the hero of *Ulysses.* "Moral pub. He doesn't chat. Stands a drink now and then. But in a leap year once in four. Cashed a cheque for me once." Given its impeccable literary connections, it's no surprise that many writers make this pub a pilgrimage spot when they're in town. Joyce himself was a regular, although the food has improved since his day—the menu of pub classics and sandwiches is actually pretty good, and reasonably priced. *Ulysses* fans will be delighted to hear that you can still order a gorgonzola sandwich, Bloom's snack of choice. 21 Duke St., off Grafton St., Dublin 2. www.davybyrnes.com. ℂ **01/677-5217.** Bus: 11, 11A, 11B, 14, 14A, 15A, 15C, 15X, 20B, 27C, 33X, 39B, 41X, 46B, 46C.

Doheny and Nesbitt ★★★ From the outside, this pub brings to mind a Victorian medicine cabinet, all polished wood with a rich blue-and-gold sign. Its proximity to the political heart of the capital makes it a perennial hangout for politicos, lawyers, economists, and those who write about them—which can make for some spectacularly good eavesdropping. (Its name inspired a catchphrase, "the Doheny and Nesbitt School of Economics," to describe the movers and shakers who used to shoot the breeze here during Ireland's boom years of the 1990s and 2000s.) To admire its cozy interior, a midweek daytime visit is best—this place gets packed in the evenings (especially summer weekends), even more so when a big sports match is on. 5 Baggot St. Lower, Dublin 2. www.dohenyandnesbitts.ie. © **01/676-2945.** Bus: 10, 10A, 25X, 51D, 51X, 65X, 66D, 66X, 67X, 77X.

Grogan's Castle Lounge ★★★ There's a friendly, chatty vibe at this satisfyingly old-fashioned place, considered one of Dublin's "quint-essential" pubs. You'll find little modern about the dimly lit, atmospheric interior, save for the incongruous art collection on the walls (if you like a piece, ask—most of it is for sale). Grogan's reputation rests mostly on its eclectic clientele, ranging from grizzled old folks who've been coming here for years to hipsterish artsy types in search of a low-fi hangout. 15 S. William St., Dublin 2. www.groganspub.ie. © **01/677-9320.** Bus: 15, 32X, 33X, 39X, 41X, 51X, 58X, 70X, 84X.

Kehoe's ★★ This lovely old pub is virtually sepia-toned, with its burnt-orange walls and acres of polished walnut. That's an appropriate analogy for the atmosphere, too—easy-going and frequently packed in the evenings. Kehoe's is best enjoyed in daylight hours, when you can observe the local characters and soak up the old-school Irish pub atmosphere. A particularly appealing feature is the original "snugs"—tiny private rooms, almost like booths. 9 South Anne St., Dublin 2. www.kehoesdublin.ie. © **01/677-8312.** Bus: 15A, 15B, 44, 61, 140.

The Long Hall ★★★ The gorgeous, polished walnut-and-brass interior of this Victorian pub is liable to elicit purrs of delight from thirsty patrons as soon as they walk in the door. Undoubtedly one of Dublin's most . . . well, *Irish* of pubs, the Long Hall is named for the bar that runs the entire length of the interior. Regulars have to fight for space alongside the tourist crowd, but it's more than worth squeezing in for a look at the interior. Not that staying here for a few pints is anything like a chore. 51 S. Great George's St., Dublin 2. © **01/475-1590.** Bus: 11E, 15F, 16, 16A, 19, 19A, 39X, 65, 65B, 65X, 83, 122.

Neary's ★ A favorite hangout of Dublin's theatergoers—and actors, stage crews, and just about everyone else from the Gaiety Theatre (p. 171) behind it—it's full of Victorian features, such as the wonderful globe lanterns out front, held aloft by a brass arm emerging from the brickwork. The upstairs bar is a quiet retreat during the day. 1 Chatham St., Dublin 2. www.nearys.ie. © **01/677-8596.** Luas: St. Stephen's Green. Bus: 15A, 15B, 61, 140.

SPINNING AN IRISH yarn OR TWO

The concept of the wonderful **An Evening of Food, Folklore & Fairies** ★★★ is timeless, yet brilliant in its simplicity. No high-tech smoke and mirrors, just compelling tales from Irish folklore, passionately told by masters of the storytelling craft. To be clear, this is storytelling for all ages, not just children, and it's a brilliant revival of an ancient art. The whole thing takes place in an atmospherically lit room inside **O'Shea's pub** on Talbot Street. During dinner, the storytellers spin their absorbing yarns. The meal, included in the price, is suitably traditional as well: beef-and-Guinness stew or bacon and cabbage with mashed potatoes. If you haven't had your fill of Irish tradition by the end of it all, you can go and listen to live music in the bar.

The storytelling evenings are held nightly at 6.30pm, every night of the week from March to October. Tickets are €54 adults, €50 seniors and students, €29 children (minimum age 6). Contact www.irishfolktours.com (✆ **01/ 218-8555**).

The Porterhouse ★★ This lovely pub in Temple Bar was the first in Dublin to sell only microbrewery beers. Most are produced by the Porterhouse's own mini-chain, and the range is constantly updated, so you never know what you'll get from one visit to the next. A relaxed, jovial vibe and hearty pub lunches make it a perfect pit stop on a long day's sightseeing. There's also live music every night. 16–18 Parliament St., Dublin 2. www. porterhousebrewco.ie. ✆ **01/679-8847.** Bus: 13, 27, 37, 39.

Theater

Abbey Theatre ★ Since 1903, the Abbey has been the national theater of Ireland, and it remains one of the most respected and prestigious theaters in the country. The original theater, destroyed by fire in 1951, was replaced in 1966 by the current functional, although uninspired, 492-seat house. In addition to its main stage, the theater has a 127-seat basement studio, the **Peacock,** where it presents newer, more experimental work. 26 Lower Abbey St., Dublin 1. www.abbeytheatre.ie. ✆ **01/878-7222.** Ticket prices generally €13–€40. Event times vary; call ahead. Rail: Tara St., Connolly. Luas: Abbey St. Bus: 27, 39A, 4, 41, 46A, 61, 7, 84X

Gaiety Theatre ★ The elegant little Gaiety, opened in 1871, hosts a varied array of performances, everything from opera to classical Irish plays and Broadway-style musicals. (The Gaiety's annual pantomime, or Christmas show, is a big event on the city's theatrical calendar.) And when the thespians leave, the partygoers arrive: On Friday and Saturday from midnight on, the place turns into a nightclub, with four bars hosting live bands and DJs, spinning R&B, indie, blues, or hip hop. There are even occasional cult movie showings. Don't forget to check out the ornate decor before you get too tipsy. The Gaiety Theatre, South King St., Dublin 2. www.gaietytheatre.ie. ✆ **081/871-9388.** Ticket prices generally €15–€50. Event

4

times vary; call ahead. Luas: St. Stephen's Green. Bus: 11, 11A, 11B, 14, 14A, 15A, 15C, 15X, 20B, 27C, 33X, 39B, 40A, 40C, 41X, 46B, 46C, 46N, 46X, 51X, 58X, 67X, 70X, 84X.

The Gate Theatre ★   Just north of O'Connell Street off Parnell Square, this 370-seat theater was founded in 1928 by Irish actors Hilton Edwards and Micheál Mac Liammóir to provide a venue for a broad range of plays; its program today still includes a blend of modern works and the classics. Although less known by visitors, the Gate is easily as distinguished as the Abbey. Cavendish Row, Parnell Sq., Dublin 1. www.gatetheatre.ie. ℰ **01/874-4045.** Ticket prices generally €20–€30. Event times vary; call ahead. Luas: O'Connell St. Bus: 1, 2, 14, 14A, 16, 16A, 19, 19A, 33X, 39X, 40, 40A, 40B, 40C, 41X, 48A, 58X, 70B, 70X, 120. 123.

DAY TRIPS
FROM
DUBLIN

5

D riving in or out of Dublin, through suburbs and then out along big, bland, modern highways, it would be easy to assume the region immediately surrounding the capital is a little . . . dull? But don't be fooled. The Dublin hinterland is like the safety curtain at a Broadway show. Might not look like much, but just wait until you see what's on the other side. Within an hour's drive north, south, or west of Dublin, you will find some of Ireland's most iconic sites, including ancient ruins, historic homes and castles, and miles of beautiful countryside. And while it's possible to see any of those listed in this chapter on a quick day trip from the capital, the area has plenty of fine hotels and restaurants should you want to spend more time here. And who could blame you?

North of Dublin: You'll find the remnants of Ireland's most ancient civilizations at prehistoric sites such as Newgrange and Knowth. A short distance away, the green hills of the Boyne Valley hold the long-lost home of early Irish kings, who once reigned with a mixture of mysticism and force.

West of Dublin: This is Kildare, Ireland's horse country. Even if you're not into horse-racing, some handsome historic homes and other sites make this area worth checking out.

South of Dublin: The Wicklow Mountains rise from the low, green countryside, dark and brooding. This is a beautiful region, dotted with early Christian ruins, gardens, forests, and peaceful river valleys. The hills are perfect for a day trip from Dublin and make a good starting point for a driving tour of the south of Ireland.

ESSENTIALS

Arriving

BY CAR   Most of the attractions listed in this chapter are easily accessible by car in about an hour from Dublin. The roads are good in the regions around the city, although traffic can be a problem—particularly during rush hour, when all roads around Dublin slow to a crawl. In reasonable traffic, Newgrange and Knowth are about an hour north of the city, Kildare Town and its nearby attractions are just under an hour to the southwest,

PREVIOUS PAGE: **Sailing in Wicklow.**

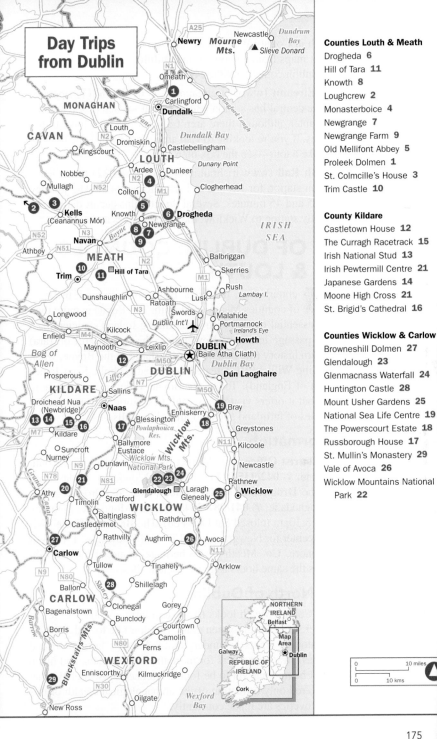

Day Trips from Dublin

Counties Louth & Meath

Drogheda **6**
Hill of Tara **11**
Knowth **8**
Loughcrew **2**
Monasterboice **4**
Newgrange **7**
Newgrange Farm **9**
Old Mellifont Abbey **5**
Proleek Dolmen **1**
St. Colmcille's House **3**
Trim Castle **10**

County Kildare

Castletown House **12**
The Curragh Racetrack **15**
Irish National Stud **13**
Irish Pewtermill Centre **21**
Japanese Gardens **14**
Moone High Cross **21**
St. Brigid's Cathedral **16**

Counties Wicklow & Carlow

Browneshill Dolmen **27**
Glendalough **23**
Glenmacnass Waterfall **24**
Huntington Castle **28**
Mount Usher Gardens **25**
National Sea Life Centre **19**
The Powerscourt Estate **18**
Russborough House **17**
St. Mullin's Monastery **29**
Vale of Avoca **26**
Wicklow Mountains National Park **22**

and Glendalough in County Wicklow is about an hour's drive south. You can get excellent maps from any one of the **Dublin Tourism** visitor centers (www.visitdublin.com; ✆ **1890/324-583**).

BY BUS **Bus Éireann** (www.buseireann.ie; ✆ **01/836-6111**) operates services from the central bus station (Busáras) out to each of the regions listed in this chapter, although there aren't always practical links to the more remote sites. If you're looking to visit attractions by bus, the best bet is probably to take a tour—see the box on p. 177.

BY TRAIN **Irish Rail** (www.irishrail.ie; ✆ **1850/366-222**) trains leave Dublin's Heuston station for Kildare at least once an hour. The journey takes between 25 and 45 minutes. Several direct trains depart daily from Dublin's Connolly station to Wicklow; the journey takes an hour.

NORTH OF DUBLIN: COUNTIES MEATH & LOUTH

North of Dublin's conurbation, the River Boyne rolls through the rich, fertile countryside of counties Meath and Louth. The Boyne is more than a river—it's an essential part of Irish lore, linking Ireland's ancient past (the prehistoric passage tombs of Newgrange, the storied Hill of Tara) with more modern history (the infamous 1690 Battle of the Boyne, when the Protestant King William III defeated the exiled Catholic King James II for the crown of England). Today the Boyne Valley is a much more peaceful place, but it offers visitors a wealth of historic treasures tucked away among miles of farmland and smooth, rolling hills.

Visitor Information

The **Dundalk Tourist Office** is on Market Square, Dundalk, Co. Louth (www.visitlouth.ie; ✆ **042/935-2111**). It's open Monday to Friday from 9am to 5pm. The **Drogheda Tourist Office** (West St., Drogheda, Co. Louth; www.drogheda.ie; ✆ **041/987-2843**) is open Monday to Saturday from 9:30am to 5:30pm (closed Sat Oct–Feb). The **Brú na Bóinne Visitor Centre,** the center for Newgrange (p. 177) and Knowth (p. 178), is at Newgrange, Donore, Co. Meath (www.heritageireland.ie; ✆ **041/988-0300**), and keeps the same hours as those ancient sites.

Exploring North of Dublin

On the surface, County Meath looks like placid farm country—little but rolling hills covered in emerald-green grass. But don't be fooled. Its most breathtaking historical sights lie underground. Meath's fertile soil and rich river land has attracted settlers for more than 8,000 years, and much of what they left behind has yet to be found. Archaeologists believe that they have uncovered only a fraction of the archaeological wealth of this region; new discoveries are made constantly.

bus trips FROM DUBLIN

Although you'll need a car to fully explore what the regions around Dublin have to offer, it's possible to see virtually all of the big attractions by taking guided bus tours. Most leave from central Dublin, quite early in the day, and deposit you back around 5 or 6pm. Book tours directly with the operator. Here are a few of the most popular ones.

Newgrange Tours by Mary Gibbons (www.newgrangetours.com; ✆ **086/355-1355**) are among the most respected of the guided tours that visit the ancient burial site. Mary is an excellent guide, and her tours have an allocated entry slot at Newgrange, meaning you don't have to wait. Tours run daily from several pickup points in Dublin, between 9:30am and 10am Monday to Friday (returning about 4:30pm); and 7:30am and 8:15am Saturday and Sunday (returning about 3:15pm). This includes a break for lunch (not included in the price). The tour costs €45.

Glendalough Bus (www.glendaloughbus. com; ✆ **01/281-8119**) runs day trips from the north side of St. Stephen's Green to Glendalough every day at 11:30am. Return tickets cost €20, and you buy them from the driver. You can also catch the bus from Bray at 12:10pm; the return fare from there is €15.

The **Wild Wicklow Tour** (www.wildwick low.ie; ✆ **01/280-1899**) takes in Dún

Laoghaire Harbour and Dalkey, before heading to Glendalough and the Sally Gap. They even take you to a pub for lunch (not included in the price). The tours—which are perhaps skewed toward youthful travelers—leave from several points in Dublin, "early but not too early" (8:50am–9:40am), and return at around 5:30 or 6pm. Tickets cost €33 adults and €28 seniors, students, and children.

Paddy Wagon Tours (www.paddywag ontours.com; ✆ **01/823-0822**) runs a number of rather touristy trips from Dublin to places all over Ireland, from near (**Kilkenny** and **Glendalough**) to about the farthest you can get from Dublin and still be in Ireland (the **Dingle Peninsula, Cliffs of Moher,** and **Giant's Causeway**). Tickets start at €25 and rise to around €85. The longest day tours take about 12 hours, door to door. Paddy Wagon also runs 2- and 3-day tours that include accommodations; see the website for details.

Brú na Bóinne, Newgrange, and Knowth ★★★ ANCIENT SITE
Brú na Bóinne, which translates to "palace of the Boyne" in Irish, is home to some of Ireland's best-known prehistoric monuments: Newgrange, Knowth, and Dowth and a World Heritage Site. **Newgrange,** the most well-known, is one of the archaeological wonders of Europe. Built as a burial mound more than 5,000 years ago—long before the Egyptian pyramids or Stonehenge—it sits atop a hill near the Boyne, massive and mysterious. Newgrange is so old, in fact, that when it was built there were still woolly mammoths living in parts of Europe. The mound is 11m (36 ft.) tall and approximately 78m (256 ft.) in diameter. It consists of 200,000 tons of stone, a 6-ton capstone, and other stones weighing up to 16 tons each, many of which were hauled from as far away as County Wicklow and the Mountains of Mourne. Each stone fits perfectly in the overall pattern, and the result is a watertight structure, an amazing feat of engineering. The

question remains, though: Why? Even as archaeologists found more elaborate carvings in the stones, they deduced no clues as to whether it was built for gods, kings, or long-forgotten rituals. Inside, a passage 18m (59 ft.) long leads to a central burial chamber that sits in pitch darkness all year, except for 5 days in December. During the winter solstice (Dec 19–23), a shaft of sunlight travels down the arrow-straight passageway for 17 minutes, where it hits the back wall of the burial chamber. You can register for a lottery to be in the tomb for this extraordinary event, although competition is fierce—and these days it's livestreamed on the Internet as well.

The extraordinary prehistoric burial site at **Knowth** was only discovered in 1968, and much of it is yet to be excavated. It is mainly composed of two massively long underground burial chambers, the longer of which stretches for 40m (131 ft.). In the mound, scientists found the largest collection of passage tomb art uncovered thus far in Europe, as well as a number of underground chambers and 300 carved slabs. Surrounding the mound, 17 satellite graves are laid out in a mysterious, complex pattern. And still, no one has a definitive answer to the biggest riddle of all: What was it all for? Even now, many of Knowth's secrets have not been uncovered—excavation work is constant here, and there is no access for visitors to the inner chamber or passage.

Tip: These sites have no direct access; you have to visit as part of a tour from the Brú na Bóinne Visitor Centre near Donore, where you park and take a shuttle bus the rest of the way. You should book weeks in advance, as soon as you know the day you'll be coming—space is limited and it's one of the most popular historic sites in the country. There are two tours—the Brú na Bóinne and Newgrange chamber tour allows you inside the passage at Newgrange, where you can walk down past the elaborately carved stones and into the chamber, which has three sections, each with a basin stone that once held cremated human remains. The Brú na Bóinne "outside" tour visits the exteriors of Newgrange and Knowth only, with no access to inside the Newgrange chamber. There is no access at all to the inside chamber at Knowth.

Brú na Bóinne Visitor Centre, on N51, 2km (1¼ miles) west of Donore, Co. Meath. www.heritageireland.ie. ✆ **041/988-0300.** Brú na Bóinne tour and Newgrange chamber: €18 adults; €16 seniors; €12 students and children over 12; free for children under 12; €48 families. Brú na Bóinne tour, exterior of Newgrange and Knowth: €12 adults; €10 seniors; €8 students and children over 12; €28 families. Visitor Centre only: €5 adults; €4 seniors; €3 students and children over 12; €13 families. Visitor Centre open daily May–Aug 9am–7pm; Sept 9am–6pm; Oct 9:30–5:30pm; Nov–Jan 9am–5pm; Feb–Apr 9:30am–5:30pm. Last admission 45 min. before closing.

Drogheda ★ TOWN   A modest industrial commuter town of 30,000 people, 56km (35 miles) north of Dublin, Drogheda (pronounced *Draada* in the local accent) has two historic churches—both, confusingly, with the same name. The bigger of the two, **St. Peter's Roman Catholic Church,** in the town center, is remarkably impressive, with its French Gothic rose window and imposing 68m (222-ft.) spire. But its main claim to fame is grislier; St. Peter's contains the shrine of St. Oliver Plunkett (1625–81), the Archbishop of Armagh, who was beheaded in London for his part in an alleged plot to assassinate King Charles II—becoming the last Catholic martyr to die in England. His severed head can still be seen, shriveled and wizened inside a glass case, as the centerpiece to his shrine. The other St. Peter's, **St. Peter's Church of Ireland,** a simple gray stone church at the northern end of the town, has its own notorious backstory, dating to 1649, during Oliver Cromwell's bloody conquest of Ireland. On September 11, after an 8-day siege, around 2,000 Irish soldiers loyal to the deposed monarch, Charles I, were massacred. Fleeing the carnage, 140 took refuge in St. Peter's steeple. Refusing to heed their surrender, Cromwell ordered them burned alive using wood from the pews—an act so heinous that some of his own men refused, risking a charge of mutiny. St. Peter's has been rebuilt twice since the terrible event. (Check out the spooky carved skeletons on one tomb in the nave.) The small **Drogheda Museum** is located in the 17th-century **Millmount Fort,** overlooking the town, where the walls were finally breached at the end of the siege. Tours cost €5 (€3 seniors), but they're a little long, so stick with the self-guided version.

St. Peter's R.C. Church: West St. www.saintoliverplunkett.com. ✆ **041/983-8536.** Daily 10am–5pm. **St. Peter's Church of Ireland:** Peter and William sts. www.drogheda.armagh.anglican.org. No phone. Daily 10am–3pm. **Millmount Fort:** Off John St. www.millmount.net. ✆ **041/983-3097.** Admission €6 adults; €4 students; €3 seniors and children; €12 families. Mon–Sat 10am–5:30pm, Sun/holidays 2–5pm.

Hill of Tara ★★ ANCIENT SITE   Legends and folklore place this hill at the center of early Irish history. Ancient tombs have been discovered that date back to the Stone Age; pagans believed that the goddess Queen Maeve reigned from here. By the 3rd century, a ceremonial residence had been built here for the most powerful men in Ireland—the high kings, who ruled as much by myth as by military strength. Every 3 years they would hold a weeklong *feis* (a kind of government session/wild party twofer), at which more than 1,000 princes, poets, athletes, priests, druids, musicians, and jesters celebrated. Laws were passed, disputes settled, and matters of defense decided. After the last *feis* was held in A.D. 560, Tara went into a decline as the power shifted. Today, little is left of the hill's great heritage, save for grassy mounds and some ancient pillar stones. All that survives of the Iron Age forts are depressions in the soil. That said, it's still a great spot with views that extend for miles. You can learn the hill's history at a visitor center in the old church beside the entrance. Guided tours are available for those who want to know what lies beneath the smooth, green surface.

Signposted on N3, about 12km (7.4 miles) south of Navan, Co. Meath. www.hilloftara.org. ✆ **046/902-5903** (Visitor Centre); 041/988-0300 (off season). Admission €5 adults; €4 seniors; €3 students and children; €13 families. Hill open year-round. Visitor Centre: Mid-May to mid-Sept daily 10am–6pm.

North of Dublin: Counties Meath & Louth

A Stone Age burial ground, Knowth contains Europe's largest collection of passage-tomb art.

Loughcrew Cairns and Gardens ★★ ANCIENT SITE Loughcrew is a two-for-one deal: beautiful 19th-century pleasure gardens dotted with lakes, perfect for picnicking, and, just a short distance away, one of the biggest megalithic burial grounds in Ireland. The 30 passage tombs of Loughcrew are known locally as *Slieve na Calliaghe,* which translates as "The Hill of the Witch." With such an atmospheric name you'd expect something good to look at, and sure enough, the three hills topped like crowns with symmetrical tombs can be seen from miles away. The site is aligned with both the equinox and the pagan day of Samhain (Halloween), so that twice a year the dawn sun lights a heavily carved stone within one cairn. Crowds gather each year to see the phenomenon. Access to the cairns is free—the climb is steep, so wear appropriate footwear. From N3, take R195 through Oldcastle toward Mullingar; 2.4km (1½ miles) out of Oldcastle, look for the signposted left turn and follow signs.

Outside Oldcastle, Co. Meath. www.heritageireland.ie. © **049/854-1240.** Cairns: Free admission. Gardens (www.loughcrew.com): €7 adults; €5 seniors; €3.50 children; €20 families. May–Aug 10:30am–5pm. Garden tours €20 per person or €60 per group; available Mid-Mar to Oct Mon–Fri 9:30am–5:30pm; Sat–Sun 11am–5:30pm; Nov to mid-Mar Sat–Sun 11am–4pm (book in advance).

Monasterboice ★ RELIGIOUS SITE This atmospheric monastic site holds a peaceful cemetery, one of the tallest round towers in Ireland, ancient church ruins, and two excellent high crosses, all surrounded by trees and green fields. The site is said to have been founded in the 4th century by a follower of St. Patrick named St. Buithe. The name "Buithe" was corrupted to Boyne over time, and thus the whole region is named after him. A small monastic community thrived here for centuries, until it was seized and occupied by Vikings in the 10th century. The Vikings were, in turn, defeated by Donal, the high king of Tara, who is said to have single-handedly killed 300 of them. Today only a little is left, but the **Muiredeach's High Cross** is worth the trip all on its own. Dating from 922, the near-perfect cross is carved with elaborate scenes from the Old and New Testaments (see box, below). Two other high crosses are more faded, and one was smashed by Cromwell's forces. The site is now accessible to wheelchair users.

Off the main Dublin road (N1), 9.7km (6 miles) NW of Drogheda, near Collon, Co. Louth. Free admission. Daily dawn–dusk.

Newgrange Farm ★ FARM   After all that history, the kids will thank you for bringing them to this busy farm, where farmer Willie Redhouse and his family offer a 1½-hour tour. You can feed the ducks, groom a calf, and bottle-feed the lambs and kid goats. Children can hold a newborn chick, pet a pony, play with the pigs, and look at pheasants and rare birds in the aviaries. Tractor rides cost an extra €2.50. The high point of the week occurs every Sunday afternoon (and on Irish national holidays), when the sheep take to the track with teddy bear jockeys for the weekly derby. (Call to check race times.) Demonstrations show farm skills such as threshing and horseshoeing, and sheepdogs show off their herding skills. The farm has kids' play areas, a coffee shop, and plenty of picnic space. The price is a little steep, but family discounts kick in at just one adult and one child.

Off N51, 3.2km (2 miles) east of Slane (signposted off N51 and directly west of New-grange monument), Co. Meath. www.newgrangefarm.com. ⓒ **041/982-4119.** Admission €9 adults; €4 seniors; €3 students and children; family rate is €8 per person. Open Mar 17–Sept 3 daily 10am–6pm. Last admission 5pm.

Old Mellifont Abbey ★ RELIGIOUS SITE/RUINS   Founded in the 12th century, this was the first Cistercian monastery on the island, and it grew to be the most important. Much of it is gone now, but enough is left to give you an idea of what Mellifont was like in its day, when it was the center of Cistercian faith in Ireland, with more than 400 monks living and working within its walls. You can see the outline of the cross-shaped nave, as well as the remains of the cloister, refectory, and the warming room (the only part of the monastery with heating—after all, monks were supposed to live lives of suffering). Mellifont was closed in the 16th

The ruins of Old Mellifont Abbey in County Louth, the first Cistercian monastery in Ireland.

HIGH CROSSES: icons OF IRELAND

You see them all over Ireland, often in the most picturesque rural surroundings, standing alone like sentries: high Celtic crosses with faded stories carved into every inch of space. Haunting and ancient as they seem to us today, when they were created, these carved stones served a practical purpose: They were books, of sorts, in the days when books were rare and precious. Think of the carvings, which illustrate biblical stories, as cartoons explaining the Bible to an illiterate population. Originally, the crosses were probably brightly painted, but the paint has long been lost to the wind and rain.

Muiredeach's High Cross (see above) at Monasterboice has carvings telling, from the bottom up, the stories of Adam and Eve, Cain and Abel, David and Goliath, and Moses, as well as the wise men bringing gifts to the baby Jesus. At the center of the old cross, the carving is thought to be of Revelations, while at the top St. Paul stands alone in the desert. The western side of the cross tells the stories of the New Testament, with, from the top down, a figure praying, the Crucifixion, St. Peter, Doubting Thomas, and, below that, Jesus's arrest. On the base of the cross is an inscription of the sort found often carved on stones in ancient Irish monasteries. It reads in Irish, "a prayer for muiredach for whom the cross was made." Muiredach was the abbot at Monasterboice until 922, so the cross was probably made as a memorial after his death.

Another excellent example of a carved high cross is the **Moone High Cross** ★, which is not too far away (p. 189). Really intrigued by high crosses? Then head southwest to the **Ahenny High Crosses** in County Tipperary (p. 369).

century during Henry VIII's dissolution of the monasteries, and a manor house was soon built on the site for an English landlord, using the abbey stones. A century later, that house would be the last place where Hugh O'Neill, the final Irish chief, stayed before surrendering to the English and then fleeing to Europe in 1607 (see "English Power & the Flight of the Earls," p. 53). At the informative visitor center next door, you can find out more about the monastery and its long, complex history.

Tullyallen, signposted off R168, 9.7km (6 miles) west of Drogheda, Co. Louth. www.heritageireland.ie. ℂ **041/982-6459** or 041/988-0300 (out of season). Admission €5 adults; €4 seniors; €3 students and children; €13 families (free admission mid-Sept to mid-May). Visitor center late May to early Sept daily 10am–5pm; last admission 45 min. before closing.

Proleek Dolmen ★ ANCIENT SITE This huge dolmen is said to resemble a giant's finger when viewed from a distance. That is subjective, to say the least. But fingerlike or not, it's an impressive sight. A massive 35-ton capstone looks alarmingly precarious, balanced on top of three smaller stones like a crude, misshapen tripod. The top of the capstone is invariably covered with pebbles, thanks to a local legend that says if you can throw a stone and it stays there, your wish will come true. You can reach the dolmen down a paved footpath from the parking lot of the

Ballymascanlon House Hotel (www.ballymascanlon.com; ✆ **042/935-8200**) near Dundalk; the dolmen is a 5-minute walk away. To find the hotel from Dublin, take exit 18 for Dundalk North off the M1, then take the N52 off the first roundabout, and the road to Ballymascanlon from the second. The hotel is about 3km (1¾ miles) down this road.

On the grounds of Ballymascanlon House Hotel, Dundalk, Co. Louth. No phone. Free admission.

St. Colmcille's House ★ RELIGIOUS SITE

Sitting incongruously near more modern houses in Kells, like a memory of Ireland's distant past, this narrow gray stone house is all that's left of a long-lost monastic settlement that once stood where the town now sprawls. Most of the nearly windowless building dates to the 10th century, although some sections predate that by another hundred years. Some experts believe it was once a scriptorium, where monks wrote and illuminated books—and quite possibly where the Book of Kells (p. 92) was produced. The first-floor room still contains traces of an ancient fireplace and entryway; a narrow staircase ascends to a dark vault just under the roof.

About 180m (590 ft.) NW of St. Columba's Church, Church Lane, Kells, Co. Meath. No phone. Free admission. June–Sept 10am–5pm. Ask for key from caretaker, Mrs. Carpenter, who lives next door to the oratory on Church Lane, opposite the churchyard.

Trim Castle ★ CASTLE

A skeletal reminder of the clout once wielded by Anglo-Normans in Ireland, this ruined edifice is an inspiring sight. The Norman lord Hugh de Lacy occupied the site in 1172 and built the enclosed cruciform keep. In the 13th century, his son Walter enlarged the keep, circled it with a many-towered curtain wall, and added a great hall as an upgraded venue for courts, parliaments, and feasts. After the 17th century, though, it was abandoned and lay in ruins for hundreds of years. Few paid much attention to it, until Mel Gibson chose to use it as a setting for the 1995 film *Braveheart.* The Irish Heritage Service restored it as a "preserved ruin." Entry to the main part of the castle is by guided tour only, but arrive early if you're visiting in summer—space is limited and the tour can't be booked in advance, so it often sells out. *Note:* The hour-long tour is unsuitable for small or unruly children, and for anyone unable to maneuver steep climbs or afraid of formidable heights.

Castle St., Trim, Co. Meath. www.heritageireland.ie. ✆ **046/943-8619.** Admission €5 adults; €4

> ### A Gruesome Find at Trim Castle
>
> In 1971, when excavation work was underway at Trim Castle, workers made a macabre discovery: While digging to the south of the central keep, they uncovered the remains of 10 headless men. Historians believe that the bodies date from the 15th century. During a time of high crime in 1465, King Edward IV ordered that all robbers be beheaded, and their heads displayed on spikes to intimidate those who might be considering a career in crime. Presumably, these men had all suffered that fate.

seniors; €3 students and children; €13 families. Mid-Mar to Sept daily 10am–5pm; Nov to early Feb weekends 9am–4pm; mid-Feb to mid-Mar and Oct daily 9:30–4:30pm; last admission 1 hr. before closing.

Where to Stay North of Dublin

Bellinter House ★★   On the banks of the River Boyne outside Navan, this imposing gray-stone Palladian country house was designed by the same man who built **Russborough House** (p. 199) and **Powerscourt** (p. 198). The hotel has been restored to resemble a 19th-century country getaway, with an atmosphere of relaxed elegance. Its drawing room is a lovely space, where you can take afternoon tea or just relax in front of the fire with a good book. Most guest rooms are less glamorous than the public areas; the more expensive rooms are, inevitably, the most beautiful. But all have large, modern bathrooms and comfortable beds. The restaurant is highly rated for its French-influenced Irish cuisine and locally sourced meat and produce. Breakfasts are huge—even the tea selection is enormous. There's a small spa (with a sauna, steam room, and outdoor hot tub), and guests are free to explore the sprawling grounds and fish on the river. Get directions from the hotel before setting out—on a tiny farm road, this place can be hard to find.

Bellinter, Navan, Co. Meath. www.bellinterhouse.com. ✆ **046/903-0900.** 42 units. €159–€279 double. Free parking. Breakfast included. **Amenities:** Restaurant; bar; spa; Wi-Fi (free).

The Cottages ★★   You can't get closer to the sea than these adorable thatched cottages on the beach in Co. Meath, just outside the village of Bettystown, where the sound of the waves will lull you to sleep. Each cottage is perfectly restored and equipped with exposed beams, comfortable beds, warm bed covers, full kitchens, and living rooms with just enough space. Bathrooms have free-standing showers and deep baths. All cottages have TVs and Wi-Fi, but long walks on the beach and strolls into the picturesque village will undoubtedly keep you busy. Book early; with just six cottages, it's understandably popular.

Coast Road., Bettystown, Co. Meath. www.cottages-ireland.com. ✆ **041/982-8104.** 6 units. €160–€400 per cottage. Minimum stay 3 nights. Free parking. Self-catering. **Amenities:** Wi-Fi (free).

D Hotel ★★   This award-winning, modern hotel on the banks of the River Boyne in the busy town of Drogheda is the perfect place to base yourself while exploring the east coast. Rooms are modern and bright, with comfortable beds and huge windows taking in the sweeping river view. The hotel restaurant, **Goodwins,** specializes in steak and seafood, while the in-house pub, **Hops,** is the perfect place to unwind with a pint after a day of exploring. All this, and reasonable prices, too.

2 Ghan Rd., Carlingford, Co. Louth. www.ghanhouse.com. ✆ **042/937-3682.** 12 units. €60–€90 double. Free parking. Breakfast included. **Amenities:** Restaurant; bar; Wi-Fi (free).

Ghan House ★★   Overlooking Carlingford Lough, Ghan House is a sweet, old-fashioned hotel. The good-size guest rooms are traditionally furnished, with antiques and sofas. Most are in the main 17th-century building, though there is also a modern extension, and many have views of the lake or mountains. "Superior" rooms have half-tester beds and deep Victorian bathtubs. The award-winning restaurant serves up excellent modern Irish cuisine, and the owners hold cooking and wine-tasting classes on-site. Check the website for special offers.

2 Ghan Rd., Carlingford, Co. Louth. www.ghanhouse.com. ✆ **042/937-3682.** 12 units. €180–€250 double. Free parking. Breakfast included. **Amenities:** Restaurant; bar; Wi-Fi (free).

Headfort Arms Hotel ★   This pleasant, cheery hotel is a 5-minute walk from St. Colmcille's House (p. 183) in the center of Kells. The picture-postcard facade—all hanging baskets and neat little shutters—gives way to a more modern interior, and bedrooms are simple but large and tidy. Executive rooms have two copper-sprung beds, and family rooms offer plenty of space for kids. The hotel restaurant, the **Vanilla Pod ★★** (✆ **046/924-0084;** see p. 187), is one of the best in the area. The small spa offers massage and beauty treatments.

Headfort Pl., Kells, Co. Meath. www.headfortarms.ie. ✆ **046/924-0063.** 45 units. €99–€189 double. Free parking. Breakfast included. **Amenities:** Restaurant (dinner only except Sun lunch); bar; room service; spa; Wi-Fi (free).

Trim Castle Hotel ★   This modern hotel is a stone's throw from the castle (you really could hit it with a rock quite easily, not that we're encouraging you). The hotel lounges and restaurants are bright and cheerful. Guest rooms are not huge but are well-appointed, with modern bathrooms. Some rooms have direct views of the evocative castle ruins. The good, bistro-style **Jules Restaurant** offers reasonably priced classic Irish fare (€30 for three courses), and a lovely rooftop patio overlooking the castle is a fine place to take a coffee and soak up the view. You can get simpler meals in the **Bailey Bar** for €22 for three courses. Or there's the **Barista Café,** which serves light bites and sweet treats. Check the website for deeply discounted deals, in the spring in particular.

Castle St., Trim, Co. Meath. www.trimcastlehotel.com. ✆ **046/948-3000.** 68 units. €119–€179 double. Free parking. Breakfast included. **Amenities:** Restaurant; bar; room service; Wi-Fi (free).

Where to Eat North of Dublin

This isn't one of Ireland's foodie regions, but that doesn't mean there aren't good options. This is a great area for simple, homey Irish food. In addition to the places listed below, plenty of places offer lighter bites.

- In Carlingford, **Ruby Ellen's Tea Rooms** (Newry St.; www.ruby ellens.com) is legendary for its decadent homemade cakes, fluffy scones, and pots of piping-hot tea. It's a wonderful place to linger on a rainy afternoon.

o In Drogheda, **Ariosa Café** (Saint Laurence St.; www.ariosacoffee. com) offers the best cup of Joe north of Dublin. Ariosa roasts its own beans to make sure each cup is perfect; you can also get croissant and pastries in the tiny town-center space.

o When you've had enough of rich food, stop in to Drogheda's **Bare Food Company** (15 West St.; www.thebarefoodcompany.ie) for a healthy break. From its creamy bircher muesli to the fresh, green salads and veg-packed sandwiches, Bare Food does its best to help clear your arteries—it's a great place for vegan food.

o In a converted barn outside Dundalk on the M1 motorway, **Strandfield House** (www.strandfield.com; ☎ **042/937-1856**) is a hybrid café/florist/bakery. Rustic and beautiful, overflowing with blooms in the summer, it uses local ingredients in all its recipes. Here you'll find obscure local cheeses, fabulous tarts and quiches, as well as fresh pizzas, bread, pastries, and, well, big bouquets of roses. Great for vegetarians. Expect a short wait—it's insanely popular.

The Bay Tree ★★★ IRISH   This restaurant isn't much to look at from the outside, but inside it's a cozy, romantic space. The cooking is top notch, allowing the freshest, local ingredients—some of which come from their own gardens—plenty of space to shine without overloading the palate. Start with a fig and Roquefort tart garnished with 25-year-old balsamic, then try the duck confit with mulled-spice red cabbage, or the salmon filet with glazed Brussels sprouts. Follow it up with a rich sticky toffee pudding with hot toffee sauce, or a super-fresh baked Alaska, straight from the oven. The Bay Tree has an attached guesthouse with pleasant, modern bedrooms, costing from €99 to €120 per night.
Newry St., Carlingford, Co. Louth. www.baytree.ie. ☎ **042/938-3848.** Entrees €23–€28. Thurs–Fri 5–8:45pm; Sat 5–8:45pm; Sun 1–7:30pm.

Burke's Restaurant ★ INTERNATIONAL   The Burke family have run this friendly, unpretentious little diner for over 25 years, making it a local institution. The enormous, overflowing full Irish breakfasts are a staple (and pretty reasonable at €8.50, given that they provide enough carbs to power you for a week). The lunch menu focuses on comfort food: fried chicken, burgers, and fresh local fish. Drop by in the afternoon for tea and sample the delicious house-recipe pancakes. The restaurant is just around the corner from St. Peter's Church on West Street.
6 Peter St., Drogheda, Co. Louth. ☎ **041/984-3498.** Entrees €6–€15. Mon–Sat 9:30am–6pm.

The Glyde Inn ★ IRISH   Overlooking scenic Dundalk Bay, this waterfront pub and restaurant in Annagassan is famed for its clever way with local seafood. Dishes are simple and classic. The seafood chowder is creamy and rich, served with warm, homemade bread. Regulars come for the lobster—caught that morning—but there are plenty of options. From

North of Dublin: Counties Meath & Louth

fish and chips to the catch of the day (if the razor clams are on the menu, definitely try them), this is hearty fare in a relaxed setting.

Main St., Annagassan, Co. Louth. www.theglydeinn.ie. © **042/937-2350.** Entrees €14–€25. Daily 11am–11pm.

Vanilla Pod ★★ MODERN EUROPEAN   Imaginative Irish cooking with international influences is the focus of this great little restaurant in Kells. The menu is seasonal and showcases regional flavors in dishes like herb crumbed scallops with gin and lemon thyme; honey- and plum-glazed duck breast; or rack of local lamb with pea and lettuce gratin. Vanilla Pod is in the popular **Headfort Arms Hotel** (p. 185).

The Headfort Arms Hotel, John St., Kells, Co. Meath. www.headfortarms.ie. © **046/924-0084.** Entrees €16–€29.50. Thurs–Sat 5–10pm; Sun 12:30–9:30pm. Closed Mon–Wed.

WEST OF DUBLIN: COUNTY KILDARE

The flatlands of Kildare are rich in more ways than one. The fertile soil produces miles of lush pastures perfect for raising horses, and the population is one of the most affluent in the country, with plenty of cash for buying horses. Driving through the smooth rolling hills, home to sleek thoroughbreds, you might notice a similarity to the green grass of Kentucky—in fact, the county is twinned with Lexington, Kentucky. This is the home of the Curragh, the racetrack where the Irish Derby is held, and smaller tracks at Naas and Punchestown.

Once the stronghold of the Fitzgerald Clan, Kildare is named after the Irish *cill dara,* or "Church of the Oak Tree," a reference to St. Brigid's monastery, which once sat in the county, surrounded by oak trees. Brigid (see box on p. 190) was a bit ahead of her time as an early exponent for women's equality—she founded her co-ed monastery in the 5th century.

Visitor Information

The **Kildare Heritage Centre** is in Market Square, Kildare Town (www. kildareheritage.com; © **045/530672**). It's open Monday to Saturday from 10am to 1pm and 2 to 4:45pm (closed Sun).

Exploring West of Dublin

Castletown House ★★ HISTORIC HOUSE   The fine, symmetrical architecture of this spectacular Palladian-style mansion has been imitated many times across Ireland over the centuries. Made of clean, white stone, with elegant rows of tall windows, Castletown was built between 1722 and 1729, designed by Italian architect Alessandro Galilei for then-speaker of the Irish House of Commons, William Connolly. Today, it's beautifully maintained, and the fully restored interior is worth the price of admission. Entry is by guided tour only, though you're free to wander around the surrounding parkland at your leisure. Two interesting follies on the estate were built as make-work for the starving population during the Famine: One is a graceful obelisk, the other an extraordinarily playful barn, created as a higgledy-piggledy inverted funnel, around which winds a fanciful stone staircase. It is aptly named the Wonderful Barn.

Signposted from R403, off main Dublin-Galway Rd. (N4), Celbridge, Co. Kildare. www.castletown.ie. ✆ **01/628-8252.** House: €10 adults; €8 seniors; €5 students and children; €25 families. Grounds: Free admission. House: Mar to early Nov daily 10am–5pm (last admission 1 hr. before closing) by guided tour only; call ahead or check tour times online. Grounds: 7am–7:30pm year-round.

The Curragh ★ RACECOURSE   The country's best-known racetrack, the Curragh has hosted races for hundreds of years. The first recorded race took place here in 1727, but historians believe races were held at this site long before then. Today it's a modern flat track—there's nothing left of whatever may have stood here centuries ago. But its place in history is assured, and it is home to the **Irish Derby,** the premier horse race of Ireland, held every year on the last Saturday of June. Races take place at least one Saturday a month from March to October. The Curragh website has full details on all races and tickets, including premium packages. Derby day tickets are inevitably more expensive than for other races; expect to pay upwards of €30 or €50 with transport to and from Dublin (prebooking is essential). On non-race days, the Curragh runs 90-minute "behind the scenes" tours, where you can visit locations like the weigh rooms and parade rings. The nearest train station is Kildare Town (a free shuttle runs from there to the track on race days); trains run direct from Waterford, Cork, Limerick, Galway, and Dublin's Heuston station, with fares starting at around €15. **Dublin Coach** (www.dublincoach.ie; ✆ **01/465-9972**) runs a "Race Bus" from Westmoreland Street in central Dublin on race days; fares start at around €10.

Dublin-Limerick Rd. (N7), Curragh, Co. Kildare. www.curragh.ie. ✆ **045/441205.** Standard race days €15–€20 adults; discount for seniors and under 25; children under 18 (with adult) free. Hours vary; 1st race usually 1:30pm (or 5pm for evening races), but check newspapers or website. Behind the Scenes tours €25–€55.

Irish National Stud with Japanese Gardens & St. Fiachra's Garden ★ FARM/GARDENS   Many of Ireland's fastest horses have been bred on the grounds of this famous stud farm. Horse lovers and racing fans will be in heaven, walking around the expansive grounds and watching the well-groomed horses being trained. There are exhibits on racing, steeplechase, hunting, and show jumping, plus a rather macabre display featuring the skeleton of Arkle, one of Ireland's most famous horses. The tranquil **Japanese Garden,** dating from 1906, has pagodas, ponds, and trickling streams, and the beautifully designed visitor center has a restaurant and shop. A garden dedicated to St. Fiachra—the patron saint of gardeners—lies in a beautiful natural setting of woods and

A mare and foal at the Irish National Stud, home of many of Ireland's finest thoroughbred racehorses.

wetlands, and a reconstructed hermitage features a Waterford crystal garden of rocks and delicate glass orchids.

Off the Dublin-Limerick Rd. (N7), Tully, Kildare, Co. Kildare. www.irishnationalstud.ie. *℗* **045/521617.** Admission €14 adults; €11 seniors and students; €8 children 5–15; €32.50 families (off-peak tickets cheaper Nov–Dec). Daily 10am–6pm (to 4pm Nov–Dec); last admission 1 hr. before closing. Tours daily 10:30am, noon, 1, 2, 3, and 4pm (off-peak tour times Nov–Dec 11am and 2pm). Car park closes 6:15pm.

Irish Pewtermill Centre ★ CRAFT FACTORY   In an 11th-century mill originally constructed for the nunnery of St. Moling, Ireland's oldest pewter mill makes a nice diversion. It has a little museum devoted to the craft, but the skilled artisans who work here are the main attraction, still casting pewter in antique molds, some of which are 300 years old. Casting takes place most days, usually in the morning—make an appointment in advance if you want to watch the craftsmen or visit the museum (both are free). The showroom has a wide selection of high-quality, hand-cast pewter gifts for sale, from bowls to brooches, at reasonable prices.

Timolin-Moone Rd. (signposted off N9 in Moone), Co. Kildare. *℗* **087/909-0044.** Free admission. Mon–Fri 10am–4:30pm, Sat–Sun 11am–4pm. Museum and workshop open by appointment only.

Moone High Cross ★ RELIGIOUS SITE   Amid the picturesque ruins of Moone Abbey, this magnificent high cross (see box on p. 182) is nearly 1,200 years old. The abbey, established by St. Columba in the 6th century, lies in evocative ruins around it. The cross features finely crafted

local hero: **ST. BRIGID**

Modern-day feminists have embraced this 5th-century Irish saint, and for good reason. Brigid was a headstrong girl who fought against the oppressive, patriarchal rules of her time. When her father picked a husband for her, she refused to marry him. Legend holds that when her father insisted that the wedding should go forward, she pulled out her own eye to prove she was strong enough to resist his plans. He backed down, and the mutilated girl joined a convent. When she took her vows, however, the bishop accidentally ordained her as a bishop rather than a nun. It is said that as soon as that happened, she was miraculously made beautiful again.

As she grew older, Brigid remained a rebel. She founded a monastery in Kildare but insisted that it be open to both nuns and monks—something unheard of at that time. Word of the monastery, and of its unusual abbess, soon spread throughout Europe, and she became a powerful figure in European Christianity. Her followers marked their homes with a plain cross woven from river reeds. In some Irish homes, you'll still find crosses made in precisely that way.

One of Brigid's strangest rules for her monastery was that a fire should always be kept burning, day and night, tended by 20 virgins. Long after she died, the fire at St. Brigid's burned constantly, tended as she said it should be. This continued as late as 1220, when the bishop of Dublin insisted that the tradition, which he viewed as pagan, be stopped. But there is still a fire pit at **St. Brigid's Cathedral ★** (see below), and a fire is lit in it every February 1, on St. Brigid's feast day.

Celtic designs as well as biblical scenes: the temptation of Adam and Eve, the sacrifice of Isaac, and Daniel in the lions' den. Among the carvings are several surprises, such as a carving of a Near Eastern fish that reproduces when the male feeds the female her own eggs, which eventually hatch from her mouth.

Signposted off N9 on southern edge of Moone, Co. Kildare. No phone. Free admission. Daily dawn–dusk.

St. Brigid's Cathedral ★ CHURCH   Built on the site of St. Brigid's monastery, which was founded in the 5th century, this beautiful 13th-century church dominates central Kildare. Its exquisite stained-glass windows portray Ireland's three great saints: Patrick, Colmcille, and Brigid. The round tower on the grounds is the second tallest in the country (33m/108 ft.); it dates to the 10th century, although its original pointed roof was later replaced by a Norman turret. If the groundskeeper is in, you can climb the stairs to the top for €7. Near the tower, a strange-looking stone with a hole at its top is known as the "wishing stone"—according to lore, if you put your arm through the hole and touch your shoulder when you make a wish, then your wish will come true. The cathedral is closed to visitors from October to April, but you can usually visit the grounds year-round, free, by inquiring at the Heritage Centre on Market Square (p. 187).

Market Sq., Kildare Town, Co. Kildare. ℂ **045/521229.** Cathedral €2; round tower €7. Cathedral: May–Sept Mon–Sat 10am–1pm, 2–5pm; Sun 2–5pm; last admission 15 min. before closing. Closed Oct–Apr. Grounds: daily dawn–dusk.

Where to Stay West of Dublin

Barberstown Castle ★★ Although parts of this hotel were built as recently as the early 2000s, enough genuine old castle is still on view as you approach for it to look and feel satisfyingly, well, *castle*-like. The oldest section dates from the 13th century, and the castle has had 37 owners since then—including rock star Eric Clapton, who held regular music sessions when he lived here in the 1980s. Even the modern guest rooms manage to feel pleasantly antique; some have four-poster beds. Family rooms are available, too. The formal **Barton Rooms** restaurant serves classic (and quite pricey) Irish bistro fare.

On R403, Straffan, Co. Kildare. www.barberstowncastle.ie. ℂ **01/628-8157.** 55 units. €190–€260 double; €220–€280 suite. Free parking. Breakfast included. **Amenities:** Restaurant; room service; Wi-Fi (free).

Dining in the castle's keep at Barberstown Castle.

Cliff at Lyons ★★★   This peaceful country retreat is set along the Grand Canal, with a small collection of stone buildings containing a boutique hotel, a spa, the two-Michelin-starred restaurant **Aimsir** (p. 193), and the less formal **Mill** restaurant, which serves country classics (much of the produce is grown on-site) and is named after an old mill, also on the grounds. There are bicycles if you wish to cycle along the canal. Rooms are all different and spread around the buildings; some have four-poster beds and free-standing baths. The Lily Pond rooms all face the inn's gorgeous main water feature. Check the website for special stay-and-dine or spa offers.

Lyons Rd., Celbridge, Co Kildare. www.cliffatlyons.ie. ℂ **01/630-3500.** 38 units. €260–€400 double. Free parking. Breakfast included. **Amenities:** 2 restaurants, bar; bikes; spa; Wi-Fi (free).

Martinstown House ★★   An elegant country house getaway near the famous Curragh racecourse (p. 188), Martinstown dates mostly from the 1830s. Bedrooms are decorated with more than a few nods to its early Victorian origins, with heritage color schemes and antique-style furniture. Excellent four-course dinners (€60) are served around a single, long, candlelit table, which gives the appealing sense of an upper-class house party from a bygone age. Expect seasonal fare such as roast duck with spiced red cabbage, or grilled sole with lemon and caper butter. The downside is that you have to reserve 24 hours in advance, and a minimum of 12 guests are required at dinner. So unless you're traveling in a large group, it might be worth determining if any of your fellow guests want to eat here on the same night as you. *Note:* Although the Curragh is just 8km (5 miles) away, a frustrating road layout means that driving between the Martinstown and the racecourse takes up to a half-hour each way. *Note:* This place can get booked up *really* far in advance.

Off L6078 (follow signs for Martinstown), Ballysaxhills, Curragh, Co. Kildare. www.martinstownhouse.com. ℂ **045/441269.** 6 units. €175–€295 double. Free parking. Breakfast included. **Amenities:** Restaurant; Wi-Fi (free).

Where to Eat West of Dublin

County Kildare is beloved by Dubliners for its horses and outlet shopping, but the restaurants aren't too shabby, either. In addition to the options below, if you're looking for coffee, head to Celbridge and try **Baobab** (92 English Row; www.baobab.ie), owned by two native Kenyans who are passionate about coffee. Everything is done well here, from roasting to serving, and there are fabulous pastries and cakes to go with the coffee. For lunches and light dinners, try the **Green Barn** at the Burtown House and Gardens (Athy, Co. Kildare; www.burtownhouse.ie). Inside an actual converted barn, this light-filled restaurant grows much of its food in the beautiful gardens here, which are also open to the public. Try the leek and kale pie or the warm goat cheese and honey fritter, and then wander the grounds.

local hero: **SILKEN THOMAS**

Nobleman and rebel rolled into one, Silken Thomas was an unlikely revolutionary. More properly known as Thomas FitzGerald, the 10th Earl of Kildare, he was born in 1513 to illustrious parents—his father was governor of Ireland—and spent much of his childhood at the court of King Henry VIII in England.

Thomas returned to Ireland as a young man, to follow in his father's footsteps and rule on behalf of the king. However, when word reached him that his father had fallen out with Henry and been executed, Thomas raised a rebellion. It began with a blistering attack on Dublin Castle. It failed, but the English were rattled. Thomas and his men retreated to the relative safety of County Kildare, expecting a counter-attack at any moment. And indeed it came . . . but by stealth. While Thomas was temporarily absent from his garrison, a guard was bribed to let in a small group of English soldiers, who massacred everybody inside.

Thomas and his remaining men fought valiantly for a while longer. The struggle was futile, however, and Thomas eventually agreed to surrender in return for a promise that he and his closest compatriots would be spared. But King Henry wasn't one for keeping his word. Thomas and his men were sentenced to death by hanging, drawing, and quartering.

On a bleak February morning in 1537, Thomas and the others were hanged by the neck, but cut down before they died. Then they were cut open, their bowels and genitals removed and then burned in front of their eyes. They were finally killed by beheading, after which their corpses were cut into quarters and placed on spikes. Such was the wrath of kings.

Despite this chilling end, Thomas remains a folk hero. But why the unusual nickname? The sobriquet "Silken Thomas" comes from the fact that Thomas always dressed in the height of fashion. And when his army of 200 men rode into battle, they wore ribbons of silk streaming from their helmets.

Aimsir ★★★ MODERN IRISH   This restaurant is such a hit it was awarded two Michelin stars just 4 months after opening. Aimsir is set on the gorgeous Cliff at Lyons estate (p. 192), and Chef Jordan Bailey, who hails from Cornwall in England, celebrates that powerful Irish force—the Irish climate (Aimsir means "weather" in Irish)—with food from the island's best producers and growers. A creatively imagined seasonal tasting menu takes you on a tour of land and sea, with lots of tasty surprises among the 18 servings. A Connemara surf clam might be served with winter apple, preserved pine spruce, and celeriac juice; Donegal halibut comes with charred pickled onion, lemon verbena, and fermented artichoke cream. It's expensive at €210, but this is a one-off experience. You can also sample a four-course snack in the lounge for €18.50 from 3pm. Aimsir is a popular spot with foodies—book well ahead.

Cliff at Lyons, Lyons Road, Celbridge, Kildare. www.aimsir.ie. © **01/630-3500.** Tasting menu (18 servings) €210. Wed–Sat, seatings at 7pm or 8pm.

The Brown Bear ★★ EUROPEAN   In the pretty village of Two Mile House outside Naas, this multi-award-winning restaurant located on the owner's family farm offers local produce and innovative cooking in a relaxed environment. Expect starters like scallops with pumpkin and black pudding, or foie gras with apple and walnut. Main dishes could include duck breast with red cabbage and pickled carrots, or cod with white bean and prawn. The chefs use a light touch and let the fresh produce sing.

Two Mile House, Naas, Co. Kildare. www.thebrownbear.ie. ✆ **045/883561.** Entrees €18–€34. Wed–Thurs 6–9pm; Fri–Sat 6–9:30pm.

Cunningham's ★ THAI/PUB FOOD   Inside and out, Cunningham's is a fairly traditional, run-of-the-mill Irish pub—which makes it all the more unlikely that it also serves some of the best Thai food in the area. Delicious authentic-style meals are prepared by the Thai chef, Chock, and served in the bar nightly. You could go for a spicy red, green, or panang curry, made with coconut and chilis; or a classic pad Thai served with crispy wontons. The menu also has a selection of traditional pub options, such as burgers and steaks, but it's the Thai food that packs in the crowds. Some nights include live music.

Main St., Kildare, Co. Kildare. www.cunninghamskildare.com. ✆ **045/521780.** Entrees €14.50–€19. Mon–Sat 5:30–9:30pm; Sun 3:30–7:30pm.

Hartes ★ GASTRO PUB   A multiple winner for "Best Restaurant in Co. Kildare," Hartes looks like a traditional pub from the outside, but expect no Irish stew here. The owners are dedicated to locally grown produce and sustainable farming practices, and the chefs can tell you where every piece of meat or seafood came from in dishes like the local goat cheese and fig tart, or the chicken wings with dry chili rub and mint yogurt. For mains, try the chicken and chorizo cassoulet, or the halloumi fritters with chickpea tagine—but save room for dessert. The chocolate fondant with 70% dark chocolate is a personal favorite of ours.

Market Square, Kildare, Co. Kildare. www.harteskildare.ie. ✆ **045/533557.** Entrees €17.50–€25.50. Tues 5–8:45pm; Wed 12:30–3:45pm, 5–8:45pm; Thurs 12:30–3:45pm, 5–9pm; Fri–Sat 12:30–3:45pm, 5–9:30pm; Sun 12:30–8:30pm.

Silken Thomas ★ INTERNATIONAL   Named for a real-life knight and dashing rebel (see above), this atmospheric pub offers simple, tasty, unfussy meals in a jovial atmosphere. The menu is something of a global tour, with Mexican fajitas, Chinese stir-fries, and Indian curries happily served alongside burgers, salads, fish and chips, and other familiar Irish fare. There's also a carvery (buffet-style station serving roast meat and vegetables) from noon daily and a substantial breakfast menu.

The Square, Kildare, Co. Kildare. www.silkenthomas.com. ✆ **045/522232.** Entrees €15–€18. Daily Mon–Sat 9am–9pm.

Sports & Outdoor Pursuits in Kildare

GOLF The flat plains here create excellent parkland layouts, including the Arnold Palmer–designed, par-72 **K Club** in Straffan, Co. Kildare (www.kclub.ie; ℭ **01/601-7200**). The club has two courses, with greens fees ranging from €90–€120 (South course) and €120–€175 (North course).

WALKING The way-marked **Grand Canal Way,** a long-distance walking path that cuts through part of Kildare, passes through such scenic towns as Sallins, Robertstown, and Edenderry, where you can find a room and stock up on provisions. For more information, go to **www.irishtrails.ie/Trail/Grand-Canal-Way/18**, or contact the Kildare tourist office.

SOUTH OF DUBLIN: COUNTIES WICKLOW & CARLOW

Wicklow's northernmost border is just a dozen or so miles south of Dublin, making it one of the easiest day trips from the city. The centerpiece of the region is the beautiful **Wicklow Mountains,** traversed by the well-marked **Wicklow Way** walking path, which wanders for miles past mountain tarns and secluded glens. Tucked into the mountains are the isolated monastery and lakes of **Glendalough** and picturesque villages such as **Roundwood, Laragh,** and **Aughrim.** Along the coast, the busy town of **Bray** is 12.6km (7¾ miles) south of Dún Laoghaire. Farther south is the coastal town of **Greystones** and, just inland, the charming villages of **Enniskerry** and **Avoca.** A handful of historic stately homes and gardens dot the countryside.

Just over the border of County Wicklow lies **County Carlow,** one of Ireland's smallest counties, bordered to the east by the Blackstairs Mountains and to the west by the fertile limestone land of the Barrow Valley and the Killeshin Hills. Its most prominent feature is the 5,000-year-old granite formation known as **Browne's Hill Dolmen.**

Visitor Information

The **Wicklow Tourist Office,** Fitzwilliam Square, Wicklow Town (www.visitwicklow.ie; ℭ **040/469117**), is open Monday to Friday year-round between 9am and 5pm (closed weekends). The **Carlow Tourist Office,** Library Building, College Street, Carlow Town (www.carlowtourism.com; ℭ **059/913-0411**), is open year-round Monday to Friday 9:30am to 1pm and 2pm to 5pm. Both are usually open all weekend in summer.

Exploring South of Dublin

Browneshill Dolmen ★ ANCIENT SITE Resembling an elephant about to topple slowly to one side, this megalithic stone table has crouched in this green field in Co Carlow for millennia. No one knows its purpose, though archaeologists suspect the dolmen was built as a portal tomb to mark the burial place of a long-dead king. The gigantic stack of stones is estimated to be 5,000 years old, and for many centuries, people believed it had been built by giants. Today, archaeologists say the vast capstone—believed to weigh a colossal 100 tons—was likely rolled into place up an earthen ramp that was then destroyed. Faced with the sheer massiveness of these stones, you may prefer to stick with the tale about the giants.

Off Rathvilly Rd., Carlow, Co. Carlow. No phone. Free admission. Daily dawn–dusk. Access via parking lot and enclosed pedestrian pathway.

Glendalough ★★★ RELIGIOUS/NATURE SITE Tucked away amid deep forests and surrounded by rolling hills, this evocative, misty glen is a truly magical place. Glendalough means "valley of the two lakes," and you can easily walk around both lakes, or climb the hills to take in the beauty of this extraordinary site from above (you can get maps at the visitor center at the entrance). The area is part of Wicklow Mountains National Park. Each of the many walking trails traversing the area takes in scenic vistas and wildlife, as well as some hidden ruins. The oldest ruins are **Teampall na Skellig,** across the lake at the foot of towering cliffs (unfortunately, there's no boat service and they cannot be visited), and the cave known as **Kevin's Bed,** believed to be where St. Kevin lived when he first arrived at Glendalough. More accessible are the ruins of the monastic village and round tower—accessed from the main road or along

A reflective moment above the lakes of Glendalough.

the path from the upper lake to the lower lake. Here, there's a nearly perfect round tower, 31m (102 ft.) high and 16m (52 ft.) around the base, as well as hundreds of timeworn Celtic crosses and several chapels. One of these is St. Kevin's Chapel, often called **St. Kevin's Kitchen,** a fine specimen of an early Irish barrel-vaulted oratory with a miniature round belfry rising from a stone roof. First established by a monk known as St. Kevin in the 6th century, Glendalough was originally devoted to Christian worship and scholarly learning. Sacked first by the Vikings and later by the English, it was eventually abandoned by the monks who sought refuge here. Those beautiful round towers were actually hideouts with retractable ladders that the monks would pull up after them when the raiders arrived. Most of the buildings were destroyed in repeated attacks, but enough survives to ensure the ruins are a striking and atmospheric spectacle in this peaceful valley.

Signposted from R756, 2km (1⅓ miles) west of Laragh, Co. Wicklow. www.heritage ireland.ie. ℂ **040/445-352.** Admission to National Park, lakes, and Glendalough monastic village is free. Visitor Centre admission €5 adults; €4 seniors; €3 students and children; €13 families. Mid-Mar to mid-Oct daily 9:30am–6pm; mid-Oct to mid-Mar daily 9:30am–4pm; last admission 45 min. before closing.

Glenmacnass Waterfall ★ NATURE SITE   A wide strip of silver running down a rugged hill, the Glenmacnass Waterfall is more pretty than spectacular. It doesn't plummet so much as slip through the rugged countryside and down Mt. Mullagheleevaun. From the parking lot near the top of the hill there's a well-signposted path to the falls, but take care on the rocks, which can be slippery.

Laragh, Co. Wicklow. Follow Military Rd. through the Sally Gap and Laragh to the top of Glenmacnass Valley, and then watch for signs to the waterfall. Free admission.

Huntington Castle ★★ CASTLE   This place has all the makings of a spectacular haunting. It's built on the site of a 14th-century abbey, which was itself built on top of a Druid temple (a modern shrine to the Egyptian Goddess Isis lies in the basement, in what used to be the kitchens and dungeons). The rambling, 17th-century crenelated manor house is overgrown with vines that turn blood-red in the fall. It should come as no surprise then that the castle claims to be the most haunted building in Ireland. The owners say it is plagued by ghosts of Druids who cause mists in the fields and showers of blood. Other than that, it's very nice. The interior can only be seen by guided tour, which includes areas that were closed until recently, such as the old kitchens and drawing room. The gardens are beautiful—many of the plants date back to the 18th century—and the unusual 17th-century water features have been restored to working condition. Don't miss the walking path guarded on either side by ancient yew trees. An adventure playground keeps little ones busy. If you're not afraid of ghosts, the castle offers bed-and-breakfast and self-catering accommodations in the elegant Georgian gatehouse; call or e-mail info@

Counties Wicklow & Carlow

huntingtoncastle.com for prices and information.

Clonegal, Co. Carlow (off N80, 6.5km/4 miles from Bunclody). www.huntington castle.com. *℃* **053/937-7160.** Guided tours: €10 adults; €9 seniors and students; €5 children 11 and under. May–Sept daily tours hourly 2–5pm. Gardens and playground only: €6 adults, €3 children. May–Sept daily 10am–5pm. May, Sept weekends only (same hours). Gardens and playground only: €5 adults, €3 children. May–Sept daily 10am–5pm; last admission 1 hr. before closing.

Mount Usher Gardens ★★

GARDENS   Spreading out on 8 hectares (20 acres) at the edge of the River Vartry, this peaceful and romantic site was once an ancient lake. Since 1868 it's been a riverside garden, designed in a distinctively informal style, with fiery rhododendrons, fragrant eucalyptus trees, giant Tibetan lilies, and snowy camellias competing for your attention. Attuned to their

Armor and hunting trophies line a hallway in rambling Huntington Castle.

natural setting, these gardens have an almost untended feel—a sort of floral woodland. A spacious cafe, run by the fantastic Avoca chain, overlooks the river and gardens.

Ashford, Co. Wicklow (off the N11). www.mountushergardens.ie. *℃* **040/449672.** Admission €8 adults; €7 seniors and students; €4 children 4–16; free for children under 4. Daily 10am–6pm; last admission 1 hr. before closing. Avoca Garden Café: Mon–Fri 9:30am–5pm, Sat–Sun 10am–5pm.

Powerscourt Estate ★★★ GARDENS/HISTORIC HOUSE   The

gardens of this magnificent estate are truly gorgeous, with classical statuary, a shady grotto made of petrified moss, a peaceful Japanese garden, and a massive, over-the-top fountain from which statues of winged horses rise. Landscaper Daniel Robertson designed the gardens between 1745 and 1767, and they take full advantage of splendid views of the Sugarloaf mountain and surrounding countryside. Legend has it that thanks to crippling gout, Robertson oversaw the work while being carted around in a wheelbarrow, sipping port as he went. When the bottle was dry, work was done for the day. The whole thing is impressive enough that in 2014 *National Geographic* magazine named Powerscourt's the third-greatest gardens in the world. At the estate's garden center you can learn everything there is to know about the plants that thrive here, and even pick up

A WALK FROM bray

At the southern terminus of the DART line from Dublin, the town of **Bray** is within reach for an afternoon excursion from the city. Its chief attraction is the **National Sea Life Centre** aquarium (Strand Rd.; www.visitsealife.com/bray; ℂ **01/286-6939**), at the center of a seafront boardwalk that was popular in Victorian times and still has a handful of amusement arcades and pubs. Bray's greatest pleasure is probably the stunning coastal view of Killiney Bay, Dalkey Island, and Bray from the rocky promontory of **Bray Head.** Follow the beachside promenade south through Bray; at the outskirts of town, the promenade turns left and up, beginning the ascent of Bray Head. Shortly after the ascent begins, a trail branches to the left—this is the cliffside Bray to Greystones walk, which continues another 5km (3 miles) along the coast to Greystones. From the center of Greystones, a DART train (check times on www.irishrail.ie) will take you back to Bray. It's an easy walk, about 2 hours each way, but don't attempt it in bad weather or strong winds, when the cliffside path becomes treacherous.

seeds to take home (although beware of Customs rules for such things). Sadly, the 20th century was not kind to the Palladian house itself, when it was abandoned and then gutted by fire. It has since been partially restored, and a few rooms are open to the public, but only on Sundays and Mondays May through September. You can visit the high-tech **Cool Planet Experience,** a visitor center aimed at teaching children about human-made climate change and how the world might combat it. The estate also has a playground and gift shops. If you feel energetic, follow the well-marked path over 7km (4 miles) to the picturesque **Powerscourt Waterfall**—the highest in Ireland at 121m (397 ft.); you can also drive here, following signs from the estate. Powerscourt is only about 20km (12½ miles) south of Dublin and can be reached by city bus 44 or 185 to Enniskerry village, approximately a 25-minute walk from the estate.

On R760, Enniskerry, Co. Wicklow. www.powerscourt.ie. ℂ **01/204-6000.** Gardens: €11.50 adults (€8.50 Nov–Feb); €9 seniors and students (€7.50 Nov–Feb); €5 children (€4) children and €26 families (€18). Cool Planet: €10.50 adults; €9 seniors and students; €7 children; €31 families. Waterfall: €6.50 adults; €5.50 seniors and students; €3.50 children under 16; €16 families. Gardens: Mar–Oct Daily 9:30am–5:30pm (or at dusk if earlier). Last admission ½ hr. before closing. Garden Pavilion: daily 9:30am–5:30pm. Ballroom and Garden Rooms: May–Sept Sun–Mon 9:30am–1:30pm. Cool Planet: daily 10am–5pm (last tour 4pm); check if open before visiting. Powerscourt Waterfall: May–Aug 9:30am–7pm (last admission 6pm); Mar–Apr and Sept–Oct 10:30am–5:30pm (last admission 5pm); Nov–Feb 10:30am–4pm (last admission 3:30pm).

Russborough House ★★ HISTORIC HOUSE Sprawling low across the green landscape, this somber gray stone villa was built between 1741 and 1751. The designer was Richard Cassels, the same man who designed the much more fanciful Powerscourt House (see above). Today, however, Russborough is known not for its architecture but for housing a

Children admiring a model interior of a room in the Powerscourt Estate.

small but mighty art gallery. In the 1950s, the house was bought by Sir Alfred Beit, a member of the De Beers diamond family, specifically to hold his massive personal art collection, and it displays one of the most exquisite small rural art collections you're likely to find anywhere. Although many of the most valuable paintings have been moved to other museums after a series of robberies, you can still view works by Vermeer, Gainsborough, and Rubens. The house can be explored only by guided tour, and there is certainly a lot to see: ornate plaster ceilings by the Lafranchini brothers, huge marble mantelpieces, and fine displays of silver, porcelain, and furniture. Kids will be amused by a fiendish maze, a "fairy trail" on the grounds that tells the story of Russborough's resident fairy. The grounds also contain traditional craft workshops where you can see artisans in action The estate's other main attraction is the **National Bird of Prey Centre** (www.nationalbirdofpreycentre.ie; ℗ **045/857-755**), home to hawks, owls, falcons, and eagles from different parts of the globe. Check the website for details on how to book a private "hawk walk" through the grounds with a trainer and one of the resident big birds. The center is open daily July to September, Wednesdays to Sundays April to June, and weekends only October to March.

Signposted from N81, 3.2km (2 miles) south of Blessington, Co. Wicklow. www.russborough.ie. ℗ **045/865-239.** House: €12 adults; €9 seniors and students; €6 children 6–15; free children 5 and under; €30 families (includes maze entry). Maze: €3, or €12 families. Outdoor family ticket: maze, parklands, and fairy trail, €15. Fairy trail €3. National Bird of Prey Centre: €9 adults; €7 seniors; €6 students and children 6–15; €25 families. House Mar–Dec daily 10am–4pm (tour times vary). Parklands daily 9am–6pm. Cafe and shop 10am–5pm daily. National Bird of Prey Centre: Sat–Sun 11am–5pm. All-day parking €3.

St. Mullin's Monastery ★ RELIGIOUS SITE   This monastery's idyllic setting—in a sleepy hamlet beside the River Barrow, surrounded by low hills—is reason enough for a visit. These are the ruins of a monastery founded by St. Moling (Mullin) in roughly A.D. 614. Plundered again and again by the Vikings in the 9th and 10th centuries, it was annexed in the 12th century by a nearby Augustinian abbey. Here, too, are a steep grassy motte (the mound on which a castle was built) and the outline of a bailey (the outer wall or court of a castle) constructed by the Normans in the 12th century. In the Middle Ages the monastery ruins were a popular destination, especially at the height of the Black Death in 1348. By tradition, pilgrims would cross the river barefoot, circle the burial spot of St. Mullin nine times, and drink from the healing waters of the saint's well. These waters are still the subject of an annual pilgrimage on or near July 25. Adjoining the monastery buildings is an ancient cemetery, where, contrary to common practice, Protestants and Catholics have long lain side by side. A number of rebels from the 1798 Rising are buried here.

On the Barrow Dr., 12km (7½ miles) north of New Ross, St. Mullins, Co. Carlow. Free admission. Daily dawn–dusk.

Vale of Avoca ★ NATURE SITE   Basically a peaceful, green river valley, the Vale of Avoca is the "Meeting of the Waters" where the Avonmore and Avonbeg rivers join to form the Avoca River. Pleasant as it is, we'd probably never have heard of it were it not for the 19th-century poet Thomas Moore, who wrote, "There is not in the wide world a valley so sweet / As the vale in whose bosom the bright waters meet. . . ." Just 3km (2 miles) away, the charming riverside village of **Avoca** makes a good stop. Here you can tour the traditional mills where **Avoca Handweavers** (www.avocahandweavers.com) still make their coveted blankets, sweaters, and other beautiful homewares, nearly 300 years after they spun their first looms. Watch the weavers at work on a free tour of the woolen mill, which also has a wonderful gift shop (of course) and cafe. The mill is signposted on the R754 road heading north out of the village

Rte. 755, Avoca, Co. Wicklow. Daily 9am–6pm summer, 9:30am–5:30pm winter.

Wicklow Mountains National Park ★★★ NATURE SITE   Stretching into the mountains around Glendalough, this hilly national park is popular with hikers walking the Wicklow Way, a trail that cuts across the park (see p. 204). In the high season, you'll find an information station at the Upper Lake at Glendalough where you can get maps and route guides. Behind the center is a sweet little "sensory garden" (free admission), containing a variety of plants chosen for their scent, texture, and even the sounds of the wildlife they attract. The closest parking is at Upper Lake, where you'll pay a few euro per car. *Note:* The Irish National Parks & Wildlife Service warns that ticks carrying Lyme disease are known to live in the hills. Although the risk of contracting the disease is small, you should dress in long sleeves, wear a hat, avoid hiking in shorts, and check

Heathlands mantle the panoramic Wicklow Mountains.

for ticks afterward. Don't panic too readily if you find one, though; ticks need to be attached for at least 24 hours for infection to take place, and fewer than 100 cases are reported annually in the whole of Ireland. In the parks service's reassuring words, "Remember, be aware, but don't worry."

Glendalough, Co. Wicklow. www.wicklowmountainsnationalpark.ie. © **076/100-2667.** Free admission to national park. Glendalough Visitor Centre: €5 adults; €4 seniors; €4 students and children; €13 families. Park open 24 hours. Visitor Centre open mid–Mar–mid-Oct daily 9:30am–6pm; mid–Oct–mid-Mar 9:30am–4pm. Last admission to center 45 min. before closing.

Where to Stay South of Dublin

BrookLodge & Macreddin Village ★★   A winning combination of top-end hotel, spa, and holiday village, BrookLodge is a luxurious hideaway. Guest rooms are understated and contemporary in design, while suites—which come with a stylish mezzanine level—offer plenty of extra room for not much greater cost. The hotel is surrounded by an entire village of activities, from golf, hiking, and horseback riding to an artisan baker, deli, and crafts store. The peaceful spa, **Wells,** is worth trying out—most 1-hour treatments cost around the €75 mark. The main restaurant, the excellent **Strawberry Tree ★★★** (p. 205), was the first in Ireland to gain full organic certification.

Macreddin Village (btw. Aughrim and Aghavannagh), Co. Wicklow. www.brooklodge.com. © **040/236444.** 86 units. €120–€260 double; €280–€360 suite. Free parking. Breakfast included. **Amenities:** 2 restaurants; 2 pubs; golf course; gym; pool; room service; spa; Wi-Fi (free).

The Lord Bagenal ★   This cheerful, modern hotel on the banks of the River Barrow loses points for character, but the air-conditioned bedrooms are spacious and comfortable. Ask for a room with a view of the river. This is a good choice for families; in addition to family rooms that cost very little more than doubles, the staff here will help organize activities, such as kayaking or fishing on the Barrow. The in-house restaurant serves rich, French-influenced cuisine in a formal setting, while the bar, with its cozy open fires and relaxed atmosphere, offers a simple, crowd-pleasing menu (steaks, burgers, local fish, and the like).

Main St., Leighlinbridge, Co. Carlow. www.lordbagenal.com. © **059/977-4000.** 39 units. €115–€155 double; €127–€149 suite. 2-night minimum on summer weekends. Breakfast included. **Amenities:** Restaurant; bar; room service; Wi-Fi (free).

Powerscourt Hotel ★★★ The grand, sweeping Palladian-style frontage of this gorgeous hotel, part of the Marriott chain, is almost as impressive as its historic namesake, Powerscourt House (p. 198). Guest rooms are large and elegantly furnished. The lounges are gorgeous, with soaring ceilings, beautiful furniture, and exquisite views. The spa is positively sci-fi in its sleek design—the pool is lit by illuminated Swarovski crystals—and the list of treatments includes everything from hot stone treatments to a "shillelagh massage" in which you are, we kid you not, rubbed down with a lucky stick. The hotel has three eateries of varying levels of formality: The **Sika** restaurant serves outstanding modern Irish menus (€65 for three courses). The **Sugar Loaf** lounge is marginally less formal and offers a lavish afternoon tea (€45 per person). If you're looking for something casual, **McGill's Pub** is the place.

Be aware: This is a lovely hotel, but it's not intimate—200 rooms can make it feel crowded, and service can slip. The child-friendly policy, while great for families, is not conducive to pure relaxation. People come here for the style and the luxury—but not peace.

Co. Wicklow. www.powerscourthotel.com. © **01/274-8888.** 200 units. €220–€430 double; €400–€630 suite. Free parking. Rates include breakfast. **Amenities:** 2 restaurants; bar; gym; pool; pub; room service; spa; Wi-Fi (free).

Wicklow Way Lodge ★★ This B&B looks unassuming from the outside, but step inside and you'll find a simple haven of tranquility and charm. Guest rooms are tastefully furnished, with lots of polished wood and toasty underfloor heating. Enormous windows take advantage of the glorious view—a fantasia of rolling hills and verdant green in spring, while in the fall, the mist rolls in across a blanket of autumnal hues. Breathe in the air and feel your soul relax—this is the Ireland you came for, isn't it? There's one family room, though note that very young kids aren't allowed because of the split-level layout of the house. Hosts Marilyn and Seamus are a joy, genuinely kind and helpful and full of tips for the best walking paths. Glendalough (see p. 196) is just 6km (4 miles) from here. There's homemade bread at breakfast, with fresh local eggs— and try the porridge, too! Those seeking even more seclusion may be interested in the self-catering cottage next door, which sleeps up to four. Plan ahead, though, as it can get booked up almost a year in advance.

Oldbridge, Roundwood, Co. Wicklow. www.wicklowwaylodge.com. © **01/281-8489.** 5 units. €110–€120 double. Free parking. Breakfast included. **Amenities:** Wi-Fi (free in lounge only).

WALK THIS WAY: hiking IN COUNTY WICKLOW

Loved by hikers and ramblers for its peace, isolation, and sheer beauty, the **Wicklow Way** is a 132km (82-mile) signposted walking path that follows forest trails, sheep paths, and country roads from the suburbs south of Dublin up into the Wicklow Mountains and down through country farmland to Clonegal in County Carlow.

It takes about 5 to 7 days to walk its entirety, with overnight stops at B&Bs and hostels along the route. You can also organize baggage transfers and guides. Most people, however, choose to walk sections as day trips. (*Tip:* The southern section, through Tinahely, Shillelagh, and Clonegal, is much gentler and less hilly.) You can pick up information and maps at the Wicklow Mountains National Park Visitor Centre at Glendalough, or get more information on the Wicklow Way, including maps and suppliers at **www.visitwicklow.ie**.

St. Kevin's Way, an ancient pilgrims' route more than 1,000 years old, has recently been restored. The path runs for 30km (19 miles) through scenic countryside from Hollywood to Glendalough. As it winds among roads, forest paths, and open mountainside, the route visits many of the historical sites associated with St. Kevin.

Leaflets containing maps and route descriptions for other walks can be found at tourist offices. Folks who prefer less-strenuous walking may enjoy the paths around the lakes at **Glendalough.**

Where to Eat South of Dublin

Wicklow is close enough to Dublin for residents to commute, so it has a gentrified restaurant scene. In addition to the options listed below, there are many small, independent places to stop for lunch or light food. In the charming village of Delgany, **Firehouse Bakery** (Old Delgany Inn; www.thefirehouse.ie) will ruin your diet with its freshly baked pastries, tarts, and cakes. It's the perfect place to grab breakfast or lunch on the go. In Wicklow Town, **Halpin's Bridge Café** (Bridge St.; www.halpinscafe.com) offers simple hot meals. Start the morning with avocado on toast with egg and bacon, or simple porridge with honey. For lunch you can grab wraps, sandwiches, or salads to have in, or take with you for a picnic later. In Enniskerry, **Poppies** (The Square; www.poppies.ie) is a terrific quick stop for light lunches eaten in, and picnic fodder to take away out. Freshly made sandwiches, quiches, and cakes are the specialty.

Chakra by Jaipur ★★★ INDIAN   If you need a break from Irish food, this outstanding Indian restaurant is one of the best in the area. It's not the most idyllic location, in a concrete-and-glass shopping mall down a rather nondescript street in Greystones, but that's about the only disappointing thing about it. The food is excellent: Indian cuisine, with all its spice, infused with the flavors of Ireland. You might start with a plate of Barbary duck breast tikka with passionfruit and orange, before following on to a traditional butter chicken made with local honey. It's a must-visit for lovers of Indian food.

1st floor, Meridian Point, Church Rd., Greystones, Co. Wicklow. www.chakra.ie. © **01/201-7222.** Entrees €20–€26.50. Tues–Sat 5:30–9:45pm; Sun 2–8:30pm.

Fika ★★ GRILL   In the seaside Dublin suburb of Bray, this restaurant perches amid a rooftop garden, overlooking the rugged coastline. Its charcoal-fueled Josper grill gives a wonderful, smoky edge to the food. Choose from tacos with pulled chicken, lime cream, and mango salsa or more meaty mains like wild boar with white bean cassoulet or low-cooked beef short rib. Locals come here for brunch and cocktails as well as dinner, and the atmosphere is lively.

7 Strand Rd., Bray, Co. Wicklow. www.fikarooftop.ie. © **01/563-9940.** Entrees €10–€24. Wed–Sun 5–9:45pm; Sat–Sun 11am–2:45pm.

The Fish Man ★★ SEAFOOD   This popular restaurant on the quay in Wicklow is one of the best places in the area for fresh, local seafood. The restaurant occupies a picturesque spot right over from the quay—you might even catch sight of a friendly seal crossing the street for a visit. All we can say is, if it's on account of the cooking, we wouldn't be one bit surprised, because the excellent food surpasses expectations. Try an appetizer of smooth and creamy fish chowder, then choose from a host of fresh-as-can-be fruits of the sea: prawns, either grilled or tempura-battered, or a perfectly prepared lemon sole.

South Quay, Wicklow. © **040/462567.** Entrees €12–€25. Thurs–Fri 6–9pm; Sat 12:30–3:30pm and 6–9pm; Sun 12:30–3:30pm and 6–7:30pm. Closed Mon–Tues and all of Jan.

The Pigeon House ★★★ MODERN IRISH   This award-winning restaurant in Delgany village is renowned for its innovative but unpretentious approach. In an old converted inn, the dining room has an airy feel. Best of all, it's open from breakfast through dinner, and all meals are delicious. Breakfast has everything from pancakes to poached eggs with veggies. Lunch options vary from light salads to sturdy meals. But dinner is when this place shines. Starters might include bacon rib with elderberry and apple, or baked local camembert sweetened with apricot. Mains are deceptively simple: chargrilled sea bass with fennel, succulent roast pork with mashed local potatoes, roast squash gnocchi with local greens. Everything is understated and absurdly fresh.

Delgany, Co. Wicklow. www.pigeonhouse.ie. © **01/287-7103.** Entrees €15–€24. Mon–Fri 8:30am–8:45pm; Sat–Sun 9am–8:45pm.

The Strawberry Tree ★★★ MODERN IRISH   The main restaurant of the excellent **BrookLodge** complex (p. 202) is rightly regarded as one of the best places to dine in the region. The beautiful, blue-tinged dining room makes a wonderful setting for any gathering. This was the first restaurant in Ireland to receive full organic certification, and that ethos guides

Counties Wicklow & Carlow

the outstanding modern Irish menu, which takes localism seriously. Depending on the season, you might dine on wild Kilmore Quay sole with Jerusalem artichoke and fermented whey, or beef filet with seasonal vegetables and bone gravy. If you're feeling gregarious, book a place at the "big table"—a communal table that seats up to 40, at which you're served a set menu in the style of a feast.

At the BrookLodge, Macreddin Village (btw. Aughrim and Aghavannagh), Co. Wicklow. www.brooklodge.com. ⓒ **040/236444.** Fixed-price menu €69. Wed–Sun 5:30–9:30pm (days sometimes vary).

Sports & Outdoor Pursuits in Wicklow

CYCLING   **Cycling Safaris** (www.cyclingsafaris.com; ⓒ **01/260-0749**) offers a weeklong tour of Dublin and Wicklow starting at €845 per person, including bed, breakfast, and 1 night's dinner.

HORSEBACK RIDING   The hillside paths of Wicklow are perfect for horseback riding. More than a dozen stables and equestrian centers in the area offer horses for hire and riding lessons. Rates average around €40 to €50 per hour. **Brennanstown Riding School,** Hollybrook, Kilmacanogue, Co. Wicklow (www.brennanstownrs.ie; ⓒ **01/286-3778**), offers beginner's treks up picturesque Little Sugar Loaf Mountain.

WATERSPORTS & ADVENTURE SPORTS   Deep in the Wicklow Mountains, the Blessington Lakes are a 2,000-hectare (4,940-acre) playground of tranquil, clean, speedboat-free water. At the Hidden Valley Holiday Park in Rathdrum, **Wicklow Adventures** (www.wicklowadventures.ie; ⓒ **086/727-2872**) offers high-octane outdoor activities, including laser tag. A standard daily ticket costs €22.50 per child and €15 per adult.

Hiking the Wicklow Way.

THE
SOUTHEAST

6

t doesn't take long to feel like you're deep into the Irish countryside as you travel to the counties south of Dublin. For a start, the accent changes—subtly but unmistakably, a mellifluous dialect creeps in, with a musical lilt all its own. The three main counties of the Southeast—**Waterford, Wexford,** and **Kilkenny**—are close enough together that you could use any as a base for exploring the region by car. (It's a little trickier by public transport, unless you stick to the main towns.) Waterford's current tourism slogan is "Where Ireland Begins," which definitely has a grain of truth to it. Waterford City, the eponymous capital, is Ireland's oldest, founded by Viking invaders 1,100 years ago. Wexford and Kilkenny are both rich in medieval heritage, including Kilkenny Castle, one of Ireland's most impressive medieval buildings.

ESSENTIALS

Arriving

BY BUS Bus Éireann (www.buseireann.ie; © **01/836-6111**) operates direct service several times a day from Dublin's central bus station (**Busáras**) into Kilkenny, Wexford, and Waterford. The journey to Kilkenny takes upwards of 2 hours; to Wexford and Waterford, closer to three.

BY TRAIN Irish Rail (www.irishrail.ie; © **1850/366-222**) operates several trains daily between Dublin and Kilkenny, Wexford, and Waterford. The journey to Kilkenny takes about 90 minutes; to Waterford, a little over 2 hours; and to Wexford, 2½ hours.

BY FERRY Ferries from Britain sail to Rosslare Harbour, 19km (12 miles) south of Wexford Town. Contact **Irish Ferries** (www.irishferries. ie; © **0818/300-400**) or **Stena Line** (www.stenaline.com; © **01/907-5555**) for bookings and information.

BY CAR The journey from Dublin to Kilkenny, Waterford, or Wexford is nearly all via motorway. From Dublin to Wexford, take N/M11 south. For Kilkenny, take the M7 southwest out of Dublin, then split off onto M9. If you're heading to Waterford, stay on M9 for another 50km (31 miles) after the turnoff for Kilkenny. The drive to Kilkenny is about 1½ hours,

PREVIOUS PAGE: **The Emigrant Flame is an eternal flame commemorating Irish emigrants.**

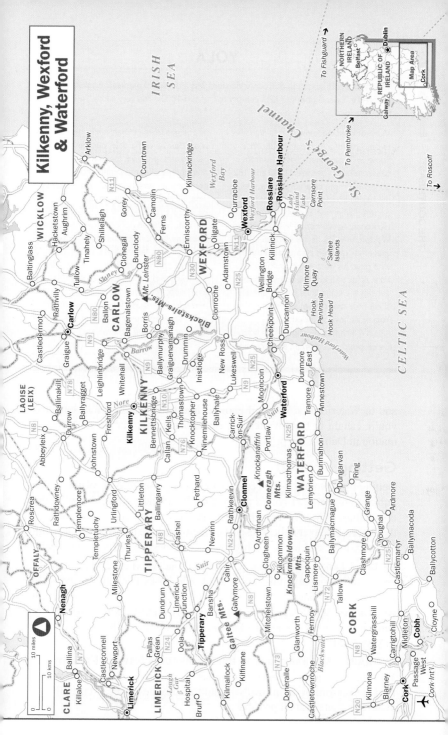

Kilkenny, Wexford & Waterford

ghost language: **YOLA**

The extinct Yola language of County Wexford was a dialect of medieval English that survived in Ireland from the 12th century to the mid-1800s. The very name "Yola" is, in fact, Yola for "old."

Much of what we know of Yola is thanks to the work of a man named Jacob Poole, who compiled glossaries from native speakers between 1800 and 1827. Somewhat more celebrated, however, is the happy accident of history that occurred when the Earl of Mulgrave, Lord Lieutenant (governor) of Ireland, visited Wexford in 1836. To his surprise, Mulgrave was greeted by a local dignitary who gave his welcome speech entirely in Yola. A full transcript survives, and its evocative closing lines are enough to show how strange, yet slightly familiar, Yola must have sounded:

"Wi Irishmen ower generale houpes be ee-boud, az Irishmen, an az dwellerès na cosh an loyale o' Baronie Forthe, w'oul daie an ercha daie, our meines an oure gurles, praie var long an happie zins, shorne o'lournagh an ee-vilt wi benisons, an yersel and oure gude zover-eine, till ee zin o'oure daies be var aye be ee-go to'glade. . . ."

With Irishmen our common hopes are inseparably bound up, as Irishmen, and as inhabitants, faithful and loyal, of the Barony Forth, we will daily and every day, our wives and our children, implore long and happy days, free from melancholy and full of blessings, for yourself and our good sovereign, until the sun of our lives be gone down the dark valley. . . .

and to Waterford or Wexford about 2 hours, but considerably longer if you're caught in Dublin's terrible rush-hour traffic. For car-rental information in Dublin, see p. 91.

Getting Around

Getting from Dublin to the centers of Kilkenny, Wexford, or Waterford by public transport is easy. It's also relatively simple to travel between the three cities. However, as with most rural areas in Ireland, getting *around* the countryside by public transport once you're here is extremely difficult. Unless you're sticking to the big towns, your best option is to rent a car.

BY BUS   Direct buses connect Waterford and Wexford every couple of hours; most journeys take an hour. A few buses per day run between Kilkenny and Waterford; the journey takes 1 to 2 hours, depending on whether you have to change buses (which you almost always do). No convenient bus routes connect Kilkenny and Wexford; you'll have to change in Waterford.

BY TRAIN   A half-dozen or so trains daily travel between Kilkenny and Waterford; the journey takes 35 minutes. Getting from Kilkenny or Waterford to Wexford by train involves multiple changes and can take all day; avoid this route if at all possible.

BY CAR If you take public transport to the Southwest and then want to drive around the countryside, you can easily pick up a rental car in one of the main towns. In Kilkenny, **Enterprise-Rent-a-Car** has a branch at the Kilkenny Car Complex, Dublin Road (www.enterprise.ie; ✆ **056/775-3318**). **Hertz** has a branch in Wexford Town, on Ferrybank (✆ **053/915-2500**), or you can try **Budget** at Rosslare Ferryport (www.budget.ie; ✆ **053/913-3318**). In Waterford, **Enterprise** has a branch on Cork Road (www.enterprise.ie; ✆ **051/304-804**).

BY FERRY Driving between Waterford and Wexford involves a circuitous route via New Ross—unless you cut the distance in half by taking the handy car ferry from the poetically named **Passage East,** about 12km (7½ miles) east of Waterford (www.passageferry.ie; ✆ **051/382-480**). Regular crossings run June to August Monday to Saturday 7am to 9pm, Sunday and public holidays 9:30am to 9pm; September to May Monday to Saturday 7am to 8pm, Sunday and public holidays 9:30am to 8pm. Tickets per car are €8 one-way, €12 round-trip. Discounts are available if you plan to make more than six trips.

COUNTY WATERFORD

County Waterford is set along Ireland's southeast coastline, with plenty of rolling countryside as well as bays and beaches dotted along the way. Waterford City itself is a small but vibrant city set slightly inland on the River Suir, near the head of Waterford Harbour. It is the oldest city in the country, founded by Viking invaders in the 9th century.

Visitor Information

The **Waterford Tourist Information Centre** is at 120 Parade Quay, Waterford (www.discoverireland.ie; ✆ **051/875-823**). It's open Monday to Friday 9am to 5pm (sometimes later in summer) and on summer weekends only.

Exploring Waterford City

Bishop's Palace ★★ MUSEUM One of three separate museums that are known collectively as **Waterford Treasures,** the Bishop's Palace focuses on life in the city from 1700 until the mid–20th century. Costumed guides show you around the collection, which includes impressive displays of 18th-century furniture, art, and fashion. The Georgian drawing room is dominated by Willem Van der Hagen's fascinating 1736 landscape painting of Waterford City—the oldest landscape of an Irish city in existence—depicting long-vanished Waterford landmarks such as the medieval Christ Church Cathedral, demolished in 1773. Appropriately, given its close proximity to the famous factory (p. 215), the museum also holds the earliest surviving pieces of Waterford Crystal, including a decanter dating from 1789. The new, 4-D *Masterpieces in Glass* exhibit

211

The Georgian drawing room at the Bishop's Palace.

uses virtual reality to explore the storied history of glassmaking in Waterford.

The Mall. www.waterfordtreasures.com/bishops-palace. **076/110-2501.** Admission €10; free for children under 12 with paying guest. The combined Freedom of Waterford ticket (including the Medieval Museum and Epic walking tour; see p. 214) €15; free for children under 12. Mon–Fri 9:15am–5pm; Sat 10am–5pm; Sun and public holidays 11am–5pm. Last admission 4:20pm.

Christ Church Cathedral ★ CATHEDRAL   Waterford's most important church building is a beautiful example of late-18th-century architecture. Corinthian columns top grand marble plinths, rising up to meet the stucco, with its delicate filigreed detail. The current building, designed by John Roberts, was finished in 1773, replacing one built by the Vikings in the 11th century. (One solitary pillar remains from the original building.) This was where Strongbow, the first English lord to invade Ireland, married an Irish princess—thus gaining a permanent foothold into Irish nobility. Christ Church's Catholic counterpart, the Holy Trinity Cathedral (also designed by John Roberts), is on Barronstrand Street (see below).

Cathedral Square. www.christchurchwaterford.com. **051/858958.** Free admission. Easter–Oct Mon–Fri 10am–5pm, Sat 10am–4pm; Oct–Easter Mon–Sat 12:30–2:30pm.

City Hall ★ MUSEUM   Headquarters of the local city government, this late-18th-century building houses a few pieces of interesting local memorabilia, including an exhibit on the extraordinary life of Thomas Francis Meagher. Convicted of treason against the British in 1848, he was

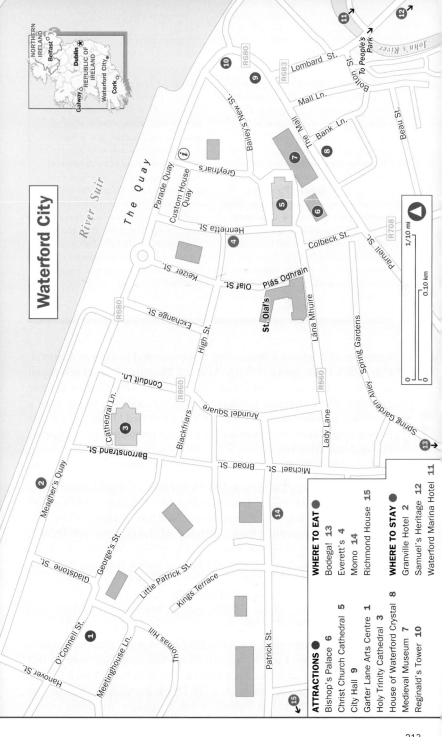

Waterford City

NORTHERN IRELAND
Belfast ⋆
REPUBLIC OF IRELAND
Galway○ Dublin ⋆
Waterford City○
Cork○

River Suir

The Quay

Parade Quay

Custom House Quay

Greyfriars

Henrietta St.

Keizer St.

Olaf St. Plás Odhráin

St. Olaf's

Lána Mhuire

Exchange St.

High St.

Conduit Ln.

Arundel Square

Blackfriars

Cathedral Ln.

Barronstrand St.

Broad St.

Michael St.

Lady Lane

Spring Gardens

Spring Garden Alley

Meagher's Quay

George's St.

Gladstone St.

O'Connell St.

Hanover St.

Little Patrick St.

Kings Terrace

Meetinghouse Ln.

Thomas Hill

Patrick St.

Bailey's New St.

The Mall

Lombard St.

Mall Ln.

Bank Ln.

Bolton St.

Beau St.

Colbeck St.

Parnell St.

John's River

To People's Park

R680
R683
R680
R708
R860
R860

0   1/10 mi
0   0.10 km

ATTRACTIONS ●
Bishop's Palace **6**
Christ Church Cathedral **5**
City Hall **9**
Garter Lane Arts Centre **1**
Holy Trinity Cathedral **3**
House of Waterford Crystal **8**
Medieval Museum **7**
Reginald's Tower **10**

WHERE TO EAT ●
Bodega! **13**
Everett's **4**
Momo **14**
Richmond House **15**

WHERE TO STAY ●
Granville Hotel **2**
Samuel's Heritage **12**
Waterford Marina Hotel **11**

213

EPIC TOURS to go

For those who like their history entertaining and fast, the **Epic Tour of the Viking Triangle** walking tour offered by the Waterford tourism office takes in 1,100 years of local history in 45 minutes. Enthusiastic guides take you to several points of interest within the so-called "Viking Triangle" of central Waterford, starting at the **Bishop's Palace** (see above) and moving swiftly through **Reginald's Tower** (p. 216), the **Chorister's Hall** (p. 216), and **Christ Church Cathedral** (p. 212). You don't get to linger inside any of these places (some you won't see further than the lobby), so think of it as a whistle-stop history primer rather than anything in depth, but the ticket allows you access to the Medieval Museum, Bishop's Palace, Irish Museum of Time and Irish Silver Museum so you can visit these in more depth after the tour. The tour's raucous style is heavy on audience participation, which may not be to everybody's taste, but kids get a kick out of the wacky vibe. The Freedom of Waterford ticket is €15 (the walking tour on its own is €10 adults and free for children 12 and under). Tours operate daily year-round at noon, 2pm, and 4pm. Meet outside the Bishop's Palace on the Mall. For details, see www.waterford treasures.com and select the "Freedom of Waterford" option.

sentenced to death—a sentence that was commuted to exile in Australia, from which he escaped and fled to America. The wily Meagher resurfaced in the Civil War as a senior Union officer, and by 1867, he had become governor of the Montana Territory, only to die suddenly, falling from a steamboat into the Missouri River. Or was he pushed? Rumor had it that he was assassinated in retaliation for military campaigns he led against Native American tribes.

The Mall. © **051/309900.** Free admission. Mon–Fri 9am–5pm.

Garter Lane Arts Centre ★ ARTS CENTER One of Ireland's largest arts centers, the Garter Lane occupies two buildings on O'Connell Street. Number 5 holds exhibition rooms and artists' studios, and no. 22a, a former Friends meeting house, is home of the Garter Lane Theatre, along with an art gallery and courtyard. The gallery showcases works by contemporary and local artists, and hosts a varied program of music, dance, and films.

O'Connell St. www.garterlane.ie. © **051/855038.** Many events and exhibits free; ticketed events around €9–€20. General opening: Tues–Sat 11am–5:30pm; individual performance and event times vary.

Holy Trinity Cathedral ★ CATHEDRAL Waterford has two impressive cathedrals, one Catholic and the other Protestant, both built by one equal-opportunity architect, John Roberts (the other being Christ Church Cathedral in Cathedral Square; p. 212). This is the Catholic version, the only baroque cathedral in Ireland. It has 10 unique Waterford crystal chandeliers. Roberts lived 82 years (1714–96), fathered 22 children with his beloved wife, and built nearly every significant 18th-century building in and around Waterford.

Barronstrand and Henrietta sts. www.waterford-cathedral.com. © **051/875166.** Free admission. Open daily; hours vary but generally 7:30am–7pm (except during Mass times).

House of Waterford Crystal ★ FACTORY TOUR One of the best-known Irish brands in the world, Waterford Crystal has been made in the city (with significant periods of hiatus) since 1783. In 2009, the company filed for bankruptcy—perhaps Ireland's most high-profile victim of the global financial crisis—and for a while it looked as if this iconic brand might disappear for good. But new owners were found, and with them came this factory and visitor center. You can tour the factory to watch the glittering products being molded, blown, cut, and finished, using traditional methods that have changed little in 200 years. If you'd rather just drop in for souvenirs, you can hit the enormous gift shop without taking the tour.

The Mall. www.waterfordvisitorcentre.com. © **051/317000.** Admission €16 adults; €14 seniors; €13 students; €8 children under 18; free for children under 10; €35 families. Tour: Mon–Fri 10am–3pm. No tours Sat and Sun. Store: Mon–Sat 9:30am–5pm. Closed Sun.

Watch fine crystal being blown in the Waterford Crystal factory.

Medieval Museum ★★ MUSEUM The fascinating Medieval Museum has many artifacts from the city's medieval period, including richly embroidered cloth-of-gold vestments, intricate metal badges worn by pilgrims to the Holy Land, and the lavishly illustrated Charter Roll of Waterford dating from 1373. In common with the other duo of sites that together make up the Waterford Treasures (the Bishop's Palace [p. 211] and Reginald's Tower [p. 216]), costumed guides are on hand in corny but enjoyable fashion, to add medieval flavor. The building itself is as much a treasure as the items on display. Though a modern design, the museum incorporates two medieval structures that were inaccessible for years: the 15th-century Wine Vault and the impressive 13th-century Chorister's Hall, with its vaulted stone ceiling.

Cathedral Square. www.waterfordtreasures.com/medieval-museum. ✆ **051/849501.** Admission €10; free for children under 12 with paying guest. The combined Freedom of Waterford ticket (including the Bishop's Palace and Epic walking tour; see p. 214) €15; free for children under 12. Mon–Fri 9:15am–5pm; Sat 10am–5pm; Sun 11am–5pm. Last admission 40 min. before closing.

Reginald's Tower ★★ MUSEUM This Viking-era stone tower was built around the year 1000, making it Ireland's oldest building still in day-to-day use. Today it houses a museum devoted to that period in Waterford's history. While much of it is interpretive in nature, a number of items are on display too: fragments of Viking pottery, coins, and jewelry, including the stunning Waterford Kite Brooch—an ornamental clasp dating from the late 11th century, intricately patterned with fine threads of gold and silver. Be careful when climbing the old stone staircase—in order to confound attackers, these "stumble steps" were designed to be deliberately uneven, hence easy to trip over (also oriented in such a way to make wielding a sword impossible if you're right-handed—so better leave yours behind).

The Quay. www.waterfordtreasures.com/reginalds-tower. ✆ **079/110-2501.** Admission €5 adults; €4 seniors; €3 students and children; €13 families. Late Mar to mid-Dec daily 9:30am–5:30pm; Jan to early Mar Wed–Sun 9:30am–5pm; last admission 30 min. before closing.

Waterford City Walking Tours ★★ TOURS Local guide Jack Burtchaell is well versed in the history, folklore, and witty anecdotes of his home city. From mid-March to October he conducts this engaging hour-long tour of the old city twice daily, leaving from the tourist office at 11:45am and 1:45pm, and the reception area of the Granville Hotel on the Quay at noon and 2pm. You don't have to book in advance—just show up a little before departure time.

The Quay. www.jackswalkingtours.com. ✆ **051/873711.** Tour €7. Mid-Mar to Oct daily 11:45am, 1:45pm.

The modern Medieval Museum showcases some impressive chambers from the Middle Ages.

Waterford City Walking Tours, led by the knowledgeable Jack Burtchaell.

Farther Afield in County Waterford

Ardmore High Cross ★ RELIGIOUS SITE Ardmore (Irish for "the great height") is a very ancient Christian site—St. Declan, its founder, is said to have been a bishop in Munster as early as the mid–4th century, well before St. Patrick came to Ireland. Tradition has it that the small stone oratory in a cemetery high above Ardmore marks his burial site. St. Declan's Oratory is one of several stone structures composing the ancient monastic settlement. The most striking is the perfectly intact 30m-high (98-ft.) round tower. Onsite are also ruins of a medieval cathedral and, nearby, St. Declan's well and church. A lovely 4km (2.5-mile) cliff walk takes around an hour. Ardmore is near the border with County Cork, about 70km (43 miles) southwest of Waterford City.

On R673, Ardmore, Co. Waterford. Free admission. Daily dawn–dusk. From the main N25 road, turn onto R673 and follow signs to Ardmore.

Lismore Castle Gardens and Arts ★★ GARDENS/GALLERY High above the River Blackwater, this turreted medieval fortress dates from 1185, when Prince John of England (later the infamous King John who signed the Magna Carta) established a castle on this site. The grounds, surrounded by thick defensive walls dating from 1626, are spread across nearly 7 acres. They're peaceful and quite lovely to stroll, dotted with sculptures and offering views of the massive castle (which is, sadly, not open to the public). Also on the grounds is **Lismore Castle Arts** (www. lismorecastlearts.ie; ✆ **058/54061**), a gallery devoted to contemporary

217

visual arts, with a good program of exhibitions and big-name featured artists such as Ai Weiwei and Dorothy Cross. Entry is included in the price for the gardens. The gallery has a second space at **St. Carthage Hall,** located on Chapel Street in Lismore (✆ **058/54061**), open Friday to Sunday noon to 5pm, during exhibition periods only (call or go online to check the schedule). Admission is free.

Lismore, Co. Waterford (6.5km/4 miles west of Cappoquin via N72). www.lismore castlegardens.com. ✆ **058/54061.** Gardens and gallery: €8.50 adults; €7 seniors and students; €6.50 children; €20 families. Mid-Mar to mid-Oct daily 10:30am–5:30pm; last admission 1 hr. before closing.

Turreted Lismore Castle dates to the 12th century.

Where to Stay in County Waterford

Cliff House Hotel ★★★   This award-winning luxury boutique hotel just outside Waterford will wow you from the start with extraordinary sweeping coastal views. Inside, things get even better, because this place is known for its superb service, innovative food, and elegant rooms. Standard rooms are not huge, but they are well appointed, with king beds and bathrooms with rainforest showers and free-standing baths. Many have private balconies with breathtaking views. If you need more privacy and money is no object, you can rent a cottage on the grounds. The Michelin-starred **House Restaurant** melds fresh local seafood and produce with cutting-edge techniques. There's also a more casual bar restaurant for relaxed dining and afternoon tea. Finally, the peaceful spa and pool will work away any tension you have left.

Middle Rd., Ardmore. www.cliffhousehotel.ie. ✆ **024/87800.** 39 units. €240–€525 double. Free parking. **Amenities:** Restaurant; bar; room service; Wi-Fi; pool; spa.

Granville Hotel ★★   With its elegant, sienna-colored frontage, this welcoming hotel was built in the late 1700s and has been in business continuously since 1865. The interior retains something of a manor house feel, with rich color schemes, deep red carpeting, and antique furniture. Guest rooms are comfortable and reasonably spacious—although not all have air-conditioning, so make sure you request this when you book if it's important to you. Some rooms overlook Waterford Quay, with its field of gently bobbing yacht masts. The hotel bar is popular with locals, and the

Bianconi Restaurant offers excellent Irish and European cooking. Staff could hardly be friendlier or more helpful.

Meagher's Quay. www.granvillehotel.ie. © **051/305555.** 98 units. €119–€184 double. Breakfast not included in lower rates. Dinner, bed-and-breakfast packages available. Parking at Clock Tower lot (opposite the hotel) free 5pm–noon the next day. Other hours, hotel will validate ticket for flat rate of €3. **Amenities:** Restaurant; bar; room service; Wi-Fi (free).

Samuel's Heritage ★★ This charming B&B on the outskirts of Waterford (just a little too far to be considered walking distance from the center) overlooks open fields on one side and the River Suir on the other. Sally, Des, and family have converted their home into a modern, well-equipped lodging, with surprisingly good amenities for a countryside B&B, such as a mini-gym and infrared sauna. The bright and cheery guest rooms have ample space and a few extras, such as flatscreen TVs and free Wi-Fi. Family rooms sleep up to four. The delicious breakfast options include smoked salmon with eggs from their own hens.

Halfway House, Dunmore Rd. www.samuelsheritage.com. © **051/875094.** 6 units. €85–€95 double. Rates include breakfast. Free parking. **Amenities:** Gym; sauna; Wi-Fi (free).

Waterford Marina Hotel ★ This modern, well-run hotel overlooking the River Suir isn't particularly characterful, but it's in a great location, a short walk from the center of Waterford. Rooms are clean and have everything you need, including comfortable beds. Family rooms are an exceptionally good value and sleep up to four, usually for just €10 or €20 more than the standard double rates. Some bedrooms have lovely views over the water. Special offers are often listed on the website, including packages that cover dinner in the excellent restaurant. *Tip:* Ask for an upper-floor room—the views are better, and you're a bit above the ruckus when there's street noise at night.

Canada St. www.waterfordmarinahotel.com. © **051/856-600.** 81 units. €79–€187 double. Free parking. Breakfast not included in lower rates. **Amenities:** Restaurant; bar; room service; accessible rooms; Wi-Fi (free).

Where to Eat in County Waterford

Waterford's restaurant scene is pretty impressive for such a small city. Luxury restaurants abound (many of the best listed here), but there are also a number of small eateries that are perfect for light meals. In Kilmacthomas, **Coach House Coffee** (The Workhouse; www.coachhousecoffee.ie) offers fantastic coffee, sandwiches, and light lunches in the historic environment of a converted workhouse and is a great stop on the Waterford Greenway (p. 222). In Tramore, the **Seagull Bakery** specializes in sourdough bread and the freshest baked goods to take with you (4 Broad St., Tramore; www.seagullbakery.ie).

A WALK TO mahon falls

The point where the narrow Mahon River reaches the top of the Comeragh Mountains makes for a beautiful, rugged view, as it tumbles hundreds of feet down the rocky slopes in a spray of silvery white. The walk to the falls is popular with hikers, both for the sheer stony loveliness of it (you can see all the way from the falls to the sea) and because it's a fairly short distance—about a 15-minute walk in each direction. The 80m (262½ ft.) waterfalls are on the R676 between Carrick-on-Suir and Dungarvan. At the tiny village of Mahon Bridge, 26km (16 miles) south of Carrick-on-Suir, turn west on the road marked for Mahon Falls, then follow signs for the falls and the Comeragh Drive. In about 5km (3 miles), you reach a parking lot along the Mahon River (in fact, just a tiny stream). The trail begins across the road. Follow the stream along the floor of the valley to the base of the falls. From here you can see the fields of Waterford spread out below you, and the sea a glittering mirror beyond. Walking time is about 30 minutes round-trip.

Hiker takes in Mahon Falls in the Comeragh Mountains.

Bodega! ★★ MODERN IRISH/EUROPEAN A restaurant with an exclamation point in the name isn't really the sort of place you'd expect to sit up straight, and Bodega! certainly does its best to cultivate a funky vibe. Order a cocktail from the extensive list while you peruse the menu, then go all out with some local beer-battered fish and chips, or roast corn-fed chicken with roasted garlic and Madeira sauce. Sink yourself into a food coma with a luscious dessert of warm chocolate fondant.

54 John St., Waterford. www.bodegawaterford.com. © **051/844177.** Entrees €17–€30. Tues–Thurs 4:30–9:30pm; Fri–Sat 4:30–10pm. Closed Sun and Mon.

Everett's ★★★ MODERN IRISH/EUROPEAN Food critics sing the praises of this Waterford restaurant, which opened in 2018 and immediately began stacking up the awards. An eponymous venture by respected chef Peter Everett, it's tucked inside a humble fifteenth century building in the medieval quarter. The food is a modern take on Irish cuisine with the ingredients so fresh and local, expect to see the farmer's name on the menu. Try the creamy goat's cheese with pickled pear and roast onion to start, or freshly caught crab with cucumber and shallot, followed by roast duck with black pudding and elderberries, or feather-blade of local beef with horseradish. The dessert plate of Irish cheeses is lush, or you can dive into chocolate fondant with homemade malt ice cream. Book early online.

22 High St., Waterford. www.everetts.ie. *C* **051/325174.** Fixed-price menu €38–€48. Lunch €32. Tues–Sat 5:30–9:30pm; Fri–Sat 12:30–2:30pm.

Momo ★★ IRISH   Chosen as one of the best restaurants in Ireland by *The Sunday Times* newspaper, Momo is a sure bet for interesting, innovative cooking without pretensions. Although the menu always features a few interesting vegetarian options (and plenty of gluten-free as well), the emphasis is on meaty dishes like slow-cooked lamb shank, or pork steak medallions with herb potato croquettes. Appetizers might include slow-cooked pork belly with black pudding (it doesn't get meatier than that!), or crispy brie cheese with spiced plums. The lunch menu is similar, but also includes an array of sandwiches (€8.50 each) and a burger with local smoked cheese (€14). The light-filled dining room is artfully designed, the perfect place to linger over a glass of wine.

47 Patrick St., Waterford. www.momorestaurant.ie. *C* **051/581509.** Entrees €17.50–€27. Tues–Sat noon–3pm, 5–9pm; Sun 1–8pm. Closed Mon.

Richmond House ★★★ MODERN IRISH   The grounds of this 18th-century mansion hide away a bountiful produce patch, where the chef gets most of the fruit and vegetables for the restaurant's kitchen. This is something of a dining destination for people in this part of Ireland, and it's easy to see why—the food is a hugely successful combination of Irish and Continental flavors. Menus change daily, according to what's fresh and in season, but you're likely to find locally sourced lamb, beef, and seafood served with sides like champ (mashed potato and spring onion) or something freshly picked from the garden. The wine list includes a better-than-average selection of wines by the glass. An early-bird menu (€36–€44) is served until 7:30pm daily. Richmond House also has a few guest rooms (around €140–€190 per night).

Signposted from N72, Cappoquin. www.richmondhouse.net. *C* **058/54278.** Fixed-price menus €46–€58. Daily 6–9pm. Closed Dec 22–Jan 10.

The Tannery ★★ IRISH   This restaurant and cookery school in a converted 19th-century leather factory has been racking up awards for innovative cuisine since 1997. Its fresh approach to fine dining—all food, no pretention—has earned it loyal fans around the world. The menu changes constantly, but expect starters like whiskey-smoked salmon, or crab crème brûlée with pickled cucumbers. Mains include quail and foie gras pie with roast cabbage, or mountain lamb with glazed turnip. If you don't order the warm chocolate mousse with pecan ice cream for dessert, we want to know why. Chef Paul Flynn also offers master classes in cooking (from €180 per day). You can stay nearby in one of the elegant rooms in a restaurant-owned townhouse (from €130 per night).

10 Quai St., Dungarvan, Co. Waterford. www.tannery.ie. *C* **058/45420.** Fixed-price menu €65. Early bird (5:30–6:30pm) €36.50. Wed–Sat 5:30–9pm; Sun 12:30–2:30pm. Closed Mon–Tues.

cycling THE GREENWAY

Off-road greenways—special walking or cycling trails along former railway lines—have become popular in Ireland in recent years, and more are in development. The 46km (28-mile) Waterford Greenway is on the old railway line between Waterford city and Dungarvan, taking in rolling countryside, bridges, viaducts, and the Ballyvoyle tunnel, which dates from 1878 and is a quarter-mile long. You will also pass old railway stations, medieval ruins, and Norman castles and see the Viking settlement at Woodstown, taking in plenty of scenic and seaside views along the way.

There are various bike hire companies, and some will also shuttle your luggage and/or bring you back to your starting point. Rates start at around €25 per day or €45 for an e-bike. Check out **Waterford Greenway Bike Hire** (www. waterfordgreenwaybikehire.com; ✆ **051/295-955**) or **Waterford Greenway** (www.waterfordgreenway.com; ✆ **085/111-3850**).

Beyond the Southeast, other scenic greenways include the **Great Western Greenway** in Mayo (p. 434) and the **Limerick Greenway** (p. 367).

Sports & Outdoor Pursuits in Waterford

CYCLING From Waterford City, you can ride 13km (8 miles) to Passage East and take the ferry (fare with bicycle €2 one-way, €3 round-trip) to Wexford and the beautiful Hook Peninsula (p. 226). Or continue on from Passage East to Dunmore East, a picturesque seaside village with a small beach hemmed in by cliffs. For a scenic cycling route along an old railway line, try the **Waterford Greenway** (see above).

FISHING **Knockaderry Reservoir** is an enormous 28-hectare (70-acre) fishery 12km (7½ miles) southwest of Waterford City, great for catching rainbow trout. You can purchase permits (€25) from the Centra supermarket on the main R680 road in Kilmeaden; boat hire from €40, see www. waterfordflyfishing.ie). The **Fort William Fishery,** Glencairn, Lismore (www.fortwilliamfishing.ie; ✆ **087/855-7218**), is renowned for its wild salmon; permits cost between €50 and €100 per day, depending on the month. They also rent cottages, sleeping up to 8, for €1,000 to €1,200 per week; see the website for details.

GOLF County Waterford has rich pickings for golf fans. Clubs and resorts include three 18-hole championship courses. **Waterford Castle Hotel & Golf Resort,** The Island, Ballinakill, Waterford (www.water fordcastleresort.com/golf-home.html; ✆ **051/878203**), is a par-72 parkland course on a small island; greens fees are around €35 to €50. **Faithlegg Golf Club,** Faithlegg House, Waterford (www.faithlegg.com; ✆ **051/382000**), a par-72 parkland course beside the River Suir, charges greens fees of €20 to €50. **Dungarvan Golf Club,** Knocknagranagh,

Dungarvan (www.dungarvangolfclub.com; ℭ **058/43310**), a par-72 parkland course, has greens fees of €15 to €30.

SAILING, PADDLEBOARDING & SEA KAYAKING   From May to September, the **Dunmore East Adventure Centre,** Dunmore East (www.dunmore adventure.com; ℭ **051/383783**), offers sailing taster sessions for €55 as well as a variety of sailing lessons. A 1-hour kayaking or stand-up paddleboarding session is €30. Summer programs for children are also available.

COUNTY WEXFORD

The countryside in this area feels so peaceful and bucolic, Dublin might as well be hundreds of miles away. Wexford is known for its long stretches of pristine beaches and for the evocative historic monuments in Wexford Town and on the Hook Peninsula. The modern English name of Wexford evolved from *Waesfjord,* which is what the Vikings called it when they invaded in the 9th century. The Normans captured the town at the end of the 12th century; you can still see remnants of their fort at the Irish National Heritage Park.

Visitor Information

The **Wexford Tourist Office** is on Crescent Quay, Wexford (www.visit wexford.ie; ℭ **053/912-3111**). It's open Monday to Saturday from 9am to 5:30pm. From late July to mid-August it's also open on Sundays from 9am to 5:30pm.

Exploring Wexford Town

The Bull Ring ★ SQUARE/STATUE   In the 17th century, this town square was a venue for bull baiting, a sport introduced by the butcher's guild. (Tradition maintained that after a match, the hide of the ill-fated bull was presented to the mayor and the meat was used to feed the poor.) But it played a greater part in history in 1798, when the first declaration of an Irish republic was made here. A memorial statue honors the Irish pikemen who fought for the cause. Today, activity at the ring is much tamer: An excellent outdoor market is held every Friday from 9:30am to 2pm and Saturday from 9:30am to 1pm.
Off N. Main St.

Cornmarket ★ SQUARE   Until a century ago, this central marketplace buzzed with the activity of cobblers, publicans, and more than 20 other businesses. Today it's just a wide street dominated by the Wexford Arts Centre, a structure dating from 1775.
Off Upper George's St.

Irish National Heritage Park ★★ HERITAGE SITE   On the banks of the River Slaney, just outside of Wexford Town, this 14-hectare

(35-acre) living-history park is great fun. It provides an ideal introduction for visitors of all ages to life in ancient Ireland, from the Stone Age to the Norman invasion. Each reconstructed glimpse into Irish history is well crafted and has its own natural setting and wildlife. There's also a nature trail and interpretive center, complete with gift shop and cafe. Kids can easily be kept amused for half a day here.

Ferrycarrig (about 4.8km/3 miles W of Wexford, signposted from N11). www.irish heritage.ie. © **053/912-0733.** Admission €11 adults; €9 seniors and students; €6 children 5–17; free for children 4 and under; €25–€30 families. May–Aug daily 9:30am–6:30pm (last admission 5pm); Sept–Apr daily 9:30am–5pm (last admission 3pm).

John Barry Monument ★ STATUE   This bronze statue, a gift from the American people in 1956, faces out to the sea as a tribute to the titular Mr. Barry, a Wexford native who became the father of the American Navy. Born at Ballysampson, Tacumshane, 16km (10 miles) southeast of Wexford Town, Barry immigrated to the colonies while in his teens and became one of the U.S. Navy's first commissioned officers. In 1797, George Washington appointed him head of the U.S. Navy.

Crescent Quay.

St. Iberius Church ★ CHURCH   Erected in 1660, St. Iberius was built on hallowed ground—the land has been used for houses of worship since Norse times. The church has a lovely Georgian facade and an interior known for its superb acoustics. Concerts are sometimes held here; see local listings for details.

N. Main St. No phone. Free admission. Mon–Sat 9:30am–4pm.

The Twin Churches: Church of the Assumption and Church of the Immaculate Conception ★ CHURCHES   Dominating Wexford's skyline, a pair of 69m (226-ft.) spires top these twin Gothic Revival structures (1851–58), designed by architect Robert Pierce, a pupil of Augustus Pugin (designer of the Houses of Parliament in London).

Bride and Rowe sts. © **053/912-2205.** Free admission; donations welcome. Daily 8am–6pm.

Westgate Heritage Centre and Selskar Abbey ★ RELIGIOUS SITE/MUSEUM   The **Westgate Heritage Centre** is housed in what was once a tollgate on the western approach to the city, part of the town's 12th-century defensive walls. At the time of writing, the center was undergoing renovation, so check if it has reopened before visiting. Adjacent to the center is the picturesque **Selskar Abbey,** where the first Anglo-Irish treaty was signed in 1169; it's said that Henry II spent Lent 1172 at the abbey doing penance for (unintentionally, so the story goes) having Thomas à Becket murdered. The abbey is mostly in ruins, its choir is part of a Church of Ireland edifice, and a portion of the original tower is a vesting room.

Westgate St. Undergoing renovation; check before visiting.

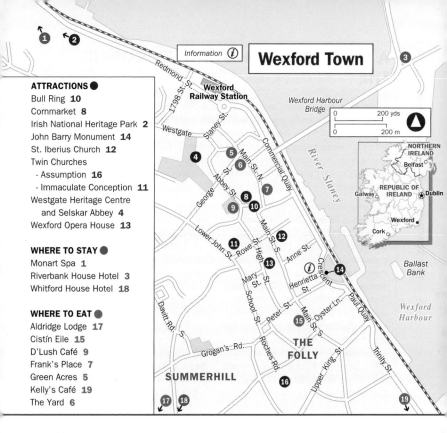

Wexford Town

Information ⓘ

Wexford Railway Station

Wexford Harbour Bridge

River Slaney

THE FOLLY

SUMMERHILL

Wexford Harbour

Ballast Bank

NORTHERN IRELAND
Belfast
REPUBLIC OF IRELAND
Galway
Dublin
Wexford
Cork

Wexford Opera House ★ CONCERT HALL   This modern opera house is a somewhat awkward addition to the Wexford skyline, with its large but rather garish copper-plated tower. The biggest event in the opera house's calendar is the prestigious **Wexford Festival Opera** (**www. wexfordopera.com**), held for 2 weeks each October/November, attracting aficionados from all over Ireland and beyond. Opera lovers will be in heaven—but book early if there's something you really want to see. Tickets start at around €10, rising to €100 for the best seats.

High St. www.wexfordoperahouse.ie. ⓒ **053/912-2144.** Ticket prices vary; generally between €15–€35. Event times vary; call ahead.

Wexford Walking Tours ★★ TOURS   Proud of their town's ancient streets and antique buildings, the people of Wexford began conducting guided tours for visitors more than 30 years ago. Now the tourist office runs the tours on a more formal basis, but they're still led by locals, whose knowledge of the town and its history is unrivaled. The regular 90-minute historical tour runs generally between April to October and departs from the Tourist Office (p. 223), which also handles booking. Other tours, such

A TRIP THROUGH HISTORY: EXPLORING THE ring of hook

A wild and rugged place of rocky headlands and secluded beaches, the **Hook Peninsula** juts out between Bannow Bay and Waterford Harbour in southwest County Wexford. In medieval times, these inlets were significant landing spots for travelers from Britain to Ireland, as archaeological remains attest. Today, the peninsula is a popular driving or cycling route (see map on p. 227), as well as a magnet for hikers on the Wexford Coastal Pathway (p. 234) and for birders watching the spring and fall passerine migration.

Start your exploration at the town of **Wellington Bridge,** 22km (14 miles) southwest of Wexford Town via R7333. Just west of Wellington Bridge on R733 is a roadside stop on the left by a cemetery; from here you can look across Bannow Bay to the ruins of **Clonmines,** a Norman village established in the 13th century. It's a fine example of a walled medieval settlement, with remains of two churches, three tower houses, and an Augustinian priory. You can drive to the ruins—just follow R733 another mile west to a left turn posted for the Wicklow Coastal Pathway and continue straight on this road where the pathway turns right. The ruins are on private land, so ask permission at the farmhouse at the end of the road.

Continuing west on R733, turn left on R734 at the sign for the Ring of Hook, and turn right at the sign for **Tintern Abbey** ★ (p. 230). Founded by Welsh monks in the 13th century, its beautiful grounds contain a restored stone bridge that spans a narrow sea inlet.

As R734 continues south, you come to **Baginbun Head,** where the Norman presence in Ireland was first established with a victory over the Irish at the Battle of Baginbun. Today it's a peaceful scene, with a fine beach nestling against the

cliffs, but from the beach you can still see the outline of the Norman earthwork fortifications on the head.

The **tip of the peninsula,** with its line of low cliffs eroded in places for blowholes, has been famous for shipwrecks since Norman times. Its historic **lighthouse** (p. 227) has been on this site since the early 13th century.

The Ring of Hook road returns along the western side of the peninsula, passing the beaches at **Booley Bay** and **Dollar Bay.** On a promontory overlooking the town of **Duncannon** is a **fort** built in 1588 to protect Waterford Harbour from the Spanish Armada. Just north of Duncannon, along the coast at the village of **Ballyhack,** a ferry runs to County Waterford (p. 211), and there's a Knights Hospitallers castle on a hill.

A visit to the Hook Peninsula wouldn't be complete without a stop at **Dunbrody Abbey,** in a field beside the road about 6.5km (4 miles) north of Duncannon. The abbey, founded in 1170, is a magnificent ruin and one of the largest Cistercian abbeys in Ireland. Despite its grand size, it bears remarkably little ornamentation. Tours are sometimes available; inquire at the visitor center across the road.

as ghost walks or visits to Selskar Abbey, are sometimes available at certain times of year; check online.

Departs from Wexford Tourist Office on Crescent Quay. www.visitwexford.ie. ☏ **053/919-6555.** Check for updated tour times and costs online.

The Ring of Hook

↑
11

Dunbrody Abbey **10**
Campile
KILKENNY
Gorteens
Cheekpoint
Coole
Ballycullane
R736
Wellington
Bridge
WEXFORD
Clonmines
1
R733
Rosetown
R734
R733
Barrystown
R736
Little I.
9 Ballyhack
Ballintry
**Tintern
Abbey**
3
St. Kierans
Suir
Passage East
Car Ferry
Arthurstown
R737
Bannow Bay
Grange
R683
R684
8 Duncannon
R734
Bannow I.
Bannow
2 →
WATERFORD
Brandane
Woodstown
Booley Bay **7**
Hook Peninsula
Clammers
Point
Keeragh Is.
*Waterford
Harbour*
6
Dollar
Bay
Fethard
Ingard Pt.
*Ballyteige
Bay*
Creadan
Head
Ramstown
Kilea
Templetown
Baginbun Head
4
R684
*Dunmore
Bay*
Sandeel Bay
Dunmore East
Patrick's Bay
Slade
Churchtown
Slade Bay
Swines Head
5
Hook Head **Hook Head Lighthouse**

1 Wellington Bridge
2 Irish Agricultural Museum
and Famine Exhibition
3 Tintern Abbey
4 Baginbun Head
5 Hook Lighthouse
6 Dollar Bay
7 Booley Bay
8 Duncannon
9 Ballyhack
10 Dunbrody Abbey
11 SS *Dunbrody* Famine Ship
Experience

NORTHERN
IRELAND
Belfast
REPUBLIC OF
IRELAND
Dublin
Galway
Map Area
Cork

0 _____ 3 miles
0 _____ 3 kms

Farther Afield in County Wexford

Hook Lighthouse & Heritage Centre ★★ LIGHTHOUSE   The
Hook Peninsula (p. 226) is one of southern Ireland's loveliest drives, full
of captivating vistas and hidden byways to discover. Nestled at the end of
it all is this picturesque old lighthouse, the oldest part of which dates from
the 13th century, making it the world's oldest lighthouse still in continuous use. Guided tours do an excellent job of telling the history of the lighthouse and of the surrounding peninsula, which has been occupied since at
least the A.D. 5th century. There is an active program of special events,

too, from art courses to ghost tours. *Tip:* The drive from Waterford is drastically shorter if you take the Passage East car ferry (p. 211).

Hook Head. www.hookheritage.ie. © **051/397-055.** Admission €10 adults; €9 seniors and students; €6 children 5–18; free for children 4 and under; €14–€30 families. Visitor center: July–Aug daily 9:30am–6pm; Sept–Jun daily 9:30am–5pm. Lighthouse tours: July–Aug half-hourly 9:30am–6pm, last tour 6pm; Sept–June half-hourly 10am–4pm. It's 30km (18⅔ miles) SE of Waterford, 47km (29 miles) SW of Wexford.

Hook Lighthouse.

Irish Agricultural Museum and Famine Exhibition ★★

MUSEUM Absorbing and at times deeply affecting, this excellent museum on the grounds of Johnstown Castle illuminates how important agriculture has been to the history of this region. Exhibits are devoted to, among other things, traditional crafts, dairy farming, country furniture, and historic machinery. Of course, no farming museum in

Johnstown Castle, home of the Irish Agricultural Museum.

local hero: JFK, GREAT-GRANDSON OF NEW ROSS

U.S. President John F. Kennedy was born in America, but Patrick Kennedy (1823–58), his great-grandfather, was a son of Ireland, raised in the small waterfront city of New Ross in County Wexford. That connection to the Kennedy family history draws thousands of visitors a year.

The house near New Ross where he lived until 1848 has been converted into a museum dedicated to the Kennedy family's Irish history. The **Kennedy Homestead** (www.kennedyhomestead.ie; ℂ 051/388264) in the tiny village of Dunganstown, 8km (5 miles) south of New Ross, is a humble, one-story traditional stone building. John F. Kennedy himself visited the homestead in June 1963, meeting his cousins during what he reportedly called "the happiest 4 days of my life." The story of that visit is one of the exhibits at the modern visitors' center on the grounds, where you can see also rare memorabilia (some acquired through the Kennedy Library archival collection in Boston) and learn what the family's life was like in the dangerous world of 19th-century Ireland, as

well as the circumstances that led to Patrick Kennedy's decision to emigrate. It's open daily 9:30am to 5:30pm (last admission 5pm); entry costs €8 adults, €7 seniors, €6 children and students, and €25 families.

Another nearby JFK site of interest is the **JFK Memorial Park & Arboretum** (www.heritageireland.ie; ℂ 051/388171), a beautiful lakeside garden and wildlife haven dedicated to the late president. It's signposted from R733, about 12km (7½ miles) south of New Ross. Opening times are May to August daily 10am to 8pm; April and September daily 10am to 6:30pm; and October to March daily 10am to 5pm. Last admission is 1 hour before closing. Entry costs €5 adults, €4 seniors, €3 students and children, and €13 families.

Ireland would be complete without mention of its greatest catastrophe: the Great Famine, which killed about a million people in the mid–19th century (and was responsible for the emigration of a million more).

Johnstown Castle Estate, Bridgetown Rd., off Wexford-Rosslare Rd. (N25). www.johnstowncastle.ie/irish-agri-museum. ℂ 053/918-4671. Gardens and museum: €9 adults; €7 seniors and students; €4 children 5–16; children under 5 free; €24 families. Castle tours (extra): €4 adults; €3 seniors and students, €2 children 5–16; €11 families. Museum: daily 9am–4:30pm; last entry 3:30pm. Castle tours noon and 2pm. Gardens: 9am–4:30pm.

SS Dunbrody Famine Ship Experience ★★★ MUSEUM This huge, life-size reconstruction of a 19th-century tall ship is exactly the kind of vessel on which a million or more people emigrated from Ireland to escape the Great Famine. An interpretive history center, the SS *Dunbrody* offers an engaging way to learn about that history—particularly for youngsters, who will find it less stuffy than a conventional museum. Actors in period dress lead the tours, describing in great detail what life

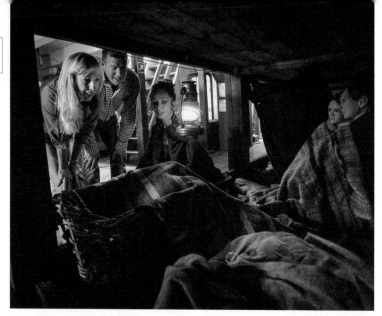

Costumed interpreters at the SS *Dunbrody* Famine Ship Experience bring to life the emigrant experience of the Famine years.

on board was like for the passengers. It's a moving experience. The SS *Dunbrody* is in New Ross, 36km (22⅓ miles) west of Wexford.

The Quay, New Ross. www.dunbrody.com. ℭ **051/425239.** Admission €12 adults; €10 seniors; €6 students and children; €25–€34 families. Apr–Sep 9am–6pm (last tour 5pm); Oct–Mar 9am–5pm (last tour 4pm).

Tintern Abbey ★ HISTORIC SITE   In a lovely rural setting overlooking Bannow Bay, Tintern Abbey was founded in the 12th century by William Marshall, the Earl of Pembroke, as thanks to God after he nearly died at sea. The parts that remain—nave, chancel, tower, chapel, and cloister— date from the early 13th century, though they have been much altered since. The grounds are extraordinarily beautiful and include a stone bridge spanning a narrow sea inlet. A visitor center has exhibitions on the history of the abbey, as well as a small cafe. Don't miss a stroll in the restored Colclough Walled Garden on the grounds.

Note: This is not the Tintern Abbey that William Wordsworth wrote about in his famous poem of the same name; however, the monks who named this abbey were Cistercians from the other Tintern, located in Wales; they simply gave this one the same name.

Saltmills, New Ross. ℭ **051/562650.** Admission €7.30 adults; €5.80 seniors; €4.50 students and children; €21.20 families. Daily Mar–Oct 9am–5pm; Nov 9am–4pm. Last admission 30 min. before closing. Closed Dec–Mar. Signposted 19km (12 miles) S of New Ross off of R733.

Where to Stay in County Wexford

In Wexford, choice within the town is limited; you'll do much better opting for a place in the countryside, where there's a satisfying mixture of bucolic farmhouses and luxurious getaways.

Monart Spa ★★★   A luxurious, restorative, grown-up retreat, Monart is consistently named among the top spas in Ireland (Condé Nast even once declared it the third best in the world)—and for good reason. It's a sumptuous, impeccably designed place, nestled beside a lake and a verdant forest. Guest rooms are surrounded by woodland, and some have little balconies overlooking the grounds. The restaurant is excellent, and the heavenly spa has a thermal suite equipped with two pools, a salt grotto, indoor and outdoor saunas, and an aroma steam room. Check the website for package deals, particularly midweek specials. To maintain the air of serenity, no children are allowed.

On L6124, The Still (about 5.2km/3⅓ miles W of Enniscorthy). www.monart.ie. ℗ **053/923-8999.** 68 units. €280–€500 double; €500–€600 suite. Minimum 2 nights on some summer weekends. Free parking. Rates include breakfast. Dinner, bed-and-breakfast, and spa packages available. **Amenities:** 2 restaurants; bar; afternoon tea; cafe; pool; room service; spa; Wi-Fi (free).

Riverbank House Hotel ★★   This cozy midsize hotel just outside the town center in Wexford has lovely views of the River Slaney. Rooms overlooking the river have suitably huge picture windows. Beds are comfortable and very large; some are four-posters. There are also family rooms with one double and one single bed. The bar and restaurant are pleasant spaces, filled with natural light. The casual pub-style food is good, too—unfussy, international dishes of the something-for-everyone variety—and in good weather, you can dine on the terrace overlooking the river. The genuinely cheerful staff helps it all run smoothly.

The Bridge. www.riverbankhousehotel.com. ℗ **053/912-3611.** 23 units. €68–€148 double. Free parking. Breakfast not included in lower rates. **Amenities:** Restaurant; bar; room service; Wi-Fi (free).

Whitford House Hotel ★★   Located a few miles outside Wexford town center, the Whitford House Hotel makes a relaxing getaway for the whole family. Rooms are moderate in size and pleasant in decor, with neutral color schemes and a mix of modern and traditional furnishings. The lounges and bar are popular and often busy—the hotel has a friendly, social vibe. It offers plenty of amusements for small children, including a playground and a kiddie pool. For the grown-ups, an adults-only pool area has a Jacuzzi, steam room, and sauna. The **Seasons Restaurant** produces solid fare—nothing too innovative but reliably good. It's the kind of place where local families go for meals on special occasions. The hotel bar and bistro is perfect for more casual fare around the wood-burning stove.

New Line Rd., Wexford. www.whitfordhotelwexford.ie. ℗ **053/914-3444.** 36 units. €79–€199 double. Free parking. Lower rates do not include breakfast. Spa packages available. **Amenities:** Restaurant; bar; pool; gym; spa; Wi-Fi (free).

Woodbrook House B&B ★★ This grand Georgian mansion is reached down a long, private road, tucked away at the foot of the Blackstairs Mountains near Enniscorthy. Owners Giles and Alexandra FitzHerbert bought the house in ramshackle condition and have coaxed it back to regal beauty. Soaring ceilings, curving staircases, long hallways, original wood and stone floors, light tumbling through towering windows, breathtaking mountain views—expect all of that and comfortable beds. The decor is eclectic, with lots of antiques; everything looks loved and lived-in. The owners are excellent cooks, so we highly recommend booking **dinner** (€50) during your stay. Make some time to wander the gorgeous grounds and breathe that fresh air.

Woodbrook, Killanne, Enniscorthy, Wexford. www.woodbrookhouse.ie. ✆ **053/925-5114.** 3 units. €170–€180 double. Free parking. Rates include breakfast. **Amenities:** Wi-Fi (free).

Where to Eat in County Wexford

Wexford isn't as famous for its cuisine as Cork or Waterford, but a growing foodie movement may change that. Along with the restaurants listed below, plenty of places offer lighter cuisine. **D'Lush Café** (Cornmarket, Wexford) in the Wexford Arts Centre claims to have the best coffee in Wexford, and we believe them. It also uses fresh, seasonal ingredients in sandwiches, tarts, soups and breakfasts. In Drinagh, at the edge of Wexford Town, **Kelly's Café** (Drinagh Retail Park; www.kellyscafe.ie) is an outpost of the popular Kelly's Resort Hotel and Spa, and it's a handy

Creative cuisine at Aldridge Lodge in Duncannon, County Wexford.

option for homemade breakfast and lunch, with a gourmet twist—we love the scrambled eggs on sourdough toast and the poached eggs with avocado, but the homemade pastries are even better. The mood is casual, the food is great, the coffee is strong. When you don't know what you want, try popping into **Green Acres** (Selskar St., Wexford; www.greenacres.ie), an upscale food hall with a delicatessen, restaurant, art gallery and wine cellar, all featuring carefully selected food to eat in or take out. It's the perfect place to put together a picnic.

Aldridge Lodge ★★★ IRISH   This wonderful restaurant near the village of Duncannon has been wowing diners for over a decade. The menu very much relies on what's in season, but specialties of the talented chef, Billy Whitty, include fried monkfish with fennel cream and rack of lamb with spinach and kumquats. The tasting menu is a delight, bucking the trend for an endless procession of bite-size plates in favor of four balanced and well-designed courses (reasonable, too, at just €40 per head). Aldridge Lodge also has three elegant bedrooms for €120 per night; dinner, bed-and-breakfast packages are good value for the money.

Duncannon, Co. Wexford. www.aldridgelodge.com. ℂ **051/389116.** Set menu €40. Reservations essential. Thurs–Sun 6–9:30pm.

Cistín Eile ★★ MODERN IRISH   The Irish words painted on the dining room wall, *"is maith an t-anlann an t-ocras,"* translate to "hunger makes a great sauce"—a wry nod to tradition that nicely sums up this place. Wexford native and rising star chef Warren Gillen deeply embraces the flavors of his home region yet gives them a contemporary edge. Haddock with wild garlic pesto, 10-hour-cooked local beef, crispy polenta with pumpkin and mushrooms—all are elegantly presented without a hint of pretension. One of the nicest things about Cistín Eile is how relaxed it feels; Warren often greets guests at the door personally and chats with them at their tables. *Tip:* Lunch here is surprisingly affordable.

80 S. Main St., Wexford, Co. Wexford. ℂ **053/912-1616.** Lunch entrees €6–€14.50; dinner set menu €40. Reservations recommended. Tues–Sat noon–3pm; Fri–Sat 6–9pm. Closed Sun and Mon.

Frank's Place ★★ MODERN IRISH   This is a food and wine bar, deli, market, and cafe set in a former bakery that goes back five generations in the owner Frank's family. The atmosphere is both buzzing and relaxed. At lunch, small plates include smoked mackerel pate with horseradish and pickled veg, or tomato seafood chowder. The dinner menu has dishes like spinach and feta stuffed lemon sole with chorizo and chickpea hot pot or a rump steak with thyme polenta chips and roast mushroom. A great wine list includes a number of fine and rare vintages.

54 N. Main St., Wexford, Co Wexford. www.franksplace1860.ie. ℂ **053/918-9109.** Lunch entrees €6–€20; Dinner entrees €25–€29. Mon–Wed 9am–6pm; Thurs–Sat 9am–9pm; Sun 10am–6pm.

walk this way: THE WEXFORD COASTAL PATHWAY

Along the entire coastline you'll see brown signs with a picture of a hiker on them, marking the **Wexford Coastal Pathway,** which meanders along the coast via pristine beaches and country lanes—and, unfortunately, some stretches of busy roads. At the north end, however, there's a peaceful beach walk from **Clogga Head** (County Wicklow) to **Tara Hill,** 14km (8 miles) south, ending with panoramic views from atop Tara Hill. South of Wexford town, another good section runs from **Rosslare Harbour** around Carnsore Point to **Kilmore Quay.**

Yet another fine coastal walk is near Wexford town in the **Raven Nature Reserve,** an area of forested dunes and uncrowded beaches. To get there, take R741 north out of Wexford, turn right on R742 to Curracloe village, and at Curracloe turn right to drive just over a mile to the beach parking lot. The nature reserve is to your right. By car it's a half-mile south, but you can also walk there along the beach. It's 5km (3 miles) to Raven Point, where at low tide you can see the remains of a shipwreck, half-buried in the sand.

Sports & Outdoor Pursuits in Wexford

BEACHES   County Wexford's beaches at **Courtown, Curracloe, Duncannon,** and **Rosslare** are good for walking, jogging, and swimming.

BIRD & WILDLIFE WATCHING   Besides the **Wexford Wildfowl Reserve ★,** bird-watchers head for **Hook Head** (p. 226), a good spot in spring and autumn for seeing the passerine migration. In addition to swallows, swifts, and warblers, look out for the less common cuckoos, turtledoves, redstarts, and blackcaps.

Kilmore Quay Angling (www.kilmoreangling.com; ✆ **087/213-5308**) offers an "eco-cruise" around the Saltee Islands, to see seals and birds (without landing); expect to pay around €30 adults, €15 children.

In May, June, and July, **Great Saltee Island** is excellent for watching seabirds, when the island's southern cliffs become mobbed with nesting birds and their young. Plentiful species include puffins, which nest in underground burrows, as well as graceful guillemots, cormorants, kittiwakes, gannets, and Manx shearwaters. The island is privately owned, but visitors are welcome as long as they do not disturb the bird habitat and the island's natural beauty. A daily ferry to the islands from Kilmore Quay runs between April and September (www.salteeferry.com; ✆ **087/252-9736;** €30 adults, €15 children under 12). You may need to walk on slippery stones or seaweed or in shallow water when you land. Landings don't take place in rough weather.

CYCLING   From Wexford, the road north up the coast through Curracloe to Blackwater is a scenic day trip. You can rent bikes or take tours with **Cycle Wexford,** Curracloe (www.cyclewexford.com; ✆ **053/913-7560**).

234

DIVING   The Kilmore Quay area, south of Wexford Town, offers some of the most spectacular diving in Ireland, especially around the Saltee Islands and Conningbeg rocks. Wrecks off the coast lie at depths of around 60m (200 ft.). For all your diving needs, consult the **Pier House Diving Centre,** Kilmore Quay (✆ **053/29703**).

COUNTY KILKENNY

Like so many Irish towns, Kilkenny City stands on the site of an old monastery from which it takes its name. A priory was founded here in the 6th century by St. Canice; in Gaelic, *Cill Choinnigh* means "Canice's Church." In medieval times, it was a prosperous walled city. Much of its medieval architecture has been skillfully preserved, including long sections of the medieval wall. Farther afield from the county seat, the gentle countryside is full of captivating old ruins, from the majestic **Kells Priory** to the haunting remains of **Jerpoint Abbey.**

Visitor Information

The **Kilkenny Tourist Office** is at Shee Alms House, Rose Inn Street, Kilkenny (www.kilkennytourism.ie; ✆ **056/775-1500**). It's open Monday to Saturday 9am to 5:15pm. It sometimes closes for lunch on quieter days, and hours can vary in winter.

Exploring Kilkenny City

Black Abbey ★ CHURCH   Nobody is quite sure why this Dominican church, founded in 1225, is named Black Abbey. It may be because the Dominicans wore black capes over their white habits, or perhaps because the Black Plague claimed the lives of eight priests in 1348. The abbey's blackest days came in 1650, when Oliver Cromwell used it as a court from which to dispense summary justice, before destroying it completely; by the time he left, all that remained were the walls. The abbey was rebuilt and opened in 1816 as a church; a new nave was completed in 1866, and the entire building was fully restored in 1979. Among the elements remaining from the original abbey are an alabaster sculpture of the Holy Trinity that dates from 1400, and a pre-Reformation statue of St. Dominic carved in Irish oak, which is believed to be the oldest such piece in the world. The huge Rosary Window, a stained-glass work of nearly 45 sq. m (484 sq. ft.) representing the 15 mysteries of the rosary, was created in 1892 by Mayer of Munich.

Abbey St. (off Parliament St.). ✆ **056/772-1279.** Free admission; donations welcome. Apr–Sept Mon–Sat 7:30am–7pm, Sun 9am–7pm; Oct–Mar Mon–Sat 7:30am–5:30pm. No visits during worship (Mass times Mon–Sat 10:30am and 1:05pm; also Sat vigil 6:10pm; Sun 9am, noon, and 6pm).

Kilkenny Castle ★★★ CASTLE   Standing majestically beside the River Nore on the south side of Kilkenny City, this stunning medieval castle was built in the 12th century and remodeled in Victorian times.

Art gallery in Kilkenny Castle.

From its sturdy corner towers to its battlements, Kilkenny Castle retains the imposing lines of an authentic fortress. The exquisitely restored interior includes a library, drawing room, and bedrooms, all decorated in 1830s style. The former servants' quarters are now an art gallery. The 20-hectare (49-acre) grounds include a riverside walk, extensive gardens, and a well-equipped children's playground. This is a very busy site, so arrive early (or toward the end of the day) to avoid waiting.

The Parade. www.kilkennycastle.ie. © **056/770-4100.** Admission €8 adults; €6 seniors; €4 students and children; children 5 and under free; €20 families. June–Aug daily 9am–5:30pm; Apr–May and Sept 9:30am–5:30pm; Oct–Feb 9:30am–4:30pm; Mar 9:30am–5pm. Guided tours only Nov–Jan. Last admission 30 min. before closing (45 min. Nov–Jan).

Kilkenny Walking Tours ★★ TOURS   Local historian Pat Tynan leads you through the streets and lanes of medieval Kilkenny on this lively walking tour. Tall-sounding (but 100% true) tales are really Pat's strong point; he's a mine of trivia, much of it rather sensational (his own website sells the tour with promises of "black death, whippings, burnings, crime, jails, theft and prostitutes"—now how's *that* for a pitch?). Tours depart daily from the tourist office, Rose Inn Street, and last about 70 minutes.

c/o Kilkenny Tourist Office, Rose Inn St. www.kilkennywalkingtours.ie. © **087/265-1745.** Tickets €10 adults; €8 seniors and students; €32 families. Mid-Mar to Oct Mon–Sat 11am and 2pm; Sun and all tours from Nov–Feb must be prebooked; call for availability.

St. Canice's Cathedral ★★ CATHEDRAL   The church that gave Kilkenny its name stands at the northern end of the city. Built in the 12th century, it was restored after the English invasion led by Oliver Cromwell in the mid–17th century. It is noteworthy for the rich interior timber and stone carvings, its colorful glasswork, and the structure itself. On the

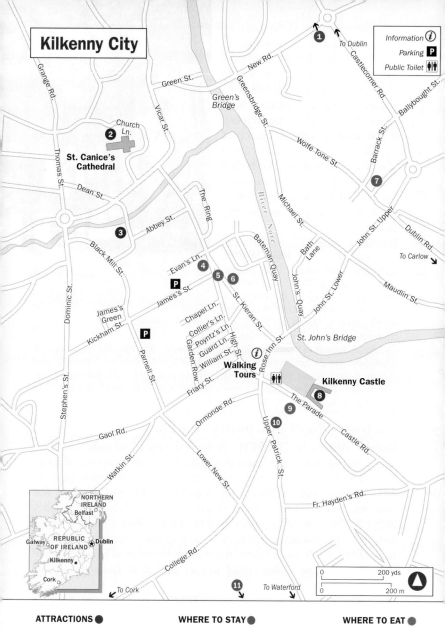

Kilkenny City

Information ⓘ
Parking P
Public Toilet 🚻

To Dublin

New Rd.

Green St.

Castlecomer Rd.

Ballybought St.

Green's Bridge

Greensbridge St.

Vicar St.

Church Ln.

2

St. Canice's Cathedral

Wolfe Tone St.

Barrack St.

7

Thomas St.

Dean St.

Michael St.

John St. Upper

Dublin Rd.

To Carlow

The Ring

Abbey St.

3

River Nore

Bath Lane

Black Mill St.

Bateman Quay

John's Quay

John St. Lower

Maudlin St.

Dominic St.

Evan's Ln.

4

P

5 **6**

St. Kieran St.

St. John's Bridge

James's St.

James's Green

Chapel Ln.

Collier's Ln.

Poyntz's Ln.

Kickham St.

P

Garden Row.

Guard Ln.

William St.

High St.

Rose Inn St.

ⓘ

Walking Tours

🚻

Kilkenny Castle

8

Friary St.

9

The Parade

Parnell St.

Stephen's St.

Ormonde Rd.

10

Upper Patrick St.

Castle Rd.

Gaol Rd.

Watkin St.

Lower New St.

Fr. Hayden's Rd.

NORTHERN IRELAND

Belfast

Galway

REPUBLIC OF IRELAND

Dublin

Kilkenny

Cork

College Rd.

To Cork

11

To Waterford

| 0 | | 200 yds |
| 0 | | 200 m |

237

ATTRACTIONS ●
Black Abbey **3**
Kilkenny Castle **8**
St. Canice's Cathedral **2**

WHERE TO STAY ●
Lawcus Farm Guesthouse **11**
Pembroke Kiklenny **10**
Rosquil House **1**

WHERE TO EAT ●
Campagne **7**
Foodworks **4**
Gourmet Store **5**
Kyteler's Inn **6**
Ristorante Rinuccini **9**

grounds, amid the tombstones in the churchyard, looms a massive round tower, believed to be a relic of the ancient church (although its original conical top has been replaced by a slightly domed roof). If you want to climb to the top of the tower, it will cost you a couple of euro and burn more calories than you can count. *Note:* The cathedral has no parking, so use the lot on Dean Street or park in the city center.

The Close, Coach Rd. www.stcanices cathedral.com. ✆ **056/776-4971.** Cathedral: €4.50 adults; €3.50 seniors, students, and children; €12 families. Round Tower: €4 adults; €4 seniors, students, and children; €12 families. Combined ticket: €7 adults; €6.50 seniors, students, and children; €15 families.

Buskers in Kilkenny City.

Cathedral: June–Aug Mon–Sat 9am–6pm, Sun 1–6pm; Apr–May and Sept Mon–Sat 10am–5pm, Sun 2–5pm (closes at 4pm Oct–Mar); Oct–Mar Mon–Sat 10am–1pm and 2–4pm. Round Tower (weather permitting): June–Aug Mon–Fri 9am–6pm, Sun 1–6pm. Last climb 30 min. before closing. **Note:** You must be over 140cm (4½ ft.) to climb the tower.

Farther Afield in County Kilkenny

Duiske Abbey ★ CHURCH A fine example of an early Cistercian abbey, Duiske Abbey was founded in 1204. Although it was officially suppressed in 1536, monks continued to occupy the site for many years. In 1774, the tower of the abbey church collapsed. In 1813, the roof was replaced, and religious services returned to the church, but the abbey didn't approach its former glory until the 1970s, when a group of locals mounted a reconstruction effort. Now, with its fine lancet windows and a large effigy of a Norman knight, the abbey is the pride of Graiguenamanagh. The adjacent visitor center has an exhibit of Christian art and artifacts.

Upper Main St., Graiguenamanagh. ✆ **059/972-4238.** Free admission; donations welcome. Daily 8am–6pm.

Dunmore Cave ★ UNDERGROUND CAVERNS This gloomy series of chambers, formed over millions of years, contains some fine calcite formations. The caves have been known to humans for at least a millennium; they are first recorded in written records from the 9th and 10th centuries. These records, known as the *Triads of Ireland,* indicate that a bloody Viking massacre took place here in the year A.D. 928. No conclusive proof has ever been found, but evidence unearthed by archaeologists in more recent years confirms that Vikings used the caves. Exhibits at the visitor center tell the story. Access to the cave is by guided tour only. Dunmore is about 11km (7 miles) from Kilkenny City.

Off Castlecomer Rd. (N78), Ballyfoyle. www.heritageireland.ie. © **056/776-7726.** Admission €5 adults; €4 seniors; €3 students and children; €13 families. June–Aug daily 9:30am–6pm (last tour 5pm); Mar–May and Sept–Oct daily 9:30am–5pm (last tour 4pm); Nov–Feb Wed–Sun 9:30am–5pm (last tour 3pm). Tours may end early in winter depending on sunset.

Jerpoint Abbey ★★★ CHURCH   About 18km (11 miles) southeast of Kilkenny, this atmospheric Cistercian monastery dates from the 12th century. Highlights of the ethereal ruins, which are preserved in a peaceful country setting, include a sculptured cloister arcade, Romanesque architecture in the north nave, and unique stone carvings on the medieval tombs (some of which have traces of original paint on them). The staff is quite friendly and knowledgeable about the local area. Ask for details of where to find the mysterious, ghostly ruins of the **Church of the Long Man,** about 16km (10 miles) away. If you're lucky, they'll be able to direct you—it's very hard to find otherwise, and a local secret you may find yourself sworn to keep. *Tip:* If you're here in spring or autumn, plan

Jerpoint Abbey dates from the 12th century.

your visit toward the end of the day. Wandering around these ancient places as the setting sun blushes the walls in peach and gold is an unforgettable experience.

On N8, 2.5km (1½ miles) SW of Thomastown. www.heritageireland.ie. ✆ **056/772-4623.** Admission €4 adults; €3 seniors; €2 students and children; €10 families. Early Mar–Sept daily 9am–5:30pm; Oct daily 9am–5pm; Nov daily 9:30am–4pm. Closed Dec to early Mar (except for prebooked tours).

Jerpoint Glass Studio ★ CRAFT STUDIO   Here you can witness the creation of Jerpoint glass, which you've probably been admiring in shops all across Ireland. The lines of the glasses, goblets, and pitchers are simple and fluid, highlighted by swirls of color. Watch the glass being blown and then blow your budget next door at the shop.

Stoneyford. www.jerpointglass.com. ✆ **056/772-4350.** Shop and gallery: Apr–Sept Mon–Sat 10am–5:30pm; Sun and public holidays noon–5pm. Oct–Mar Mon–Sat 10am–5pm (closed Sun). Glassblowing demonstrations Mon–Thurs 10am–4pm, Fri 10am–1pm. No demonstrations on public holidays.

Kells Priory ★★ RELIGIOUS RUINS   With its encompassing fortification walls and towers, Kells is a glorious ruined monastery enfolded into the sloping south bank of the King's River. In 1193, Baron Geoffrey FitzRobert founded the priory and established a Norman-style town beside it. The current ruins date from the 13th to 15th centuries. The priory's wall has been carefully restored, and it connects seven towers, the remains of an abbey, and foundations of chapels and houses. You can tell by the thick walls that this monastery was well fortified, and those walls were built for a reason—it was frequently attacked. In the 13th century, it was the subject of two major battles and burned to the ground. (Despite the similar name, this is not the same monastery where the famous Book of Kells [p. 92] was stored for years.) The priory is less than half a mile from the village of Kells, so if you have time to spare, cross the footbridge behind it, which takes you on a beautiful path across the river and to riverside walk leading to a picturesque old mill.

Kells. ✆ **056/775-1500.** Free admission. Take N76 S from Kilkenny, follow signs for R699/Callan and stay on R699 until you see signs for Kells.

Where to Stay in County Kilkenny

Lawcus Farm Guesthouse ★★★   Perfect peace and tranquility await you at this gorgeous farmyard B&B, deep in the Kilkenny countryside. Make no mistake: This is the real deal ("Helping us on the farm at feeding time is greatly appreciated," says the website), but hosts Mark and Anne Marie go out of their way to welcome guests. The early-19th-century farmhouse has been beautifully renovated. Guest rooms are decent-size, with plenty of natural light. It's a pastoral setting to die for—you're right next to a river, where you can go wild-water swimming or try your hand at fishing for trout. Home-cooked breakfasts are delicious, but you'll have to fend for yourself at dinner. (Your hosts can recommend nearby

The ruins at Kells Priory.

places.) They've also opened a self-contained lodge for couples, the Tree House, which sits on a rocky outcrop down by the river, and costs €250 for 2 nights, including breakfast in the main house. The only snag in this rural idyll? Lawcus Farm doesn't accept credit cards, but you can send payment by PayPal (without having an account).

Stoneyford. www.lawcusfarmguesthouse.com. ✆ **086/603-1667.** 6 units. €100–€120 double. Free parking. Breakfast included. Discounts for stays of 3 or more nights. Children under 5 free (1 per party). **Amenities:** Wi-Fi (free). From the R713, pass Stoneyford sign and turn to the right of the small bridge; follow signs to B&B.

Mount Juliet Estate ★★★   Tucked away on a 500-acre estate in the lush Kilkenny countryside, Mount Juliet offers a choice of two rural hideaways: the historic Manor House, which dates from 1757, or Hunter's Yard, a gorgeous conversion of the former stables. At both, rooms are spacious and decorated with elegant restraint—large beds are swathed in fine linens, bathrooms are bang up to date, and all have peaceful, bucolic views. You're walking distance from charming Thomastown, with its pretty churches and sweet cafes. The Manor House is the more well-known, formal and expensive of the two, renowned for its service and Michelin-starred restaurant, **Lady Helen ★★★**. But we like Hunter Yard's low-key vibe. **The Hound** restaurant **★★** is bright and relaxed, with a chilled-out gastro-pub approach that features fresh, local ingredients without pretension. It's also significantly cheaper across the board. Whichever property you choose, though, it's very unlikely you'll be disappointed.

Mount Juliet Estate, Thomastown. www.mountjuliet.ie. ✆ **056/777-3010.** 32 units (Manor House); 93 units (Hunter's Yard). €90–€150 double (Hunter's Yard); €230–€420 Manor House. Free parking. Rates include breakfast. **Amenities:** Restaurant; bar; spa, pool; room service; Wi-Fi (free).

Pembroke Kilkenny ★★   Just a few streets away from Kilkenny Castle (from the upper floors you can see the castle's turrets poking up over rooftops), this is a cosmopolitan hotel in the center of Kilkenny City. Bedrooms are modern and comfortable, with plenty of room, if not a great deal of character. The in-house **Statham's** restaurant serves good modern Irish cooking, and certain nights in summer features barbecue. The **Mint Medispa** offers treatments including Bio-Penta infusion facials and massages (prices start at around €90 for half an hour). The sophisticated bar is a lively spot for a cocktail or glass of wine.

11 Patrick St. www.kilkennypembrokehotel.com. © **056/778-3500.** 73 units. €129–€249 double. Free parking. Rates include breakfast. **Amenities:** Restaurant; bar; Medispa; room service; Wi-Fi (free).

Rosquil House ★★   Comfortable and friendly, this modest little B&B is great value for the money. Your hosts, Rhoda and Phil, greet guests with genuine warmth and enthusiasm, making them feel immediately at home. The house was purposely built as a B&B, so the bedrooms are spacious and well-proportioned. One room is fully accessible for those with mobility problems, and family rooms are available. Public areas, including a large guest lounge, are tastefully decorated in color schemes of chocolate and cream, with polished wood floors. The breakfasts cooked by Phil are delicious. The only downside is that you're a little far from the action, with central Kilkenny about a 15-minute walk away.

Castlecomer Rd. www.rosquilhouse.com. © **056/772-1419.** 7 units. €100–€200 double. Free parking. Rates include breakfast. **Amenities:** Wi-Fi (free).

Where to Eat in County Kilkenny

Kilkenny has a small but growing restaurant scene, and among the options are excellent coffee shops and cafes. One of the best is **Gourmet Store** (56 High St.), a sunny cafe/deli in Kilkenny town. It's the perfect stop for breakfast or lunch on the go, offering freshly made bagels, sandwiches, salads, and soups, as well as all the ingredients for a picnic. Another spot to try is **Foodworks** (7 Parliament St.; www.foodworks.ie), an airy, modern eatery that's winning awards for its fresh approach to light cuisine. Think glorious salads, towering sandwiches, and cakes you'll dream of for days. There's also a great wine list—you're on vacation, you know. For richer fare, try the places below, or check out **Lady Helen** at Mount Juliet (p. 241), a Michelin-starred restaurant tucked away in the countryside.

Campagne ★★★ BISTRO   The chef at this outstanding French-Irish restaurant, about a 10-minute walk from Kilkenny Castle, once ran the kitchen at Dublin's superlative **Chapter One** ★★★ (p. 146). The sleek and atmospherically lit dining room has colorful modern art on the walls. The three-course fixed-price menus are short but subtly inventive, showcasing dishes like wild duck and bacon with elderberries, stuffed black sole with creamed leeks, or roast partridge with pumpkin gnocchi. A full vegetarian menu is always available. For dessert, try the butterscotch poached pears (delicious), or salted caramel custard (pudding) with popcorn and popcorn ice cream (crazy, but it works). The extensive wine list is well chosen, with particularly strong French options. Locals make this their top choice for special occasions—but if you find the prices too high, come for the early-bird menu, priced at €45 for three courses.

5 The Arches, Gashouse Lane. www.campagne.ie. ℂ **056/777-2858.** Three-course fixed-price menu €70. Dinner Wed–Thurs 5:30–9pm; Fri–Sat 5–9:30pm; lunch Fri–Sun 12:30–2:30pm. Open Sun nights on Bank Holiday weekends 6pm–8pm. Closed Mon and Tues.

Kyteler's Inn ★ PUB In business for over 6 centuries, this vintage inn serves decent pub food—sandwiches, Irish stew, burgers, fish and chips—but it's the atmosphere you really come for. With all the exposed flagstones and cozy nooks, it's hard to think of a more satisfyingly Irish-looking pub. The place is named after noted hellraiser Alice Kyteler, who died in 1324. She poisoned at least three of her husbands, ran the inn as a den of debauchery, and was sentenced to be burned as a witch. But she escaped, and nobody saw or heard from her again. Unless, that is, you believe some of the more colorful tales about this place after dark. . . .

Kieran St. www.kytelersinn.com. ℂ **056/772-1064.** Lunch entrees €6.50–€15.50. Dinner entrees €14.50–€26. Mon–Thurs 10:30am–11:30pm; Fri–Sat 10:30am–1:30pm; Sun 12:30–11pm (food served until about 10pm).

Ristorante Rinuccini ★★★ ITALIAN This extremely popular restaurant opposite Kilkenny Castle packs in diners for delicious Italian food with an Irish accent. The basement-level dining room gets very busy, but the food more than makes up for it. The homemade pasta is as good as you'd expect, and on the specials board, local produce really comes into its own: catch of the day fresh from Kilmore Quay; Silver Hill duck baked with sweet aurum (an Italian liqueur); or spinach and ricotta ravioli in a tomato sauce. Desserts are equally good—try the classic tiramisu filled with zabaglione. Make reservations, especially if you're coming on a weekend.

1 The Parade. www.rinuccini.com. ℂ **056/776-1575.** Lunch two courses €25, three courses €20. Dinner entrees €26–€35. Reservations recommended. Mon–Fri noon–2:30pm, 5–9:30pm; Sat noon–2:30pm, 5–9:30pm; Sun noon–8:30pm.

Sports & Outdoor Pursuits in Kilkenny

GOLF Mount Juliet Golf and Country Club in Thomastown (www. mountjuliet.ie; ℂ **056/777-3000**) is an excellent course 16km (10 miles) south of Kilkenny City. The 18-hole, par-72 championship course, designed by Jack Nicklaus, charges greens fees of €55. Even closer to the city is the 18-hole championship course at the **Kilkenny Golf Club** in Glendine (www.kilkennygolfclub.com; ℂ **056/776-5400**), an inland par-71 layout with greens fees from €35 to €40.

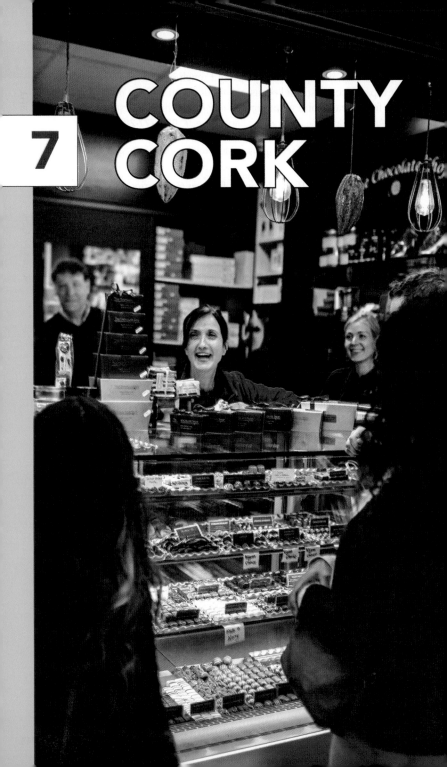

7

COUNTY CORK

W ith its lively capital city, quiet country villages, rocky hills, picturesque beaches, as well as long, peaceful miles of lush, green farmland, it's easy to see why Cork is one of Ireland's most popular destinations. St. Fin Barre is credited with the name—in the 6th century, he built a monastery on a swampy estuary of the River Lee, giving it the Irish name *Corcaigh* (marsh). Stop in **Cork City** for wonderful restaurants and good hotels. Keep going to see the pretty harbor town of **Kinsale,** famous for its gourmet food scene; the storied seaport of **Cobh** in East Cork; or the barren beauty of **Cape Clear Island** in craggy West Cork. Cork is also the start (or end) point of the **Wild Atlantic Way** (p. 477).

ESSENTIALS
Arriving

BY BUS **AirCoach** (www.aircoach.ie; ✆ **01/844-7118**) runs a regular direct service from Dublin to Cork City. You can catch the bus either at Dublin Airport or Aston Quay in Dublin city center; from there, the journey to St. Patrick's Quay in the center of Cork takes 3 hours, traffic permitting. Buses start at 7:25am, 5 minutes later from Terminal 1, and then on the hour from Aston Quay. There are around nine services a day, with the last bus leaving Terminal 2 at 25 minutes past midnight (from Aston Quay at 1am). One-way tickets are €20 adults, €14 children under 13; round-trip tickets are €30 adults, €20 children. Tickets may be purchased in advance online.

   Bus Éireann (www.buseireann.ie; ✆ **01/836-6111**) runs regular services from all parts of the Republic to Cork Bus Station (Parnell Place). The trip from Dublin takes around 3 hours and 30 minutes. One-way tickets are €14.75 adults, €9.50 children, and €12.50 students. From Parnell Place Bus Station, Bus Éireann buses run to the rest of the county. Bus 226 connects Cork with Kinsale. Buses also arrive on Pier Road.

BY TRAIN **Iarnród Éireann/Irish Rail** (www.irishrail.ie; ✆ **1850/366-222**) travels to Cork City from Dublin and other parts of Ireland. Trains arrive at Kent Station, Lower Glanmire Road, in eastern Cork City (✆ **021/455-7277**). Kinsale does not have a train station.

BY FERRY There are no longer any direct ferry routes into Cork from Britain. However, **Brittany Ferries** (www.brittany-ferries.com; ℂ **021/427-7801**) sail a few times per week between Roscoff, in France, and Cork's Ringaskiddy Ferryport.

BY CAR Cork is easily reachable on the M8 from Dublin, N25 from Waterford, and N22 from Killarney. To rent a car in Dublin, see p. 91; to rent a car at Shannon Airport, see p. 344. To hire a car in Cork, try **Enterprise Rent-A-Car,** Kinsale Road (ℂ **021/497-5133**), or **Hertz** at Cork Airport (ℂ **021/496-5849**).

BY PLANE **Cork Airport (ORK),** Kinsale Road (www.corkairport. com; ℂ **021/4313131**), is served by several airlines, including **Aer Lingus, British Airways, Air France** and **Ryanair.** Cork is the Republic of Ireland's second busiest airport (and the fourth in Ireland overall, after Dublin and the two airports in Belfast). It has direct flights to and from several European countries, including the U.K. and France.

Visitor Information

Cork Tourist Information Centre (www.discoverireland.ie; ℂ **021/605-7700**) is at 125 St. Patrick St., Cork. It's open Monday to Saturday 9am to 5pm (closed Sun). **Kinsale Tourist Information Office** at Emmet Place, Kinsale (www.kinsale.ie; ℂ **021/477-2234**), is open Monday to Saturday 9am to 5pm (closed Sun). **Cobh Tourist Office,** in Market House, Casement Square, Cobh (ℂ **021/481-3301**), is open Monday to Friday 9am to 5pm. There are year-round tourist offices in Youghal, Midleton, Fermoy, Mallow, Bandon, and Macroom, and seasonal tourist offices in Clonakilty, Skibbereen, Baltimore, Schull, Bantry, and Glengarriff.

CORK CITY

While Cork City has a population of only 125,000 residents, it's a busy, attractive, cultured place with the feel of a much larger city. The presence of University College Cork keeps the population young, the creative class dynamic, the pubs interesting, and the number of affordable restaurants plentiful. It has its flaws—traffic congestion, for one, and some areas can feel gritty and crowded. But lose yourself in the narrow lanes of the old Huguenot Quarter or wander MacCurtain Street at night and you'll understand the unique spirit of this real Irish city, which is not a tourist trap. Cork City is compact and best seen on foot. So park the car and strike out.

City Layout

Cork City center is set on an island, so don't be confused if you come across not one River Lee but two. These two channels divide the city into three sections:

FLAT OF THE CITY The downtown core is bounded by two channels of the River Lee. Its main shopping thoroughfare is bustling **St. Patrick**

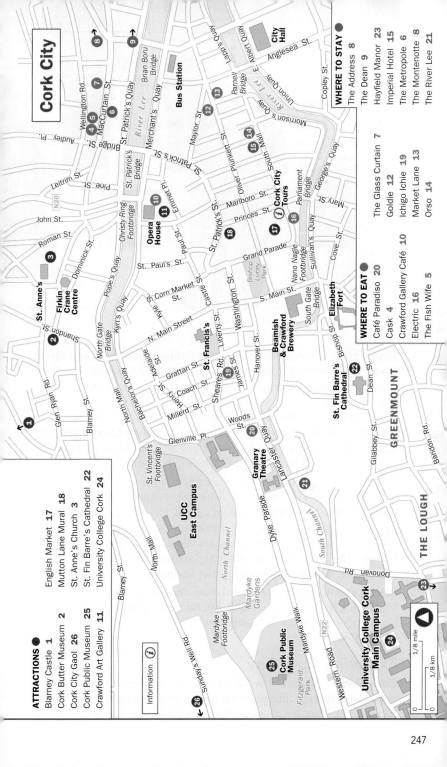

Cork City

ATTRACTIONS ●

Blarney Castle 1
Cork Butter Museum 2
Cork City Gaol 26
Cork Public Museum 25
Crawford Art Gallery 11

English Market 17
Mutton Lane Mural 18
St. Anne's Church 3
St. Fin Barre's Cathedral 22
University College Cork 24

WHERE TO EAT ●

Café Paradiso 20
Cask 4
Crawford Gallery Café 10
Electric 16
The Fish Wife 5

The Glass Curtain 7
Goldie 12
Ichigo Ichie 19
Market Lane 13
Orso 14

WHERE TO STAY ●

The Address 8
The Dean 9
Hayfield Manor 23
Imperial Hotel 15
The Metropole 6
The Montenotte 8
The River Lee 21

247

Sculptures in the Crawford Art Gallery in Cork.

Street, which curves up to **St. Patrick's Bridge. Oliver Plunkett Street** is also full of shops and cafes. Nearby, **South Mall** is a wide, tree-lined street with attractive Georgian architecture and a row of offices; linking them at their western end is **Grand Parade,** a spacious thoroughfare that blends 18th-century bow-fronted houses with the remains of the old city walls. It holds businesses and shops as well as **Bishop Lucey Park.** The pedestrianized lanes around French Church Street and Carey's Lane, the old **Huguenot quarter,** are lined with cafes, restaurants, and small shops.

NORTH BANK   St. Patrick's Bridge leads over the river's north channel to the hilly north side of the city, where St. Patrick Street becomes **St. Patrick's Hill.** And is it ever a hill! It's got an incline so steep it'll remind you of San Francisco. East of St. Patrick's Hill, the lively **MacCurtain Street** runs past the train station and out to the M8 motorway. West of St. Patrick's Hill is Shandon, one of the city's oldest neighborhoods, with the tall spire of **St. Anne's Church** its chief landmark.

SOUTH BANK   Across the river's south channel, the largely residential South Bank is where you'll find **St. Fin Barre's Cathedral,** the site of St. Fin Barre's 6th-century monastery, and, farther west, the campus of **University College Cork.**

Exploring Cork City

Cork Butter Museum ★ MUSEUM   With a name like this, it's no surprise that this fun little place has turned up on several "world's quirkiest museums" lists, but it's more than just a celebration of tasty Irish dairy produce. From 1770 until the 1920s, Cork was the largest exporter of butter in the world, peaking at half a million casks annually by the turn of the 20th century. The museum chronicles that industrial past, using butter as a springboard to explore wider stories about Irish farming, society, and industry, from the Middle Ages onward. It's surprisingly enlightening.

John Redmond St. www.corkbutter.museum. ℭ **021/430-0600.** Admission €4 adults; €3 seniors and students; €1.50 children under 18; children under 12 free. Tues–Sat 10am–4pm; Sun 11am–4pm.

Cork City Gaol ★ HERITAGE SITE   Like something out of a Victorian novel, this early-19th-century jail is an austere and highly atmospheric building. It opened in 1824 as a women's prison. Famous inmates included the extraordinary Countess Constance Markievicz (1868–1927). The first woman elected to the British parliament, she was sentenced to death for her part in the 1916 Easter Rising (her sentence was commuted because of her sex, to which she reportedly responded, "I do wish you had the decency to shoot me"). Earlier in its history, the jail was the last place in Ireland many convicts were held before being shipped off to Australia. This colorful past is well-presented, with the aid of costumed mannequins in key positions. Somewhat incongruously, in 1927, after the building ceased to be used as a prison, it became the site of Ireland's first radio

The atmospheric Cork City Gaol.

station. A small museum tells this story, complete with a restored studio from the period.

Convent Ave., Sunday's Well. www.corkcitygaol.com. ℰ **021/430-5022.** Admission €10 adults; €8.50 seniors and students; €6 children, €30 families. Wed–Mon 10am–4pm. Closed Tues.

Cork Public Museum ★ MUSEUM   This simple, rather endearing civic museum is a good place to get an overview of the city's history. Displays include a few objects from Cork's ancient past—including an Iron Age helmet and some of the oldest tools ever discovered in Ireland. But it's strongest when it comes to the traditional crafts made in the city during the 19th and 20th centuries, including silverware and intricate lace from the Victorian period. There are also very good collections relating to the lives of local revolutionaries, including Michael Collins (p. 282). The museum is located on the west side of Cork, in the middle of Fitzgerald Park—near the Western Road, about a 10-minute walk from the city center.

Fitzgerald Park. www.corkcity.ie/en/cork-public-museum. ℰ **021/427-0679.** Free admission. Tues–Fri 10am–4pm; Sat 11am–4pm. Closed Mon, Sun, and bank holidays.

Crawford Art Gallery ★★★ ART MUSEUM   One of the top art galleries in Ireland, the Crawford has impressive collections of sculpture and paintings. The Irish School is particularly well-represented with works from John Butts (1728–65), including his fine 1755 panorama of Cork City, and Dublin-born Harry Clarke (1889–1931), one of the most celebrated illustrators of the early 20th century, who also produced some extraordinary, early Deco–influenced stained glass. The gallery has a strong collection of works by female Irish artists from the mid–19th century onward; check out the extraordinary abstract work of Mainie Jellett (1897–1944) and the Cubist painter Norah McGuinness (1901–80). The gallery also has a program of temporary exhibitions. The **Crawford Gallery Café** ★★ (p. 258) is a good spot for a light lunch.

Emmet Place. www.crawfordartgallery.ie. ℰ **021/480-5042.** Free admission. Mon–Sat 10am–5pm; Sun and bank holidays 11am–4pm. Last entry 15 minutes before closing.

English Market ★★ MARKET HALL   The name of this bustling food market harks back to the days of English rule—it was first granted a charter in 1610 during the reign of King James I. The current market building dates from 1788, although it was redesigned after being gutted by fire in the 1980s. Inside is a cornucopia of fresh produce, including super-traditional Cork delicacies—some of them tempting, others less palatable to outsiders. (Mmm, tripe! Pig's trotters? Anyone?) Happily, there are lots of tasty treats too like local cheeses, handmade cakes, and a specialist chocolate shop, with plenty of takeaway snacks.

Grand Parade; enter from Patrick St., Grand Parade, Oliver Plunkett St., or Princes St. www.englishmarket.ie. ℰ **021/492-4258.** Free admission. Mon–Sat 8am–6pm.

CORK: THE rebel CITY

Travel in County Cork today, and all that appears in front of you are rolling green hills and bucolic farmscapes. But this county was once at the heart of the battle for Ireland's soul.

For centuries, the county had a reputation for defiance and revolt. Once the seat of power in South Munster, it changed hands many times as the English and Irish battled for control. Devastated by the Great Famine, Cork became a center of the 19th-century Fenian movement, when the label "Rebel Cork" was first widely used. It certainly lived up to the name during Ireland's early-20th-century battle for independence. It was a battle of wills, and Cork refused to surrender.

The British troops occupying Cork at the time—a paramilitary force nicknamed the "Black and Tans" for the color of their uniforms—were among the most repressive in the country. The struggle came to a head in 1920 when Thomas MacCurtain, mayor of Cork City, was killed by the Black and Tans. His successor, Terence MacSwiney, was arrested, and later died in a London prison after a hunger strike lasting 75 days.

On December 11 of that year, after an attack by the IRA, the British forces set fire to Cork city center, apparently as payback. The library, the City Hall, and almost all the buildings on St. Patrick Street were burned to the ground. More than 300 buildings were destroyed in the ensuing conflagration—virtually the entire city was smoldering rubble. As the fires blazed, two men suspected to be members of the IRA were shot as they slept, also allegedly by the occupying military troops.

The atrocity's bitter legacy ensured that fighting would rage on in Cork, even as peace talks took hold elsewhere in Ireland. Cork resisted peace agreements to the end, even a treaty negotiated by Cork native son Michael Collins (p. 282). And it ensured that Cork natives would embrace their identity as Rebel Cork forevermore.

Mutton Lane Mural ★ PUBLIC ART This riotously colorful mural along the walls of Mutton Lane, down one side of the Mutton Lane Inn, is intended to represent the essence of Cork. It depicts musicians performing the traditional "Pana Shuffle," and all of the characters featured are real local people. It is a vivid evocation of peace and community spirit, beloved locally—so much so, claim the owners of the pub, that it has never been vandalized by graffiti (impossible to prove, of course). The mural was painted by local artist Anthony Ruby in 2004. Its historical provenance can be dated by the following message, which is hidden within the colorful scene: "dedicated to everyone except george bush." The lane leads into the English Market.
Mutton Lane, off St. Patrick St.

St. Anne's Church and Shandon Tower ★ CHURCH Cork's most recognizable landmark, also known as Shandon Church, is famous for its giant pepper-pot steeple and eight melodious bells. Pretty much wherever you stand in the downtown area, you can see the stone tower crowned with a gilt ball and distinctive fish weathervane. The clock, added in 1847, made it the first four-faced clock tower in the world (beating London's Big Ben by just a few years). Until fairly recently, due to a quirk of clockworks, it was known as "the four-faced liar" because each side showed a different time—except on the hour when they all somehow managed to synchronize. Disappointingly, perhaps, that charming oddity has now been repaired. Climb the 1722 belfry tower for a chance to ring the famous Shandon Bells. (Be warned, though: It's 132 steps up to the belfry, and the gap narrows to a claustrophobic half-meter—that's just over 1½ ft.—near the entrance to the belfry.) If you continue on the somewhat precarious climb past the bells, you'll be rewarded with spectacular views over the surrounding countryside.

Church St., Shandon. www.shandonbells.ie. © **021/450-5906.** Free admission. Clock tower €6 adults; €5 seniors and students; €3 children; €15 families. June–Sept Mon–Sat 10am–4:30pm, Sun 11:30am–4:00pm; Mar–May and Oct Mon–Sat 10am–4pm, Sun 11:30am–4pm; Nov–Feb Mon–Sat 11am–3pm, Sun 11:30am–3pm. Public holiday hours same as Sun. Last entry to tower 30 min. before closing.

St. Fin Barre's Cathedral ★ CATHEDRAL   With its three soaring spires dominating the Cork skyline, this Church of Ireland cathedral sits on the very spot St. Fin Barre chose in A.D. 600 for his church and school (according to legend). A much smaller medieval tower was demolished to make way for the current building, which dates from the early 1860s—

there's nothing left of the original aside from a few pieces of decorative stonework inside. In this building, the architect, William Burges (1827–81), embraced the French Gothic style popular at the time. The interior is highly ornamented with some stunning mosaic work. The bells were inherited from a 1735 church that also previously stood on this site. The cathedral hosts occasional exhibitions; check the website for listings of what's on.

Bishop St. www.corkcathedral.webs. com. © **021/496-3387.** Admission €6 adults; €5 seniors and students; €3 children under 16. Mon–Sat 10am–1pm, 2–5:30pm; bank holidays 10am–5:30pm, closed Sun.

University College Cork and Glucksman Gallery ★★ UNIVERSITY   Part of Ireland's national university, with about 21,000 students, this center of

The Gothic Revival St. Fin Barre's Cathedral stands atop Cork City's monastic foundations.

learning is housed in a pretty quadrangle of Gothic Revival–style buildings. Colorful gardens and wooded grounds grace the campus. An audio tour of the campus takes in the **Crawford Observatory,** the Harry Clarke stained-glass windows in **Honan Chapel,** the landscaped **President's Garden,** and the **Stone Corridor,** a collection of stones inscribed with the ancient Irish *ogham* written language. You can also join an hour-long guided tour, given by students, leaving from the visitor center at 3:30pm every Wednesday or 3pm on Saturday. Also on the campus, the innovative **Lewis Glucksman Gallery** (www.glucksman.org; ✆ 021/490-1844) has an excellent program of exhibitions. Expect to see cutting-edge photography, painting, sculpture, and a few items from the university's ever-expanding permanent collection. A good cafe and shop are also on-site. Admission to the Glucksman is free, though a donation of €5 per person is requested.

Visitor center: North Wing, Main Quad, Western Rd. www.ucc.ie/en/discover/visit/centre. ✆ **021/490-1876.** Free admission (€5 suggested donation). Visitor center: Mon–Fri 9am–5pm, Sat noon–5pm. Glucksman Gallery: Tues–Sat 10am–5pm, Sun 2–5pm.

Outside Cork City

Blarney Castle ★ CASTLE   Though the runaway favorite for the hotly contested title of "cheesiest tourist attraction in Ireland," Blarney Castle is nonetheless an imposing structure beloved by many. Constructed in the late 15th century, it was once much bigger; the massive square tower is all that remains of the vast medieval building. But, be honest, that's not why you've heard of this place, right? Its most famous attraction, and probably the most disappointing magical rock you'll ever kiss in your life, is the eponymous "Blarney Stone." Whoever first decided that this particular slab had mystical powers certainly didn't have the convenience of visitors in mind; after trudging up a series of narrow, poorly lit staircases, you'll find it wedged underneath the battlements, far enough to make it uncomfortable to reach, but not so far that countless tourists cannot lie down, stick their heads outside, and kiss it in hopes of achieving lifelong loquaciousness. There's no extra charge for kissing the Blarney Stone, though it's customary to tip the attendant who holds your legs (you might want to do it *before* you're slung over the edge). Thanks to Covid, a special cleaning spray is used on the stone after each person. Have we sold you on the experience yet? Snark aside, there is definitely more to see here. Take time to explore the atmospheric dungeons beneath the castle, and if you need a break from the tour-bus groups, the gardens are not only very pretty, but much less crowded. On the grounds is the later **Blarney House,** built in 1874 in the then-fashionable Scottish Baronial style with imposing gray stone and filigreed turrets that make it resemble a mini-Hogwarts. It's still a private residence, but you can tour the interior (June–Aug only, Mon–Sat 10am–2pm). Blarney Castle is 8km (5 miles) outside

An attendant hoists tourists to kiss the Blarney Stone at Blarney Castle.

the city on R617. You can easily get here by taxi or bus—the number 215 stops about twice an hour (once per hour on Sun). Ask the driver to let you off at the stop nearest the castle. *Tip:* Save a few euro on the castle admission price by booking online.

Blarney, Co. Cork. www.blarneycastle.ie. ✆ **021/438-5252.** Admission €18 adults; €14 seniors and students; €8 children 8–16; €45 families. Daily 9am–5:30pm. Last admission 30 min. before closing; times can change due to bad weather/poor light.

ORGANIZED TOURS

Cork City Tours ★   Riding on open-top buses, you can hop on and off to explore the sights of Ireland's second city. The buses run all day in a loop from March through October (as frequently as every half-hour July–Aug). Tour highlights include the Cork City Gaol, St. Anne's Church (Shandon Bells), and U.C.C. (University College, Cork). While the tour begins at the tourist office (42 Grand Parade), you can buy a ticket on the bus at several stops; check out the route on the Cork City Tours website.

www.corkcitytour.com. ✆ **021/430-9090.** Tickets €15 adults; €13 seniors and students; €5 children 5–18; free for children under 5; €35 families. Number of tours according to seasonal demand. June–Aug daily tours every half-hour 9am–4:30pm; Apr–May and Sept–Oct daily tours every 45 min. 9:30am–4:15pm; Mar and Nov daily tours every 90 min. 9:30am–3:30pm. Times refer to start of tours at Grand Parade, which depart from St. Patrick St. 5 min. later; complete circuit takes about 75 min.

Where to Stay in Cork City

There's a good selection of hotels in Cork City, with many new openings plus refurbishments of old favorites in recent years, giving a decent range of options for all budgets and tastes, from no-frills to stylish design statements. Choose the city center if you plan to walk around, or somewhere on the outskirts with parking if you plan to do a bit of sightseeing in the county by car. Book ahead for the best room rates and try to avoid busy festival times.

EXPENSIVE

Hayfield Manor ★★★   Everything about this elegant manor house is plush, from the sofas, decor, and grand piano in the lobby to comfy rooms where old-fashioned glamour meets all five-star luxuries. Located just outside town and right beside U.C.C. (University College Cork), Hayfield has two restaurants, **Orchids** for afternoon tea and fine dining, and the less formal **Perrotts** in the conservatory, for lunch and dinner. The indoor pool, outdoor hot tub, and courtyard garden provide a welcome retreat after a day in the city. In the evening, cozy up with a book after dinner in the library or drawing room. Nice touches are a local brand of cosmetics in the **Beautique Spa** and a golf putter in every room.

Perrott Ave, College Rd (beside U.C.C.). www.hayfieldmanor.ie. © **021/484-5900.** 88 units. €239–€559 double; €660–€1,500 suite. Dinner and other packages available. Free parking. **Amenities:** 2 restaurants; bar; valet parking; gym; room service; spa; swimming pool; outdoor hot tub; Wi-Fi (free).

The River Lee ★★   A 5-minute walk from the city center, this shiny, modern hotel overlooks the River Lee (as you may have guessed). Guest rooms are quietly chic, with an understated modern style and huge windows that make the most of city or river views. Executive rooms have access to a private lounge with panoramic views of the city. The **River Club** terrace is the place to be in good weather; there's also a restaurant and a stylish cocktail bar with rare whiskeys from the Midleton Distillery in East Cork. The health club includes an indoor 20m (65-ft.) swimming pool, with complimentary Pilates and spin classes for guests.

Western Rd. www.doylecollection.com/hotels/the-river-lee-hotel. © **021/425-2700.** 182 units. €208–€420 double. Underground parking (check for charges). Breakfast not included in lower rates. Dinner, bed-and-breakfast packages available. **Amenities:** Restaurant; bar; gym; parking; room service; swimming pool; Wi-Fi (free).

The Gift of Gab (or Is It Just Blarney?)

Can being held upside down and backwards from the top of a tall castle to kiss a rock really bring you the ability to talk up a storm? Well, Blarney Castle's association with the gift of gab does go back a long way. The popular version has it that Queen Elizabeth I (1533–1603) invented the notion in a fit of exasperation at then–Lord Blarney's tendency to prattle on at great length without ever agreeing to anything she wanted. The custom of actually kissing the stone, though, is less than a century old. Nobody knows quite when, how, or why it started, but around here they've got a thousand possible tales, some involving witches and others the crusaders. But don't believe them—it's all a bunch of...

MODERATE

The Dean ★★   While its Horgan Quay setting beside the Kent train station is not in the center of town (it's about a 15-min. walk), you might feel as if you're in the heart of the action simply while checking in. The emphasis here is on "fun," and the lobby buzzes with a cocktail and spritz bar and pumping tunes. Rooms are compact but feature retro-style gadgets and generously sized showers. Rooftop restaurant **Sophie's** has an outdoor terrace with views over the developing docklands area. There's a well-equipped Power Gym and studios (fitness classes cost extra), plus a small relaxation pool and steam room, on the ground-floor level.

Horgan Quay. www.thedean.ie/cork. ℂ **021/234-1200.** 114 units. €150–€300 double. €350–€1,025 suite. Parking at Kent Station €8.50/24 hrs. **Amenities:** Restaurant; bar; gym; hydrotherapy pool; room service; steam room; Wi-Fi (free).

The Metropole ★★   Handily located in the historic Victorian Quarter and dating from 1897 itself, the Met is an elegant redbrick building with Hogwarts-like roof peaks and turrets. Despite its age, the 112 small-ish rooms are up to sparkling modern standards, with marble bathrooms, comfortable beds, and fast Wi-Fi. The smallest rooms are tiny indeed—branded "cozy" by the hotel, these singles come with a twin bed and just enough room for you and a suitcase. The standard double isn't huge, but it's pleasantly decorated, and the executive room has a king-size bed and seating area. Downstairs is a pretty, statue-surrounded swimming pool, with sauna and Jacuzzi. The ground-floor bar is popular with locals as well as guests. The breakfast earns raves from regulars, but there are plenty of other restaurants nearby if you crave variety.

MacCurtain St. www.themetropolehotel.ie. ℂ **021/464-3700.** 112 units. €105–€275 double. Nearby parking €7.50. **Amenities:** Restaurant; bar; gym; pool; room service; Wi-Fi (free).

The Montenotte ★★   Those who like to stay perched above the action, rather than right in the thick of it, will doubly appreciate one of the chief selling points of the stylish Montenotte: fantastic views across Cork City and the River Lee. Recently renovated from top to bottom, the hotel is now a sophisticated place to stay. The hotel's **Bellevue Spa** offers treatments in an elegant setting, as well as a hair salon and nail bar. The cool, modern color schemes in the good-size guest rooms are offset with traditional patterns. Beds are new and very comfortable. The **Panorama Bistro** offers topnotch bistro cooking—with a superb view from the dining room, of course. There's even an in-house cinema, where dinner-and-movie specials are offered a few nights each month.

Middle Glanmire Rd. www.themontenottehotel.com. ℂ **021/453-0050.** 108 units. €139–€254 double. Free parking. Breakfast not included in lower rates. Dinner, bed-and-breakfast packages available. **Amenities:** Restaurant; bar; cinema; gym; swimming pool; room service; spa; Wi-Fi (free).

INEXPENSIVE

The Address ★   The impressive redbrick exterior of this hilltop 1870s mansion on the northeast outskirts of Cork gives way to a snazzy lobby, with black-and-white checkered floors. The guest rooms continue the stylish theme, based around traditional-style furniture. Pay the extra for an upper-floor room with a city view or balcony. **McGettigans Cookhouse** is a bright bar and restaurant filled with floor-to-ceiling bookcases, and a comfy outdoor terrace comes with heaters. The fitness center has a sauna. Be aware that the hotel can get booked up by wedding parties in the summer.

Military Hill. www.theaddresscork.com. © **021/453-9000.** 70 units. €109–€230 double. Free parking. Breakfast included. **Amenities:** Bar/restaurant; gym; room service; Wi-Fi (free).

Imperial Hotel ★★   This city-center hotel is surprisingly affordable for the amenities it offers, with elegantly restored public areas that are redolent of a much more expensive kind of hotel altogether. The guest rooms are perhaps a little plain by comparison, and the most basic rooms are small, but upgrading just a little gets you ample space and a bit more style. The hotel has four restaurants; among them, the **Pembroke** specializes in local meats and seafood. Unwind in the **Escape Spa,** which offers a long list of indulgent, revitalizing treatments, starting at about €85 for a 50-minute facial or a back, neck, and shoulder massage.

76 South Mall. www.flynnhotels.com. © **021/427-4040.** 125 units. €150–€280 double. Parking at nearby lot (€10/24 hr.). Breakfast included. Dinner, bed-and-breakfast, and spa packages available. **Amenities:** 4 restaurants; bar; room service; spa; Wi-Fi (free).

Where to Eat in Cork City

Cork City is smattered with trendy eateries. The latest development is the happening outdoor dining scene, with tables along pedestrianized streets (such as Princes St.) off Oliver Plunkett Street. Cafes around the city range from old-fashioned spots serving traditional fry-ups to hipster joints with high-energy brunches and in-house roasteries. Whether casual or high-end, Cork's restaurants take advantage of the county's abundant supplies of fresh farm produce, cheese, and seafood.

In the Victorian quarter, take a stroll along MacCurtain Street for excellent take-away fish and chips at the **Fish Wife** (45 MacCurtain St.; www.the fishwife.ie) or try cocktails and sharing plates at either **Cask** (48 MacCurtain St.; www. caskcorkcom) or the **Glass Curtain** (Thompson House, MacCurtain St.; www.theglass curtain.ie), located in the old

> ### Brewing Up Loyalty
>
> There is a definite sense of civic loyalty when it comes to drinking stout in this town. Yes, Ireland is known for its love of Guinness, but in Cork you're more likely to find locals drinking the two locally brewed stouts—Murphy's or Beamish. In fact, walk into any pub and order a "home and away" and you'll be presented with a pint of Murphy's (or Beamish) and one of Guinness.

Thompson's Bakery. Another popular option in town is the charming **Crawford Gallery Café** (Emmet Place; www.crawfordgallerycafe.com), in the Crawford Art Gallery, offering hot breakfasts and lunch, plenty of vegetarian options, and devastatingly good cakes and scones. It's the perfect place to take a sightseeing break.

Cafe Paradiso ★★★ VEGETARIAN   An inventive, classy vegetarian restaurant on the Western Road strip, Cafe Paradiso does such magnificent things without meat that even passionate carnivores will find plenty to love. Try the grilled cauliflower and cashew korma starter, or the parsnip and lemongrass soup, and then move on to the feta and pistachio couscous with smoky greens. Desserts are heavenly; if it's on the menu, try the dark chocolate mousse served with popcorn and whiskey salted caramel. *Note:* The restaurant does not allow infants or small children.
16 Lancaster Quay. www.paradiso.restaurant. ✆ **021/427-7939.** Three-course menu €46.50. Tues–Sat 5:30–9:30pm. Closed Sun.

Electric ★★ MODERN IRISH/SEAFOOD   You could easily get swept up in the romance of this trendy but unpretentious restaurant, with a dining room overlooking the river and the city skyline beyond. The smallish menu focuses on casual but upscale comfort food: roast chicken with red wine jus, short ribs with duck-fat roast potatoes, or perhaps a juicy burger served with chips and pink peppercorn coleslaw. You can also order from a slightly more casual selection in the bar. In addition, there is the **Fish Bar** (evenings only), where you dine on super-fresh seafood while perched on bar stools overlooking the river. Despite its popularity, you can usually get a table at Electric if you arrive early—a full fifth are held back every night.
41 South Mall. www.electriccork.ie. ✆ **021/422-2990.** Entrees €12–€40. Wed–Sun and bank holidays 3–10pm. Fish Bar open evenings only; no children in the Fish Bar.

Goldie ★★★ IRISH/SEAFOOD   The food here is all about wild Irish seafood with a "whole catch" approach (they use everything the boat brings), so the menu changes daily. Sea vegetables are foraged by the chefs, vegetables come straight out of a community garden, and there's a zero-waste policy. The setting is informal; go for counter seating for views of the open kitchen or the plant-filled upstairs. Prepare for delicious snacks like Achill Island sea salt and vinegar *parnisse* with crème fraîche tartar, or mains like oak-smoked jerk mackerel with rhubarb and apple salsa, or steamed Roaringwater Bay mussels with creamed leek and dashi broth—made with foraged seaweed. Ales (brewed with no additives) from Elbow Lane brewery across the road are crafted to suit the food.
128 Oliver Plunkett St. www.goldie.ie. ✆ **021/239-8720.** Main courses €18.50–€24.50. Wed–Sat 5–9:45pm.

Ichigo Ichie ★★★ JAPANESE   After it earned a Michelin star back in 2019, this simple, elegant dining room quickly became the hottest ticket in town. Run by Takashi Miyazaki, the restaurant offers a simple proposition—manage to get one of the 25 seats, and you will be served a 12-course meal prepared by Miyazaki himself. No substitutions, no changes. The set menu is €120 if you sit in the dining room and €135 to sit at the chef's table. The draw is Miyazaki's precise blending of Japanese techniques and Irish touches. Dishes change with the season, but you might be served pistachio tofu with beetroot miso, Bantry Bay sea urchin with wasabi and akazu rice, or Lough Neagh eel with taro potato. This is haute cuisine, quite formal in style. Be sure and read the terms and conditions on the restaurant's website before booking—Miyazaki is fierce about no-shows, serves one or two seatings each night, and allows no children under 12.

5 Fenn's Quay, Sheares St. www.ichigoichie.ie. ℂ **021/427-9997.** Set menu €120–€135. Tues–Sat 6pm and 9pm.

Market Lane ★★ IRISH   This friendly, informal downtown restaurant serves Irish-inflected bistro food. It's a let-down-your-hair kind of place, with the menu consisting mostly of traditional, unpretentious cooking, done very well. Think sophisticated comfort food: seafood bouillabaisse with haddock, shrimp, and mussels, served with confit potatoes. Or a local goat cheese and roast squash quiche. There are plenty of vegetarian and vegan options and lighter choices at lunch. But don't miss dessert!

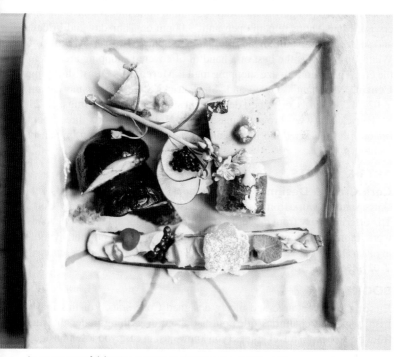

An assortment of delicacies composes a Hassun starter at Ichigo Ichie.

Try the delicious marmalade and vanilla bread and butter pudding. Gourmet sandwiches are served at lunch.

5–6 Oliver Plunkett St. www.marketlane.ie. ☎ **021/427-4710.** Entrees €14.50–€26. Mon–Wed noon–9:30pm; Thurs noon–10pm; Fri–Sat noon–10pm; Sun 1–9:30pm.

Orso ★★★ IRISH/MEDITERRANEAN   This place is like a ray of warm Mediterranean sunshine in downtown Cork City. Traditional flavors of southern Europe and North Africa meet Irish influences, and the result is nothing short of delightful. It's open all day, so you can pop in for a breakfast of Syrian *manoushi* bread with poached egg and caramelized onion, or smoked salmon and scrambled eggs. The lunch menu is long and varied, but it's really at dinnertime when the excellent cooking comes into its own. Plates might include scallops with samphire and sumac, or *sfeehas*—small Lebanese pies made with spiced lamb and fennel. Nearly everything on the wine list is available by the glass, and the small cocktail menu is intriguing—try the delicious house Bellini.

8 Pembroke St. www.orso.ie. ☎ **021/243-8000.** Entrees €7–€22. Mon–Wed 9am–3pm; Thurs–Sat 9am–10pm; closed Sun and bank holidays.

Cork City Shopping

St. Patrick Street is the main shopping thoroughfare, though many stores are scattered throughout the city on side streets and in lanes. In general, shops are open Monday to Saturday 9:30am to 6pm, unless indicated otherwise. Many shops remain open until 9:00pm on Thursday and Friday, and some are open on Sunday from noon to 5pm. **Winthrop Arcade,** off Winthrop Street, is the best of a handful of covered shopping arcades in the city. The main full-size shopping mall is **Merchant's Quay Shopping Centre,** Merchant's Quay and St. Patrick Street (www.mqsc.com; ☎ **021/427-5466**). Cork's best department store is **Brown Thomas,** 18-21 St. Patrick St. (www.brownthomas.ie; ☎ **021/480-5555**), its three floors filled with the same kind of upscale items found in the main branch in Dublin (p. 157).

ARTS & CRAFTS

Cork Craft & Design ★   This spacious, airy shop on the city's outskirts features work from dozens of craftspeople living in County Cork. The offerings vary from modern to traditional, and include pottery, woodwork, fabric, paintings, and sculpture. The offerings are constantly evolving. 27a St. Patrick's Woollen Mill, Douglas, Cork. www.corkcraftanddesign.com. ☎ **021/436-8365.** Open until 5pm Mon–Sat.

BOOKS

Easons ★   The large and nicely designed Cork branch of this major Irish bookstore chain has titles on just about everything under the sun, from bestsellers to travel guides (you know, just in case you lose this one). 113–115 St. Patrick's St. www.easons.com. ☎ **021/427-0477.**

Vibes and Scribes ★ This cheery secondhand bookstore stocks titles in a huge array of genres, as well as gifts and crafty knick-knacks. A second branch, also selling stationery and art and craft supplies, is at 3 Bridge St. (℃ **021/450-5370**). 21 Lavitt's Quay. www.vibesandscribes.ie. ℃ **021/427-9535.**

FASHION & CLOTHING

Blarney Woollen Mills ★ On the grounds of **Blarney Castle ★** (p. 253), this is the flagship outlet of an Irish chain that specializes in traditional Irish gear: Aran sweaters, cashmere and other knitwear, tweeds, country clothing, capes, and accessories. It also stocks a large range of Irish crafts, such as Waterford crystal and Celtic-style jewelry. It's open until 6pm daily. On the grounds of Blarney Castle, Blarney. www.blarney.com. ℃ **021/451-6111.**

Monreal ★★ Designer handbags, belts, and other accessories are for sale at this boutique in the Winthrop Arcade. The gorgeous stock of shoes includes some rather cool lace-up Wellington boots—a handy way of staying stylish, whatever the Irish weather throws at you. Winthrop Arcade, off Winthrop St. www.monreal.ie. ℃ **021/480-6746.**

Cork City After Dark
PUBS

An Spailpin Fánac ★★ One of Cork's oldest pubs (it opened in 1779), this is a wonderful spot to hang out with a pint and while away an hour or two. It's also one of the best pubs in the city for live music (p. 262). 28–29 S. Main St. ℃ **021/427-7949.**

The Idle Hour ★ This is the sort of place you go if you want some good lively craic (fun), loud music, and a young crowd. It's an extremely popular pub, especially during sports matches, shown here on huge TVs. Albert Quay. ℃ **021/496-5704.**

John Henchy & Sons ★★ Full of appealing Victorian features, this fantastic pub looks as if it has hardly changed since it first opened in 1884. It's got a private area ("snug") that was originally built to allow ladies to visit the pub without fear of impropriety. St. Luke's Cross. ℃ **021/453-0432.**

The Long Valley ★★ A cheerful, gregarious air pervades at this long-standing favorite of the Cork pub scene. The crowd is a good mix of stalwart locals and hip young things. It also has a good program of live music and spoken word. 10 Winthrop St. ℃ **021/427-2144.**

> ### The Guinness Cork Jazz Festival
>
> Held every year since 1978, this is Ireland's biggest and most prestigious jazz festival. Big names such as Ella Fitzgerald, Oscar Peterson, and Stephane Grappelli have played here over the years, with more than 1,000 performers from all over the world taking part annually. It's held at various city-wide venues in late October. Visit **www. guinnessjazzfestival.com** for details. Tickets go on sale in early September; prices vary and some events are free.

a tuneful pint: **CORK'S MOST MUSICAL PUBS**

Cork has a deserved reputation as home to some of Ireland's best pubs for live, traditional music. It's virtually a rite of passage to catch a session while enjoying a pint or two (and it's stout in these parts, by the way—Murphy's or Beamish, not Guinness—if you really want to fit in).

You can just follow your ears to find the best places, but to get you started, here are a few of the most respected spots. **An Bodhrán** (the name refers to a type of drum made from goatskin), 42 Oliver Plunkett St. (© **021/427-4544**), has live sessions nightly, as does the cozy **An Spailpín Fánach** (which means "the wandering labourer"), 27 S. Main St. (© **021/427-7949**). The succinctly named **Sin é** (literally, "That's It"), 8 Coburg St. (© **021/450-2266**), has been one of Cork's top live-music pubs for decades. It has sessions most nights at 7pm, but those on Tuesday, Friday, and Sunday are particularly good. There's traditional Irish music every Thursday night at the atmospheric **Long Valley Bar,** 10 Winthrop St. (www.thelongvalleybar.com; © **021/427-2144**)—but if you've had your fill of the tin whistle by this point, come on Monday nights at 9:30 to catch the lively program of spoken-word events; see www.obheal.ie for more details.

THE PERFORMING ARTS

Cork Opera House ★ Near the river on Emmet Place, the Cork Opera House is the region's preeminent venue when it comes to opera and other live concerts (classical, trad, folk, rock, country), plus dance, standup, and more. Emmet Place. www.corkoperahouse.ie. © **021/427-0022.** Tickets around €18–€50.

The Firkin Crane Cultural Centre ★★ Named after two Danish words for measurements of butter, the Firkin Crane is set in a quirky Victorian-era rotunda on the North Bank, just downhill from St. Anne's Church/Shandon Bells. It's one of Ireland's major centers for contemporary dance, hosting touring companies in addition to showcasing new talent. Many performances are free. The only downside is that performances are infrequent—usually just a handful per month—and the most headline-grabbing tend to be during the Guinness Jazz Festival (p. 78). John Redmond St., Shandon. www.firkincrane.ie. © **021/450-7487.** Ticket prices and performance times vary by event.

Sports & Outdoor Pursuits in Cork City

GAELIC GAMES Hurling and Gaelic football are both played on summer Sunday afternoons at Cork's **Páirc Uí Chaoimh Stadium,** Marina Walk (© **021/201-9200**). The stadium recently underwent a €30-million redevelopment. Check the local newspapers for match listings or visit the **Gaelic Athletics Association** website at www.gaa.ie.

STAND-UP PADDLEBOARDING See the city from the water on a 2-hour stand-up paddleboarding tour with **Cork City SUP** (www.corkcitysup.ie; ✆ **086/259-7688**) on the River Lee from St. Mary's Priory Church on Popes Quay. After a short lesson (beginners welcome), you'll paddle past famous landmarks and under the city bridges while hopefully remaining balanced on the board. All equipment is provided (but there are no changing facilities on-site). The cost is €40 per person.

URBAN KAYAKING A lovely way to see the city from the water is on a relaxed 2.5-hour under the bridges kayaking tour with **Atlantic Sea Kayaking** (www.atlanticseakayaking.com; ✆ **028/21058**), where you'll glide past historical sites and hear stories of the Rebel City's history. You can also a sunset tour. The cost is €60 per person (over 12s only; Thurs–Sun Apr–Sept). Atlantic Sea Kayaking also offers guided kayaking trips in West Cork (p. 287).

DAY TRIPS TO EAST CORK

Along the coast just east of Cork City are a number of attractions worth venturing away from the city for, most within an easy hour's drive. While families will probably make a beeline for **Fota Wildlife Park** on the shore of Lough Mahon, foodies will love **Ballymaloe House** and its famous cooking school, both farther east near Shanagarry. A vital piece of Ireland's history is told at the harbor town of **Cobh,** which under its former name Queenstown was once Ireland's chief port of emigration and the last port of call for the *Titanic.* If you have more time to spend, stay on an extra day or two and visit the village of **Ballycotton** for cliff walks and to tour its island lighthouse or the beach town of **Youghal** (pronounced *yawl*) near the Waterford border.

Arriving

If you're driving from Cork City, take the main Waterford road (N25) east. Exit at R624 for Fota and Cobh; exit at Midleton for Ballycotton and Shanagarry; Youghal has its own signposted exit. **Irish Rail** (www.irishrail.ie; ✆ **021/455-7277**) operates a daily train service between Cork City and Cobh via Fota Island. The journey takes about half an hour. **Bus Éireann** (www.buseireann.ie; ✆ **021/450-8188**) also provides a daily service from Cork City to Cobh and other points in East Cork.

Exploring East Cork

Ballymaloe Cookery School ★★ SCHOOL Professional and amateur cooks flock here from all over the world to sit near the whisk of Darina Allen. It all started with Darina's mother-in-law, Myrtle, whose evangelization of Ireland's bounty of fresh produce at **Ballymaloe House** ★★★ restaurant (p. 266) elevated Irish "country house" cooking to gourmet status. The Allen family's success led to the founding of this cooking school, the most famous in Ireland, which offers dozens of courses ranging in length from a half-day to 12 weeks. Prices start at about €50. The extensive **gardens** on the grounds are open to visitors all year. The **Ballymaloe Shop,** open 10am to 5pm daily, sells kitchen produce (including Ballymaloe's own delicious brand of relish) and craft items, while the **Ballymaloe Café** offers light lunches, afternoon tea, and lip-smackingly good cakes. Weather permitting, you can usually get a guided tour of the gardens for—from €7.50 per person, depending on group size.

Shanagarry. www.cookingisfun.ie. ℂ **021/464-6785.** Half-day courses from €60–€215. Open year-round; schedule varies. Admission to gardens and farm: €8.50 adults; €7 seniors and students; €6.50 children; €25 families. Gardens and farm Mon–Sat 11am–5:30pm (closed Sun).

Fota House & Gardens ★★ HISTORIC HOUSE   This is one of two popular attractions on Fota Island, a small island in Cork Harbour that is fully accessible by road. Built in the 1820s, Fota House is considered to be one of the finest example of a Regency mansion in Ireland. You can wander the elegant, classically influenced interior by yourself, or take a tour between 12:30 and 3:30pm (booking advised). The house maintains a working Victorian kitchen garden, which you can also explore. Meanwhile **Fota Arboretum** is a must-see for horticulturalists. Laid out at around the time the house was built, the 27-acre grounds include walled gardens, with a number of exotic plants that defy the odds and thrive here, thanks to the island's unusually mild microclimate. For overnight stays and golf, check out nearby **Fota Island Resort** (www.fotaisland.ie; ℂ **021/488-3700**), a five-star resort with three championship golf courses and a spa.

Fota Island, Carrigtwohill. www.fotahouse.com. ℂ **021/481-5543.** House: €10 adults; €8 seniors and students; €3.50 children; €25 families. Arboretum: €3. House: Mar–Sept daily 10am–5pm; Feb and Oct–Nov weekends only. Garden: Apr–Sept Mon–Fri 10:30am–3pm,Sun 1–4pm.

Fota Wildlife Park ★★ ZOO   If only all zoos were like this thoughtfully designed park. Many of the animals—including kangaroos, macaws, and lemurs—have the run of 16 hectares (40 acres) of grassland, free to roam without any apparent barriers and mingling with human visitors and each other. Only the more dangerous animals, such as cheetahs and gibbons, are behind conventional fencing. Besides close contact with a menagerie of exotic creatures, kids can be entertained by a tour train, picnic area, and gift shop. The **Savannah Café** (one of two in the park) has a view of the meerkat exhibition, so you may find yourself being watched by curious eyes while you eat your lunch.

Fota Island, Carrigtwohill. www.fotawildlife.ie. ℂ **021/481-2678.** Admission €16.90 adults; €12.50 seniors and students; €11.50 children under 16, children 2 and under free; €49.50–€66 families. Daily 9:30am–6pm. Last entry 1½ hr. before closing.

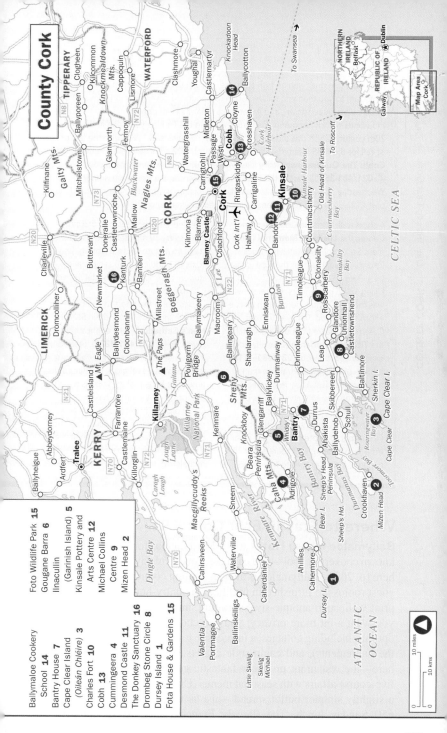

County Cork

NORTHERN IRELAND
Belfast
REPUBLIC OF IRELAND
Galway
Dublin
Cork
Map Area

To Swansea →
← To Roscoff

Ballymaloe Cookery School **14**
Bantry House **7**
Cape Clear Island (Oileán Chléire) **3**
Charles Fort **10**
Cobh **13**
Cummingeera **4**
Desmond Castle **11**
The Donkey Sanctuary **16**
Drombeg Stone Circle **8**
Dursey Island **1**
Fota House & Gardens **15**

Foto Wildlife Park **15**
Gougane Barra **6**
Ilnacullin (Garinish Island) **5**
Kinsale Pottery and Arts Centre **12**
Michael Collins Centre **9**
Mizen Head **2**

265

point of departure: **A DAY IN COBH**

If you're a foreigner with an Irish surname, this bustling seaside town could be more important to you than you realize. Cobh (pronounced *cove*, meaning "haven") used to be called Queenstown, and it was once Ireland's chief port of emigration. For thousands of Irish emigrants, particularly during the Famine years and in the early 20th century, Cobh was the last bit of Ireland they ever saw. It was also the last port of call for the RMS *Titanic* before it sank in April 1912. That story is expertly told at **Cobh: The Queenstown Story** (Deepwater Quay; www.cobhheritage.com; ℗ **021/481-3591**). Part of the Cobh Heritage Centre, the exhibition is open Wednesday to Sunday 10am to 4pm. Last admission is 1 hour before closing. Tickets cost €12 adults, €10 seniors and students, €6 children, and €30 families.

A short walk from the Cobh Heritage Center, the **Lusitania Memorial** (Casement Sq.) commemorates the British luxury liner sunk just off the Cork coast by a German U-boat on May 7, 1915, killing 1,198 passengers. Queenstown was the base for the heroic Irish rescue efforts that saved 764 lives. Across Casement Square from the memorial, the **Titanic Experience** (www.titanic experiencecobh.ie; ℗ **021/481-4412**) is more of a themed attraction than a museum—it's just a few re-created rooms from the ship and a series of exhibits about the ill-fated voyage, emptying into a very busy gift shop. From April to September it's open daily from 9am to 6pm, with tours every 15 minutes; from October to March the opening times are 10am to 5:30pm, tours every 30 minutes. The last tour starts 45 minutes before closing. Entry costs €11 adults, €9.50 seniors and students, €7.50 children under 16, and €22 to €38 families.

It's worth the effort to climb the hill to the handsome neo-Gothic **St. Colman's Cathedral** (www.cobhcathedral parish.ie; ℗ **021/481-3222**). Started in 1868, the cathedral was the country's most expensive religious building of its time. The largest of its 47 bells weighs 3½ tons, and the organ has nearly 2,500 pipes. The interior is vast and ornate, including a beautiful nave and precipitously high chancel arch. It is also a popular venue for concerts and recitals.

Where to Stay in East Cork

Ballymaloe House Hotel ★★   Most famous for being Ireland's best-known cookery school—you can take wonderful day and half-day courses here (p. 263)—Ballymaloe is also an inviting country hotel. Comfortable guest rooms are furnished in traditional country-house decor, with floral-print wallpaper, antique-style furniture, and original art on the walls. If you want a bit more privacy, you can choose from several self-catering options, including cottages, a faux castle tower (complete with balcony on the battlements), and cabin-style chalets. The kitchen is the real draw here—the restaurant produces fantastic gourmet dinners nightly, lavish five-course affairs with seasonal menus (€80 per person); Sunday features a slightly simpler buffet spread—just as well if you've already had the €50 Sunday lunch. The (largely French) wine list is extensive and

If you want to discover more about Cobh's role in the *Titanic* story, an hour-long **Titanic Trail** walking tour visits several related sites, putting it all into the context of the town's maritime history. In truth, this is a general historical tour of the town with just a couple of *Titanic* connections, but it's informative, nonetheless. The tour departs from the Commodore Hotel, 4 Westbourne Place, at 11am and 2pm daily. (From Oct–Mar, the tour only runs if there are prebookings.) It costs €15 adults, €7.50 children ages 11 and under (plus a booking fee). Call ℂ **087/276-7218** or book tickets at **www.titanic.ie**.

Harbor view of historic Cobh.

unusually high-tech—ask to be given the iPad version to check out video information pages.

Shanagarry, Midleton. www.ballymaloe.ie. ℂ **021/465-2531.** 33 units. €280–€345 double. Breakfast included. Dinner, bed-and-breakfast packages available. Closed early Jan to early Feb. **Amenities:** Restaurant; room service; Wi-Fi (free).

Bayview Hotel ★ If ever there was a view that qualified as "wow factor," this would be it: miles of coastline dotted with islands and headlands, and boats bobbing gently in the harbor. Guest rooms are basic but pleasant, with modern furnishings. Each room has a view of the sea. The **Capricho** restaurant serves good modern Irish cuisine, using plenty of local produce, including fish direct from the pier and meat from local and regional farms; prices are high (€25–€28 for a main course) but there aren't a lot of alternatives around here. Hotel guests have free use of the

Students cooking up a storm at Ballymaloe Cookery School.

spa and health club at sister property the **Garryvoe Hotel** (www.garry voehotel.com; ℭ **021/464-6718**), a 10-minute drive away. Check the Bayview's website for deals and special offers, including dinner, bed-and-breakfast packages and senior discounts.

Ballycotton. www.thebayviewhotel.com. ℭ **021/464-6746.** 35 units. €100–€200 double, €170–€230 suite. Breakfast included. 2-night minimum on summer weekends. **Amenities:** Restaurant; bar; use of nearby health club; room service; Wi-Fi (free). Closed Nov–Easter.

Where to Eat in East Cork

Don't miss the nightly five-course gourmet dinners at the **restaurant at Ballymaloe House** ★★★ (p. 266), its food sourced from local producers and Ballymaloe's own farm. It also serves a Sunday buffet.

Sage ★★ IRISH/EUROPEAN   Although Midleton town is not on the main tourist track, locals flock to Sage for its food store and restaurant, where you can choose to sit in the indoor dining room or the lovely out-door garden. Meat, fish, dairy, and vegetables are all local to within a few miles and lovingly prepared into dishes like cured mackerel with house crème fraîche, cucumber, and chile or East Cork chargrilled sirloin steak with celeriac gratin and chard.

The Courtyard, 8 Main St, Midleton. www.sagerestaurant.ie. ℭ **021/463-9682.** Wed–Sat 4–8:45pm; Sun 12:30–8pm. Entrees €18–€29.

KINSALE

A half-hour's drive south of Cork City (take N27 to the R600, aka Kinsale Rd., or N71 to the R607), **Kinsale** is a charming fishing village sitting on a picturesque harbor, surrounded by green hills. Considered the gateway to West Cork, Kinsale is also the start of the **Wild Atlantic Way** (p. 477). This artsy town of 5,000 residents enchants with its narrow winding streets, well-kept 18th-century houses, imaginatively painted shopfronts, window boxes overflowing with flowers, and a harbor full of sailboats. Picturesque as it is, however, Kinsale has a more eventful history than you might think. In 1601, it was the scene of a major sea battle between Protestant England and Catholic Spain—one in which Irish rebels played a covert part. You can learn all about this fascinating conflict on one of local man Don Herlihy's absorbing Kinsale Historic Strolls (p. 270).

Exploring Kinsale

Charles Fort ★ HISTORIC SITE   Southeast of Kinsale, at the head of the harbor, this coastal landmark dating from the late 17th century was named after Charles II, who was king of England and Ireland at the time it was built. A classic star-shaped fort, it was constructed after the Battle of Kinsale (1601) to replace medieval Ringcurran Castle, which had been reduced to rubble by the English army. The building was strengthened throughout the 18th and 19th centuries, and the fort remained in use as a military garrison right up until the British left in 1921. It suffered extensive damage during the civil war and has only recently been restored.

Kinsale's historic harbor is a welcome haven for sailboats.

Across the river, the smaller **James Fort** dates to the reign of King James I (1603–25) and was later captured in 1690 by the forces of (Protestant) King William I during his war with the deposed (Catholic) James II—part of the same conflict that is still commemorated by Protestant "Orange marches" in Northern Ireland.

Summercove. www.heritageireland.ie. ℂ **021/477-2263.** Admission €5 adults; €4 seniors; €3 students and children; €13 families. Daily 11am–5pm. Last admission ½ hr. before closing.

Desmond Castle ★ MUSEUM This small, squat stone fortress doesn't really look like a castle, in part because it sits incongruously halfway up a residential street. Built around 1500 as the Customs house for Kinsale Harbour, in the late 17th century it was turned into a prison—at which time its history took several dark detours, including a fire that gutted the building in 1747, roasting alive the 54 French soldiers imprisoned within. Later, during the Great Famine, it was used as a workhouse. There is a small museum inside.

Cork St. www.heritageireland.ie. ℂ **021/477-4855.** Admission €5 adults; €4 seniors; €3 students and children; €13 families. Mid-Apr to early Oct daily 10am–6pm. Closed early Oct to mid-Apr. Last admission 45 min before closing. **Note:** The castle and museum are under renovation, so check website before visiting.

Kinsale Historic Stroll ★★★ TOURS One of the most pleasant ways to spend an hour in these parts is to take local resident Barry Moloney's excellent walking tour—or "historic stroll," as he prefers to call it—of Kinsale town. Barry and his fellow guides have been leading visitors around the main sights since the mid-1990s, and their local knowledge is second to none. Highlights include the 12th-century St. Multose Church; a walk past Desmond Castle (see above); and the harbor, where the 17th-century Battle of Kinsale is recounted with an enthusiasm only found in people who really love their subject. Barry asserts that the battle was perhaps the most significant turning point in Irish history. The tour starts outside the tourist office at 11:15am every day. From May to September, there's also an

Biking the hilly streets of Kinsale.

THE scilly WALK

Effectively a miniscule suburb across the harbor from Kinsale, the village of Scilly—pronounced "silly"—clings to a strong sense of its own identity. Its unusual name is thought to hark back to fishermen from the Scilly Isles (off the coast of Cornwall, England) who settled here during the 17th century.

To explore the area, follow the signposted pedestrian path that runs along the sea from Scilly to Charles Fort. (You can pick up maps of the full route at the Kinsale tourism office.) Take the right-hand road around the village, skirting along the coast, and join the marked pedestrian trail by the waterside. Along here are lovely views across the harbor to Kinsale and the stout remains of **James Fort** (p. 270).

You'll pass another tiny hamlet on the outskirts of Kinsale, **Summer Cove,** which is as sweet a place as its halcyon name suggests. Black-and-white toy-town houses, with splashes of green and red, face the harbor as gulls circle overhead and the waves froth and bubble along the harbor walls.

A short walk uphill from Summer Cove lies **Charles Fort** (p. 269), built to defend the port from foreign invaders. Local lore has it that until the 19th century, access to this stretch of water was controlled by a massive chain floating on timber kegs between the two shores that could be drawn tight at a moment's notice.

The Scilly Walk ends here, but if you continue south along the sea, you'll find another path that follows the headland to the tip of **Frower Point,** which affords great views across the harbor to the Old Head of Kinsale. The total distance from Kinsale to Frower Point is 8km (5 miles) each way, and every part of it is rewarding.

earlier tour at 9:15am (except Sun). You pay at the end or, in their words, "drop out for free if you're not delighted." That probably doesn't happen very often.

Departs from Kinsale Tourist Office, Pier Rd. www.historicstrollkinsale.com. ✆ **021/477-2873** or 087/250-0731. Tours €8 adults; €1 children. May–Sept Mon–Sat 9:15 and 11:15am, Sun 11:15am; Mar–Oct daily 11:15am. Nov–Feb prebooking only.

Kinsale Pottery and Arts Centre ★ ART STUDIO   This excellent ceramics workshop outside of Kinsale sells beautiful, original items of pottery from delicate tea sets and tableware to ornamental masks. The shop is full of surprises, and prices aren't too steep. A two-floor gallery always has some interesting pieces on display. If you're looking for an alternative way to spend a day or more, the workshop also runs pottery courses where you can learn the basics of the craft and go home with your own creations. Prices start at around €50 for a half-day adult course (plus the cost of shipping what you make after it's fired, finished, and glazed, if you're unable to pick it up in person a week later). All materials are included in the price, as is lunch for the adult courses. From Pearse Street in Kinsale, turn left at the junction with the Blue Haven hotel on your right, then follow signs to Bandon and Innishannon. Take this road up the big hill, past the Kinsale sports ground, and look for signs to Kinsale Pottery on the left.

Ballinacurra. www.kinsaleceramics.com. ✆ **021/477-7758.** Free admission. Daily 10am–5pm.

Where to Stay in Kinsale

Actons Hotel ★   Built in the mid–19th century, this pleasant, well-run property overlooking Kinsale Harbour has been a hotel since the 1940s, and a renovation has added a few modern touches. Guest rooms aren't huge, but they're nicely designed, with very large beds and lovely harbor views. In a town where it's easy to find accommodations with character but lacking modern conveniences, you'll welcome the few extras such as an elevator (rare around here) and a swimming pool. The hotel's two restaurants are good, but you've also got Kinsale and all its wonderful restaurants on your doorstep.

Pier Rd. www.actonshotelkinsale.com. ✆ **021/477-9900.** 77 units. €145–€220 double; €250–€380 suite. Free parking. Breakfast included. Dinner, bed-and-breakfast packages available. **Amenities:** 2 restaurants; bar; room service; gym; pool; Wi-Fi (free).

Blue Haven Hotel ★★   There's something wonderfully old-school about this chic town house hotel in the middle of Kinsale. The rooms are traditionally decorated with antique-style furniture and heritage print wallpaper. Appropriately enough for a hotel in such a foodie town, the hotel has three restaurants, all of them good: a bar and bistro, a seafood cafe, and a tapas bar. The only snag is street noise, so ask for an upper-floor room if you're a light sleeper.

3–4 Pearse St. www.bluehavenkinsale.com. ✆ **021/477-2209.** 16 units. €160–€220 double. Parking at nearby lots around €1 per hr. Breakfast included. Dining packages and other deals available. **Amenities:** 2 restaurants; bar; room service; Wi-Fi (free).

Desmond House ★★   This lovely, historic B&B is one of the best places to stay in Kinsale. Desmond House was built in the mid–18th century, making it one of the oldest and best-preserved Georgian buildings in town. Grainne and Paddy Barnett Byrne bought the building several years ago and have only made it better. Guest rooms are generously sized with big, comfortable beds, and the modern bathrooms are furnished with whirlpool tubs. Many of the ingredients for the delicious breakfasts come straight from the **English Market ★★** in Cork (p. 250), and the building is sustainably run with solar panels, full recycling, and an eco-friendly approach.

42 Cork St. www.desmondhousekinsale.com. ✆ **021/477-3575.** 4 units. €160–€170 double. Parking at nearby lots around €1 per hr. Breakfast included. 2-night minimum on summer weekends. **Amenities:** Wi-Fi (free).

Pier House ★★ There's something wonderfully bright and cheerful about this sweet place. Hosts Pat and Ann have done a beautiful job converting the 19th-century townhouse into a B&B, with a maritime feel and subtle splashes of modern art. A few of the rooms have little balconies, and guests are welcome to bring wine back with them if they want to spend a leisurely hour admiring the views of the harbor or garden. Breakfasts are delicious and plentiful. You'll have to fend for yourself at dinner, but this is hardly a chore in foodie-friendly Kinsale.

Pier Rd. www.pierhousekinsale.com. ℭ **021/477-4169.** 10 units. €130–€140 double. Parking for bikes and motorbikes only; car parking at nearby lots around €2 per hr. Breakfast included. **Amenities:** Wi-Fi (free).

Where to Eat in Kinsale

Kinsale is famous as a foodie hub, and for good reason—there's an excellent restaurant on every corner. But if you're looking for lighter fare, the town has plenty of outstanding options. These include **Flying Poet** (44 Main St.; www.flyingpoet.ie), a small aviation-themed cafe serving light-as-air scones and tea, or fresh sandwiches and coffee. It also sells books to take with you on the road. Serving breakfast, lunch and dinner, **9 Market Street** (Market St.; www.ninemarketstreet.ie) offers creamy, steaming-hot porridge or perfectly cooked eggs in the morning. Lunch

The "Dog Walk" at the Kinsale Arts Festival.

could be pork bao buns or local Wagyu beef burger, and the steaks at dinner are excellent. Also the coffee and desserts are addictive. The **Lemon Leaf Café** (70 Main St.; www.lemonleafcafe.ie) has a great menu and space for families with young children—on sunny days, kids are drawn to the courtyard, while parents will welcome the lunchtime seafood chowder or Mediterranean salad piled high with falafel and a litany of fresh veggies. **Kinsale Food Tours** (www.kinsalefoodtours.com; ℂ **085/107-6113**) will take you on a 2.5-hour culinary odyssey around the town on foot, with lots of stories and tastings, from €60 per person.

Bastion ★★★ IRISH   This funky, creative restaurant is a big hit with local diners, and it got international attention when it snagged a Michelin star in 2019. An eight-course tasting menu brings updated Irish flavors to the fore, from the tender filet served with smoked potato cream and onion crumble to the melt-in-your-mouth confit duck. The exquisitely presented desserts are a treat—try the poached pear with mascarpone, perhaps washed down with a sweet glass of orange muscat. *Note:* Children are only allowed in the restaurant until 7 p.m.

Corner of Main St and Market St. www.bastionkinsale.com. ℂ **021/470-9696.** Tasting menu €100 (vegetarian version available); optional wine pairing €65. Wed–Sat 5–9pm. Closed Sun–Tues.

Black Pig Winebar ★★★ BISTRO/TAPAS   This charming cafe-bar has won hearts as much for its warm atmosphere as for the excellent food and wine. Gently flickering candlelight and bookcases filled with well-thumbed tomes set the laidback tone. The menu has constantly changing local specialties: smoked duck breast served with a salad of orange and rocket (arugula); rich and creamy Dingle crab ravioli; or perhaps a delicious plate of scallops from Kilmore Quay. The wine list is outstanding, with over 170 vintages on offer. This is a popular spot, especially on weekends, so booking is advisable.

66 Lower O'Connell St. www.theblackpigwinebar.com. ℂ **021/477-4101.** Entrees €8–€17.50. Wed–Sun 5:30–11:30pm.

Finns' Farmcut ★★★ MODERN IRISH   The menu here is ambitious without being overly complicated, with a focus on the seasons and plenty of space to let the ingredients breathe. Grass-fed beef and lamb come direct from the Finns' family farm in Mitchelstown in north County Cork, all prepared in the charcoal oven affectionately known as "Bertha." As you'd expect from Kinsale, the seafood on the menu comes directly from the harbor, so you never know exactly what will end up in the kitchen for the daily special.

6 Main St. www.finnsfarmcut.com. ℂ **021/470-9636.** Entrees €22.50–€36. Tues–Fri 6–9pm; Sat 5–9pm.

Fishy Fishy ★★★ SEAFOOD   Widely respected, hugely popular, and yet brilliantly simple, Fishy Fishy is one of the best restaurants in Kinsale.

The owners also have a gourmet store and fish-and-chips shop on Guardwell Street, but this is their flagship. The skillfully prepared fresh seafood comes from a small number of trusted local suppliers. Exactly what's cooking depends on the day's catch, but you can expect to find the signature Fishy Fishy pie of salmon and shellfish in a creamy sauce, and a plate of classic fish in tempura batter with homemade chips (thick-cut fries). Reservations are only taken for dinner, so this place gets packed during lunchtime.

Kinsale Food Festival

Food lovers from all over Ireland—and even farther afield—descend on Kinsale for a weekend each October when the **Kinsale Gourmet Festival** takes over town. The event's calendar changes every year but always includes plenty of cooking demonstrations and other lively activities. Restaurants join in the fun by hosting parties, special tastings, "meet the chef" events, and other culinary happenings. Many of these are free, although some of the bigger events and banquets charge €20 to €100 per ticket. It's magnificent, Bacchanalian fun. Learn more and book tickets at www.kinsale restaurants.com.

Crowleys Quay. www.fishyfishy.ie. ✆ **021/470-0415.** Entrees €19–€28. Mar–Oct daily noon–9pm; Nov–Feb Sun–Wed noon–4pm, Thurs–Sat noon–9pm. Closed Jan.

High Tide ★ MODERN IRISH   This restaurant is scoring big with the locals in Kinsale, who are impressed by the quality of the cooking and the owners' dedication to sourcing their fish, meat, and produce locally. The result is fresh, innovative cooking in a homey space. Sit by the fire and start with the lightly fried calamari, then try the creamy seafood chowder, the mildly spiced monkfish curry, or the rich stewed lamb. At lunch expect soups, wraps, salads, or toasted sandwiches. Most dishes are gluten-free, and there are plenty of vegetarian options.
3 Main St. www.hightidekinsale.com. ✆ **083/044-5676.** Entrees €15.50–€25.50. Daily noon–3pm and 5:30–9:30pm.

Man Friday ★★★ MODERN IRISH/SEAFOOD   The dining room at Man Friday overlooks the bay in Scilly, a perfect setting for the reliably excellent food served here. We can't resist the seafood—smoked salmon rolls stuffed with shrimp, plaice with crab and lemon butter, and a delightfully retro-style sole Colbert—although the beef and lamb options are excellent, too. For dessert, try the sticky toffee pudding with butterscotch sauce. Sunday lunch (€31 for three courses) is quite an event, and always very popular—be sure to book ahead. Ask to sit in the conservatory for the most heavenly views.
Scilly. www.manfridaykinsale.ie. ✆ **021/477-2260.** Entrees €20–€35. Mon–Tues and Thurs–Sat 5–9:30pm; closed Wed and Sun.

Max's ★★★ MODERN IRISH   A husband-and-wife team has run Max's since the '90s and has a way of making diners feel welcome that looks effortless. The menu costs €39 for two courses and changes seasonally, but the main flavors are all local. There's usually a lamb dish on the menu, and fish dishes depend on the local catch—sea bass and monkfish are favorites.

48 Main St. www.maxs.ie. ℂ **021/477-2443.** Two courses €39. Daily 6–10pm. Closes periodically between Nov and March.

The Spaniard ★★ BISTRO   The portrait on the sign of this atmospheric old inn shows Don Juan de Aguila, the Spanish commander who led a force of 4,000 men against the English at the Battle of Kinsale in 1601. The English won, but Don Juan became a hero in local folklore. The inn dates from around 50 years after the battle, and it's a popular place for good, homey pub food like fish pie or fish and chips, with roasts on Sunday. An eclectic program of live music runs nightly.

Junction of Scilly and Lower Rd. www.thespaniard.ie. ℂ **021/477-2436.** Entrees €11–€24. Mon–Thurs 10:30am–11:30pm; Fri–Sat 10:30am–12:30am; Sun 12:30–11:30pm. (Food served until about 9pm daily.)

Sports & Outdoor Pursuits in Kinsale

FISHING   Kinsale is one of the southern Irish coast's sea-angling centers. The area has numerous shipwrecks for wreck fishing (not the least of

Dating from the 17th century, the Spaniard serves up homey pub food.

them the *Lusitania,* near the Old Head of Kinsale). Try **Kinsale Angling** (1 Rampart Lane, The Ramparts; www.kinsale-angling.com; ℰ **021/242-9000**) for charter boats. They also run whale- and dolphin-watching trips. Prices vary widely, so call or e-mail for more information.

GOLF   Embraced by the sea on three sides, the nothing-short-of-spectac-ular **Old Head Golf Links** (www.oldhead.com; ℰ **021/477-8444**) is Tiger Woods's favorite Irish course. Named one of *Golf Magazine*'s "Top 100 Courses in the World" in the 2000s, it is hauntingly beautiful, rain or shine. The course retains a resident environmentalist to ensure that crucial wildlife habitats are not disturbed. But golfing here costs big money: Greens fees in summer are a whopping €375 for one 18-hole round (closed Nov to mid-Apr).

SAILING   There's excellent sailing out from Kinsale Head. **Sovereign Sailing** (www.sovereignsailing.com; ℰ **021/477-4145** or 086/858-6212) offers a full range of yacht-sailing options for all ages and levels of experi-ence. Between March and November, full- or half-day sails from Kinsale leave every day. Rates vary widely based on the kind of sailing you try, but a half-day trip on a 27-foot day yacht costs €195 for up to four people, or a 40-foot yacht is €365 for up to eight people.

WATERSPORTS   The **Oysterhaven Activity Centre** (www.oysterhaven. com; ℰ **021/477-0738**), 8km (5 miles) from Kinsale, rents kayaks, SUPs (stand-up paddleboards), windsurfing gear, and sailing dinghies. The prices start from €20 for windsurfing equipment, €12 to €18 for kayaks, €30 for dinghies and €15 for SUPs (stand-up paddleboards). Sailing, SUP, kayaking, and windsurfing lessons are also available and cost from €30 to €120. Things get pretty busy during summer, so try to book ahead as much as possible.

WEST CORK

You might say that West Cork is like County Kerry without the crowds. Like Kerry, it's got a photo-friendly craggy topography and jagged Atlan-tic coastline; and also as in Kerry, it's impossible to make good time on the narrow, sinuous roads here, as they twist along rivers, through valleys, around mountains, and through lovely small towns. Those willing to slow down and go with the flow are amply rewarded. In places, the route that hugs the coast narrows to just one lane and delivers heart-stopping views.

   Some of the most beautiful coastal scenery (and severe weather) is on West Cork's islands. **Cape Clear,** home to a bird-watching observatory, is also a well-known Gaeltacht: Schoolchildren and adults alike come here to work on their Irish language skills each summer. **Dursey Island,** off the tip of the Beara Peninsula, is accessible by cable car. The sheltered **Garin-ish Island** in Glengarriff is the site of Ilnacullin, an elaborate Italianate garden.

Arriving

The N71 is the main road into West Cork from north and south, looping around its coast; the east-west N22, on its way from Cork City to Killarney, also passes through some of West Cork. **Bus Éireann** (www.bus eireann.ie; © **021/450-8188**) provides daily bus service to and from the principal towns in West Cork. Find bus schedules online.

Exploring West Cork

Bantry House ★★ HISTORIC HOUSE   Built around 1750 for the earls of Bantry, this Georgian house is filled with exquisite furniture and objets d'art from all over Europe, including Aubusson and Gobelin tapestries said to have been made for Marie Antoinette. The gardens, with original statuary, are beautifully kept—climb the steps behind the building for a breathtaking panoramic view of the house, gardens, and Bantry Bay. Inside, stop by the exhibition on the ill-fated Spanish Armada, which, led by the Irish rebel Wolfe Tone, attempted to invade the country near Bantry House in 1769. Fully guided tours (included in the ticket price) take place daily at 2pm; otherwise, you're free to wander by yourself. And if you really love it here, you can spend the night (doubles €180–€230).

Bantry. www.bantryhouse.com. © **027/50047.** Admission €11 adults; €8.50 seniors and students; €3 children under 16; €26 families. Gardens only: €6. June–Aug daily 10am–5pm; mid-Apr to May and Sept–Oct Wed–Sun and public holiday Mon 10am–5pm. Closed Nov to mid-Apr.

Cape Clear Island (Oileán Chléire) ★★ HERITAGE/NATURE SITE
The southernmost inhabited point in Ireland, 13km (8 miles) off the mainland, Cape Clear Island has a permanent population of just a hundred residents. It is a bleak place with a rock-bound coastline and no trees to break the rush of sea wind, but it's also starkly beautiful. In early summer, wildflowers brighten the landscape, and in October, passerine migrants, some on their way from North America and Siberia, fill the air. Seabirds are abundant during the nesting season, especially from July to September. A bird observatory is at the **North Harbour,** with a warden in residence from March to November. You can stay at the observatory overnight, on a self-catering basis (www.birdwatchireland.ie; €25 per night). There are no hotels on the island, so other accommodation is based around house rentals, small B&Bs or yurt glamping at **Chléire Haven** (www.chleire-haven.com; © **086/197-1956**).

You can get to the island by ferry with **Cape Clear Ferries** (www.capeclearferries.com; © **028/39159;** return tickets €18 adults, €9 children, €45 families) and explore it all at your own pace; alternatively, take the Fastnet Rock Lighthouse Tour with the same ferry company (www.fastnettour.com; €42 adults, €12 children, €27 seniors and students, €90 families), which runs a couple of times a week from June to August, weather permitting (call for current sailing times). It starts at Baltimore or Schull

walk this way: THE SHEEP'S HEAD LOOP

A jagged strip of land reaching out into the Atlantic on the western side of County Cork, the Sheep's Head Peninsula is well worth a visit. It's a place of wild, rocky scenery, ice-blue lakes, and spectacular coastal views. It is also an isolated place; you'll likely find yourself alone for large stretches of time, with the expansive sea views all to yourself. Which, in bustling modern Ireland, is enough to make it worth the trip.

To see it the easy way, drive the **Sheep's Head Loop,** which begins just outside Bantry along the tiny road to Kilcrohane. It takes you through the coastal village of **Ahakista,** where you can stop to explore a Bronze Age stone circle, and on to tiny **Durrus,** home to the rocky ruins of the Cool na Long Castle. The main draw here, though, is the natural beauty. The north side of the peninsula is all sheer cliffs and stark, rocky scenery, unmarred by modern development (the sunsets on this side are unbelievable), while the more lush south-side road runs right along the wondrous Dunmanus Bay.

To explore the peninsula in more depth, however, you could walk the **Sheep's Head Way,** voted "Best Walk in Ireland" by *Country Walking* magazine a few years ago. The windy coastal walk is certainly ambitious, making an 89km (55-mile) loop around the peninsula. Most walkers choose to explore only the tip, from the point where the road ends down to the stumpy 1960s-era lighthouse, which keeps oil tankers from running aground. If you try the longer walk, be aware that the route is rough in places, particularly on the north side. The south side of the peninsula is greener and the path well-traveled.

The *Guide to the Sheep's Head Way* by Stephen Bosch (2003), available in local shops and tourist offices, combines history, poetry, and topography in a fantastic introduction to the region. The lavishly illustrated guide *Walking the Sheep's Head Way* by Amanda Clarke (2014) helpfully breaks the walk into all its various stages.

on the mainland and stops at Cape Clear for 2 to 3 hours, enough time to stroll around and also take in the island's heritage center, before a boat ride out to sea that circles **Fastnet Rock.** Home to nothing but a magnificent lighthouse, Fastnet was traditionally known as "Teardrop Island," not for its shape but because it was the last piece of Ireland emigrants saw on their way to America.

Cape Clear Island. www.oilean-chleire.ie.

Drombeg Stone Circle ★★ ANCIENT SITE   This ring of 13 standing stones is the finest example of a megalithic stone circle in County Cork. The circle dates from 153 B.C., and little is known about its ritual purpose. However, the remains of two huts and a cooking area just to the west of the circle, give some clue; it is thought that heated stones were placed in a water trough (which can be seen adjacent to the huts), and the hot water was used for cooking. This section has been dated to sometime between A.D. 368 and 608.

Signposted off R597 btw. Rosscarbery and Glandore, just east of Drombeg village. No phone. Free admission (open site).

Walk to Abandoned Cummeengeera

Stark and eerie, **Cummeengeera** ★ is an abandoned village in a wild, remote valley near Lauragh, on the Kerry side of the Beara Peninsula. The walk to the village gives you a taste for the rough beauty of this mountainous area, and a sense of the extent to which people in pre-Famine Ireland would go to find a patch of arable land. To get to the start of the walk, take R571 from Castletown up along the coast toward the town of Lauragh. Just west of Lauragh, turn onto the road for Glanmore Lake, signposted on the right. After approximately 1km (⅔ mile), turn right at a road posted for "stone circle." Continue 2km (1¼ miles) to the point at which the road becomes dirt, and park on the roadside. From here, there is no trail—just walk up the valley to its terminus, about 2km (1¼ miles) away, where the ruins of a village hug the cliff's base. Where the valley is blocked by a headland, take the route around to the left, which is less steep. Return the way you came. The whole walk—4km (2½ miles)—is of moderate difficulty.

Dursey Island ★★ HERITAGE/NATURE SITE   This is a real adventure; a barren promontory extending into the sea at the tip of the Beara Peninsula. The island offers no amenities for tourists, but the adventurous will be rewarded with beautiful seaside walks, a 200-year-old signal tower, and a memorable passage from the mainland via cable car. To get there, take R572 past Cahermore to its terminus. As you sway wildly in the wooden cable car, you'll wonder whether or not to be reassured that someone saw fit to place some holy water and the text of Psalm 91 inside. ("If you say 'the Lord is my refuge,' and you make the most high your dwelling, no harm will overtake you.") At this point you might be wondering whether a ferry would have been a wiser option. It wouldn't: Apparently the channel between the island and mainland is just too treacherous to permit regular crossing by boat. Cable cars run all year, 7 days a week. Crossings can't be prebooked—it's always first come, first served—and you can only pay with cash. The island has no shops, pubs, restaurants, or lodging of any kind. Bring food, water, and warm clothing. The crossing is very popular in summer, and numbers are sometimes restricted on the island on particularly busy days. **Dursey Boat Trips** (www.durseyboat trips.com; ℰ **083/898-9999**) runs a 1.5-hour trip around the island from Garinish Pier but does not actually land on the island.

Dursey Island. www.durseyisland.ie. ℰ**027/73851.** Cable-car round-trip €10 adults; €5 children; cash payment only. Mar–Oct daily 9:30am–7:30pm; Nov–March 9:30am–4:30pm. Closed 1–1:30pm. About 21km (14 miles) west of Castletownbere (follow R572). Dursey Boat Trips €50 adults; €25 children ages 6–12.

Gougane Barra ★★ HERITAGE/NATURE SITE   One of County Cork's most beautiful spots, Gougane Barra (which means "St. Fin Barre's Cleft") is the name of both a tiny old settlement and a forest park a little northeast of the Pass of Keimaneigh, 24km (15 miles) northeast of

Bantry, and well signposted off R584. If you're coming from the east, it's about 30km (18½ miles) southwest of Macroom. Its loveliest feature is a still, dark, romantic lake, which is the source of the River Lee. This is where St. Fin Barre founded a monastery, supposedly on the small island connected by a causeway to the mainland. Though nothing remains of the saint's 6th-century community, the setting is idyllic, with rhododendrons spilling into the still waters where swans glide by. The island now holds an elfin chapel and eight small circular cells dating from the early 1700s, as well as a modern chapel. Signposted walks and drives lead through the wooded hills.

7km (4½ miles) west of Ballingeary (signposted off R584). Park admission €5 per car (in coins).

Ilnacullin (Garinish Island) ★★ GARDEN Officially known as Ilnacullin, but usually referred to as Garnish (or "Garinish"), this little island is a beautiful and tranquil place. It used to be little more than a barren outcrop, whose only distinguishing feature was a Martello tower left over from the Napoleonic Wars of the early 19th century. Then, in 1919, the English landscaper Harold Peto was commissioned to create an elaborately planned Italianate garden, with classical pavilions and myriad unusual plants and flowers. The island's unusually mild microclimate

allows a number of subtropical plant species to thrive here; George Bernard Shaw is said to have written *St. Joan* under the shade of its palm trees. The island can be reached for €10 per person round-trip (€5 children 6–15) on a covered ferry operated out of Glengarriff by **Harbour Queen Ferries** (www.harbourqueenferry. com; ✆ **027/63116**). Boats run back and forth about every 20 to 30 minutes. *Note:* The Harbour Queen doesn't take credit cards. The nearest ATMs are in Bantry.

Glengarriff. www.garnishisland.com. ✆ **027/63040**. Admission (gardens) €5 adults; €4 seniors; €3 students and children; €13 families. July–Aug Mon–Fri and Sun 9:30am–5:30pm, Sat 9:30am–6pm. June Mon–Fri and Sun 10am–5:30pm, Sat 10am–6pm. Apr–May and Sept–Oct daily 10am–5:30pm. Last landing 1 hr. before closing. No landings Nov–Mar.

St. Fin Barre's Oratory in Gougane Barra Forest Park.

Among the heroes of Ireland's struggle for independence, Michael Collins seems to be Cork's favorite native son. Affectionately referred to as "the Big Fella," Collins was the commander-in-chief of the army of the Irish Free State, which finally won the Republic's independence from Britain in 1921.

Collins was born in 1890, and, along with seven brothers and sisters, he was raised on a farm in Sam's Cross, just outside the little town of **Clonakilty.** He emigrated to England at 15, like many other young Irish men seeking work in London. In his 20s, he joined the Irish revolutionary group, the Irish Republican Brotherhood (I.R.B.) and first came to fame in 1916 as one of the planners and leaders of the Easter Rising (p. 59). Although it aroused passions among the population, the Rising was in fact a military disaster, and Collins—young but clever—railed against its amateurism. He was furious about the seizure of prominent buildings—such as Dublin's

General Post Office (p. 112)—that were impossible to defend, impossible to escape from, and difficult to get supplies into.

After the battle, Collins was arrested and sent to an internment camp in Britain, along with hundreds of other rebels. There his stature within the I.R.B. grew, and by the time he was released, he had become one of the leaders of the Republican movement. In 1918, he was elected a member of the British Parliament, but like many other Irish members, he refused to go to London, instead announcing that he would sit only in an Irish parliament in Dublin. Most of the rebel Irish MPs (including Eamon de Valera) were arrested by British troops for their actions, but Collins avoided arrest, and he later helped de Valera escape from prison. Over the subsequent years, de Valera and Collins worked together to create an Irish state.

After lengthy political wrangling and much bloodshed (Collins orchestrated an

Mizen Head ★★ VIEWS   At Mizen Head, the very extreme southwest tip of Ireland, the land falls precipitously into the Atlantic breakers in a procession of spectacular 210m (689-ft.) sea cliffs. You can cross a suspension bridge to an old signal station, now a visitor center, and stand on a rock promontory at the southernmost point of the mainland. The sea view is spectacular, and it's worth a trip regardless of the weather. On wild days, tremendous Atlantic waves assault the cliffs, while on clear days, you might see dolphins leaping from the waves and seals basking on the rocks. A huge renovation in the early 2010s added new bridges, viewing platforms, and a simulated ship's bridge. On the way out to Mizen Head, you'll pass Barleycove Beach, a gorgeous stretch of sand and rock.

From Ballydehob, take R592 and then R591 to Goleen and follow signs to Mizen Head. www.mizenhead.ie. ✆**028/35000.** Admission €7.50 adults; €6 seniors and students; €4.50 children under 14; free for children under 5; €25 families. June–Aug daily 10am–6pm; Sept–Oct daily 10:30am–5pm; Nov–Mar Sat–Sun 11am–4pm.

assassination that essentially wiped out the British secret service in Ireland), Collins was sent by de Valera in 1921 to negotiate a treaty with the British government. In the meeting, British Prime Minister David Lloyd George agreed to allow Ireland to become a free republic, as long as that republic did not include the largely Protestant counties of Ulster, which would stay part of the United Kingdom. Knowing he could not get more at the time and determined to end the violence, Collins reluctantly agreed to sign the treaty, hoping to renegotiate later. After signing the document Collins said, "I have just signed my death warrant."

As he'd expected, the plan tore the new Republic apart, dividing the group now known as the IRA into two factions: those who wanted to continue fighting for all of Ireland, and those who favored the treaty. Fighting soon broke out in Dublin, and the civil war was underway.

The battles stretched on for 10 months. In August 1922, Collins, weary

of the war, was on a peace mission in his home county. Stopping at a pub near his mother's birthplace, he and his escort were on the road near Béal na Bláth when Collins was shot and killed. Precisely who killed him—his own men or the opposition—was never known. On his rapid rise to the top, he'd made too many enemies. He was 31 years old.

The **Michael Collins Centre** (www. michaelcollinscentre.com; © **023/884-6107**), located on the farm where he grew up, is a good place to learn more about the man. In addition to an hour-long tour, featuring a film and a visit to the actual ambush site, the center runs in-depth guided trips around the local area. (These last 3½ hr. are probably for Collins devotees only.) The center is signposted off N71, 5.6km (3½ miles) west of Clonakilty. It's open mid-June to mid-September, Monday to Friday 11am to 4pm, and there is one tour on Saturday at noon. Admission €6 adults; €3 children; €15 family.

North Cork

The Donkey Sanctuary ★ ANIMAL SANCTUARY   A real tear-jerker, this one: a charity that rescues abandoned and abused donkeys and nurses them back to health. A few here have been voluntarily relinquished by owners who are no longer able to care for them, but the majority have sadder histories. The donkeys live out their days at this quiet, bucolic place, where they receive medical aid and plenty of TLC. Visitors can meet the gentle patients and learn their stories. The emphasis is on happy endings. Seeing these animals given a new lease on life can be a touching and even profound experience for kids.

Liscarroll, near Mallow, North Cork. www.thedonkeysanctuary.ie. © **022/48398.** Free admission. Mon–Fri 9am–4:30pm; Sat, Sun, and public holidays 10am–5pm.

Where to Stay in West Cork

Eccles Hotel & Spa ★★   This charming hotel has a gorgeous setting overlooking Bantry Bay. The building has been open to guests since 1745 and has undergone many renovations and additions since then, welcoming famous guests along the way including writers. **Garnish Restaurant**'s Chef Eddie Attwell is passionate about local food; he forages and grows his own produce and guests are welcome to join him on morning walks. The **Harbour Bar** serves casual eats, and the spa is divine—one treatment room has a bath overlooking the bay. This is a great base for exploring the area—the hotel has bicycles for guests and can arrange everything from golf to kayaking. Some rooms are on the small side but are priced accordingly so check when booking—ask for a bay rather than a forest room for sea views.

Glengarriff Harbour. www.eccleshotel.com.✆ **027/63093.** 57 units. €150–€210. Breakfast included. Check website for offers. Free parking. **Amenities:** Restaurant; bar; spa; Wi-Fi (free).

Glebe Country House ★   About halfway between Cork and Kinsale, this place was built as a rectory in the late 17th century. Bedrooms are comfortable and traditionally furnished, with views of the idyllic gardens. The owners are real foodies—the breakfast menu is longer and more imaginative than most places this size, with lots of organic produce, homemade preserves, and tasty buttermilk waffles.

Balinadee (off Balinadee center), Bandon. www.glebecountryhouse.ie.✆ **021/477-8294.** 4 units. €120–€130 per night per double. Minimum 2-night stay. Breakfast included. Free parking. **Amenities:** Wi-Fi (free). Closed in winter.

Inchydoney Lodge & Spa ★★★   So close to the beach you could almost dive into the Atlantic from your balcony, this famously luxurious spa hotel is dreamy. The spa specializes in thalassotherapy treatments, using seawater, and the full list of what's offered may relax you just by reading it. Guest rooms are sophisticated and modern, with huge windows that open out onto amazing views of the sea. The **Gulfstream Restaurant** serves French- and Mediterranean-influenced cooking, with fresh seafood a particular specialty. The hotel also has a pub and bistro if you're after something simpler. Unlike some high-end spas, Inchydoney is a great option for families, with its dedicated Children's Lounge; the hotel can also arrange family-friendly activities such as kayaking, whale-watching, surfing, and cycling.

Clonakilty. www.inchydoneyisland.com.✆ **023/883-3143.** 67 units. €170–€320 double. Free parking. Breakfast included. Dinner, bed-and-breakfast packages available. **Amenities:** 2 restaurants; bar; pool; room service; spa; Wi-Fi (free).

Longueville House ★★   This is North Cork rather than West, but worth a detour for a Georgian country house experience with exquisite dining. The house dates from 1720, and its spacious bedrooms reflect the building's heritage, with traditional furniture and a homey feel. You'll have plenty of grounds on the estate to wander and explore and log fires to relax over. Chef William O'Callaghan—who runs the house along with his wife, Aisling—trained under famed French chef Raymond Blanc and puts his skills to wonderful use here. Stays are 2 nights and include a four-course dinner nightly with a set menu and set (7:30pm) dining time. Local ingredients, many grown on Longueville's own farm and kitchen garden, feature heavily in the Irish-French menus, including Castletownbere cod and honey from the house hive.

Mallow. www.longuevillehouse.ie. ☎ **022/47156.** 22 units. Minimum 2-night stay. Dinner, breakfast and afternoon tea included. €680–€800 double. Free parking. Closed Mon and Tues. Weekends only Oct–Mar. **Amenities:** Restaurant; Wi-Fi (free).

Where to Eat in West Cork

With its microclimate and clear waters, West Cork has a wealth of food artisans producing everything from cheese, preserves, and smoked fish to whiskey and mead made in the area. Weekly farmer's markets are a great source for local foods and often a hive of social activity. Look out for meet-the-maker experiences while you're there. You can also take master classes, do tastings, or go on foraging tours at **Woodcock Smokery** (www.woodcocksmokery.com; ☎ **028/36-232**); drop into **Clonakilty Black Pudding** visitor center to learn more about the Irish breakfast staple (www.clonakiltyblackpudding.ie; ☎ **023/883-4835**); or visit **Clonakilty Distillery** (www.clonakiltydistillery.ie; ☎ **023/887-8020**) to learn about whiskey distilling or blend your own gin.

West Cork has lots of food trucks (many in converted horseboxes) as well—look for the **Beara Barista** caravan on Ballydongan Beach in Allihies for hot dogs made with Gubbeen Smokehouse sausages; **Bean & Berry** at Garretstown beach for açai smoothie bowls; or the food truck park at **Quills** in Glengarriff for treats like woodfired pizza from **Boxed** or pulled pork baps from **Wild Hogs.**

Blairscove ★★ IRISH   This has to be one of the most picturesque dining rooms in Ireland—a former barn, which may have originated as an 18th-century watchtower. The menu isn't cutting-edge, but that's kind of the point. Instead, what you get (after a charmingly retro buffet of appetizers) are traditional Irish flavors elegantly updated, such as rack of lamb with braised chicory and sorrel pesto, or hake served in a mustard, dill, and white-wine sauce. Desserts are rich and delicious. If you want to make even more of a night of it, Blairscove offers B&B lodging for €190 to €260 a night for two people sharing.

Barley Cove Rd., Durrus. www.blairscove.ie. ☎ **027/61127.** Three-course fixed-price menus €65. Mid-Mar to Nov Tues–Sat 5:30–9:30pm. Closed Nov to mid-Mar.

The Heron's Cove ★★ SEAFOOD   It's all about the bounty of the sea at this laid-back restaurant about 15km (9 miles) from **Mizen Head** (p. 282). All the seafood is caught on the West Cork coastline; expect Bantry Bay organic salmon, tempura monkfish, or perhaps some lemon sole filet prepared in a creamy white-wine sauce. You can sit outside on a terrace overlooking the harbor if the weather's good. It also offers B&B

lodging in pleasant guest rooms with views of the harbor for €90 to €100 per night (€100–€140 per night for family room).

Harbour Rd., Goleen. www.heronscove.com. ✆ **028/35225.** Entrees €17–€27. June–Sept daily 7–9:45pm. Bookings only Oct–May. Essential to call ahead in winter: Restaurant closes in quiet periods and hours may vary at other times.

Mary Ann's ★ SEAFOOD/PUB FOOD   The handsome exterior of this friendly pub in Castletownshend, near Skibbereen—in fact, the *only* pub in the village—is a photo op waiting to happen. The ochre paint and neat black windows look so satisfyingly publike that it may as well be on the front of a postcard (for all we know, it might well be). Fortunately, the food is just as good. This being the West Cork coast, the seafood is often what stands out—fresh, local crab salad, local scallops, fish pie with plenty of, guess what, local ingredients—but there are meatier choices as well, such as roast duck in a sauce of blood orange and star anise, or lamb chops. You can eat in a little courtyard terrace if you're blessed with sunshine.

Castletownshend. ✆ **028/36146.** Entrees €15–€27. Daily 11am–11pm (food served until about 9pm).

Pilgrim's ★★★ MODERN IRISH   Don't let the simple, rustic setting—wood tables, whitewashed walls, and dried wildflowers—fool you. This is where you'll find some of West Cork's finest ingredients, grown and foraged from land and sea, crafted together with finesse daily for a tasty menu that changes with the seasons. Expect dishes like Roaring Water Bay mussels with house miso and lovage, or sole parcels with a crab and ricotta filling, sun gold tomato broth, braised leek, and hazelnut crumb. Desserts often include local berries.

6 South Square, Rosscarbery. www.pilgrims.ie. ✆ **023/883-1796.** Three-course set menu €50. Thurs–Sat 6–9pm; Sun 1–4pm.

Restaurant Chestnut ★★★ FRENCH/IRISH   This tiny (18 seats at six tables) former pub earned sudden fame when it received a Michelin star in 2019. It's an unassuming place, with ceilings so low that tall customers have to stoop to get inside. But size isn't everything, and here it's all about the food. The opener is homemade smoked butter with warm, sourdough bread just out of the oven. The eight-course tasting menu is ever-evolving but features dishes such as paper-thin slices of celeriac wrapped around local Young Buck cheese; fresh local mussels with seaweed and tapioca; and crisp scallops with parsley and yeast. This is experimental cooking, playful and unpredictable—tiny, complex dishes designed to challenge your expectations. The Michelin reviewers believe it to be one of the best restaurants in the country. *Note:* Vegetarians and anyone with dietary restrictions should notify the restaurant when they book to request substitutions.

Staball Hill, Ballydehob. www.restaurantchestnutwestcork.ie. ✆ **028/25766.** 8-course set menu €100. Reservations essential, well in advance. No children under 12. Wed–Sat 6:30–9pm. Closed mid-Dec to mid-Feb.

Sports & Outdoor Pursuits in West Cork

BEACHES   **Barleycove Beach** is a vast expanse of pristine sand with a fine view out toward the Mizen Head cliffs; despite the trailer park and holiday homes on the far side of the dunes, large parts of the beach never seem to get crowded. Take R591 to Goleen and follow signs for Mizen Head. **Inchydoney Beach,** on Clonakilty Bay, is famous for both its gorgeous beach and the luxe **Inchydoney Lodge & Spa** (p. 284).

CYCLING   The **Mizen Head, Sheep's Head,** and **Beara peninsulas** offer fine roads for cycling, with great scenery and few cars. The loop around Mizen Head, starting in Skibbereen, is a good 2- to 3-day trip; a loop around the Beara Peninsula from Bantry, Glengarriff, or Kenmare takes at least 3 days at a casual pace. In Skibbereen, 18- and 21-speed bicycles can be rented from **Roycroft Cycles,** Heron Court, Town Car Park (www.westcorkcycles.ie; ✆ **028/21235**); expect to pay around €15 to €20 per day, €70 to €80 per week.

DIVING   The **Baltimore Diving Centre** in Baltimore (www.baltimorediving.com; ✆ **086/241-2855**) provides equipment and boats to certified divers to explore the many shipwrecks, reefs, and caves off Cork's western coast. Cost is €40 to €65 per dive. Various 3-hour to 14-day certified PADI courses are available for all levels of experience.

FISHING   The West Cork coast is known for its many shipwrecks, making this one of the best places in Ireland for wreck fishing. **Courtmacsherry Sea Angling Centre,** Woodpoint House, Courtmacsherry (www.courtmacsherryangling.ie; ✆ **086/825-0905** or 023/884-6427), offers packages that include bed-and-breakfast in an idyllic 18th-century stone farmhouse, plus a day's sea angling aboard an Aquastar fishing boat that can reach the wreck of the *Lusitania* in about 40 minutes. A day's fishing costs around €70 per person (€80 to go out to a wreck). Rod hire is €10 per day. They also run dolphin- and whale-watching excursions for €50 per person. B&B rates starts at €45 per person. **Bantry Bay Charters** (www.bantrybaycharters.ie; ✆ **083/089-6828**) offers everything from 3-hour mackerel fishing trips to full-day sea angling trips, whale-watching, and diving. Trips start from €40 to around €130 for a full day at sea (minimum six people).

KAYAKING   With hundreds of islands, inviting inlets, and sea caves, the coast of West Cork is a sea kayaker's paradise. **Lough Hyne,** one of the largest saltwater lakes in Europe, offers warm, still waters for beginners, a tidal rapid for the intrepid, and access to a nearby headland riddled with caves. **Atlantic Sea Kayaking** (www.atlanticseakayaking.com; ✆ **028/21058**) specializes in guided trips on Lough Hyne as well as along the coastal bays and inlets from Castlehaven Bay near Skibbereen. They also run night kayaking trips in both locations, starting at dusk.

WALKING   A spectacular coastal walk begins along the banks of **Lough Hyne,** cupped in a lush valley of exceptional beauty. To get there, follow signs for Lough Hyne along R595 between Skibbereen and Baltimore; a parking lot is at the northwest corner of the lake. The wide trail proceeds gradually upward from the parking lot through the woods on the west slope of the valley; once you reach the hilltop, you'll see a sweeping view of the coast from Mizen Head to Galley Head. Walking time to the top and back is about 1½ hours.

WHALE-WATCHING   The Atlantic waters off the southwest coast are some of the best for spotting dolphins, porpoise, and basking sharks, plus—if the season is right—fin, humpback, and minke whales, who all come here to feed. On a whale-watching boat trip you can also see lots of bird life and seals and admire the bays, cliffs, and caves from the water. Try **Atlantic Whale and Wildlife Tours** for a 3- to 4-hour trip from Courtmacsherry (www.atlanticwhaleandwildlifetours.com; ✆ **087/774-4401**) or **Cork Whale Watch,** which runs from Reen Pier near Union Hall (www.corkwhalewatch.com; ✆ **086/385-05680**). Trips with **Baltimore Sea Safari** range from 20 minutes to 2 hours and take in a seal colony (www.baltimoreseasafari.ie; ✆ **028/207-53**).

COUNTY KERRY

olling green fields, lakes and mountains, picture-postcard towns, and craggy ocean vistas . . . there's a reason why so many visitors to Ireland put County Kerry
at the top of their itineraries. Charming, colorful towns
like Kenmare and Dingle make perfect stops on any
Irish tour. Kerry's peaceful green valleys are just what everyone
hopes for when they come to Ireland. And therein lies the rub!
With massive popularity comes massive crowds. The height of
summer is incredibly busy here—if it's peace you want, ideally, you
should hit these hills in the late spring or fall, when it's much quieter (but still just as beautiful). There's an antidote for even the
busiest times, however: Should you find that the tour bus traffic on
the **Ring of Kerry** is getting to you, simply turn off onto a small
country lane, and within seconds you'll find yourself virtually alone
in the peaceful Irish countryside.

ESSENTIALS
Arriving

BY BUS   **Bus Éireann** (www.buseireann.ie; ✆ **064/663-0011**) operates
regularly scheduled service into Killarney and Dingle from all parts of
Ireland.

BY TRAIN   Trains from Dublin, Cork, and Galway arrive daily at **Killarney Railway Station** (www.irishrail.ie; ✆ **064/663-1067**), Railway Road,
off East Avenue Road, and **Tralee Casement Station** (www.irishrail.ie;
✆ **066/712-3522**). Kenmare and Dingle do not have train stations.

BY CAR   Getting to Killarney from Cork is easy—just head northeast
out of Cork City on N22; the distance is about 85km (53 miles). To get
to Killarney from Dublin, take M7 southwest to Limerick, then N21
(which also leads to Tralee, gateway to the Dingle Peninsula), and N22
to Killarney. The total journey is about 310km (193 miles). Kenmare
and Killarney are connected by the main N71 Ring of Kerry Road;
they're only 33km (20½ miles) apart, but allow plenty of time because
of the winding nature of the road (and, in summer, tour-bus traffic). To
hire a car in Killarney, try **Budget** at the International Hotel on Kenmare

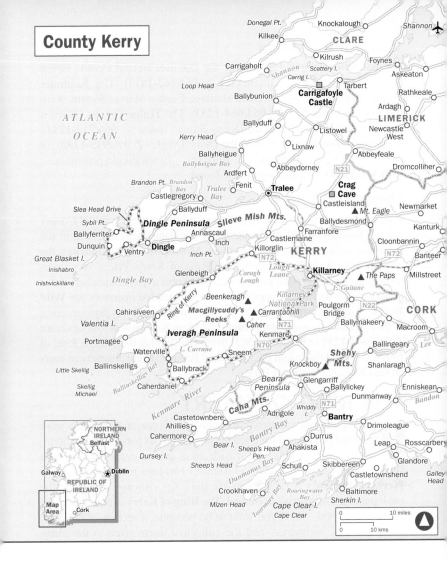

County Kerry

Place (www.budget.ie; ☎ **064/663-4341**). For details on car rentals in Dublin, see p. 91; for Shannon Airport car rentals, see p. 344.

BY PLANE   Aer Lingus (www.aerlingus.com; ☎ **081/836-5000**) has two flights per day from Dublin into the miniscule **Kerry County Airport** in Farranfore (www.kerryairport.ie; ☎ **066/976-4644**), about 16km (10 miles) north of Killarney. A handful of flights fly every week from London's Luton and Stanstead airports, Manchester, Frankfurt, Berlin, Faro in Portugal and Alicante in Spain, operated by **Ryanair** (www.ryanair.com; ☎ **0871/246-0000** in the U.K. or 1520/444-004). Fewer flights are scheduled in winter.

Visitor Information

The **Killarney Tourist Office** is at the Discover Ireland Centre, Beech Road, Killarney (www.killarney.ie; © **064/663-1633**). The **Kenmare Tourist Office** is at the Kenmare Heritage Centre, Market Square, Kenmare (www.kenmare.ie; © **064/664-1233**). The **Tralee Tourist Office** is at the Ashe Memorial Hall on Denny Street, Tralee (© **066/712-1288**). The **Dingle Tourist Office** is on the Quay, Dingle (© **066/915-1188**), or contact **Dingle Peninsula Tourism** (www.dingle-peninsula.ie; © **064/9152248**). All stay open year-round.

Organized Tours

If you're not confident in hiring a car and driving yourself around County Kerry's tourist-clogged roads, plenty of companies will take you to see the major sights on organized bus tours. Most depart from **Killarney,** the most popular base for exploring the Ring of Kerry. Prices vary enormously according to what you choose, but expect to pay somewhere in the region of €25 to €50 per person. Two recommended operators are **Wild Kerry Day Tours,** 100 New St. (www.wildkerrydaytours.com; © **064/663-1052**), and **Dero's Tours,** 22 Main St. (www.derostours.com; © **064/663-1251** or 064/663-1567). Both run full-day tours of the Ring of Kerry, tours to Dingle and the Slea Head Peninsula, and a variety of tours around Killarney National Park.

THE RING OF KERRY

This green and beautiful stretch of countryside is one of the world's most photographed places, and for good reason: Gorgeous panoramas of mountains, valleys, rolling hills, and seaside await around every curve. It's no surprise, then, that the 178km (110-mile) two-lane road encircling the **Iveragh Peninsula** is such a massive draw for visitors—it's by far the most popular scenic drive in Ireland. The **Ring of Kerry** is both the actual name of the road—or, if you want to be pedantic, a section of the N70, N71, and N72 highways—and the collective name given to the many attractions in the area. Nearly all of County Kerry's most popular sights are either on or within a short distance of the Ring, including the stunning **Killarney National Park.**

What you won't find, at least in the summertime, is much in the way of peace. Bicyclists avoid the route because of the scores of tour buses thundering down it from early morning until late in the day. You can drive either way along the Ring of Kerry, but a counterclockwise route gives you the best views. Very large vehicles are always meant to travel this way to avoid accidents and nasty traffic jams around the Ring's perilously narrow bends.

Of course, if you yearn for peace and quiet, you can simply skedaddle off that busy highway and onto the many narrower country roads.

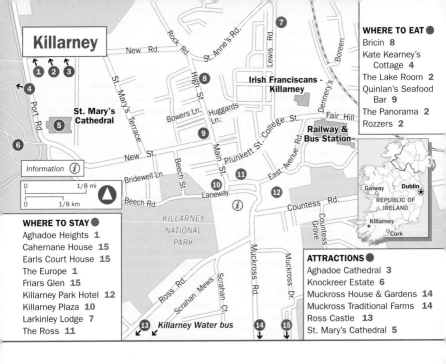

Killarney

WHERE TO EAT ●
Bricin **8**
Kate Kearney's
  Cottage **4**
The Lake Room **2**
Quinlan's Seafood
  Bar **9**
The Panorama **2**
Rozzers **2**

Irish Franciscans -
Killarney

St. Mary's
Cathedral

Railway &
Bus Station

Information (i)

Galway   Dublin
REPUBLIC OF
IRELAND
Killarney
Cork

KILLARNEY
NATIONAL
PARK

WHERE TO STAY ●
Aghadoe Heights **1**
Cahernane House **15**
Earls Court House **15**
The Europe **1**
Friars Glen **15**
Killarney Park Hotel **12**
Killarney Plaza **10**
Larkinley Lodge **7**
The Ross **11**

ATTRACTIONS ●
Aghadoe Cathedral **3**
Knockreer Estate **6**
Muckross House & Gardens **14**
Muckross Traditional Farms **14**
Ross Castle **13**
St. Mary's Cathedral **5**

Killarney Water bus

There's so much beauty here, it doesn't really matter how you choose to see it. Often the greatest pleasures can be found during a scenic drive along a side road or on a quiet byway just begging to be explored.

The small but busy town of **Killarney** is the area's main hub. It's conveniently sited on the edge of spectacular **Killarney National Park,** which includes the breathtaking **Killarney Lakes** and the scenic **Gap of Dunloe.** Most people traveling the route start and finish at Killarney, but smaller, quieter **Kenmare** makes for a good alternative base.

Killarney & Killarney National Park

Killarney's ample stock of restaurants, pubs, and hotels keeps it buzzing with visitors throughout the year. Given this, tourism is a bit more in-your-face here than anywhere else in Kerry—in the summer its narrow streets are prone to tour-bus traffic jams. That aside, Killarney has much to offer, and plenty of beauty to go with the bustle.

The main attraction is the valley in which Killarney nestles—a verdant landscape of mist-wreathed lakes and rugged hills so spectacular that "even an ad man would be ashamed to eulogize it," as author and playwright Brendan Behan once said. Escaping the crowded streets to explore the quiet rural splendor of the 65-sq.-km (25-sq.-mile) **Killarney National Park** could hardly be easier. The main visitor center is at **Killarney House and Gardens** (p. 294), which leads into the park.

A huge, rambling wilderness with breathtaking scenery, **Killarney National Park ★★★** is an essential stop along the Ring of Kerry. Within the park's limits are lakes, mountains, and two estates—**Muckross** and **Knockreer** (p. 300). The main visitor center for the park, located in **Killarney House and Gardens** (www.killarney nationalpark.ie; ☎ **064/663-1440**), is just a 5-minute walk from Main Street in the town center. Stop by here to pick up maps and take in an exhibition before you get started. The visitor center is open daily from 8am to 6pm in summer and from 9am to 5:30pm in winter.

Cars are banned from most of the trails that traverse the park, so you'll have to explore it on foot—or else hire a **"jarvey,"** or "jaunting car," an old-fashioned horse-and-buggy. Jarveys can be booked from **Killarney Jaunting Cars,** Muckross Close (www.killarneyjaunting cars.com; ☎ **064/663-3358**). Drivers also often congregate in one of the small parking lots on the main N72 Ring of Kerry Road, between the edge of Killarney Town and the entrance to Muckross House, and at Kate Kearney's Cottage at the Gap of Dunloe.

Three lakes dot the park. The largest, the **Lower Lake,** is sometimes called Lough Leane or Lough Lein, translated as "the lake of learning." It's more than 6km (3¾ miles) long and holds 30 small islands that seem to rise from the mist. The most celebrated of Killarney's islands, the lovely **Innisfallen ★★** (p. 296), can be found on the Lower Lake. Nearby are the **Middle Lake** or Muckross Lake, and the smallest of the three, the **Upper Lake.**

Here are several marked trails for exploring the beauty of Killarney Park:

Blue Pool Nature Trail: Starting behind the Muckross Park Hotel, this trail winds for a relaxing 2.3km (1.5 miles) through coniferous woodland beside a small lake. The trail is named for the lake's unusually deep blue-green color, a result of copper deposits in the soil.

Cloghereen Nature Trail: Incorporated into a small section of the Blue Pool

An easy way to get around the park is on the **Killarney Shuttle Bus** (www.killarneyshuttlebus.com; ☎ **087/138-4384**), which starts at the Tourist Office on Beech Road and stops at Ross Castle, Muckross Abbey, Muckross House, Torc Waterfall, and Ladies View. Tickets are €5 for one journey or €10/€20 for the day. The **Killarney Tour** guided hop-on/hop-off bus (www.killarneytour.com; ☎ **087/250-8122**) runs to Ross Castle, Torc Waterfall, Muckross House, and Muckross Abbey; single tickets are €5 to €6 and day tickets are €12.50.

TOWN LAYOUT

Killarney may be the most important town in the region, but this is Ireland, so this "metropolis" is much smaller than you'd expect, with a full-time population of only about 14,500. Of course this number can swell considerably at the height of tourist season—and it feels like it. The town trail, this walk is fully accessible to blind visitors. A guide rope leads you along the route, lined by plants identifiable by scent and touch. An audio guide is available from the Muckross House visitor center for a small deposit.

Mossy Woods Nature Trail: One of the park's gentler trails, this route starts from Muckross Lake and runs just under 2km (1.2 miles). The moss-covered trees and rocks it passes are a major habitat for bird life. You'll also see several strawberry trees (*Arbutus*), something of a botanical mystery—they're common in these parts but found almost nowhere else in Northern Europe. The route offers incredible mountain views.

Old Boat House Nature Trail: This short lakeside walk begins at the 19th-century boathouse below Muckross Gardens and goes .8km (.5 mile) around a small peninsula by Muckross Lake.

Arthur Young's Walk: Starting on the road to Dinis Island, this longer (4.8km/3 miles) hike traverses natural yew woods,

then follows a 200-year-old road on the Muckross Peninsula.

Audioguides for all trails can be obtained at the Muckross House visitor center.

Jaunting cars, or "jarveys," bustle around Killarney National Park.

is laid out around one central thoroughfare, **Main Street,** which confusingly changes its name to **High Street** at the northern end. The principal cross streets are **New Street** and **Plunkett Street** (which becomes **College St.**). The Deenagh River edges the western side of town, and **East Avenue Road** edges the eastern side. The busiest section of town is at the southern tip of Main Street, where it curves to meet East Avenue Road, then curves again to head south to the Muckross road and the entrance to Killarney National Park.

There is limited local bus service, but the best and fastest way to get around town is almost always on foot. (Those with mobility problems might find it easier to call a taxi than look for a bus—nowhere is all that far from anywhere else in this town, so fares are low.) A signposted **Tourist Trail** visits all the highlights; it takes less than 2 hours to complete. Pick up a booklet outlining the trail's sights at the tourist office.

TOP ATTRACTIONS IN KILLARNEY & KILLARNEY NATIONAL PARK

Gap of Dunloe ★★★ VIEWS   A narrow pass between the Purple Mountains and the dark, rocky hills known as MacGillycuddy's Reeks, the winding Gap of Dunloe rises through mountains and wetlands just west of Killarney National Park. The route through the gap (called Gap of Dunloe Road, naturally) passes craggy hills, meandering streams, and deep gullies, and it ends in the park at the Upper Lake. Some of the roads can be difficult around here, so many people choose to explore by bicycle (see p. 308) or by "jarvey" (see above). While cars are not strictly banned from this road (which is not technically part of Killarney National Park), it's not advisable to drive all the way through the Gap. Drive into the scenic countryside—perhaps as far as **Kate Kearney's Cottage** (p. 306)—park your car, and then proceed on foot or by bike or rent a jarvey car from one of the drivers here.

Signposted from N72 (Ring of Kerry Rd.), Killarney.

Innisfallen ★★ HERITAGE/NATURE SITE   Shrouded in forest, this small island appears to float peacefully on the Lower Lake in Killarney National Park. Behind the trees is what's left of a 7th-century monastery that flourished for 1,000 years. It's thought that Brian Boru, the great Irish

Biking is the best way to explore the Gap of Dunloe, just outside Killarney National Park.

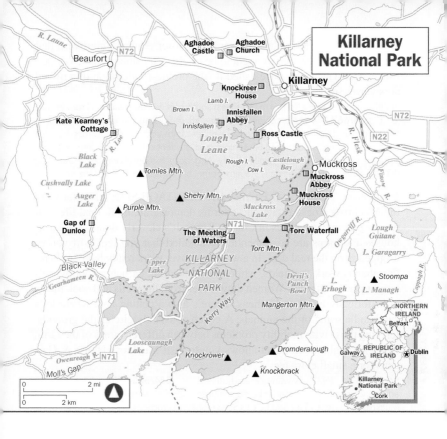

chieftain, and St. Brendan the Navigator received their education here. From 950 to 1320, the "Annals of Innisfallen," a chronicle of early Irish history, was written at the monastery. You can reach Innisfallen by rowboat in the summer season only, available for rental at **Ross Castle ★** (p. 298).

Lower Lake, opposite Ross Castle, Ross Rd. (signposted from N71, Ring of Kerry Rd.), Killarney.

Muckross House & Gardens ★★ HISTORIC HOUSE   This elegant, neo-Gothic Victorian house at one of the entrances to Killarney National Park was built in 1843. Guided tours offer an enlightening glimpse at how both masters and servants of the house once lived—the grand, *Downton Abbey*–like formal dining room contrasts starkly with the Victorian kitchens and servants' quarters below stairs. The landscaped gardens are beautiful and a riot of color in high summer. The pleasant cafe, overlooking some manicured flowerbeds, is a lovely spot to linger over a cup of tea. A traditional weavers' and craft shop is also on the grounds, along with the evocative ruin of the 15th-century **Muckross Abbey,** founded about 1448 and burned by Cromwell's troops in 1652.

The abbey's central feature is a vaulted cloister around a courtyard that contains a huge yew tree, thought to be as old as the abbey itself. William Makepeace Thackeray once called it "the prettiest little bijou of a ruined abbey ever seen."

On N71 (Ring of Kerry Rd.), 6km (3¾ miles) south of Killarney. www.muckross-house. ie. ℗ **064/667-0144.** Admission €9 adults; €8 seniors and students; €6 children 6–18; free for children under 5; €29–€33 families. Joint ticket with Muckross Traditional Farms: €15.50 adults; €13.50 seniors and students; €10.50 children 6–18; €6 children under 5; €40–€45 families. July–Aug daily 9:30am–6pm; Sept–Oct daily 9:30am–5:30pm; Nov–Dec daily 9:30am–5pm. Last admission 1 hr. before closing.

Muckross Traditional Farms ★★ HERITAGE SITE   Not far from the Muckross House estate, these farms demonstrate traditional life as it was in previous centuries in County Kerry. It's cleverly done—the farmhouses and barns are so authentically detailed that you feel as if you've dropped in on the real deal. In a way, you have. Work really happens here: Farmhands work the fields, while the blacksmith, carpenter, and wheelwright ply their trades. Women draw water from the wells and cook meals in historically accurate kitchens. There's also a petting zoo, where kids can handle some of the animals. A coach constantly circles the grounds, ferrying those with mobility problems between different areas of the farm. *Note:* A combination ticket allows you to visit Muckross House & Gardens for a small extra fee.

Kenmare Rd. (N71). www.muckross-house.ie. ℗ **064/663-0804.** Admission €9 adults; €8 seniors and students; €6 children; €29–€33 families. Joint ticket with Muckross House: €15.50 adults; €13.50 seniors and students; €10.50 children 6–18; €6 children under 5; €40–€45 families. June–Aug daily 10am–6pm; May and Sept daily 1–6pm; Mar–Apr, and public holidays 1–6pm. Last admission 1 hr. before closing. Closed Oct–Feb.

Ross Castle ★ CASTLE   Just outside Killarney Town, this 15th-century fortress still guards the edge of the Lower Lake. Built by the O'Donoghue chieftains, the castle was the last stronghold in Munster to surrender to Cromwell's forces in 1652. But it could not withstand time and the English army: All that remains of it today is a tower house surrounded by a fortified *bawn* (walled garden) with rounded turrets. The tower has been furnished in the style of the late 16th and early 17th centuries. The tours are a little overlong for the amount of information there actually is to impart, but it's worth it to see inside. Luckily, you can wander the grounds at leisure. In good weather, the best way to reach the castle is via a lakeside walk (it's 3km/2 miles from Killarney). From the castle, you can also take boat tours of the lake (see p. 299).

Ross Rd., signposted from N71 (Ring of Kerry Rd.). www.heritageireland.ie. ℗ **064/663-5851.** Admission €5 adults; €4 seniors; €3 students and children; €13 families. Mar to mid-Nov daily 10am–5pm. No photography on tour.

Torc Waterfall ★★ NATURE SITE   A walk through sylvan woods, populated with red deer, brings you to this popular beauty spot. The 18m

What's in a Name: MacGillycuddy's Reeks

This marvelously named mountain range just west of Killarney is quite a sight to behold. Formed of red sandstone, the mountains were gradually shaved down by glaciers until the peaks reached the gentle shape they hold today. The name, however, sounds anything but dignified. It may help to know that the mountains were named after an ancient and noble clan that once predominated in this area, the Mac Gilla Machudas, and the word "reek" is an old Irish term for a peaked hill.

(60-ft.) falls are impressive, and well worth the 5-minute walk from the dedicated parking lot on the Ring of Kerry Road. More strenuous but even more rewarding is the climb up the 100 or so steps next to the Falls, which take you up to **Friar's Glen**—so-called because it was a hideout for priests during Cromwell's invasion—with its sweeping views across the Killarney Lakes. The river that feeds the Falls rises on a mountainside a few miles away; the source is evocatively known as the Devil's Punchbowl.

Off N71, about 1.5km (¾ mile) S of Muckross House (in the direction of Kenmare), Killarney.

OTHER ATTRACTIONS IN THE KILLARNEY AREA

Aghadoe Cathedral ★ RUINS/RELIGIOUS SITE   These evocative ruins look more like a crumbling parish church than a cathedral, but that's exactly what stood here until the hamlet of Aghadoe was sacked by the forces of Oliver Cromwell in 1652. Ivy grows along a roofless nave, and decaying stone walls give way to a hillside graveyard. The tiny round tower, a few yards away, is the sole remnant of a monastery dating from 1027. Adjacent to the ruins is a viewpoint with breathtaking views over the Lower Lake, 1.6km (1 mile) away. Squint and you can also see Ross Castle on the far shore. There's a small (free) parking lot next to Aghadoe Heights Hotel (p. 300), just across the street. It's worth booking afternoon tea at the hotel—the dining room has extraordinary views of the lake. And the scones and cakes are to die for.

About 5km (3 miles) NW of Killarney off N22/L2019; Ard Na Be Rd., Aghadoe. Follow signs for Aghadoe Heights. Free admission. Daily dawn–dusk.

Killarney Water Bus ★ BOAT TOURS   From the harbor at **Ross Castle ★** (see above), the *MV Pride of the Lakes* takes you on an hour-long waterborne cruise. The covered boat ride is a little on the touristy side, but the views of the park from the lake are gorgeous. You can also take a tour that combines a lake cruise with a "jaunting car" ride around the park. *Tip:* You can get to the pier by Ross Castle on a free shuttle bus from Killarney town center. It leaves Scotts Street (by the junction with E. Avenue Rd.) a quarter of an hour before each sailing—check in advance to see if the shuttle is operating. Lake cruises are strictly limited to 80 people, so you may want to book ahead at busy times—but be sure to bring a printout of the confirmation or they won't let you board.

The Pier, Ross Castle, Ross Rd., off N71 (Ring of Kerry Rd.), Killarney. www.killarney laketours.ie. © **064/663 2638.** €12 adults; €10 seniors, €6 children under 12. Mar–Oct daily 11am, 12:30, 2:30, and 4pm. Times may change according to weather.

Knockreer Estate ★ GARDENS The grand old house that once stood here burned down in the early 20th century; what you see today is a modern building of the same name on the same site, which serves as the park's education center. Still, the estate's lovely old gardens remain, with 200-year-old trees setting off sweet wildflowers and azaleas to fragrant effect. A signposted walk takes you past beautiful views of the Lower Lake and the valley; a pathway leads down to the River Deenagh. Main access to Knockreer is through Deenagh Lodge Gate, opposite St. Mary's Cathedral in Killarney town.

Main entrance on Cathedral Place, off New St., Killarney. Free admission.

The Meeting of the Waters ★ NATURE SITE One of the most tranquil spots in Killarney National Park (and not to be confused with the more famous place with the same name in County Wicklow; see p. 201), this is where the Upper, Middle, and Lower lakes converge. You can hike from Muckross House (about 5km/3 miles), or park at the unmarked lot about 1.6km (1 mile) south of the Torc Waterfall (p. 298) parking area on the main Ring of Kerry Road. From here, the walk down a signposted path takes about 15 minutes, although "unofficial" side paths also lead you to the shore at different points. These can give you just as lovely views, and be free of people, but take care—the ground is uneven in places. Good, sturdy walking shoes are recommended.

Off N71, about 2.4km (1½ miles) S of Muckross House, Killarney.

St. Mary's Cathedral ★ CATHEDRAL If you think this limestone cathedral looks more Castle Dracula than local church, it may be because New Street was once the home of Bram Stoker, who spent summers in Killarney while he was a student at Trinity College Dublin. Officially known as the Catholic Church of St. Mary of the Assumption, it's designed in the Gothic Revival style and laid out in the shape of a cross. Construction began in 1842, was interrupted by the Famine, and concluded in 1855 (although the towering spire wasn't added until 1912).

Cathedral Place, off New St. © **064/663-1014.** Free admission. Daily 9am–6pm.

WHERE TO STAY IN KILLARNEY

Expensive

Aghadoe Heights ★★★ Luxurious, welcoming, and with one of the best views in Ireland, this is among the country's top spa hotels. Perched on a hill to the north of Killarney Town, this modernist building boasts floor-to-ceiling windows that take in the full, glorious panorama of Lough

Views of Lough Leane from a lakeside room in the Aghadoe Heights hotel.

Leane in Killarney National Park. (In winter, an atmospheric fluke can mean that you're literally above the clouds here, an effect that's nothing short of fairy tale.) The **Lake Room** (p. 305) serves French-influenced seasonal Irish cuisine with an emphasis on fresh seafood in an elegant atmosphere. Alternatively, you can graze on lighter fare in the adjacent lounge and piano bar. When you're not out sightseeing, take a relaxing break in the opulent **Voya** spa and thermal suite. The staff is, to a person, delightful. Take time to explore the ethereal ruins of **Aghadoe Cathedral,** directly across the street from the hotel (p. 299).

About 5km (3 miles) NW of Killarney, signposted off N22; Ard Na Be Rd., Aghadoe. www.aghadoeheights.com. ℂ **064/663-1766.** 74 units. €230–€500 double, €499–€650 suite. Free parking. Rates include breakfast. Spa and dinner, bed-and-breakfast packages available. **Amenities:** 2 restaurants; bar; pool; room service; spa; tennis court; Wi-Fi (free).

Cahernane House ★★ A neo-Gothic mansion on the outskirts of Killarney National Park, Cahernane is a luxurious retreat. The decor is authentically grandiose: Public areas have the feel of a traditional gentlemen's club, filled with antique furniture, stag heads on the wall, and the scent of a peat fire hanging heavy in the air. Guest rooms are more modern, though no less elegant, and some bathrooms have deep claw-foot tubs. Many of the rooms have private patios. The house has two restaurants: the excellent, formal **Herbert Restaurant,** which has beautiful views of two mountain ranges; and the more relaxed **Cellar Bar,** where you can take lighter meals among the beautifully lit arches of an old wine cellar. Check the website for special offers, including dinner, bed-and-breakfast deals.

Muckross Rd. www.cahernane.com. ☎ **064/663-1895.** 38 units. €170–€390 double, €270–€420 suite. Free parking. Rates include breakfast. **Amenities:** Restaurant; bar; room service; Wi-Fi (free). Closed Jan–Feb.

The Europe ★★★   Tucked away at the edge of the Lakes of Killarney, and with splendid lake and hill views from every floor, the Europe is widely seen as one of the best hotels in Ireland. The modern white building looks plain from the outside, but inside it is exceptional. Guest rooms are spacious, most overlooking the glorious Lakes of Killarney. Beds are enormously comfortable, and rooms are quiet. The hotel has two dining options: the gastropub-like **Brasserie** and the elegant **Panorama,** with its jaw-dropping views and highly rated five-star French-influenced cuisine. There are numerous lounges where you can sip tea, read a book, savor a whiskey. Downstairs, you can soak in the indoor/outdoor pool at the award-winning spa while taking in more lake and mountain views or walk right down to the lake's edge. This is one of our favorites.

Fossa Rd. www.theeurope.com. ☎ **064/667-1300.** 187 units. €300–€520 double, €800–€1,900 suite. 2-night minimum stay in high season. Free parking. **Amenities:** 2 restaurants; bar; room service; spa; gym; Wi-Fi (free).

Killarney Park ★★   Conveniently located in the center of town, the lemon-yellow, five-story building has appealing arched attic windows. Rooms are not huge, but they're comfortable and up to date. Premium rooms are larger and have king beds and separate seating areas. Afternoon tea is popular with visitors and locals alike. The **Park Restaurant** offers upscale, French-influenced Irish cuisine in an elegant atmosphere. On cool nights, open fires bring warmth to the dining room. The **Elemis spa** is an oasis with an indoor pool and outdoor hot tubs overlooking the hills outside the town. Indulge in a treatment if you can.

East Ave. www.killarneyparkhotel.ie. ☎ **064/663-5555.** 67 units. €210–€480 double, €520–€1,500 suite. Free parking. Breakfast not included in lower rates. **Amenities:** Restaurant; bar; room service; spa; Wi-Fi (free).

Moderate

Earls Court House ★★   Just outside the center of Killarney, on a quiet street with views of the mountains, Earls Court House is a pleasingly old-fashioned kind of B&B. Guest rooms are simple but pleasant, featuring polished wood furniture and buttermilk-colored walls. A few have four-poster beds and Jacuzzi baths. American visitors also take note: It has ice machines! (Very few hotels in Europe do.) You can have afternoon tea in one of the two guest lounges, and optional light suppers are offered.

Woodlawn Rd. www.killarney-earlscourt.ie. ☎ **064/663-4009.** 24 units. €94–€185 double. Free parking. Rates include breakfast. 2-night minimum summer weekends. **Amenities:** Library; Wi-Fi (free).

spa life, **IRISH STYLE**

It's fair to say Ireland is blessed with more than a few top-rated spas—and some of the top spas cluster around Kenmare and Killarney. The best spas use the beautiful natural settings to spectacular effect and borrow their treatments from the Irish countryside. Everything from Irish spring water to peat mud and local river stones are used to coax forth beauty from tired, work-dulled skin and hair. None of these spas are cheap, but they're a wonderful way to treat yourself on the road.

All guests at the **Aghadoe Heights Hotel & Spa** ★★★ outside Killarney are welcome to spend an hour in its exquisite thermal suite for the relatively small fee of €15. With a wide array of steam rooms, saunas, tropical showers, cooling rooms, and hot tubs, that's a luxuriant 60 minutes. Sample one of the spa's massages or facials. Treatments range from about €90 to €165.

The **Easanna Spa** at the **Sheen Falls Lodge,** off N71, Kenmare (www.sheen fallslodge.ie; ☏ **064/664-1600**), features a pool shaped like a flower, each petal forming a kind of relaxation space. You can have a hot stone massage or facial and then float off in total relaxation. Room rates here start at around €455 in high season. Treatments range from about €85 to €130.

The spa at the **Killarney Park Hotel,** off East Avenue in the center of Killarney (www.killarneyparkhotel.ie; ☏ **064/663-5555**), is a modern, peaceful oasis, with a soothing pool and such exotic treatments as the thousand flower detox wrap, in which you are soaked in green tea balm and wrapped up cozily while it gets to work, or the lime and ginger salt

scrub, designed to revitalize tired skin. Rooms here start at around €250 (not including breakfast). Treatments range from about €80 to €145.

The **Sámas spa** in the elegant **Park Hotel Kenmare,** Shelbourne Street, Kenmare (www.parkkenmare.com; ☏ **064/664-1200**), has won awards for its unique design. You can soak in the warm spa pool while gazing out over the mountains nearby. Spend an hour relaxing in the thermal suite (rock sauna, ice fountain, tropical mist shower), before moving on to your facial, wrap, or massage. Unlike the other spas here, this thermal suite is strictly for spa guests only, but they sometimes make exceptions when it's not too busy. Rooms start at about €310; treatments range from around €125 to €200.

The artfully lit **ESPA spa** in the **Europe** hotel (p. 302) offers exquisite views of the lake and the hills from the indoor/outdoor pool. There's a full thermal suite to steam your cares away, and the massages and facials here earn raves from regulars. Rooms start at about €300; treatments range from €125 to €390.

Friars Glen ★★★   Nestled in the cleft of a lush and verdant glen inside Killarney National Park, this delightful B&B could hardly be friendlier or better run. Hosts John and Mary (and their two dogs) welcome guests like old friends; they really take pride in their region, and love to help visitors plan explorations of the park and the Ring of Kerry. They will organize tours on your behalf and can even provide babysitting in the evenings with a bit of notice. The building looks like an old farmhouse, but is actually contemporary and very well-designed, with exposed stone. Ask for a room with a view; the vistas across the surrounding glen are inspiring, and deer sometimes visit the garden.

Mangerton Rd., Muckross. www.friarsglen.ie. © **064/663-7500.** 10 units. From €115–€130 double. Free parking. Rates include breakfast. **Amenities:** Wi-Fi (free).

Killarney Plaza ★   This large, modern hotel couldn't have a better location if you like to be in the thick of the action—it's right in the middle of Killarney town center. The accommodations are functional, contemporary, and comfortable rather than luxurious—think U.S. chain hotel and you're close enough. (Indeed, this place is big with tour groups, from the U.S. and elsewhere.) The buffet breakfast offers a vast selection, and there are two in-house restaurants—although being this centrally located in Killarney, you're hardly short of choice at your doorstep.

Town Centre, Killarney. www.killarneyplaza.com. © **064/662-1111.** 198 units. €150–€250 double; €215–€320 suites. Free parking. Rates include breakfast. **Amenities:** 2 restaurants; 3 bars; pool; spa; Wi-Fi (free).

Larkinley Lodge ★★   A great option just a few blocks from the center of Killarney, Larkinley Lodge is a modern B&B in a beautifully converted townhouse. Toni and Danny Sheehan are gregarious hosts with an eye for detail. Guest rooms are small but just the right mix of traditional and modern, with minimal clutter and muted color schemes. Triple rooms only cost a little more than doubles. Don't miss the home-baked scones at breakfast. The location is only about a 10-minute walk into central Killarney, not far from great pubs and restaurants, yet in a quiet neighborhood where you can escape the evening street noise.

Lewis Rd. www.larkinley.ie. © **064/622-2447.** 6 units. Doubles from €120. Free parking. Rates include breakfast. **Amenities:** Wi-Fi (free).

The Ross ★★   This charming small hotel in the middle of Killarney packs lots of personality into four walls. Within easy walking distance to most of the town's sights and shops, it's beautifully designed, especially downstairs in the dramatic **Cellar Restaurant,** a great place to stop for dinner, and the snazzy **Pink Lounge,** which prides itself on offering 50 types of gin. If you're looking for a coffee or a light bite, the relaxed **Lane Café Bar** is fabulous and bright. Beds are comfortable, and rooms are big enough to easily accommodate families with kids; many have views of the town. Room decor is simple but pleasant.

East Ave. www.theross.ie. © **064/663-1855.** 29 units. €180–€250 double. Rates include breakfast. **Amenities:** Restaurant; bar; Wi-Fi (free).

WHERE TO EAT IN KILLARNEY

A bustling tourist town, Killarney offers lots of food options. In addition to the restaurants listed below, there are ample places to stop for a quick coffee, a light meal, or a freshly made sandwich. The **Lane Café Bar** at the Ross Hotel (theross.ie; see above) is a stylish, airy bar and coffee shop with a good menu of salads, sandwiches, and burgers, ideal for lunch.

Their desserts are something else—try the Smores Skillet, if you dare. For your morning caffeine, along with something a little special, head straight to **Jam** (Old Market Lane; ℂ 064/662-1444). The coffee here is the best in town, and the scones, croissants, quiches, and tarts are perfect for breakfast or lunch on the go. In the summer, don't miss out on **Murphy's Ice Cream** (Main St.; www.murphysicecream.ie)—it's one of the best things Ireland has to offer on a sunny day.

Expensive

The Lake Room ★★★ MODERN IRISH   The main restaurant at the **Aghadoe Heights Hotel** (p. 300) overlooks the Lower Lake, a special-occasion view if ever there was one—with sumptuous cooking to match. Local seafood is, of course, a specialty, with a constantly changing menu that might include poached sea trout with caviar. For a meatier choice, try the Kerry beef, cooked to perfection, perhaps finished with black currant jus. The wine list is excellent. While this undoubtedly qualifies as fine dining, the friendly staff add a relaxed air.

At Aghadoe Heights Hotel, about 5km (3 miles) NW of Killarney, signposted off N22. www.aghadoeheights.com/dining/the-lake-room. ℂ **064/663-1766.** Fixed-price menu: 2 courses €59, 4 courses €69. Daily 6–9pm. Smart casual dress. No children after 7pm.

The Panorama ★★★ INTERNATIONAL   The glorious views of Lough Leane and the McGillycuddy Reeks at this aptly named restaurant inside the Europe hotel are not the main draw, but they certainly come a close second. The primary draw is the perfectly prepared European/Irish cuisine. Everything is locally sourced and might include something like foie gras mousse with raisins, spiced grapes, and truffle meringue; turbot with squash puree; or lamb and bean cassoulet. The wine list is unsurprisingly excellent. A place to celebrate.

At the Europe Hotel, Fossa Rd. www.theeurope.com/panorama-restaurant. ℂ **064/667-1300.** Entrees €21–€39. Daily 7–9:30pm June–Aug; closed Sun Sept–May.

Moderate

Bricín ★★ IRISH   Located above a craft store on Killarney's main street, this is a long-standing favorite on the local dining scene. *Bricín* means "little trout" in Irish, and seafood is one of the strong points of the traditional Irish menu. Locally reared meat is also often on the menu, served with interesting sauces, such as supreme of chicken with thyme jus and cinnamon. It is the house specialty for which this place is renowned, however: boxty, a savory pancake stuffed with several different types of filling (see box on p. 139). The dining room is an old-fashioned kind of place, complete with stained-glass windows and an open fireplace. *Tip:* Bricín serves a great-value early-bird menu (€23 for two courses) from 6pm until 6:45pm.

26 High St. www.bricin.ie ℂ **064/663-4902.** Fixed-price menus €30–€38. Tues–Sat 6–9:30pm. Closed early Jan to early Mar.

Rozzers ★★★ MODERN IRISH   This is a popular spot with a simple menu combining the best local Irish ingredients with classic French influences—Kerry beef might be served with a celeriac gratin wild mushroom fricassee, sweet carrot puree and a port and wine sauce. There's often roast rack of Ring of Kerry lamb as well as oysters, salmon and monkfish, or chateaubriand with Irish beef for a treat. Décor is old-style—the building is an old Edwardian rectory from 1838—but the country house hotel setting is charming. You can also stay over, there are 23 bedrooms, doubles cost from €160–€230, check for dinner and B&B packages.

At the Killeen House Hotel, Aghadoe. ℭ **064/663-1711.** Fixed-priced menu: 2 courses €39.50, 3 courses €49.50. Daily (Apr–Nov) seatings at 6:30 and 8:30pm. Check website for dinner and B&B specials.

Inexpensive

Kate Kearney's Cottage ★ INTERNATIONAL   Unofficially considered the gateway to the Gap of Dunloe, this cheerful pub is hugely popular. It's more than a little touristy, but the stick-to-your-ribs pub food is pretty tasty. The menu offers steaks, burgers, and bistro-style classics, best washed down with a restorative pint. Semi-regular "Irish Nights" offer a package of dinner and a show of traditional music; call or check the website for upcoming dates. The pub is named after a feisty local woman who carved out a reputation as a maker of illegal *poitín* (moonshine) that she called Mountain Dew.

Gap of Dunloe, Beaufort, signposted from N72 (Ring of Kerry Rd.). www.kate kearneyscottage.com. ℭ **064/664-4146.** Entrees €14–€20. Daily noon–11pm (food until 8pm).

Quinlan's Seafood Bar ★ SEAFOOD   With a seafood counter up front selling right off the boat, the fare here is simple and straightforward. Fish and chips, with a light batter and a giant portion of chunky fries, come hot from the fryer. Have it with mushy peas, and you're deep into a true Irish dinner. If you fancy more sophisticated dishes, the menu obliges, with scallops in butter, boiled Irish lobster, lemon sole in a buttery sauce, or prawns so fresh they all but swim off the plate. Also run by the Quinlan brothers is the slightly more upscale **The Mad Monk** (21/22 Plunkett St.), serving delicious Portmagee crab claws, Dingle Bay squid, and Atlantic prawns as well as fish and chips and wine.

77 High St. www.kerryfish.com/seafoodbar-killarney. ℭ **064/662-0666.** Entrees €10–€18. Sun–Thurs 1–8pm; Fri–Sat 1–9pm.

KILLARNEY SHOPPING

Shopping hours in Killarney are usually Monday to Saturday 9am to 6pm, but from May through September many stores are open every day until 9 or 10pm. Although Killarney has more souvenir and craft shops than you can shake a shillelagh at, here are a few of the best.

Aran Sweater Market ★   Rows of soft wool sweaters, skirts, hats, and scarves in colors ranging from traditional cream to bright blues, reds, and ochre await in this town center store. All are Irish made, most from pure wool. College Square. www.aransweatermarket.com. © **064/662-3102.**

Bricín ★ This little craft store sells traditional ceramics, jewelry, and clothes. Many of the wares on sale here were made locally. Upstairs is one of the town's best restaurants (p. 305). 26 High St. © **064/663-4902.**

The Dungeon Bookshop ★ One of Killarney's most popular independent bookstores, the Dungeon stocks a good range of secondhand books. 99 College St. © **064/663-6536.**

Killarney Art Gallery ★★ This gallery showcases work from respected Irish artists as well as new and local talent. 32 Main St. www.killarneyartgallery.com. © **087/276-7999.**

Mr. McGuire's Olde Sweet Shop ★★ This charming traditional candy store is a delight for kids of all ages. Candy is measured out from tall jars into little bags, or you can pick out some very giftable packages straight from the shelf. Closed weekdays in winter. College Square. © **064/667-1764.**

Muckross Craft Centre ★★ Part of the Walled Garden, a small shopping complex on the grounds of **Muckross House** ★★ (p. 297), this place has a good stock of Irish crafts, pottery, clothing, cards, and quality gifts—and many items are made locally. Muckross House, Muckross Rd. www.muckross-house.ie. © **064/667-0147.**

KILLARNEY AFTER DARK

The mainstay of nightlife in Killarney is the lively pub scene. The town has more than its fair share of good places to enjoy a pint and some live traditional music. All of these places can get pretty packed on a busy summer's night—so come early to stand a chance of getting a seat.

Charlie Foley's ★★ Every trip to Killarney should include at least one pint at Charlie Foley's. The old pub is a local institution, one of the places in town where you might actually meet Irish people instead of tourists. Take a seat in the snug or at the bar and wait for the local gossip to flow. New St. © **064/663-4311.**

Killarney Grand ★★ This hugely popular pub is one of the best places in the region to hear traditional Irish music—and for free. Nightly live sessions start at 9pm; after 11pm it turns into a nightclub. The atmosphere gets pretty raucous, and the crowds can really pack in here (definitely standing-room-only), but the music is always good. Some of the biggest names in Irish music have played here over the years; you never know when you might catch the next big thing. A "neat" dress code is enforced at the door—meaning you don't have to wear your best duds, but don't walk in looking too scruffy, either. Main St. www.killarneygrand.com. © **064/663-1159.**

The Laurels ★ Another very popular pub for live music, here the traditional music sessions take place several times a week, usually starting at around 9pm. The pub also serves good food, including stone-baked pizzas. Main St. www.thelaurelspub.com. ℰ **064/663-1149.**

O'Connors ★★ At this traditional-feeling pub, the program of live music is extensive, with bands playing every night—scheduled and, occasionally, spontaneous. It doesn't stop there, either; you might catch a play, some standup comedy, or even a spoken-word event. 7 High St. ℰ **064/663-9424.**

Tatler Jack ★ For Gaelic sports fans, this is the place to go. Football and hurling matches are shown on big-screen TVs, and traditional music is played on many nights in summer. Expect to find a raucous atmosphere. 23–29 Plunkett St. ℰ **064/663-2361.**

OUTDOOR PURSUITS IN THE RING OF KERRY

CYCLING   Killarney National Park, with its lakeside and forest pathways, trails, and roads, is a paradise for bikers. Bike rental charges average around €15 to €35 per day, €85 to €95 per week. Bicycles can be rented from **Killarney Rent-a-Bike,** Lower New Street or 49 High St. (www.killarneyrentabike.com; ℰ **064/663-1282**).

FISHING   Fishing for salmon and brown trout in Killarney's unpolluted lakes and rivers is a popular pastime. Brown trout fishing is free on the lakes, but a permit is necessary for the rivers Flesk and Laune. Salmon fishing anywhere requires a permit. Permits, tackle, bait, rod rental, and other fishing gear can be obtained from **O'Neill's,** 6 Plunkett St. (ℰ **064/663-1970**). The shop (which was started in 1947) also arranges boat rentals and *ghillies* (fishing guides) for around €100 to €150 per day on the Killarney Lakes, leaving from Ross Castle.

GOLF   Overlooking the Atlantic Ocean, on the southwestern part of the Ring of Kerry, the par-72 **Waterville Golf Links,** Waterville (www.water villegolflinks.ie; ℰ **066/947-4102**), is considered one of the best courses in Ireland. The 6,200-yard course also has the distinction of containing a "Mass Hole," a relic of the days when Catholic Mass had to be celebrated in secrecy. Greens fees are €250 April to October, €75 November to March. Daily second rounds are €100 to €110; early or late €150 and November to March €75. Visitors are always welcome at the twin 18-hole championship courses of the **Killarney Golf & Fishing Club,** Killorglin Road (N72), Fossa (www. killarneygolfclub.ie; ℰ **064/663-1034**), 5km (3 miles) west of the town center. Widely praised as one of the most scenic golf settings in the world, it has two 18-hole courses—Killeen and Mahony's Point—with gorgeous lake and mountain layouts. There is also a 9-hole course, **Lackabane.** Greens fees are €45 to €150, depending on the course and the time of day.

HORSEBACK RIDING   Many trails in the Killarney area are suitable for horseback riding. Hiring a horse costs from €50 per hour at **Killarney Riding Stables,** N72, Ballydowney (www.killarneyridingstables.com; ℰ **064/663-1686**). Lessons and weeklong trail rides can also be arranged.

Kenmare

Kenmare is a sweet little town with flower boxes at every window, lots of restaurants, and plenty of places to stay. Originally called Neidin (pronounced Nay-*deen,* meaning "little nest" in Irish), Kenmare is indeed a little nest of verdant foliage and colorful buildings nestled between the River Roughty and Kenmare Bay. And while it certainly gets more than its fair share of visitors in the summer, Kenmare isn't as frenetic as Killarney. If you crave a quieter life, this can make it a more pleasant place to stay—especially if you have the freedom of a car.

EXPLORING KENMARE

Kenmare Druid Circle ★ PREHISTORIC SITE On a small hill near the market square, this large Bronze Age druid stone circle is magnificently intact, featuring 15 standing stones arranged around a central boulder that still bears signs (circular holes, a shallow dent at the center) of having been used in ceremonies. To find it, walk down to the market square and follow signs on the left side of the road. There's no visitor center and no admission fee; it's just sitting in a small paddock.

Off the Square, Kenmare.

At Kenmare's annual Fair Day, every August 15, local livestock, horses, and sheepdogs for sale throng the town streets.

The Best Drive in Ireland?

It takes about 45 minutes to drive between Killarney and Kenmare, but it's one of the most picturesque routes in the country. It's easy enough to find—just follow signs for N71 through Killarney National Park, taking care not to get onto the quicker but infinitely less romantic back roads instead (your GPS may try and take you this way by default). If you're setting out from Kenmare, the drive begins along gentle foothills; from Killarney, it's sun-dappled, sylvan woods. Either way, before long you hit wide, sweeping vistas of lakes and mountains, guaranteed to catch your breath and steal your heart. Fortunately, there are plenty of places to pull over and gawp at the scenery, including **Ladies View**—so-called because it was, apparently, a favorite of the ladies-in-waiting to Queen Victoria. The viewpoint has a handy **cafe** (www.ladiesview.com) with a solid menu (homemade soups, Guinness stew, fresh pastries), a craft shop, bar, and a rooftop alfresco terrace for panoramic views. All of the best viewpoints have small, free parking areas, so don't be tempted to pull over illegally on the narrow road—and don't forget to leave time to take all those dreamy pictures.

Kenmare Farmer's Market ★ MARKET   If you're visiting midweek, be sure to check out this small but lively open-air market held every Wednesday in Kenmare's main square. The emphasis is on food from small, artisan producers from across the region. Traders may come here from quite far afield to sell their wares, although the bulk of what's for sale is locally sourced. It's a fun market to browse your way through.

The Square. Kenmare. Wed 10am–4pm. Some stalls may close in bad weather.

Seafari ★★ BOAT TOUR   A good option for families, this 2- to 3-hour cruise aboard a 19m (65-ft.) covered boat makes for an engaging introduction to Kenmare Bay and its wildlife—specifically the dolphins, sea otters, and gray seals you'll most likely see frolicking nearby. Boats depart from the pier next to the Kenmare suspension bridge. The family ticket includes coffee, tea, a lollipop for kids, and a glass of rum for the grownups. Reservations are recommended.

3 The Pier, Kenmare. www.seafariireland.com. (✆ **064/664-2059**. €25 adults; €20 students; €15 teenagers; €12.50 children 11 and under; €60 families and then €7.50 per extra child. Apr–Oct 2 sailings daily; call or check website for departure times.

Tom Cream Brewery ★★ BREWERY TOUR   The famous Irish Antarctic explorer Tom Crean was from Annascaul on the Dingle Peninsula in County Kerry, and his granddaughter Aileen, a trained chef, set up this brewery, restaurant, and guesthouse. On the 1-hour tour you'll learn all about how the beer is brewed and the family history of exploration before sampling some of the brew. You can also stay overnight in a room above the pub; doubles start at €80 (✆ **064/664-1589**).

Main St., Kenmare. www.tomcreanbrewerykenmare.ie. (✆ **087/161-2929**. €15 adults; €12 seniors and students; €6 under-18s; €35 family. Tours Mar–Oct Fri–Mon 3pm; book online.

WHERE TO STAY IN KENMARE
Expensive

Park Hotel Kenmare ★★★   This circa-1897 hotel is an elegant option. Large, traditionally decorated rooms with open fireplaces, grand oil paintings, and imposing staircases fill the ground floor. All around are spectacular views of the lake and green hills. This is a formal place—the staff is polite but not snobbish and will help arrange anything you need. Bedrooms are quiet and spacious; some have four-poster beds. There's a 12-seater cinema where you can watch a movie of your choice from the hotel library. The restaurant has lavish modern European à la carte menus or a seven-course tasting menu for €110. But the extraordinary **Sámas spa** (p. 303) might prove so distracting that you forget to do anything else at all.

Kenmare High St., Kenmare. www.parkkenmare.com. ✆ **064/664-1200.** 46 units. €310–€555 double. Free parking. Rates include breakfast. **Amenities:** Restaurant; bar; cinema; golf course; pool; room service; spa; Wi-Fi (free).

Sheen Falls Lodge ★★★   This elegant hideaway on the River Sheen outside Kenmare was built in the 17th century as a nobleman's hunting lodge, but now it is a hotel more famous for its massages than its venison. Expect spacious rooms with luxurious decor (all have views of the grounds or the dappled river). **The Falls** restaurant offers exceptional Irish-influenced European cuisine in formal surroundings. The endless grounds offer opportunities for horseback riding, shooting, fishing, golf, and tennis. You can have high tea in the sun lounge or champagne in the cocktail bar, but it's the spa that most people rave about. Try one of the exclusive treatments, then soak in the heated pool. Bliss.

Knockduragh, Kenmare. www.sheenfallslodge.ie. ✆ **064/664-1600.** 66 units. €255–€550 double; €475–€1200 suite. Free parking. **Amenities:** Restaurant; bar; cinema; golf course; pool; tennis; horseback riding; room service; spa; Wi-Fi (free).

Moderate

Brook Lane Hotel ★★   Just a mile outside of Kenmare, this hotel doesn't look like much from the outside but offers a lot on the inside. Attractively designed rooms made cozy by underfloor heating, plus big, comfortable beds topped with soft linens, are just the answer after a long day of exploring. The in-house **Casey's** bar and restaurant is run by the outstanding team behind sister restaurant **No. 35** (p. 313), so no need to go out for dinner. Handy, quiet, and affordable.

Sneem Rd., Kenmare. www.brooklanehotel.com. ✆ **064/664-2077.** 22 units. From €135–€205 double. **Amenities:** Restaurant; bar; Wi-Fi (free).

Sallyport House ★★   This peaceful 1930s mansion-turned-B&B in Kenmare is filled with antiques, lending a touch of old-school luxury to its already abundant charms. Guest rooms are comfortable and spacious, and a few have four-poster beds. The house is surrounded by countryside, and some rooms look out over an idyllic lake. Breakfasts are delicious, and the service is warm and accommodating without ever being intrusive.

Shelbourne St., Kenmare (just S of junction with Pier Rd.). www.sallyporthouse.com. ☎ **064/664-2066.** 5 units. From €145–€155 double. Open May–Oct. Free parking. Rates include breakfast. **Amenities:** Wi-Fi (free).

Shelburne Lodge ★★ This 18th-century house was originally the country home of William Petty, the Lord Shelburne (1737–1805), a Dublin-born landowner who was responsible for building much of the modern town of Kenmare. He later became Prime Minister of Great Britain and Ireland, and in 1783 he signed the Treaty of Paris, which formally ended the American War of Independence. His home is in good hands, thanks to hosts Tom and Maura Foley. Rooms are decorated with antique furniture, huge beds, and color schemes of cream and peach. Public areas have a similar feel. The center of Kenmare is only a short walk away.

Cork Rd., Kenmare. www.shelburnelodge.com. ☎ **064/664-1013.** 9 units. €140–€170 double. Free parking. Rates include breakfast. Open 7 days Easter–Sept; weekends only in Oct; closed Nov–Easter. **Amenities:** Wi-Fi (free).

Inexpensive

Rockcrest House ★★ This is a typical Irish B&B where you get a homely welcome from hosts Marian and David. It's a 5-minute walk from the town center—enough to be close to restaurants and shops but also to enjoy a rural feel in a quiet country setting. Rooms are spacious if basic, and the full Irish breakfasts will set you up for the whole day.

Gortmullen, Kenmare. www.visit-kenmare.com. ☎ **064/664-1248.** 6 units. €85–€99 double. Free parking. Rates include breakfast. Open all year. **Amenities:** Wi-Fi (free).

WHERE TO EAT IN KENMARE

Kenmare is a lovely place to linger over a cup of tea or a light lunch, and there are plenty of places to do just that. If you're looking for a hot breakfast or a chilled-out lunch, **Rookery Lane** (Bridge St.; www.rookerylane.ie) is a good spot for poached eggs, fluffy pancakes, and cinnamon buns. Burrito bowls are popular, and vegetarian options include vegan tacos and a Buddha bowl with potatoes, beetroot, hummus, lentil, kale, and pickled veg. (It also has four guest rooms; €120–€150 double.) Another terrific breakfast and lunch option, **Poffs** (New Rd.; ☎ 064/664-0645) serves sandwiches piled high with fixings. We love the scrambled eggs on toasted brioche. You can also eat your way around town with **Kenmare Foodie Tours** (www.kenmarefoodies.com), where local food enthusiast Karen Coakley introduces you to the town's food producers with some tasty samples over 2.5 to 3 hours. Tours are €65 and run every Wednesday in summer from around 10am.

Expensive

Anois ★★ IRISH Anois is popular with both locals and visitors for its relaxed dining in a casual atmosphere, with lots of small plates and sharing options. Bloody Mary oysters and seafood chowder are favorites. You might also find pan-seared scallops, seabass with creamy leeks and clam sauce, or a slow-cooked beef brisket with gratin dauphinois on the menu. If you still have room after that, desserts are tempting. There are also cheese options and a good selection of reasonably priced wines and ports by the glass.

Henry St., Kenmare. www.anoiskenmare.ie. © **064/664-1508.** Entrees €14–€20. Mar–Apr and Oct–Dec Thurs–Sat, June–Sept Wed–Sat 5:30–9pm. Closed Jan and Feb.

The Lime Tree ★★ MODERN IRISH This internationally praised restaurant in a charming historic building offers an elegant twist on Irish comfort food. The menu is smart and varied without being overly complicated, with plenty of locally sourced ingredients—black pudding from Sneem, salmon from Kenmare, County Kerry lamb. You might start with a "deconstructed prawn cocktail" with cognac-infused sauce, then go on to a baked filet of salmon with lemon crumb crust, or breast of free-range duck with a spicy ginger and rhubarb chutney. Try the crepes for dessert, served with pralines and a rich butterscotch sauce.

Shelbourne St., Kenmare. www.limetreerestaurant.com. © **064/664-1225.** Set menu: 2 courses €43, 3 courses €49. Thurs–Mon 6–9pm. Closed Tues–Wed.

Moderate

The Boathouse Bistro ★ BISTRO/SEAFOOD This casual seafood bistro at Dromquinna Manor has an outside seating area overlooking Kenmare Bay, making it perfect for a warm summer night. The menu serves dishes like pan-seared salmon or the house-special fishcakes with mango salsa. Or you could just have a burger and sea-salted French fries while you take in the wonderful view. This is a good stop for lunch on a sunny day, especially when the weather's fine and you can sit outside. It closes for much of the winter.

On N70, 5km (3 miles) W of Kenmare. www.dromquinnamanor.com. © **064/664-2889.** Entrees €16–€35. July–Aug daily 12:30–9pm; May–June and Sept Tues–Sun 12:30–9pm; Oct Thurs–Sun 12:30–9pm; Mar–Apr weekends 12:30–9pm. Closed Nov–Feb.

The Boathouse Bistro, at Dromquinna Manor.

No. 35 ★★ IRISH/INTERNATIONAL "Local produce" is a term you see a lot in the best restaurants, but this place really takes it a step further—all the meat it serves was reared on its own farm. The menu is short and simple; you might start with some pork sausages served with pumpkin puree, followed by catch of the day with smoked almonds or Irish duck with Jerusalem artichoke, hazelnut, and dill. The dining room is small, and this place can get packed, so reserve ahead.

35 Main St., Kenmare. www.no35 kenmare.com. 📞 **064/664-1559.** Dinner menu €39.95. Mon–Tues and Fri–Sun 5–9:30pm. Closed Wed and Thurs.

Inexpensive

Maison Gourmet ★ BAKERY A little touch of *la vie Parisienne* on the very un-French streets of

Maison Gourmet and its owners, Emma and Patrick Puech.

Kenmare, this artisan bakery serves freshly made sandwiches, salads, soups—and excellent coffee. The patisserie is so tempting it's hard even to walk past it without dreaming of a delicious slice of cake or tart. Eat in or take out.

26 Henry St., Kenmare. www.maisongourmetkenmare.com 📞 **064/664-1857.** All items €2–€17. Tues–Sun 8am–6pm.

Pyro ★ PIZZA This funky little pizza place is tucked away down a small alleyway, right next door to Anois (p. 312). And we do mean little—it has just a handful of tables, so this might be a better takeout option. The pizzas have quirky names like the "Pizza of Knowledge" (salmon, zucchini, and cream sauce) or the "Will Flog It" (smoked chicken, spinach, and barbecue sauce). Lots of veggie options.

Henry Court, off Henry St., Kenmare. www.pyro.ie. 📞 **064/664-8441.** Entrees €8–€14. Daily 4–9pm (Thurs–Sat Oct–Mar).

KENMARE SHOPPING

The Ring of Kerry has many good craft and souvenir shops, but those in and around Kenmare offer some of the best choices in terms of quality. Kenmare shops are open year-round, usually Monday to Saturday 9am to 6pm. From May to September, many shops remain open until 9 or 10pm, and some open on Sunday from noon to 5 or 6pm.

Avoca at Moll's Gap ★★ Creative, colorful, and with what must be one of the world's best appointed parking lots, this branch of Avoca is on a mountain pass just off the main Ring of Kerry Road, 10km (6 miles) north of Kenmare. Though quite small, it sells a good selection of the crafts, knitwear, and upscale knick-knacks for which the Wicklow-based company is famous. The cafe upstairs is also a great pit stop for a light lunch or cup of tea. Moll's Gap (on R568, signposted from main N71 Ring of Kerry Rd.). www.avoca.ie. ⓒ **064/663-4720.** Mon–Fri 10am–5:30pm; Sat–Sun 10am–6pm.

Lorge Chocolatier ★★★ Benoit Lorge makes exquisite artisanal chocolates in every form, from bars and boxes to truffles, hot chocolate, chocolate spreads, and nougat. They're wonderful creations, elegantly presented—the gift boxes are little works of art in themselves. Too bad their precious, tasty cargo must be eaten. All of it. Right now. 18 Henry St. and N71, Bonane. www.lorge.ie. ⓒ **064/667-9994.**

Quills Woollen Market ★ Housed in a delightfully multicolored row of shops in the center of Kenmare, this long-standing business specializes in traditional Irish knitwear—particularly heavy-knit Aran sweaters, coats, and cardigans. It also sells Irish tweeds, shawls, linens, and various decor pieces like plush sheepskin rugs. It's a great place to stock up on authentic souvenirs. Other branches of Quills are in Killarney, Glengarriff, Ballingeary, and Sneem. Main St. www.irishgiftsandsweaters. com. ⓒ **064/664-1078.**

SPORTS & OUTDOOR PURSUITS IN KENMARE

ADVENTURE SPORTS Eclipse Ireland, Blackwater Bridge, Kenmare (www.eclipseireland.com; ⓒ **064/668-2965**), offers a host of high-thrills activities and outdoor fun, including kayaking, archery, raft building, fishing, and trekking. See the website for the full list.

CYCLING You could conceivably cycle directly from Kenmare to Killarney National Park (about 13.2km/8½ miles), although the main Ring of Kerry Road is narrow, with sharp bends, and can get clogged with tour-bus traffic in summer. Ask for alternative cycling routes when you rent bikes, either from **Finnegan's Corner** at 37 Henry St., Kenmare (www.finneganscorner.com; ⓒ **064/664-1083**), or **Eclipse Ireland,** Blackwater Bridge, Kenmare (www.eclipseireland.com; ⓒ **064/668-2965**). Rates are around €20 per day.

KAYAKING & SUP Take a guided kayaking or SUP (stand-up paddleboarding) tour of Kenmare Bay with **Emerald Outdoors** (www.emerald outdoors.ie; ⓒ **083/031-7011**). On the 2.5-hour night kayaking tour, look for bioluminescent plankton lighting up the water beneath you as you paddle under the silhouette of the Caha mountains.

Driving the Ring of Kerry Road

Whether you're setting out from Kenmare or Killarney, it's best to follow the Ring of Kerry tourist route in a counterclockwise direction. This means that you'll begin by heading west out of Killarney on the N72 road. (The road number will change to N70 for most of the loop as it

You can drive either way along the Ring of Kerry, but we recommend a **counter-clockwise** route for the most spectacular views. Drivers of very large vehicles also stick to this direction in order to avoid bottlenecks on the perilously narrow bends. This all worked fine for years—until modern technology intervened with the spread of GPS technology and mapping apps. Now some drivers unfamiliar with the route are being sent by their devices in a clockwise direction, thus causing all sorts of chaos, including some of the worst traffic jams ever seen on the Ring. These problems are rare, but expect high traffic in the summer.

circumnavigates the Iveragh Peninsula; it becomes N71 when you swing back through Kenmare.) About 22km (16½ miles) northwest from Killarney is the next major stop: **Killorglin,** a smallish town that lights up in mid-August when it hosts a traditional horse, sheep, and cattle fair called **Puck Fair** (see box above). For the rest of the year, Killorglin is a pretty, quiet town, well worth a wander, with the River Laune running straight through the town center.

As you continue on what is now the N70, glimpses of Dingle Bay will soon appear on your right. **Carrantuohill,** Ireland's tallest mountain at 1,041m (3,414 ft.), is to your left, and bleak vistas of open bog land constantly come into view. Along this coast, the Ring winds around cliffs and the edges of mountains, often with nothing but the sea below—another reason you will probably average only 50kmph (31 mph), at best. As you travel along, you'll notice the remnants of many stone cottages dotting the fields along the way. Most date from the mid-19th-century Great Famine, when millions of people starved to death or were forced to emigrate. This area was particularly hard hit, with the Iveragh Peninsula alone losing three-quarters of its population.

Glenbeigh is next on the Ring, a sweet little seafront town with a sandy beach and streets lined with palm trees. Continue along the sea's edge to **Cahirsiveen,** where you can branch off the N70 onto R565 to visit the lovely seaside town of **Portmagee,** which is connected by a bridge to leafy **Valentia Island,** where you can visit the lighthouse (p. 320). In the 18th century, the Valentia harbor was notorious as a refuge for smugglers and privateers; it's said that John Paul Jones, the Scottish-born American naval officer in the War of Independence, also anchored here quite often.

From Valentia you can book a seat on a ferry to arguably the most magical site of the Ring of Kerry, an island just off its shore: **Skellig Michael ★★★** (p. 320), a rocky pinnacle towering over the sea, where medieval monks built a monastery in exquisite isolation. Today, the ruins of their church, reached by way of rambling stone staircases up the sides of cliffs at the edge of the cobalt sea, still convey a sense of deep spirituality. Seabirds nest here in abundance, and more than 20,000 pairs of gannets inhabit neighboring **Little Skellig** during the summer nesting season.

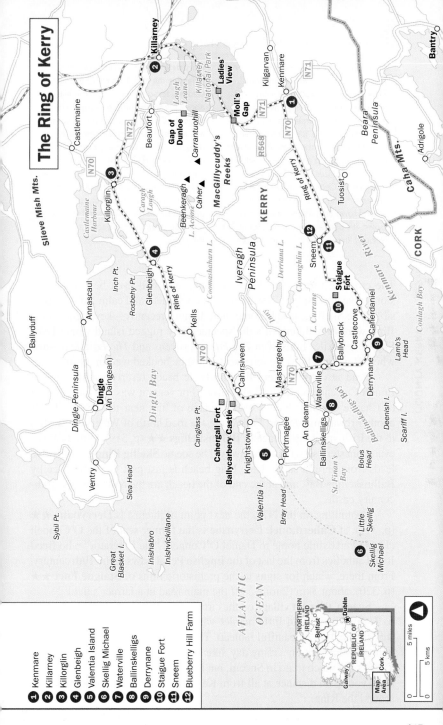

The Ring of Kerry

Slieve Mish Mts.

Castlemaine

N70

N72

Beaufort

Killarney

Gap of Dunloe

Carrantuohill

MacGillycuddy's Reeks

Beeneragh ▲

L. Acoose

Caher ▲

Coomashaharn L.

Iveragh Peninsula

KERRY

Killarney National Park

Lough Leane

Ladies' View

Moll's Gap

N71

Kilgarvan

Kenmare

R568

Ring of Kerry

N70

Tuosist

Beara Peninsula

Adrigole

Caha Mts.

CORK

Bantry

Kenmare River

Coulagh Bay

Kilgarvan

Killorglin

Caragh Lough

Caragh L.

Castlemaine Harbour

Dingle (An Daingean)

Dingle Peninsula

Dingle Bay

Annascaul

Ballyduff

Inch Pt.

Rossbehy Pt.

Glenbeigh

Kells

Cahirsiveen

Mastergeehy

N70

Cloonaghlin L.

Derriana L.

Sneem

Staigue Fort

Caherdaniel

Lamb's Head

Ballybrack

Castlecove

Derrynane

L. Currane

Inny

Ballybrack

Ballinskelligs Bay

Waterville

An Gleann

Portmagee

Ballinskelligs

Bolus Head

St. Finan's Bay

Deenish I.

Scariff I.

Knightstown

Valentia I.

Cahergall Fort

Ballycarbery Castle

Canglass Pt.

Bray Head

Little Skellig

Skellig Michael

ATLANTIC OCEAN

Sybil Pt.

Sea Head

Great Blasket I.

Inishabro

Inishvickillane

Ventry

① Kenmare
② Killarney
③ Killorglin
④ Glenbeigh
⑤ Valentia Island
⑥ Skellig Michael
⑦ Waterville
⑧ Ballinskelligs
⑨ Derrynane
⑩ Staigue Fort
⑪ Sneem
⑫ Blueberry Hill Farm

NORTHERN IRELAND

Belfast

REPUBLIC OF IRELAND

Galway

Dublin

Cork

Map Area

0   5 miles
0   5 kms

317

Killorglin: The Puck Stops Here

Sleepy little **Killorglin** wakes up every year on August 10, when the annual **Puck Fair** (www.puckfair.ie) incites a 3-day explosion of merrymaking and pageantry. One of Ireland's last remaining traditional fairs, it's technically an agricultural show; the apex of the event involves capturing a mountain goat (which symbolizes the *puka* or *puki,* a mischievous Celtic sprite), which is then declared "King Puck" and paraded around town on a throne, wearing a crown. It's bonkers, but quite a lot of fun. Nobody knows how it began, but one story dates to Cromwell's invasion of Ireland in the mid–17th century. English soldiers, foraging for food in the hills above the town, tried to capture a herd of goats. One goat escaped to Killorglin and alerted the villagers to mount a defense. Others say the fair is pre-Christian, connected with the Pagan feast of Lughnasa on August 1. As you cross the old stone bridge over the River Laune, look out for the whimsical statue of the goat on the eastern side—and know that it stands in honor of this town's love for the *puka.*

The crossing to the island can be rough and will even be canceled in stormy weather, so you'll want to visit on as clear and calm a day as possible. The Skelligs have become more famous recently—key parts of *Star Wars* were filmed here (it's the spectacularly rugged island where Luke Skywalker exiles himself in *The Force Awakens* and *The Last Jedi*—and where Rey finds him), so ferry seats must be booked well in advance.

Head next for **Waterville,** an idyllic beach resort located between Lough Currane and Ballinskelligs Bay. For years it was a favorite retreat of Charlie Chaplin; there's even a statue of him near the beach. Here's another rewarding detour: Follow the sea road north of Waterville (R567) to the Irish-speaking village of **Ballinskelligs** ★★ (p. 319), with its medieval monastery slowly rotting away. The scenic **Skellig Ring** coastal drive leads from here; a sandy Blue Flag beach is just past the post office by Ballinskelligs Bay, and at the end of the beach are the remnants of a 16th-century castle.

Continuing on the N70, the next point of interest is **Derrynane** ★★ (p. 319), at **Caherdaniel.** Derrynane is the former seat of the O'Connell clan and erstwhile home to Daniel O'Connell, "the Liberator" who freed Irish Catholics from the last of the English Penal Laws in the 19th century. From there, watch for signs to the prehistoric ruins of **Staigue Fort** ★★ (p. 320), about 3km (2 miles) off the main road in a farmer's field.

Sneem, the next village on the circuit (see **Blueberry Hill Farm** ★★; p. 319), is a colorful little hamlet where houses are painted in vibrant shades, creating a beautiful tableau. The colors—blue, pink, yellow, and orange—burst out on a rainy day, like a little touch of the Mediterranean. There's not much to do in Sneem, but it's worth a stop just to see it. From here, you're no distance at all from Kenmare, and you've made your way around the Ring.

TOP ATTRACTIONS ON THE RING OF KERRY DRIVE

Ballinskelligs & the Skellig Ring ★★ RUINS/RELIGIOUS SITE
West of Waterville, across a small bay, the coastal village of Ballinskelligs contains the absurdly picturesque ruins of **St. Michael Ballinskelligs,** a medieval priory overlooking the sea. A beautiful sandy beach also features the remnants of a 16th-century castle. Ballinskelligs is a starting point for the so-called **Skellig Ring,** a stunning coastal drive that takes in some of the best viewpoints of the mysterious Skellig Islands (see box on p. 320). It also passes through some of the most dramatic scenery in the county, and with the merest fraction of the traffic that can clog the Ring of Kerry. Be warned, however: Its very remoteness means that this route can be tough going, and the roads are very mountainous in places. This is also the edge of Gaeltacht territory, where Irish is the primary language on road signs. To find the Ring, head south through Ballinskelligs. About 0.5km (⅓ mile) after the pink An Post building, you'll come to a crossroads. The Skellig Ring (*Morchuaird na Sceilge* in Irish) is signposted to the right. The signs continue throughout the route.
Visitor Information Point: Cafe Cois Trá, Ballinskelligs Beach, Ballinskelligs. ℂ **066/947-9323.** Cafe open daily 9am–6pm (hours may be reduced in winter).

Blueberry Hill Farm ★★ HERITAGE SITE   Looking for a way to amuse younger children for half a day? Try this working farm, which still follows traditional farming methods. As part of the half-day tours, you can help milk cows, make butter, and take part in a treasure hunt. Book ahead in the high season, as tours are limited to small groups.
Signposted from R568 (Sneem-Killarney Rd.), Sneem. www.blueberryhillfarm.ie. ℂ **087/364-7371.** Admission €20 adults and children; family groups (4 or more) €15 per person. Tours daily 10am and 3pm. Tours may not run in winter or bad weather; call ahead.

Derrynane House National Historic Park ★★ HISTORIC HOUSE   Irish political leader and Parliament member Daniel O'Connell (1775–1847) became known as "the Great Liberator" for his successful campaign to repeal the laws that barred Catholics from holding office. He became particularly famous in his lifetime for his so-called "monster meetings," vast public rallies held across the country (one, on the Hill of Tara, was reckoned to have been attended by nearly a million supporters). His house at Caherdaniel contains a museum devoted to his life. Not everything will be of interest to those unfamiliar with his story, but a few items—such as the gilded carriage from which he greeted crowds after a spell as a political prisoner—are worth seeing.
Signposted from N70 (Ring of Kerry Rd.), approx. 3.5km (2 miles) from Caherdaniel. www.derrynanehouse.ie. ℂ **066/947-5113.** Admission €5 adults; €4 seniors; €3 students and children; €13 families. Mid-Mar to Sept daily 10:30am–6pm; Oct daily 10am–5pm; Nov to early Dec weekends 10am–4pm. Last admission 45 min. before closing.

a great, mysterious wonder:
A TRIP TO THE SKELLIG ISLANDS

"Whoever has not stood in the graveyard on the summit of that cliff, among the bee-hive dwellings and beehive oratory, does not know Ireland through and through. . . .

—George Bernard Shaw

The craggy, inhospitable Skellig Islands rise precipitously from the sea. Here gray skies meet stormy horizons about 14km (8 miles) off the coast of the Iveragh Peninsula. From the mainland, Skellig Michael and Little Skellig appear impossibly sharp-angled and daunting even today—just imagine how perilous the mere act of getting there would have been in the 6th and 7th centuries. Back then, a group of monks built a community on the steepest, most wind-battered peaks. Over time, they carved 600 steps into the cliffs and built monastic buildings hundreds of feet above the ocean. The complex is now a UNESCO World Heritage Site.

There is something tragic and beautiful about the remains of the ancient oratories and beehive cells there. Historians know very little about these monks and how they lived, although they obviously sought intense isolation. Records relating to the Skelligs indicate that even here, all but completely hidden, the monastery was discovered by Vikings, who attacked it as they did all the Irish monastic settlements. Monks were kidnapped and killed in attacks in the 8th century, but the settlement always recovered. To this day, nobody knows why the monks finally abandoned the rock in the 12th century.

Landing is only possible on **Skellig Michael ★★★**, the largest of the islands on clear, sunny days. Due to its protected status, there's an annual quota for the number of visitors allowed. Although the island has always been a popular attraction, this was rarely a problem in the past—until a little film franchise called *Star Wars* came along. After *The Force Awakens* and *The Last Jedi* were filmed here in 2014 and 2016 respectively, demand to visit Skellig Michael skyrocketed. What was once a small, rural site is now massive business . . . but one that's still run like a small, rural site. So, if you want to have the unique experience of making landfall on Skellig Michael in the summer, it takes a bit of planning. Boat tours to the island are run by individual local companies rather than a central ferry operator.

Staigue Fort ★★ ANCIENT SITE   This well-preserved, surprisingly large prehistoric fort is built of rough stones without mortar of any kind. The walls are 4m (13 ft.) thick at the base. Historians are not certain what purpose it served—it may have been a hilltop fortress or a kind of prehistoric community center—but experts think it dates from around 1000 B.C. It's an open site with no visitor center. Look for signs and hike up the path through the field. It's quite something to see.

Off N70 just outside Castlecove, on a small farm road (follow signs 4 km/2½ miles to site). Daily 9am–7pm.

Valentia Lighthouse ★★ HERITAGE SITE   There's something fascinating about the lonely life of a lighthouse keeper. The last keeper lived

There are about a dozen of them, most contactable only via their cellphones or their websites, or at their stalls on the beach near Portmagee. Bookings need to be made as far in advance as possible. *Do not assume that you can get a place on the day.* Our advice is to book as soon as you know your travel dates.

The Skellig Michael Cruises Company is one of a few boat services currently offering online booking, and it has a good word-of-mouth reputation (www.skelligmichaelcruises.com; © **087/617-8114**). Another recommended option with online booking is **Casey's Skellig Island Tours,** which also offers an eco-tour of the puffins and other rare birds that inhabit the islands (www.skelligislands.com). The Cork and Kerry tourism offices can also assist, as can your hotel.

Most, though not all, tours leave from Portmagee harbor; be sure to check when you book.

Whether or not you're making the trip out there, the **Skellig** Experience (www.skelligexperience.com; © **066/947-6306**) is an excellent visitor center devoted to the islands and their history. It tells you all about the extraordinary history of these ancient edifices and also offers boat trips out to see the islands. The center, which is on Valentia Island (reached via a road bridge from Portmagee), is open daily 10am to 6pm in May, June, and September; 10am to 7pm in July and August; and weekdays only 10am to 4:30pm in March, April, October, and November. Last entry is 1 hour before closing. Admission costs €5 adults, €4 seniors and students, €3 children, and €14 families.

The visitor center also offers boat trips around the Skelligs; the cost of admission plus a cruise is €40 adults, €36 seniors and students, €25 children, and €125 families. Note that these trips only cruise *around* the Skelligs, however, and **do not make landfall.** If you want to see the ruins on Skellig Michael up close, you'll have to go with one of the independent boat operators listed above.

Here's a last little fun fact for *Star Wars* fans: The porgs from *The Last Jedi* were a late addition because it proved impossible to keep all the puffins who live on Skellig Michael out of the shots. Instead of trying to digitally remove the hundreds of inquisitive birds, it was decided to paint over them—and thus, the fluffy little porgs were born.

here with his family until the lighthouse was automated in 1947, and you can learn more about the conditions and the isolation they must have faced during a visit here. As well as the stunning location overlooking the sea on Valentia Island, the lighthouse has lots of history—it was built on the site of Fleetwood Fort, which dates way back to 1653. The lighthouse opened in 1841. On a 45-minute guided tour you can explore the fort, visit the lightkeeper's house, and climb the 21 steps of the lighthouse tower. Cromwell Point, Valentia Island. www.valentialighthouse.ie. © **066/947-6985.** Admission €7.50 adults; €6.50 seniors and students; €4 children under 12; €20 families. Mar–Oct 10:30am–6pm. Last tour at 5pm.

WHERE TO STAY ALONG THE RING OF KERRY

Although the Ring of Kerry is easily driven as a day excursion from Killarney or Kenmare, don't overlook the option of staying overnight in the countryside or in one of the small towns along the Ring—and it just may save you a few euros, too.

Expensive

Ard na Sidhe Country House ★★★   Ard na Sidhe means "Hill of the Fairies" in Irish, and this beautiful arts-and-crafts house does look quite magical as it appears in the folds of the green Irish hills near Killorglin. With only 18 bedrooms and tucked away on gorgeous grounds, it's the perfect place to hide away from the world. Rooms are done in muted shades with firm, king-sized beds, modern bathrooms, and peaceful views. The lounges are like elegant living rooms, with sofas clustered around wood-burning fireplaces. The in-house restaurant is simply fabulous, with European-influenced Irish cuisine, using locally sourced, seasonal produce in a relaxed but delightful setting. This place is well worth the drive.

Caragh Lake, Killorglin. www.ardnasidhe.com. ✆ **066/976-9105.** 18 units. €235–€330 double. Free parking. Rates include breakfast. **Amenities:** Restaurant; croquet; Wi-Fi (free).

Guest room in the Art na Sidhe Country House.

Moderate

Kells Bay House & Gardens ★★ Anyone who loves gardens, bird-song, and the sea will fall in love with this place. It's on the Ring of Kerry overlooking Dingle Bay, making it a great stop if you are driving the Ring. The 17 hectares (42 acres) of gardens are famed for exotic plants and ferns, and owner Billy Alexander, a renowned horticulturist, won a gold medal at the prestigious Chelsea Flower Show in England in 2021. Rooms are cozy, and most in the main house have garden views; others have mountain or bay views, and some have all three. Private suites to the side of the house are adjacent to a primeval forest and walled garden. What's nice about an overnight stay here is that you can roam the gardens freely when the day visitors have left, and you have direct access to a beach. Breakfast is €12.50 extra.

Kells, Cahersiveen, Co Kerry. www.kellsbay.ie. 𝄢 **066/947-7975.** 8 units. €98–€145 double. Rates do not include breakfast. Free parking. Closed Jan. **Amenities:** Bar license; restaurant; Wi-Fi (free).

Picín Cottage ★ Romantic and secluded, Picín is a place to live out your Irish country-cottage fantasy. It's just one double room, but guests have a private entrance, with a garden-facing terrace and their own sitting room with a wood-burning stove. Upstairs, the bedroom is an oasis of peace and calm. Hosts Amelia and Nick Etherton are a delight and so considerate. The only snag is that you have to fend for yourself at dinner, but Caherdaniel is a short drive away. Picín is just off the Ring of Kerry Road, between Caherdaniel and Castlecove.

Off N70, about 3.8km (2⅓ miles) E of Caherdaniel. www.picincottage.com. 𝄢 **066/947-5894.** 1 unit. €110–€120 suite. Free parking. Rates include breakfast. **Amenities:** Wi-Fi (free).

Quinlan & Cooke ★★ More of a restaurant-with-rooms than a small hotel, this is a stylish and unique place to stay. Bedrooms are open-plan contemporary spaces with a minimalist vibe: polished wood floors, huge skylights, and clawfoot tubs, plus a few high-tech extras such as Bose stereos. The guest lounge looks as if it's tumbled from the pages of a decor magazine, with deep velvet sofas and a cozy wood-burning stove. The superb restaurant **QC's** specializes in fresh local seafood (such as Valentia scallop Mornay) and steaks cooked to perfection, accompanied by sides like scallion mashed potatoes.

3 Main St., Cahersiveen. www.qc.ie. 𝄢 **066/947-2244.** 10 units. €135–€250 double. Free parking. Rates include breakfast. **Amenities:** Gym; Wi-Fi (free).

Inexpensive

River's Edge ★ A bright, cheery building overlooking the River Laune in the center of Killorglin, Coffey's is a sweet little guesthouse. Most rooms are decently sized (one upstairs is quite small, though), with double beds and contemporary wood furniture. Breakfasts are served in a dining room overlooking the river and picturesque stone bridge. No evening meal is served, but pretty Killorglin is right at your doorstep. Owners Finbarr and Anne are both keen golfers and will happily arrange a game for you at a local course.

The Bridge, Killorglin. www.riversedge.ie. ✆ **066/976-1750.** 11 units. €85–€100 double. Free parking. Rates include breakfast. **Amenities:** Wi-Fi (free).

WHERE TO EAT ON THE RING OF KERRY DRIVE

Some of the best foodie options are found in the area hotels—**Ardh na Sidhe Country House** in Killorglin (p. 322) has one of the finest restaurants on the Ring of Kerry. Similarly, Quinlan & Cooke's **QC's** in Cahersiveen (www.qc.ie; p. 323) is a stellar gastropub, with gorgeous seafood sourced by the owner's own fishing fleet.

Expensive

Jack's Coastguard Restaurant ★★ SEAFOOD/MODERN IRISH This cheery restaurant lists "Water's Edge" as its address. That's not so much a street name as a description; it's right on the harbor in Cromane, a tiny village near Killorglin. The dining room is a bright, modern space boasting beautiful views of the bay, while a pianist plays away in the corner. As you can imagine, the specialties are mostly seafood, but the menu always finds room for some meatier options too. For dessert, try the delicious poached pear and frangipane tart.

Water's Edge, Cromane Lower, Killorglin. www.jackscromane.com. ✆ **066/976-9102.** Entrees €19–€36. Light menu Mon and Wed–Sat 1–3pm; dinner Mon and Wed–Sun 6–9pm; Sun lunch 1–3pm. Closed Tues. Reservations encouraged.

Kingdom 1795 ★★ MODERN IRISH This gorgeous restaurant takes its casual style from its former life as a pub—1795 is the date of the first lease—and it has been given a stylish contemporary update by its owners, host Suzi and chef Damien, with informal seating and marble-topped tables. The food is exquisite: creative dishes largely based on seasonal ingredients from local suppliers. You might see Wagyu beef blade and brisket served with cabbage, stout mustard, and house butter, as well as seafood and duck on the menu, or a kohlrabi pie with truffle ketchup, ramsons, and coolattin cheese.

Main St., Killorglin. www.kingdom1795.com. ✆ **066/979-6527.** Set menu: 2 courses €43, 3 courses €50. Wed–Sun 6:30–9pm.

Nick's Restaurant & Gastro Bar ★★ SEAFOOD Nick's is quite famous in this part of Ireland—it's been here since 1976, and a recent change of ownership has done nothing to dent its reputation. Choose from two dining areas: the formal restaurant or the **Gastro Bar,** where a simpler selection is served in more relaxed surroundings. In the main restaurant, expect dishes like freshly caught grilled sole, a monkfish and prawn thermidor, or a classic seafood platter. The bar menu offers simpler, pub-style

Serious hikers test their chops on the **Kerry Way**, a long-distance trail that traverses extraordinary scenery while roughly following the Ring of Kerry. Ireland's longest marked hiking trail, the 202km (126-mile) route includes several "green roads" (old, unused roads built as Famine relief projects and now converted into walking paths).

The first stage, from Killarney National Park to Glenbeigh, travels inland over rolling hills and past pastoral scenes. The second stage circles the Iveragh Peninsula and takes in spectacular ocean views, passing through picturesque towns including Cahersiveen, Waterville, colorful Sneem, and lovely Kenmare. The final inland walk brings you via the old Kenmare Road back to Killarney.

The walk is steep in places—the highest point is 385m (1,200 ft.) in a section known as Windy Gap. There are long stretches of wilderness between civilization—walkers attempting the entire path, or even substantial portions of it, need to prepare carefully. But some short stretches can be easily accessed and make for gentle afternoon walks, suitable for amateurs.

Maps outlining the route, and the best short walks, are available from the Killarney and Kenmare tourist offices. For details, see **www.kerryway.com**.

8

COUNTY KERRY | The Ring of Kerry

---

fare (fish and chips, seafood mornay, supreme of chicken). Everything is served to the gentle melodies of live piano music. Same as it ever was.
Lower Bridge St., Killorglin. www.nicks.ie. © **066/976-1219.** Entrees €26–€36. Tues–Sun 4:30–10pm.

Moderate

Bianconi ★ GASTROPUB   In a rambling Victorian pub, this restaurant has a surprisingly modern menu. In the bar you can have light meals, toasted sandwiches on sourdough bread, huge, fresh salads, and chilled seafood platters. In the restaurant, the dishes are true gastropub fare. Start with the hot and cold salmon with crispy capers, or the baked mushrooms stuffed with black pudding. Or stay light and have the fresh salad with cashel blue cheese and poached pear. Mains might include duck leg confit with orange brandy sauce, pan-fried chicken with Irish barley stew, or polenta-coated fish of the day. Upstairs, the stylish guest rooms (€95–€130) are a great option if you need a place to base yourself.
Lower Bridge St., Killorglin. www.bianconi.ie. © **066/076-1146.** Entrees €14–€30. Daily 9am–10pm.

The Blind Piper ★ IRISH   This friendly, lively pub is one of the top places to eat in Caherdaniel. The menu is straightforward comfort food—toasted sandwiches, beer-tempura hake, or beef and Guinness casserole with champ potatoes (mashed with scallions and butter). Live traditional music sessions liven up the place on Tuesday and Thursday nights in July and August from 9:30pm. *Note:* The Blind Piper is a bit hard to find. Turn off N70 road in Caherdaniel next to the big red building in the center of the village. The pub is bright yellow.

Off main Ring of Kerry Rd. (N70), Caherdaniel. www.blindpiperpub.ie. ✆ **066/947-5126.** Entrees €12.50–€17. Wed–Sun 12:30–8pm. Closed Mon and Tues.

The Blue Bull ★ IRISH This great little pub in tiny, picturesque Sneem serves traditional fare in cozy dining spaces. The menu doesn't deviate too far from Irish pub classics, but it does it all very well: Irish stew, fish and chips, mussels in garlic sauce, steaks, sandwiches, and salads. The crowd, a good mix of hungry tourists and easygoing locals, makes for a congenial atmosphere. This is a straight-up traditional pub with a bar area in the front separate from the dining rooms—a great spot for eavesdropping on local conversations.

South Sq., Sneem. www.bluebullsneem.com. ✆ **064/664-5382.** Entrees €14–€24. Wed–Sun 4–11pm. Closed Mon and Tues.

Inexpensive

Beachcove Cafe ★★ CAFE This Waterville eatery is a sunny place to stop for breakfast or lunch while touring the Ring of Kerry. The food here is unpretentious and fabulously fresh. Expect sandwiches made with sourdough bread and local cheese, big salads with falafel, sweet potato, and quinoa, homemade soups, and hot plates like fish and chips or burgers. The coffee is excellent, and the hot chocolate is absolutely decadent. The cakes are fresh. A find.

Upper Waterville, Waterville. ✆ **086/947-4733.** Entrees €6–€12. Daily 10am–6pm. Hours may be reduced in winter.

Wharton's Traditional Fish & Chips ★★ FISH & CHIPS Not actually a restaurant at all, but a food truck on the roadside at Templenoe, between Sneem and Kenmare (it's around 6km/3.5 miles from Kenmare), and an outstanding "chipper," with a traditional menu of (usually) cod and hake—although asking if you'd prefer your fish battered or fried in breadcrumbs is a nice twist. It's nothing fancy, but that's half the point—this is real Irish fast food.

Greenane, Templenoe. ✆ **083/348-7505.** Entrees €11–€12.50 (half portions from €6). Wed–Sun 4–8pm.

TRALEE

While it's near both the Ring of Kerry and the Dingle Peninsula, Tralee doesn't quite live up to its singsong pretty name. Mostly it's a place you go *through,* rather than to. With a population of 24,000, the town is nearly twice the size of Killarney, but this is a workaday place, rather than a tourist center, and there's not much here for visitors. In fact, it can feel a bit rough at times—especially on weekend nights, when the town's many bars are packed. However, it has some attractive Georgian architecture and a few sights worth seeing, with a couple more offerings in the countryside nearby.

COULD YOU BE THE rose OF TRALEE?

This International Rose of Tralee is a unique festival that sets out each year to find and crown the famous **Rose of Tralee.**

A 19th-century song about a local girl named Mary O'Connor is at the root of this world-famous contest. William Mulchinock's tear-jerker tune about the girl he was stopped by fate from marrying so caught the public's imagination that more than 100 years later, it is still performed in Irish pubs worldwide. Thus, in 1959 the idea was born for a contest to find the loveliest lass in Tralee and crown her.

The competition has evolved from a beauty pageant to an international event that celebrates all that's good about Irish culture and heritage, and while many Irish people view it as slightly cheesy, it does connect the global Irish community around the world—the winner takes on an ambassadorial role to represent Ireland and the festival with a year-long international tour that includes charity work.

Every August, the town fills with the 32 young women vying for the title, many flying in from around the world. The contest rules are fairly generous in terms of who is Irish, not to mention Traleean—the rules require contestants to be of Irish birth or ancestry, so past winners have been from places as far-flung as the U.S. and Australia. Each "rose" is accompanied by a designated male escort for the festival (escort in the old-fashioned sense—they provide support and companionship for the Roses and that's it), and to reward the best escort, there is even an "Rose Escort of the Year" award.

The festival lasts 5 days, during which time the entire town becomes somewhat obsessed with it—restaurants, pubs, and theaters all get involved in hosting events related to the Rose of Tralee.

If you want to join in the fun, or if you know a girl with an Irish last name who would make a good Rose, contact the **Rose of Tralee Festival Office** (www.roseoftralee.ie; ☏ **066/712-1322**).

Exploring In & Around Tralee

Blennerville Windmill ★★ LANDMARK   Reaching 20m (66 ft.) into the sky, this snow-white windmill must surely be the most photographed object in Tralee. Perched at the edge of the river, the windmill has blades that still turn, which makes it rare in this part of the world. Built in 1800, it flourished until 1850, when it was largely abandoned. After decades of neglect, it was restored and is now fully operational. You can climb to the top and see some of its complex inner workings in detail. The visitor complex has an exhibition on the Famine years (when Blennerville was a major point of emigration), and a cafe. The windmill is about a mile outside of central Tralee on the N86.

Windmill St., Blennerville. www.blennerville-windmill.ie ☏ **066/712-1064.** Admission €8 adults; €6 seniors and students; €4 children; free for children under 5; €22 families. June and Oct Tues–Sun 9:30am–5pm; Jul–Aug and Sept daily 9:30am–5pm. Closed Nov–May.

Crag Cave ★★ UNDERGROUND CAVERNS Although they are believed to be more than a million years old, these limestone caves were not discovered until 1983. The guides accompany you 3,753m (12,310 ft.) into the well-lit cave passage on a 35-minute tour revealing massive stalactites and fascinating caverns. It's very touristy, but interesting, nonetheless. There is a children's play area (endearingly called **Crazy Cave**), although it costs extra. The **Garden Restaurant** is a useful stop for lunch if you need a quick bite.

College Rd., Castleisland (turn left off N21 onto Main St., then left onto College Rd.). www.cragcave.com. ℂ **066/714-1244.** Caves: €15 adults; €12 seniors and students; €6 children; €35–€40 families. Crazy Cave: €9 per child for 2 hr. play (accompanying adults free), or €11 including cave tour; €7 children 2 and under. Mid-Mar to Oct daily 10am–6pm; Jan to mid-Mar Fri–Sun 10am–6pm. Nov–Dec Wed–Sun 10am–6pm. Tour times: May–Aug, every half-hour; off-season, no set times.

Kerry County Museum ★ MUSEUM Spanning several thousand years of history, up to the present day, this museum's galleries cover Kerry's ancient past; the coming of the Normans and the medieval period; the Famine years; and the struggle for independence. In the Knight's Hall and Medieval Experience, you can wander around a re-created medieval town, with requisite sound effects, dressed-up mannequins, and the like. The museum is in the same building as the Tralee tourism office.

Ashe Memorial Hall, Denny St., Tralee. www.kerrymuseum.ie. ℂ **066/712-7777.** Admission €5 adults; free for accompanying children; €10 families. June–Aug daily 10am–5pm; Sept–Mar Tues–Sat 10am–5pm. Last admission 4pm.

The Seanchaí: Kerry Writers' Museum ★ MUSEUM This imaginative museum's innovative displays often feel more like art installations devoted to the life and work of various Kerry writers from the past and present. Life-size statues sit hunched over books and even propping up a bar, with the text of their best-known works covering them from head to toe. Listowel is 26km (16 miles) northeast of Tralee on N69.

24 The Square, Listowel. www.kerrywritersmuseum.com. ℂ **068/22212.** Admission €8 adults; €6.50 seniors and students; €3 children 8 and over; €13 families. June–Sept Mon–Fri 9:30am–5pm, Sat 10:30am–4pm; Oct–May Mon–Fri 10am–4pm. Closed Christmas holidays.

Where to Stay & Eat in Tralee

Ballygarry House ★★ On the outer edge of Tralee, this pleasant country inn is ensconced amid lush gardens. Built as a manor house in the 18th century, it has retained plenty of its original features. Elegant guest rooms maintain the country-mansion air, and superior rooms are surprisingly spacious, with king-size beds. Family rooms are an excellent value at usually the same price as doubles. The fantastic in-house spa is a relaxing, revitalizing hideaway, while the outdoor hot tub, overlooking fields and distant mountains, is a calming oasis. Special inclusive spa offers change monthly—massage, facial, and access to the spa facilities for around €110 to €140 is the kind of deal you can expect. The **Brasserie** restaurant serves excellent modern Irish food. Check the website for dinner, bed-and-breakfast offers.

Signposted off N21, Leebrook, approx. 3.3km (2 miles) W of central Tralee. www.ballygarryhouse.com. (℗ **066/712-3322.** 46 units. €95–€255 double; €215–€455 suite. Free parking. Breakfast not included in lower rates. **Amenities:** Restaurant; bar; spa; Wi-Fi (free).

The Yellow Door ★ BISTRO   A good option for a quick breakfast or lunch in Tralee, the Yellow Door does everything from light pastries and muffins to omelets, pancakes, and the full Irish breakfast. For lunch there's a deli menu or a full carvery lunch, including roast pork or roast turkey and ham with all the trimmings. Or try the delicious hot roast sandwich of the day.

Denny Lane, 11 Denny St., Tralee. (℗ **087/182-6969.** Breakfast €6–€10. Lunch €10–€12. Mon–Fri 9am–3pm

Sports & Outdoor Pursuits in Tralee

GOLF   The Arnold Palmer–designed **Tralee Golf Club,** Fenit/Churchill Road, West Barrow, Ardfert (www.traleegolfclub.com; (℗ **066/713-6379**), overlooking the Atlantic 13km (8 miles) northwest of town, is one of the most spectacularly situated courses in Ireland. Greens fees are a pricey €250 in high season (May–Oct), although this also allows you to play a second round within a week of the first for €180.

About 40km (25 miles) north of Tralee in the northwest corner of County Kerry is former U.S. President Bill Clinton's favorite Irish course, **Ballybunion Golf Club,** Ballybunion (www.ballybuniongolfclub.ie; (℗ **068/27146**). This facility has two challenging 18-hole seaside links, both on cliffs overlooking the Shannon River estuary and the Atlantic. Tom Watson has rated Ballybunion's Old Course one of the finest in the world, while the Cashen Course was designed by Robert Trent Jones, Sr. Greens fees are €80 for the Cashen Course and €230 for the Old Course (or play both for €300).

THE DINGLE PENINSULA

North of the Iveragh Peninsula, the less-visited Dingle Peninsula also has much to offer. To call it "undiscovered" would be a stretch—in the summer, little Dingle Town can get busy with travelers. Out of the high season, this is a sleepy little place, filled with color and wonderful to explore. The peninsula is also in the Gaeltacht or Irish-speaking area so road signs and place names will be in Irish.

West of Dingle Town, a stunning coastal drive known as the **Slea Head Drive** is lined with archeological sites. (It's also a memorable route for cycling.) Some of Ireland's finest beaches line both sides of the peninsula (see p. 340), and the views are spectacular. Walkers can tackle the challenges of the **Dingle Way** (p. 341).

Dingle Town

A charming, brightly colored little town at the foot of steep hills, **Dingle** (also known as *An Daingean*—the town is in the Gaeltacht or Irish-speaking area) has plenty of hotels and restaurants and makes a good base for exploring the region. The town's most famous former resident, Fungie the dolphin, put the town on the map when he appeared in 1983 and began escorting fishing boats in and out of the bay. He soon drew the dolphin-loving crowds and interacted with swimmers, kayakers, and tour boats. Sadly, this heartwarming story came to an end when he disappeared from Dingle Bay in October 2020, thought to have either moved on or died. But Fungie's legacy lives on and there is still plenty to see on a boat trip (including dolphins). The town's busiest time is in August, when the **Dingle Races** draw crowds to watch the horses run every other weekend. (The racetrack is just outside town on the N86.) In the last week of August, the **Dingle Regatta** fills the harbor with traditional Irish currach boats in a vivid display of color and history.

EXPLORING DINGLE TOWN

Boat Tours ★★ BOAT TOUR   While trips out to see Dingle's famous dolphin Fungie are no longer possible (he disappeared in late 2020 after living in the bay for 37 years), you can still enjoy a fantastic 3-hour boat trip out to Dingle Bay and the stunning coastline of the Blasket Islands, where you might spot seals, dolphins, whales, and basking sharks depending on the season and weather. You can also take a 1-hour harbor cruise (adults €15, children €10; tours run approx. every hour) and see tunnels, cliffs, and Fungie's Cave, where the dolphin was often spotted.

The Pier, Dingle Town. www.dingledolphin.com. (𝒞 **066/915-2626.** €55 adults; €40 children 12 and under. May–Oct Daily 11am and 2:30pm, weather permitting. Closed Nov-Apr.

Dingle Oceanworld Aquarium ★ AQUARIUM   This is a nicely designed aquarium, although it's quite small, given the ticket price. As is the norm at such places, it's home to lots of sea critters in creatively designed tanks. You can walk through an aquarium tunnel with fish swimming above and around you, and members of the young staff carry around live lobsters, crabs, starfish, and other "inner space" creatures for kids to touch and pet. The aquarium also has some super-cute Antarctic Gentoo penguins. This compact, hands-on, interactive place makes a good reward for your kids for being so patient while you took pictures of a pile of rocks back up the road.

Dingle Harbour, Dingle Town. www.dingle-oceanworld.ie. (𝒞 **066/915-2111.** Admission €16 adults; €12.50 seniors and students; €11 children 4–16; €50–€57 families. Daily 10am–5pm. Last admission 1 hr. before closing.

Eask Tower ★ LANDMARK/VIEW   Built in 1847 as a Famine relief project, this 12m-tall (39-ft.) tower built of solid stone nearly 5m (16 ft.)

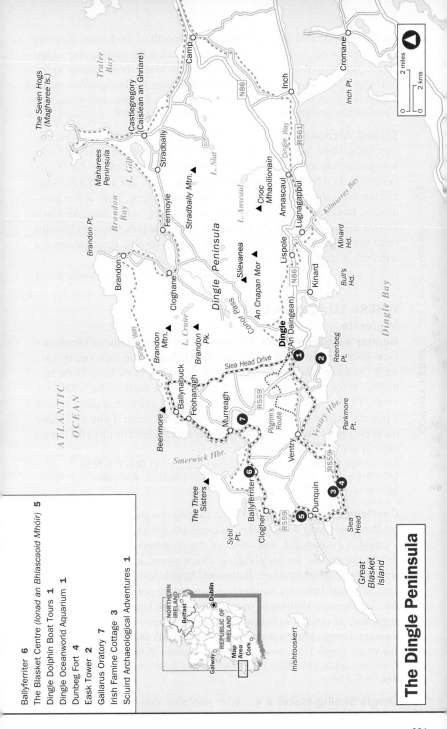

The Dingle Peninsula

Ballyferriter **6**

The Blasket Centre (Ionad an Bhlascaoid Mhóir) **5**

Dingle Dolphin Boat Tours **1**

Dingle Oceanworld Aquarium **1**

Dunbeg Fort **4**

Eask Tower **2**

Gallarus Oratory **7**

Irish Famine Cottage **3**

Sciuird Archaeological Adventures **1**

thick with a wooden arrow pointing to the mouth of the harbor. It is certainly interesting to look at, but the main reason for making the 1.6km (1-mile) climb to the summit of Carhoo Hill is to see the incredible views of Dingle Harbour, and, on the far side of the bay, the Iveragh Peninsula.

Carhoo Hill. From Dingle, follow Slea Head Rd. 3.2km (2 miles), turn left at road signposted for Colâiste Ide, and continue another 3.2km (2 miles).

Sciúird Archaeological Adventures ★★ TOUR   For serious history buffs, these tours are a great opportunity to get deeper insight into how prehistoric settlers and early Christians left their mark on the Dingle Peninsula. Led by local expert historians, the tours last about a half-day and involve a short bus journey and some easy walking. Four or five monuments, from the Stone Age to medieval times, are on the route. All tours, limited to 8 to 10 people, start from the top of the pier, although pickups from your hotel are possible if you're staying locally. Reservations are required, at least a day or so in advance if possible.

Holy Ground, Dingle Town. ℰ **066/915-1606.** Tour €30 per person. Apr–Sept daily 10:30am and 2pm; rest of year by appointment.

WHERE TO STAY IN DINGLE
Moderate
Benner's Hotel ★   This 300-year-old inn in the middle of Dingle is a local institution, with plenty of traditional charm. The location, an easy walk from everything in Dingle Town, is the big draw here. Done in a neutral decor, rooms have a modern look, and most come with town views. The bar downstairs is popular with locals and a great place to have a pint after a day of sightseeing. It serves a good menu if you don't have the energy to go out to dinner. Or you can retreat with a drink to the library room if you prefer some quiet.

Main Street, Dingle Town. www.dinglebenners.com. ℰ **066/915-1638.** 52 units. €89–€304 double. Free parking. Rates include breakfast. **Amenities:** Bar; library; Wi-Fi (free).

Castlewood House ★★★   Overlooking the glassy expanse of Dingle Bay, this lovely whitewashed house is filled with art and antiques. Its location is exceptional, and views of the shimmering water, framed by distant mountains, are breathtaking. Guest rooms are chic and comfortable, with designer furniture. Bathrooms have Jacuzzi tubs. Breakfasts (in fact, all meals here) are outstanding—including porridge with a dash of whiskey, homemade breads, oranges in caramel, kippers with scrambled eggs, and an omelet with smoked salmon. Despite the rural feel to the location, Dingle Marina is only a 10-minute walk away.

The Wood, Dingle Town. www.castlewooddingle.com. ℰ **066/915-2788.** 14 units. €96–€180 double; €160–€225 suite. Free parking. Rates include breakfast. **Amenities:** Wi-Fi (free).

Dingle Skellig Hotel ★★   With sweeping views of Dingle Bay, this modern hotel at the edge of town is a great option for those looking for a

The Greenmount House on Dingle Bay.

little relaxation or a place with space for kids. The hotel decor is up to date but has a classic style, with firm king-sized beds in the sizeable guest rooms and walk-in showers in the ensuite bathrooms. Everything's done in neutral tones—some rooms have balconies with fabulous views. Breakfast is served buffet style, and the **Coastguard** restaurant has bay views. The **Peninsula Spa** and pool offer relaxation with a sea view.

Farran Dingle Bay, Dingle Town. www.dingleskellig.com. © **066/915-0200.** 50 units. €200–€350 double, €360–€610 suite. Free parking. Rates include breakfast. **Amenities:** 2 restaurants; bar; lounge; pool; spa; Wi-Fi (free).

Greenmount House ★★★   A luxurious B&B overlooking Dingle Bay, Greenmount House is one of the best places to stay in the area. The view from the front is like a cliché of what you might imagine all of Ireland to be: rolling green slopes falling gently into the sea with the streets of quaint Dingle town curving around the coastline below. The public areas are arranged at the front as much as possible, so that you can admire the view from the guest lounge or breakfast room. The garden has an enclosed hot tub where you can savor a glass of wine. Guest rooms are bright and spacious; some have polished wood floors and others have skylights, letting the daylight pour in. Breakfasts are delicious and plentiful—try the tasty smoked salmon and scrambled eggs. Hosts Mary and John Curran are incredibly friendly and will even arrange personal tours of the area for you, escorted by a member of their own family.

Upper John St., Dingle Town. www.greenmounthouse.ie. © **066/915-1414.** 14 units. €100–€170. 2-night minimum on summer weekends. Free parking. Rates include breakfast. **Amenities:** Wi-Fi (free).

Expensive

The Chart House ★★ IRISH   This friendly bistro is one of the most popular places to indulge in the local produce. The menu is short, but dishes are expertly prepared, filled with regional flavor and a smattering of global influences. Monkfish medallions are served with chile and cilantro salsa; hake comes with chorizo and lemon; and the free-range roast chicken is accompanied by a delightfully rich parmesan gnocchi. Almost everything on the menu is sourced from providers within the Dingle Peninsula. The three-course early-bird special (6–7pm) has almost as much choice as the evening service for €38.

The Mall, Dingle Town. www.thecharthousedingle.com. ☎ **066/915-2255.** Entrees €25–€31. Mon–Sat 7–10pm, Sun 9am–9pm. Times may vary in winter.

Doyle's Seafood Restaurant ★★ SEAFOOD   Doyle's is simply one of the best places in the region for seafood, and a lot of what you find on the menu depends on the catch of the day. Although there's a small selection of mains, the focus of the menu is around 15 small sharing plates featuring delicacies like crispy crab cakes, chorizo and tomato mussel, Glenbeigh gigas oysters, and roasted Blasket crayfish. Vegetarians are well-served with a menu of starters and entrees, while dishes like duck spring rolls and pan-seared ribeye steak satisfy the carnivores. The wine list is extensive.

4 John St., Dingle Town. www.doylesrestaurantdingle.ie. ☎ **066/915-2674.** Small plates €2.50–€26; entrees €12–€50. Daily 5–9pm. Closed Jan to mid–Feb.

Out of the Blue ★★ SEAFOOD   The name of this much-loved restaurant could refer to the sea it sits next to or the bright blue building it occupies. There's nothing here but seafood, but it's some of the freshest in the country. The menu is entirely dependent on the day's catch, which is listed on blackboards outside. If no fish is caught that day, the restaurant doesn't open. The place is casual, but the cooking isn't. The seafood chowder is creamy and rich, chargrilled tuna is served with lentil salad, and the smoked salmon is house-cured. There are only a few tables, so booking is essential, but you can do it online.

Waterside, Dingle Town. www.outoftheblue.ie. ☎ **066/915-0811.** Entrees €21–€37. Daily 5–9:30pm.

Inexpensive

Bean in Dingle ★★ CAFE   A little slice of metropolitan cool right in the middle of Dingle, Bean serves one of the finest cups of joe we've had in Ireland. Bean hand-roasts its own specialty coffee, and you can buy it in bags to bring home—try the house blend "An Fear Marbh," named after the Blasket island that looks like a sleeping giant. Have your coffee to go or sit at the long, communal wooden table and linger over a black pudding sausage roll or a slice of tasty cake—baked by the owner's mother and grandmother.

Green St., Dingle Town. www.beanindingle.com. ✆ **087/299-2831.** Items €3–€6. Mon–Sat 8:30am–5pm; Sun 10am–4pm.

Reel Dingle Fish ★★ FISH & CHIPS Dingle is not short of an authentic "chipper" or two, and this is one of the best in town. Everything's cooked the traditional way—fish in batter, with piping-hot chips, and no messing around—but the menu has a greater-than-average choice of fresh fish to choose from, including hake, monkfish, pollock, and locally smoked haddock, in addition to the usual cod and plaice. It also sells homemade burgers crafted from local beef.

Bridge St., Dingle Town. ✆ **066/915-1713.** Fish and chips €9.90–€13.50. Daily 1–10pm.

DINGLE TOWN SHOPPING

Brian de Staic Jewellery Workshop ★★ Brian is a respected jewelry designer who has built up quite a following since he first appeared on the scene more than 30 years ago. He specializes in modern interpretations of ancient Celtic motifs, and you'll find everything from pendants and brooches to earrings, bracelets, and crosses. Some of his work is based on instantly recognizable designs; others are more subtle and abstract. Green St., Dingle Town. www.briandestaic.com. ✆ **066/915-1298.**

Greenlane Gallery ★★ A great selection of new, contemporary art is on sale at this interesting gallery. Styles vary from abstract watercolors and oils to challenging sculpture. Prices vary, inevitably, but several pieces are really quite affordable. Holyground, Dingle Town. www.greenlane gallery.com. ✆ **086/8211-225.**

Lisbeth Mulcahy: The Weavers' Shop ★★ Lisbeth Mulcahy is a talented weaver and fashion designer who creates lovely, colorful items of knitwear, hats, throws, and wall hangings. It's all exquisite quality, and the designs are true originals—elegant and distinctive. She also sells a selection of pottery from her husband's workshop (see below). The shop is closed on Sundays from October to May. Green St., Dingle Town. www. lisbethmulcahy.com. ✆ **066/915-1688.**

Louis Mulcahy Workshop ★★ Husband of weaver Lisbeth Mulcahy (see above), Louis Mulcahy is a big name in handmade Irish pottery. It's all beautifully made, from Deco-influenced vases to kitchenware, tea sets, and ornaments. Considering what a name he is, Louis's prices are pretty reasonable. Everything can be shipped worldwide, and we say with experience that the shopworkers are experts in packing breakable things so they arrive without a scratch! The workshop, which sprawls over a two-story building with gorgeous views down to the coast, also has a handy cafe. The shop is open daily year-round—until 8pm in the midsummer months. Clogher is 16.5km (10⅓ miles) northwest of Dingle. On R559, Clogher, Ballyferriter. www.louismulcahy.com. ✆ **066/915-6229.**

The Slea Head Drive & Other Dingle Diversions

Looping around the western tip of the Dingle Peninsula, the magnificent **Slea Head Drive ★★★** offers rugged coastal vistas, unspoiled islands, and mossy archaeological sites—some of the Wild Atlantic Way at its best. At any tourist information center, you can get a guide to the various ruined abbeys and old forts along the way. Sights below are listed in the order you'll pass them when you drive the loop clockwise (the road is narrow, and you need to drive it clockwise to avoid bottlenecks where only one vehicle can pass). This way, you also get the wow factor of sweeping coastal views as soon as you leave Dingle. *Note:* This is in the Gaeltacht (Irish-speaking) area, so by law, all signs—even road-hazard signs—are in Irish.

Leaving Dingle by car, head southwest along R559 through the town of Ventry, following the **Slea Head Drive** road markers. **Slea Head (Ceann Sléibhe),** at the southwestern edge of the peninsula, has pristine beaches, great walks, and extensive archaeological remains such as **Dunbeg Fort (*Dún Beag*) ★**; see p. 338. After rounding the Head, go north to the village of **Dunquin (*Dún Chaoin*),** stunningly situated between Slea Head and Clogher Head, where you can catch ferries to the abandoned **Blasket Islands (*Na Blascaodaí;* see p. 337),** inhabited these days only by seals and seabirds.

Coumeenoole Beach and Bay on Slea Head.

After this, the scenery opens up to take in some stark moorland on your right, in contrast to the ever-spectacular coastal views on the left. There are plenty of spots to safely pull over for pictures on this stretch. If the sun is out, this section is jaw-dropping. The weather is also dramatic; incoming squalls can hit you suddenly, like an icy, wet wall. Pause for coffee and a browse of the excellent pottery and crafts at **Louis Mulcahy** ★★ (p. 335), which looks out toward **Clogher Strand,** a pretty coastal inlet (at the 2 o'clock position if you're standing outside the pottery).

A few miles north and east along the coast, the sleepy village of

Abandoned dwellings dot the Blasket Islands off of Dunquin Bay.

Ballyferriter (*Baile an Fheirtear-aigh***)** ★ has an Iron Age fort with a particularly grim backstory (see box on p. 339). Continue along R559 and you'll soon see signs for the **Gallarus Oratory** ★, a beautifully preserved early Christian church. From here, continue on the loop back to Dingle, 8km (5 miles) farther along R559, and you've completed the Slea Head Drive.

The Blasket Islands ★★ HERITAGE/NATURE SITE Overshadowed by the more famous Skelligs (p. 320), the Blaskets are another group of mysterious, abandoned islands off the Kerry coast, but with more recent stories to tell. For hundreds of years these were home to an isolated community with a rich tradition of storytelling and folklore—all in Irish, of course—that was well documented in the late 1800s. In 1953, however, the islands were considered too dangerous for habitation and the Irish government ordered a mandatory evacuation. The individual islands have wonderfully evocative names like the **Sleeping Giant** and **Cathedral Rocks,** but the only island you can actually visit is the largest, **Great Blasket,** where a few crumbling buildings and skeletal edifices remain— an eerie ghost town in an outstandingly beautiful setting. See it all in a stunning 13km (8-mile) walking route that stretches to the west end of the island, passing sea cliffs and beaches of ivory sand. You can pick up maps and other information from the **Blasket Centre** on the mainland in Dunquin. Trips aboard the *Peig Sayers* (www.greatblasketisland.net/ boat-trips; ✆ **086/315-5098**), a rigid inflatable vessel, include a 3-hour stop on Great Blasket; it leaves from Dingle Marina (below the tourist office) at 11am daily from March to October. The cost is €65 per person (no reduction for kids or seniors). Alternatively, **Marine Tours** (www.

marinetours.ie; ℂ **086/335-3805**) runs full- and half-day tours leaving Ventry at 10am or 1pm daily April to October. Their tour includes 3 hours on Great Blasket; the rest of the time is spent cruising around the other islands without making landfall. Tickets are €45 for a morning tour, €75 for a full day. It also runs a 4-hour **Eco Marine Tour** for €60, but this one is designed for spotting seals, sharks, and whales and doesn't make landfall.

The Blasket Centre (*Ionad an Bhlascaoid*): Dunquin (*Dún Chaoin*). www.blasket.ie. ℂ **066/915-6444.** Admission €5 adults; €4 seniors; €3 students and children; children under 8 free; €13 families. Late Mar–end Oct daily 10am–6pm. Last admission 45 min. before closing.

Dunbeg Fort (Dún Beag) ★ RUINS   Sitting atop a sheer cliff just east of Slea Head, outside the village of Ventry, this 5th-century fort's stony walls rise from the cliff edge as if they were always part of it. The round Iron Age structure's stone walls are still mostly sturdy, although part of the fort fell into the sea during storms in 2014 and 2017. Walk around the fort to see where other fortifications and "beehive" huts were built inside the walls thousands of years ago. There's also a mysterious underground passage. A short video at the visitor center gives more information about the fort's history.

Dunbeg Fort, Slea Head Dr. www.dunbeagfort.com. ℂ **086/173-7724.** Admission €3 adults; €2.50 students and seniors; €1.50 children. Mar–May and Oct daily 9am–6pm; June–Sept daily 9am–7pm.

Gallarus Oratory ★ RELIGIOUS SITE   This tiny, beehive-shaped chapel is one of the best-preserved pieces of early Christian architecture in Ireland. Built sometime between the A.D. 7th and 9th centuries, its walls and roof are made entirely of dry stones without mortar—yet the interior stays remarkably dry. (Not quite dry enough, sadly, to avoid damage during the heavy floods that hit Ireland in 2014, though the repairs are seamless.) If the visitor center is closed, you can just walk around back and straight up the little path to the next field, where the Oratory is located. You can't get any closer than this by car, and the uphill walk takes a minute or two from the parking lot. Nearby is the single surviving tower of 15th-century **Gallarus Castle.** Tours of the castle can be prebooked at the visitor center—not that there's much to see inside.

Gallarus. www.gallarusoratory.ie. ℂ **066/915-5333.** Free admission. Visitor center Apr–Oct daily 10am–6pm or on request during off-season. Signposted down small farm road off R559, 7km (4⅓ miles) NW of Dingle, 4.8km (3 miles) W of Ballyferriter.

Irish Famine Cottage ★ HERITAGE SITE   This cottage isn't a replica; it's a real dwelling, maintained as it would have been at the time it was abandoned during the Great Famine years of the mid–19th century. The humble stone building, scattered with pieces of furniture, is a stark and haunting sight, perched on a windswept cliff overlooking the coast. You can't go inside, but looking in through the windows gives a powerful

A gruesome TALE IN BALLYFERRITER

The unassuming village of **Ballyferriter** (**Baile an Fheirtearaigh**), part of the Slea Head Drive, is named after a local rebel named Piaras Ferriter, a poet and soldier who fought in the 1641 rebellion and ultimately became the last area commander to surrender to Oliver Cromwell's English troops.

Just north of the village, however, lie relics of an even darker chapter of the village's history. Follow signs to the moody ruins of the **Dún an Oir Fort,** a defensive citadel dating from the Iron Age. A small memorial is dedicated to 600 Spanish and Irish troops who were massacred here by the English in 1580. Most were beheaded—a fact commemorated by the highly gruesome local names for two adjacent fields nearby. The first, where the executions were carried out, is called "The Field of the Cutting." The second, where their partial remains were buried, is "the Field of the Heads."

enough impression of what life was really like for the rural poor. Kids get a little bowl of feed to give to the animals in the field. *Note:* The cottage is a short walk uphill from the parking lot, so it may not be suitable for those with mobility problems. They also run **Sheepdog demonstrations** (www.dinglesheepdogs.com), where you can see a farmer herding sheep with his dogs (€7 per person; year-round; call the below number to book). Signposted from R559, Slea Head Dr., Fahan, Ventry. www.famine-cottage.com. © **087/762-2617.** Admission €3 adults €2 children under 12. Apr–Oct daily 9:30am–6:30pm.

OTHER SCENIC DRIVES

If you're heading back toward Killarney and the Ring of Kerry from here, there are two routes—the main N86 (known locally as the "Low Road"), which is pretty enough, or the smaller but more memorable "High Road," which goes over the mountains via the **Conor Pass.** The road is narrow and lacks passing places at a few points you really wish it didn't, but the views are nothing short of incredible. The best viewpoint is a small parking area next to a waterfall, just after you begin descending through the pass. To go this way, take R559 (Spa Rd.) east out of Dingle; on the outskirts of town, when you hit a fork in the road, follow signs for Conor Pass and Tralee, to the right.

The High Road eventually meets up with the main N86, just after the nothing-much village of **Camp**—where there's another scenic alternative for the adventurous. Instead of going the way your GPS or maps app will probably steer you, around dull and trafficky Tralee, veer off down the tiny, unnamed road signposted for **Aughils,** on the right as you pass through Camp. This lovely route takes you first by a stretch of modern but idyllic houses (you'll probably dream briefly about moving here), before crossing beautiful moorland, then through another picturesque mountain pass. It then joins up with the R561 coast road, just 10 minutes or so from Castlemaine on the Ring of Kerry. But beware—although this way can definitely be a shortcut, especially in rush hours, we mean it when say the road is tiny! The last time we took this route the receptionist at our hotel raised an eyebrow and exclaimed "in a *rental car?*" (And we do not recommend either this or the Conor Pass in heavy rain or icy weather.) But remember, fortune favors the brave. Especially those with good tires.

Sports & Outdoor Pursuits in the Dingle Peninsula

SPECTATOR SPORTS

HORSE RACING   The **Dingle Races** are a major event in the Irish horse-racing calendar, with 20 or so events taking place over a long weekend in mid-August. The incredibly picturesque Ballingtaggart Racecourse is just outside Dingle, on the road to Tralee. For more information, visit www.dingleraces.ie.

ROWING   Held over a couple of days in mid-August, the **Dingle Regatta** is where you'll see Currach or *naomhóg* racing in traditional wooden boats covered with canvas (formerly animal skins) and tar. See the regatta's Facebook page for dates—search for "Dingle Regatta." Also check **www.dingle-peninsula.ie** for information on annual rowing regattas in Ballydavid (June), Ventry (July), and Brandon (Aug).

OUTDOOR PURSUITS

BEACHES   The Dingle Peninsula is home to several spectacular beaches. The most famous is **Inch Strand**—a 5km-long (3-mile) creamy stretch of sand dunes in the town of Inch (*Inse*). It makes for a beautiful stop on the coast road into Dingle, with a beach cafe (open summer only) and a colony of semi-wild ginger cats that live among the slopes of its parking lot, ever hopeful for scraps. On Kilmurray Bay, **Minard Beach,** in the shadow of Minard Castle, giant sandstone boulders form a beach unlike anything you've ever seen. It's definitely *not* safe for swimming, but ideal for a stroll or a picnic.

The calmest beaches for swimming in this area are east of Castlegregory, on the more protected west side of Tralee Bay. The beach at **Maherabeg** has a coveted European Blue Flag (meaning it is exceptionally unpolluted and environmentally safe), and the beaches of **Brandon Bay** are particularly scenic—great for walking and swimming. These beaches are all popular surfing spots when the wild Atlantic is doing its thing.

CYCLING   Traditional and electric bikes can be rented at **Dingle Bikes** (www.dinglebikes.com; ✆ **086/084-8378**); they will deliver to your hotel or B&B. Regular bikes are €25 and e-bikes €49 for the day (8:30am–7pm), and you are provided with maps, a helmet, and lock. Or try **Paddy's**

The **Dingle Way** begins in Tralee and circles the peninsula, covering 153km (95 miles) of gorgeous mountain and coastal landscape. The most rugged section is along Brandon Head, on the peninsula's north coast, where the trail passes between Mount Brandon and the ocean. Farther west, the section between Dunquin and Ballyferriter (24km/15 miles) follows an especially lovely stretch of Atlantic coast. For more information, pick up maps from local tourist offices.

Ireland Walk Hike Bike (www.irelandwalkhikebike.com; © **066/718-6181**) has a selection of self-guided walks and hikes on the Dingle Way, ranging between 3 and 10 days. Prices include maps/apps, accommodation, and luggage transfers. They also run fully guided hiking trips on both the Dingle Peninsula and the Kerry Way (p. 325).

A Dingle Way itinerary is also offered by **Hidden Ireland Tours,** Dingle (www.hiddenirelandtours.com; © **251/751-3087** in the U.S., or 087/235-5293), which offers guided hiking tours around the Kerry Way and Killarney National Park (p. 294).

8

COUNTY KERRY

The Dingle Peninsula

Bike Shop, Dykegate Lane (www.paddysbikeshop.com; © **066/915-2311**), where regular bikes are €18 per day, e-bikes €42. Both hire shops can suggest a number of day trips or overnight touring options.

DIVING & WATER SPORTS   On the north coast of the Dingle Peninsula, Castlegregory on protected Tralee Bay is the region's go-to place for water sports. **Waterworld,** Harbour House, Scraggane Pier, Castlegregory (www.waterworld.ie; © **066/713-9292**), is a diving center that offers packages including diving, room, and board at good rates. Classes for beginners are available. The house is a short boat ride from most of the diving sites. You can take surfing, SUP, or windsurfing lessons at **Jamie Knox Watersports,** Brandon Bay, Castlegregory (www.jamieknox.com; © **066/713-9411**), on the road between Castlegregory and Fahamore. Surfing lessons start at €25 and windsurfing lessons cost from €40, including all equipment.

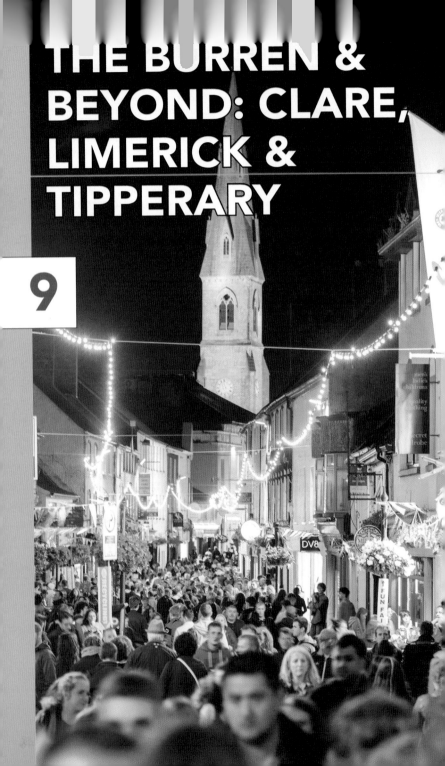

THE BURREN & BEYOND: CLARE, LIMERICK & TIPPERARY

9

N orth of County Kerry, the west coast of Ireland has long drawn visitors entranced by its stunning landscapes. From the verdant farmland of the Shannon River Valley, head north to the towering Cliffs of Moher, drive winding roads to the extraordinary alien landscape of the Burren National Park, or travel inland and wander through the ancient ruined fortress known as the Rock of Cashel. However far you go, whether it's along the Wild Atlantic Way coast or past lush farmland, there's always something wonderful to catch your eye.

Bordering Kerry to the north, but entirely separated by the broad Shannon Estuary, **County Clare** is a rugged and beguiling county. Its principal draw is the region known as the Burren, a stark and desolate rocky landscape filled with mysterious, ancient stone dolmens—it's quite unlike anywhere else in the country. As if that wasn't enough to impress, Clare also has the famous coastal Cliffs of Moher, a place of high drama and majestic beauty. The contrast with its neighbor, and rural **County Limerick,** could hardly be more pronounced. Limerick is distinguished by the swirls and eddies of the Shannon River and its verdant valley. To the east, **Tipperary** is filled with pleasant, emerald-green farmland. In truth, Tipperary doesn't contain much that's worth going out of the way for, with one major exception: the Rock of Cashel, one of Ireland's most spectacular medieval ruins. It's worth a trip across the county all on its own.

ESSENTIALS
Arriving

BY PLANE   Several of the big airlines operate regular scheduled flights into **Shannon Airport,** off the Limerick–Ennis road (N18), County Clare (www. shannonairport.com; ✆ **061/712000**), 24km (15 miles) west of Limerick city. If you need a taxi, you can catch one at the airport or prebook with **Shannon Airport Taxis** (www.shannonairportcab.com; ✆ **061/471-538**). Alternatively, **Bus Éireann** (www.buseireann.ie; ✆ **1850/836-611**) provides regular bus service from Shannon Airport to **Colbert Station** in Limerick.

BY BUS   **Bus Éireann** (www.buseireann.ie; ✆ **1850/836-611**) provides regular bus service from all parts of Ireland to most towns listed in this chapter, although service isn't frequent in the most rural areas, and many of the sights located outside of towns and villages are not served by public transportation.

FACING PAGE: **Fleadh Ennis in County Clare.**

BY TRAIN   **Irish Rail** operates direct trains from Dublin, Cork, and Killarney, with connections from other parts of Ireland, to Limerick's **Colbert Station,** Parnell Street (www.irishrail.ie; ℰ **061/315555**). **Irish Rail** also runs trains to **Clonmel** and **Thurles** in County Tipperary (www.irishrail.ie; ℰ **01/836-6222**) and to **Ennis** in County Clare.

BY CAR   Although several of the major sights in this region can be reached on public transportation, you really need a car for the more remote places. Shannon Airport has offices for international car-rental chains **Avis** (www.avis.ie; ℰ **061/715600**), **Budget** (www.budget.ie; ℰ **061/471361**), **Hertz** (www.hertz.ie; ℰ **061/471369**), and **Enterprise** (www.enterprise.ie; ℰ **061/704914**). Several local firms also maintain desks at the airport; among the most reliable is **Dan Dooley Rent-A-Car** (www.dan-dooley.ie; ℰ **061/471098**).

COUNTY CLARE

With its miles of pasture and softly rolling fields, at first glance Clare seems a pleasantly pastoral place. But head to the coast and a dramatic landscape awaits, with plunging cliffs and crashing waves. Turn north from there and you'll find visual drama of a different kind, courtesy of the stark, rocky landscapes of the Burren.

Visitor Information

The **Burren Centre** in Kilfenora (www.theburrencentre.ie; ℰ **065/708-8030**) is the place to go for information on the Burren region. In addition, visitor information points are on Main Street in **Ballyvaughan** (ℰ **065/707-7464**) and at the **Cliffs of Moher** (ℰ **065/708-6141**).

Exploring the Burren

The **Burren National Park ★★★** (p. 348) is far and away the county's greatest attraction. You could spend several days exploring its profound wilderness, although a day is plenty to hit the high points. One of the best ways to explore the Burren is to take the R480. Through a series of corkscrew turns, the road curves from **Corofin** through gorgeous scenery north to **Ballyvaughan,** a delightful little village overlooking the blue waters of Galway Bay. **Lisdoonvarna,** on the park's western edge, is a small and charmingly old-fashioned town that has long been known for its natural mineral springs. Each summer, it draws thousands of people to bathe in its sulfuric streams, iron creeks, and iodine lakes (see box on p. 354).

Aillwee Cave ★★ CAVES   The story of how this deep cave system came to be discovered starts with a curious dog. In 1944, a local farmer followed his dog into a small crevice in the hillside. The man was astonished to find that it opened into a huge cavern with 1,000m (3,280 ft.) of passages running straight into the heart of a mountain. The publicity-shy farmer kept it to himself for decades before eventually spreading the

Counties Clare, Limerick & Tipperary

345

word. Professional cave explorers later uncovered its magnificent bridged chasms, deep caverns, frozen waterfall, and hollows created by hibernating brown bears (which have been extinct in Ireland for 10,000 years). Guided tours are excellent here, usually led by geology students from area universities. Enjoy the spookiness when they turn out the lights for a minute so you can experience the depth of the darkness inside. Tours last approximately 30 minutes and are conducted continuously. On the same site, the **Burren Birds of Prey Centre** is a working aviary designed to mimic the natural habitat of the buzzards, falcons, eagles, and owls that live there. For €95 per person you can take a private, 45-minute "Hawk Walk," where a handler shows you the birds up close and teaches you how to handle a hawk for yourself. It culminates in a guided forest walk, where you learn how to release the bird and call it back. (The handlers need at least a day's notice, ideally more, to arrange a Hawk Walk—you can't book on the day. Tickets include admission to the cave and the Birds of Prey Centre.) A couple of on-site craft shops sell Aillwee's own brand of cheese, among other things.

Off R480, near Ballyvaughan, Co. Clare. www.aillweecave.ie. ℂ **065/707-7036.** Admission to caves: €15 adults; €7 children; €34–€46 families. Birds of Prey Centre: €15 adults; €7 children; €34–€46 families. Combined ticket: €22 adults; €12 children; €52–€64 families. Daily July–Aug 10am–6:30pm; Mar–June and Sept–Oct 10am–5:30pm; Nov–Feb 10am–5pm. Times are first and last tours.

Wildflower spotting in the Burren.

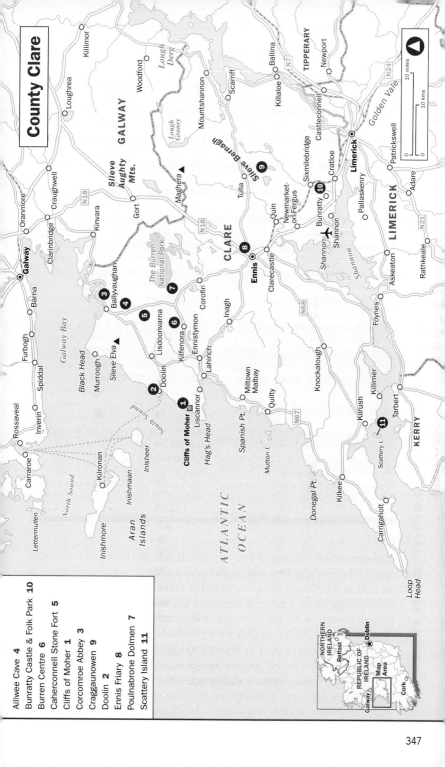

County Clare

Allwee Cave **4**
Bunratty Castle & Folk Park **10**
Burren Centre **6**
Caherconnell Stone Fort **5**
Cliffs of Moher **1**
Corcomroe Abbey **3**
Craggaunowen **9**
Doolin **2**
Ennis Friary **8**
Poulnabrone Dolmen **7**
Scattery Island **11**

THE burren NATIONAL PARK

The otherworldly landscape of the **Burren National Park** spreads across 1,653 hectares (4,083 acres) carved by nature from bare carboniferous limestone, both desolate and beautiful. Sheets of rock jut and undulate in a kind of moonscape as far as you can see. Amid the rocks, delicate wildflowers somehow find enough dirt to thrive; ferns curl gently around boulders, moss softens hard edges, orchids flower exotically, and violets brighten the landscape. With the flowers come butterflies that thrive on the rare flora. Even the Burren's animals are unusual: The pine marten (small weasels), stoat (ermine), and badger, all rare in the rest of Ireland, are common here.

The Burren began to develop 300 million years ago when layers of shells and sediment were deposited under a tropical sea. Many millions of years later, those layers were exposed by erosion and poor prehistoric farming methods. Since then, it's all been battered by the Irish rain and winds, producing the haunting landscape you see today.

Humans first began to leave their mark here about 7,000 years ago. The park is particularly rich in archaeological remains from the Neolithic through the medieval periods—dolmens and wedge tombs (approximately 120 of them), ring forts (500 of those), round towers, ancient churches, high crosses, monasteries, and holy wells.

Though there's no official entrance, the park is centered at Mullaghmore Mountain—and like all national parks in Ireland, it's completely free to enter (www.burrennationalpark.ie; *C* **065/682-7693**). The **Burren Centre** (www.the burrencentre.ie; *C* **065/708-8030**), on R476 to Kilfenora, provides an informative overview with films, landscape models, and interpretive displays. Admission to the center is €6 adults, €5 seniors and students, €4 children ages 6 to 16, and €20 families (free for children 5 and under). It's open daily June to August from 9:30am to 5:30pm; mid-March to May and September to October 10am to 5pm. A craft shop and tearoom are also on-site. In June, July, and August, local guide **Tony Kirby** (www.heartofburren walks.com; *C* **087/2925487**) leads 2½-hour guided walks from outside the center at 10:30am on Tuesday, Wednesday, and Thursday, and 2:15pm on Friday. The cost is €35, including entry to the exhibition. The center is next to the ruins of **Kilfenora Cathedral,** which has some interesting wall carvings—look for the heads above what's left of the doors and windows.

Caherconnell Stone Fort ★ ANCIENT SITE Built sometime around the year A.D. 950, this rugged early medieval ring fort was used on and off as a defensive structure until the 1600s. It's one of the best-preserved ruins of its kind in Ireland; the dry stone walls are around 3m (approximately 9 ft.) tall in places, and equally as thick. Evidence of a much earlier structure, possibly dating to the Neolithic period, have been found nearby (though there's very little to see). The site is rich in artifacts, thanks to the high-caliber metalwork that was produced here in the Middle Ages, and you'll often see archaeology students at work here. A visitor center has a cafe and an exhibition focusing on the Burren's forts, dolmens, and other ancient monuments. More entertainingly, you can also see sheepdog "trials" (demonstrations, that is—they haven't done anything wrong) at the fort from March to October. See the website for a weekly calendar of when the trials are scheduled to take place.

On R480, 1km (¾ mile) N of the Poulnabrone Dolmen (see below), near Carran, Co. Clare. www.caherconnell.com. ℂ **065/708-9999.** Admission to fort: €6 adults, seniors, and students; €4 children under 12; €18 families. Sheepdog demos: €6 adults, seniors, and students; €3 children under 12; €15 families. Joint ticket fort & demos: €10 adults, seniors, and students; €5.60 children under 12; €24.50 families. July–Aug 10:30am–5pm; May–June and Sept–Oct 10:30am–4:30pm. Last tour 45 min. before closing.

Corcomroe Abbey ★★ RELIGIOUS SITE/RUINS   Set jewel-like in a languid green valley bounded by rolling hills, the jagged ruins of this Cistercian abbey are breathtaking. Donal Mór O'Brien founded the abbey in 1194, and his grandson, a former king of Thomond, is entombed in the structure's northern wall. Some interesting medieval and Romanesque carvings are set in the stone, including one of a bishop with a crosier. Corcomroe is a lonely spot, except for Easter morning, when people come from miles around to celebrate Mass. On your visit, look for a mound, surrounded by trees, beside the road on the way out—it's the remains of an ancient ring fort.

Signposted from L1014, near Oughtmama, Co. Clare. No phone. Free admission (open site).

Poulnabrone Dolmen ★ ANCIENT SITE   This portal tomb is an exquisitely preserved prehistoric site, made all the more arresting by the alien Burren landscape in which it sits. Its dolmen (stone table) is huge and surrounded by a natural pavement of rocks. The tomb has been dated back 5,000 years. When it was excavated in the 1980s, the remains of 16 people were found. And yet, it's still a mystery how the gigantic boulders were moved and lifted—the capstone alone weighs 4½ tonnes (5 tons). In summer, you shouldn't have much trouble finding this sight—just look for all the tour buses; at times they literally block the road.

On R480, 1km (¾ mile) S of Caherconnell Stone Fort (see above), near Carran, Co. Clare. Free admission (open site).

Exploring the Clare Coast

One of Ireland's most photographed places, the **Cliffs of Moher** draw thousands of visitors to Clare's remote reaches every day of the year, rain or shine. Rising to vertiginous heights above the Atlantic Ocean, the cliffs are undeniably impressive. The site is well worth a visit, but be aware that in the high season, the crowds can rather spoil the effect.

Farther along the Clare Coast, **Lahinch** is an old-fashioned Victorian seaside resort, with a wide beach and long promenade curving along the horseshoe bay. The beach is great for surfing, and golfers love the outstanding links course (p. 359).

Traditional Irish music is always on heavy rotation in Clare, which has a vibrant music scene. The secluded fishing village of **Doolin,** near Lahinch, is the unofficial capital of Irish traditional music. The village is also a departure point for the short boat trip to the beautiful and isolated **Aran Islands** (p. 384).

The Clare Coast is dotted with seaside resorts with varying degrees of crowds and beauty, such as **Kilrush, Kilkee, Miltown Malbay,** and **Ennistymon.** You'll also stumble across places with quirky names, like Puffing Hole, Intrinsic Bay, Chimney Hill, Elephant's Teeth, Mutton Island, and Lover's Leap.

Bunratty Castle & Folk Park ★★ HERITAGE SITE   Built in 1425 and restored in the 1950s, Bunratty is an impressive early-15th-century castle, and home to two major tourist attractions: a "living-history" re-creation of a 19th-century village, and a riotous nighttime medieval banquet. You can tour the interior of the castle, which is surprisingly complete, including a fine collection of medieval furniture and art. The restored walled garden is a beautiful place to wander around. However, the folk park is probably the bigger draw here. Actors in period costume wander around as you walk through the authentic-looking village center, complete with everything from a post office and schoolroom to a doctor's office. You can go inside

Entertainers and diners at a medieval banquet in Bunratty Castle.

walk this way: **THE BURREN WAY**

With its unique terrain and meandering walking paths, the Burren lends itself beautifully to walking. The **Burren Way** is a 42km (26-mile) signposted route stretching from Ballyvaughan to Liscannor, incorporating old "green roads"—unpaved former highways that crisscross the Burren landscape in inaccessible areas. (Most were created during the Great Famine as work projects for starving locals.) An information sheet outlining the route is available from any tourist office. You can also download trail maps of marked Burren walks at the **Burren National Park**'s website (**www.burrennationalpark. ie**)—they run free guided walks during the summer season. Marie McGauran of **Burren Experience** (www.mullaghmore-burren.com; ✆ **086/821-9441**) will take you on a 2- to 3-hour guided nature walk to some remote and beautiful areas in the park that you can only reach on foot. Walks cost €25 for an adult; accompanying children under 16 can join free.

each and chat with the occupants. Meanwhile, professional craftspeople work their trades, using traditional methods. There's even a Victorian-style pub. It's all great fun, and a brilliant way to imbue kids with a sense of history. In the evenings, the medieval banquet takes over the castle's Great Hall. After a full, sit-down meal, actors and musicians in medieval garb put on a lively show of music, dancing, and folk stories. The banquet starts at 5:30pm and booking is essential—it can sell out months in advance.

Signposted from N18 (Shannon-Limerick Rd.), Bunratty, Co. Clare. www.bunratty castle.ie. ✆ **061/711-222.** Admission €16.95 adults; €11.50 seniors and students; €11.50 children 4–18; free for children 3 and under; €49.95–€62.50 families. Book online for discounts. Medieval banquet: €63–€70 adults; €35 children 2–18. Castle: Daily 9:30am–5:30pm. Last admission to castle 1½ hr. before closing.

Cliffs of Moher ★★ NATURAL SITE   The cries of nesting seabirds are faintly audible over the roar of the Atlantic crashing against the base of these breathtaking cliffs. Undulating for 8km (5 miles) along the coast, the cliffs tower as high as 214m (702 ft.) over the sea. In bad weather, access is (understandably) limited—the wind can be dangerous here. When the weather is fine, a guardrail offers you a small sense of security as you peek over the edge. (Some visitors always insist on climbing over it for a better view of the sheer drop—needless to say, this is against the rules and extremely dangerous.) On a clear day, you can see the Aran Islands in Galway Bay as misty shapes in the distance. Look the other way, however, and you'll see a constant throng of tour groups, coaches, and cars. The enormous visitor center houses gift shops, a high-tech "Cliffs of Moher Experience," and various other exhibits that feel designed to wring every last cent out of this natural wonder. Furthermore, the visitor center has the only (legal) parking, which you can't use without buying entry tickets to the visitor center—effectively turning it into a steep

The Cliffs of Moher, a perennial tourist attraction.

per person parking charge. (You may see places beside the narrow road where you could illegally park and walk straight up to the cliffs for free, but this is very much at your own risk.) Because of the overwhelming popularity of the cliffs, in summer it can be crowded. In July and August, the cliffs stay open until 9pm, and arriving late in the day is a good way to see the view without a crowd. Head up the path beside the visitor center to **O'Brien's Tower** for the best view of the cliffs. The 19th-century tower is a knockout spot for photos, although—surprise!—you'll have to pay an extra €4 to climb the stairs. Another way to see the cliffs (for free) is to walk along the Coastal Walk North from either **Doolin** or **Liscannor.** The entire walk is 20km (12.4 miles) and takes around 4½ hours, but for a shorter version you can just walk to the visitor center and then take a shuttle bus back to where you started—the shuttle runs eight times a day between the starting points and visitor center. Shuttle fares start at €4 (see www.cliffsofmoher.ie for timetable).

Near Liscannor, Co. Clare. www.cliffsofmoher.ie. ✆ **065/708-6141.** Admission €7 adults, seniors, and students; free for children 15 and under; family €16. Price includes parking and visitor center admission. May–Aug daily 8am–9pm; Mar–Apr and Sept–Oct daily 8am–7pm; Nov–Feb daily 9am–5pm. Tower and cliffs may be inaccessible in bad weather.

Craggaunowen ★★ HERITAGE SITE   Following the successful castle-plus-open-air-museum template of **Bunratty Castle** (see above), Craggaunowen focuses on what life would have been like for the Bronze Age inhabitants of Ireland. A reconstructed "crannog" shows how Celts lived, worked, and defended themselves from the Iron Age right through to the middle of the first millennium. (Records indicate, in fact, that scattered communities lived like this as late as the 1600s.) Other reconstructions to explore here include a 4th-century ring fort and underground passages known as souterrains, thought to have been used for cool storage. (Incidentally, some archaeologists believe there are real souterrains at **Caherconnell Stone Fort**—see p. 348—that have yet to be excavated.) Costumed historian-guides provide demonstrations of the techniques inhabitants of such settlements would have used to cook, build, weave, and so on. Also on display is the Brendan Boat, a replica of the kind of vessel Vikings are believed to have sailed to America; it was built in 1976 by explorer Tim Severin, who used it to do just that—a 4,500-mile journey that took him and his crew just over a year. The 16th-century **Craggaunowen Castle** is also on the grounds (included in the price).

Kilmurray, near Quin, Co. Clare. www.craggaunowen.ie. (C) **061/711-222.** Admission: €10 adults; €7.50 students; €8 seniors and €7 children 4–18; free for children under 3; €30–€40 families. Easter to early Sept daily 10am–5pm. Last admission 1 hr. before closing. Closed mid-Sept to Easter.

Doolin ★★ VILLAGE   Doolin's old pubs and restaurants ring with the sound of fiddle and accordion all year long, earning this secluded fishing village a reputation as the unofficial capital of Irish traditional music. Most famous among them is **Gus O'Connor's Pub** (Fisher St.; www.gusoconnorsdoolin.com; (C) **065/707-4168**), set among a row of thatched fisherman's cottages, about a 10-minute walk from the seafront. Great though the craic is here, the pub's fame inevitably draws crowds, and it can get packed to the rafters on a busy night. If you're looking for something a little more authentic, head up the road to **McGann's** (Main St.; www.mcgannspubdoolin.com; (C) **065/707-4133**); it's less well-known and not so unrelentingly jammed as Gus O'Connor's. In fact, on many nights, there are no locals in Gus's at all—they're all here, downing pints of Guinness and listening to the fiddles. Feel free to join them. Doolin is on R479, about 7.8km (4¾ miles) west of Lisdoonvarna.

Tourist Information Centre: Next to the Hotel Doolin, Fitz's Cross, Doolin, Co. Clare. www.doolin.ie (C) **065/707-5649.**

Ennis Friary ★ RELIGIOUS SITE/RUINS   When you walk around what's left of Ennis Friary, it can be hard to get a sense of its original scale. Records show, however, that in 1375 it was the home and workplace for no less than 350 friars and 600 students. Founded in 1241, this Franciscan abbey was a famous seat of learning in medieval times, making Ennis a focal point of Western Europe for many years. It was finally forced to close in 1692, and thereafter fell into ruin, but it's been partly restored, and contains many beautifully sculpted medieval tombs, decorative fragments, and carvings, including the famous McMahon tomb, with its striking representations of the Passion. The nave and chancel are the oldest parts of the friary, but other structures, such as the 15th-century tower, transept, and sacristy, are also rich in architectural detail.

Abbey St., Ennis, Co. Clare. www.heritageireland.ie. (C) **065/682-9100.** Admission €5 adults; €4 seniors; €3 children and students; €13 families. Easter–Sept daily 10am–6pm; Oct daily 10am–5pm. Last admission 45 min. before closing.

Scattery Island ★ ISLAND/RUINS   Atmospheric monastic ruins dating from the 6th century perch upon this unspoiled island in the Shannon Estuary near Kilrush, on Clare's south coast. A high, round tower and several churches are all that remain of an extensive settlement founded by St. Senan. Ferries depart multiple times a day and take around 30 minutes

THE BURREN & BEYOND: CLARE, LIMERICK & TIPPERARY

County Clare

LOVED UP IN lisdoonvarna

If you've been looking for love in all the wrong places, clearly you've never been to Lisdoonvarna. This County Clare town lives for l'amour.

There's a Matchmaker Pub on the main street (inside the Imperial Hotel) and local resident Willie Daly is a professional matchmaker. Every autumn, the town hosts the month-long **Lisdoonvarna Matchmaking Festival** (www.match makerireland.com). Thousands of lovelorn singletons come in search of The One, and locals cheer them on. Up and down each street, every atmospheric corner is used for mixers and minglers.

Residents stir the pot by hosting romantic breakfasts, dinners, games, and dances. There's music in every pub, and crowds on the narrow village streets. So good are their intentions and so charming is their belief in true love—in the idea that there really is somebody out there for everybody, and that they might find each other in a far-flung corner of western Ireland—that you, too, may believe.

to cross to the island. Island visits are usually 2 or 2.5 hours—tickets include a 1-hour guided monastic village walking tour and free time for a walk, picnic, or swim. A longer Great Island Experience gives visitors 4 to 5 hours on the island (on selected dates only). You can also prebook a packed lunch with the ferry company.

Kilrush Marina, Kilrush, Co. Clare. www.scatteryislandtours.com. © **085/250-5512.** Return ferry and tour tickets €25 adults; €16 children 13–17; €12 children 3–12; €20 seniors and students; €65 family. Sat–Sun May and Sept: 2 tours per day between 8am–4pm. Daily June–Aug: up to 4 tours per day between 9am–4pm. The island is tidal, so tour times vary each day thanks to tide times; call in advance or book online.

Where to Stay in County Clare

County Clare contains the most unique and special places to stay in the region. That said, it's perhaps a little surprising that there aren't more of them. Fortunately, there are some real gems among their number.

Aran View Country House ★★   The clue's in the name at this small and friendly country house in Doolin: There's a glorious view across 100 acres of rolling green farmland and icy blue sea, out to the fog-wreathed Aran Islands in the distance. The Georgian country house was built in the mid–18th century and later expanded, and its good-size guest rooms maintain a traditional feel. The lounge wisely takes full advantage of the amazing view out front, making this a lovely spot for an early evening glass of wine as the sun goes down. Breakfasts are good and fresh in the beautiful, vaulted-ceiling dining room. Doolin is about a 10-minute drive up the coast from the Cliffs of Moher.

Coast Rd., Doolin, Co. Clare. www.aranview.com. © **065/704-5004.** 11 units. €120–€150 double. Free parking. Rates include breakfast. **Amenities:** Wi-Fi (free). Closed Oct–Easter.

Dromoland Castle ★★ If you've always wanted to stay in a real Irish castle, Dromoland might just fit the bill, with its huge grey stone walls, battlements, and Gothic features, right down to suits of armor in the hallways. It's a five-star hotel so it's pricey—but if you can splash out for a night of luxury, it's worth it. A castle has stood here since 1014 and was rebuilt over the years. The current buildings date to the 1700s and 1800s but have been fully modernized. Dinner at the **Earl of Thomond** dining room is worth dressing up for (and gentlemen will need a jacket), with a tasting menu (€95) or à-la-carte options. You can also have afternoon tea in the **Gallery** or arrange a picnic basket and explore the 450-acre grounds for the day—it has an 18-hole golf course, lake fishing, tennis, falconry, and a spa—plus a pool and gym in the golf club (just a short walk or golf-buggy ride from the main castle), hone to the **Fig Tree Restaurant,** a less formal option for dinner.

Newmarket-on-Fergus, Co. Clare. www.dromoland.ie. ⓒ **061/368-144.** 97 units. €310–€680 double, €845–€2,800 suite. Check website for 2-night and other offers. Rates include breakfast. Free parking. **Amenities:** 2 restaurants; bar; concierge; gym; golf course; pool; room service, Wi-Fi (free).

Fergus View ★★ There are breathtaking views to be had at this sweet B&B near Corofin, one of the gateways to the Burren. You could sit for ages marveling at the long vista of rolling fields and rambling hills, joined by the wonderful owner, Mary, as she brings you a fortifying tray of tea to sip by the open fire. Mary is also an expert on the Burren and all this area has to offer visitors and will happily share her encyclopedic knowledge. Guest rooms are small and simple, but the beds are comfortable. On the grounds is a self-catering lodge that sleeps five. Fergus View is closed from November to Easter.

On R476 in Kilnaboy, 3.2km (2 miles) N of Corofin, Co. Clare. www.fergusview.com. ⓒ **065/683-7606.** 6 units. €84 double. Discounts for 2 nights or more. Free parking. Rates include breakfast. **Amenities:** Wi-Fi (free). Closed Nov–Easter.

Gregans Castle Hotel ★★★ An elegant 18th-century house in an extraordinary setting, Gregans is not in fact at all castle-like, but don't let that bother you. The unique location, deep in the Burren, makes this one of the most peaceful hotels in Ireland. It's been delighting guests for decades, including J. R. R. Tolkien, who was apparently so inspired by the otherworldly views that he drew on them to describe Mordor in *The Lord of the Rings.* Guest rooms are design-magazine chic, with modern furnishings and bay windows. There are no televisions, to enable guests to get maximum peace from their stay. If you can't stretch to the cost of a night here, consider booking a table in the superb restaurant, **Gregans Castle** ★★★ (p. 357). Chef Robbie McCauley's modern Irish cooking is utterly superlative—though if you don't want to splurge, the excellent bar menu is much cheaper. Check the website

THE BURREN & BEYOND: CLARE, LIMERICK & TIPPERARY

County Clare

for some attractive dinner, bed-and-breakfast packages and midweek deals.

Ballyvaughan, Co. Clare. www.gregans.ie. ℭ **065/707-7005.** 22 units. €250–€340 double; €375–€540 suite. Free parking. Rates include breakfast. **Amenities:** Restaurant; bar; Wi-Fi (free).

Sheedy's ★★   Less than an hour from Shannon Airport and 10 minutes from the Cliffs of Moher, Sheedy's location could hardly be better. It lies at the edge of the charming country town of Lisdoonvarna. The owners pride themselves on offering rural charm with all the comforts of any urban home. Spacious guest rooms are all done in low-key classic country-house style, with armoires (called wardrobes here) and armchairs. It's not fussy; instead, it's pleasantly home-like. There are fireplaces to sit by with hot tea on a cold day. The award-winning in-house restaurant prides itself on using local meat and seafood in its French-influenced cooking. Try this place and you'll undoubtedly become a regular.

Main St., Lisdoonvarna, Co. Clare. www.sheedys.com. ℭ **065/707-4026.** 11 units. €185 double. Free parking. Check website for offers and 2-night walking breaks. Rates include breakfast. **Amenities:** Restaurant; bar; Wi-Fi (free).

Where to Eat in County Clare

Historically County Clare doesn't have the foodie reputation of somewhere like Cork, but that seems to be changing. In addition to the restaurants listed below, there are many stellar places to get light meals. The **Wooden Spoon** in Killaloe (Bridge St.; no website) is so popular with locals for its cakes, sandwiches, quiches, and salads that there is almost always a line out the door at lunchtime. Regulars believe it's worth the wait for fresh, homemade meals, and excellent coffee. If you're in Ballyvaughan and craving lunch, look no further than the **Larder Deli** (Ballyvaughan Enterprise Centre; no website), which uses locally baked sourdough bread and local cheeses in its sandwiches and the freshest produce in its hearty salad plates (lentil and carrot with sesame dressing is a favorite). The homemade sausage rolls are legendary, but there's lots for vegetarians here as well. In Lisdoonvarna, the **Burren Storehouse** (Kincora Rd.; burrenexperiences.ie) is a microbrewery and eatery whose humble setting (picnic tables on a concrete floor) belies its elevated cooking. The wood-fired pizzas are crisp-edged with local toppings, meats are chargrilled to perfection, and local oysters are so fresh they might pick a fight. Well worth a stop if you're in town.

Barrtrá Seafood Restaurant ★ SEAFOOD   A friendly, family-run place with a good lineup of simple, tasty seafood, this restaurant looks out over Liscannor Bay. Just look at a map and you'll quickly see why that makes this such a lovely spot in the late evening—the sun sets over the sea on a virtually direct line to the dining room. You can order à la carte or opt for the "surprise" menu. You decide whether you want fish, meat, vegetarian, or a mixture and specify anything you *don't* want (or can't eat), and the chef prepares a five-course dinner for your table. Otherwise, your à la carte choices might include oysters or fisherman's broth, perhaps, followed by a juicy steak or pan-fried haddock with caper berries and lime butter.

Miltown Malbay Rd., Lahinch, Co. Clare. www.barrtra.com. ☎ **065/708-1280.** 5-course menus €45–€50. Entrees €26–€30. Mar–Apr and Oct–Dec Fri–Sat 5:30–9pm, Sun noon–7pm; May–Sept Wed–Sat 5:30–9pm, Sun noon–7pm; July–Aug lunch 12:30–4:30pm. Closed Jan–Feb.

Durty Nelly's ★ IRISH/PUB FOOD   You don't walk into a pub called Durty Nelly's expecting haute cuisine, but some welcome surprises are to be found here. It serves hearty pub food—fish and chips, steak sandwiches, burgers, and salads. Those who don't mind a bit of cheesy tourist novelty can have their picture taken while pouring their own pint of Guinness. Durty Nelly's actually has three dining rooms—the main pub area, the more refined Oyster Restaurant, and the Loft. The latter two offer an upscale version of the same food (good steaks, Thai curries, fresh seafood, and so on). And if you're wondering about the name, "Durty Nelly" was a somewhat ribald heroine of Irish folklore, said to have invented the magical cure-all (and highly alcoholic) variety of moonshine, poitín or potcheen (see box on p. 410).

Next to Bunratty Castle, Bunratty, Co. Clare. www.durtynellys.ie. ☎ **061/364-861.** Pub: Entrees €15–€30. Daily noon–10pm. Oyster Restaurant: Entrees €20–€30. Daily noon–10pm. The Loft: Entrees €20–€30. Daily 5:30–10pm.

Gregans Castle ★★★ MODERN IRISH   The inhouse dining room at **Gregans Castle Hotel** in Ballyvaughan (p. 355) is the perfect place for an elegant meal with an exquisite view of the wild countryside. Everything is locally sourced; a six-course tasting menu might include scallops or whipped goat curd, followed by halibut with sea purslane (similar to spinach), or perhaps a beef filet with white garlic and bordelaise. The atmosphere is friendly, and the service is excellent.

Ballyvaughan, Co. Clare. www.gregans.ie. ☎ **065/707-7005.** Fixed-price menu: 7 courses €80; 10 courses €95. Daily 6–9pm. Bar food 12:30pm–2:30pm. Closed Dec–mid-Feb. Children under 7 only allowed at 6pm sharp.

Vaughan's Anchor Inn ★★ SEAFOOD   A 10-minute drive from the Cliffs of Moher, this excellent pub specializes in topnotch seafood. Liscannor Bay crab claws come with creamy garlic butter and fresh bread, while the fish and chips are indulgently fried in pure beef drippings. At lunch you'll find a few lighter mains alongside the heartier options. Vaughan's Anchor Inn is on the main street in Liscannor; look for the long white building with the small parking lot on the right, not long after you round the bend and see the small town center ahead of you.

Main St., Liscannor, Co. Clare. www.vaughans.ie. ☎ **065/708-1548.** Entrees €21–€34. Daily noon–9pm.

A fire crackles in the bar at the Wild Honey Inn.

Wild Honey Inn ★★★ MODERN IRISH   This gastropub in tiny Lisdoonvarna was recently awarded a Michelin star, and it only takes one meal here to see why. In a 19th-century pub, Chef Aidan McGrath and Kate Sweeney are producing extraordinary, unique cuisine, with an emphasis on wild local produce, and they are doing it in an atmosphere as relaxed as your grandmother's kitchen. A wood fire crackles at the hearth while diners who have traveled from all over the world sample charred organic salmon with capers and gravadlax, or duck and foie gras terrine with wild mushrooms and roasted wild hazelnuts, topped with puree of local apples. Expect whatever is in season, locally sourced, gorgeously cooked with a light touch. The wine list is small but well chosen. Make sure to stay over—double rooms cost €180 to €250 (including breakfast), and the ground-floor rooms open onto a little patio.

Kincora Rd., Lisdoonvarna, Co. Clare. www.wildhoneyinn.com. ℂ **065/707-4300.** Fixed-price menu €80. Tues–Sat 6–9pm, Mar–Oct. Bookings essential.

Sports & Outdoor Pursuits in County Clare

BIRD-WATCHING   The **Bridges of Ross,** on the north side of **Loop Head,** is one of the prime autumn bird-watching sites in Ireland, especially during northwest gales, when several rare species have been seen with some consistency. The **lighthouse** at the tip of the head is also a popular spot for watching seabirds.

DOLPHIN-WATCHING   The **Shannon Estuary** is home to about 70 bottlenose dolphins, one of four such resident groups of dolphins in Europe. **Dolphinwatch** (www.dolphinwatch.ie; ℂ **087/917-5984**) runs 2- to

3-hour cruises costing €35 adults, €20 children 15 and under. Advance booking is essential.

GOLF   One of the region's most famous golf courses is at **Lahinch Golf Club,** Lahinch (www.lahinchgolf.com; ✆ **065/708-1003**). Of its two 18-hole links courses, the "Old Course"—the longer championship links course—is the one that has given Lahinch its worldwide repute. This course's elevations, especially at the 9th and 13th holes, make for great views, but it also makes wind an integral part of play. Watch the goats, Lahinch's legendary weather forecasters: If they huddle by the clubhouse, it means a storm is approaching. Visitors are welcome to play, especially on weekdays; greens fees are €200 to €250 for the Old Course and a more affordable €35 to €40 for the newer Castle Course.

NATURE WALKS   The Burren is full of rare plants and flowers and interesting patches of shoreline that make it a wonderful place for a guided walk or tour. Forage for different seaweeds on the rocky shores of The Burren on a 1.5-hour tour with **Wild Kitchen** (www.wildkitchen.ie; tours €30). Or take a "Shuck Off" oyster tour with **Flaggy Shore Oyster** to see how oysters grow and how to shuck them, following up with an **oyster picnic** (www.flaggyshoreoysters.ie; class and picnic €25). On a 2.5-hour herb walk, herbalist and naturopath **Lisa Guinan** (www.irishherbalroots.ie; €80 per person) points out the various medicinal flowers and trees that grow in the area. For something sweeter, the free guided tour at **Burren Perfumery** (www.burrenperfumery.com; 3pm tours daily June–Sept) shows visitors how local flowers and scents are transformed into lovely perfumes, skincare, and soap.

SURFING   If you've always wanted to try surfing, here's your chance: **Lahinch Surf School** (www.lahinchsurfschool.com; ✆ **087/960-9667**), set up in a hut on Lahinch promenade, specializes in getting people suited up and out on the waves—whether you surf every weekend or have never hit a board in your life. They're friendly and know their stuff. Wetsuits and surfboards are included with the lessons. Average water temps in late summer are 16°C (60.8°F)—so wetsuits are advised for the length of time

The Mass Hole

To say golf is a religious experience in Ireland wouldn't just be hyperbole. Only in Ireland can you experience the unique hazard of the "Mass hole." When the celebration of Mass was outlawed during penal times, secret Masses were often held in hidden dales, culverts, and gorges, out of sight of the British. A few golf links have incorporated such places into their courses. For example, hole 5 at the **Lahinch Golf Course** (p. 359) has a uniquely hidden spot that could easily have served this purpose. Another example is at **Waterville Golf Course** in County Kerry (p. 308), where the 12th hole is still universally known as the Mass hole.

Surfing students in training at the Lahinch Surf School.

you're in the water. Private lessons are €120; you can join a group lesson for €40 for an adult; €36 for a student; €32 for a teen. A family of two adults and two kids pay €120 (€30 per extra child) for one 2-hour lesson.

COUNTY LIMERICK

Most of County Limerick is peaceful, pleasant farmland. The picture-postcard village of **Adare** is definitely worth a visit (although you'll likely see it amid a row of tourist buses), and the number of good restaurants and hotels nearby make it a good choice for an overnight base. **Limerick City** (see box on p. 362) is not as scenic but has a rich history, and it's worth spending time in the city's medieval quarter and seeing **King John's Castle** (see box on p. 362). If your time is limited, a full day or one overnight in the city should definitely cover the highlights. Elsewhere, **Lough Gur** is also well worth a visit, with its lovely lakeside scenery and intriguing ancient sites.

Visitor Information

The **Limerick Tourist Information Centre** on Arthur's Quay, Limerick (www.limerick.ie; ℂ **061/317522**), is open Monday to Saturday 9am to 5pm; in summer it's also often open weekends (call for hours).

Another office inside the **Adare Heritage Centre,** Main St., Adare (www.adareheritagecentre.ie; ℂ **061/396-666**), is open daily year-round from 9am to 6pm.

Exploring County Limerick

Adare ★★ VILLAGE   Looking like a village plucked from a book of fairy tales, Adare has thatched cottages, black-and-white timbered houses, lichen-covered churches, and romantic ruins, all strewn along the banks of the River Maigue. Unfortunately, all of this means that Adare has been seriously discovered by the tour-bus crowds—even by May, which is still officially off-season, the roads can get clogged at times—but it's absolutely worth a stop, nonetheless. Drop in at the **Adare Heritage Centre** on Main Street, roughly in the middle of the village. Part visitor center, part museum on the history of the town, it also has a small craft store and a shop selling Irish woollens. From June to September the center also runs bus tours to Desmond Castle (p. 270), costing €10 adults; €8 seniors, students, and children; and €22.50 families.

Adare Heritage Centre, Main St., Adare, Co. Limerick. www.adareheritagecentre. ie. ℂ **061/396-666.** Free admission. Daily 9am–6pm.

Thatched cottages in the picture-postcard town of Adare.

Foynes Flying Boat Museum ★★ MUSEUM   When Shannon Airport was just a remote patch of undeveloped farmland, this was the center of international aviation in Europe. The first commercial flight from the U.S. to Europe touched down at Foynes Airport, one hot July morning in 1937. Five years later, this became one end of the first-ever regular service between the two continents. (In the same year, Foynes was also the birthplace of the Irish coffee: After a particularly violent storm turned back a New York–bound flight, the bartender was asked to serve something that would both warm up and calm down the rattled passengers—so he served hot coffee and threw shots of whiskey in for good measure.) At this engaging museum, you can see a replica of the original Pan Am "flying boat," which may make you swear never to complain about a modern flight again. Leave lots of time for your visit. There's a Maritime Museum; a Maureen O'Hara exhibition, with fashion and memorabilia from the late

It's synonymous the world over with a type of lively verse, but Limerick itself is a fascinating city with a rich history. With a population of 95,000, it's the Republic of Ireland's third-largest city (only Dublin and Cork are bigger), but the city center itself is tiny and perfectly walkable. Set along the River Shannon, Limerick has had its high and low points over the years—it has been home to Irish kings, a walled medieval city, and a prosperous Georgian town. Bleaker times in the 20th century (some of which are featured in Frank McCourt's memoir *Angela's Ashes*) have given the city a gritty, urban feel usually associated with much bigger cities. Limerick has been undergoing a regeneration in recent years, however, and the atmosphere is relaxed, lively, and safe. There's lots to see and do here. If you are spending a day or two in the city and plan to take in a number of sights, the best way to get your bearings and see the highlights is to take a guided walking tour—see **www.limerick.ie** for a list of tours and guides.

Start at **King John's Castle** ★★ (Nicholas St.; www.kingjohnscastle.com; *C* **061/711-222**), a magnificent riverside fortress dating from 1210, and the centerpiece of Limerick's historic quarter. A walk through the castle will take you through the history of Ireland via high-tech interactive displays, videos, costumed characters, and fun medieval games, and you can also explore the massive towers. Admission costs €13 adults, €9.50 seniors, students, and children 4 to 18 (free for children under 4), and €38 to €50 families. It's open April to September from 10am to 5pm (last admission 1 hr. before closing).

Also in the medieval quarter is **Saint Mary's Cathedral** ★★ (Bridge St.; www.saintmaryscathedral.ie; *C* **061/310-293**), which dates to 1168 and has quirky

star's personal collection; an Irish coffee lounge; and a fun flying boat flight simulator, plus a restaurant. Foynes, Co. Limerick. www.flyingboatmuseum.com. *C* **069/65416.** Admission €12 adults; €10 seniors and students; €6 children 5–13; free for children under 5; €30 families. Daily June–Aug 9:30am–6pm; mid-Mar to May 9:30am–5pm; Oct to mid-Nov 10am–5pm. Last admission 1 hr. before closing. Closed mid-Nov to mid-Mar.

Lough Gur ★★ LAKE/ANCIENT SITES Occupied continuously from the Neolithic period to late medieval times, this lovely lake's shores hold an unusual preponderance of ancient sites, most of which are well-signposted on the R512, the drive that skirts around the lake's edge. Archaeologists have uncovered foundations of a small farmstead built around the year 900; a lake island dwelling built between 500 and 1000; a wedge-shaped tomb that was a communal grave around 2,500 B.C.; and the extraordinary Grange Stone Circle, a 4,000-year-old site with 113 upright stones forming the largest prehistoric stone circle in Ireland. An interesting Visitor Centre helps put it all into context, with exhibits explaining why Neolithic people chose this area to settle. To find the center, turn east off R512 at Reardons Pub in Holycross, take the first left features like the Leper's Squint (a wall opening from medieval times) and "mercy seats" from the 15th century, which allowed clergy to rest while standing. It has countless small chapels and stained-glass windows, but just stepping through the doors gives you a feel of ancient history. Admission is €5.

Located in an 18th-century Customs building with a fine Palladian front, the **Hunt Museum** ★★ (Rutland St.; www. huntmuseum.com; ℂ **061/312833**) has a magnificent medieval collection, plus exhibits on ancient Greece and Rome and paintings by Picasso and Renoir. Admission costs €7.50 adults, €5.50 seniors and students, €5.50 children, and €22 families. It's open Monday to Saturday 10am to 5pm, Sunday and public holidays 2 to 5pm. For more modern art, the **Limerick City Gallery of Art** ★ (Pery Square; www.gallery.limerick.ie; ℂ **061/310633**) has contemporary art exhibitions plus a permanent collection

with work by Irish painter Jack B. Yeats. It's open Monday to Saturday 10am to 5:30pm (until 8pm on Thurs) and Sunday noon to 5:30pm (closed on public holidays). Admission is free.

A 1-hour **Treaty City Brewery tour** ★★ (www.treatycitybrewery.ie; ℂ **061/546-549**) in the medieval quarter takes you through the city's history of brewing, which dates back to the 1700s. Tours includes tastings and run between Friday and Sunday (€21 per person). If you're in town on a weekend, don't miss the **Milk Market Limerick** ★★ (www. milkmarketlimerick.ie; ℂ **061/214782**), a lively farmer's market offering everything from fruits and veggies to local cheeses, jams, and bread on Saturdays; street food, live music, and vintage shops join the offerings on Fridays and Sundays. It's a great place to sample produce from the rest of the county and collect snacks and treats for day trips. Check website for details; admission is free.

afterward, and follow Lough Gur Road. The lake itself is a great place to explore and have a picnic.

11km (6¾ miles) SE of Limerick City on R512, Lough Gur, Co. Limerick. www. loughgur.com. ℂ **061/385186.** Free access to Lough Gur itself; Visitor Centre €5 adults; €4 seniors and students; €3 children; €15 families. Visitor Centre Mar to late Oct Mon–Fri 10am–5pm, Sat–Sun and public holidays noon–6pm. Late Oct to late Feb Mon–Fri 10am–4pm, Sat–Sun and public holidays noon–4pm.

Where to Stay in Limerick City & County

Some of the larger hotels and recent builds in Limerick City feel somewhat impersonal, but many of the real finds are in the rural parts of County Limerick, where you can hide away in a lovely old cottage on a tranquil farm, or splurge on a night in a grand country-house retreat.

Adare Manor ★★★ We've long been big fans of this sumptuous place, and so it came as no surprise at all in 2019 when *Condé Naste Traveller* named it the best resort in Europe (and fifth in the world overall). The beautifully restored and converted Victorian Gothic manor house is set in a whopping 240 hectares (840 acres) of landscaped grounds. It's a

The Oak Room at Adare Manor in Limerick.

golfer's paradise, with a championship standard course, as well as archery, clay pigeon shooting, and horseback riding. The hotel has three restaurants, including the Michelin-starred **Oak Room ★★★** (p. 367). It might break the bank, but you'll have fun on the way.

Adare, Co. Limerick. www.adaremanor.com. ℭ **061/605200.** 104 units. €450–€925 double; €1,985–€1,700 state room; €3,450–€4,350 suite; €1,450–€1,700 cottage. Free parking. Rates include breakfast. **Amenities:** 2 restaurants; bar; gym; golf course; pool; room service; spa; Wi-Fi (free).

Courtyard Cottage ★ A former cowshed may not sound like the height of glamour, but this is a beautifully converted, elegant space, a short drive east of Foynes and 15 minutes' drive from Adare. You really feel away from the herd (no pun intended), with 202 hectares (500 acres) of farmland between you and civilization. This is a self-catering option set on an organic farm—guests can join in whatever farm activities are going at the time, collect eggs, feed the chickens, or play with the dogs. There's no website, but e-mail **donnaghogrady@yahoo.com.**

Askeaton, Co. Limerick. ℭ **061/392112** or 087/213–3698. Self-catering. 2 units. €150 per night, 2 nights minimum, further nights €110 per night. Free parking. **Amenities:** kitchen; tennis court; no Wi-Fi.

Echo Lodge ★★ This place was once a convent before being converted into a chic and stylish country house hotel with a relaxed, homely feel. Guest rooms are relatively small but decorated in old-world style with antiques, vintage-print wallpapers, flowing curtains, and pleasantly eccentric objets d'art such as mini-Ionic columns for bedside tables.

Dining is the highlight here—the **Mustard Seed** ★★★ restaurant is one of the best in the region (p. 367). There's usually a handful of special offers on the website, including dinner, bed-and-breakfast packages.

Ballingarry, Co. Limerick (13km/8 miles south of Adare). www.mustardseed.ie. © **069/68508.** 18 units. €140–€340 double; €340 suite. Free parking. Rates include breakfast. **Amenities:** Restaurant; bar; room service; Wi-Fi (free in public areas only).

Fitzgerald's Woodlands House Hotel ★★

The rooms at this pleasant, modern hotel aren't particularly fancy, but they're enormous—rare for a place that charges just a little more than €100 a night in low season. The hotel makes a big deal out of how good its beds are, thanks to a full 10cm (4 in.) down mattress topper on each of the beds. The in-house **Revas Spa** offers relaxation treatments and a thermal suite to while away the last hint of travel fatigue. Deals are available that include dinner, bed-and-breakfast packages and senior discounts.

Adare, Co. Limerick. www.woodlands-hotel.ie. © **061/605100.** 94 units. €105–€250 double; €250–€375 suite. Free parking. Rates include breakfast. **Amenities:** Restaurant; bar; room service; spa; Wi-Fi (free).

No. 1 Pery Square ★★

This gorgeous restored Georgian townhouse is on one of the elegant streets of the Georgian part of Limerick city, opposite People's Park and around 10 minutes' walk from the city center. For the full experience, opt for one of the six period bedrooms at the front of the house, which have roll-top and copper baths, sash windows, and views of the park. This part of the house also a lovely drawing room for guests, plus a large underground spa and an excellent restaurant where the chef uses local produce from Limerick, including gourmet meats, cheeses, and breads from suppliers at the Milk Market.

1 Pery Square, Georgian Quarter, Limerick City. www.oneperysquare.com. © **061/402-402.** 21 units. €195–€275. Free parking. Check website for dinner and spa packages. **Amenities:** 2 restaurants; bar; terrace; room service; spa; Wi-Fi (free).

Where to Eat in Limerick City & County

An exciting food scene in Limerick has emerged in the past few years in both the city and along the rural byways of the county, with places to eat that would be serious contenders on any "best of" lists for the whole of Ireland. In addition to the options listed below, for light bites and coffee in the city, check out **Rift Coffee** (30 Mallow St.; www.riftcoffee.com) or **Jack Monday's** (Thomond Bridge House, Thomondgate), while **Bean a Tí** (1 Little Catherine St.) is the place to go for cakes—the bakery has been run by the same family for three generations.

Cornstore ★★ MODERN IRISH This is a gorgeous space with a lively atmosphere. At lunch the menu is casual, featuring pub grub like sourdough pizza, gourmet burgers, and fish and chips. In the evening the lights are dimmed, candles are lit, and the menu goes upscale with dishes like braised short ribs, oven-roasted pork belly, and a selection of grilled

THERE ONCE WAS A poet FROM LIMERICK . . .

So how exactly did a genre of bawdy pub poetry come to be associated with Limerick? The answer seems buried nearly 300 years in the past. Nobody really knows who wrote the first sharply worded, five-line poem, but the format became popular in the 18th century, thanks to a group of poets who lived in the town of Croom in County Limerick. Known as the *Fili na Maighe*, or "Poets of the Maigue," the poets wrote sardonic, quick-witted poems in Irish that soon became all the rage. Their style was adopted across the region, and within a century, everybody was doing it. Anthologies on the subject list 42 poets and Irish scholars in the county in the 19th century, whose limerick-style compositions covered a range of topics: romance, drinking, personal squabbles, and politics.

But it's possible that the scathing, satiric limerick style we know today rose from an 18th-century battle of wills between poet and pub owner Sean O'Tuama and his boyhood friend Andrias MacCraith. O'Tuama and MacCraith grew up in County Limerick, but after a spectacular falling-out (nobody quite remembers over what), they vented their wit in a series of castigating verses about each other. These became enormously popular, thus birthing the modern limerick. In retrospect, they're kind of cute, although the meter sometimes feels a little stretched. As MacCraith once wrote:

O'Tuama! You boast yourself handy,
At selling good ale and bright brandy
But the fact is your liquor
Makes everyone sicker,
I tell you this, I, your good friend,
Andy.

local dry-aged beef (tasty sides include truffle or crab mac-n-cheese with a Parmesan crust). There's a decent wine and cocktail list too. Thomas St., Limerick. www.cornstore.ie. ✆ **061-609-000.** Entrees lunch €14–€24, dinner €18–€26. Wed–Thurs 4–10pm Fri–Sun noon–10pm.

1826 Adare ★★★ MODERN IRISH   It's set in a rustic thatched cottage with plenty of old-world charm (1826 is the year the first Lord of Dunraven built the cottage), but there's nothing twee or old-fashioned about the cooking here. Chef Wade Murphy has worked in some of the world's top kitchens and was awarded best chef in Limerick, and with a menu that changes every month, he works his culinary magic with the county's best produce. Expect dishes like warm chicken liver salad, served with piccalilli, pickles, and greens, or free-range pork with squash and beer mustard cream, all served in a relaxed setting. Book well in advance. Main St., Adare, Co. Limerick. www.1825adare.ie. ✆ **061/396-004.** Entrees €18.50–€35. Thurs–Sat 5–9pm; Sun 3–9pm.

Foley's at the Pike ★ PUB FOOD/GRILL   Nearly 16km (9 miles) southwest of Adare, just off the main N21 road, this friendly little bar and grill focuses on hearty, unpretentious comfort food, such as steak, fish, and grilled lamb, alongside a more international selection "from the wok" (stir-fries, fajitas, curries). Heading west from Adare on N21, take the R523 turnoff signposted for Athea.

Reens Pike, Ardagh, Co. Limerick. www.foleyspub.ie. © **069/64416.** Entrees €13–€19. Wed–Sat noon–9pm, Sun noon–8pm.

The Mustard Seed ★★★ MODERN EUROPEAN   Not so much the in-house restaurant of the excellent **Echo Lodge ★★** (p. 364) as the main attraction with guest rooms upstairs, this is one of the best-loved, and most widely known, restaurants in the region. The Mustard Seed's own kitchen garden supplies many of the ingredients. The four-course menus are imaginative and scintillating; after a starter of pecorino and egg-cream pasta with pomegranate, you could go for the monkfish prepared with seaweed and prawn bisque, or beef filet with aubergine (eggplant) and miso. An eight-course tasting menu is €75; or come before 7:30pm any night except Saturday for the Twilight Dinner, a slightly pared-down version of the main menu for €49.

Echo Lodge, Ballingarry, Co. Limerick (13km/8 miles S of Adare). www.mustardseed.ie. © **069/68508.** Fixed-price 4-course dinner €67. Daily 7–9:30pm.

The Oak Room ★★★ MODERN IRISH   The first restaurant to gain a Michelin star in this part of Ireland, the Oak Room is part of **Adare Manor ★★★** (p. 363). This is a place where you're expected to sit up straight and dress right. The food certainly lives up to the elegant surrounds; the five-course set menu may include Dexter beef and wild garlic, squab with salsify and Madeira, or perhaps a filet of John Dory, delicately flavored with hazelnut and verjus (a type of grape juice). And if you're enjoying the place too much to leave at the meal's end . . . well, you probably should anyway, since an overnight stay here can cost about the same as your transatlantic airfare home.

Adare, Co. Limerick. www.adaremanor.com. © **061/605200.** Fixed-price menus €120–€160. Wine pairings €70–€80. Daily 6–9:30pm.

Sports & Outdoor Pursuits in County Limerick

CYCLING   The **Limerick Greenway** (www.limerick.ie/greenway) is a 40km (24-mile) walking and cycling trail through bucolic rural Limerick countryside on the old Limerick-to-Kerry railway line. Don't expect jaw-dropping, dramatic scenery: This is a gorgeous, gentle jaunt past trees, farms, rivers, and old train stations, soaking up the country feels (and smells), going through a small tunnel, and perhaps stopping off for coffee and cake. It's well set up, with free parking, and a number of bike and e-bike hire companies will also take you back to your car or shuttle your luggage; rental starts from €20.

FISHING   **Celtic Angling,** in Ballingarry, just south of Adare (www.celtic angling.com; © **069/68202**), offers daylong salmon-fishing excursions on the Shannon, including pickup from Limerick City, equipment, and licenses. A day's fishing costs on average €180 to €300 per person, plus

IF THE story FITZ . . .

"Honey Fitz" was the nickname of John Fitzgerald (1863–1950), maternal grandfather to President John F. Kennedy. Born in America to Irish immigrants (his father was from Limerick), Fitzgerald was twice elected mayor of Boston.

According to the biographer Robert Dallek, Fitz had a reputation for being "the only politician who could sing "Sweet Adeline" sober and get away with it"—hence the nickname, in praise of his sweet singing voice. Between Adare and Limerick, the small town of

Patrickswell is home to the bijou **Honey Fitz Theatre** (www.loughgur.com/honeyfitz; ℭ **061/385386**). This is the main venue for the **Lough Gur Storytelling Festival,** a 5-day event in late October that celebrates the art of the good yarn, through a program of music, drama, and poetry. The theater was opened in 1994 by Fitzgerald's granddaughter, Jean Kennedy Smith (who was then U.S. ambassador). Naturally, "Sweet Adeline" was sung during the ceremony.

€50 to €100 for each additional person in a group. (Owner Paddy Dunworth also offers guided sightseeing trips and hillwalking excursions; check the website for details.)

HORSEBACK RIDING The county's fields provide good turf for horseback riding. Rates run about €25 to €30 per hour. The **Clonshire Equestrian Centre** in Adare (www.clonshire.com; ℭ **061/396770**) offers riding holidays for adults and children. It's also one of the only riding schools in Ireland to offer riding for disabled visitors.

COUNTY TIPPERARY

"It's a long way to Tipperary" as the song goes, and it can certainly feel true when you have the map spread out before you, trying to plan your itinerary. Tipperary's big attractions are few and far enough between that they don't always work conveniently as day trips. (Though the one truly essential site, the **Rock of Cashel,** can easily be worked into a road trip on the M8 between Dublin and Cork.) The relative quietness of Tipperary, however, is also part of its appeal. Far from the tour buses and selfie sticks, it just may be the welcoming, unspoiled Ireland everyone is looking for.

Visitor Information

The **Clonmel Tourist Office** at 6 Sarsfield St., Clonmel (ℭ **052/612-2960**), is open year-round Monday to Friday 9:30am to 1pm and 2 to 4:30pm. The small **Cashel Tourist Office** at the Heritage Centre, Main St., Cashel (www.cashel.ie; ℭ **062/61333**), is open 9:30am to 5:30pm daily from March to October and Monday to Friday November to February. A **seasonal office** at Castle Street, Cahir (ℭ **052/744-1453**), is open April to September only, Tuesday to Saturday from 9am to 5:15pm.

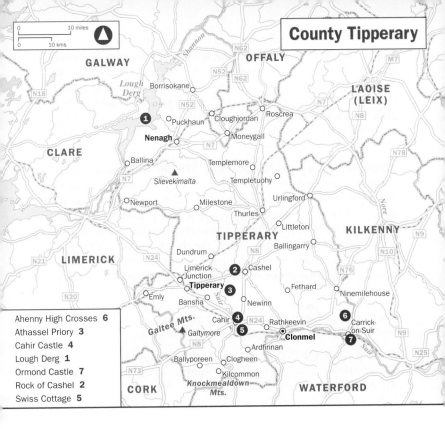

0   10 miles
0   10 kms

GALWAY

OFFALY

L'AOISE (LEIX)

CLARE

TIPPERARY

KILKENNY

LIMERICK

Lough Derg

Borrisokane

Puckhaun   Cloughjordan   Roscrea

Nenagh

Moneygall

Ballina

Templemore

Slievekimalta

Templetuohy

Newport   Milestone

Urlingford

Thurles

Littleton

Dundrum

Ballingarry

Limerick Junction

2 Cashel

Tipperary **3**

Fethard

Ninemilehouse

Emly

Bansha

Newinn

Galtee Mts.   Cahir **4**   N24   Rathkeevin   **6** Carrick-on-Suir

Galtymore   **5**   ● **Clonmel**   **7**

Ardfinnan

Ballyporeen   Clogheen

CORK

Kilcommon

Knockmealdown Mts.

WATERFORD

Ahenny High Crosses **6**
Athassel Priory **3**
Cahir Castle **4**
Lough Derg **1**
Ormond Castle **7**
Rock of Cashel **2**
Swiss Cottage **5**

Exploring County Tipperary

Clonmel, the capital of Tipperary, is the unassuming gateway to the region. A working town largely unspoiled by tourism, Clonmel (whose name in Irish, *Cluaín Meala,* means "Meadows of Honey") makes a pleasant strategic touring base. Looking at this sleepy place on the banks of the Suir, it's hard to believe that it once withstood a Cromwellian siege for 3 brutal months.

North of Clonmel and deep in the Tipperary countryside, **Cashel,** with its monastic buildings and dramatic setting, is not to be missed. From Cahir, there's a gorgeous drive north through the Galtee Mountains to the pristine 11km (7-mile) **Glen of Aherlow,** a secluded and scenic pass between the plains of counties Tipperary and Limerick (see p. 376 for hiking and walking suggestions in this area).

Ahenny High Crosses ★ RELIGIOUS SITE   You're likely to have this little-known and rarely visited site to yourself, except for the cows whose pasture you cross to reach it. On a bright day, the setting is idyllic and gorgeous. The well-preserved Ahenny high crosses date from the 8th or 9th century. Tradition associates them with seven saintly bishops, all brothers said to have been waylaid and murdered. Their unusual stone "caps," thought by some to represent bishops' miters, more likely suggest the transition from wood crosses, which would have had small roofs to shelter them from the rain. Also note their intricate spiral and cable ornamentation in remarkably high relief, which may have been inspired by earlier Celtic metalwork.

Kil Crispeen Churchyard, Ahenny, Co. Tipperary. 8km (5 miles) N of Carrick-on-Suir, signposted off R697. Free admission (box for donations).

Athassel Priory ★ RELIGIOUS SITE/RUINS Many delightful details still remain from the original medieval priory that once stood here. An Augustinian priory, founded in the late 12th century, it was once elaborately decorated. The main approach is over a low stone bridge and through a gatehouse. The church entrance is a beautifully carved doorway at the west end, while to the south of the church you can see the graceful arches of the cloister, eroded by time. Look for a carved face protruding from the southwest corner of the chapel tower, about 9m (30 ft.) above ground level.

3km (2 miles) S of Golden, Co. Tipperary, 7km (4 miles) from Cashel. Take signposted road from Golden, on the N74; the priory is in a field just east of the road. You will need to climb over a stile and walk through a field to reach it.

Cahir Castle ★★ CASTLE On a rock in the middle of the River Suir, this remarkably complete medieval fortress can trace its history from the 3rd century, when a fort was first built on the rock—hence the town's Irish name, "City of the Fishing Fort." The present structure, which belonged to the Butler family for 600 years (1375–1961), is Norman. It has a massive keep, high walls, spacious courtyards, original gateways with a portcullis still intact, and a fully restored great hall. The interpretive center offers an engaging 20-minute video introduction to the region's major historic sites, and you can take a guided tour of the castle grounds.

Castle St., Cahir, Co. Tipperary. www. heritageireland.ie. ✆ **052/744-1011.** Admission €5 adults; €4 seniors; €3 students and children; €13 families. Mid-June to Aug daily 9am–6:30pm; Mar to mid-June and Sept to mid-Oct daily 9:30am–5:30pm; mid-Oct to Feb daily 9:30am–4:30pm. Last admission 1 hr. before closing.

The massive Norman keep of Cahir Castle towers over the River Suir.

petticoat loose & OTHER SCENIC DIVERSIONS

Driving up from County Waterford, you might want to travel via the **Vee Gap,** an 18km-long (11-mile) road winding through the Knockmealdown Mountains from Lismore and Cappoquin in County Waterford to Clogheen in County Tipperary. It's a dramatic drive, which peaks at the Tipperary-Waterford border, where the two slopes of the pass converge to frame the patchwork fields of the Galtee Valley far below.

At this point, numerous walking trails lead to the nearby peaks and down to the mountain lake of **Petticoat Loose**— named after a, shall we say, lady of flexible morals. A more edifying local character was Samuel Grubb, who so loved these slopes that he left instructions to be buried upright overlooking them. Look for the rounded stone cairn off the road between Clogheen and the Vee Gap, where Samuel does indeed stand entombed, facing the Golden Vale of Tipperary.

The Vee Gap also has some terrific walking paths. About 2km (1¼ miles) north of R669 and R668, you reach the highest point in the gap; a parking lot is here, as well as a dirt road continuing down to a lake—**Bay Lough**—nestled into the slope below. This dirt road, once the main thoroughfare over the gap, now offers a fine walk to the shores of the lake, with outstanding views of the valley to the north. For a panoramic perspective of the region, start walking due east from the gap parking lot to the summit of **Sugarloaf Hill;** the hike is extremely steep, but well worth the effort—the views from the ridge are superb.

Ormond Castle ★★ CASTLE   This mid-15th-century castle built by Sir Edward MacRichard Butler on a strategic bend of the River Suir has laid in ruins for centuries. What still stands, attached to the ancient battlements, is the last surviving Tudor manor house in Ireland. Trusting that "if he built it, she would come," Thomas Butler constructed an extensive manor in honor of his most successful relation (and childhood friend), Queen Elizabeth I. He was to be disappointed, however—Elizabeth never did visit. But many others have, especially since the Heritage Service partially restored this impressive piece of Irish history. The manor's plasterwork, carvings, period furniture, and collection of original 17th- and 18th-century royal charters will make you glad you came and leave you wondering why Queen Bess never did.

Signposted from the center of Carrick-on-Suir, Co. Tipperary. www.heritageireland. ie. © **051/640787.** Guided tours hourly; prebook by phone. Admission €5 adults; €4 seniors; €3 students and children; €13 families. April to late Oct 10am–6pm. Closed Nov to Feb. Last admission 45 min. before closing.

The Rock of Cashel ★★★ RELIGIOUS SITE/RUINS   One of Ireland's most iconic medieval ruins, this dramatically craggy abbey atop a hill in the center of Cashel dominates views for miles around. The so-called "Rock"—an outcrop of limestone reaching some 60m (197 ft.) into the sky—tells the tales of 16 centuries. It was the seat of the kings of Munster at least as far back as 360, and it remained a royal fortress until 1101, when King Murtagh O'Brien granted it to the church. Among Cashel's many great moments was the legendary baptism of King Aengus by St. Patrick in 448. Remaining on the rock are the ruins of a two-towered chapel, a cruciform cathedral, a 28m (92-ft.) round tower, and a cluster of other medieval monuments. Inside the cathedral, extraordinary and detailed ancient carvings survive in excellent condition. The views of and from the Rock are spectacular. Guided tours are available most days; check with the visitor center for times. Cashel is just off the N8 motorway. *Note:* Check the site's Facebook page for info on upcoming light shows that bathe the ruins in color: It's been green (St. Patrick's Day week), purple (International Day of People with Disability), and gold (National Autism Day).

Cashel, Co. Tipperary. www.heritageireland.ie. © **062/61437.** Admission €8 adults; €6 seniors; €4 children and students; €20 families. Early June to mid-Sept daily 9am–7pm; mid-Mar to early June and mid-Sept to mid-Oct daily 9am–5:30pm; mid-Oct to mid-Mar daily 9am–4:30pm; last admission 45 min. before closing.

Swiss Cottage ★ HISTORIC HOUSE   A hunting and fishing lodge for the earls of Glengall from around 1812, the Swiss Cottage is a superb example of *cottage orné:* a rustic house embodying the ideal of simplicity

The Rock of Cashel, County Tipperary's most iconic heritage site.

THE lough derg DRIVE

At the meeting point of counties Clare, Limerick, and Tipperary, the Shannon River's largest lake, Lough Derg—virtually an inland sea—creates a stunning waterscape 40km (25 miles) long and almost 16km (10 miles) wide. The road that circles the lake for 153km (95 miles), the **Lough Derg Drive,** is one of Ireland's great scenic drives, a continuous photo op with panoramas of glistening waters, gentle mountains, and hilly farmlands unspoiled by commercialization.

The drive is also a collage of colorful shoreline towns, starting at the lake's south end with **Killaloe,** County Clare, and **Ballina,** County Tipperary. They're so close that they are essentially one community—only a splendid 13-arch bridge over the Shannon separates them. In the summer, its pubs and bars fill with weekend sailors. **Killaloe** is a picturesque town with lakeside views at almost every turn and restaurants and pubs perched on the shore. **Kincora,** on the highest ground at Killaloe, was traditionally said to be the royal settlement of Brian Boru

and the other O'Brien kings, although no trace of any buildings survives.

Memorable little towns and harborside villages, like **Mountshannon** and **Dromineer,** dot the rest of the Lough Derg Drive. Some towns, like **Terryglass** and **Woodford,** are known for atmospheric old pubs where spontaneous sessions of traditional Irish music are likely to break out. Others, like **Puckane** and **Ballinderry,** offer unique crafts. On the north shore of the lake in County Galway, **Portumna** is worth a visit for its forest park and castle.

The best way to get to Lough Derg is by car or boat. Because the area has limited public transportation, you will need a car to get around the lake. Major roads that lead to Lough Derg are the main Limerick–Dublin road (N7) from points east and south; N6 and N65 from Galway and the west; and N52 from the north. The Lough Derg Drive, which is well signposted, is a combination of R352 on the west bank of the lake and R493, R494, and R495 on the east bank.

that so appealed to the Romantics of the early 19th century. The thatched-roof cottage has extensive timberwork, usually not seen in Ireland, and is believed to have been designed by royal architect John Nash. The interior has some of the first wallpaper commercially produced in Paris. A guided tour (the only way to see the building) lasts approximately 40 minutes. Off R670 Ardfinnan Rd., Cahir, Co. Tipperary. www.heritageireland.ie. © **052/744-1144.** Guided tour €5 adults; €4 seniors; €3 students and children; €13 families. Mid-Mar to late Oct daily 10am–5pm; last tour 45 min. before closing.

Where to Stay in County Tipperary

Anner Hotel ★★   This elegant boutique hotel just outside the bustling town of Thurles has an idyllic location on extensive, manicured grounds. Rooms are bright and spacious if not huge, with comfortable beds, tasteful decor, and views of the gorgeous grounds. It's well located for exploring the Rock of Cashel and Kilkenny, but you may want to stay in for formal afternoon tea in one of the sunny lounges or to try out the swimming pool and steam room. You'll definitely want to stay in for dinner at

Seasons Restaurant, which specializes in using Tipperary produce in everything they make; the hotel also has a more casual bar and bistro.

Dublin Rd., Co. Tipperary. www.annerhotel.ie. ✆ **050/421799.** 92 units. €99–€165 double. Free parking. Rates include breakfast (room-only rates also available). **Amenities:** Restaurant; bar/bistro; gym; indoor pool; Wi-Fi (free).

Bansha House ★ This vine-covered Georgian manor house in tiny Bansha, in the shadow of the Galtee Mountains, is just a few miles south of Cashel. Guest rooms are simple and old-fashioned—not all have private bathrooms, for instance, so be sure you ask for one if that's important—but it's cheerful, cozy, and well-run. Guests are free to wander the enormous grounds, and the friendly owners also run a horse-breeding stable next door—ask and they'll take you to meet the occupants. A self-catering cottage on the ground sleeps up to five.

Bansha, Co. Tipperary. www.banshahouse.com. ✆ **062/54194.** 6 units. €100 double. Free parking. Rates include breakfast. **Amenities:** Wi-Fi (free).

Hotel Minella ★★ The River Suir babbles along in front of this modern hotel in Clonmel, overlooked by a distant mountain range. Guest rooms are properly spacious, with large, comfortable beds and modern (if rather uninspiring) decor. Some rooms even have their own hot tubs. The hotel has a small spa with a swimming pool, though you'll need to book ahead for treatments. If you want slightly more space, the hotel also has 10 well-equipped apartments on the grounds that can be rented on a self-catering basis. The only real downside to this place is that it's a popular venue for weddings, reunions, and parties, especially in summer.

Coleville Rd., Clonmel, Co. Tipperary. www.hotelminella.com. ✆ **052/612-2388.** 90 units. €170–€180 double. Free parking. Rates include breakfast. Check website for special offers. **Amenities:** Restaurant; bar; gym; pool; Wi-Fi (free).

Where to Eat in County Tipperary

Befani's ★ MEDITERRANEAN/TAPAS This cheerful little restaurant in Clonmel is a pleasant surprise in a region where Irish cooking is king. The tapas lunch menu is short but satisfying—including *patatas bravas,* fritto misto (calamari and king prawns), and serrano ham with vegetable salad, all for around €6.50. In the evening, the menu combines Irish and Mediterranean influences, ranging from a rich seafood linguini to a succulent filet of lamb. Befani's also has simple guest rooms available for €80 per night, including breakfast.

6 Sarsfield St., Clonmel, Co. Tipperary. www.befani.com. ✆ **061/617-7893.** Tapas €6–€8; entrees €16–€29. Thurs 5–9pm; Fri–Sat 12:30–2:30pm, 5–9pm; Sun 12:30–3pm, 4–8pm.

Chez Hans ★★ EUROPEAN Located in a beautiful converted church building—which was purchased in the 1860s with a thousand-year lease on terms of 1 shilling per year—Chez Hans is one of the most reliably good restaurants in Cashel. Menus change several times a week, based on what's freshest. Seafood features heavily (king scallops with crab and lemon butter, or maybe Dover sole with caramelized cauliflower), or you could opt for a cassoulet of wild pheasant, served with bread sauce. Reservations are recommended. The restaurant is a 2-minute walk from the Rock of Cashel.

Rockside, Cashel, Co. Tipperary. www.chezhans.net. © **062/61177.** Entrees €20–€35. Fri–Sat 5:30–9:30pm; Sun 12:30–3:30pm, 5:30–8pm.

The Lazy Bean Café ★ CAFE   This is a place that takes coffee and tea seriously. In addition to an exceptionally fine cup of coffee, you can order tea that comes in a traditional Japanese *suki* teapot. The cafe serves very good wraps, bagels, and focaccia sandwiches at lunchtime, and has a varied all-day breakfast menu. The cafe also has free Wi-Fi.

The Square, Cahir, Co. Tipperary. www.thelazybeancafe.com. © **052/744-2038.** Lunch €4–€7. Daily 9am–5pm.

Quimby's Café and Deli ★ CAFE/DELI   This cute little cornerside cafe serves tasty snacks, cakes, and brasserie-style lunches. The menu has plenty of traditional favorites—potato and leek soup, Irish stew, deliciously fluffy potato pancakes—or you could opt for a simple chicken salad or toasted sandwich. It also does a great breakfast if you're tired of hotel fare.

98 Irishtown, Clonmel, Co. Tipperary. © **052/618-0255.** Entrees €8–€14. Mon–Sat 9am–5:30pm.

Sports & Outdoor Pursuits in Tipperary

BIRD-WATCHING   As many as 15 species of Irish water birds—including mute swans, coots, gadwalls, and gray herons—can be seen at the **Marlfield Lake Wildfowl Refuge,** several miles west of Clonmel in Marlfield. On your way, you'll pass signposts for **St. Patrick's Well,** less than 1.6km (1 mile) away, a tranquil spot with an effervescent pool of reputedly healing crystalline water and an ancient Celtic cross rising from the middle of the pool. Legend has it that St. Patrick himself visited here.

CYCLING   Centered around the town of Nenagh, the **North Tipperary Cycle Network** consists of three scenic cycling routes around the north Tipperary countryside. Signposted routes pass Lough Derg, small riverside villages, and farmland, before looping back to Nenagh. They vary in length from 30km (18½ miles) to 67km (41½ miles). Maps and other information can be found under **Nenagh Cycling Hub** at **www.nenagh. ie**. To hire a bike, contact **Moynans,** 4 Cecil Walk, Nenagh (www. moynans.com; © **067/31293**).

WALKING   In the Clonmel area, you'll find some excellent river and hill walks, some more challenging than others. The most spectacular is the ascent of famed **Slievenamon,** a mountain rich in myth. Inexpensive, detailed trail maps for at least a half-dozen walks are available at the Clonmel Tourist Office on Sarsfield Street, Clonmel.

The **Galtee Mountains,** northwest of the Knockmealdowns, offer some great long and short walks. For trail maps and other assistance, contact the **Glen of Aherlow Fáilte Society,** Coach Road, Newtown (www. aherlow.com; © **062/56331**). It's open daily June to October from 9am to 6pm (hours vary the rest of the year). One particularly beautiful trail—a 3-hour round-trip—loops around the sparkling waters of **Lake Muskry,** on the north side of the range. (Ask for directions in Rossadrehid, west of Bansha on the R663.)

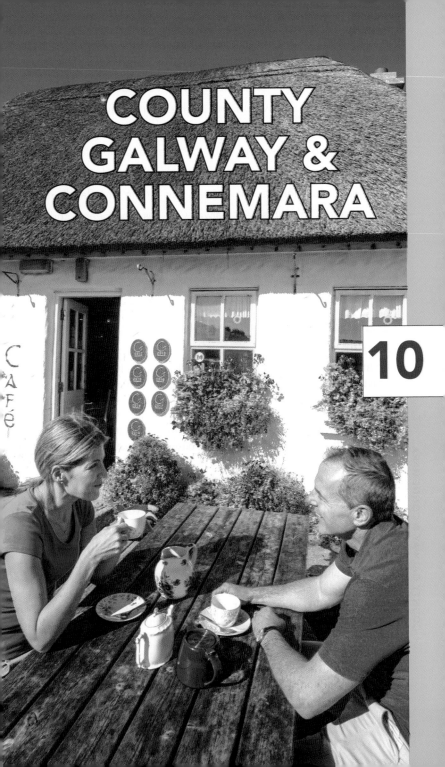

COUNTY
GALWAY &
CONNEMARA

10

W hether you arrive from the north, south, or east, you will notice the scenery change dramatically once you get to County Galway. Parts of the county have bleak bogs, stone walls, windswept trees, and extraordinary light; you will also find lakes, beaches, and mountains in this wild place. And yet, just near the edge of the windswept, boggy expanse of Connemara, on Galway Bay, is one of Ireland's most vibrant cities. Though small, Galway City has long been a thriving center for the arts—it was even the designated European Capital of Culture in 2020. Exploring this lovely city's colorful lanes and taking in its electric atmosphere may be one of the highlights of your trip.

ESSENTIALS

Arriving

BY BUS Buses from all parts of Ireland arrive daily at **Bus Éireann Travel Centre,** Ceannt Station, off Eyre Square in Galway City (www.buseireann.ie; ☏ **091/562-000**). It also provides daily service to Clifden. Buses to rural areas sometimes run only a handful of times per day, and remote sites may be completely inaccessible without a car. **CityLink** (www.citylink.ie; ☏ **091/564-164**) runs buses to Galway from Cork, Limerick, Dublin, and Dublin Airport.

BY TRAIN Trains from Dublin and Limerick arrive daily at Ceannt Station in Galway City, off Eyre Square. That's pretty much the end of the line, however; to explore the Galway countryside, you'll need a car.

BY CAR Galway City is on the main M18, N17, N63, N67, and M6 roads. Journey time from Dublin is 2 or 2½ hours; from Killarney it's about 3 hours; and from Cork it's about 2½ hours. Outside of Galway City, your options in this region get pretty limited if you don't have a car. To hire one in Galway, try **Budget,** 12 Eyre Square (www.budget.ie; ☏ **091/564-570**), or **Europcar** at Motorpark, Headford Road (www.europcar.ie; ☏ **091/396-555**). For car rental options in Dublin, see p. 91; for Shannon airport, see p. 344.

BY PLANE Galway has an airport, but it is not used for scheduled flights or commercial services. See **www.galwayairport.com** for information. The nearest airport is Shannon (p. 343).

PREVIOUS PAGE: **Inishmore in the Aran Islands.**

Galway City

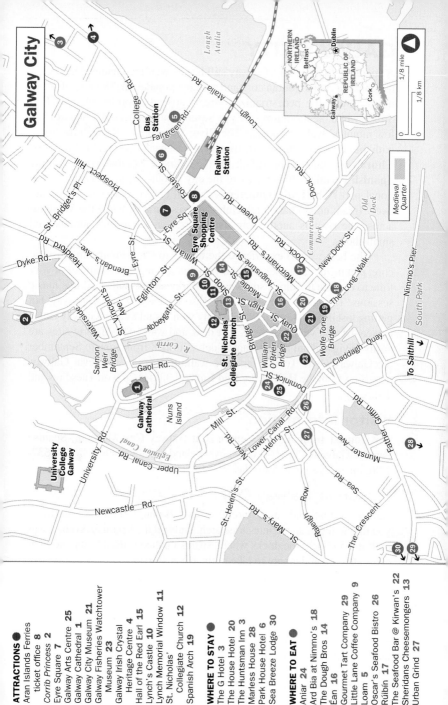

GALWAY CITY

A small but thriving city, Galway still has its winding medieval lanes, but it also has a cosmopolitan core and a young population. The hub of activity is around the pedestrianized streets around Shop Street and High Street, while the more formal **Eyre Square** (pronounced *Air* Square) is a few minutes' walk from here. The **River Corrib** runs through the town, with the city's artsy historic district on its east bank between **St. Nicholas' Church** and the harbor. (Look for the riverside **Spanish Arch** and the **Spanish Parade,** which testify to the city's 16th-c. heyday as an international port.) The **Latin Quarter** is a small but vibrant area, filled with lively (read: noisy) bars, nightclubs, and restaurants, while the **Westend** across the river is another creative quarter with bars, restaurants, and small shops.

The best way to experience the city is to stroll around the historic core, picking out a few key sites to visit, but leaving the remainder of your time to explore the city's small cafes, quirky shops, pubs, and live music sessions. The area is tiny but tangled, so it's easy to lose your way, but getting lost is half the fun. You certainly won't want a car in Galway City's center—if you've driven here, just park and walk. The historic sites are easily navigated but if you want to delve further, from June to September the Galway Civic Trust offers free walking tours of medieval Galway, departing from the **Hall of the Red Earl** (p. 382) at 2pm on Tuesdays and Thursdays.

Visitor Information

The **Tourist Information Centre** is at Galway City Museum, Spanish Parade, Galway City (www.discoverireland.ie/galway-city; ✆ **091/537-700),** open Tuesday to Saturday 9am to 5pm.

Exploring Galway City

Galway is small and best explored on foot. If you start on the waterfront, you might notice an ancient stone arch. Dubbed the **Spanish Arch,** it was built in 1594 near the docks where Spanish galleons used to unload their cargo. It's a popular spot to take in the River Corrib.

Galway Arts Centre ★★ CULTURAL CENTER   Once the home of W. B. Yeats's patron, Lady Gregory, this attractive town house held local governmental offices for many years. Today it offers an excellent program of concerts, readings, and exhibitions by Irish and international artists—returning the house to a purpose that Lady Gregory would have appreciated. Usually two or three exhibitions run at any one time.

47 Dominick St., Galway City. www.galwayartscentre.ie. ✆ **091/565-886.** Free admission. Tues–Sat 10am–5pm; Sun noon–5pm. Closed Mon.

Galway City

COUNTY GALWAY & CONNEMARA

GALWAY FESTIVAL OF arts

Held over 2 weeks at the end of July, the prestigious **Galway International Arts Festival** has been an annual fixture on the country's cultural calendar since 1978. It came from somewhat humble beginnings—in its first year, the festival took place in a building that is now a cheesemonger (a very good one too, as it happens; see p. 390). Now around 250,000 people attend every year, with nearly 40% of visitors coming from outside Ireland.

The lively program of music, theater, talks, and visual arts is usually announced in May, although they often tease out many events (and big names) in advance of that. Headline music acts for the 2022 festival included the Pixies and Sinead O'Connor, and major speakers of recent years have included the former Irish President Mary Robinson.

Ticket prices vary, but many events are free. Check out **www.giaf.ie** for more information.

Galway Cathedral ★ CATHEDRAL Officially the "Cathedral of Our Lady Assumed into Heaven & St. Nicholas," Galway's cathedral has an impressive domed exterior that looks Romanesque in style, although it was actually built in the 1960s. The striking interior has rows of symmetrical stone archways and dramatic lighting. Contemporary Irish artisans designed the statues, colorful mosaics, and stained-glass windows. The limestone for the walls was cut from local quarries, while the polished floor is made from Connemara marble.

University and Gaol rds., Galway City (by west end of Salmon Weir Bridge). www.galwaycathedral.ie. ℂ **091/563-577** (select option 4). Free admission, €2 donations encouraged. Daily 8:30am–6:30pm.

Galway City Museum ★ MUSEUM Permanent galleries downstairs relate to Galway's prehistoric and medieval periods, while the upper levels deal with the city's more recent past, including its relationship with the arts. Highlights include a large collection of intricate embroidered textiles, made by a local order of nuns between the 17th and 20th centuries. A lively program of special events includes talks, touring exhibitions, and arts workshops.

Spanish Parade, Galway City. www.galwaycitymuseum.ie. ℂ **091/532-460.** Free admission (book online). Easter–Sept Tues–Sat 10am–5pm, Sun noon–5pm. Oct–Easter Tues–Sat 10am–5pm (closed Sun).

Galway Fisheries Watchtower Museum ★ MUSEUM This tiny, free museum is worth visiting for the views of the River Corrib alone. The symmetrical yellow tower was built in 1852 as a lookout from which fishing boats on the river could be monitored; it was in use until commercial net fishing died out in the 1970s. Exhibits tell the story of Galway's fishing heritage and the role it played in the city's industry.

Wolfe Tone Bridge, off Father Griffin Rd., Galway City. www.galwaycivictrust.ie. No phone. Free admission. Mon–Fri 10am–4pm. Closed Sat and Sun. Open summer only; heck opening hours online before visiting.

The Tribes of Galway

By the 15th century, 14 wealthy merchant families ruled Galway Town, giving it a nickname it still bears today—"City of Tribes." These families, mostly of Welsh and Norman origins, ruled as an oligarchy. As you walk around Galway City, look for these names on storefronts and businesses: Athy, Blake, Bodkin, Browne, Darcy, Deane, Font, French, Joyce, Kirwan, Lynch, Martin, Morris, and Skerret.

Galway Market ★★ MARKET   There has been a regular street market of some kind in Galway for hundreds of years, and its vibrant modern iteration shows no sign of letting the tradition slide. Galway Market is a great place to shop for locally made crafts and homewares, but it's the scent of the food stalls that often brings people in. The market takes place next to St. Nicholas' Church (p. 383) every Saturday from 8am to 6pm and Sundays and bank holidays from noon to 6pm. It also runs Wednesday to Friday in July and August from noon to 6pm, and daily from noon to 6pm during the Galway Arts Festival (p. 381). The **Galway Christmas Market** runs daily in Eyre Square from mid-November to December 22 9am to 6pm.

Church Lane, Galway City. www.galwaymarket.com.

Hall of the Red Earl ★★ ANCIENT SITE   This fascinating site is what's left of a baronial hall from the Middle Ages, built by the powerful de Burgh family, Anglo-Norman earls who ruled this region in the 13th century. In the late 1200s, they erected what must have been a lavish hall in which to hold court, receive subjects, settle disputes, and generally live it up in true medieval style. The earls were eventually overthrown by local tribes and the building abandoned. Time slowly covered any trace of the building, until the foundations were found during building work in 1997. You can view the site on glass gangways and see some of the artifacts that were also unearthed during the excavation.

Custom House, Druid Lane, Galway City. www.galwaycivictrust.ie. ✆ **091/564-946.** Free admission. May–Sept Mon–Fri 9:30am–5:30pm; Oct–Apr Mon–Fri 9:30am–4:30pm. Closed Sat and Sun.

Lynch's Castle ★ HISTORIC HOUSE   Dating from 1490 and renovated in the 19th century, this impressive structure was once home to the Lynch family, who ruled the city for many years. One of the oldest medieval town houses in Ireland, it's now a branch of the Allied Irish Bank. Gargoyles preside over the exterior, while inside is a small display describing the building's history.

Abbeygate and Shop sts., Galway City. ✆ **091/567-041.** Free admission. Mon–Fri 10am–4pm.

St. Nicholas' Collegiate Church ★★ CHURCH   Galway's oldest church, St. Nicholas' was established about 1320. It's claimed that Christopher Columbus prayed here in 1477 before one of his early attempts to reach the New World, although there's no real evidence to suggest it's true. Over the centuries, it has changed from Roman Catholic to Church of Ireland and back again at least four times. Inside are a 12th-century crusader's tomb with a Norman inscription, a carved font from the 16th or 17th century, and a stone lectern with barley-sugar twist columns from the 15th century. You can explore alone or arrange guided tours conducted by a church representative. Ask at the church for details.

Mainguard and Lombard sts., Galway City. www.stnicholas.ie. ℭ **091/564-648.** Free admission (donations requested). Mar–Dec daily 9am–7pm; Jan–Feb daily 9am–5pm (opening times may vary in winter). No tours Sun morning.

Outside the City

Corrib Princess Cruise ★ TOUR   Sit back and take in the view from this 157-passenger, two-deck boat as it cruises along the River Corrib out of Galway City. The journey along the river takes in castles, historical sites, and wildlife. It's not for those averse to the full tourist treatment, but the 90-minute trip is very picturesque. You can buy tickets at the dock or online.

Departs from Woodquay, Galway City. www.corribprincess.ie. ℭ **087/806-5366.** €17 adults; €15 seniors and students; €8 children; €42 families (2 adults, 3 children). Sailings Wed–Sun May–June and Sept 12:30pm and 2:30pm; July–Aug 12:30, 2:30, and 4:30pm.

Galway Irish Crystal Heritage Centre ★ FACTORY TOUR   It might not be as well-known as its feted Waterford rival, but Galway Crystal is just as distinctive and beautiful. At this visitor center, you can observe master craftspeople at work blowing the molten glass and cutting the finished product (weekdays only). But most people just come to browse the factory shop, with its glittering array of crystal and other craft items, such as fragile Belleek pottery.

East of the city on main Dublin Rd. (N6), Merlin Park, Co. Galway. www.galwaycrystal. ie. ℭ **091/757-311.** Free admission. Mon–Fri 9am–5:30pm, Sat 9:30am–5:30pm, Sun and public holidays 9:30–5:30pm.

The Tragic Tale of Lynch's Window

One block away from Eyre Square on Market Street, the **Lynch Memorial Window** sits in a wall above a built-up Gothic doorway. It commemorates the tragic story of the 16th-century Galway mayor James Lynch FitzStephen, who condemned his own son to death for the murder of a Spanish merchant. After finding no one to carry out the deed, he executed the boy himself. The act destroyed him, and he retreated into a life of seclusion.

THE aran islands

When you see the ghostly shapes of the Aran Islands floating 48km (30 miles) out at sea like misty Brigadoon, you instantly understand why these sea-battered and wind-whipped isles have been the subject of fable, song, and film for thousands of years.

All three islands—**Inishmore (*Inis Mór*)**, **Inishmaan (*Inis Meáin*)**, and **Inisheer (*Inis Oírr*)**—are rather strange looking, with a ring of rocks around their outer edges and, inside, small farms surrounded by soft green grass and wildflowers. Life on the islands is isolated but has been modernized—only a handful of the 1,500 inhabitants still maintain the traditional island lifestyle, fishing from *currachs* (small crafts made of tarred canvas stretched over timber frames), living in stone cottages, and speaking Irish. Some islanders wear the classic, creamy, handmade Aran *bainín* sweaters that originated here and are now popular in Irish gift shops.

Inishmore is the largest island and the easiest to reach from Galway. Most visitors disembark from the ferries at **Kilronan (*Cill Rónáin*)**, the island's main town (though it's only the size of a village). From there, it's easy to arrange transportation around the island: Horse-drawn buggies are available for islands tours as you step off the boat, minivans stand at the ready, and bicycle-rental shops are within sight. Drop in at **Oifig Fáilte (Aran Island Tourist Information)** in Kilronan (*C* **099/61263**) to pick up walking maps, ask questions, and generally get yourself going. It's open daily year-round from 10:30am to 5pm.

The islands have some excellent geological sights, including the magnificent **Dún Aengus ★★** on Inishmore. A ruined 2,000-year-old stone fortress, on the edge of a cliff that drops 90m (295

Where to Stay In & Around Galway City

Prices have gone up quite a bit in Galway City in recent years, and it's hard to find a bargain. Even B&Bs often run over €200 a night, especially in summer season or during festivals and race week. The hotels listed below are the best options for location and quality.

The G ★★   Chic designer flourishes, bright color schemes, and contemporary art grace this modern hotel overlooking the waters of Lough Atalia and Galway Bay, about a 10-minute walk northeast of the city center. Many bedrooms have floor-to-ceiling windows to take full advantage of those views. Beds are big and comfortable, and bathrooms are modern. **Gigi's** restaurant is a delightful space serving excellent modern Irish cuisine, with plenty of local meats and seafood. Treatments in the hotel spa aren't cheap, but check for special offers online.

Wellpark, Galway City. www.theghotel.ie. *C* **091/865-200.** 101 units. €169–€299 double; €289–€609 suite. Free parking. Rates include breakfast. **Amenities:** Restaurant; bar; gym; room service; spa; Wi-Fi (free).

The House Hotel ★★   This upbeat, funky hotel is right in the heart of the Latin Quarter. Public areas have stylish design with polished wood

384

10

Galway City

COUNTY GALWAY & CONNEMARA

ft.) to the sea, Dún Aengus is among the most dramatic ancient ruins in the west. Its original purpose is unknown—some think it had a military purpose, others say it was a ceremonial theater. From the top are spectacular views of Galway Bay, the Burren, and Connemara. Nearby, in what looks like an Irish country cottage, the charming, thatched-roofed cafe/restaurant **Teach Nan Phaidi ★★ (ℂ 099/20975)** offers sandwiches, salads, excellent Irish stew, cakes, pies—comfort food, in other words, and incredibly welcome after a blustery day on the island.

Aran Island Ferries (www.aran islandferries.com; ℂ **091/568-903**) runs daily service to all three islands, Inishmore, Inishmaan, and Inisheer. Boats leave from **Rossaveal (Ros a' Mhíl),** 37km (23 miles) west of Galway City. The crossing takes 50 minutes to Inishmore and 1 hour to Inishmaan or Inisheer. For all three islands, there are two crossings a day, at 10:30am and 6pm (an extra 1pm crossing to Inishmore runs Apr–Aug), but always call ahead to check the schedule, and make sure you know the time of the return ferries. The ticket office is at 37 Forster St. in Galway; a shuttle bus goes from nearby Queen's Street to the ferry port (to take the shuttle, you must check in at the booking office at least 90 min. before sailing time). The round-trip crossing costs €30 adults, €25 seniors and students, €15 children. The shuttle bus costs €9 adults, €8 seniors and students, €6 children, round-trip.

Although visiting the Aran Islands is a thoroughly doable day trip from Galway City, if you're tempted to stay overnight, a handful of good B&Bs and restaurants are available—see listings, p. 386.

floors and retro-style seating, while guest rooms are more muted, with oatmeal, white, or green color schemes. The restaurant is good and surprisingly reasonable for a hotel of this size in the center of the city. That said, you're spoiled for choice when it comes to nightlife in this neighborhood—Galway's buzzing center is literally on your doorstep. The hotel does not have parking, but a car park a few minutes' walk away offers a discount rate of €9 per 24 hours.

Spanish Parade, Galway City. www.thehousehotel.ie. ℂ **091/538-900.** 40 units. €69–€299 double; €299–€439 suite. Parking at nearby lot (€9/24 hr.). Breakfast not included in lower rates. **Amenities:** Restaurant; bar; room service; Wi-Fi (free).

The Huntsman Inn ★★ This smart, modern inn and restaurant on Lough Atalia, a 20-minute walk from the city center, is a good option. Rooms are surprisingly big—some have super-king beds—and decorated with clean, neutral colors. Bathrooms are modern. A well-rated restaurant and stylish bar, both popular with locals, are located downstairs. There's live music on Saturday evenings, so this may not be one for light sleepers, but the pub quiz on Mondays is good *craic,* as the Irish say.

164 College Rd., Galway City. www.huntsmaninn.com. ℂ **091/562-849.** 12 units. €80–€170 double. Rates include breakfast. **Amenities:** Restaurant; bar; Wi-Fi (free).

Marless House ★   This pleasant, friendly B&B in Salthill, a small seaside commuter town immediately west of Galway, is good value for the money. Guest rooms are spacious and clean, though some have slightly overwhelming floral color schemes. Hosts Mary and Tom have arrangements with several local tour companies, so if you want to book a trip to sights in the region—including the Aran Islands or the Cliffs of Moher—the tour bus will pick you up from here and drop you back at the end of the day. Mary is a fount of useful sightseeing information.

8 Threadneedle Rd., Salthill, Co. Galway. www.marlesshouse.com. ✆ **091/523-931.** 6 units. €80–€90 double. Free parking. Rates include breakfast. **Amenities:** Wi-Fi (free).

Park House Hotel ★★   This friendly, traditional hotel is just 5 minutes' walk from Eyre Square at the heart of Galway City. The lobby is a bit fussy, with heavy drapes and marble statues, but rooms are simply designed in warm colors with comfortable beds and modern bathrooms. The in-house restaurant does excellent European-influenced Irish food, with an emphasis on fresh seafood. A smaller menu is served all day in **Boss Doyle's Bar**—a relaxed, publike space, perfect for a pint.

Forster St., Co. Galway. www.parkhousehotel.ie. ✆ **091/564-924.** 99 units. €160–€269 double. Rates include breakfast. Check website for dinner, bed and breakfast packages. **Amenities:** Restaurant; bar; Wi-Fi (free).

Sea Breeze Lodge ★   This stylish option in Salthill, just outside Galway City, has a lot to offer. The modern gray exterior gives way to contemporary lounges inside. Guest rooms are spacious, with polished wood floors and windows looking out over the bay or garden. Beds are king-sized and comfortable with memory-foam mattresses. Breakfasts are served in a pleasant conservatory overlooking the garden. The B&B can arrange tours of the area, including an all-day trip to the Aran Islands or to Connemara for €35 per person (€30 students and seniors). There's no restaurant, and the center of Galway is 5km (3 miles) by car or taxi.

9 Cashelmara, Salthill, Co. Galway. www.seabreezelodge.org. ✆ **091/529-581.** 6 units. €174–€212 double. 2-night minimum on certain dates. Free parking. Rates include breakfast. **Amenities:** Wi-Fi (free).

Where to Stay on the Aran Islands

Inis Meáin Restaurant & Suites ★★★   Hosts Ruairi and Marie-Thérèse have created a special place to stay and eat on the least-visited of the Aran Islands, Inis Meáin. Indeed, for many who spend time here, this experience is one of the main reasons to visit the island. The *Financial Times* declared the restaurant one of the 12 best in the world a few years ago, and dining here certainly is a memorable experience. Ruairi creates simple, fresh, delicious meals from produce as local as it comes—including the garden outside and the sea around you. It all depends on what's best that day, but the four-course set menu (€80) might include periwinkle with wild garlic, scallop tartare with toasted hazelnuts, or John Dory with baby carrot. Five modern guest suites make the most of the stunning views of Galway Bay with huge windows. The only drawback is the 2-night minimum stay, but that won't feel like a problem once you get here, breathe in the air, and feel the peace wash over you.

Inis Meáin, Aran Islands, Co. Galway. www.inismeain.com. ℂ **086/826-6026.** 5 units. €1080–€1,500 suite. Free parking. Rates include breakfast and HotPot lunch. **Amenities:** Restaurant; Wi-Fi (free). Closed Oct to mid-Mar.

South Aran House ★ This whitewashed stone house seems to fit the rugged landscape on Inisheer, the smallest of the Aran Islands. Low and sturdy enough to withstand the windswept winters, inside it's snug, with comfortable, lived-in furniture and a fireplace warming the lounge. Rooms are on the small

Inis Meáin, a sought-after restaurant and B&B on the remote Aran Island of the same name.

side but spotless, with modern beds, underfloor heating, and power showers—and each room has its own entrance. The house is owned by Enda, a former lighthouse keeper, and it has plenty of books around for anyone to read. Reserve your space early; with only four rooms, this place gets booked up fast.

Inisheer, Aran Islands, Co. Galway. www.southaran.com. ℂ **087/340-5687.** 4 units. €84 double. Rates include breakfast. No children. **Amenities:** Wi-Fi (free).

Where to Eat in Galway City

This west coast foodie hub offers endless places to eat—you can hardly walk two steps in the city center without passing a cafe or restaurant. In addition to the options listed below, you'll find delicious breakfasts, lunches, and cakes all day at the charming **Gourmet Tart Company** (www.gourmettartco.com). It has branches all over town (Headford Rd., Newcastle Rd., Lr. Abbeygate St., St. Francis St.) if your tart craving arrives suddenly. Some of the best coffee in Galway is at **Urban Grind** (8 William St. W; www.urbangrind.ie), which also serves epic breakfasts (organic bread with grilled sausage and poached egg), or **Little Lane Coffee Company** (10 Abbeygate St. Upper, www.littlelanecoffee.com), which takes its coffee seriously, with brews from Irish specialty coffee roasters. If you need help navigating the city's culinary offerings, take a 2.5-hour food tour with **Galway Food Tours** (daytime €65, evening €95; www.galwayfoodtours.com) to sample local artisan products and visit the city's best dining spots.

September's Galway International Oyster and Seafood Festival draws foodies from far and near.

Aniar ★★★ MODERN IRISH   This Michelin-starred restaurant in the lively Westend of Galway City is one of the best, and most fashionable, places to eat in the region. Head chef Ultan Cooke changes the tiny menu constantly around what's best that day, and it's deeply imbued with the produce of the region: smoked cheese with kelp; beef with nasturtium; pork with sorrel and buttermilk. It doesn't come cheap, but legions of fans think it's worth it. Needless to say, reservations are essential.

53 Lower Dominick St., Galway City. www.aniarrestaurant.ie. ℰ **091/535-947.** Tasting menu €89. Tues, Fri–Sat 5:30–9:30pm; Thurs 6–9:30pm. Closed Sun–Mon.

Ard Bia at Nimmo's ★★ SEAFOOD/BISTRO/CAFE   The rustic dining room at this fashionable restaurant in Galway City doubles as a popular cafe during the day. At any time, the emphasis is the same: simple cooking using local produce. Stop in for a breakfast or brunch of buttermilk pancakes or a vegan fry-up with mushroom, avocado, spinach, and hummus. At lunch sample creative salads and sandwiches. In the evening, when the atmosphere gets cozy with candlelight, expect local fish with roasted veggies and lemon yogurt, or a tender rib-eye served with roast potatoes, kale, broccoli, and Crozier Blue butter. The wine list is excellent and reasonably priced, and some tables even have river views.

Spanish Arch, Long Walk, Galway City. www.ardbia.com. ℰ **091/561-114.** Breakfast €6–€12.50; lunch €5–€13.50; dinner entrees €21–€30. Breakfast and lunch daily 10am–3pm; Dinner Wed–Sun 6–9pm.

The Dough Bros ★★ PIZZA   The young, the trendy, and the just plain hungry stand in line for a table at this popular pizza joint in the middle of Galway City. It's a heartwarming tale: Three local boys, in love with Italian cooking, start a food truck after one of them loses his job. Fast-forward a few years and that truck has become a restaurant, serving wood-baked pizza to hordes of locals. You might go for a classic Neapolitan, with tomato, fresh basil, and mozzarella, but if you're feeling a bit adventurous, how about the "Hail Caesar," with lemon chicken, bacon lardons, and rocket (arugula)? They don't take reservations, so you will probably have to stand in line on Friday and Saturday nights.

Cathedral Bldgs., 1 Middle St., Galway City. www.thedoughbros.ie. ⓒ **091/395-238.** Entrees €9–€13. No reservations. Thurs 5–10pm, Fri–Sun noon–10pm.

Éan ★★ MODERN IRISH   The word éan is the Irish for bird, an appropriate name for the selection of delicate pastries and exquisite savory plates here. This is a bakery by day and a wine bar by night, serving sharing plates like squid toast with blonde miso and bonito, or mackerel with beetroot, fermented blackcurrant, and horseradish. Food is local—if it's not grown in Ireland, you won't find it on the menu. The relaxed setting, in a lovely old stone building on Druid Lane (with a few outdoor tables), is ideal for a pre-theater nibble or a glass of wine (it even has a connecting door to the theater).

Druid Lane, Galway City. www.eangalway.ie. ⓒ **091/374-154.** Entrees €4–€26. Bakery and cafe: Thurs–Sun 10am–3pm. Wine bar: Thurs–Sat 6–9pm.

Loam ★★★ EUROPEAN   This spartan restaurant with bare, polished wood tables does not look like a Michelin-starred restaurant until the food starts to arrive. Chef Enda McEvoy is a master of taking humble food and making it spectacular. The mutton is served velvety-soft and prepared as if it were the finest steak. The crab comes with a subtle garnish of radish and cabbage and creamy yogurt. Mains might be served with a simple bowl of boiled, organic potatoes, to balance the other flavors. Everything is exceptional. Book in advance.

Fairgreen Rd., Galway. www.loamgalway.com. ⓒ **091/569-727.** Tasting menus: 7-course €78, 9-course €99. Tues–Sat 6–10pm.

Oscar's Seafood Bistro ★★★ SEAFOOD   Specializing in seafood, the menu at Oscar's depends on what's fresh and in season, but you could start with some oat-coated fish cakes, smoky and delicious, followed by

COUNTY GALWAY & CONNEMARA

Galway City

The Galway Oyster Festival

On the main road south (N18) of Galway you'll pass two unremarkable small fishing villages, **Clarenbridge** and **Kilcolgan.** If you're here at the end of September, however, these villages become an essential stop, when they host the annual

Galway Oyster Festival (www.galway oysterfest.com; ⓒ **091/394-637**). The 5-day festival, held every year since 1954, is packed with traditional music, song, dancing, sports, art exhibits—and, above all, oyster-tasting events.

prawns cooked simply in garlic and butter, followed by filet of monkfish with a chipotle and chorizo sauce. Ingredients are local, and the seafood is excellent.

Dominick St., Galway City. www.oscarsbistro.ie. ℒ **091/852-180.** €11–€25.50. Mon–Sat 5:30–9:30pm.

Rúibín ★★ MODERN IRISH   This is a relaxed and bright restaurant set over two floors, with views out over the Galway docks from the upper level. The emphasis is on local Irish food—with dishes like smoked black pudding with grilled sweetheart cabbage, and lemon sole with chicken butter, chanterelles, and greens. Lunch is served on both floors by day; in the evening the downstairs becomes a wine bar with sharing plates and upstairs is for fine dining. It's got a great cocktail menu.

1-3 Docks Rd., Galway City. www.ruibin.ie. ℒ **091/399-200.** Lunch €8–€14. Dinner €22–€31. Mon–Sat noon–3pm, 5–9:45pm.

The Seafood Bar @ Kirwan's ★ SEAFOOD   The exposed stone walls of this elegant downstairs dining room speak to the building's medieval origins. Open the menu, however, and everything suddenly seems bang up to date—this is one of the most popular and reliable restaurants in Galway City for good seafood, dishes like shrimp and clams with chili, fish and chips, steamed mussels, or a generous cold seafood platter. Tucked down a narrow lane, this place can be hard to find, but it's worth the search.

Kirwan's Lane, Galway City. ℒ **091/568-266.** Entrees €18–€27. Mon–Sat 12:30–2:30pm, 6–10pm; Sun 6–10pm.

Sheridans Cheesemongers ★★ DELI/WINE BAR   This is a delightful idea: an artisan cheese shop and deli, doubling as a bar where you can order a glass of wine and some nibbles. Food comes in the form of cheeseboards and charcuterie, much of it locally produced. So simple, and hugely popular, too—you might struggle to get one of the few tables during busy times. This is a really good alternative to heavy restaurant food when all you really want is a chat and a sophisticated snack.

Church Yard St., Galway City. www.sheridanscheesemongers.com. ℒ **091/564-832** or 091/564-829 (shop). Entrees €5–€12. Wine bar: Tues–Fri 1pm–midnight, Sat noon–midnight, Sun 5pm–midnight. Shop: Mon–Fri 10am–6pm, Sat 9am–6pm, Sun noon–5pm.

Shopping in Galway City

Given its status as both a tourist hub and a vibrant arts community, it's no surprise that Galway has great shopping. Some of the best is in tiny clusters of shops in historic buildings, such as the **Cornstore** on Middle Street or the **Grainstore** on Lower Abbeygate Street, but most stores are concentrated along the aptly named Shop Street, which runs into High Street and Quay Street, and the laneways off these. **Eyre Square Centre,** the downtown area's largest shopping mall, rather incongruously incorporates a section of Galway's medieval town wall into its complex of 50 shops.

The daily bustle of Shop Street in Galway City.

Most shops are open Monday to Saturday 9 or 10am to 5:30 or 6pm. In July and August, many stay open late, usually until 9pm on weekdays, and some also open on Sunday from noon to 5pm.

BOOKS

Bell, Book and Candle ★★
You'll find not only a good selection of secondhand books here, but a host of collectible vinyl and CDs, some of them very rare. It's a quirky place (there's even a car inside—long story) and great for a browse. Small Crane, Sea Rd. ℂ **091/589-060.**

Charlie Byrne's Bookshop ★★
Packed floor-to-ceiling with books—secondhand, antiquarian, and new—this wonderfully chaotic bookshop has a huge stock, covering just about anything. It's so beloved that the *Irish Times* once named this the best bookshop in Ireland. It also sells very fetching little cotton tote bags. The Cornstore, Middle St. www.charliebyrne.com. ℂ **091/561-766.**

Kenny's Book Shop and Galleries Ltd ★
Another long-standing favorite of Galway bibliophiles, Kenny's, which is outside the city, has a great selection of new books on all topics, plus secondhand and hard-to-find antiquarian titles. (***Tip:*** It delivers anywhere in the world, if you prefer to order online.) The bookstore also an interesting little art gallery. Liosbán Retail Park, Tuam Rd. www.kennys.ie. ℂ **091/709-350.**

CRAFTS & DESIGN

Mishnóc ★★
You can buy beautiful handmade handbags, backpacks, briefcases and a host of other leather accessories here, many of them unique and Irish-made. 3 Cathedral Buildings, Lower Abbeygate St. www.mishnoc.com. ℂ **091/563-859.**

My Shop . . . Granny Likes It ★★
Irish-made crafts, jewelry and homeware are for sale as this darling little boutique, run by a nice lady named Rona and her dog. A great place to browse for gifts and high-quality keepsakes. 29–31 Upper Abbeygate St. ℂ **091/534-877.**

CRYSTAL, CHINA & SOUVENIRS

Galway Irish Crystal ★★
This local brand of fine crystal rivals Waterford Crystal. At the factory on the edge of town, you can watch the craftspeople at work and purchase armfuls of the stuff yourself. See p. 383 for more details. Merlin Park, Dublin Rd. www.galwaycrystal.ie. ℂ **091/757-311.**

Treasure Chest ★   This large craft store and gift emporium in the town center sells china (including Belleek and Royal Doulton), plus Aran sweaters, Irish linens, handicrafts, and a host of other souvenirs. 31–33 William St. www.treasurechest.ie. ✆ **091/563-862.**

JEWELRY

Blacoe ★★   This popular jeweler in the Eyre Square Centre sells Claddagh rings, engagement rings, and a large range of jewelry featuring traditional Irish motifs. Plenty of pieces sell for well under €100. 212 Eyre Square Centre. www.blacoe.ie. ✆ **091/561-003.**

Claddagh Jewellers ★   In a crowded field, this purveyor of Claddagh rings and other fine Celtic jewelry has something extra: a (free) visitor center next door, the **Legend of the Claddagh Ring,** where you can watch the jewelers at work. 25 Mainguard St. www.thecladdagh.com. ✆ **091/562-554.**

Cobwebs ★★   Located opposite the Spanish Arch, this great little store sells antique and modern jewelry, plus curios, antiques, and objets d'art. 7 Quay Lane. www.cobwebs.ie. ✆ **091/564-388.**

Fallers of Galway ★   Fallers makes and sells the Claddagh ring, a traditional Galway souvenir that symbolizes love and friendship (see box above). It also has a large stock of other jewelry with Celtic motifs. Williamsgate St. www.fallers.com. ✆ **091/561-226.**

Hartmanns of Galway ★   Another maker of Claddagh rings, Hartmanns also specializes in watches and diamonds. This is one of Galway's real high-end jewelry stores. 27–29 William St. www.hartmanns.ie. ✆ **091/562-063.**

Thomas Dillon's Claddagh Gold ★   This chirpily colored little store makes two bold claims: to be the original maker of Claddagh rings (they're the only ones allowed to stamp the rings with "original") and to be the oldest jewelry store in all of Ireland. If the date it was established—1750—is anything to go by, it's probably true. The shop has a tiny little museum displaying Claddagh rings from the 1700s. 1 Quay St. www.claddaghring.ie. ✆ **091/566-365.**

MUSIC & MUSICAL INSTRUMENTS

P. Powell & Sons ★   Usually just called Powell's, this is an excellent source for instruments—including pennywhistles, bodhráns, and the like—as well as a good range of traditional music CDs. 53 William St. www.powellsmusic.ie. ✆ **091/562-295.**

TWEEDS, WOOLENS & CLOTHING

Galway Woollen Market ★   This colorful store is one of the best for traditional, hand-loomed Aran knits, plus lace and other traditional textiles. Visitors who live outside the European Union don't have to pay sales tax on items bought from here. 21 High St. www.aranislandsknitwear.com. ✆ **091/562-491.**

ESSENTIAL SOUVENIR: THE claddagh RING

Known worldwide as a symbol of love and friendship, the delicate **Claddagh** (pronounced *Clad*-uh) ring is probably a design you'll recognize—two hands holding a heart topped with a crown—even if the name is new to you. Over the years this iconic design has also become a symbol for Ireland and its diaspora.

Claddagh rings first appeared sometime in the 17th century, although the design was based on a much older European tradition, dating back to Roman times. The hands are said to represent friendship, the crown loyalty, and the heart love—the three ingredients of a perfect marriage.

Originally, the ring was a wedding band worn facing out for engagement and facing in for marriage. Though no longer widely worn as a symbol of marriage, it is still frequently worn as a friendship ring and makes a lovely memento. The first rings were made in Galway—or more precisely, just over the Father Griffin Bridge, on the west bank of the River Corrib, in the town of Claddagh. It's now a residential satellite to Galway, but in ancient times it was a kingdom with its own laws, fleet, and customs.

Irish Tweeds ★   Although not the oldest tweed maker in town by any means, Irish Tweeds has a great selection of traditionally made garments, including snazzy hats, jackets, and nightwear. They also ship worldwide, free of charge. 51 William St. www.irishtweeds.com. ©**091/539-745.**

O'Máille (O'Malley) ★   Another excellent place to buy Aran knitwear and other Irish knits, this store has a claim to fame of its own—when *The Quiet Man* was filmed near here in 1951 (p. 444), it provided costumes for all the actors, including John Wayne. 16 High St. www.omaille.com. ©**091/562-696.**

Galway City After Dark
THEATER
Druid Theatre ★★ THEATER   Highly respected across Ireland and beyond for its original, cutting-edge productions, the Druid has been one of the region's foremost arts institutions since the 1970s. It's particularly known for premiering new work from up-and-coming writers, so expect to find challenging, intelligent material staged here. The theater also produces new versions of classic plays by Irish, British, and European dramatists. Shows can sell out some time in advance and are often out on the road (the Druid is a touring company), so it's advisable to check what's on and make bookings as far ahead as possible. Ticket prices range from around €15 to €45. Flood St. www.druid.ie. ©**091/568-660.** Performance times vary by show.

PUBS & BARS

The Crane Bar ★★★   Considered one of the best pubs in the city for traditional music, the Crane Bar has live bands nightly from 9:30, and on some weekend afternoons, too. Admission is usually free, but some sessions in the upstairs bar cost anything from a couple euro to €20. 2 Sea Rd. www.thecranebar.com. ℰ **091/587-419.**

The Front Door ★★   This cheerful pub, which sprawls over two floors, is a wonderfully social place where you can saunter in at lunchtime for a tasty sandwich and a pint and find yourself staying for hours. It sometimes shows Irish sports on big-screen TVs. 8 Cross St. at High St. www.frontdoorpub.com. ℰ **091/563-757.**

Halo ★★   Playful decadence is the vibe at this popular nightclub, which pitches itself at a young-but-not-too-young demographic (under 23s are not admitted). It has five bars and a good, slightly retro cocktail menu. 36 Upper Abbeygate St. www.halonightclub.com. ℰ **091/565-976.**

Murty Rabbitt's ★★   This charming and unspoiled late-19th-century pub has a delightfully old-school feel. (It's still run by the same family who owned it all the way back then, too. How's that for tradition?) Rabbitt's sometimes has live music in the evening. 23 Forster St. ℰ **091/566-490.**

Kirwan's Lane in the historic Latin Quarter of Galway City.

A DAY AT THE races

"As I went down to Galway Town/To seek for recreation. . . ." So goes the famous folk song "Galway Races," and the **Galway Races** are still a big deal in the Irish horse-racing calendar—and almost as big a social event as a sporting one.

People dress up in posh frocks and big hats, and the crowds cheer enthusiastically as competing racehorses pound the turf. Horse lovers and high rollers pour in from around the country for the race weeks in July, September, and October. The animals are the best around, and the atmosphere is electric.

Since 1869, the action has taken place at the **Galway Racecourse**

(www.galwayraces.com; ✆ **091/700-100**), just outside Galway City in Ballybrit, less than 3km (2 miles) north-east of town. Ticket prices vary depending on the event and day of the week, but expect to pay from a round €20 to upwards of €40 for a ticket. Multi-day and season tickets are also available.

Galway horse races at the Ballybrit race course.

The Quays ★★   Another good place to hear live music, The Quays has the unusual distinction of having interior decor that was reclaimed from a medieval French church. The what's-on list is a real mixed bag—you could find anything from trad to 80s rock, hip hop to indie. Expect the fun to kick off around 9pm. 11 Quay St. ✆ **091/568-347.**

Róisín Dubh ★★   As much a concert venue as it is a bar, this place gets great acts—expect to see a few famous names crop up among the packed program of live music and standup comedy. 9 Dominick St. www.roisindubh.net. ✆ **091/586-540.**

Side Trips from Galway City

On the main road inland from Galway City you'll find a number of attractions perfectly geared toward families: the well-preserved medieval town of **Athenry** (p. 398), the giant fish tanks of the **Galway Atlantaquaria** (p. 397), and ye-olde-tyme-funne feasting at **Dunguaire Castle** (see below). Meanwhile, more literary types may be interested in a string of sites related to one of Ireland's greatest poets, W. B. Yeats (see "A Poetic Soul," p. 448).

Heading west out of Galway City, the R336 coast road makes for a lovely scenic drive, snaking along the edge of Galway Bay. The first stop will be the city suburb and beach resort of **Salthill** (*Bóthar na Trá*). It has a boardwalk and a fine beach, plus lots of bars, fast food, amusement rides, and game arcades, a good respite from the city if you've got kids (as long as you don't mind the crowds). Farther along the R336, you will also be entering the Gaeltacht or Irish-speaking area, with some charming historic towns such as Irish-speaking **Spiddal** (*An Spidéal*). The road continues as far as **Inverin** (*Indreabhán*), then turns northward, with signposts for **Rossaveal** (*Ros an Mhíl*), ferry port to the **Aran Islands** (p. 384). Continuing north on R336, you can branch off on R340 to visit **Ros Muc,** site of the **Padraig Pearse Cottage ★** (p. 398).

Dunguaire Castle ★ CASTLE   This gray and forbidding fortress on the shore of Galway Bay, between Gort and Kilcolgan, was once the royal seat of the 7th-century King Guaire of Connaught. It was at its peak in the 1500s, though, when most of what you see now was constructed. Later, it fell into disrepair, until it was purchased by the Irish writer Oliver St. John Gogarty (1878–1957), who restored it to glory. Today, you can climb the square tower for views of the nearby Burren and Galway Bay. The castle

Jumping off the Blackrock diving board at the Salthill Promenade.

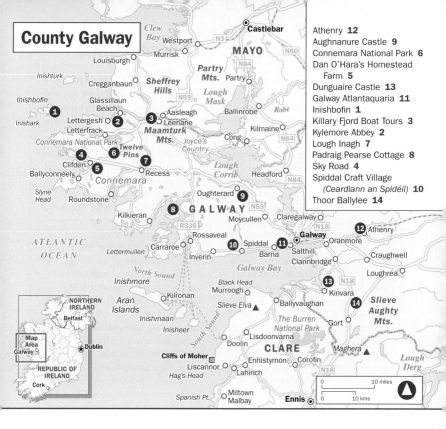

County Galway

| Athenry **12** |
| Aughnanure Castle **9** |
| Connemara National Park **6** |
| Dan O'Hara's Homestead Farm **5** |
| Dunguaire Castle **13** |
| Galway Atlantaquaria **11** |
| Inishbofin **1** |
| Killary Fjord Boat Tours **3** |
| Kylemore Abbey **2** |
| Lough Inagh **7** |
| Padraig Pearse Cottage **8** |
| Sky Road **4** |
| Spiddal Craft Village (*Ceardlann an Spidéil*) **10** |
| Thoor Ballylee **14** |

throws a popular **medieval banquet** from April to September—expect mead, a traditional supper, and a show featuring song and poetry. Shows are nightly at 5:30pm, with an additional show at 8:45pm in the summer months. Reservations are essential. Dunguaire is near Kinvara, approximately 26km (16 miles) southeast of Galway.

On N67 (Ballyvaughan Rd.), Dunguaire, Co. Galway. www.dunguairecastle.com. © 061/711-222. Apr–Sept daily 10am–5pm; last admission 30 min. before closing. **Castle:** €8 adults; €5.50 seniors, students, and children 4–18; children 3 and under free; €24–€30 families. **Banquet:** €63 adults; €35 children 4–18; children 3 and under free. Reservations essential.

Galway Atlantaquaria ★ AQUARIUM This is a fantastic change of pace for kids who are tired of trudging around historic ruins. Highlights of the exhibits include an enormous two-story **ocean tank** housing a couple hundred sea creatures; a **wreck tank** that's home to dangerous conger eels; and **touch pools** where kids can handle tame starfish and hermit crabs. The schedule for what gets fed when is displayed at the entrance.

The Promenade, Salthill, Co. Galway. www.nationalaquarium.ie. © 091/585-100. Admission €13 adults; €9.50 seniors; €10 students; €8.50 children 3–16; €24–€35 families. Mon–Fri 10am–5pm, Sat–Sun 10am–6pm. Last admission 45 min. before closing.

ATHENRY: FADED medieval SPLENDOR

Remarkably intact after more than 6 centuries, the medieval town walls of **Athenry**—about 25 minutes' drive east from Galway—surround a charming small town that feels like a time-warp experience. Those walls are some of the best-preserved in Ireland, constructed in the 1300s, with well over half of the original 2km (1⅓ miles) circuit still surviving—up to 5m (16½ ft.) tall in places.

Start with a visit to the **Athenry Heritage Centre** on The Square, in the town center (www.athenryheritagecentre.com; ℂ **091/844-661**). As well as providing all the usual orientation—including maps for walking routes—it has a lively **Medieval Experience.** Aimed mostly at kids, it has plenty of interactive exhibits, dress-up areas, and re-creations of a torture dungeon and medieval street. Admission costs €8 adults, €6 children, and €26 families. You can also play Robin Hood by trying your hand at archery; hour-long lessons cost €25. The center is open June to August daily 10am to 4:30pm, and April to May weekdays 10am to 4:30pm (closed Oct–Mar). A winter wonderland is open on weekends in December.

Just a 10-minute walk away, on Court Lane, is the medieval **Athenry Castle.** Inside its modest tower keep—the only substantial part that survives—are interesting carvings on the main doorway and window arches. Admission costs €5 adults, €4 seniors, €3 students and children, and €13 families. From April to September it's open daily 9:30am to 6pm; last admission 5:15pm. In October, it's open Monday to Thursday 9:30am to 5pm; last admission 4:15pm (closed Nov–Mar).

Just around the corner from the castle on Bridge Street, check out the ruins of a **Dominican Priory,** built in the mid–13th century and comprehensively destroyed by Cromwell's forces 400 years later. Today it's just a picturesque ruin, incongruously surrounded by modern houses; to medievalists, however, it's of particular interest because of its elaborately carved gravestones.

To reach Athenry from Galway, take the M6 motorway east about 25km (15½ miles) to junction 17, signposted for Athenry and Craughwell. There's also train service hourly from Galway City; the trip takes between 15 and 30 minutes and costs around €6 round-trip.

Pearse Cultural Centre and Padraig Pearse Cottage ★ MUSEUM/ HISTORIC HOUSE   This small but engaging center is devoted to Padraig Pearse (1879–1916), one of the leaders of Ireland's 1916 Easter Rising. Dublin-based Pearse, who read the Declaration of Independence from the steps of the G.P.O. in Dublin (p. 112), made Connemara his countryside home. The center uses that as a springboard from which to celebrate the region's culture, and of course there's plenty to say about Pearse's all-too-short life, which ended tragically when he was executed for his part in the rebellion.

Inbhear, near Ros Muc, Co. Galway. www.heritageireland.ie. ℂ **091/574292.** Admission €5 adults; €4 seniors; €3 children/students; €13 families. Mid-Mar to Sept daily 9:30am–6pm; Oct to mid-Mar daily 9:30–4pm; last admission 45 min. before closing.

Spiddal Craft Village (Ceardlann an Spidéil) ★★ CULTURAL CENTER   On the main road as you enter Spiddal from Galway, this is a fantastic collection of cottage-style crafts stores and workshops. The artists-in-residence here change regularly, but selection is always diverse. Plenty of the work is affordable without stretching the budget too far. Even if you're not buying, it's an inspiring place to browse. The **Builín Blasta Café** sells bakery goods, snacks, and light meals in addition to deli items. You can contact the individual artists via the main website.

About 15km (9 miles) W of Galway on R336, Spiddal, Co. Galway. www.spiddalcrafts. com. No phone. Mon–Sat 10am–5:30pm; Sun 11am–5pm. Often closes earlier in the winter.

Thoor Ballylee ★★ HISTORIC HOUSE   This restored 15th-century Norman tower house was once part of the estate of the Earls of Clanricarde. It probably still exists today because it was part of the property owned by the family of Lady Gregory, a close friend and patron of the poet W. B. Yeats. He bought the castle from her family for £35 in 1916 and set about restoring it. The building inspired his poems "The Winding Stair" and "The Tower." It was Yeats who renamed it, from Ballylee

IN THE footsteps OF POETS

In the early 1900s, every summer the area southeast of Galway City became a sort of Bloomsbury Society West, as Dublin's greatest literary minds decamped to a cluster of nearby manor homes. About 36km (22⅓ miles) southeast of Galway City, near the northern border of the Burren (see chapter 9), you'll see signs to the beautiful **Coole Park National Forest** (www.coolepark.ie; ☏ **091/631-804**). This was once the country home of the dramatist and arts patron Lady Augusta Gregory (1852–1932), who, along with W. B. Yeats and Edward Martyn, founded the **Abbey Theatre** ★ in Dublin (p. 171). Sadly, her house no longer stands, but her influence is memorialized in a tree on the grounds on which the following people carved their initials while visiting with her: George Bernard Shaw, Sean O'Casey, John Masefield, Oliver St. John Gogarty, W. B. Yeats, and Douglas Hyde, the first president of Ireland. Clearly, she was an exceptional woman, and this is an exceptional place. The visitor center shows a number of films on Lady Gregory and Coole Park, and has a tearoom, picnic tables, and some lovely nature trails. The visitor center is open daily 10am to 6pm from June to August and 10am to 5pm in April, May, and September (closed last weekend in Sept). Admission is free.

Not too far from the home of his friend, the great poet W. B. Yeats (1865–1939) had his own summer home in Gort at **Thoor Ballylee** (see above). The restored 15th-century Norman tower house served as an inspiration for his poetry and is now a museum to Yeats, with exhibitions and events such as poetry readings.

Nearby **Dunguaire Castle** (p. 396) was rescued from ruin by Oliver St. John Gogarty (1878–1957), Irish surgeon, author, poet, and wit. He restored the stone structure to glory and made a home here. His great friends Yeats and Lady Gregory were frequent guests.

Castle to Thoor (or "Tower") Ballylee. Today it serves as a Yeats museum, with displays on his life and a bookshop specializing in Anglo-Irish literature.

Off N18 at Ballylee, Gort, Co. Galway. www.yeatsthoorballylee.org. ✆ **091/631-436.** Tickets €7 adults; €5 seniors; €4 children. June–Aug daily 10am–6pm; April–May and Sept–Oct Mon–Fri 10am–4pm, Sat 11am–5pm.

CONNEMARA

If you look for Connemara on road signs, you may be looking forever, because it's not a city or county, but rather a region—and one with a particularly distinct identity. Like the Burren in County Clare, the boundaries are a bit hazy. Most agree that Connemara is west of Galway City, starting at Oughterard and continuing toward the Atlantic. Anyway, you know it when you see it: It's an area of breathtaking barrenness and unique beauty, with dark bogs and tall jagged mountains punctuated by curving lakes dotted with green islands. The desolate landscape is caused, in part, by an absence of trees: Most native stands were felled and dragged off long ago for building ships, houses, and furniture. As Oscar Wilde wrote, "Connemara is a savage beauty."

It's a varied place—in fact, you could say that there are two Connemaras. South of the Galway–Clifden road (N59) is a vast bog-mantled moorland dotted with lakes, with a low, indented, rocky coastline. North of the Galway–Clifden road, tall quartzite domes and cones form the Maumturks and the Twelve Bens (also called the Twelve Pins), rising to the Killary fjord—the only fjord in this part of Europe.

Note that Connemara is part of the **Gaeltacht,** or Irish-speaking area; many signs are in Irish only (see p. 470).

Visitor Information

The **Clifden Tourist Office** is on Galway Road, Clifden (✆ **095/21163**). Its opening hours are a little unpredictable—generally daily 9am to 5pm in summer, but you might find it closed on spring and fall weekends, and it's closed altogether from mid-October to mid-March. Also see **www.visitclifden.com** for local information.

Getting Around

The main road through Connemara—the N59 highway up from Galway City to **Clifden** and **Leenane** (*Leenaun*)—is hardly a crowded superhighway, but you'll still want to branch off from it to explore the region's wild and rugged coast. Loops such as the Sky Road from Clifden (p. 404), the R341 from Ballyhinch to Roundstone, or the Connemara Loop from Letterfrack reward travelers who have time to get off the beaten track. Regular **buses** run from Galway to Clifden; the route takes around half an hour longer than by car. Make sure you check the time of the last return journey—they tend to stop quite early in the evening.

Exploring Connemara

Much of the attraction of Connemara is the wild countryside, but when you're ready to come in from the cold, the seaside town of **Clifden (*An Clochán*)** has an enviable location at the edge of the blue waters of Clifden Bay, where miles of curving, sandy beaches skirt the rugged coastline. It's an attractive Victorian town with colorful shop fronts and church steeples thrusting skyward, well provided with restaurants, shops, hotels, and pubs, which makes it a handy base for exploring the area. If you prefer a quieter location, seek out one of the many smaller towns and villages in the area, such as the little fishing port of **Roundstone (*Cloch na Rón*)** ★ on the south coast about 24km (15 miles) away, which also has all the essentials: pristine beaches, comfortable guesthouses, good restaurants, shops, and more than its share of natural charm. North of Clifden, the little community of **Letterfrack (*Leitir Fraic*)** sits at the edge of **Connemara National Park** (p. 401), close to the extraordinary Gothic **Kylemore Abbey** (p. 403). The tiny village, founded by Quakers, has a handful of pubs and B&Bs in a glorious natural setting. It's near the bright white sands of **Glassillaun Beach** and **Lettergesh,** where horses raced across the sand in the film *The Quiet Man* (p. 444). North and east of Letterfrack, on the shore of Killary Fjord, **Leenane (*Leenaun*)** is the starting point for a number of excellent scenic hikes.

Aughnanure Castle ★ CASTLE Standing on an outcrop of rock surrounded by forest and pasture, this sturdy fortress is a well-preserved Irish tower castle with an unusual double *bawn* (fortified enclosure) and a still-complete watchtower that you can climb. It was built around A.D. 1500 as a stronghold of the "Ferocious" O'Flaherty clan, who dominated the region and terrified their neighbors. The castle's fireplaces are so big that you could fit a double bed in them. Aside from the tower the site is mostly a ruin, although you can wander through what remains of the banqueting hall. The grounds also contain the remnants of a dry harbor.

Oughterard, Co. Galway. www.heritageireland.ie. © **091/552-214.** Admission €5 adults; €4 seniors; €3 children; €13 families. Apr–Oct daily 9:30am–6pm. Last admission 45 min. before closing. Closed Nov–Mar.

Connemara National Park ★★★ NATURE SITE This gorgeous national park encompasses more than 2,000 hectares (4,940 acres) of mountains, bogs, grasslands, and hiking trails. Some of the best trails lead through the peaceful *Gleann Mór* (which means "Big Glen"), through which flows the **River Polladirk,** or up to the **Twelve Bens** (also called the "Twelve Pins"), a small, quartzite mountain range north of the Galway–Clifden road. None of the Twelve Bens rises above 730m (2,392 ft.), which makes their summits quite accessible to those who don't mind walking at a steep incline. Nearby are the lesser-known, equally lovely **Maumturk** range and the breathtaking **Killary Fjord**—the only fjord in

Ireland, indeed this entire region of Europe. Frequent rainfall produces dozens of tiny streams and waterfalls, and the views are spectacular. The excellent visitor center south of the crossroads in **Letterfrack** dispenses general information on the park, as well as providing sustenance in the form of tea, sandwiches, and fresh baked goods.

Visitor center signposted from N59, Letterfrack, Co. Galway. www.connemara nationalpark.ie. ℂ **076/100-2528.** Free admission. Visitor center: Daily 9am–5:30pm. Park: Daily year-round.

Dan O'Hara Homestead Farm ★★ HERITAGE SITE   This open-air museum tells the story of Connemara, its people, and how they worked this rocky and inhospitable land. Dan O'Hara was a real person who farmed the land for his family, until the potato famine destroyed their livelihood. The reconstructed farmstead is set up exactly as it would have been in the years before the Famine, complete with farm dwellings. Also on the grounds of the museum is a dolmen and prehistoric tomb.

About 6.5km (4 miles) E of Clifden off N59 in Lettershea, Co. Galway. www.connemara heritage.com. ℂ **095/21808.** Admission €8.50 adults; €7.50 seniors and students; €4.25 children; €22 families. Mar–Nov daily 10am–6pm; last admission 1 hr. before closing.

Inishbofin ★★ ISLAND   A place of seclusion and spectacular beauty, this small emerald-green gem lies 11km (6¾ miles) off the northwest coast of Connemara. Try to come here on a day when the skies are clear enough to deliver the unforgettable views. Once the domain of monks, then the lair of pirate queen Grace O'Malley (see p. 438), later Cromwell's infamous priest prison—you can still see his original, star-shaped barracks—Inishbofin is currently home to just 180 year-round human residents, a seal colony, and a seabird sanctuary. Numerous ferries to the island operate from the port of Cleggan (13km/8 miles northwest of Clifden off N59) daily April through October. **Inishbofin Ferry** (www.inishbofinferry.ie; ℂ **095/45819** or 086/171-8829) sails twice a day, or three times a day from late March to mid-October. Round-trip fares are €25 adults, €15 students, €10 children 5 to 18, and €5 children 3 to 5; it's free for seniors and children 2 and under. *Note:* Reservations are essential, and evening sailing times can change in bad weather.

Inishbofin, Co. Galway.

Dare You Take . . . the Spooky Shortcut?

If you're planning a drive across the Connemara National Park to Clifden, you may want to make a shortcut on the rough but striking "bog road" (to find it, drive south from Clifden on the R341 and turn left at Ballinaboy). Unless you're traveling at night, that is. A hotel manager in these parts once told us that some locals consider the road to be haunted and won't take it after dark. Spooks or not, that's probably good advice at night, especially in bad weather.

Cruising on the magnificent Killary Fjord

Killary Fjord Boat Tours ★★ CRUISE This pleasant 90-minute cruise gives you ample time to enjoy the gorgeous views, across smooth waters to where green hills seem to cascade down to the shoreline. Weather permitting, you should be able to see three major mountain ranges: the Maumturk and Twelve Bens to the south, and the Mweelreas in County Mayo to the north. The boat—designed, they claim, to avoid seasickness, or your money back—has viewing decks inside and out, so the tour can be taken in all weather. Boats depart from Nancy's Point, about 2.7km (1½ miles) west of Leenane (Leenaun). Book online for a slight discount on ticket prices.

Signposted on N59, Leenane, Co. Galway. www.killaryfjord.com. ✆ **087/235-9136.** Tickets €23.50 adults; €19.50 seniors and students; €12.50 children 11–17; free for children 10 and under; €47–€59 families. Book online for discounts. Departures daily June–Aug 10:30am, 12:30, 2:30, and 4pm; May 10:30am, 12:30, and 2:30pm; Apr, Sept and Oct 12:30 and 2:30pm. Closed Nov–Mar.

Kylemore Abbey ★ RELIGIOUS SITE As you round yet another bend on the particularly wild stretch of country road around Kylemore, this extraordinary neo-Gothic abbey looms into view, at the base of a wooded hill across mirrorlike Kylemore Lake. The vast, crenelated 19th-century house was donated to the Benedictine nuns in 1920, and the sisters have run a convent boarding school here ever since. You can see a little of the interior, but it's surprisingly plain; the exterior and the grounds are the real reason to visit, especially that breathtaking view across the lake. The highlight is the restored Gothic chapel, an exquisite cathedral in miniature with a plain, somber cemetery to one side; don't miss the lavish Victorian walled garden. Free, short history talks take place inside the abbey at 11:30am, 1pm, and 3pm daily. From June to August a free guided tour of the walled gardens is given daily at noon. The complex includes a restaurant that serves produce grown on the nuns' farm, a shop with a working pottery studio, and a visitor center. The abbey is most atmospheric when the bells are rung for midday office or for vespers at 6pm.

Kylemore, Co. Galway (follow signs from N59). www.kylemoreabbey.ie. ⓒ 095/52001. Admission €15 adults; €12.50 seniors and students; children 16 and under free; €38 families. July–Aug daily 9am–7pm; Apr–June daily 9am–6pm; Sept–Oct daily 9:30am–5:30pm; Nov–Mar daily 10am–4:30pm.

The Sky Road ★★ SCENIC ROUTE   One of the most picturesque drives in the west, the Sky Road is the name given to a mountain pass that rises from Clifden and loops around the Kingstown Peninsula. The vistas over the hills and cliffs to the wide Atlantic Ocean are spectacular, and there are plenty of viewpoints where you can pull over to take it all in. The Sky Road starts and ends just off the N59 highway. The route is signposted (perhaps a little too discreetly), and you can go in either direction, but we suggest counterclockwise. Starting in the center of Clifden, turn down Church Hill (second left after the tourism office, facing north). Stay

The neo-Gothic Kylemore Abbey perches on its lakeside site.

Cycling Lough Inagh in Connemara.

left at the fork and you're on the Sky Road. About 2.5km (1½ miles) later, you'll pass the remains of **Clifeden Castle,** a Gothic folly dating from 1818. It's completely derelict, but you can visit for free by passing through the marked gate and walking across the pasture. The whole Sky Road takes about 40 minutes to drive, but you may double that with stopping time. And be warned—it is very narrow, little more than a paved track in places, so we don't recommend it in bad weather, and always be prepared to meet oncoming cars traveling in the other direction.

Clifden, Co. Galway.

Where to Stay in Connemara
EXPENSIVE

Abbeyglen Castle ★★   This is how a stay in a castle should be. The gray stone fortress perched on a low hill might look stern and unforgiving from a distance, but inside it's all welcoming charm. It has an ambience of slightly faded nobility, with roomy lounges where chairs are grouped around warming fireplaces and huge windows overlook the grounds. At night, guests gather in the piano bar to chat over brandies. Rooms are spacious, with four-poster beds. The staff can arrange fishing trips and packed lunches, and to give you tips on local sights. Dinners are convivial and chatty, and the food is delicious.

Sky Rd., Clifden, Co. Galway. www.abbeyglen.ie. ✆ **095/21201.** 45 units. €178–€325 double. €170–€350 suite Rates include breakfast. Closed Jan. Free parking (if booked online). **Amenities:** Restaurant; bar; Jacuzzi; outdoor pool; sauna; spa; tennis court; Wi-Fi (free).

Ballynahinch Castle ★★   At the side of Owenmore River, near the foot of Ben Lettery, this gabled manor house looks too good to be true. It's a postcard setting, perfect in almost every way. The 16th-century building, once the seat of the O'Flaherty chieftains, is now a casually elegant hotel. Lounges have towering ceilings and warming fireplaces. Guest rooms are just modern enough, in muted shades of cream and toast, and all have orthopedic mattresses. The river is known for its trout and salmon, and your catch can be weighed up each evening in the wood-paneled **Fishermen's Bar.** Dinner in the beautiful **Owenmore Restaurant** is a highlight of any stay.

Recess, Co. Galway. www.ballynahinch-castle.com. ✆ **095/31006.** 40 units. €235–€370 double; €470–€605 suite. Rates include breakfast. **Amenities:** Restaurant; bar; babysitting; limited room service; tennis courts; Wi-Fi (free).

Delphi Lodge ★★ This vine-covered 18th-century country house dwarfed by mountains on a 1,000-acre lakefront estate was made for Instagram. Calling this place a "lodge" isn't just cute nomenclature; this is very much an actual hunting lodge, and a veritable paradise for fishing. Everything is arranged to make fishing easy—boats, *ghillies,* and licenses are all taken care of. If you don't fish, you can just enjoy the utterly splendid countryside, spending the day hiking the enormous grounds, where filling your lungs with the fresh air is like a balm for the soul. Afterward, relax by the fire in the cozy library with a sherry from the honor bar, or try your hand at a game of snooker. Guest rooms are comfort-

Hunts Room, a guest lounge at Ballynahinch Castle Hotel & Estate.

able and generously proportioned (though note that the doors don't have locks). The pricier rooms have views of the lake. The excellent dinners here are an event, eaten at a long dining table to encourage conversation.

The Delphi Estate and Fishery, Leenane, Co. Galway. www.delphilodge.ie. ℂ **095/42222.** 12 units. €320–€370 double. Rates include breakfast. Closed Christmas and New Year's holidays. **Amenities:** Restaurant (guests only); honor bar; Wi-Fi (free).

MODERATE

Currarevagh Country House ★★ This elegant Italianate manor house, built in 1842, sits just outside tiny Oughterard, in the middle of a huge private park, at the edge of the clear blue waters of Lough Corrib. The house is a perfect retreat—its spacious lounges have fires crackling at the hearth, ideal for relaxing on a rainy day. There's also a lakeside sauna. Rooms are large, with floral curtains, and beds are comfortable. The guesthouse can help you plan activities, from pony trekking and hiking to fishing on the Lough (you can even borrow one of the house's traditionally made boats). Meals in the pink-hued dining room are excellent and often feature the day's catch. There's a 2-night minimum stay.

Oughterard, Co. Galway. www.currarevagh.com. ℂ **091/552-312.** 9 units. €175–€230 double. 2-night minimum stay. Closed Dec–Feb. Rates include breakfast. **Amenities:** Restaurant; bar; sauna; Wi-Fi (free).

Renvyle House Hotel ★★ The poet W. B. Yeats honeymooned here when it was a family home; Winston Churchill was also a regular guest.

This grand old house on the rocky edge of the Atlantic Ocean seems to be in the middle of nowhere, although it's close to Connemara National Park. Still, it's worth the journey, and not just for the breathtaking sea views and warm hospitality. You'll have miles of pristine Irish wilderness to explore; there's a lake you can go boating on, an outdoor pool, and an outdoor hot tub overlooking the beach. Decor is old-school, with sprawling, wood-floored lounges warmed by open fires. Guest rooms vary in size and decor—some are grand and spacious, others small and cozy. The in-house restaurant offers divine European-inspired Irish cooking.

Renvyle, Co. Galway. www.renvyle.com. © **095/46100.** 68 units. €150–€220 double; €175–€270 suite. Rates include breakfast. Closed Jan–Feb. **Amenities:** Restaurant; bar; hot tub; outdoor pool; 2 tennis courts; Wi-Fi (free).

INEXPENSIVE

The Anglers Return ★ Surrounded by beautiful gardens, this lovely, artsy retreat was built as a hunting lodge in the 19th century; today it's a quiet and relaxed B&B run with great charm by Lynn Hill. Bedrooms are simple and modestly sized, furnished in traditional style. Two of the rooms are en-suite; the others have the use of one of two bathrooms located down the corridor—robes are thoughtfully provided. You can cook your own dinner in the fully equipped kitchen or on the grills out-

side. There are log fires and pleasant river or garden views from bedrooms—guests are free to wander the gardens, which are practically an attraction by themselves. *Note:* The Anglers Return doesn't accept credit cards.

Toombeola, Roundstone, Co. Galway. www.anglersreturn.com. © **095/31091.** 5 units. €120–€150 double. 3-night minimum stay. Free parking. Rates include breakfast. No credit cards. No children under 14. Closed Dec–Jan. **Amenities:** Guest lounge; Wi-Fi (free).

Doonmore Hotel ★ This waterfront hotel on Inishbofin Island might not be fancy, but the views are extraordinary—from every window you see stunning vistas of the sea and High Island. Guest rooms are quite basic, but families will be pleased to find the spacious units with children's bunk beds. Rooms in the modern

Front Hall in the Currarevagh Country House.

extension are furnished with pine furniture and flooded with light. Older rooms in the main house are a little worn but still pleasant. Staff are cheerful, and the restaurant offers good, unpretentious cooking.

Inishbofin Island, Co. Galway. www.doonmorehotel.com. ℰ **095/45804.** 25 units. €140–€190 double. Rates include breakfast. 2-night minimum on some dates. Closed Nov–Apr. **Amenities:** Restaurant; bar; Wi-Fi (free).

Rockmount House ★ It should come as no surprise that the views from this little cozy B&B are pretty amazing, given its location on the Sky Road (p. 404). Rooms are basic but cheerful, with comfortable beds. Hosts Anne and Paddy are delightful and filled with knowledge about the region. Equally charming are their two collies, who have been known to accompany guests on long walks. The grounds contain a private clifftop path with spectacular views across the bay. Rockmount House is on the Lower Sky Road, which branches off the main Sky Road about 5km (3 miles) west of Clifden.

Lower Sky Rd., Clifden, Co. Galway. www.rockmounthouse.com. ℰ **095/21763.** 4 units. €88–€120 double. Rates include breakfast. Closed Sept–Apr. **Amenities:** Wi-Fi (free).

10 Where to Eat in Connemara

In addition to the area's great restaurants, some of the tastiest finds in Connemara are from food trucks. The **Misunderstood Heron** (Derrynacleigh, Leenane; www.misunderstoodheron.com) has been winning awards for its creative menu of fresh seafood, local lamb, and foraged foods assembled in wraps, flatbreads, and savory pastries, all served in an amazing setting overlooking the fjord at Killary Harbour. Or check out the tasty seaweed bread, cold-smoked salmon, and delicious cakes from **The Pink Wagon** at Derrigimlagh, on the R341 between Clifden and Roundstone.

The Carriage Restaurant ★ MODERN CONTINENTAL Locals flock to this restaurant, hidden away in the courtyard at the rear of the Clifden Station House Hotel. The draw is imaginative cooking that manages to infuse even the simplest dish with zest and originality. Look for dishes like roasted hoisin pork belly, filet of Connemara salmon with hollandaise, and turbot served with smoked oysters and grilled mushrooms. More casual dining is available in the adjacent bar, the **Signal.**

At the rear of the Clifden Station House Hotel, on the N59, Clifden, Co. Galway. www.clifdenstationhouse.com. ℰ **095/21699.** Reservations essential. Entrees €16–€32. Daily 6:30–9:30pm. Closed Oct–Apr.

O'Dowd's of Roundstone ★★ SEAFOOD There's not much room in this tiny pub in Roundstone, which means you'll be fighting for space with dozens of hungry locals. But trust them, for they know exactly what

THE BEST smell IN ALL OF IRELAND?

"Níl aon tinteán mar do thinteán féin (there is no fireside like your own fireside)."
—Irish proverb

You might experience the strong, smoky, slightly sweet smell of burning turf—dried bricks of peat taken from bogs—on your travels in the West of Ireland. There are plenty who don't care for this quintessentially Irish smell, and for sure it can be quite overpowering. But for the rest of us, there's nothing else like it. In fact, if there's another smell so instantly redolent of this land—of cozy evenings by smoky hearths, of tales told and faraway friends—well, we've yet to find it.

A full third of the Connemara countryside is classified as bog, and these stark and beautiful boglands—formed over 2,500 years ago—have long been an important source of fuel. (During the Iron Age, the Celts also found other use for the bogs, using them to store perishable foods such as butter.) Although no longer the lifeline it once was, cutting and drying turf is still an integral part of the rhythm of the seasons in Connemara.

Cutting requires a special tool, a spade called a *slane*, which slices the turf into bricks about 46cm (18 in.) long. The bricks are first spread out flat to dry, and then stacked in pyramids for further drying—you might see stacks of turf as you pass.

The climate crisis means that, along with other smoky fuels, turf burning is being reduced. Where it was used commercially in the peatlands, alternative uses are now being examined.

they're here for: extremely good, fresh seafood, simple and beautifully prepared. Start with some Roundstone crab claws with garlic butter, followed by a local catch of the day, served in classic style with lemon and tartar sauce. The creamy seafood chowder is always a crowd-pleaser. A simpler bar menu is also available. Needless to say, booking is advisable.

Roundstone, Co. Galway. www.odowdsseafoodbar.com. ✆ **095/35809.** Entrees €14–€24. Daily 10am–9:30pm.

Paddy Coyne's Pub ★★★ IRISH It can be hard to find this lovely pub in tiny, blink-and-you'll-miss-it Renvyle—just outside blink-just-a-little-bit-longer-and-you'll-miss-it-too Tullycross—but it's worth the trek. Aside from the postcard-worthy frontage, dating from 1811, this doesn't *look* like the kind of place that's going to wow you with its cooking. But the numbers of people making their way here for dinner should provide a clue. There's nothing pretentious about the cooking—it's just wonderful, classic Irish fare, done extremely well. Seafood is a specialty—the daily specials are chalked up outside, but expect hake, salmon, mussels, and maybe some Clew Bay oysters, served as they come. Wash it all down with a pint of Guinness (of course). Desserts are avowedly traditional (try the homemade trifle). *Note:* They don't take reservations, so arrive early or expect to wait.

Tullycross, Renvyle, Co. Galway. www.paddycoynespub.com. ✆ **095/43499.** Reservations not accepted. Entrees €16–€28. Daily 5–9pm (but times vary—call to check).

Steam Cafe ★ CAFE   This cute and simple little cafe is one of the best places in Clifden for lunch. The menu isn't fancy, but it's all good: wraps, sandwiches, light meals, and daily specials, everything made with quality ingredients. The cakes and desserts are great to wash down with the excellent coffee.

Station House Courtyard, off N59 (Galway Rd.), Clifden, Co. Galway. ✆ **095/30600.** Entrees €4–€12. Tues and Sat 9:30am–5:30pm. Wed–Fri 10am–5:30pm. Closed Sun–Mon.

Veldon's Seafarer ★★ SEAFOOD   The fishermen's nets, captain's wheels, and assorted sailing paraphernalia plastered across the polished wooden walls of this friendly bar and restaurant leave no doubt as to the specialty of the house. You can eat from a fairly simple bar menu—traditional fish and chips, hamburgers, Irish stew—or retreat to the restaurant area. Local crab is a specialty, although if you want to go all out, the seafood platter has a bit of everything. Try the cheesecake of the day for dessert.

On the N59, Letterfrack, Co. Galway. www.veldons.ie. ✆ **095/41046.** Entrees €11.50–€24. Bar daily noon–9pm; restaurant daily 6–9pm (Fri–Sat only in off-season).

TAKING A (moon) SHINE TO POITÍN

"Keep your eyes well peeled today, the excise men are on their way, searching for the mountain tay, in the hills of Connemara. . . ."

Poitín (sometimes written as poteen) is a potent form of Irish moonshine, traditionally brewed from grain or potatoes. It was banned by the English crown in 1661, in an act that effectively criminalized thousands of distillers overnight. That didn't stop people from making the stuff, however, and after 336 years on the wrong side of the law, poitín was finally made legal again in 1997.

One 17th-century writer said of poitín that "it enlighteneth ye heart, casts off melancholy, keeps back old age and breaketh ye wind." Its usefulness didn't stop there, evidently, as history records the drink being used as everything from a bath tonic to a substitute for dynamite.

Poitín has long been used in fiction as a symbol of Irish nationalism, its contraband status rich with rebellious overtones. The traditional folk song "The Hills of Connemara" describes poitín being secretly distributed right under the noses of excise men.

In 2008, the European Union awarded the drink "Geographical Indicative" protection. This means that only the genuine Irish product is allowed to carry the name (the same status enjoyed by Champagne and Parma ham).

There are many commercial or "legal" versions of poitín on the market now, although these versions are less potent than the moonshine version. Like most liquors, it can be drunk straight, on the rocks, or with a mixer, but at anything from 80 to a massive 180 proof, poitín packs a mean punch, so enjoy . . . cautiously.

walk this way: THE WESTERN WAY

Nestled between the Maumturk and the Twelve Bens mountains in the heart of Connemara, the waters of **Lough Inagh** lie cupped in a spectacularly beautiful valley, where mountain slopes rise precipitously from the valley floor and small streams cascade into the lake in a series of sparkling waterfalls. The **Western Way,** a walking route that traverses the high country of Galway and Mayo, follows a quiet country road above the R344 through the Lough Inagh Valley.

To reach the beginning of the walk, drive north on the R344, turning right on a side road—look for the sign for Maum Ean—about 200m (656 ft.) before the Lough Inagh Lodge Hotel. Continue on this side road for about 6km (3¾ miles) to a large gravel parking lot on the left. Park here and follow the well-worn trail 2km (1.25 miles) to the top of the pass, through glorious mountain scenery.

At the top of the pass, which has long been associated with St. Patrick, a small oratory has been built. There's a hollow in the rock known as **Patrick's Bed,** a life-size statue of the saint, and a series of cairns marking the Stations of the Cross. Together, these monuments make a striking ensemble, strangely eerie when the mists descend and conceal the far slopes in their shifting haze. A clear day offers great views, with the Atlantic Ocean and Bertraghboy Bay to the southwest and more mountains to the northeast. The round-trip walking time is about 1 hour.

Sports & Outdoor Pursuits in Connemara

WALKING Connemara National Park ★★★ (p. 401) has excellent walking trails, some of which lead up the sides of the Twelve Bens. You can get maps at the park's visitor center. From the town of **Leenane (*Leenaun*),** there's an exhilarating 4km (2.4 miles) walk to the picturesque Aasleagh Waterfall (*Eas Liath*) northeast of the Killary Fjord harbor. A 2- to 3-hour walk around the fjord follows the Green Road, a sheep track that was once the primary route from the Renvyle Peninsula to Leenane; along the way you'll even pass a ghost town (a village abandoned after the Famine), where the fields rise at a devilishly steep slope from ruined cottages clustered at the water's edge.

Archery at the Delphi Adventure Resort.

CONNEMARA pony TREKKING

The sturdy yet elegant Connemara pony is the only horse breed native to Ireland, though it has received an infusion of Spanish blood over the centuries. Often raised in tiny fields with limestone pastures, the ponies are known for their stamina and gentleness, which make them ideal for amateur riders and young people. Born and bred to traverse the region's rugged terrain, they are adept at scaling short, steep hills and delicately picking their way along rocky shores.

Because much of the countryside is well off the beaten track, pony trekking is actually a fantastic way to cover ground. It gets you off the busy roads and out into the countryside, even onto the white-sand beaches near Roundstone and elsewhere along the coast. The **Cleggan Beach Riding Centre,** Cleggan (✆ **083/388-8135**), offers beach and mountain treks, the most popular being a 3-hour ride to Omey Island at low tide. And near Loughrea, the peat **Cross Equestrian Centre** (✆ **091/843-968**) can set you up with guided treks for all levels of ability.

WATERSPORTS & ADVENTURE SPORTS   One-stop shopping for outdoorsy activities—kayaking, waterskiing, hill and coastal walking, rock climbing, archery, you name it—can be found at the **Killary Adventure Company** in Leenane (www.killary.com; ✆ **095/43411**). Rates start at around €35 per session. The **Delphi Adventure Resort** in Leenane (www.delphiadventureresort.com; ✆ **095/42208**) offers courses in kayaking, windsurfing, and raft building, as well as mountaineering, abseiling, hiking, and archery. Everything is reasonably priced, and the atmosphere is laid-back and friendly.

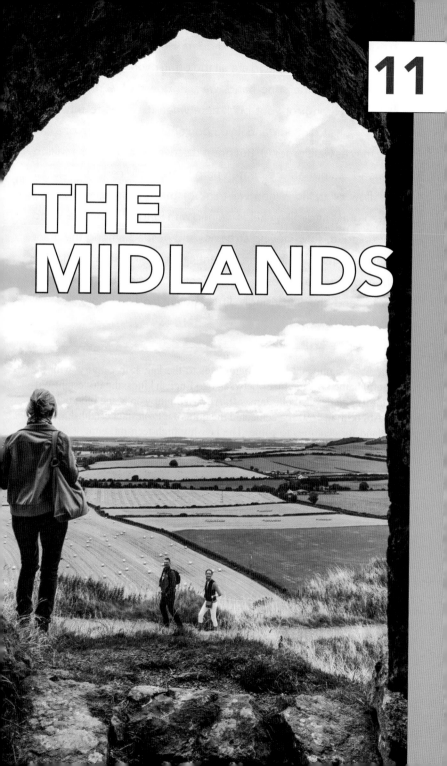

11

THE
MIDLANDS

Promoted as the "Hidden Heartlands," the middle parts of Ireland are all too often overlooked by visitors. On the sone hand, we can guess why. You get less bang for your buck here when it comes to must-see attractions (and if you don't have the freedom of a car, you may as well forget it). But great discoveries await those willing to head . . . not off the beaten path exactly, but certainly *against* the flow of traffic. When we think of the Midlands, we picture green grass and rolling fields, veined with long, winding rivers and picturesque, slow-moving streams. And nestled among them are a few real gems, such as the romantic medieval castles at Charleville and Birr, the atmospheric ancient monastic site at Clonmacnoise, and the surprisingly little-known (and *very* old indeed) Corlea Trackway.

The most significant history here dates to the late 17th century, with the fateful battle for supremacy between two English kings: the Protestant William III and the Catholic James II. After William won at the bloody Battle of Aughrim in 1691, he cemented the hold of a Protestant establishment in Ireland for centuries to come. The lavishly high-tech museum at Athlone Castle is the best of several in the region that tell this important story.

ESSENTIALS

Arriving

BY CAR By far the best way to get to and around the Midlands is by car. Although Athlone is easy to reach by public transportation from Galway or Dublin, you'll need a car to see the smaller towns and remote sites. Major roads that lead to this area are the main Galway–Dublin road (M6) from points east and west, N62 from the south, and N55 and N61 from the north. For car rentals in Dublin, see p. 91; for rentals from Shannon airport, see p. 344.

BY BUS Bus Éireann (www.buseireann.ie; © 061/313333) runs buses every half-hour to 90 minutes, from Galway City to Athlone (journey time 80–100 min.). From the main bus station in Dublin, buses also go to Athlone about every hour (journey time 2–3 hr.) and a handful of times a day to Birr (3–4 hr.).

PREVIOUS PAGE: **The Rock of Dunamase is a popular historic attraction.**

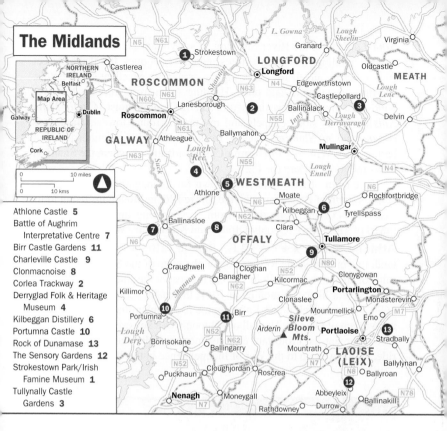

The Midlands

NORTHERN
IRELAND
Belfast

Map Area

Galway
★Dublin

REPUBLIC OF
IRELAND

Cork

| 0 | 10 miles |
| 0 | 10 kms |

Athlone Castle **5**
Battle of Aughrim
Interpretative Centre **7**
Birr Castle Gardens **11**
Charleville Castle **9**
Clonmacnoise **8**
Corlea Trackway **2**
Derryglad Folk & Heritage
Museum **4**
Kilbeggan Distillery **6**
Portumna Castle **10**
Rock of Dunamase **13**
The Sensory Gardens **12**
Strokestown Park/Irish
Famine Museum **1**
Tullynally Castle
Gardens **3**

BY TRAIN **Irish Rail** operates direct trains from Galway to Athlone Station, Southern Station Road (www.irishrail.ie; ℰ **090/647-3300**), every 1 to 2 hours; the journey takes 90 minutes. From Dublin, trains go to Athlone about every hour; most journeys take just over an hour.

A Note on Listings

Officially the Midlands region covers the counties of Laois, Longford, Offaly, and Westmeath; we've also included a couple of sights in the far eastern part of County Galway, because of their close proximity. Attractions in this region are widely spread out—hiring a car is the only practical way to see the Midlands' best sights without spending excessive amounts of time on public transport, which is scarce in rural areas. Therefore, we present the sights as one list, not split up by county, allowing travelers to pick and choose according to their interests.

EXPLORING THE MIDLANDS

The area's most appealing town of any size—although it's hardly a teeming metropolis, with a population of just over 20,000—is **Athlone** (*Baile*

Átha Luain)**,** on the River Shannon. It's a vibrant place where brightly painted buildings house craft stores and cool boutiques. It's also a perfect spot to base yourself for exploring the area, with excellent small hotels, charming restaurants, and pubs. Heading south from Athlone, the river winds past the early Christian settlement of **Clonmacnoise (***Cluain Mhic Nóis***),** with its stone chapels and mysterious round towers; **Banagher (***Beannchar na Sionna***),** a sleepy working town with a picturesque river harbor; and eventually **Portumna Castle,** artfully set where the Shannon flows into Lough Derg (p. 422).

The town of **Birr (***Biorra***),** known for its magnificent historic gardens, is south of Banagher, with the Slieve Bloom Mountains rising to its east; the N52 angles northeast from Birr, passing through the county towns of **Tullamore** (County Offaly) and **Mullingar** (Westmeath).

Athlone Castle ★★ CASTLE   Built in 1210 for King John of England, this mighty stone fortress sits on the edge of the Shannon, atop the ruins of an earlier fort built in 1129 as the seat of the chiefs of Connaught. Besieged for almost 6 months in 1641, the castle was attacked again in 1690 and finally fell in 1691 after an intense bombardment by forces sent by William of Orange. The fall of Athlone was a key event in the war that would cement the Protestant establishment in Ireland and ensure British rule, all the way up to the War of Independence in the 1920s. (The Dutch

Birr Castle.

THE GREAT telescope

At noble **Birr Castle** ★★ (p. 418), one of the key attractions is not the historic castle itself, nor the beautiful grounds, but a fascinating exhibition on 19th-century science. William Parsons, the 3rd Earl of Birr, was a scientist and astronomer, obsessed with discovering all he could about the night sky. Under his leadership, Birr Castle became an unlikely hub of research into astronomy, photography, and botany. One of his inventions—now known as the Great Telescope—was built in 1845 and soon nicknamed (somewhat sarcastically) the "Leviathan of Parsonstown." Until the 20th century, it was the largest telescope in the world.

The huge astronomical machine may resemble a medieval siege engine, but the key thing about it was that it worked. Using it, Parsons discovered and documented numerous nebulae, some of which were later determined to be hitherto unknown galaxies. He found and named the Crab Nebula, among others. He also discovered that certain galaxies were shaped like spirals. Birr Castle was the only place in the world where the phenomenon could be observed until 1914, when new, more advanced telescopes were developed.

To this day, the Great Telescope is kept in full working order, and demonstrations of its power are held regularly in summer. If you want to witness one of these displays for yourself, call ahead to check times.

military commander who took the town, Godard van Glinkel, was rewarded for his efforts with the earldom of Athlone.) Three centuries later, in 2012, the castle underwent a multimillion-euro renovation; it now houses eight separate galleries on the history of Athlone, particularly the 1690-91 siege, using plenty of high-tech wizardry. The castle's original medieval walls have been preserved, as have two large cannons dating from the reign of George II, and a pair of 25cm (10-inch) mortars cast in 1856.

Athlone, Co. Westmeath. www.athlonecastle.ie. © **090/644-2130.** Admission €9 adults; €6.50 seniors and students; €4.50 children under 15; free for children 3 and under; €23–€28 families. June–Aug Tues–Sat 9:30am–6pm, Sun 10:30am–6pm; Sept–Oct Tues–Sat 10am–5:30pm, Sun 11am–5:30pm; Mar–May Wed–Sat 10am–5:30pm, Sun 11am–5:30pm; Nov–Feb Wed–Sat 10:30am–5pm, Sun 11:30am–5pm. Last admission 1 hr. before closing.

Battle of Aughrim Interpretative Centre ★ BATTLEFIELD

About midway between Galway City and Athlone, just off the M6 motorway, lies this interesting little museum, dedicated to a battle between two kings that took place here in 1691. When James II became king of England in 1685, his days on the throne were already numbered. He had a "flaw" that the Protestant establishment simply couldn't live with: He was a convert to Catholicism. In 1688, James was deposed by Parliament in favor of his own son-in-law—the Protestant William III. Retreating to Ireland, James led a rebellion that was to have far-reaching consequences for Irish history. Aughrim wasn't the most famous nor arguably the most

An open-air market stall in the lively town of Athlone.

important battle of that war, but it was the last. With the defeat of the so-called Jacobite forces loyal to James, the prospect of a Catholic Ireland was crushed for almost 2½ centuries. The center does a competent job of telling the story through displays and exhibits, plus the obligatory visitor-center film.

R446, Aughrim, near Ballinasloe, Co. Galway. © **090/967-3939.** Admission €5 adults; €4 seniors and students; €3 children 11 and under; €12 families. June–Aug Tues–Sat 10:30am–4:30pm, Sun 2–5pm. Closed early Sept–May.

Birr Castle Gardens ★★ GARDENS This magnificent 90-room, 17th-century castle stands amid gorgeous sprawling gardens, beautifully crafted as a kind of wonderland. The great house is still lived in by the same family that has owned it for centuries. It is only open to the public from May to August, 6 days a week—and even then for just a handful of pricey guided tours, limited to 15 adults, so advance booking is essential. But the real reason to come to Birr is to see the extraordinary grounds, which are open year-round. The *demesne* (estate) of the Parsons family, now the earls of Rosse, wraps around a peaceful lake and stretches over miles of pastures and wild woodland. There's much to discover—beautiful topiaries, huge box hedges, a lovely wrought-iron bridge, a newly renovated science exhibition, and even a steampunk-esque, 19th-century telescope (see above). There's also a charming tea shop and a play area for kids.

Birr, Co. Offaly. www.birrcastle.com. © **057/912-0336.** Admission to grounds €10 adults; €8 seniors, €7.50 students; €5 children 5–16; free for children 4 and under; €26 families. Outdoor tour €12. Castle tours €20 per person; no children under 12 on tours. Garden tour €15. Grounds: Daily 9am–4:30pm, last admission 1 hour before closing. Castle tours: May–Aug Mon–Sat 10am, 11:30am, 1pm. Outdoor tour Fri noon, Sat noon and 3pm.

Charleville Castle ★★★ CASTLE   Now, *this* is a castle. Designed in 1798 by Francis Johnston, the crenellated Gothic Revival masterpiece took 12 years to build. Today it's considered one of the best of Ireland's early-19th-century castles, with fine limestone walls and plenty of towers, turrets, and battlements—and those who believe in such things say it is haunted. (It has been featured on the TV shows *Ghost Hunters* and *Most Haunted.*) Inside you'll find spectacular plasterwork and hand-carved stairways, as well as secret passageways and dungeons. The castle is open year-round. It's quite a casual set-up—ring the bell and someone will come let you in. Tours run daily from May to August. For the rest of the year, try and book tours a couple of days in advance. Charleville is run by volunteers, so opening times can be a little unpredictable. The volunteers are as accommodating as possible, but do bear in mind that they're running it out of love rather than for profit. ("Tourists who drop in generally find one of the volunteers and get a tour in any case," they explained to us recently.) Prices are a little on the high side, but the money is obviously

Performers at Charleville Castle's annual Castlepalooza festival.

needed for restoration. The fact that the staff, so dedicated and enthusiastic, is all unpaid, makes it easier to justify paying that little bit extra.

Off Birr Rd. (N52), Tullamore, Co. Offaly. www.charlevillecastle.ie. © **057/932-3040.** Guided tour €20 adults; €12 students ages 17–18; €6 children 6–16; free for children under 6. Castle open year-round; June–Aug tours daily 1–5:30pm; Sept–May tours by appointment.

Clonmacnoise ★★★ RELIGIOUS SITE/RUINS   Resting somberly on the east bank of the Shannon, this is one of Ireland's most profound ancient sites. St. Ciaran founded the monastic community of Clonmacnoise in 548 at the crucial intersection of the Shannon and the Dublin-Galway land route, and it soon became one of Europe's great centers of learning and culture. For nearly 1,000 years, Clonmacnoise flourished under the patronage of Irish chiefs; the last high king, Rory O'Connor, was buried here in 1198. Clonmacnoise was raided repeatedly by native chiefs, Danes, and Anglo-Normans. It was finally destroyed by English troops in 1552. Previously the monks always had something to rebuild, but this time the English looted everything. In a report written by a monk from that time, "There was not left a bell, small or large, an image or an altar, or a book, or a gem, or even glass in a window, from the wall of the church out, which was not carried off." Today you can see remnants of the cathedral, a castle, eight churches, two round towers, three sculpted high crosses, and more than 200 monumental slabs. On some stones, the old carvings can still be seen with thoughtful messages in ancient Irish, such as "A prayer for Daniel."

On R357, 6.5km (4 miles) N of Shannonbridge, Co. Offaly. © **090/967-4195.** Admission €8 adults; €6 seniors; €4 students and children; €20 families. 10am–5:30pm. Last admission 30 min. before closing.

Corlea Trackway ★★ ANCIENT SITE   This is one of those places that makes you stand back, scratch your head, and marvel at just how *old* Ireland is. The fairly unassuming, modern interpretive center, situated in a bog, contains what at first glance looks like an elevated platform of planks nailed onto rails, like a boardwalk through a marsh or swamp. It is, in fact, an excavated wooden trackway that has been carbon dated to the year 148 B.C. Roughly 18m (59 ft.) of original track has been uncovered so far and can be seen on a (free) guided tour. The center also contains an exhibition and a film to put the whole thing into context. A replica version crosses a starkly beautiful section of bog, roughly where the rest of the track is believed to be buried. The weird thing is that the modern version really doesn't look all that different. Was the track built merely as a bridge over the bog, or did it have some religious significance—perhaps enabling people to reach a part of the bog considered sacred for some long-forgotten reason? Archaeologists disagree, but it's fascinating to contemplate the possibility.

Kenagh, Co. Longford. www.heritageireland.ie. © **043/332-2386.** Free admission. Early Apr to early Nov daily 10am–6pm. Last admission 1 hr. before closing.

walk this way: **THE SLIEVE BLOOM WAY**

11

Linking counties Laois and Offaly, the lush and gentle Slieve Bloom mountain range is great hillwalking territory—its tallest peak is just 527m (1,729 ft.), which clocks in at about the same as the 44th tallest in the Wicklow Mountains (p. 201). The Slieve Blooms also have the great advantage of being decidedly undervisited, so peace and solitude are easy to come by.

The Slieve Bloom Mountains Nature Reserve—Ireland's largest state-owned nature reserve—has several looped hiking trails, including several around **Lough (Lake) Boora;** one of them has its own sculpture trail. Another takes you through the tiny but charming village of **Clonaslee,** and up to the **Rickets Rock waterfall.** For a touch of scenic wilderness, walk a portion of the **Slieve Bloom Way,** a circular 34km (21-mile)

signposted trail that begins and ends in Glenbarrow, County Laois; see **www.slievebloom.ie** for details. Several trained guides live locally and will offer their services if you'd prefer to be taken around by an expert; a list with contact details is available at **www.slievebloom.ie** (click "Walking").

The terrain also lends itself particularly well to horseback riding; the **Birr Equestrian Centre,** Kingsborough House, Birr, County Offaly (www.birr equestrian.ie; ℂ **087/244-5545**), organizes regular treks and special trips.

Several castles lie within the boundaries of the Slieves, including **Charleville** ★★ (p. 419) and **Portumna** ★★ (p. 422).

For more information, visit **www.slievebloom.ie**.

Derryglad Folk & Heritage Museum ★ MUSEUM   For a highly concentrated dose of mid-20th-century nostalgia, visit this sweet little museum just outside Athlone. You walk through a series of re-created businesses, each little building jam-packed with memorabilia and antiques—a "medical hall" (drugstore), grocery store, hardware store—and a few farmer's crofts. The intriguing **McCormack Photography Room** preserves the collection of a real photography studio that operated in Athlone from 1948 until 2002. As well as antique cameras and developing equipment, it displays photographs from the decades the shop was in operation. Museum guides could hardly be keener to impart their encyclopedic knowledge.

Curraghboy, Co. Roscommon (13.8km/8½ miles NW of Athlone on R362). www.derrygladfolkmuseum.com. ℂ **090/648-8192.** Admission €7 adults; €4 children; €20 families. May–Oct Mon–Sat 10am–6pm. Closed Oct–Apr.

Kilbeggan Distillery ★ FACTORY TOUR   The oldest licensed distillery in Ireland, Kilbeggan has been producing whiskey here since 1757. Well, almost—it closed in 1957 and was virtually derelict for 25 years, until locals revived it as a small-time distillery and museum. Full production resumed in the late 2000s, in part using traditional methods and equipment, including oak mash tuns (vats) and a 2-century-old copper still—thought to be the oldest still in day-to-day use anywhere in the world. (They also have a working waterwheel and a steam-powered

421

Sampling whiskeys at the Kilbeggan Distillery.

engine, although these are mostly for show.) Unlike most distilleries, you can wander around yourself, or choose one of the guided tours. The daily **Apprentice Tour** (€14 per person; Apr–Oct hourly 10am–4pm and 4:30pm, Nov–Mar hourly 11am and noon) includes a master-class tasting of three whiskeys and a dram glass to take home. The daily **Distillers Tour** (€50 per person; Apr–Oct 1:30pm, Nov–Mar noon) allows you to meet the distillers themselves and take part in a four-whiskey master-class tasting. True enthusiasts can opt for the **Artisan Tour** (€100 per person; Apr–Oct 12:30pm, Nov–Mar 12:15pm), a 2-hour experience that includes a whiskey and cheese pairing and the chance to bottle your own blend. Private 30-minute master-class tastings are also available (prices vary).

On M6 (Junction 5), Kilbeggan, Co. Westmeath. www.kilbegganwhiskey.com. ✆ **057/933-2134.** Apr–Oct daily 9am–6pm; Nov–Mar daily 10am–4pm.

Portumna Castle and Forest Park ★★ CASTLE/PARK   Built in 1609 by Earl Richard Burke, this massive, noble structure on the northern shores of Lough Derg is a particularly fine manor house. Had it not been gutted by fire in 1826, who knows what billionaire might own it now? The fire spared much of the impressive exterior, including its decorative Dutch-style gables and rows of stone mullioned windows; the ground floor is open to the public and contains exhibits on the history of the castle, particularly the so-called "Flight of the Wild Geese," when James II's Jacobite supporters fled Ireland in defeat. The grounds contain a restored walled kitchen garden and a willow maze. Surrounding the castle, the beautiful 560-hectare (1,383-acre) expanse of **Portumna Forest Park** offers trails and signposted walks, plus viewing points, picnic areas, and the remains of a 13th-century Cistercian abbey.

Off N65, Portumna, Co. Galway. ☎ **090/974-1658.** Castle €5 adults; €4 seniors; €3 children and students; €13 families. Free admission to gardens and Forest Park. Castle: Mar to late Oct daily 10am–6pm; late Oct to late Nov daily 10am–4pm. Last admission 45 min. before closing. Castle closed Nov–Mar.

The Rock of Dunamase ★ RUINS   There isn't much left of the castle that once stood atop this rocky outcrop overlooking a valley near the town of Portlaoise; what remains, however, is quite an impressive sight. The ruins were once **Dunamase Castle** (though nobody calls it that anymore), built during the 12th century. It clearly didn't last long; records indicate that it was a total ruin by as early as 1350. A much earlier fort is believed to have once stood on the same site. A few arched gateways survive intact, and the scattered remains of walls and turrets give a good idea of how large it must have once been. The stunning view from among the ruins, over rolling green fields toward the Slieve Mountains in the distance, is worth the visit alone. The Rock is signposted from the main road, but it's very easy to get lost. So to get there, follow these directions: Leave Portlaoise on N80, heading southeast toward Carlow. Shortly after crossing over the M7 motorway, just outside the town limits, you'll pass some large green industrial sheds. Approximately 1.8km (just over 1 mile) after this you will come to some scattered houses, with a turning on the left, next to a triangular patch of lawn and a telegraph pole. Take this turning; you will start to see the Rock on the hill to your left in about 0.5km (550 yards).

Off of N80 (Portlaoise-Carlow Rd.), about 9km (5½ miles) E of Portlaoise, Co. Laois. Free admission. Daily dawn–dusk.

The Sensory Gardens ★ GARDENS   On the grounds of a convent in the town of Abbeyleix, not far from the border between counties Laois and Kilkenny, these gardens were designed by people with learning difficulties. They are intended to be not only accessible but also stimulating to disabled visitors. Plants are chosen for their particularly strong effect on the senses, whether it be their vibrant colors, powerful scent, or tactile appeal. Touches like wind chimes here and there, and even an innovative "humming stone," make this an ingenious and pleasant place to wander.

At Dove House, Main St., Abbeyleix, Co. Laois. ☎ **057/873-1325.** Free admission (donations requested). June–Sept Mon–Fri 9am–4pm, Sat–Sun and public holidays 2–6pm; Oct–May Mon–Fri 9am–4pm.

Tullynally Castle Gardens ★ CASTLE/GARDENS   A turreted and towered Gothic Revival manor, this creamy white castle is dazzling. It has been the home of the Pakenham family, the earls of Longford, since 1655.

A somber SORT OF GRANDEUR: STROKESTOWN & ITS FAMINE MUSEUM

For nearly 4 centuries, from 1600 to 1979, **Strokestown Park House** (www.strokestownpark.ie; ☏ 071/963-3013) was the seat of the Pakenham-Mahon family. After the Restoration, King Charles II granted the vast estate, which stretches for miles in every direction, to Nicholas Mahon in appreciation for supporting the House of Stewart during the bloody English Civil War. (Quite a reward indeed!) Nicholas's grandson, Thomas, considered the original house, completed in 1697, too small and unimposing, so he upped the ante by hiring Richard Cassels—aka "Richard Castle," the architect behind Russborough House (p. 199) and Powerscourt House (p. 198)—to build him something more impressive. The result? This stunning 45-room Palladian mansion, a monument to upper-class privilege. In the north wing, note Ireland's last existing galleried kitchen (where the lady of the house could observe the culinary activity without being part of it), and in the south wing, a vaulted stable so magnificent it has been described as an "equine cathedral."

These days Strokestown is also the permanent home of the **Irish National Famine Museum,** one of the country's very best museums devoted to that deadly period in Irish history. It dramatically sets forth not only the natural disaster, but also the shocking cruelty of the British establishment's response. Exhibits include letters penned by some of the tenants of Strokestown during the Famine years.

The pairing of these two historic attractions may seem incongruous, until you learn a little more of Strokestown Park's history—particularly the behavior of Major Denis Mahon, the landlord at Strokestown during the 1840s. When the potato blight struck and famine started to spread, Mahon and his land agents could have done many things to help the hundreds of starving people who lived and worked on the property. Instead they evicted them as soon as it became clear they couldn't pay their rent; callously, Mahon even chartered ships to send his own tenants away from Ireland. In 1847, Major Mahon was shot to death near Strokestown. Two men

Frustratingly, the building itself is only open to prebooked groups of 20 or more. But the 12-hectare (30-acre) grounds are an attraction in themselves. Highlights include a large kitchen garden, where the grass is kept short by grazing llamas; forest trails and a riverside walk; and an idyllic path leading to a Victorian grotto. Tullynally is near Lough Derravaragh, a tranquil spot featured in the legendary Irish tale *The Children of Lir.* Check the website for events listings, including classical concerts—the only way you're likely to get inside the castle without being part of a large group.

About 32km (20 miles) E of Longford and 21km (13 miles) N of Mullingar, off the main Dublin-Sligo Rd. (N4), Castlepollard, Co. Westmeath. www.tullynallycastle.ie. ☏ **044/966-1856.** Gardens €7 adults; €3 children; €18 families. Castle open for prebooked group tours—call for information. Garden open Apr–Sept Thurs–Sun and public holidays 11am–5pm. Open daily during Heritage Week in Aug.

were hastily (and dubiously) convicted of the crime, but it seems clear that many hungry people had motives.

Strokestown Park is on the main Dublin-Castlebar Road (N5). Admission costs €9.25 (one attraction) and €12.50 (two attractions) adults, €12.50 seniors and students, €6 children, and €29 families. It's open daily from mid-March to October 10:30am to 5:30pm (from Nov to mid-Mar 10:30am–4pm). The house can only be seen on a 45-minute guided tour, at noon, 2:30, and 4pm (2pm only in winter).

Manager John O'Driscoll in an elegant drawing room inside the 17th-century Strokestown Park House.

WHERE TO STAY IN THE MIDLANDS

Athlone, on the southern tip of Lough Ree and almost halfway between Galway and Dublin, makes a natural base from which to explore the Midlands region. It's a colorful waterside town, small enough to explore on foot, with good hotels and eateries and some gorgeous old pubs.

Athlone

Bastion ★★ This delightful B&B is run by the lovely Anthony and Vinny McCay, who have converted an old Athlone townhouse into a chic, rather bohemian getaway. The decor fills the place with light and cheer, from the whitewashed walls and polished wood floors in the bedrooms to the sophisticated furniture and Eastern-influenced accent pieces strewn here and there. Breakfasts are served across the street at the **Bastion Kitchen** (p. 428). Two minor downsides: Two of the bedrooms have shared bathrooms, and those with mobility problems should be sure to ask for a room on the lower floors—there are quite a few stairs to climb.

2 Bastion St., Athlone, Co. Westmeath. www.thebastion.net. ⓒ **090/649-4954.** 7 units. €65–€85 double. No parking (street parking nearby). Breakfast not included in lower rates. **Amenities:** Wi-Fi (free).

Hodson Bay Hotel ★★   The deep blue waters of Lough Ree stretch out before this modern spa hotel just outside Athlone. Views of the lake are stunning, which somewhat makes up for what the guest rooms lack in character, with their rather plain, corporate look. (Needless to say, you should ask for a room on the lake side.) Rooms in the "Retreat" wing are better designed, but more expensive. The spa is excellent, with a huge list of treatments. The hotel has two good restaurants and a pub, and the center of Athlone is only a 10-minute drive away.

Signposted off N61, 7km (4½ miles) NW of Athlone, Co. Westmeath. www.hodsonbayhotel.com. ⓒ **090/644-2004.** 176 units. €100–€200 double. Free parking. Breakfast not included in lower rates. Check website for special offers. **Amenities:** 2 restaurants; bar; pool; room service; spa; Wi-Fi (free).

Wineport Lodge ★★   This romantic, modern hotel overlooking Lough Ree is a truly relaxing getaway. The contemporary bedrooms have plenty of space, and balconies offer glorious views of the lake—perfect for watching the clear waters turn to amber as the sun goes down. The hotel has a spa if you're worn out from exploring. The restaurant is highly rated and offers a modern take on Irish/French cuisine, with an emphasis on seafood—this is one of best eateries in the region.

Glasson, Athlone, Co. Westmeath. www.wineport.ie. ⓒ **090/643-9010.** 29 units. €220–€370 double, €270–€490 suite. Free parking. **Amenities:** Restaurant; bar; room service; spa; Wi-Fi (free).

Birr

Emmett House ★   A corner terrace house with a cozy, authentic interior, Emmett House is a satisfyingly traditional B&B. Guest rooms are a bit of a mixture; some nicely reference the 18th-century origins of the house, with antique-style furniture (including a beautiful four-poster in one room), but others are plainer and more modern. They're a decent enough size, though (given their age), and everything is spotlessly clean. Breakfasts are tasty and filling, and the welcome from host Maureen is genuine and friendly.

Emmett Sq., Birr, Co. Offaly. www.emmethouse.com. ⓒ **087/242-6965.** 7 units. €90–€110 double. 2-night minimum stay in summer. No parking (street parking nearby). Breakfast included. **Amenities:** Wi-Fi (free).

leprechauns: **YOU'RE DOING IT ALL WRONG**

For better or worse, leprechauns have long been known around the world as a symbol of Ireland. Usually portrayed as little green creatures, grinning broadly, they are absurd, cartoonish figures, with which we've all grown up.

Originally, though, they were something much different. The word "leprechaun" comes from the Irish *leath bhrógan*, meaning "shoemaker." And in early folklore, leprechauns were often depicted as cobblers by trade. Though they were elven, mischievous creatures, they weren't evil exactly—just prone to the occasional malicious practical joke.

In those days, different regions of Ireland had their own versions of the Leprechaun folklore. Back then, all leprechauns were portrayed as wearing *red*

coats, not the green you see today. The green coats came much later in the 20th century, probably invented by foreigners to denote their Irishness.

Where that pot of gold came from, though, is anybody's guess, but many people believe that some of the modern image of leprechauns was created by Disney for the movie *Darby O'Gill and the Little People* in 1959.

Nowadays, Irish people view leprechauns as a tourist concept rather than something authentic, and indeed, the description is sometimes used by the Irish to describe the crass side of the tourism industry. So bear all this in mind when you consider buying that figurine of a leprechaun wearing an Irish flag.

Longford

Viewmount House ★★ Tranquil, elegant gardens await at this country-house B&B just outside Longford. Guest rooms are done in a pleasingly old-fashioned style, with antique wood furniture and plenty of space. Some have little sitting areas and roll-top tubs in the bathrooms. Viewmount also has a deserved reputation as one of the best places to eat in the area; the **VM Restaurant** serves superb modern Irish meals (entrees €24–€35); they also do Sunday lunch (€40). Check the website for special offers, including good midweek dinner, bed-and-breakfast deals.

Dublin Rd., Longford, Co. Longford. www.viewmounthouse.com. ℰ **043/334-1919.** 12 units. €160–€190 double. Free parking. Breakfast included. **Amenities:** Restaurant; Wi-Fi (free).

WHERE TO EAT IN THE MIDLANDS

Most small towns in this area have little in the way of restaurant life. In some villages, the only place in town serving food at all is the pub. But **Athlone** has some good restaurants, plus a couple of quality coffee shops. Along with the choices below, most of the hotels listed above have excellent restaurants.

Abbeyleix

The Gallic Kitchen @ Bramley ★ BREAKFAST/LUNCH   If you've come this way from Dublin, there's a good chance you've already sampled Gallic Kitchen's tasty pies, quiches, and desserts—these folks started out running a stall at Dublin's **Temple Bar Food Market** (p. 160), which is still very popular. This is the main HQ, however, and it's a great spot for breakfast or a light lunch. Everything's fresh and homemade, and don't even think about leaving without trying a slice of cake or delicious tart for dessert.

Main St., Abbeyleix, Co. Laois. ✆ **086/605-8208.** All items €3–€8. Thurs 9am–5pm; Fri–Sat 9:30am–8pm; Sun 10am–5pm.

Athlone

Al Mezza ★★ MIDDLE EASTERN/MEDITERRANEAN   Athlone is an unlikely location in which to find a topnotch Lebanese restaurant, but Al Mezza has fast become one of the best places to eat in the area. After seating you at one of the nicely shabby-chic tables (ours was an old sewing table), the staff helpfully takes you through the options—especially useful if you're not familiar with Middle Eastern food. Order off the menu for healthy, delicious meat and fish dishes (try the chicken shawarma, or the sea bream, simply served with cilantro and garlic), or go for the *mezza* plate, filled with tasty small servings of traditional Lebanese dishes (the hummus is a must, of course). Plenty of vegetarian options are available. Round the meal off with some sweet baklava and ice cream. There's a good wine list, too.

6 Bastion St., Athlone, Co. Westmeath. www.almezza.ie. ✆ **090/649-8765.** Entrees €12–€22. Mezza plates (for 2 people) €52–€64. Wed–Sun 5–9pm; Closed Tues.

Bastion Kitchen ★★ CAFE   Delicious, healthy meals are the main focus at this charming little cafe and deli. Its specialty is organic pita sandwiches, served in a variety of interesting ways (turkey and cranberry; chicken with fresh hummus; organic yams with pepper and pesto). You can also make your own combinations with "No hassle!" as the menu says. There are also salads and excellent daily soups—try the pea, kale, and coconut broth served with spelt bread, if it's on offer. Lots of vegetarian options, too. Most items can be ordered to go.

1 Bastion St., Athlone, Co. Westmeath. www.bastionkitchen.com. ✆ **090/649-8369.** All items €5–€12. Wed–Fri 9am–5pm, Sat 9am–4:30pm. Closed Sun–Tues.

Beans & Leaves ★ CAFE   This cheerful cafe/deli is another great place for a quick, healthy lunch in Athlone. In addition to excellent sandwiches, it offers tasty light meals: fishcakes, seafood chowder, and specials such as a steaming-hot plate of tasty chicken curry. Desserts are well worth checking out.

23 Lloyds Lane, Athlone, Co. Westmeath. ✆ **090/643-3534.** Lunch entrees €5–€12. Mon–Wed, Fri, and Sun 9:30am–4:30pm; Sat 9am–5pm. Closed Tues.

Who can lay claim to the title of Ireland's oldest pub? It's a vexing question, with several contenders battling it out. **The Brazen Head ★★★** in Dublin (p. 168) has been serving customers since 1198, making it an oft-cited candidate for the honor—although detractors would scoff that most of the building was replaced in the 17th century, thus disqualifying it. The other big contender is **Sean's Bar ★★**, Main Street in Athlone (www.seansbar.ie; ☎ 090/649-2358). Records show that a drinking establishment of some kind or another has been on this site since the astonishingly far-away date of A.D. 900. The fact that a section of wall is believed to be original further strengthens the claim—but again, the extent to which it can be considered *the same pub* is debatable.

The dispute was finally settled when the *Guinness Book of Records* ruled in favor of Sean's. Presumably this means that it's now acceptable to call it officially Ireland's oldest pub. And, although some of the decor is modern, the fact that you still have to duck low to get in the door gives it an *olde* feel. All the same, to look at the place you'd certainly never guess that it's been serving customers since half a millennium before Columbus sailed to America.

The Fatted Calf ★ MODERN IRISH   The most recent upscale restaurant to gain attention in Athlone, the Fatted Calf is an attractive place with a sustainable, local approach. Run by a husband-and-wife team, the restaurant has a glossy, modern look, with rows of tables lined up against dark gray walls—it's elegant without being fussy. The cooking is just the same. Expect inventive appetizers like remoulade of mango and kohlrabi, or Dublin Bay prawn wontons with spiced pineapple jam. For the main event, try the seared Irish duck breast with anise poached pear—tender and sweet. The lovely desserts are an Instagram post waiting to happen. Reservations for dinner are recommended.
Church St., Athlone. www.thefattedcalf.ie. ☎ **090/643-3371.** Entrees €21–€34. Wed–Fri 5–9pm; Sat 12:30–3pm, 5–9pm; Sun 3–8pm. Closed Mon and Tues.

Hatters' Lane Bistro ★★ BISTRO   Black-and-white portraits of movie stars adorn the walls of this friendly little bistro in the center of Athlone. The menu doesn't present too many surprises, but it's all done very well—roast pork glazed with honey and mustard, lamb shank with garlic and herb mashed potatoes, or perhaps roast duck with plum sauce. For dessert, try the Toblerone cheesecake and warm chocolate sauce—it's made with a Swiss chocolate-bar brand that's been popular here since the '70s. The set menu is a pretty good deal at €25 for two courses, 309 for three (served all night Mon–Thurs or until 7:30pm Fri–Sat).
Strand St., Athlone, Co. Westmeath. www.hatterslane.ie. ☎ **090/647-3077.** Entrees €17–€27. Mon–Sat 5–10pm; Sun 3–10pm.

Thyme ★★★ MODERN IRISH   Offering fine dining without being overly fussy or formal, this excellent bistro is one of the best places to eat in Athlone—or anywhere in the Midlands, come to that. Local ingredients feature heavily on the imaginative menu; to start, you may be offered young buck cheese mousse with candied walnuts, then maybe a loin of Wagyu beef, cooked to perfection, with smoked Gubeen cheese, or wild venison served with *cavolo nero* (Tuscan kale) salsa and elderberry ketchup. The "value menu," served all night Wednesday and Thursday, 5 to 6pm on Friday and Saturday, and 5 to 7pm on Sunday, offers similar dishes at €38 for three courses. Be sure to make reservations, especially on weekends.

Costume Place, Athlone, Co. Westmeath. www.thymerestaurant.ie. © **090/647-8850.** Set dinner menu €58. Entrees Sun lunch €18–€28. Mon–Sat 5–10pm; Sun 1–8pm.

Tullamore

The Blue Apron ★★★ IRISH   This great little bistro is in Tullamore, about 3.4km (2 miles) northeast of **Charleville Castle** (p. 419). Start with a plate of tender king scallops with prawn toast or a spiced pear and Cashel blue cheese salad, before choosing from honey-and-thyme-glazed duck breast or slow-roasted lamb with garlic potatoes and rosemary jus. A full vegetarian menu is always available (try the sweet roast vegetable and honey log with goat cheese). There's a set menu for dinner on Wednesday and Thursday (€26 for two courses, €32 for three) and a set menu for Sunday lunch (€25 for two courses, €30 for three) is also a great, and very filling, choice—don't expect to get much done afterward.

Harbour St., Tullamore, Co. Offaly. www.theblueapronrestaurant.ie. © **057/936-0106.** Entrees €20–€31. Wed–Thurs 5:30–9pm; Fri–Sat 5:30–10pm; Sun 12:30–9pm. Closed Mon–Tues.

COUNTIES
MAYO &
SLIGO

The strikingly beautiful landscapes of northern Galway become even more rugged and mountainous as you segue into County Mayo. This is a land of dramatic scenery, with stark, craggy hills, ancient woodlands, boglands, and rocky cliffs plunging down into the opaque blue waters of the icy sea. Picture-postcard villages lie nestled among lush valleys and the kind of mountainous vistas that make your soul soar. Northeast of Mayo lies County Sligo. An altogether gentler sort of landscape, Sligo is still very much associated with the great Irish poet William Butler Yeats, who drew much of his inspiration from its unique character. Though Sligo is dotted with fairy-tale castles and mysterious prehistoric sites, its biggest gift to the visitor is tranquility.

ESSENTIALS

Arriving

BY BUS   **Bus Éireann** runs daily bus service to Sligo Town from Dublin, Galway, and other points including Derry in Northern Ireland. It provides daily service to major towns in Mayo. The bus station in Sligo is on Lord Edward Street.

BY CAR   Mayo can be reached by four major highways: N84 from the south; N59 from the south and north; and N5 and N60 from the east. Four other major roads lead to Sligo: N4/M4 from Dublin and the east, N17 from Galway and the south, N15 from Donegal to the north, and N16 from Northern Ireland.

BY PLANE   **Ireland West Airport Knock** in Charlestown, County Mayo (www.knockairport.com; ✆ **094/936-8100**), is becoming quite a popular hub for budget airlines from the U.K. and mainland Europe. **Ryanair** (www.ryanair.com; ✆ **0871/246-0000**) is the main airline operating from the airport. Year-round, there are at least a handful of scheduled flights per week to and from Edinburgh, Manchester, and Liverpool in the U.K.; Barcelona in Spain; and Cologne in Germany. Additional routes open up between April and October. As befits Knock's own status (p. 441), you can also catch occasional flights to other major pilgrimage sites in Europe, such as Lourdes, Cadiz, Fátima, and Medjugorje.

Trains from Dublin and other major points arrive daily at **Westport** in Mayo, and **Sligo Town** in Sligo. The train station in Westport is on Altamont Street, about a 10-minute walk from the town center; in Sligo it's on Lord Edward Street, next to the bus station.

COUNTY MAYO

For experienced Ireland travelers, Mayo is the place they escape to after visiting Galway—its rugged coastal scenery is similar, but it has less of the traffic and tourist overload from which Galway suffers in the summer. It's a delightfully unpredictable place, where the terrain changes at the turn of a steering wheel, from lush and green to stark, desert-like, boggy, and mountainous. This region was hit so hard by the Great Famine that, in certain ways, it has never quite recovered. Starvation and emigration emptied it then, and that emptiness is still palpable.

In 1951, the tiny village of **Cong** became the setting for the John Ford film *The Quiet Man,* starring John Wayne and Maureen O'Hara (see box on p. 444). Surprisingly, the county still vigorously celebrates this 70-year-old connection to cinematic stardust—the townsfolk of Cong even paid for a bronze statue of the film's stars in 2013. More recently, Ashford Castle was one of the main locations for the popular CW series *Reign.*

Among Mayo's other attractions are the mysterious 5,000-year-old settlement at **Céide Fields,** the religious shrine at **Knock,** and some of Europe's best fishing waters at **Lough Conn, Lough Mask,** and the **River Moy** (p. 449). It's such a storied angler's destination that **Ballina (*Béal an Átha*),** Mayo's largest town, calls itself the home of the Irish salmon.

Visitor Information

The main tourist information center for County Mayo is the **Westport Tourist Office,** Bridge Street, Westport (www.mayo.ie; ✆ **098/25711**). Other offices are on Pearse Street, **Ballina** (✆ **096/72800**), and in the Old Courthouse on Abbey Street in **Cong** (✆ **094/954-6542**).

Exploring County Mayo

Because it's a rural county with no major cities or many large towns, County Mayo feels a bit like a place without a center. Towns such as Castlebar, Claremorris, and Ballinrobe in the southern part of the county, and Ballina in the northern reaches, make good places to stop, refill the tank, and have lunch, but they offer little to make you linger. The county's attractions lie in the countryside, and in smaller communities like Foxford, Ballycastle, and Louisburgh.

County Mayo's loveliest town, **Westport (*Cathair na Mairt*)** ★, nestles on the shore of Clew Bay and makes an excellent touring base. Once a major port, it was designed by the famed architect Richard Cassels (he of Leinster House [p. 112] and Powerscourt House [p. 198]) with a tree-lined mall, rows of Georgian buildings, and an octagonal central mall.

12

COUNTIES MAYO & SLIGO

County Mayo

take the **GREENWAY**

The dedicated walking and cycle trail the **Great Western Greenway** traverses a 44km (26-mile) route between Westport and Achill Island. The trail, which completely avoids public roads, roughly follows the line of an old railway that closed in the 1930s. It takes in some stunning scenery, particularly around Clew Bay and is divided into three stages:

Westport to Newport, Newport to Mulranny, and Mulranny to Achill. You can either do the route in stages or all in one go. Bike hire companies will shuttle your luggage or deliver you back to your car. Hills are gentle, but if you need a little help, e-bikes are available to rent. For maps and further details, see **www.greenway.ie**.

From here, you can take a scenic drive west to **Achill Island** (*An Caol;* p. 440), walk in **Wild Nephin National Park** (p. 442), or catch a ferry to the bay's **Clare Island,** once the home of Mayo's legendary "Pirate Queen," Grace O'Malley (p. 438). Southeast of Westport, **Croagh Patrick,** a 750m (2,460-ft.) mountain, dominates the views of western Mayo for miles. St. Patrick is said to have spent the 40 days of Lent praying here in the year 441. To commemorate that, on the last Sunday of July, thousands of Irish people make a pilgrimage to the site, which has become known as St. Patrick's Holy Mountain.

A short drive inland from Westport, in **Castlebar,** you can pick up the R310 road, which swings north past the clear, mountain-ringed waters of **Lough Cullin** and **Lough Conn** and eventually to **Ballina** (*Béal an Átha*). A dramatic coastal drive runs along the R314 from Ballina to Downpatrick Head, passing through the secluded harbor village of **Killala** (*Cill Alaidh* or *Cill Ála*) and on to **Céide Fields** (p. 439). Outside Killala on the road R314, several ruined friaries are worth a stop, particularly **Moyne Abbey** ★ (p. 442) and **Rosserk Abbey** ★ (p. 442).

IN & AROUND WESTPORT

Ballintubber Abbey ★★ CHURCH   This abbey is a real survivor—one of only a few Irish churches in continuous use for almost 800 years. Founded in 1216 by Cathal O'Connor, king of Connaught, it has endured fires, numerous attacks, pestilences, and anti-Catholic pogroms. Although Oliver Cromwell's forces thoroughly dismantled the abbey—they even carried off its roof in 1653 in an effort to finally suppress it—clerics continued discreetly conducting religious rites. Today it's an impressively restored church, with 13th-century windows on the right side of the nave and a doorway dating to the 15th century. Guided tours are available weekdays (and on weekends by prior arrangement) from 9:30am to 5pm; there's no charge, but donations of €4 per person are requested. The **Celtic Furrow** visitor center illuminates the abbey's troubled and fascinating

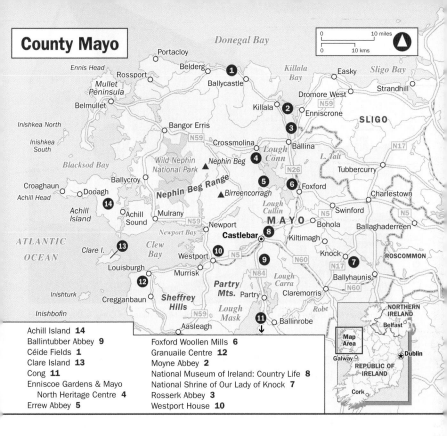

County Mayo

Donegal Bay

Portacloy

Belderg ❶

Ennis Head
Rossport

Ballycastle

Killala
Bay

Easky

Sligo Bay

Mullet
Peninsula

Killala ❷

Dromore West

Strandhill

Belmullet

Enniscrone

Bangor Erris

SLIGO

Inishkea North

Crossmolina ❸

Inishkea
South

Lough
Conn

Ballina

L. Talt

Blacksod Bay

Wild Nephin
National Park

Nephin Beg ❹

N26

Tubbercurry

Croaghaun
Achill Head

Ballycroy

Nephin Beg Range

❺

Birreencorragh

Foxford ❻

Charlestown

Dooagh

N5

Swinford

Achill
Island

❶⁴

Achill
Sound

Mulrany

Lough
Cullin

Bohola

Ballaghaderreen

ATLANTIC

Newport

M A Y O

Kiltimagh

OCEAN

Clare I.

❶³

Clew
Bay

Newport Bay

Castlebar ❽

Knock

Louisburgh

Westport ❶⁰

N5

❾

N60

❼

ROSCOMMON

Murrisk

N84

Lough
Carra

Ballyhaunis

Inishturk

❶²

Cregganbaun

Partry
Sheffrey
Hills

Partry

Claremorris

N60

Inishbofin

Lough
Mask

Robe

NORTHERN
IRELAND

N59

Aasleagh

❶¹

Ballinrobe

Belfast

Achill Island **14**

Ballintubber Abbey **9**

Céide Fields **1**

Clare Island **13**

Cong **11**

Enniscoe Gardens & Mayo
    North Heritage Centre **4**

Errew Abbey **5**

Foxford Woollen Mills **6**

Granuaile Centre **12**

Moyne Abbey **2**

National Museum of Ireland: Country Life **8**

National Shrine of Our Lady of Knock **7**

Rosserk Abbey **3**

Westport House **10**

Map
Area

Galway

Dublin

REPUBLIC OF
IRELAND

Cork

history as part of a wider examination of spiritual life in Ireland dating back 5,000 years.

Ballintubber, Co. Mayo, off the Galway-Castlebar Rd. (N84), about 21.5km (13½ miles) E of Westport. www.ballintubberabbey.ie. ℭ **094/903-0934.** Free admission; donations requested. Abbey: Daily 9am–midnight. Celtic Furrow: July–Aug daily 10am–5pm.

Clare Island ★★ ISLAND   Floating about 5km (3 miles) off the Mayo coast, just beyond Clew Bay, Clare Island is a place of unspoiled splendor. Inhabited for 5,000 years and once quite populous—1,700 people lived there in the early 19th century—Clare is now home to only about 150 year-round islanders, plus perhaps as many sheep. But the island is best known as the haunt of Grace O'Malley, the "Pirate Queen," who controlled the coastal waters 400 years ago (p. 438). O'Malley's modest castle and the partially restored Cistercian abbey where she is buried are among the island's few attractions—the main draw is the island's remote natural beauty. Two ferry services operate out of Roonagh Harbour, 29km (18 miles) south of Westport: **O'Malley Ferries** (www.omalleyferries. com; ℭ **098/25045**) and **Clare Island Ferries** (www.clareislandferry.

Among the relics of the movie *The Quiet Man*, set in the Mayo village of Cong, is this re-created crofter's cottage.

com; ☏ **098/23737** or 086/851-5003). The round-trip fare for the 15-minute journey is €17.

Co. Mayo. www.clareisland.info.

Granuaile Centre ★ MUSEUM This small but rather charming museum is devoted to a particularly cool local hero: Grace O'Malley, also known as "the Pirate Queen" (p. 438). Today she is feted as a defender of the rights of the people of Mayo as much as for being a ruthless pirate—but the pirate stuff is more fun. The center, set in a former church building, is old-style but offers a historical film, some engaging exhibits that tell the story of O'Malley's life, and displays on the wider history of the area, particularly during the Great Famine. A short drive from the Roonagh Harbour ferry to Clare Island (p. 435), it makes a worthwhile introduction to O'Malley's life and times, but call ahead first if getting here involves more than a minor detour—opening times can be a little unpredictable, especially in winter.

Church St., Louisburgh, Co. Mayo, 21km (13 miles) W of Westport on R334. ☏ **098/66341.** Admission €5 adults; €2.50 seniors and students; children free. Mon–Fri 10am–4pm. Call ahead to check times, particularly in winter.

The National Museum of Ireland: Country Life ★★ MUSEUM The countryside outpost of Ireland's multi-site national museum (the others are all in Dublin—see chapter 4), this one specializes in Irish life, trade, culture, and tradition since the mid–19th century. Absorbing exhibits deal with folklore; the natural environment and how local communities have relied on it for survival; political and social upheaval, particularly in the years preceding the Great Famine; traditional trades and crafts; and the changing life of the Irish people at home and at work. You could easily spend 3 hours wandering around here especially if you include the grounds. The museum also has a thoughtful program of changing exhibitions. As at all the National Museum sites, entry is completely free. On the grounds opposite the museum is **Turlough Park House,** a moderately sized country house built for the wealthy Fitzgerald family in the 1860s—there are two rooms on view, which have been kept much as they would have been in the house's Victorian heyday, complete with original furniture.

Signposted from N5, Turlough Park, about 8km (5 miles) E of Castlebar, Co. Mayo. www.museum.ie/Country-Life. ℂ **094/903-1755.** Free admission. Tues–Sat 10am–5pm; Sun–Mon 1–5pm.

Westport House and Pirate Adventure Park ★★ HISTORIC HOUSE/THEME PARK

This is the sort of family-friendly attraction that requires a deep breath before listing everything there is to do here. It's all centered around an elegant late-18th-century residence—the home of Lord Altamont, the Marquess of Sligo and a descendant, it is said, of Pirate Queen Grace O'Malley (hence the bronze statue of her on the grounds). The work of Richard Cassels and James Wyatt, the house has a graceful staircase of ornate white Sicilian marble, unusual Art Nouveau glass and carvings, family heirlooms, and silver. The grandeur of the residence is undeniable, but during the summer months a large proportion of visitors come here without even setting foot in the building—just follow the whoops and cheers of a thousand excited children and you'll find the sprawling **Pirate Adventure Park.** Here kids can burn off energy on the swinging pirate ship, log ride, go-karts, swan-shaped pedal boats, and a giant bouncy castle. When that's over you can all tour the gardens together in a Toytown-sized express train. Very young children can enjoy some slightly gentler fun at the **Pirate's Den** play area (an extra €5–€7 per child, depending on age). Upping the ante even further, the **Adventure Activity Centre** piles on bungee jumping, zip wires,

British two-tone band the Selecter at the Westport Festival, Westport House.

local hero: **GRACE O'MALLEY, THE PIRATE QUEEN**

By all accounts, Grace O'Malley—aka the "Pirate Queen"—was a woman ahead of her time. Born in 1530 on **Clare Island** (p. 435), she grew up to be an adventurer, pirate, gambler, mercenary, traitor, chieftain, noblewoman, and general badass. And while she is remembered now with affection, at the time she was feared and despised in equal measure.

Even as a child, Grace was fiercely independent. When her mother refused to let her sail with her father, she cut off her hair and dressed in boys' clothing. Her father called her *"Grainne Mhaol,"* or "Bald Grace," later shortened to Granuaile (pronounced Graw-nya-*wayl*), a nickname she'd carry all her life.

At 16, Grace married Donal O'Flaherty, second in line to the O'Flaherty clan chieftain, who ruled all of Connacht. Her career as a pirate began a few years later when the city of Galway, one of the largest trading posts in northern Europe, refused to do business with the O'Flahertys. Grace used her fleet of fast galleys to waylay slower vessels on their way into Galway Harbour. She then offered safe passage for a fee in lieu of pillaging the ships.

She is most fondly remembered for refusing to trade her lands in return for an English title, a common practice of the day.

When the English captured her sons in 1593, she went to London to try to win their release. In an extraordinary turn of events, she actually secured a meeting with Queen Elizabeth I herself. History records that the two women got on quite well (although legend has it that Grace initially tried to smuggle a knife in with her, in case things went differently). A deal was struck: Elizabeth agreed to release Grace's sons and to return some captured lands if Grace would agree to renounce piracy. This she did and returned to Ireland triumphantly.

The truce did not last, however. Grace got her sons back, but not her property—so she took up piracy again and continued her legendary seafaring career until her death from natural causes in 1603.

tree climbing, archery, and a host of other high-adrenaline amusements. The house turns into a festive Winter Wonderland in November/December. *Note:* Pirate Adventure Park passes do not cover entry to Westport House, but the cost is heavily discounted to €5 per person as an add-on. The estate grounds are open to walkers during daylight hours year-round.

The Westport Demense, Westport, Co. Mayo. www.westporthouse.ie. ✆**098/27766.** **House and Gardens:** €13.50 adults; €11 seniors and students; €6.50 children. Admission reduced to €5 with Pirate Park ticket. **Pirate Adventure Park:** €25 adults; €20 seniors, students, and children; €70–€90 families. **House and Gardens:** June–Aug daily 10am–6pm; Sept–Oct and Mar–Apr daily 10am–4pm; May Mon–Fri 10am–4pm, Sat–Sun 10am–6pm; Nov–Dec: Open for Winter Wonderland event only. Closed Jan–Feb. **Pirate Adventure Park:** May Sat–Sun 11am–6pm; June–Aug daily 11am–6pm; July–Aug daily 11am–6pm; Apr and Oct open for Easter and Halloween holidays (check website for times). Closed Jan–Mar and Sept.

IN & AROUND BALLINA

Céide Fields ★★ ANCIENT SITE   In a breathtaking setting above huge chalk cliffs that plunge hundreds of feet down into a deep blue sea, an ancient people once lived, worked, and buried their dead. But nobody knew this until the 1930s, when a local farmer noticed the stones in his fields were piled in strange patterns. More than 40 years later, his archaeologist son discovered Stone Age fields, megalithic tombs, and the foundations of a village. Standing amid it now, you can see a pattern of farm fields as they were laid out 5,000 years ago (predating the Egyptian pyramids). Preserved for millennia beneath the bog, the site is both fascinating and inscrutable. To a casual observer, it's little more than piles of stones, but the visitor center makes it meaningful in a series of displays, films, and tours. It has just undergone renovation and also contains a cafeteria, which comes as a relief since this hilly, rocky site is miles of winding roads from anywhere.

On R314, 8km (5 miles) W of Ballycastle, Co. Mayo. www.heritageireland.ie. ✆ **096/43325.** Admission €5 adults; €4 seniors; €3 students and children; €13 families. June–Sept daily 10am–6pm; mid-Mar to May and Oct to mid-Nov daily 10am–5pm; last tour 1 hr. before closing. Closed mid-Nov to mid-Mar.

Enniscoe Gardens & Mayo North Heritage Centre ★ GENE-ALOGY CENTER   Part of the huge Enniscoe estate—where you can stay in the charming manor house (**Enniscoe House** ★★; see p. 444)—

Exhibit at the Céide Fields Visitor Centre, where installations interpret the megalithic relics and Stone Age fields found on this remote clifftop site.

A TRIP TO achill island

The rugged, bog-filled, sparsely populated coast of counties Mayo and Sligo makes for scenic drives to secluded outposts. Leading the list is **Achill Island,** a heather-filled slip of land with sandy beaches and spectacular views of waves crashing against rocky cliffs.

Once you've crossed the bridge from the mainland, follow a winding road across the island to the little village of **Keel,** a trip that requires patience but rewards you with a camera full of photos. About 5.7km (3½ miles) west of Keel, you'll find the secluded Blue Flag beach of **Keem Bay** (it was once a major fishing ground—basking shark were caught here commercially up until the 1950s—but no more). You can reach the bay along a small cliff-top road, which passes by cliff faces containing rich seams of glittering amethyst. Apparently it's not uncommon to find chunks of the stuff lying loose after a heavy rainfall.

Speaking of remarkable finds: Hidden on the slopes of **Mount Slievemore,** Achill's tallest mountain, are the remains of an **abandoned village.** The hundred or so crumbling stone cottages of the nameless ghost town date back to some-time around the 12th century. It was deserted during the Great Famine, although some cottages are known to have been in occasional use until the very early years of the 20th century, a traditional practice known as "booley-ing"—seasonal occupation by farming communities, which continued here long after it had died out in the rest of Ireland. Mount Slievemore is between Keel and Doogort, in the central northeastern part of Achill Island.

At Kildavnet, between Derreen and Cloughmore, in the southeastern corner of the island, you'll find **Granuaile's Tower.** This impressive 15th-century tower house was owned by Grace O'Malley, the "Pirate Queen," who caused all manner of havoc for the English around these parts in the 16th century (see box on p. 438). There's not a great deal to see, but it's a stunning spot to admire. Nearby **Kildavnet Church** is thought by some archaeologists to date from the 8th century. From here, the Atlantic Drive north, overlooking the cliffs, is spectacular.

To get to the Achill Island bridge, take N59 heading northwest out of West-port, then join R319, signposted to Achill. The drive from Westport to the crossing is about 42km (26 miles) and should take around 40 minutes. Once you're on Achill Island, Keel is about another 14km (8⅔ miles) down the same road.

these beautiful gardens comprise woods, parkland, and part of Lough Conn. One of the highlights is an 18th-century walled garden that has been restored to the layout it had in the estate's Victorian heyday. The on-site **Mayo North Heritage Centre** (www.northmayogenealogy.com) is the ideal place to start if you're checking out your roots. It offers extensive records such as church registers (Catholic, Presbyterian, Methodist, and others); registers of births, marriages, and deaths; estate and probate records; property leases and rent rolls; school registers; emigrant rolls; and census records. Research fees, which give you access to expert gene-alogists, range from €45 for 1 hour for a basic question or to get you started, up to €350 for 10 hours for more in-depth research. A little museum displays a somewhat random collection of historic farm equipment and household items from the early to mid–20th century.

On Lough Conn, about 3.2km (2 miles) S of Crossmolina, off R315, Enniscoe, Castlehill, Ballina, Co. Mayo. www.enniscoe.com. © **096/31809.** Gardens and musem: €8 adults, €3 students and children. Gardens and Heritage Centre: Apr–Oct Mon–Fri 11am–5pm, Sat–Sun and public holidays 1:30–5:30pm. For genealogical inquiries only, year-round Mon–Fri 9:30am–4pm.

Errew Abbey ★ RELIGIOUS SITE   This atmospheric ruined 13th-century Augustinian church sits on a tiny peninsula in Lough Conn. The cloister is well-preserved, as is the chancel with altar and *piscina,* a stone basin used for disposing of the water used during Mass. An oratory of massive stone walls in fields adjacent to the abbey stands on the site of a church founded in the 6th century. It's known locally by the marvelous tongue-twisting name *Templenagalliaghdoo,* which means "Church of the Black Nun."

Near Crossmolina, Co. Mayo. No phone. Free admission (open site). Signposted about 3.2km (2 miles) S of Crossmolina on the Castlebar Rd., then 5km (3 miles) down a side road.

Foxford Woollen Mills Visitor Centre ★ FACTORY TOUR   This popular Irish brand of knitwear and tweed was founded by a nun, Mother Agnes Morragh Bernard, in the late 19th century. Mother Agnes's idea was to build a new local industry to try to ameliorate the effects of the Great Famine. Ever since then the mill has thrived, producing rugs, clothing, and the like. Not only did her scheme help to stave off poverty for the local workforce, but the brand became hugely successful in Ireland and beyond. You can tour the mills to hear the story in detail before visiting the store. There are free guided tours three times a day and they take 30 minutes or so (Be aware that the mills run Mon–Thurs only, although tours are offered daily.) Also on-site is a jewelry workshop, a cafe, and a full store where you can buy everything from woollen scarves and clothing to homewares and gifts.

St. Joseph's Place, Foxford, Co. Mayo. www.foxfordwoollenmills.com. © **094/925-6104.** Free admission and free tours. Centre: Mon–Sat 10am–5pm, Sun noon–5pm; Café Mon–Sat 10am–4pm, Sun noon–4pm. Tours: Mon–Sat 10:30am, 11:30am, and 3pm; Sun 3pm (no working mill Fri–Sun).

National Shrine of Our Lady of Knock and the Church of the Apparition ★ SHRINE   Ireland's version of Lourdes, Our Lady of Knock draws pilgrims, mostly Irish Catholic, in droves. It all stems from a day in August 1879 when two young local girls said they saw Joseph, Mary, and St. John standing in bright light in front of the southern tower of the parish church. Soon, 13 other witnesses claimed to have seen the same thing. Before long, miracles were occurring fast and furious, as sick and lame visitors to the church were pronouncing themselves healed. Knock came to the world's attention in 1979, when Pope John Paul II visited the shrine. More than 10,000 pilgrims still visit every year, and during

Novena week in August (marking the anniversary of the miracle), the shrine holds special twice-daily ceremonies and other commemorative events. There's not much to the town of Knock on the whole—it sits unspectacularly at the intersection of the N17 and R323 roads—but it's filled with increasingly large, modern religious structures, including a huge circular basilica that seats 7,000 and contains artifacts or furnishings from every county in Ireland. The grounds also hold a folk museum (with a few letters relating to the original testimonies) and a religious bookshop.

On the N17 Galway Rd., Knock, Co. Mayo. www.knockshrine.ie. ✆ **094/938-8100.** Free admission to shrine. Museum €4 adults and students; €3 seniors and children; free for children under 5. Shrine and grounds: Late May to Aug daily 9am–7:30pm (9am–8:30pm and 9:30–11pm during Novena week); Sept–Dec daily 10am–5pm; Jan to late May 9am–6pm. Museum: Daily 10am–6pm.

Rosserk Abbey and Moyne Abbey ★ RELIGIOUS SITES/RUINS These two abbeys, about 3km (2 miles) from each other, are in some ways twins. Both are evocative ruins, built in the mid-1400s and destroyed in the 16th century by the troops of Sir Richard Bingham, the English governor appointed to suppress rebellion in Connaught. Rosserk Abbey, sitting at the edge of the River Rosserk, is in much better shape than Moyne. Its chapel windows are well-preserved, and the church's *piscina* (once used for washing altar vessels) is still here, carved with angels. On its lower-left-hand column is a delightful detail: a tiny, elegant carving of a round tower that recalls its 23m-tall (75-ft.) counterpart in nearby Killala. Climb the winding stone stair for a lovely vista out across the bay.

On R314 btw. Killala and Ballina. Signposted. No phone. Free admission (open sites).

Wild Nephin National Park ★★ NATIONAL PARK Home to some of the wildest scenery in Mayo—and indeed Ireland—with 15,000 hectares (37, 000 acres) of vast boglands, rivers, mountains and forests, this is probably the least-known of Ireland's six national parks, which means it is rarely overrun with tourists. You can start your visit at the visitor center at Ballycroy, on the N59 between Mulranny and Bangor Erris, which has views over to the Nephin Beg Mountain range and Achill Island. The main park has a number of marked looped walking trails at Letterkeen, ranging from 6km (3.7-mile) to 12km (7.5-mile), around 40 minutes' drive from the visitor center, off the N59 just outside the village of Newport. Here, you're rewarded with views for miles in each direction of a landscaped untouched by roads, houses, or development—and parts of the park are being rewilded. Keep an eye out for sheep, deer, and eagles. Because it has so little light pollution, Wild Nephin is also a designated **Dark Sky Park** (www.mayodarkskypark.ie). The 2km (1¼-mile) **Claggan Mountain Coastal Trail,** just south of the Ballycroy Visitor Centre, has a boardwalk over peat bog along a gorgeous coastal route.

Visitor Centre at Ballycroy Village, Co. Mayo. www.wildnephinnationalpark.ie. ✆ **098/49-888.** Visitor center daily 10am–5pm. Free admission to park (open all year).

Where to Stay in County Mayo

This region of Ireland is not the most abundant ground for topnotch places to stay. Even some of the major towns have only a smattering of decent B&Bs and small hotels. However, some gems are to be found in the deepest reaches of the countryside. It takes effort to get to these places, but the journey will be worth it.

EXPENSIVE

Ashford Castle ★★★   This extraordinary fairy-tale-like castle has entertained plenty of famous guests over the years—Grace Kelly, Ronald Reagan, Brad Pitt, and Pierce Brosnan, to name just a few. Ashford Castle was built in the 13th century and still looks and feels every inch the palatial abode—with suits of armor and old portraits lining the hallways, plus antiques and four-poster beds in some of the guest rooms. You can walk or cycle the stunning grounds—it overlooks Lough Corrib, with acres of forest and landscaped gardens. The drawing room is the place for an elegant afternoon tea and the **George V** dining room is worth dressing up for at dinner time, although a couple of less formal eateries are on the grounds, too.

On R346, on the eastern approach to Cong, Co. Mayo. www.ashfordcastle.com. © **094/954-6003.** 83 units. €625–€995 double; €1,450–€3,000 state room; €2,250–€5,500 suite. Free parking. Rates include breakfast. **Amenities:** 3 restaurants; 2 bars; cigar terrace; gym; massage treatments; small swimming pool, estate sports including 9-hole golf course, fishing, and clay pigeon shooting; Wi-Fi (free).

Afternoon in the Connaught Room in Ashford Castle.

WHEN THE GOLDEN AGE OF hollywood CAME TO MAYO

When director John Ford descended on the sweet little village of **Cong,** County Mayo, to make his classic 1952 film *The Quiet Man,* starring John Wayne and Maureen O'Hara, the town's profile skyrocketed. Tourists were soon visiting in the tens of thousands, and Cong was transformed.

But what's really surprising is that visitors still flock here on Quiet Man pilgrimages, even though the film is more than 70 years old, and Cong merrily continues to hang its hat on its brief brush with stardust. The **Quiet Man Museum,** Circular Road (www.quietmanmuseum.com; ☎ **094/954-6089**), is a charming little thatched cottage that has been transformed into an exact replica of John Wayne's house in the movie, right down to the furniture. From April to October, it's open daily from 10am to 4pm. Admission costs €5 adults, €4 seniors, students, and children, and €15 families. The museum runs tours of the village every day from June to August on the hour between 11am and 3pm (at 11:30am, 12:30pm, and 1:30pm in April–May and Sept–Oct).

Just around the corner on Abbey Street are the ruins of **Cong Abbey.** Founded in 623, it was rebuilt in the 12th century, then comprehensively destroyed by Henry VIII in the 1540s. The ruins are an open site that you can wander at leisure—but even here there's a reminder of this town's love affair with an old Hollywood movie. The **Quiet Man Statue,** a full-size bronze of Maureen O'Hara being

whisked off her feet by John Wayne, was unveiled just outside the abbey in 2013. Since then it's become an almost obligatory focal point for souvenir selfies.

Unfortunately, the countless movie fans Cong has attracted haven't always treated the town with respect. The actual cottage used as John Wayne's house is little more than a pile of rocks now, having been gradually torn apart over the years by souvenir hunters.

Aside from *The Quiet Man,* Cong is most famous as the location of **Ashford Castle ★★★**. Built in the 13th century, it is one of Ireland's biggest and most complete medieval castles. Unfortunately, you can't tour the inside unless palatial luxury is within your price range, as it is now a super-exclusive hotel and resort (p. 443). Something that might be more budget-friendly is the more modest splurge of dinner at **Wilde's ★★★** (p. 448), an outstanding restaurant in **The Lodge** (https://thelodgeac.com), a former estate keeper's house on the castle grounds.

Cong is roughly halfway between Galway and Westport, on R344, R345, and R346.

Enniscoe House ★★ Flanked by Mount Nephin on one side and the shimmering waters of Lough Conn on the other, Enniscoe is a stunningly restored 18th-century mansion. Little has been altered from the original structure, so the place is overflowing with period detail (one room even has original silk wallpaper). Bedrooms are spacious, with big windows and half-tester beds. Bathrooms are modern. Owner Susan Kellett is a great cook, so make sure you book one of her excellent dinners. The grounds are lovely and offer enough to do that you could spend a day here (see **Enniscoe Gardens,** p. 439). There are also self-catering cottages if you want more privacy.

Castlehill, Ballina, Co. Mayo. www.enniscoe.com. ☎ **096/31112.** 6 units. €190–€270 double. Dinner €50. Free parking. Rates include breakfast. **Amenities:** Guest lounge; Wi-Fi (free) in public areas. Closed Nov–Mar.

MODERATE

The Bervie ★★★   Overlooking the Atlantic Ocean on **Achill Island** (p. 440), the Bervie is an inspiring place to stay. Husband-and-wife hosts John and Elizabeth Barrett spent years lovingly restoring the sturdy building. Elizabeth actually grew up in this house; it's been a B&B since the 1930s, although today it's a far more sophisticated place than she remembers from her childhood. Guest rooms are large and spacious, with well-chosen furniture (most of it made locally). Most rooms directly overlook the sea—and what a view! You can see islands dotted around the bay from certain rooms, while others have a dramatic view of cliffs. Light pours in from huge windows, and the whispering of the waves soothes you to sleep. The garden has direct access to the beach. Elizabeth's home-cooked breakfasts are to die for, and evening menus might offer black sole or Clare Island salmon. Worth staying in for.

The Strand, Keel, Achill, Co. Mayo. www.bervie-guesthouse-achill.com. ☎ **098/43114.** 14 units. €150–€170 double. Free parking. Rates include breakfast. Dinner entrees €22 to €32. **Amenities:** Restaurant; garden; Wi-Fi (free).

The Ice House ★★★   This boutique hotel at the edge of Ballina offers a tantalizing mixture of old and new—the main building is over a hundred years old and was once used for storing salmon, and the modern extensions are bright and warm, with panoramic views of the Moy River. Rooms are good sized and quiet, with gorgeous views and good beds. You can choose a traditional room in the old building or a modern room, but all have eiderdown bedcovers and Voya toiletries. The in-house spa is luxury personified (and has outdoor hot tubs overlooking the river), and the restaurant is a destination eatery that brings people from miles around for European/Irish cuisine served in an airy room overlooking the river.

Quay Rd., Ballina, Co. Mayo. www.icehousehotel.ie. ☎ **096/235000.** 32 units. €150–€300 double. Free parking. Rates include breakfast. Access to the thermal suite and outdoor hot tubs €25. **Amenities:** Restaurant; bar; spa; hot tubs; Wi-Fi (free).

Knockranny House ★   This modern hotel less than 15 minutes by foot from the town of Westport is a great place to base yourself while exploring the region. Decor is minimal, but guest rooms are sizeable, with firm beds and up-to-date bathrooms. The more expensive rooms and suites are more elegant than the cheaper rooms, but both are perfectly serviceable. There are pleasant lounges where you can relax with a cup of tea or a pint of beer. The **La Fougère** restaurant is highly rated for European-influenced cuisine and also offers gorgeous views over the verdant countryside. The pool and spa are lovely, and the thermal suite will work all the knots out of your aching muscles.

Castlebar Rd., Westport, Co. Mayo. www.knockrannyhousehotel.ie. ℭ **098/28600.** 97 units. €130–€240 double; €170–€440 suite. Free parking. **Amenities:** Restaurant; pool; spa; Wi-Fi (free).

INEXPENSIVE

Westport Coast Hotel ★   This pleasant, modern hotel on the Quay in Westport overlooks the smooth, dreamy waters of Clew Bay and the mountains beyond. It's worth paying a little extra for a room with a view or a spacious suite if your budget allows. The Veda spa has plenty of invigorating and affordable treatments. The top-floor restaurant, which looks out over the bay, serves tasty, crowd-pleasing fare (leg of lamb, roast chicken, steaks—you get the picture). Check the website for dinner, bed-and-breakfast deals.

The Quay, Westport, Co. Mayo. www.westportcoasthotel.ie. ℭ **098/29000.** 85 units. €60–€299 double; €120–€299 suite. Breakfast not included in lower rates. Free parking. **Amenities:** Restaurant; bar; pool; spa; Wi-Fi (free).

Where to Eat in County Mayo

While the west coast is not one of Ireland's main foodie regions, innovative chefs are using the Wild Atlantic Way's freshest seafood and produce to create top-notch dishes. In addition to the restaurants listed below, **This Must Be The Place** in Westport (High St.; www.thismustbetheplace.ie) serves gorgeous sourdough toasties, vegan curries, and sweet potato cakes, while **Christy's Harvest** (Shop St.) is a tiny, charming cafe for tea and cake. At **Mocha Beans** in Ballina (Pearse St.; www.mochabeans. com), you can get salads, wraps, and soups and good coffee. In Castlebar, **Café Rua** (New Antrim St.; www.caferua.com) is an award-winning deli that specializes in breakfast with locally sourced eggs and meats.

An Port Mor ★★ SEAFOOD/MODERN IRISH   At this multi-award-winning seafood restaurant in Westport, local catches dominate the menu—from Connemara smoked salmon to linguine made with Clew Bay lobster bisque. The seafood is excellent, but it's not all that's on the menu; expect juicy steaks served with something fresh and tasty like red onion marmalade, as well as local chicken and lamb. Everything is impeccably presented, and the atmosphere in the cheerful dining room is relaxed. Service is excellent, too.

Bridge St., Westport, Co. Mayo. www.anportmor.com. ℭ **098/26730.** Entrees €22–€38. Daily 5–9pm.

The Beehive ★ CAFE   There aren't that many places to eat on Achill Island, and this cafe is one of the best. (Technically, they say, this is a "Craft Coffee Shop," since it sells lovely knick-knacks and homewares too.) Stop and refuel on excellent sandwiches and cakes, or a bowl of homemade soup—the chowder is particularly good. The craft store isn't

The region to the east of the Mullet Peninsula has a spectacular array of sheer sea cliffs and rugged, craggy islands. The small, secluded beach at **Portacloy,** 14km (8⅔ miles) north of Glenamoy on the R314, is a good starting point for a dramatic walk. On a sunny day, its aquamarine waters and fine-grained white sand recall the Mediterranean more than the North Atlantic.

From the concrete quay at the beach's western edge, head north up the steep green slopes of the nearest hill. The sea views from here are breathtaking. Don't be too distracted by the fantastic vista or adorable little sheep—the boggy slopes on which you are walking end precipitously at an unmarked cliff edge. The walk is therefore **not** recommended for children and should not be undertaken in bad weather. Resist the urge to get a better view of the mysterious sea caves, or to reach the outermost edges of the coast's promontories. Instead, using the farmer's fence as a guide, head west toward the striking profile of **Benwee Head,** about 2.4km (1½ miles) away. This will give you gorgeous views of blue sea and rocky countryside. Return the same way to finish with a swim in the chilly, tranquil waters of Portacloy.

bad, either. The Beehive overlooks the beach at Keel, and you can sit outside with your food on a warm day.

Keel, Achill Island, Co. Mayo. ✆ **086/854-2009.** €5–€11. Daily 9:30am–5pm. Closed Nov–Easter.

The Helm ★ SEAFOOD/BISTRO   The hungriest diners are welcomed with open arms at this relaxed Westport bar-restaurant, which specializes in local seafood—tackle the delicious fisherman's platter, if it's on offer, only if you're wearing elasticated pants. In addition to the fishy options, main dishes include steaks, rack of lamb, and pork chops. Lunch service is more traditional, with Irish stew alongside fish and chips. The comfort-food desserts include pies, crumbles, and even jelly and ice cream. The Helm is also a B&B with a few self-catering apartments.

The Harbour, Westport, Co. Mayo. www.thehelm.ie. ✆ **098/26398.** Entrees €15–€26. Daily 8am–9:30pm.

The Poacher ★★★ MODERN IRISH   Fish from the Atlantic, meat and poultry from local farms, foraged finds and daily specials: The seasonal menu here features the best of local produce from land and sea. But it is the tiny, delicate surprises in each dish, like the forest berries infused with sweet port served over lamb, a flat-leaf-parsley risotto with beef, or the popcorn-fried globe artichoke with roast chicken, that take the food here to the next level. It's all set in a cozy dining space above a bakery and deli, and the wine list reasonably priced to boot.

First Floor, 4 Market Sq., Ballina. www.thepoacher.business.site. ✆ **096/77982.** Entrees €19–€28. Wed–Fri 4–9pm; Sat 4–9:30pm; Sun 1–9pm.

a poetic soul: **W. B. YEATS**

One of Ireland's greatest and most beloved writers, **William Butler Yeats** (1865–1939) had Sligo in his soul.

The first of Ireland's four Nobel laureates, Yeats (pronounced "Yates") was a poet, playwright, and politician. He was at the forefront of the Celtic Revival, which celebrated and championed native Irish culture and heritage. Drawing heavily upon the traditional folklore of Ireland, his work was steeped in myth and imagination.

Yeats grew up amid Sligo's verdant hills and dales, sometimes known as "Yeats Country." You can cruise Lough Gill while listening to a live recital of Yeats's poetry; follow Yeats trails and buy a hundred items of Yeats memorabilia; and visit dozens of his purported haunts—some reputedly still spooked by his ghost, and some of which have only tenuous connections with the man.

Yeats died in Menton, on the French Riviera, in 1939. Knowing he was ill, he stated, "If I die here, bury me up there on the mountain, and then after a year or so, dig me up and bring me privately to Sligo." True to his wishes, in 1948 his body was moved to Sligo and reinterred at **Drumcliffe Church** (p. 455).

Wilde's at the Lodge ★★★ MODERN IRISH   If, like the other 99% of us, you can't quite swing a night at **Ashford Castle** ★★★ (p. 443), then you might find this lodge on the castle grounds a viable alternative for a slice of upper-crust Irish glamour. Wilde's is overseen by Jonathan Keane, an up-and-coming star of the Irish culinary world. A lot of his ingredients come from the castle's own garden, with menus deeply rooted in the flavors of the season. Vegans are catered to with a full separate menu. The wine list is curated to be paired with the seasonal menus, with plenty of choices available by the glass. The somewhat more straightforward children's menu should please the junior palate (entrees €8). The dining room has a fantastic view of Lough Corrib, and you can also stay overnight (double rooms €166–€550).

On the grounds of Ashford Castle, Cong, Co. Mayo. www.thelodgeac.com. ⓒ **094/954-5400.** 3-course fixed-price menu €65. Entrees €21–€36. Mar–Oct Mon–Sat 6:30–9pm, Sun 1–3:30pm and 6:30–9pm; Nov–Feb Tues–Sat 6:30–9pm, Sun 1–3:30pm and 6:30–9pm.

Sports & Outdoor Pursuits in County Mayo

CYCLING   Get up close and personal with the Wild Atlantic Way on two wheels with the **Clew Bay Bike Trail** (www.clewbaybiketrail.ie), which takes in a loop around Clew Bay and includes Clare Island (by ferry) and Achill Island. The total distance is 105km (65 miles), but you can do as much or as little as you like—an overnight stay on Clare Island (p. 435) is a nice way to break up the journey. Keep in mind that some of the trail is on main roads (with traffic), but it also links in with the off-road **Great**

Western Greenway (p. 434). There are bike hire companies in Westport, Newport, Mulranny, and Achill; rentals start from €25 per day.

FISHING   The waters of the River Moy and loughs Carrowmore, Conn, and Cullin are renowned fishing destinations, particularly for salmon and trout. To arrange a day's fishing, contact **Cloonamoyne Fishery,** Castlehill, near Crossmolina, Ballina (www.cloonamoynefishery.com; ✆ **096/31928**). The fishery rents fully equipped boats and tackle, teaches fly-casting, and provides transport to and from all fishing: for brown trout on loughs Conn and Cullin; for salmon on loughs Beltra, Furnace, and Feeagh; and for salmon and seatrout on the rivers Moy and Deel. Daily rates are around €30 for a rowboat, €60 for a boat with engine, and €120 for a boat with engine and *ghillie* (guide).

Obtain a permit and state fishing license at the **Mayo Angling Advice Centre,** at the Tiernan Bros. fishing tackle shop, Upper Main Street, Foxford (www.themoy.com; ✆ **094/925-6731**). It also offers a range of services, including boat hire and ghillies.

For fishing tackle, try **Kingfisher Bates,** Pier Road, Enniscrone, County Sligo (✆ **096/36733**), or the **Ballina Angling Centre,** Unit 55, Ridge Pool Road, Ballina (✆ **096/21850**). On Achill Island, get fishing tackle at **Supervalu Supermarket,** Achill Sound (✆ **098/45211**). Also a good place to stock up on supplies, it's the smallish white-and-red building on the right, immediately after the bridge crossing from the mainland.

HORSEBACK RIDING   One of the best riding centers in the West is **Drummindoo Stud & Equestrian Centre,** Knockranny, Westport (www.drummindoo.com; ✆ **098/25616**).

WINDSURFING & OTHER WATERSPORTS   With constant winds off the Atlantic Ocean, Achill Island is ideal for breeze-dependent sports like windsurfing, surfing, and kite-surfing. The **Achill Outdoor Education Centre** on R319, between Cashel and Bunacurry (www.achilloutdoor.com; ✆ **098/47253**), can outfit you for windsurfing and surfing, as well as other water activities like kayaking and sailing. Adrenalin junkies can take kite-surfing lessons and set up wing-boarding or gentler stand-up paddleboarding sessions on Keel Lake, Achill Island, with **Pure Magic** (www.puremagic.ie; ✆ **086/265-0811**).

COUNTY SLIGO

Inland, bucolic, rural County Sligo is blessed with an extraordinary concentration of ancient burial grounds and pre-Christian sites, most of them within easy reach of the county capital, **Sligo Town.** Remnants of a distant past feel like they're everywhere here, whether or not you can visit them. Driving down the country lanes on your way to the Stone Age cemeteries at **Carrowmore** and **Carrowkeel,** you can't help spotting a standing stone or *dolmen* (ancient stone table) in some farmer's pasture or another, with sheep or ponies grazing casually around it. The countryside has been labeled "Yeats Country" in honor of the great Irish poet W. B. Yeats, who was born in Dublin but spent so much time in County Sligo that it became a part of him, and he a part of it—literally, as he is buried here. Sligo is also a coastal county along the Wild Atlantic Way with long, golden beaches—you may have one all to yourself on a walk or share the sand with surfers. The village of Strandhill is a popular surf spot; you can also watch pro surfers go for big-wave action on windy days farther north at Mullaghmore.

Visitor Information

The **Sligo Tourist Office** is on the ground floor of the Old Bank Building, O'Connell Street, Sligo Town (www.sligotourism.ie; ✆ **071/916-1201**). It's open Monday to Saturday 9am to 5pm (closed Sun).

Exploring Sligo Town

It goes to show just how rural this part of Ireland is that a small port and farming town with a population of just 20,000 is the largest urban center in the northwest—but welcome to Sligo Town! Bisected by the River Garavogue and surrounded on three sides by mountains, the most famous of which are Ben Bulben to the north and Knocknarea to the south, Sligo is a gray and solid place, with a mix of historic and less interesting modern architecture. Though few would name Sligo their favorite of Ireland's major towns, it has undergone something of a renaissance in recent years. From a visitor's perspective, the focus of this has been Sligo's new "Left Bank," where cafes and restaurants spill onto the waterfront promenade whenever weather permits. Most of its commercial district is on the river's south bank. **O'Connell Street** is the main north-south artery, while the main east-west thoroughfare is **Stephen Street,** which becomes Wine Street and then Lord Edward Street. Three bridges span the river; the **Douglas Hyde Bridge,** named for Ireland's first president, is the main link between the two sides.

The Model ★★ MUSEUM/CULTURAL CENTER   One of Ireland's most renowned contemporary art museums, the Model houses an impressive collection of paintings and other visual art. It includes probably the best collection of works by Jack B. Yeats (1871–1957) outside the National Gallery in Dublin (p. 99). Brother of William, Jack was one of the foremost Irish painters of the 20th century, painting landscapes and figures in a bold Expressionist style. Other luminaries of the Irish art world represented here include Louis le Brocquy (1916–2012), an extraordinary figurative painter; and the portraitist Estella Solomons (1882–1968). The Model is also a venue for live music and film screenings. Check the website for listings.

The Mall, Sligo Town. www.themodel.ie. ✆ **071/914-1405.** Free admission to exhibitions (suggested donation €4); tickets to other events free to around €25. Tues–Sat 11am–5pm. Closed Sun–Mon.

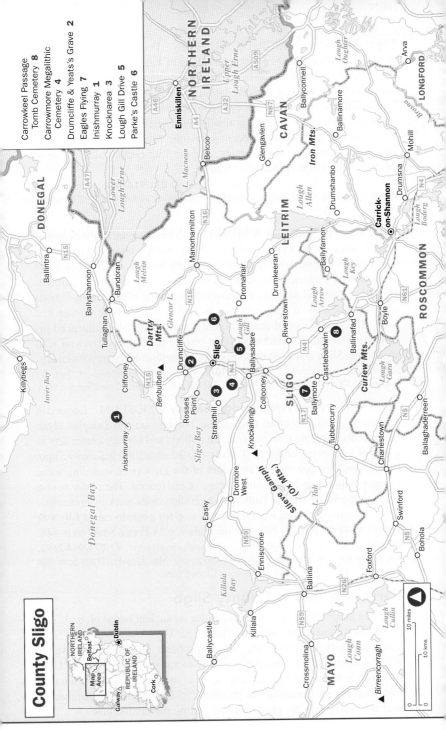

County Sligo

NORTHERN
IRELAND

Belfast

Map
Area

REPUBLIC OF
IRELAND

Galway ⊛ Dublin

Cork

DONEGAL

NORTHERN IRELAND

CAVAN

LEITRIM

ROSCOMMON

SLIGO

MAYO

Inver Bay

Donegal Bay

Sligo Bay

Killala Bay

Lough Gara

Lough Key

Lough Arrow

Lough Allen

Lough Melvin

Lough Gill

Lower Lough Erne

Upper Lough Erne

Lough Macnean

L. Gill

Glencar L.

Lough Talt

Lough Conn

Lough Cullin

Lough Oughter

Lough Boderg

Darty Mts.

Iron Mts.

Curlew Mts.

Slieve Gamph
(Ox Mts.)

Sligo Abbey ★ RELIGIOUS SITE/RUIN   Founded as a Dominican house in 1252 by Maurice Fitzgerald, Earl of Kildare, Sligo Abbey was the center of early Sligo Town. It thrived for centuries and flourished in medieval times when it was the burial place of the chiefs and earls of Sligo. But, as with other affluent religious settlements, the abbey was under constant attack, and it was finally destroyed in 1641. Much restoration work has been done in recent years; the fine cloisters contain outstanding examples of stone carving, and the 15th-century altar is one of the few intact medieval altars in Ireland.

Abbey St., Sligo Town. www.heritageireland.ie. ✆ **071/914-6406.** Admission €5 adults; €4 seniors; €3 students and children; €13 families. Apr–Oct daily 10am–6pm; last admission 45 min. before closing.

Sligo County Museum ★ MUSEUM   This museum in the center of Sligo Town presents a good overview of the county's history from ancient times to the present day. The most interesting sections cover the region's extraordinary prehistoric heritage, including a couple of ancient artifacts. The other standout sections are devoted to two of Sligo's most famous residents: the poet W. B. Yeats (see box on p. 448), whose mother was from Sligo and whose affinity with the county drastically influenced his work, and Constance Markievicz (see box on p. 454), an aristocrat who grew up in Sligo and went on to become a prominent Irish revolutionary.

Stephen St., Sligo Town. ✆ **071/911-1679.** Free admission. May–Sept Tues–Sat 9:30am–12:30pm, 2–4:50pm; Oct–Apr Tues–Sat 9:30am–12:30pm. Closed Sun and Mon.

Yeats Society and Hyde Bridge Gallery ★ MUSEUM   Located in a distinctive red-and-white town house building on the Douglas Hyde Bridge, this engaging little museum, art gallery, and heritage center acts as a kind of focal point for the W. B. Yeats–related attractions in County Sligo. Exhibitions focus on the life and work of the great poet, including some recently rediscovered color film footage of his funeral. The center is also home to the **Hyde Bridge Gallery,** which showcases work by contemporary Irish artists. It's also a good place to stop for a bite to eat, at **Lily's & Lolly's Café** ★ (p. 462). For more on Yeats, see "A Poetic Soul" on p. 448.

Douglas Hyde Bridge, Sligo Town. www.yeatssociety.com. ✆ **071/914-2693.** Admission €3. Apr–Sept Mon–Sat 10am–5pm; Oct–Mar Tues–Fri 11am–5pm, Sat 11am–4pm. Gallery: Tues–Sat 11am–4pm. Closed Sun.

Farther Afield in County Sligo

The area around Sligo Town is known for its ancient burial grounds and pagan sites, some dating from the Stone Age. These include the vast Neolithic cemetery **Carrowmore,** the atmospheric hilltop cairn grave of **Knocknarea,** and the haunting Neolithic mountaintop cemetery of **Carrowkeel.** Some lesser sites are also open to the public, but most are not. The Irish are passionate about property rights, so don't go clambering over a fence for a better photo without getting permission first.

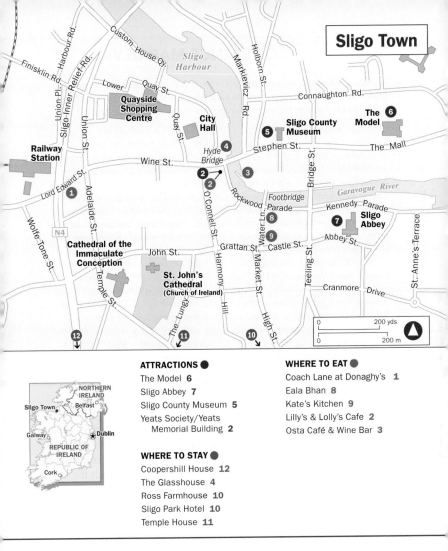

Sligo Town

Sligo Harbour

Custom House Qy.

Finiskin Rd.

Harbour Rd.

Sligo-Inner Relief Rd.

Lower Quay St.

Union Pl.

Union St.

Quayside Shopping Centre

Railway Station

Lord Edward St.

Adelaide St.

Wolfe Tone St.

N4

Cathedral of the Immaculate Conception

Temple St.

The Lungy

John St.

Wine St.

Hyde Bridge

City Hall

Quay St.

O'Connell St.

Rockwood Parade

Harmony Hill

Grattan St.

St. John's Cathedral (Church of Ireland)

Holborn St.

Markievicz Rd.

Stephen St.

Connaughton Rd.

Sligo County Museum

The Model 6

The Mall

Bridge St.

Footbridge Parade

Kennedy Parade

Garavogue River

Water Ln.

Castle St.

Market St.

High St.

Teeling St.

Abbey St.

Sligo Abbey

St. Anne's Terrace

Cranmore Drive

0   200 yds
0   200 m

Northern Ireland / Republic of Ireland map inset:
NORTHERN IRELAND
Sligo Town • Belfast
Galway
Dublin ★
REPUBLIC OF IRELAND
Cork

ATTRACTIONS ●
The Model **6**
Sligo Abbey **7**
Sligo County Museum **5**
Yeats Society/Yeats
    Memorial Building **2**

WHERE TO STAY ●
Coopershill House **12**
The Glasshouse **4**
Ross Farmhouse **10**
Sligo Park Hotel **10**
Temple House **11**

WHERE TO EAT ●
Coach Lane at Donaghy's **1**
Eala Bhan **8**
Kate's Kitchen **9**
Lilly's & Lolly's Cafe **2**
Osta Café & Wine Bar **3**

At the foot of Knocknarea is the delightful resort area of **Strandhill,** 8km (5 miles) from Sligo Town. Stretching into Sligo Bay, Strandhill has a sand dune beach that's popular for surfing (it's not possible to swim here because of the strong currents) and small island nearby called Coney Island, usually credited as the namesake of New York's amusement park. Across the bay is **Rosses Point,** popular for golf and sailing.

Carrowkeel Passage Tomb Cemetery ★★ ANCIENT SITE   Atop a hill overlooking Lough Arrow, this ancient passage-tomb cemetery is impressive, isolated, and frequently empty. Its 14 cairns, dolmens, and stone circles date from the Stone Age (ca. 5000 B.C.), and it's easy to feel

local hero: **CONSTANCE MARKIEVICZ**

Aristocrat, suffragette, revolutionary, politician, and all-round badass, Constance Markievicz (1868–1927) was one of the most influential Irish women of the 20th century and a key figure in the country's struggle for independence from Britain.

Born in London to Anglo-Irish gentry, Constance became aware of the realities of life for the poor in Ireland at an early age. Her father, Sir Henry Gore-Booth, owned Lissadell House, a great estate in County Sligo. Unlike many landowners of the time, he was widely loved by his tenants; during an outbreak of famine when Constance was eleven, he provided them with lifesaving food relief.

In 1900 Constance married a Polish count, Casimir Markievicz (1874–1932), and the two settled in Dublin. By this time she was actively involved in the fight for women's suffrage. It wasn't long before she began to move in revolutionary circles too. (One story has it that she was finally persuaded to join

Sinn Fein, the political party set up in 1905 to fight for independence, after discovering a collection of rousing pamphlets left behind at a remote country cottage.)

In 1914 her revolutionary career began in earnest when she joined the Irish Citizens Army. She became known for her leading role in gun-running missions, alongside Douglas Hyde (1860–1949), who would later become the first President of Ireland. During the Easter Rising of 1916 she manned barricades in St. Stephen's Green, Dublin, engaging in gunfights with British soldiers.

After the Rising was put down, Markievicz, along with many of her fellow revolutionaries, was sentenced to death.

a mystical connection to that history, standing among the cold, ageless rocks. The tombs face **Carrowmore ★★★** (see below) in the far distance below and are aligned with the summer solstice. The walk uphill from the parking lot takes about 20 minutes, but the exercise is worth the effort. This is a simple site—no visitor center, no tea shop, no admission fee— nothing but ancient mystery.

Signposted on N4 btw. Sligo Town and Boyle, Co. Sligo. No phone. Free admission (open site).

Carrowmore Megalithic Cemetery ★★★ ANCIENT SITE   This is one of the great sacred landscapes of the ancient world. At the center of the Coolera Peninsula sits a massive passage grave that once had a Stonehenge-like stone circle of its own. Around that were as many as 200 additional stone circles and passage graves arranged in an intricate and mysterious design. Over the years, some of the stones have been moved; more than 60 circles and passage graves still exist, although the site spreads out so far that many of them lie in adjacent farmland. Look for your first dolmen in a paddock next to the road about a mile before you reach the site. The dolmens were the actual graves, once covered in stones and earth. Some of these sites are open to visitors, and you can get a map

But the court commuted her sentence to life in prison because she was a woman. In a withering comeback, she shot back from the dock, "I wish you had the decency to shoot me."

In the end Markievicz served only a year in prison, including solitary confinement at the notorious **Kilmainham Gaol ★★★** (p. 99), although she would later be jailed again for sedition. It was while serving a sentence in 1918 that she learned she had become the first woman elected to the British Parliament. She refused to take her seat and was later elected to the Irish Dáil.

Following the War of Independence, Markievicz was to achieve another political first for women, when she was appointed Minister for Labor in the new Irish government—the first woman in Europe to serve at cabinet level.

CONSTANCE
MARKIEVICZ

MAJOR
IRISH CITIZEN ARMY
1916

to them from the visitor center. (Not all are, however; be careful not to trespass on private land.) On the main site, the oldest tomb is thought to date from around 3,700 B.C.—making it one of the oldest pieces of free-standing stone architecture in the world. From Carrowmore, you can see the hilltop cairn grave of **Knocknarea ★** (p. 457), which is about 4km (2½ miles) away. The visitor center has good exhibits and guided tours. Follow signs from Woodville Road heading west out of Sligo Town, or from R292 at Ransboro.

Carrowmore, Co. Sligo. www.heritageireland.ie. ✆ **071/916-1534.** Admission €5 adults; €4 seniors; €3 students and children; €13 families. Apr–Oct daily 10am–6pm; last admission 1 hr. before closing. Closed Nov–Mar.

Drumcliffe Church ★ CHURCH/GRAVESITE   An essential stop for Yeats fans, this square-towered village church, where Yeats' great-grand-father was once rector, was the poet's chosen burial site. (See "A Poetic Soul," p. 448.) His grave is marked with a dark, modest stone just left of the church, alongside his young wife, Georgie Hyde-Lee (when they married in 1917, he was 52 and she was 23). His epitaph, "cast a cold eye on life, on death. . . ." comes from his poem "Under Ben Bulben." While you're here, also check out the 11th-century high cross in the churchyard—

An ancient stone circle at Carrowmore Megalithic Cemetery.

its faded eastern side shows Christ, Daniel in the lions' den, Adam and Eve, and Cain murdering Abel. The site also has a little visitor center and cafe. Drumcliffe. 10km (6½ miles) N of Sligo Town, on the N15 road. www.drumcliffe church.ie. Free admission.

Eagles Flying ★★ AVIARY   Some of the biggest birds of prey in the world are displayed at this aviary and educational center near Ballymote. Eagles, vultures, owls, and falcons take part in an hour-long flying show daily at 11am and 3pm. Most of the awe-inspiring birds who live at the center can be handled by visitors. The center also has a petting zoo, home to lambs, chinchillas, donkeys, and rabbits. Ballymote, Co. Sligo. www.eaglesflying.com. ✆ **071/918-9310.** Admission €15.90 adults; €13.90 students; €8.90 children 3–15; free for children 2 and under; €45.90 families. Apr to early Nov daily 10:30am–12:30pm, 2:30–4:30pm. Bird shows 11am and 3pm. Closed early Nov to Mar.

Inishmurray ★★ ISLAND/RUINS   Northwest of Sligo Bay, this tiny, uninhabited island shelters an ancient past. The haunting ruins of St. Molaise, a 6th-century monastic settlement that was destroyed by the Vikings in 807, stands within its circular walls. You can still see the remains of several churches, beehive cells, altars, and an assemblage of "cursing stones" once used to bring ruin on those who presumably deserved it. In the 19th and early 20th centuries, however, Inishmurray harbored a different identity: a thriving illicit trade in the distilling of moonshine whiskey. The last permanent residents left the island in 1948; their ruined houses can still be seen, battered by the elements. Boat trips to the island are operated by **Inishmurray Island Trips** (www.inish murrayislandtrips.com; ✆ **087/254-0190**) and **Ewing's Sea Angling and Boat Charters** (www.sligoboatcharters.com; ✆ **086/891-3618**). Expect to pay around €55 adults, €50 children, and you may need a minimum group size of five. Call or visit the websites for details and sailing times.

NW of Sligo Bay, 6km (3¾ miles) offshore. Ferries leave from Mullaghmore or Rosses Point.

Knocknarea ★ ANCIENT SITE   From the low vantage point of **Carrowmore ★★★** (p. 454), if you study the mountain ranges that ring the surrounding valley, you'll notice a stone cairn in the center of each one. One of these is the unexcavated **Knocknarea.** Local legend has it that this is the grave of the warrior Queen Maeve or Medb—the legendary queen of Connacht, who is said to have led armies into Ulster on the Cattle Raid of Cooley. If you have the time to make the relatively gentle 30-minute climb to the top, the views are extraordinary.

Knocknarea, about 6.4km (4 miles) W of Sligo, Co. Sligo. No phone. Free admission (open site). Signposted from small farm road btw. Cullenduff and Knocknarea, and from R292 heading S from Strandhill. Follow signs for mescan meadhbha chambered cairn.

Parke's Castle ★ CASTLE   If you happen to be on the north side of the Lough Gill Drive (p. 459), just over the County Leitrim border, you'll see Parke's Castle standing out as a lone outpost amid the natural tableau of lake views and woodland scenery. Named after an English family that gained possession of it during the 1620 plantation of Leitrim (when land was confiscated from the Irish and given to favored English families), this castle was originally the stronghold of the O'Rourke clan, rulers of the Kingdom of Bréifne. Beautifully restored using Irish oak and traditional craftsmanship, it exemplifies the 17th-century fortified manor house. In the visitor center, informative exhibits and a splendid audiovisual show illustrate the history of the castle and the surrounding area.

On R286, 11.2km (7 miles) E of Sligo Town, Co. Leitrim. www.heritageireland.ie. © **086/071-6968.** Admission €5 adults; €4 seniors; €3 students and children; €13 families. Early Apr to Sept daily 10am–6pm; last admission 45 min. before closing.

Where to Stay in County Sligo

As with County Mayo, many of the best places to stay in County Sligo are hidden in the countryside.

MODERATE

Coopershill House ★★★   This is an utterly charming if rather posh country house experience—stepping through the doors here is like going back into history, with four-poster beds, original roll-top baths, and a grandfather clock chiming away in the hall. There's a homely, relaxed atmosphere in the house; guests gather beside the fire in the drawing room for a drink before dinner—perhaps with Juno the dog asleep at their feet. The house has been in host Simon's family for seven generations, and his wife, Christina, is a talented chef, creating amazing seasonal dishes, most of them with produce from the gardens and orchards of the 500-acre estate. You can stroll the grounds before dinner, wandering through woodlands and deer pastures and admiring the peaceful countryside around you.

Riverstown, Co Sligo. www.coopershill.com. ℂ **071/916-5108.** 7 units. €275 double per night (2-night minimum stay). Rates include breakfast. 4-course dinner €62. Free parking. Closed Nov–Mar. **Amenities:** Restaurant; full bar; Wi-Fi (free).

Sligo Park Hotel ★   A pleasant little park surrounds this convenient, cheap-ish hotel in Sligo Town. Guest rooms are simply furnished in a contemporary style, with muted color schemes of gray and brown, and good-size bathrooms. It won't win any awards for heart-of-Ireland atmosphere, but as a clean, modern base, it's a good option in a region that's short on choice. Families are especially well catered for, with treasure hunts, kids' pool obstacle courses, and movie nights. The hotel is also a popular venue for weddings and other events, so noise can sometimes be a problem on weekends. You might want to ask for a room as far away from the bar as possible.

Pearse Rd., Sligo Town. www.sligoparkhotel.com. ℂ **071/919-0400.** 136 units. €99–€136 double; €140–€165 suite. Free parking. Breakfast not included in lower rates. **Amenities:** Restaurant; bar; pool; room service; sauna; Wi-Fi (free).

Temple House ★★★   Along with Coopershill above, this is another one of *the* best places to stay in the northwest if you're after a unique and historic B&B experience. Make no mistake: Temple House is not a hotel, and it's not full of five-star extras—but it is full of historical authenticity,

Entrance hall at Temple House.

THE lough gill DRIVE

An essential stop on Yeats Country pilgrimages is this beautiful lake, which figured prominently in the writings of W. B. Yeats. A well-signposted drive-yourself tour around the lake's perimeter covers 42km (26 miles) and takes less than an hour.

To start, head 1.6km (1 mile) south of Sligo Town and follow the signs for Lough Gill. Within 3.2km (2 miles) you'll be on the lower edge of the shoreline. Among the sites are **Parke's Castle** (p. 457); **Dooney Rock,** with its own nature trail and lakeside walk (inspiration for the poem "Fiddler of Dooney"); the **Lake Isle of Innisfree,** made famous in poetry and song; and the **Hazelwood Sculpture Trail,** a unique forest walk along the shores of Lough Gill, with 13 wood sculptures. At the lake's east end, branch off to visit **Dromahair,** a delightful village on the River Bonet.

The road along Lough Gill's upper shore brings you back to the northern end of Sligo Town. Continue north on the main road (N15), and you'll see the graceful profile of **Ben Bulben** (519m/1,702 ft.), one of the Dartry Mountains, rising off to your right. One of

Yeats' last poems, "Under Ben Bulben," alludes to this majestic rock formation as a silent sentinel looming over Irish history.

If you prefer to see all this beautiful scenery from the water itself, **Lough Gill Cruises** take you around Lough Gill and the Garavogue River aboard the 72-passenger *Wild Rose* waterbus as you listen to the poetry of Yeats. The boat departs from Parke's Castle daily at 12:30pm; tours last around an hour. During summer only there are also 3-hour trips daily from Doorly Park in Sligo at 2:30pm. Tickets for the hour-long tour are €15 adults, €13 seniors and students, €7.50 children; for the 3-hour version it's €18 adults, €15 seniors and students, €9 children. Trips to Innisfree, sunset cruises, and dinner cruises are also scheduled. Visit www. roseofinnisfree.com or call ✆ **071/916-4266** for details and booking.

beautiful surroundings, and sheer, unforgettable charm. The delightful custodians of the estate, Roderick and Helena Perceval, are now more than a decade into their painstaking restoration of the 1665 manor house. Once a thriving country estate, it had fallen slowly into near-ruin during the turbulent years of the 20th century. (When we first stayed, the 18th-c. silk curtains in one room, now fully restored, would literally crumble to the touch.) Now the huge guest rooms are packed with interesting antiques, but have completely modern, recently renovated bathrooms. Nightly dinners are more akin to parties, with all guests seated around an enormous old table enjoying outstanding food. Breakfasts hit the spot, too, with plenty of homemade treats. The beautiful grounds include a boating lake, a walled garden, and even a ruined Knights Templar castle—hence the name. Supposedly there are a couple of resident ghosts roaming around, although they must be of a very Bacchanalian kind, with such a welcoming and convivial atmosphere as this. There is also a self-catering cottage on the grounds.

Ballymote, Ballinacarrow, Co. Sligo. www.templehouse.ie. ✆ **087/997-6045.** 6 units. €155–€210 double. 4-course dinner €59 (no dinner Sun). Free parking. Rates include breakfast. **Amenities:** Wi-Fi (free). Closed Dec–Mar.

INEXPENSIVE

The Glasshouse ★   A solid, modern option in Sligo Town, the Glasshouse overlooks the River Garavogue and resembles a gleaming, modern ship from the outside. The public areas inside either look bold and funky or like an explosion in a kitsch factory, depending on your point of view: multicolored circles on the carpet, misshapen blue sofas, and a bright orange signature color in the towering atrium. Bedrooms are a little more refined, with muted tones and modern art on the walls. There is an in-house restaurant, although you could eat more cheaply in town. The appropriately named **View Bar** looks out over Sligo Town and has live music (if you are sensitive to noise, ask for a room away from the bar when you book). A few years ago, places like this were all but unheard-of in Sligo, and the Glasshouse offers a good alternative for those who want a decently priced, convenient, and contemporary place to stay.

Swan Point, Sligo Town. www.theglasshouse.ie. ✆ **071/919-4300.** 116 units. €100–€150 double; €140–€166 suite. 2-night minimum some weekends. Parking €4 per night. Breakfast not included in lower rates. **Amenities:** Restaurant; 2 bars; room service; Internet (broadband/via TV).

Ross Farmhouse ★★   Not far from Carrowkeel (p. 453), Ross Farmhouse is a restored 1880s cottage, surrounded by acres and acres of rolling farmland. The owner, Gemma Hill-Wilkinson, took over the place from her parents in 2019 (they had been running it for a mere 60 years). Bedrooms are reasonably sized, with simple, unfussy furnishings. One is a family room, and another is fully accessible to wheelchairs. Downstairs are two lovely guest lounges, filled with antiques. An open peat fire warms the hearth in winter. Breakfasts are varied and delicious—porridge is served either "nice" (plain) or "naughty" (with a shot of Baileys Irish cream liqueur).

Riverstown, Co. Sligo. Follow signs from Drumfin on N4 or Coola on R284. www.rossfarmhousesligo.com. ✆ **071/916-5140.** 5 units. €70 double. Free parking. Rates include breakfast. **Amenities:** Wi-Fi (free).

Where to Eat in County Sligo

Some of the best places to eat in Sligo are the smaller coffee shops and restaurants that have opened in recent years. **Shell's Café** (in Strandhill opposite the beach; www.shellscafe.com) has earned legions of fans for its hearty breakfasts with names like "the simple" (two poached eggs, two slices of bacon, on buttered toast). Small but perfectly designed (and perfect for Instagram), this darling cafe offers good, freshly made food (with lots of options for vegetarians) and excellent coffee, served up with a smile. In the tiny town of Easkey, on the Wild Atlantic Way, **Pudding Row** (Main St.; www.puddingrow.ie) is *the* place to stop for breakfast or lunch. This sunny, award-winning cafe bakes everything fresh in-house, and uses all organic produce. Expect beautiful breakfasts, sandwiches, soups, and cakes. Sligo Town's **Sweet Beat Café** (Bridge St.; www.sweetbeat.ie) is a vegetarian restaurant good enough to lure even hardened carnivores for its veggie bean burgers, risotto, and falafel. it's closed in the winter.

Coach Lane at Donaghy's ★★ IRISH/INTERNATIONAL   A very popular spot with Sligo residents, Coach Lane has two dining rooms: a bar serving easy crowd-pleasers such as burgers, fish and chips, and shepherd's pie; and a more upmarket, gastropub-style restaurant. Most ingredients are regionally sourced, and the seafood is particularly good. Try the baked stuffed aubergine (eggplant), then dive into a striploin steak, or a plate of Kilmore Quay scallops served with crab claws and seaweed. Coach Lane also makes its own craft beer.

1–2 Lord Edward St., Sligo Town. www.coachlanesligo.com. ℂ **071/916-2417.** Entrees €12–€28. Bar food: Daily 3–9:30pm. Restaurant: Daily 5:30–10pm.

Eala Bhan ★★★ INTERNATIONAL   This popular brasserie has been awarded the title of "best restaurant in Ireland" by the Irish Restaurant Awards five times since 2013. The menu takes traditional brasserie classics and adds a light touch of creative flair—tender rack of local lamb comes with *courgette* (zucchini) purée and shallot mash while the trio of fish combines buttered scallops, pistachio-crumb hake, and a sea trout lemon risotto. Three-course set menus are a good value and feature many dishes from the main menus. The early-bird menu (served until 6:20pm daily) is just €27 for three courses. The lunch menu is almost as extensive as dinner, with a few lighter options such as poached chicken salad and seafood chowder.

Rockwood Parade, Sligo Town. www.ealabhan.ie. ℂ **071/914-5823.** Fixed-price menus €45–€50. Entrees €19–€30. Mon–Sat noon–3pm, 5–9:30pm; Sun 12:30–3pm, 5–9:30pm.

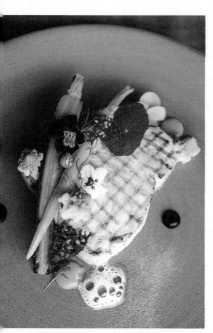

Eala Bhan, Gaelic for "white swan," offers updated brasserie classics.

Kate's Kitchen ★★ DELI   This great delicatessen has a large stock of gourmet foods, Irish cheese, fresh bread, salads, chutneys, and other tasty items that just beg to be put together to make an elegant picnic or lunch on the go. It also has a small shop selling bath products and a particularly nice range of handmade chocolates—perfect for gifts, if you can keep yourself from raiding them before the journey home.

3 Castle St., Sligo Town. www.kates kitchen.ie. ℂ **071/914-3022.** Most items €4–€8. Mon–Sat 8:30am–5:30pm.

Lily's & Lolly's Café ★ CAFE   Handy for a quick and tasty lunch, this cheery cafe inside the **Yeats Memorial Building** ★ (p. 452) serves reasonably priced wraps, panini, and light meals, in addition to homemade cakes and pies. The cafe is next to the Garavogue River; you can sit outside on a sunny little terrace when the weather's fine.

At the Yeats Memorial Building, Douglas Hyde Bridge, Sligo Town. ℂ **071/914-4727.** All items €3–€8. Tues–Sat 10am–5pm. Closed Sun and Mon.

Osta Café & Wine Bar ★★ CAFE   The owners of this sweet cafe overlooking the river in Sligo are big believers in the slow-food and organic movements, and their delicious, healthful food makes superb use of ingredients from small local producers. There are usually only a few dishes on offer every day, but you're guaranteed to find something properly, authentically Irish. Even the sandwiches qualify as local—they're made with deliciously fresh bread from a nearby bakery. In the early evening on Thursday to Saturday, the food switches to a simple but tasty tapas menu. *Tip:* A Gaelic-speaking group meets here every Friday evening, which makes it a good time to drop by if you fancy eavesdropping on some of the language used.

Garavogue Weir, off Stephen St., Sligo Town. www.osta.ie. ℂ **071/914-4639.** Entrees €5–€8. Mon–Wed and Sat 8am–6pm; Thurs 8am–8pm; Fri 8am–7:30pm; Sun 9am–5pm.

Shopping in Sligo Town

Sligo Town has some great little boutiques and independent local businesses. Most shops are open Monday to Saturday 9am to 6pm; some may have extended hours in July and August.

The Cat & the Moon ★★   Named after a Yeats poem, this is a great place to shop for Irish crafts and jewelry. They design their own silver rings and pendants with Celtic motifs. In addition, the shop stocks an interesting range of art, ceramics, candles, and other handicrafts, and always seems to offer something in the way of unique finds and souvenirs.

4 Castle St., Sligo Town. www.thecatandthemoon.com. ℂ **071/914-3686.**

Michael Quirke ★★   Michael Quirke is a real Sligo character. He used to be a butcher but got bored with it and decided to follow his real passion: woodcarving. Out went the meat and in came the artisan tools, and his shop became a studio. Now he spends his time carving and selling exquisite statues, ornaments, and objets d'art out of Irish wood, with a particular focus on figures from Irish mythology. His carvings are quite affordable for the quality. Wine St., Sligo Town. ℂ **071/914-2624.**

Wehrly Bros. Ltd ★★   The granddaddy of Sligo jewelry stores, this firm has been trading from behind its elegant black-and-gold storefront since 1875. It specializes in diamond rings, watches, and pearls, with a wide range of designer jewelry. It also sells Waterford crystal. 3 O'Connell St., Sligo Town. www.wehrlybros.ie. ℂ **071/914-2252.**

Sports & Outdoor Pursuits in County Sligo

HIKING   Explore the hills and peaks of County Sligo with **Northwest Adventure Tours** (www.northwestadventuretours.ie; ℂ **087/125-9594**). Hikes to mountains like Ben Bulben or Knocknarea start at €35; Northwest also runs biking, free-diving, and SUP (paddleboarding) tours along gorgeous waterways like Lough Gill.

HORSEBACK RIDING   Arrange an hour or a day of horseback riding on the beach, in the countryside, or over mountain trails through **Sligo Riding Centre,** Carrowmore (www.sligoridingcentre.com; ℂ **087/230-4828**). Rates average around €30 to €50 per hour. **Island View Riding Stables** (www.islandviewridingstables.com; ℂ **071/916-156**) near Grange runs gorgeous beach and bog treks from 1 to 5 hours long, starting from €35 for an adult and €25 per child.

SURFING   The beaches of County Sligo are the home of surf, with excellent waves for all levels at **Strandhill,** reef breaks for the more experienced at **Easkey,** and big waves for pros only at **Mullaghmore.** For lessons that provide all the gear including wetsuits, try **Sligo Surf Experience** at Strandhill (www.sligosurfexperience.com; ℂ **087/747-1915;** lessons €40 adult, €35 under 16).

DONEGAL

13

When the landscape opens up into great sweeping views of rocky hills and barren shores, and a freezing mist blows off the sea, you know you've reached Donegal. The beauty of this county is both austere and bleak—but it is also unforgettable. On a clear day, you can stand at the edge of the sea at Malin Head at the very top of Ireland, and, despite the sun, the sea spray will blow a chill right through you. It feels as if you're standing at the edge of the world. If you've reached this far—congratulations! You can truly say that you've seen Ireland now, in all its wild, exhilarating beauty.

County Donegal's natural wonders include the magnificent Sliabh Liag (Slieve League) cliffs and remote beaches tucked into the bays and inlets of its sharply indented coast. While Donegal is one of Ireland's least touristy counties, it does have some truly fantastic places to stay, but they tend to be hidden away amid mountainous roads and tiny seaside towns. Buildings are made of cold stone; villages sit near tiny harbors or at the foot of hills; road signs sometimes vary from cryptic to nonexistent. When you stop to take a wander, you can't help but worry whether the car's brakes will hold. But take the chance. You will spend half your time lost, but wherever you're headed, you'll get there eventually, most likely with a few adventures along the way. And the people in Donegal are as nice as can be—meeting them is worth the trip in itself.

ESSENTIALS
Arriving

BY BUS **Bus Éireann** (www.buseireann.ie; ✆ **074/912-1309**) operates daily bus service to Donegal Town from Dublin, Derry, Sligo, Galway, and other points, and runs a daily service from Dublin to Letterkenny. Buy tickets in advance online for the best price.

BY CAR The only practical way to get around the remote attractions of County Donegal is by car. If you're driving from the south, Donegal is reached on N15 from Sligo or A46 from Northern Ireland; N56 is the main road from Donegal Town circling around the rest of the county.

FACING PAGE: **Sunset at Malin Head.**

BY PLANE Donegal Airport, in Carrickfinn in northwest Donegal (www.donegalairport.ie; ✆ 074/954-8284), also known as Carrickfinn Airport, is a small budget airline hub and has been voted one of the world's most scenic landings. Currently a couple of scheduled flights connect per day with Dublin and about five flights per week with Glasgow in the U.K., all operated by **Aer Lingus** (www.aerlingus.com; ✆ **1890/800-600**) or **Loganair** (www.loganair.co.uk; ✆ **0344/800-2855**).

BY TRAIN   There are no trains to Donegal. You can catch a train as far as Sligo and then switch to bus, but it's easiest to take a bus all the way.

DONEGAL TOWN & DONEGAL BAY

Overseen by a low, gloomy castle at the edge of the picturesque estuary of the River Eske on Donegal Bay, Donegal Town is a tiny burg, with just 2,500 residents. As recently as the 1940s, the town's triangular central mall (called "the Diamond"), set at the meeting point of roads from Killybegs, Ballyshannon, and Ballybofey, was used as a market for trading livestock and goods. Today the marketing takes the form of tweeds and tourist goods, as the Diamond is surrounded by little crafts shops and small hotels of variable quality. In the center stands an obelisk erected in memory of four 17th-century Irish clerics from the local abbey (see below) who wrote *The Annals of the Four Masters,* the first recorded history of Gaelic Ireland.

Visitor Information

The **Donegal Tourist Information Centre** is on the Quay, Donegal Town (www.govisitdonegal.com; ✆ 074/972-1148), and is open Tuesday to Saturday from 9am to 5pm. The **Ardara Heritage Centre** (✆ 087/242-4590) is on the main road through Ardara and is open Monday to Saturday 11am to 4pm.

Exploring Donegal Town

Donegal Abbey ★ RELIGIOUS SITE/RUINS   Sitting in a peaceful spot on the quay in Donegal Town, where the River Eske meets Donegal Bay, this ruined Franciscan monastery was founded in 1474 by the first Red Hugh O'Donnell and his wife, Nuala O'Brien of Munster. It was generously endowed by the O'Donnell family and became an important center of religion and learning; records show that there was a great gathering of clergy and lay leaders here in 1539. It was from this friary that some scholars undertook to salvage old Irish manuscripts and compile *The Annals of the Four Masters* (1632–36). Enough remains of the abbey's glory—ruins of a church and a cloister—to give you an idea of how magnificent it once was.

The Quay, Donegal Town. Free admission (open site).

Donegal Town

To Mountcharles & Killybegs

Presbyterian Church ❶

Methodist Church ❷

Church of Ireland ❸

❹

❺

❻

❼ Old Abbey

Cemetery

Pier

Shopping Centre

To Ballyshannon & Sligo

❽

The Glebe

Railway Rd.

To Ballybofey, Letterkenny & Derry

To Lough Derg

❾

❿

L. Eske Rd.

The Mullins

Tyrconnell St.

New Row

River Eske

Waterloo Place

Killybegs Rd.

Bridge St.

New Row

Castle St.

Upper Main St.

Water St.

Main St.

Drumcliff Terrace

The Bank Walk

River Eske

Quay St.

Ballyshannon Rd.

Information ⓘ
Parking 🅿
Post Office ✉

| 0 | 200 yds |
| 0 | 200 m |

NORTHERN IRELAND
Belfast
Donegal
Galway
REPUBLIC OF IRELAND
Dublin
Cork

ATTRACTIONS ●
The Diamond **4**
Donegal Abbey **7**
Donegal Bay Waterbus **6**
Donegal Castle **2**

WHERE TO STAY ●
Ard Na Breátha **10**
The Gateway Lodge **1**
Harvey's Point Hotel **9**

WHERE TO EAT ●
Blueberry Tea Room **3**
Quay West **5**
Smugglers Creek Inn **8**

Donegal Bay Waterbus ★ BOAT TOUR   These guided 75-minute tours of Donegal Bay take place daily on a modern, two-deck boat. Points of interest along the way include the **Old Abbey** ★ (p. 466); the aptly named **Seal Island,** home to a colony of about 200 noisy seals; and **The Hassans,** a port from which many emigrants from the northern part of the country left for the New World. The guides are enthusiastic and knowledgeable; unfortunately, their commentary is nonstop (guides have even been known to play the keyboard to fill in moments of silence). The views, however, are wonderful. There's a bar on board, plus seniors get free tea,

Donegal's colorful cityscape.

coffee, and bottled water (ask for a voucher when picking up your tickets). Sailing times are usually morning and afternoon or evening but are dependent upon tides and weather, so call ahead. Buy tickets from the office on Quay Street—it's the white-and-blue building next to Dom's Pier 1 Bar.

The Pier, Donegal Town. www.donegalbaywaterbus.com. ⓒ **074/972-3666.** Tour €20 adults; €12 students 17–23 (must have student ID); €7 children 5–16; free for children 4 and under. Closed Nov–Feb.

Donegal Castle ★ CASTLE   Built in the 15th century on the banks of the River Eske, this solid gray stone castle was once the chief stronghold for the O'Donnells, a powerful Donegal clan. In the 17th century, during the Plantation period, it was taken over by Sir Basil Brook, who added an extension with 10 gables, a large bay window, and smaller mullioned windows in Jacobean style. Much of the building has survived the centuries, and both the interior and exterior of the castle were beautifully restored in the 1990s. Guided tours run hourly and are included in the admission price.

Castle St., Donegal Town. www.heritageireland.ie. ⓒ **074/972-2405.** Admission €5 adults; €4 seniors; €3 students and children; €13 families. Easter to mid-Sept daily 10am–6pm; mid-Sept to Easter Thurs–Mon 9:30am–4:30pm; last admission 45 min. before closing.

Exploring Around Donegal Bay

The coastline around Donegal Bay is wild and beautiful. Speeds much above 55kmph (35 mph) are dangerous, but that's just as well, because the spectacular views will cause you to stop again and again to take in the rolling hills, jagged mountains, bright green fields, and crashing seas.

Heading south from Donegal Town, there are few attractions besides the historic village of **Ballyshannon** (*Béal Átha Seanaidh;* p. 469) and, inland, the pilgrimage site on the shore of **Lough Derg** (p. 472). But this area's a magnet for sporty types, with fine beaches, outstanding golf courses, and some of the best surfing in Ireland (p. 477).

To the north of Donegal Town, however, the coastal scenery is breathtaking. Follow the main road (N56) west out of Donegal Town for a slow, winding, but spectacularly scenic drive along the bay. You'll often see the distinctive thatched-roof cottages typical of this area, with rounded roofs held down by ropes (called *sugans*) fastened beneath the eaves to help the thatch resist the strong sea winds.

Just before the fishing village of **Killybegs** (*Ceala Beaga*), where the main N56 road swings inland, continue on the coastal road R263 through Killybegs to **Kilcar** (*Cill Chártha*), where you can pick up Donegal tweeds at a bargain at **Studio Donegal** (the Glebe Mill; www.studiodonegal.ie). Truly spectacular photo ops await at **Sliabh Liag** (p. 473), with its perilously high sea cliffs crashing down into the waters below. (Take the turnoff for the Bunglas viewing point at Carrick.) The traditional end of the west coast drive is the heritage site of **Glencolumbkille** (*Gleann Cholm Cille*), 48km (30 miles) from Donegal Town (p. 472).

To continue touring from Glencolumbkille, follow the signs directing you on the R230 to Ardara (*Árd an Rátha*). This is a breathtaking drive through **Glengesh Pass,** a narrow, sinuous, scenic roadway that rises to a height of 270m (886 ft.) before plunging in hairpin curves into the valley below to reach the village of **Ardara (***Árd an Rátha***)**—ready to take on the rest of the county.

Ballyshannon (Béal Átha Seanaidh) ★★ VILLAGE   The first proper town you'll come to on a drive south of Donegal Town is this busy, pretty little place, built on a hill, with a 15th-century town center. Some claim that Ballyshannon is the oldest town in Ireland, in part because traces have been found of permanent settlements dating as far back as

DONEGAL | Donegal Town & Donegal Bay

Summer Fests in Donegal Town

If you're heading this way in late June or early July, check out the town's laidback annual **Summer Festival.** The program is an enthusiastic mixture of free concerts (from local bands that, in all probability, you've never heard of) and family-friendly fun and games. The festival lasts 4 days, with the biggest events scheduled over a weekend. See **www.**

govisitdonegal.com for more event details. And if you're heading this way later in the summer, you might be able to catch the **Donegal Food Festival.** Held over a weekend in late August, the festival brings together chefs, restaurateurs, and artisan food providers from all over Ireland. Visit www.atasteofdonegal.com for more details.

IRISH only!

Although English is the day-to-day language spoken by the majority of Irish people, Irish is the original Celtic language indigenous to these shores, and it is the national and first official language. You will see Irish (sometimes called Gaelic outside Ireland) on all road signs and official documents, and there are still places in Ireland where you will hear the Irish language being spoken. While only about 3% of Irish people speak Irish as their first language, it is still taught to all schoolchildren, and around 50% of the population can speak a little.

There are certain regions of Ireland, known as **Gaeltacht,** where Irish is predominantly spoken and official signage is in Irish rather than English. These areas are spread all over the country, but some of the biggest are in Donegal, Mayo, and Kerry. When you're driving around Gaeltacht districts, all the road signs will be in

Irish—even emergency signs and place names. In this book we've included the Irish names as well as the English names for those places where you're likely to encounter this. (Donegal has a high proportion of native Irish speakers—more than a third of the residents of the Rosguill Peninsula, for example, speak Irish as their main language.)

You won't have any problem communicating with locals, however—nobody in Ireland speaks *only* Irish. While use of the language is in decline, there are efforts to preserve and revive it. It was made an official language of the EU in 2007, and the number of all-Irish schools is growing (around 1 in 12 schoolchildren is educated entirely through Irish). There are Irish TV and radio stations, as well as a number of popular Irish language apps and social media accounts that promote the language and help learners.

4000 B.C. The small **Ballyshannon and District Museum,** on the second floor of Slevin's Department Store, has artifacts and information on local history. It's open Monday to Saturday from 10am to 6pm and admission is free. Ballyshannon is also the location of **The Abbey Mill** (✆ **071/985-1260**), a heritage center and craft store. Part of a ruined Cistercian abbey, the mill still has a working waterwheel. (Opening hours vary—generally Mon–Sat 10am–5pm, summer months only; entry is free, but leave a few coins in the collection box by the waterwheel to help pay for its upkeep.) While you're here, check out tiny **Catsby Cave,** about 50m (164 ft.) along the riverbank. During the years of British occupation, when Catholicism was outlawed (from the 16th c. until the mid–19th c.), priests would give Mass here in secret. You can still see the remains of an altar, chiseled from the rock. Admission is free. Ballyshannon is known for its lively pubs, many of which have reliably good traditional music—never more so than during a weekend in late July or early August, when the streets come alive for the **Ballyshannon Folk & Traditional Music Festival** (http://bally shannonfolkfestival.com).

Tourism Office: The Bridge, Ballyshannon, Co. Donegal. About 22km (13½ miles) S. of Donegal Town on N15.

County Donegal

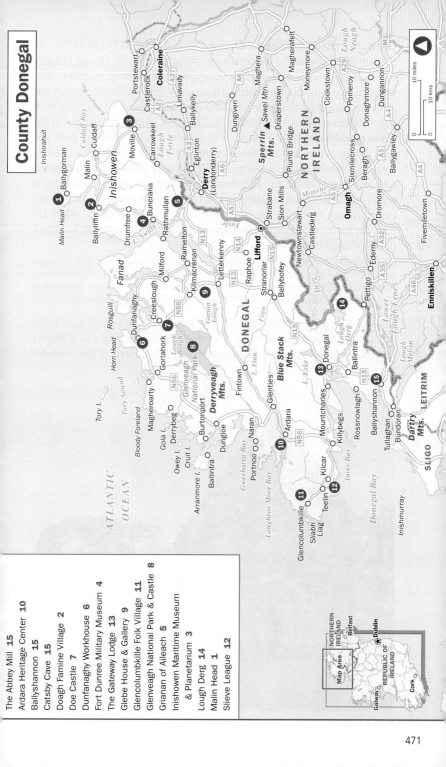

471

Glencolumbkille (Gleann Cholm Cille) ★★ HERITAGE SITE   An extraordinarily beautiful outpost overlooking the Atlantic Ocean, Glencolumbkille is sited in a lush green valley, west of the dark boglands. It is said that St. Columba established a monastery here in the 6th century and gave his name to the glen (its Irish language name—*Gleann Cholm Cille*—means "Glen of Columba's Church"). Today it's home to the **Glencolumbkille Folk Village,** a wonderful "living history" park and craft center, set up and maintained entirely by local people. In a series of small traditional cottages, the park tells the story of this remote community and of traditional life in Ireland in the 19th century, in an engaging way. Guided tours are available, or you can take it at your own pace. Don't leave without browsing the craft shop selling local products, while the tearoom serves traditional Irish stews, soups, and brown bread. Tea brack (a fruity cake) is a house specialty.

On R263, about 26km (16 miles) NW of Killybegs, Glencolumbkille, Co. Donegal. www.glenfolkvillage.com. ✆ **074/973-0017.** Admission €6 adults; €5 seniors and students; €2.50 children 7–16; free for children under 7; €15 families. Easter–Sept Mon–Sat 10am–6pm, July–Aug Sun 10am–6pm. Oct Mon–Sun 11am–4:30pm.

Lough Derg ★★ NATURE SITE   This beautiful island-dotted lake lies about 16km (10 miles) east of Donegal Town. Legend has it that St. Patrick spent 40 days and 40 nights fasting in a cavern at this secluded

Ruins in Lough Derg.

walk this way: CLIMBING SLIABH LIAG (SLIEVE LEAGUE)

There are two ways to see Sliabh Liag (also known as Slieve League)—and rarely has the phrase "the easy way or the hard way" been more appropriate.

The walking path is a truly spectacular hike across stunning countryside, about 10km (6¼ miles) in length, which takes between 4 and 5 hours. The summits of Sliabh Liag, rising almost 600m (1,968 ft.) above the sea, are often capped in clouds, and you shouldn't undertake the walk if there are high winds or any danger at all of losing visibility along the way. In any case, this is only for the fearless and fit. And we *really* mean fearless; the high point (literally) is the frankly terrifying **One Man's Pass,** a footpath so narrow that it can only take one person at a time—and it's *on top of* the cliff, with a 450m

(1,500-ft.) drop on one side and a perilously steep incline on the other. Your starting point will be the Bunglas lookout point; you'll end up at Trabane Strand in Malin Beg, a few miles southwest of Glencolumbkille. Be sure to arrange a pickup at the end.

So where does "the easy way" come into all this? The less intrepid (or possibly just "sane") can walk or take a shuttle bus from the visitor center up to the best viewing point. You won't be able to see the vista from the cliffs, but you'll get a great view *of* them.

Sliabh Liag Tours (www.sliabhliag tours.ie; © **087/671-1944**) runs a tour from Carrick and can arrange to drop you off at the best (and more manageable) walking points on the way back. Tours are all customized; call for information.

spot, and since then it has been revered as a place of penance and pilgrimage. From June 1 to August 15, thousands of Irish Catholics take turns coming to Lough Derg to do penance for 3 days at a time, remaining awake and eating nothing but tea and toast. It's considered one of the most rigorous pilgrimages in all of Christendom.

Co. Donegal. www.loughderg.org. Take R232 to Pettigo, then R233 for 8km (5 miles).

Sliabh Liag (Slieve League) ★★ NATURE SITE   It's surprising that these towering sea cliffs aren't better known, because they're almost three times the height of their far more feted southern cousins, the **Cliffs of Moher** (p. 351), and arguably even more spectacular. Needless to say, given the remote location, they also get a tiny fraction of the visitors that the Cliffs of Moher attract. During peak summer season, around July and August, you can park (free) in the lower car park and either walk up to the main viewing point (a lovely walk of around 45 min.) or take a shuttle bus up (€6 adults; €5 seniors and students; €18 families). There's also parking halfway up (€5 for 2 hr. or €15 per day) and the walk from there is about 25 minutes. During the off-season, you may be able to drive all the way to the upper viewing point, but walking is the nicest way to appreciate the surroundings. When you reach the viewpoint, you can fully take in the wild, ominous beauty of this rugged, far-flung outpost. If you really want to test yourself against the terrain, try the hike right to the top of the cliff (p. 473). There's a visitor center and cafe at the lower car park at Bunglas. You can also see the cliffs from the water with **Sliabh Liag Boat Trips** (www.sliabhleagueboattrips.com; ✆ **087/628-4688**) for €25 adults, €15 teens, and €10 ages 5 to 12. Meanwhile The **Slieve League Cliffs Centre** (www.slieveleaguecliffs.ie; ✆ **074/973-9077**) in Teelin, about 3km (1⅓ miles) southwest of Carrick, is a friendly little visitor center, run by an archaeologist and an artist, with a great cafe and a gorgeous crafts store. Admission is free and it's open daily 10:30am to 5:30pm.

Carrick, Co. Donegal (signposted from R263). www.sliabhliag.com; ✆ **074/973-9620.** Free admission. Open year-round.

Where to Stay in Donegal Town & Donegal Bay

Ard Na Breátha ★★   This peaceful B&B is located on a farm and is only a 10-minute walk from the center of Donegal Town, but the peaceful surroundings and mountain views give the feeling of rural seclusion. Bedrooms are summery and spacious, with bright colors, polished wood floors, and antique-style iron frame beds in some rooms. The lounge has a cozy fireplace and a small honesty bar and there's also a small kitchen that guests can use.

Railway Park, Middle Drumrooske, Co. Donegal. www.ardnabreatha.com. ✆ **074/972-2288.** 6 units. €85–€120 double. Free parking. Breakfast included. **Amenities:** Kitchen; Wi-Fi (free). Closed Nov–Easter.

The Gateway Lodge ★★   This stylish and contemporary lodging, just a few minutes' walk from the town center, incorporates a 19th-century house and two modern wings. Good-sized bedrooms make the most of the space, with modern furniture and just enough quirky touches to be characterful and functional at the same time. Bathrooms have what may be described as a "utilitarian chic" air to them, with white tiled walls and satisfyingly powerful showers. A little restaurant and cafe called **Blas** is located in the old house, where you can get delicious and healthful bistro-style lunches featuring plenty of local produce—or just a cup of fresh coffee.

Killybegs Rd., Donegal Town, Co. Donegal. www.thegatewaydonegal.ie. ✆ **074/974-0405.** 26 units. €89–€129 double. Free parking. Breakfast included. **Amenities:** Wi-Fi (free).

Harvey's Point Hotel ★★★   There are few more romantic views in Donegal than the glassy expanse of Lough Eske, and this wonderful lakeside resort takes full advantage of the location. Rooms and bathrooms are spacious, modern, and very comfortable. The decor is traditional throughout, with marble bathrooms, striped wallpaper, and antique reproduction beds. All guest rooms are suites, with seating areas and plenty of space to relax. Downstairs, the restaurant serves rich meals with exquisite views of the lake—afternoon tea here is absolutely decadent, with fresh-baked scones, cakes, and homemade jam. The wood-paneled bar has the feel of a private club, and a good selection of wine and whiskey to go with it. The place has the ambience of an exclusive getaway, as if you're hiding from the world. No wonder it's won so many awards.

At Lough Eske, about 7km (4½ miles) from Donegal Town, off N15, Co. Donegal. www.harveyspoint.com. ✆ **074/972-2208.** 101 units. €218–€371 double. 2-night minimum on summer weekends. Free parking. Breakfast included. **Amenities:** Restaurant; bar; room service; Wi-Fi (free).

Where to Eat in Donegal Town & Donegal Bay

Blueberry Tea Room ★ CAFE A buttermilk-colored shopfront, adorned with little baskets of azaleas, twinkling fairy lights, and walls filled with knick-knacks—and the friendliest owner in Donegal—what more could you want from a small-town cafe? If the answer is "tasty, simple lunches in huge portions," guess what, you're in luck there, too! The homemade soups are a specialty (served with or without a toasted sandwich), or you could fill up on a hearty plate of steak fajitas or breaded chicken with pasta and house special sauce. The cafe also has a little deli selling Irish cheese, breads, muffins, and other tasty treats to go.

Castle St., Donegal Town. www.theblueberrytearooms.ie. ✆ **074/972-2933.** Entrees €10–€12. Mon–Sat 9am–6pm. Closed Sun.

Tending the fire at Harvey's Point Hotel.

Quay West ★★ IRISH   Romantic, contemporary food is served up in this delightful place overlooking Donegal Bay. The food is modern without a hint of pretension. Start with a plate of local shellfish with fresh sourdough toast, then for your main course try a char-grilled steak (cooked on hot lava stones) or stick with the local seafood and opt for a creamy fish pie with a comet cheese crust. Desserts are mostly of the indulgent, comfort-food variety. If you can resist the profiteroles with dark chocolate ganache sauce, you are a better person than either of us.

Quay St., Donegal Town. www.quaywestdonegal.ie. ✆ **074/972-1590.** Entrees €16–€30. Wed–Sat 5–9pm; Sun 1–7pm. Closed Mon–Tues.

Smugglers Creek Inn ★ SEAFOOD   With a breathtakingly beautiful clifftop view of Donegal Bay, this mid-19th-century inn is a fantastic place to come and watch the sun setting over the Atlantic Ocean. See if you can get a table outside or in the conservatory. Although you can order steaks and other meaty dishes, the seafood is what's best here: chowder, smoked mackerel, scampi, crab claws, or the ever-reliable fish and chips. Vegetarians and vegans are better catered to than you might expect at a little restaurant in the back of beyond; try the delicious penne with roasted vegetables. Wash it all down with a pint of local ale.

Cliff Rd., Rossnowlagh, Co. Donegal. www.smugglerscreekinn.com. ✆ **071/985-2367.** Entrees €10–€27. Jan–Mar Fri–Sun, Apr–May and Sept Thurs–Sun, June–Aug daily 12:30–10:30pm. Oct Fri–Sun 12:30–10pm. Closed Nov–Dec.

Sports & Outdoor Pursuits Around Donegal Bay

BEACHES   Donegal Bay's beaches are wide, sandy, clean, and flat—ideal for walking. **Ballyshannon** has a good beach, but it gets crowded; **Rossnowlagh** and **Bundoran** are better options, and both are popular for surfing. On the North Donegal Bay drive, **Glencolumbkille** has two fine beaches: one a flat, sandy beach at the end of Glencolumbkille village, where the R263 swings left, the other a tiny gem of a beach surrounded by a horseshoe of cliffs, accessible from the small road signposted to Malin More (off the R263) about 1.6km (1 mile) southwest of town.

CYCLING   If you're very fit, the north side of Donegal Bay has great cycling roads—tremendously scenic but with some demanding climbs. One good but arduous route from Donegal Town follows the coast roads west to Glencolumbkille (day 1), continues north to Ardara and Dawros Head via Glengesh Pass (day 2), and then returns to Donegal (day 3). It takes in some of the most spectacular coastal scenery in Ireland along the way, but follows small, winding roads that must sometimes be shared with fast-moving cars.

GOLF   The coast around Donegal Bay is home to two outstanding 18-hole championship seaside golf courses. **Donegal Golf Club,** Murvagh, Ballintra (www.donegalgolfclub.ie; ✆ **074/973-4054**), is 5km (3

The Wild Atlantic Way

The Wild Atlantic Way is a 2,500km (1,550-mile) marked road trail stretching the entire length of the west coast. The trail, which runs from Malin Head in the north (p. 485) all the way to Kinsale in County Cork in the south, can be a handy navigator to some of the main sights, especially in more rural and isolated areas. Look for brown road signs with a thick white squiggle in a blue box (like two Ws linked together). More information, including a full list of the points of interest covered, can be found at **www.wildatlanticway.com**.

miles) north of Rossnowlagh and 11km (6¾ miles) south of Donegal Town. It's a par-73 course with greens fees of €150 May to September, €120 April to October, €50 November to March. The **Bundoran Golf Club,** off the Sligo–Ballyshannon road (N15) in Bundoran (www.bundorangolfclub.com; ✆ **071/984-1302**), is a par-69 course designed by Harry Vardon. Greens fees are around €40 weekdays, €50 weekends.

SURFING **Bundoran** is popular with surfers for its steady waves; it has hosted the European Surfing Championships. **Rossnowlagh** also has excellent surf. You can rent boards and wetsuits locally from around €20 each per day or take a lesson from around €40 per person, which includes all equipment. Try **Bundoran Surf Co.** (www.bundoransurfco.com; ✆ **071/984-968**) in Bundoran, which offers lessons year-round at Tullan Strand in Bundoran or Rossnowlagh.

WALKING The peninsula to the west of Killybegs offers some of the most spectacular coastal scenery in Ireland, much of it accessible only from the sea or on foot. Besides the **Sliabh Liag (Slieve League)** hike (p. 473), there's a spectacular coastal walk between Glencolumbkille and the town of **Maghera** (not so much a town as a small cluster of houses). Begin by hiking up to the Martello tower on Glen Head, which overlooks Glencolumbkille to the north, then continue along the cliff face for 24km (15 miles), passing only one remote outpost of human habitation along the way, the tiny town of **Port.** For isolated sea splendor, this is one of the finest walks in Ireland, but only experienced walkers with adequate provisions should undertake it, and only in fine weather.

COUNTY DONEGAL

Donegal is the most isolated county in Ireland. It doesn't get much more rugged and exhilarating, and, well . . . *isolated* than this. At a certain point when you're driving through the Gaeltacht area (p. 470), the signs switch entirely to Irish. It's disorienting—one minute you know exactly where you are and the next you haven't a clue. And at that moment—which almost always occurs on a mountainside by a rushing stream amid rocky terrain—you're in the true Donegal.

Traditional weaver in Donegal.

The best place to start a tour of County Donegal is at **Ardara (*Árd an Rátha*),** an adorable village about 40km (25 miles) northwest of Donegal Town. From there, weave your way up the coast. This drive can take 4 hours or 4 days, depending on your schedule and interests. Our advice is to take your time. You may never come this way again, and you will want to remember every moment.

Exploring County Donegal

Looking as if it were carved from stone, charming little **Ardara** is known for its exceptional tweed and wool creations. Astride a narrow river in a steep gulch, it is a pleasant place to stop, chat with the locals, and do a bit of shopping or maybe have a cup of tea in its small but useful **Heritage Centre** on the N56 main road through the village. You will also be able to see weavers at work in some of the shops—ask at the Heritage Centre.

Heading north from Ardara, the N26 passes through the neat-as-a-pin little town of **Glenties (*Na Gleanta*),** where playwright Brian Friel set his play *Dancing at Lughnasa,* and eventually curves inland to gorgeous **Glenveagh National Park ★★★** (p. 480) and **Mount Errigal,** Donegal's highest mountain. Just east of the park, the surprisingly good **Glebe House and Gallery ★★** (p. 480) sits on lovely Lough Gartan.

It would be a shame, however, not to sample some scenic coastal detours along the way. The southernmost is on R261, taking in **Naran (*An Fhearthainn*)** and **Portnoo**—beaches that are favorites with Irish families in the summer. Your next option is at Dungloe, where you can split off on coastal R259 to visit **the Rosses,** a rock-strewn land punctuated by mountains, rivers, and glassy lakes (and vacation homes). On this loop you'll pass the tiny port of **Burtonport (*Ailt an Chorrain*),** where, it's said, more salmon and lobster are landed than at any other port in the country. The next coastal loop heading north is on R257, swinging through Derrybeg and Gortahork. This is known as the **Bloody Foreland,** from the fact that its rocks take on a ruddy color when lit by the setting sun. For a remote area, it is surprisingly built-up, but if you can arrange to be driving through here at sunset on a clear day, you are in for some rewarding views.

If you follow N56 to the top rim of Donegal, you'll find a series of small peninsulas like fingers jabbing out into the sea. West to east, they are **Horn Head (*Corrán Binne*),** with spectacular cliffs towering 180m (590 ft.) above the ocean; **Rosguill (*Ros Goill*);** and **Fanad,** jutting out between Mulroy Bay and the glassy waters of Lough Swilly. Each peninsula has its own driving circuit. Horn Head's clifftop drive is the most spectacular but also rather perilous; you may want to opt instead for Rosguill's scenic 16km (10-mile) Atlantic Drive, or, if you have more time, the Fanad's 73km (45-mile) circuit, which takes in the beautiful **Fanad Head Lighthouse.** There is a bridge between Rosguill and Fanad on the R245 just beyond Carrickart. At the base of the Horn Head peninsula, pretty **Dunfanaghy (*Dún Fionnachaidh*)** can be a good option for an overnight stay, with a fine beach and an intriguing heritage center, the **Dunfanaghy Workhouse** (see below). Between Horn Head and Rosguill, **Doe Castle** (see below) is also well worth a stop. At the base of the Fanad Peninsula, the tiny village of **Rathmelton (*Ráth Mealtain*)** is eminently photographic, with its gray Georgian warehouses reflected in the mirror-like water of the lake.

About 10 minutes' drive north of Rathmelton, on the coast of Lough Swilly, the village of **Rathmullan (*Ráth Maoláin*)** is an excellent stopping point, with an evocative ruined abbey, a beautiful stretch of flat, sandy beach, and a couple of good hotels (splurge on **Rathmullan House ★★★** if you can swing it—see p. 481).

Doe Castle (Caisleán na dTuath) ★ CASTLE This little 600-year-old castle at the edge of a mirrorlike lake is so perfect it's hard to believe it's real. A battlement wall with round towers at the corners encloses the central tower house, which was once the stronghold of Clan Sweeney. Built in the early 16th century, the castle was extensively restored in the 18th century and was a used as a home until 1843. Uninhabited since then, it's now maintained by Heritage Ireland. It's a lovely little place, surrounded on three sides by the waters of Sheephaven Bay, and on the fourth by a moat carved into the bedrock that forms its foundation. The view from the battlements across the bay is superb.

5.6km (3½ miles) off N56; turnoff signposted just S of Creeslough, Co. Donegal. www.heritageireland.ie. Free admission. Daily 9am–6pm.

Dunfanaghy Workhouse ★ MUSEUM   This rather unassuming gray stone building was the scene of great hardship and fear in the 19th century, when it was one of around 100,000 workhouses set up to feed and house the poor during the Great Famine. Their approach was hardly altruistic, however; fearing that merely feeding people would engender a "something-for-nothing" culture in the poor, the authorities decreed that they should perform backbreaking labor in return for their bread. It's estimated that workhouses killed around a million people in Ireland. This particular one housed about 300 inmates. The museum does a good job of describing their daily lives, as well as providing a history of the Famine in this area. One exhibit focuses particularly on a local girl, "Wee Hannah" Herrity, who lived here and survived to tell the tale—which she did, in extensive conversation with a local biographer. Guided tours are available on request (these do not need to be prebooked except in high season).

Just W of Dunfanaghy on N56, Co. Donegal. www.dunfanaghyworkhouse.com. ℂ **074/913-6540.** Admission €5 adults; €4 seniors, students, and children over 12; free children 12 and under; €15 families. Daily 10am–5pm.

Glebe House & Gallery ★★★ ART MUSEUM   What a pleasant surprise, in such a remote location, to find an art gallery as good as this. This early-19th-century house on the shores of Lake Gartan was once home to noted English painter Derek Hill (1916–2000), who donated the house, along with his personal art collection, to the Irish state in the 1980s. And what a collection—highlights include paintings by Picasso, Renoir, Jack Yeats, and Oskar Kokoschka, along with rare Islamic and Far Eastern art and original William Morris prints. About 300 works are on display from the permanent collection, plus temporary and special exhibitions. The house itself is worth seeing, too—a handsome Regency building, surrounded by pretty woods and gardens, stretching down to the Lough. The house can only be visited on a guided tour, and space is limited to 15 people at a time.

Signposted from R251, 17km (10½ miles) NE of Letterkenny, Church Hill, Co. Donegal. www.glebegallery.ie. ℂ **074/913-7071.** Admission to House €5 adults; €4 seniors; €3 students and children; €13 families. Admission to Gallery is free. **Gallery and House:** Late May to end Sept daily 11am–6:30pm; Oct 11am–5:30pm; Last tour 1 hr. before closing. Grounds open year-round.

Glenveagh National Park and Castle ★★★ NATURE SITE/ CASTLE   This thickly wooded valley is peaceful now, but its history is dark. Nestling at its heart, **Glenveagh Castle** was originally the home of the infamously cruel landlord John George Adair, who evicted scores of struggling tenant farmers in the freezing winter of 1861, leaving many to die, ostensibly because their presence on his estate was ruining his view. If the tale is true, it's divine justice that this estate now belongs to all of the people of Ireland. Today the fairy-tale setting includes woodlands, herds of red deer, alpine gardens, a crystal-clear lake, and the highest mountain in Donegal, Mount Errigal. There's a visitor center with a little shop, and a charming tearoom in the castle. You can also explore the gardens at the castle, take walking trails along the lake, or go on ranger-led walks of the park for €10. Cars must be parked at the entrance, and a shuttle bus can take you up to the castle for €3 round-trip (€2 seniors, students, and children)—but it's also a lovely walk in nice weather.

Church Hill, Co. Donegal (signposted from R251, 24.4km/15 miles NE of Letterkenny). www.glenveaghnationalpark.ie. ✆ 076/100-2537. Free park admission. Castle: €7 adults; €5 seniors, students and children; €15 families. Visitor center and castle: Mid-Mar to Oct daily 9:15am–5:30pm; Nov–Mar daily 9am–5pm; last admission 1 hr. before closing.

Where to Stay in County Donegal

Arnold's Hotel ★   Near the harbor in Dunfanaghy, this simple but pleasant hotel overlooks Sheephaven Bay. The overly bright interior decor won't win any design awards, but guest rooms have all the basics and comfortable beds. Ask for a room with a view of the bay. There is also a horseback-riding stables on the hotel grounds.

On N56, Dunfanaghy, Co. Donegal. www.arnoldshotel.com. ✆ 074/913-6208. 31 units. €110–€205 double. Free parking. Check website for special offers. **Amenities:** Restaurant; bar; Wi-Fi (free).

Castle Grove Hotel ★★   Lancelot "Capability" Brown, the famous English landscaper who virtually invented landscape gardening in the 18th century, laid out the elegant grounds at this inviting white manor house. Inside the decor is avowedly traditional in style, with plenty of period detail and heritage hues. Rooms have antique furnishings (including a four-poster bed in one). All have views of the grounds. Breakfasts are outstanding, and the **Castle Grove restaurant** (see below) is one of the best in the region. Check the website for dinner, bed-and-breakfast packages.

Ballymaleel, off Ramelton Rd., Letterkenny, Co. Donegal. www.castlegrove.com. ✆ 074/915-1118. 12 units. €155–€220 double; €250 suite. 2-night minimum on weekends June–Aug. Free parking. Breakfast included. **Amenities:** Restaurant; bar; room service; access to nearby golf courses; tennis courts; Wi-Fi (free).

Rathmullan House ★★★   Right on the edge of Lough Swilly, this delightful mid-18th-century mansion is one of our favorite places to stay in the northwest. The guest lounges are warm and hospitable, with sumptuous period decor and fires crackling in the hearth on cold days. Bedrooms are spacious and extremely comfortable; rooms in the modern extension lose nothing in terms of style and charm to the rooms in the older section of the house. Some have fireplaces and deep roll-top bathtubs. Superior rooms have even more space. Family rooms can work out to be only slightly more expensive than standard doubles. The house has a swimming pool, but you can also take a short stroll down to the beautiful beach. The **Cook & Gardener restaurant ★★★** (see below) is outstanding, deserving its reputation as one of the top places to eat in Donegal; alternatively, **Pavilion** serves stone-baked pizza and craft beers outside under a traditional king pole canvas tent and in the garden.

On R247 (Chapel Rd.), Rathmullan, Co. Donegal. www.rathmullanhouse.com. ✆ **074/915-8188.** 34 units. €200–€320. double. 2- night minimum stay applies. Free parking. Breakfast included. **Amenities:** 2 restaurants; bar; pool; Wi-Fi (free).

Where to Eat in County Donegal

Castle Grove ★★ IRISH   This place has won plenty of awards over the years, and it's easy to see why—the food is superb and a top recommendation if you're staying here or nearby. Seasonal menus present classic Irish flavors with a modern edge: asparagus with blood-orange hollandaise, followed by beef filet with onion jam or Barbary duck prepared with honey and clove. **Castle Grove ★★** is also a very good hotel—see above for review.

Ballymaleel, off Ramelton Rd., Letterkenny, Co. Donegal. www.castlegrove.com. ✆ **074/915-1118.** Entrees €18–€32. Daily 7–9:30pm; Sun noon–2:30pm. No children under 10 allowed after 7pm.

The Cook & Gardener ★★★ IRISH   It's entirely befitting that, as one of the very best hotels in Donegal, **Rathmullan House ★★★** (see above) would also have one of its best restaurants. Many of the ingredients have come no greater distance than the house's own gardens, and most of the rest haven't traveled all that much farther. The menu changes daily, but expect delights such as seared Greencastle monkfish with fondant potato, or free-range Glin Valley roast chicken with shallot puree, cabbage, and bacon. If you're not in the mood for a formal lunch, head to the hotel bar for a more casual menu of sandwiches, burgers, and stone-baked pizza (lunch 12:30–4:30pm).

Rathmullan House hotel, R247 (Chapel Rd.), Rathmullan, Co. Donegal. www.rathmullanhouse.com. ✆ **074/915-8188.** 3-course set menu €55. Daily 1–2:30pm and 6pm–8:30pm.

The Rusty Oven ★ PIZZA   Locals love this place, hidden in a courtyard behind Patsy Dan's Pub, for delicious sourdough pizza and toasted sandwiches. The atmosphere is very casual—it's a bit like eating in someone's living room, in a good way. In the summer, dining happens outside, on the bohemian courtyard, beneath the trees. It's best to not be in a hurry, for the pizzas are made at a leisurely pace. But sometimes someone's playing guitar, and everyone sings, and the mood is chill.

Off Market Sq., behind Patsy Dan's Pub, Dunfanaghy, Co. Donegal. www.therusty oven.ie. No phone. Entrees €8–€12. Daily 5–10pm.

Horseback riding on Dunfanaghy beach.

Sheila's Coffee & Cream ★
CAFE This cozy cafe at the Ardara Heritage Centre (p. 466) is a welcome find. Drop in for a fine cup of coffee and a restorative slice of cake, or lunch—soups, Irish stew, salads, and filling sandwiches. The bread is home-baked, and the ever-present Sheila herself is quite delightful. From Wednesday to Saturday you can get supper here, too. It's all quite traditional fare—steak in peppercorn sauce, cheeseburgers, fish and chips—but it's all good, tasty, comfort-food stuff.

Ardara Heritage Centre, Ardara, Co. Donegal. ℭ **074/953-7905.** Entrees €5–€14.50. Mon–Sat 10am–6pm. Closed Sun.

Sports & Outdoor Pursuits in County Donegal

BEACHES There are Blue Flag beaches in **Portnoo** and **Navan. Magheroarty,** near Falcarragh on the northern coast, has a breathtaking beach, unspoiled by crowds or development. The same goes for **Tramore** beach on the western side of Horn Head near Dunfanaghy; you have to hike a short distance, but the rewards are seclusion and miles of creamy sand.

WALKING **Ards Forest Park,** on a peninsula jutting into Sheep Haven Bay about 5.6km (3½ miles) south of Dunfanaghy on N56, has lovely coastal boardwalks running between the beach and sand dunes, with gorgeous sea views, plus inland forest trails.

For a bit more of a challenge, try some scenic hiking on **Horn Head,** signposted off N56 just west of Dunfanaghy. From the concrete lookout point, a trail leads out to a ruined castle on the headland and continues south along a line of impressive quartzite sea cliffs that glitter in the sun.

THE INISHOWEN PENINSULA

Driving around the northernmost point of Ireland is worth doing just so you can say you did. You stood on Malin Head and felt the icy mist come in on a wind that hit you like a fist. You have felt the satisfaction that comes from knowing there is no farther to go.

There is, however, so much more to this land than that. Around the edges are ancient sites, beautiful beaches, and charming villages. At its center are gorgeous views, mountains, and quiet, vivid green pastures. If you are looking to get lost, this is a great place to do it—although the Inishowen Peninsula circuit is very well signposted, with all directions clearly printed in English and Irish.

Exploring the Inishowen Peninsula

The Inishowen (*Inis Eoghain*) Peninsula reaches out from Lough Foyle to the east and Lough Swilly to the west toward **Malin Head ★★** (p. 485), its farthest point.

From Donegal Town, take N15 through the scenic Barnesmore Gap—a vast open stretch through the Blue Stack Mountains—to N13 and on to Letterkenny (*Leitir Ceanainn*), the largest town in County Donegal, set on a hillside overlooking Lough Swilly. From there, head north on N13, then east on R238, to Buncrana, an excellent place to rest and have a meal. Near Buncrana are a couple of worthwhile stops—**Fort Dunree Military Museum ★★** (see below) to the north, and the much more ancient hilltop fort known as **Grianan of Aileach ★** (see below), a short drive south of Buncrana.

Ascend a corkscrew road (R238) from Buncrana through the Gap of Mamore, a mountain pass that rises 240m (787 ft.). Head east to the beach town of Ballyliffin for golf and surfing, and from here, take a detour for the fascinating Doagh Famine Village. Passing the cute village of Malin (Málainn), with its picturesque stone bridge and village green, it's another 20-minute drive north on R242 to Malin Head (Cionn Mhélanna), for stunning coastal views from Ireland's most northerly point (see p. 485).

From Malin Head, head back on R242/238 to **Culdaff (*Cúil Dabhcha*),** a sleepy waterfront village with a pretty beach. On its main street, the Clonca Church is a solid 17th-century structure with a fine carved high cross. The coastal road leads from here to picturesque **Inishowen Head** (follow signs off the R241 onto a side road, follow that to its end, and walk the rest of the way to the headland). It's eerily isolated, but the views are stupendous—on clear days, you can see all the way to the Antrim Coast.

Continuing around the peninsula, follow coastal road R241 southwest to **Greencastle (*An Cáisleá Nua*),** site of the quirky **Inishowen Maritime Museum and Planetarium ★** (see below).

Doagh Famine Village ★★★ MUSEUM　A visit here takes you on a fascinating and sometimes humorous journey through Irish history and culture. The village comprises original Irish thatched cottages as they would have looked during the 1840s and includes everything from an Irish wake and eviction scene to a hedge school and haunted rooms. It's all the creation of Pat Doherty, who built this village around his own family history. It's a fantastic way to understand the different periods of Irish history and worth the drive—even the views are stunning. A short guided tour includes tea and scones and a shot of *poitín* (p. 410) and then free time to explore (allow 2 hr. for the visit). At Christmas, Pat transforms the village into "Donegal Lapland," with all sorts of magical characters, Santa's Castle, and a toy factory.

Doagh Island, Inishowen, Co. Donegal. www.doaghfaminevillage.com. © **074/937-8078.** Mar 17 to mid-Oct daily 10am–5pm. Admission €12 adult; €6.50 child. **Donegal Lapland:** Nov 26–Dec 22 daily 5–9pm; tickets €15.50 adult or child.

Fort Dunree Military Museum ★★ MUSEUM   Rising precipitously from the cliffs beside Lough Swilly, this impressive-looking fort was constructed as a defensive lookout in the event of a French invasion during the Napoleonic Wars. It later became part of Irish sea defenses against German invasion during the First World War. Neither came, and today Dunree serves as an informative museum. Spread partly through subsurface bunkers, the exhibitions tell the history of the fort, and of the local area as a whole. It also serves as the starting point for scenic walks around Dunree Point along three recommended walking paths. The museum has a handy coffee shop overlooking Lough Swilly.

Signposted on the coast road, about 11km (7 miles) N of Buncrana, Co. Donegal. www.dunree.pro.ie. © **074/936-1817.** Admission €7 adults; €5 seniors and children; €15 families. Mon–Fri 10:30am–4:30pm; Sat–Sun 10:30am–6pm.

Grianan of Aileach ★★ ANCIENT SITE   Built high atop a hill outside the village of Burt, this beautifully preserved ring fort can be seen from miles away, a crown made of stone. Experts think the existing structure was built in the 6th or 7th century A.D., although the site had already been used for many centuries by then. There's evidence it may have originally been a temple of the sun as long ago as 1700 B.C. From the A.D. mid-5th century to the early 12th century, this was the seat of the kingdom of Aileach, home to the O'Neills, the chieftains of this area. The view from the top is spectacular. The waters of the two sea inlets—Lough Swilly and Lough Foyle—sparkle in the distance, and you can make out the shape of the entire peninsula. The round fort is made of stone without mortar; the walls are terraced, giving access to the top.

Signposted on N13, behind the town of Burt, about 16km (10 miles) S of Buncrana, Co. Donegal. Free admission. Mid-June to Sept daily 9am–9pm; Oct to mid-June daily 9am–7:30pm. Gate not locked out of hours mid-June to Sept Fri–Sun.

Inishowen Maritime Museum & Planetarium ★ MUSEUM/ PLANETARIUM   Overlooking Lough Foyle, this small but engaging museum packs all it can into the Old Coastguard building for the harbor town of Greencastle. It follows the town's maritime history from the armadas of the 16th century, through emigration to the modern-day lifeboat crews and their selflessly heroic work. There's also a planetarium, complete with a full-dome digital theater presenting more or less hourly shows such as "Sea Monsters—A Prehistoric Adventure" and "Dynamic Earth," plus a small shop and café.

The Harbour, Greencastle, Co. Donegal. www.inishowenmaritime.com. © **074/938-1363.** Museum only: €5 adults; €4 seniors and students; €3 children. Museum plus planetarium: €10 adults; €8 seniors and students; €6 children. June–Aug Tues–Sat 9:30am–5:30pm, Sun noon–5:30pm; last admission 4pm. Sept–May Mon–Fri 10:30am–4pm; last admission 3pm.

Malin Head (Cionn Mhélanna) ★★ NATURE SITE   On this stunning promontory, the road goes no farther. This is Ireland's most northerly point. Even on a sunny day, the wind often howls, and temperatures can be a few degrees colder than just a few miles south. To reach Malin Head, take R242 north until it turns into a small, unnamed road. Following the few signs, meander past a small cluster of houses until you reach rocky **Banba's Crown (*Fíorcheann Éireann*),** the farthest point of the headland. Winds permitting, you can even wander down to the edge of the land and catch a glimpse of some old concrete huts built in World War II as lookout points. To the west of them is the dramatically named **Hell's Hole,** a natural land formation where waves crash deafeningly against the craggy shore. To the east, a path leads to a hermit's cave known as

Aurora Borealis **above Linsfort Church at the Inishowen Peninsula.**

the **Wee House of Malin.** There's a little information board that explains all this—but you may be too busy gazing at the incredible view to notice. Malin Head, Co. Donegal.

Where to Stay on the Inishowen Peninsula

Ballyliffin Lodge ★★ With impressive views of **Malin Head** (see above), this hotel is a relaxing place to stay. Bedrooms, which take full advantage of the gorgeous views, are nice and spacious, with muted, autumnal decor. The hotel can help organize plenty of activities, from horseback riding to surfing and golf. The in-house spa, **Rock Crystal,** provides a welcome respite at the end of a long day's travel, with prices that are a lot more reasonable than they would be in an equivalent place in a more visited part of the country.

Shore Rd., Ballyliffin, Co. Donegal. www.ballyliffinlodge.com. © **074/937-8200.** 40 units. €130–€200 double. **Amenities:** Restaurant; bar; gym; pool; room service; spa; Wi-Fi (free).

Inishowen Gateway ★ This large, modern hotel is a particularly appealing choice for families. It overlooks Lough Swilly—a dramatic view that's either glorious in sunshine or stark and moody in the rain. Guest rooms are basic and quite small, but they tick enough boxes as long as you're not craving anything too fancy. This place has excellent facilities for kids—a supervised play area, Planet Active, has plenty to keep the little ones busy, including game tables, video games, and soft play for younger kids. If you book a family room package, you even get perks such as a free children's' craft workshop per child, movie nights, and so on. *Tip:* Just make sure you ask for a room away from the bar, as it can get a little noisy.

Railway Rd., Buncrana, Co. Donegal. www.inishowengateway.com. © **074/936-1144.** 80 units. €89–€171 double. Free parking. Breakfast included. **Amenities:** Restaurant; bar; gym; pool; spa; Wi-Fi (free).

The Strand ★ Another place with views of Malin Head, this modest but friendly hotel also has views of Pollan Strand, a 2-mile stretch of beach outside Ballyliffin. Accommodations aren't overly fancy, but they're modern and comfortable, with deep tubs in the bathrooms. Family rooms sleep up to four; one room is fully accessible for wheelchair users.

Shore Rd., Ballyliffin, Co. Donegal. www.ballyliffinstrandhotel.com. © **074/937-6107.** 35 units. €75–€120 double. Free parking. Breakfast included. **Amenities:** Restaurant; bar; Wi-Fi (free).

Where to Eat on the Inishowen Peninsula

The Drift Inn ★★ BISTRO/PUB FOOD   This cheerful gastropub in Buncrana only serves food from Thursday to Sunday, but when the kitchen's open, it serves some of the best pub food in the area. You could opt for a duo of Derry lamb and duck (the lamb comes as a loin, the duck as a lollipop), or catch of the day with white beans and asparagus. Try the dark

The Inishowen Gateway hotel in Buncrana overlooks Lough Swilly.

Surfing Pollan Bay.

chocolate ganache with honeycomb for dessert. On Thursday and Friday nights, you can get three courses for two people, plus a bottle of wine, for just €50.

Railway Rd., Buncrana, Co. Donegal. www.thedriftinn.ie. © **074/936-1999.** Main courses €16–€28. Thurs 2–9:30pm; Fri–Sat 1–9:15pm; Sun 1–8:45pm.

Nancy's Barn ★★★ CAFE   With its red shutters and gray stone walls, this old barn looks so pretty from the outside that on a sunny day, you may stop to take a picture and end up having lunch. You'll be so glad you did. Nancy's serves delicious sandwiches, organic salads, and other light meals—their chowder is famous for miles (Chef Kieran Doherty was crowned World Seafood Chowder Champion in 2017). They also bake their all their own breads, cakes, and scones.

On the main road through Ballyliffin, Co. Donegal. www.nancysbarn.ie. © **074/937-6556.** Entrees €7–€15.50. Mon–Fri 10am–5pm; Sat–Sun 9:30am–5:30pm.

The Rusty Nail ★★ GASTROPUB   This is one of those pubs out in the middle of nowhere, where, when you open the door, you are greeted with an open fire and maybe even a live music session. The rear part is the gastropub with tasty favorites like steaks, 6-ounce beef burgers, beer-battered cod with caper mayo, or cornfed chicken. They also do pizzas with ingredients like Fivemiletown goat's cheese.

Crossconnell, Clonmany, Co. Donegal. © **074/937-6116.** Entrees €14.50–€24. June–Aug daily 4–11:30pm; Sept–May Fri 4–11:30pm, Sat 1–11:30pm, Sun 12:30–11:30pm.

Sports & Outdoor Pursuits in the Inishowen Peninsula

GOLF   A definite center for golf in Ireland, the Inishowen Peninsula has four 18-hole golf courses. Two are at **Ballyliffin Golf Club,** Ballyliffin (www.ballyliffingolfclub.com; © **074/937-6119**). Greens fees are €140 to €160. The **North West Golf Club,** Fahan, Buncrana (www.northwest golfclub.com; © **074/936-1715**), founded in 1890, is a par-69 seaside course with greens fees of around €50 weekdays, €60 weekends. After 4pm the twilight rate is €30. **Greencastle Golf Course** in Greencastle (www.greencastlegolfclub.com; © **074/938-1013**) is a par-69 parkland course with greens fees of around €30 to €40.

KAYAKING   If you're feeling adventurous, **Inish Adventures** (www. inishadventures.com; © **074/938-5903**) will take you kayaking along some of Inishowen's most scenic coastline around Moville or under Fort Dunree at Dunree Head, where you get to see sea caves and bird life. The 3-hour trips take place Wednesday to Saturday between Easter and the end of September at 9:30am or 1:30pm and cost €50.

SURFING   The Inishowen Peninsula's northwest coast presents some of the most challenging surfing conditions in Europe. For information and classes, contact the **Inishowen Surf School,** Hill Road, Buncrana (www. inishowensurfschool.com; © **087/777-3323**).

BELFAST

14

T he beautiful and vibrant six counties of Ireland, which are part of the United Kingdom, are all the more fascinating for their complex history. At the epicenter is Belfast, the capital of Northern Ireland—a curious combination of faded grandeur and forward-looking optimism. Belfast boomed in the 19th century as prosperity flowed from its vast textile and shipbuilding industries. The 20th century was not so kind to the city, which spent decades in decline, riven with political divisions and terrorism. But an entire generation has grown up since those troubled years ended in the 1990s, and with them, Belfast has forged a new identity, complete with an energetic art and food scene.

The old Belfast is still here—both in its grand old Victorian buildings and some old-school, never-the-twain-shall-meet Protestant and Catholic neighborhoods. But new developments signal change and renewal, such as the Titanic Quarter, with its sleek new museums and modern visitor attractions. This is a lively, funky, youthful, and complicated city. Come and let it surprise you.

ESSENTIALS
Arriving

BY BUS Ulsterbus (www.translink.co.uk; ✆ 028/9066-6630) runs buses from Dublin to Belfast and towns across Northern Ireland. From Dublin Airport, **AirCoach** (www.aircoach.ie; ✆ 01/844-7118) also runs a regular nonstop service to Belfast. Round-trip tickets are €24 (or £22) and the trip takes just under 2 hours. Round-trip fare for children is €10 (or £9). (Book online for best fares.) In Belfast, the main bus station is **Europa Bus Centre** on Glengall Street.

BY CAR Driving from Dublin to Belfast is easy; just go north up the M1 motorway. From Dublin airport, the journey takes about 90 minutes in good traffic. From Sligo Town, take N16 and A4 west; from there it's 200km (124 miles), about 2½ hours.

BY PLANE Belfast has two airports: **Belfast International** (www.belfastairport.com; ✆ 028/9448-4848) and **Belfast City Airport** (www.belfastcityairport.com; ✆ 028/9093-9093). **Aer Lingus** (www.aerlingus.

FACING PAGE: **The Drawing Office Two bar in the Titanic Hotel.**

com; ☎ **01/814-1111**), **British Airways** (www.ba.com; ☎ **189/0626-747** in Ireland, or 084/4493-0787 in the U.K.), and **easyJet** (www.easyjet. com; ☎ **084/3104-1000**) operate regular scheduled flights from Britain to Belfast. Most intercontinental routes require a change in London or Manchester. You can also fly direct to Belfast from several European cities.

BY TRAIN   Belfast has two train stations: Great Victoria Street Station and Belfast Central Station on East Bridge Street. Contact **Translink** (www.translink.co.uk; ☎ **028/9066-6630**) for tickets. The journey from Dublin takes about 2½ hours; book on www.irishrail.ie.

[FastFACTS] BELFAST

ATMs/Banks   ATMs are easy to find in central Belfast. Several banks around Donegall Square include **Ulster Bank** (☎ **028/9024-4112**) and **Bank of Ireland** (☎ **028/9043-3420**).

Currency   As part of the United Kingdom, Northern Ireland uses the **pound sterling,** not the euro. The cheapest way to get local currency is to use an ATM. The pound/euro exchange rate fluctuates, but it currently hovers between parity and around €1.18.

Dentists   For dental emergencies, your hotel can contact a dentist for you. Otherwise, you could try

Dublin Road Dental Practice, 23 Dublin Rd. (☎ **028/9032-5345**), or **Lisburn Road Dental Clinic,** 424 Lisburn Rd. (☎ **028/9038-2262**).

Doctors   For medical emergencies, dial ☎ **999.** For non-emergencies, your hotel can call you a doctor. Otherwise there's **Ormeau Health Centre,** 120 Ormeau Rd. (☎ **028/9032-6030**), or the **Crumlin Road Health Centre,** 94–100 Crumlin Rd. (☎ **028/9074-1188**).

Emergencies   For police, fire, or other emergencies, dial ☎ **999.**

Pharmacies   Belfast has branches of **Boots the Chemist** at 35–47 Donegall Place (☎ **028/9024-2332**) and 17–21 Great Northern Mall (☎ **028/9031-0530**).

Post Offices   Main branches in Belfast include 16–22 Bedford St. and 12–14 Bridge St.

Taxis   You can catch a taxi at the stand in front of City Hall. Alternatively, try phoning **Value Cabs** (☎ **028/9080-9080**), **Courtesy Cabs** (☎ **028/9032-9988**), or **Gransha Taxis** (☎ **028/9060-2092**).

Visitor Information

The main tourist information center for the city is the **Belfast Welcome Centre** at 9 Donegall Square, BT1 5GJ (www.visitbelfast.com; ☎ **028/9024-6609**). From June to September it's open Monday to Saturday 9am to 7pm and Sunday 11am to 4pm; and October to May Monday to Saturday from 9am to 5:30pm and Sunday 11am to 4pm. The staff at the center can help book accommodations in the city, and they also have a bureau de change and left-luggage facility. Smaller visitor information points are at **Belfast International Airport** (☎ **028/9448-4677**) and **George Best Belfast City Airport** (☎ **028/9093-5372**).

VISITING NORTHERN IRELAND: f.a.q.

What is Northern Ireland? It's still part of Ireland, right?

Yes—and no. It's a part of the island of Ireland, but not the Republic of Ireland.

I'm confused. Is it a different country or not?

Bear with us—this is complicated. Northern Ireland is part of the United Kingdom. It has been a separate entity from the rest of Ireland since 1921. If "entity" sounds a little vague, that's because—get this—there isn't even an official term to describe what Northern Ireland is. (Trust us, we checked.) It's referred to, variously, as a country, a nation, a region, and a province. Note, however, that your mobile phone company will treat Northern Ireland as the U.K., so you may find yourself hit with extra roaming charges. Also, check that your travel insurance and any car-rental agreements are equally valid in Northern Ireland.

Will I need to show my passport at the border crossing?

No, because there really isn't a border crossing. In fact, it can be hard to tell when you've entered Northern Ireland—except that the road signs change from miles to kilometers. Signs around the border usually show both.

What are those letters and numbers at the end of Northern Irish addresses?

They're British-style postal codes and almost every address in Northern Ireland has one. This is actually a big advantage if you're driving, as it makes GPS navigation much easier.

Does Northern Ireland use the euro?

No. The currency in Northern Ireland is the **British pound (sterling).** In practice, euros are accepted in some border areas, at tourist attractions and hotels; however, you may be given change in pounds. (And just try using those pounds in the rest of Ireland!) And if you're traveling onward to Britain, be aware that Northern Irish pounds look completely different from standard ones, and many businesses won't accept them. Any bank in England will change Northern Irish pounds to English pounds for free. Just walk to the counter.

What about Brexit? Has that changed anything?

Everything and nothing. The U.K. left the EU in January 2020, and because it is part of the United Kingdom, Northern Ireland had to leave the EU as well. To avoid a hard border between Northern Ireland and the Republic of Ireland, however, Northern Ireland still adheres to EU Customs rules—an economic arrangement that at press time was causing some tension. *Practically* speaking, nothing at all should have changed about your travel arrangements, no matter what country you're from.

City Layout

Small and easily traversed, central Belfast is best explored by walking. The main tourist districts are as follows.

CATHEDRAL QUARTER North of Donegall Square, surrounding Donegall Street, **Belfast Cathedral** (p. 504) presides over this area with many vast Victorian warehouses. The district has quite a lively feel, with plenty of interesting shops.

CITY CENTER Dominated by the impressive domed City Hall (p. 498), the bustling **Donegall Square** area is the best place for shopping, particularly along **Donegall Place,** which extends north from the square, onto **Royal Avenue. Bedford Street,** which travels south from Donegall Square, becomes **Dublin Road,** which leads to:

GOLDEN MILE Southwest of Donegall Square, the stretch of **Great Victoria Street** leading to Bradbury Place is the city's best address for restaurants and pubs, although it's a bit hyperbolically named. As one local said to us, "It's not a mile and it's not golden. But it's nice enough."

TITANIC QUARTER Northeast of the city center, a series of big commercial developments have recently gone up around Belfast Harbour. Here you'll find several attractions such as **Titanic Belfast** (p. 500).

UNIVERSITY QUARTER The leafy area around Queen's University (p. 505) contains the Botanic Gardens (p. 496), art galleries, and museums, as well as a buzzing nightlife scene.

Getting Around

BY BIKE Belfast has a public bike-sharing system. "Belfast Bikes" are available at 30 unmanned rental stations around the city. You can set up an account at the station's terminal, or by downloading the *Nextbike* app for your phone. When you're done, simply return the bike to any station. Prices start at £1 per half-hour. See **www.belfastbikes.co.uk** for details.

BY BUS **Metro** (www.translink.co.uk; ✆ **028/9066-6630**) city buses depart from Donegall Square East, West, and North, plus Upper Queen Street, Wellington Place, Chichester Street, and Castle Street, and from bus stops throughout the city. The cheapest way to use the buses is to buy a Metro Day ticket, which allows unlimited travel all day for £3.50.

BY CAR If you've brought a **car** into Belfast, it's best to leave it parked and take public transport or walk. If you must drive and want to park downtown, look for a blue p sign that shows a parking lot. No parking is allowed in "control zones," marked by pink-and-yellow signs.

BY TAXI **Taxis** are available at all main rail stations, ports, and airports, and in front of City Hall. Most metered taxis are London-type black cabs with a yellow disk on the windows. You can hail a taxi on the street, although it rarely takes long for a cab to arrive if you call.

EXPLORING BELFAST

Belfast's wealthy past has left the city with some handsome industrial remnants. However, it's the more troubled, 20th-century Belfast that many visitors find most intriguing, and a **Black Taxi Tour ★★★** (see below) is a unique way to explore that history. Meanwhile, there's a whole mini-industry of attractions related to the most famous shipwreck in history. Because the SS *Titanic* was built in Belfast—a curious symbol of

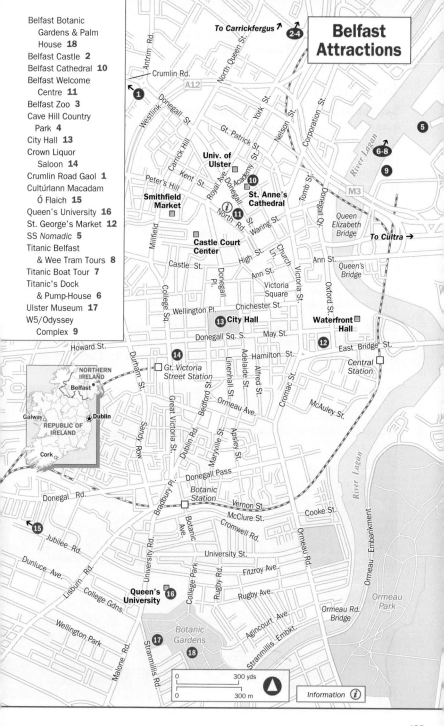

**Belfast
Attractions**

To Carrickfergus ↗
2-4

To Carrickfergus ↗

Antrim Rd.
Crumlin Rd.
A12
1
North Queen St.
Westlink
Donegall St.
York St.
Nelson St.
Corporation St.
Gt. Patrick St.
Carrick Hill
Kent St.
Royal Ave.
Donegall St.
Academy St.
River Lagan
5
Peter's Hill
Univ. of Ulster
10
Tomb St.
Donegall Qy.
6-8
9
M3
Smithfield Market
North St.
11
St. Anne's Cathedral
Waring St.
Queen Elizabeth Bridge
Millfield
Castle Court Center
High St.
Church Ln.
Ann St.
Queen's Bridge
To Cultra →
Castle St.
Donegall Pl.
Ann St.
Victoria St.
Oxford St.
College Sq.
Wellington Pl.
Victoria Square
Chichester St.
13 **City Hall**
Waterfront Hall
Donegall Sq. S.
May St.
12
East Bridge St.
Howard St.
14
Hamilton St.
Central Station
Durham St.
Gt. Victoria Street Station
Adelaide St.
Linenhall St.
Alfred St.
Croniac St.
NORTHERN IRELAND
Belfast
Great Victoria St.
Bedford St.
Ormeau Ave.
Apsley St.
McAuley St.
Galway
REPUBLIC OF IRELAND
Dublin
Sandy Row
Dublin Rd.
Maryville St.
Cork
Donegall Pass
Donegal Rd.
Bradbury Pl.
Botanic Station
Vernon St.
River Lagan
McClure St.
15
Botanic Ave.
Cromwell Rd.
Cooke St.
Ormeau Rd.
Ormeau Embankment
Jubilee Rd.
University St.
Dunluce Ave.
Lisburn Rd.
College Gdns.
Fitzroy Ave.
Rugby Rd.
Rugby Ave.
Queen's University
16
College Park Ave.
Ormeau Rd. Bridge
Ormeau Park
Wellington Park
Malone Rd.
17
Botanic Gardens
Stranmillis Rd.
Agincourt Ave.
Stranmillis Embkt.
18

0		300 yds
0		300 m

Information *(i)*

495

pride for natives of this city—shipwreck aficionados (aka "Titanoraks") are drawn to the bold **Titanic Belfast** museum (p. 500) and the **Titanic's Dock & Pump-House** (p. 501) in the newly regenerated harbor district.

Top Attractions

Belfast Botanic Gardens & Palm House ★★ GARDENS   Dating from 1828, these gardens were first laid out by the Belfast Botanic and Horticultural Society, but their most important feature came along 10 years later, when noted Belfast architect Charles Lanyon designed the beautiful glass-and-cast-iron conservatory. Now known as the Palm House, this curvilinear Victorian glasshouse contains an excellent variety of tropical plants, including sugarcane, coffee, cinnamon, banana, aloe, ivory nut, rubber, bamboo, guava, and birds of paradise. If the weather's fine, stroll in the outdoor rose gardens, which date back to 1927. The **Ulster Museum** (p. 502) is also on the grounds.

College Park, Botanic Ave., Belfast, BT7 1LP. ℭ **028/9049-1813.** Free admission. Palm House: Apr–Sept daily 10am–4:45pm; Oct–Mar daily 10am–3:45pm (check if Palm House is open before you visit). Gardens: Mid-Apr to Aug daily 10am–9pm; Sept to mid-Apr daily 10am–sunset (hours can vary in winter; call ahead).

Black Taxi Tour ★★★ TOUR   For many years, Belfast was best known for its most conflicted neighborhoods, where in the 1970s and '80s protest and violence occurred daily. Peace has held on the Catholic Falls

The Victorian-era Palm House, centerpiece of the Belfast Botanic Gardens.

the art of conflict: BELFAST'S STREET MURALS

Painted by amateur artists—albeit very talented ones—the huge street murals in West Belfast tell tales of history, strife, anger, or peace. The densest concentration is around the **Falls and Shankill roads**—the epicenter of the conflict during the Troubles, from the late 1960s to the mid-1990s. The Falls Road is staunchly Catholic and Republican (largely those who want Ireland united as a single country). Shankill, just half a mile away, is resolutely Protestant and Loyalist (those who want Northern Ireland to remain part of the United Kingdom).

While all are deeply political, there is a noticeable difference in the tone of these murals. Those on the Falls Road tend to be about solidarity with the downtrodden (and not just in Ireland—you'll see murals about war and oppression in other parts of the world, too). By contrast, the Shankill murals are more strident, featuring more violent and threatening imagery, although some of the most offensive examples were removed a few years ago.

Perhaps the most famous political mural in Ireland, if not the world, is on the corner of Falls Road and Sevastopol Street: a mural of the late hunger striker **Bobby Sands** (1954–81). Locals in all districts are very proud of their murals and are fine with visitors taking photos. Still, you should exercise the usual caution you would in any rough city neighborhood. It's best to steer clear of these parts of town on **parade days**—ostensibly celebratory events, they tend toward displays of nationalism, erupting into street violence. The biggest, and most controversial, is the Protestant "Orange Order" parade on July 12 (marking the

Battle of the Boyne in 1690, which was basically Year Zero for the big sectarian divide in Ireland; see p. 54). Any parades likely to cause trouble are well covered by the local media, so it's easy to know when one is coming up. From time to time there are P.R.-led attempts to sanitize these events, promoting them as inclusive and celebratory, but don't buy it. They remain contentious and should be avoided.

The best, safest, and certainly the most informative way to see the murals is to take a **Black Taxi Tour ★★★** (p. 496). The tours are a real Belfast highlight and could hardly be more convenient—the drivers will pick you up at your hotel and drop you off anywhere you like in the city.

Street art of a less political nature has also begun popping up around the city in recent years, particularly around the Cathedral Quarter, and the 2-hour **Seedhead Street Art Walking Tour** (www. seedheadarts.com) is led by local artists who will show you the latest masterpieces; tours cost £10.

Road and its nearby parallel, the Protestant Shankill Road, for more than 20 years. A growing industry supports this enterprising tourism initiative, with the Black Taxi Tour company's **Belfast Political & Mural** tour by far the best option. Tours are conducted in black cabs that take you through the neighborhoods, past the barbed wire, towering "peace walls" dividing communities, and partisan murals, as guides explain their significance. Drivers, who are all locals, are relaxed, patient, and unbiased, with a talent

Belfast street murals can be viewed via open-top bus tours or Black Taxi tours.

for explaining this complicated history to outsiders in an easy and engaging way. Tours aren't just limited to politics; the guides will also take you to see the *Titanic* shipyard or on a daylong tour to see the locations where *Game of Thrones* was filmed (one of many such tours that have sprung up; see box on p. 539). The standard tour lasts about 90 minutes, and guides will pick you up and drop you off anywhere in the city.

www.belfasttours.com. ℗ **028/9064-2264.** £45 for up to 2 passengers, then £20 for each additional passenger, up to 6 people.

City Hall ★ ARCHITECTURAL SITE   The clearest remaining testament to the city's grand industrial past, this domed building of granite, marble, and stained glass dominates central Belfast. Built in classical Renaissance style in 1906, it has white Portland stone walls and a soft green copper dome. Several statues dot the grounds, including a grim-faced Queen Victoria, who stands out front looking as if she wished she were anywhere else. Bronze figures around her represent the textile and shipbuilding industries that powered Belfast's success. There's also a memorial to the victims of the *Titanic* disaster. Inside the building, the elaborate entry hall is heavy with marble but lightened by stained glass and a rotunda with a painted ceiling. A 16-room exhibition center hosts changing displays on art or the city and its history. Free hour-long guided tours offer a surprisingly absorbing insight into the building's history.

Donegall Sq. North, Belfast, BT1 5GS. ℗ **028/9032-0202.** Free admission. City Hall building: Mon–Sun 8:30am–5pm. City Hall grounds: May–Sept 7am–9pm; Oct–May 7am–7pm. Closed mid–Nov to mid-Jan for Christmas market. Guided tours: Times vary; check before visiting.

Crown Liquor Saloon ★★★ ARCHITECTURAL SITE/PUB   Easily the most impressive Victorian pub in the city, and possibly the best building in Belfast, the Crown Liquor Saloon piles on the atmosphere. The old "gin palace" owes its ornate appearance to Italian workers who came to Ireland in the late 19th century to work on churches but ended up building this, in 1873. Some of the finer features definitely have something ecclesiastical about them, from the stained glass in the windows to the pewlike "snugs," their elaborately carved doors designed to shield the more refined class of Victorians from their fellow drinkers. The floors are intricately tiled, and the ceiling is gorgeous hammered copper. This place was considered so important to the iconography of Belfast that it was actually bought for the nation by the National Trust in the 1970s, ensuring its impeccable upkeep while it continues to run as a working pub.

46 Great Victoria St., Belfast, BT2 7BA. www.nicholsonspubs.co.uk/thecrownliquor saloonbelfast. ℂ **028/9024-3187.** Mon–Sat 11:30am–midnight; Sun 12:30–11pm.

Crumlin Road Gaol ★★ HISTORIC SITE   From 1846 until its closure 150 years later, Crumlin Road Gaol (known as "The Crum") was one of the most notorious prisons in Northern Ireland. Improbable though it sounds, the Crum is now used as a conference center and wedding venue (festive!), although the original structure has been excellently preserved.

Spring Market at Belfast's City Hall, on Donegall Square.

The building brings to mind the popular image of a Victorian-era prison, with its forbidding, fortresslike exterior and row upon row of cells. An informative 90-minute tour takes you around the building, filling in some fascinating details of what prison life was like. It would take a hard person indeed not to shudder as you walk down the claustrophobic underground tunnel connecting to the old courthouse across the street or stand inside the condemned cell from which prisoners made their final journeys until 1961. Book online for ticket discounts.

53–55 Crumlin Rd., Belfast, BT4 6ST. www.crumlinroadgaol.com. ℂ **028/9074-1500.** Admission £12 adults; £10 seniors and students; £6.50 children 5–15; free for children 4 and under; £30 families. Apr–Sept Sun–Thurs 10:30am–3pm, Fri–Sat 10:30am–6pm. Oct–Mar daily 10:30am–3pm.

St. George's Market ★★ INDOOR MARKET Built in 1896, the iron-and-glass **St. George's Market** has a number of different street markets with live music and food and craft stalls. It's a fun, vibrant place to visit on weekends. On Friday, the **Variety Market** (6am–3pm) is packed with 250 stalls of fresh produce, antiques, clothing, and bric-a-brac. On Saturdays, the **City Food & Craft Market** (9am–3pm) specializes in artisan foods, with plenty of tempting fresh snacks on offer, plus an assortment of local crafts. The **Sunday Market** (10am–4pm) is a happy combination of the two, although the balance tends to be in favor of crafts. It's a great place for coffee, good eats, and local atmosphere.

May and Oxford sts. ℂ **028/9043-5704.**

SS Nomadic ★★ SHIP The last working ship in the White Star Line fleet, the *Nomadic* was built in Belfast as a tender to the most famous ocean liner in history—the ill-fated SS *Titanic*. (Tenders were small steamships that ferried passengers and supplies to and from the oceangoing behemoths.) After seeing action in both World Wars—first press-ganged into service by the French Navy, then used by the British to evacuate. After a decade-long restoration, *Nomadic* has been returned to her original 1911 glory. You can tour the vessel, from the cramped and claustrophobic crew quarters to the bridge and upper deck. Daily ticket numbers are limited due to space—book in advance if possible.

Hamilton Dock, Queens Rd., Belfast, BT3 9DT. www.nomadicbelfast.com. ℂ **028/9076-6386.** Admission (includes entry to Titanic Belfast) £19.50 adults; £15.50 seniors and students Mon–Fri only; £8.75 children 5–15; free for children 4 and under; £48 families. May–June and Nov–Mar Mon and Thurs–Sun 11:30am–3:30pm; July–Aug daily 11:30am–4:30pm; Sept–Oct daily 11:30am–3:30pm.

Titanic Belfast ★★★ MUSEUM This ambitious and impressive museum, which opened to huge fanfare in 2012, tells the story of the *Titanic* in revelatory detail. Located next to the site where the doomed vessel was built, the angular aluminum-clad frontage juts out in four directions at the height of the ship's actual bow. You can explore the

Titanic Belfast discovery tour.

museum yourself or take an hour-long "Discovery Tour" of its innovative galleries. Exhibitions cover everything from the *Titanic*'s construction to her triumphant launch, disastrous sinking, and the lasting cultural phenomenon that rose in her wake. A ride takes you on a virtual tour of the shipyard to see how *Titanic* and her sister ship, *Olympic,* were built. In a split-level gallery you can even "visit" the wreck. Finally, the **Ocean Exploration Centre** offers high-tech exhibits on the science of sea exploration, including a live link to an undersea probe. Needless to say, an extremely well-stocked gift shop is at the end. Crowds can swell at busy times, so it's advisable to book ahead in summer.

1 Olympic Way, Belfast, BT3 9DP. www.titanicbelfast.com. ℂ **028/9076-6386.** Admission (includes entry to SS *Nomadic*) £19.50 adults; £15.50 seniors and students Mon–Fri only; £8.75 children 5–15; free for children 4 and under; £48 families. **Discovery Tour:** £10 adults; £8 children. Parking £2 for 1st hr., £1 per hr. afterward. May Mon and Thurs–Sun 9am–6pm; June Mon and Thurs–Sun 9am–7pm; July–Aug daily 9am–7pm; Sept daily 9am–6pm; Oct daily 9am–5pm; Nov–Mar Mon and Thurs–Sun 10am–5pm. Last admission 1 hr. 40 min. before closing.

Titanic's Dock & Pump-House ★★ MUSEUM   Another of Belfast's ship-related attractions, this fascinating self-guided tour takes you around the dry docks at the old Harland and Wolff shipyard, where *Titanic* and *Olympic* were constructed from 1909–11. Designed to appeal to a general audience, not just enthusiasts, it's a unique way to learn what it was like to work here at the turn of the last century, when Belfast was a great industrial city. The enormous Edwardian pump-house, which could drain a staggering 21 million gallons of water in just over 90 minutes, is worth the price of admission alone. An audiovisual room includes rare film footage of the *Titanic in situ* at the dock. The large visitor center has interesting exhibits, a gift shop, and a cafe. At the time of writing, a distillery was being added to the Pump-House building, scheduled to open in May 2022; check online for revised opening hours and prices.

Queen's Rd., Queen's Island, Belfast, BT3 9DT. www.titanicsdock.com. ℂ **028/9073-7813.** Admission £5 adults; £3.50 children 5–16; free for children under 5; £12 families. Parking £1.50 per hr. Apr–Oct daily 10am–5pm; Nov–Dec daily 10am–4pm; Jan–Mar daily 10:30am–5pm. Prices and times may change—check before visiting.

A brief HISTORY OF NORTHERN IRELAND

Shelves upon shelves of books have been written in an attempt to unravel the complicated history and politics of Northern Ireland. Only a fool would expect to be able to do it clearly and concisely, in just a few short paragraphs. So here goes.

In 1921, after nearly a thousand years of British occupation and more rebellions and civil wars than you could count, Ireland won its independence from Great Britain. At least, *most* of it did. Britain didn't want to give it all up, nor did the Protestant, pro-British majority in parts of the north. So a compromise was reached: The northern counties of Antrim, Armagh, Down, Fermanagh, Londonderry, and Tyrone (which are part of the province of "Ulster") were split off to form a new country called Northern Ireland. This, in turn, would be part of the United Kingdom—a U.K. state, effectively. It was a messy deal, but the violence would end. That, at least, was the plan.

It didn't work out well. The Catholic minority in Northern Ireland was treated appallingly, discriminated against in almost every aspect of life, from work and housing to elections and policing. Not unreasonably, they wondered if they would be better off in the Republic of Ireland, too. Things came to a head in the late 1960s, when the Catholic population began an intense civil rights campaign. Their marches and demonstrations were crushed by the authorities, sometimes with brute violence—which spurred the reemergence of the Irish Republican Army (IRA), a paramilitary group that had first appeared early in the 20th century.

In 1971 things reached a fever pitch in the "Bloody Sunday" massacre, when the British army opened fire on a peaceful protest in Derry (p. 553). After that, the IRA launched a terror campaign aimed at civilians, both in Northern Ireland and the British mainland. Bombs

Ulster Museum ★★★ MUSEUM One of Ireland's best museums, the Ulster Museum has a comprehensive collection of everything from dinosaur bones and prehistoric artifacts to art and other treasures from Ireland and around the world. Highlights include 16th- to 18th-century Dutch and Italian paintings; a hoard of priceless 16th-century Spanish jewelry, recovered off the coast near Belfast in the 1960s; clothes, textiles, and ceramics from Asia and Africa. The Life and Death in Ancient Egypt exhibit has about 2,000 artifacts from Pharaonic times, as well as items from ancient Mesopotamia, Rome, and Greece.

At the Botanic Gardens, Belfast, BT9 5AB. www.nmni.com/um. © **028/9044-0000.** Free admission; book online in advance. Tues–Sun 10am–5pm. Closed Mon (except public holidays).

The Wee Tram Tour ★★ TOUR A fun way to see the Titanic Quarter, this lively tour takes you around the docks in about half an hour—including a few areas you can't see any other way. The guides are adept at telling the history as a story. The circular route includes all the highlights of the docks, including the museums, **HMS *Caroline***, the last surviving were planted in bus stops, cafes, schools, pubs, and shopping malls, killing many innocent people. Politicians were assassinated. (In 1985, Prime Minister Margaret Thatcher was inches away from being killed by a bomb.) The British army, meanwhile, patrolled Northern Irish streets and colluded with pro–U.K. terrorist groups. People were thrown in jail for crimes they didn't commit. Those in jail went on hunger strikes to protest their treatment. There were shootings and bombings almost weekly, far too many to list here. Over 3,000 died, both here and in Britain, and tens of thousands were injured—mostly just ordinary folks who were in the wrong place at the wrong time.

The struggle continued for decades, until the so-called "Good Friday Agreement" was negotiated, with the help of U.S. President Bill Clinton, in 1997. While it didn't end all political and religious violence, it did change the atmosphere considerably. A massive constitutional overhaul, the agreement ended institutional discrimination against the Catholic minority, installed power sharing, and devolved government. Paramilitary groups such as the IRA agreed to disarm. Mortal enemies agreed to share power together, peacefully.

Skip forward 24 years, and the region is still at peace. Sporadic flare-ups of violence do happen, the "Orange" marches still stir up bad feelings, but nothing remotely approaching what it was. Meanwhile, Brexit has opened a whole new can of worms. Northern Ireland voted heavily to remain in the E.U. but was forced to leave along with the rest of the U.K.— leading some to speculate that, were it ever put to a vote, the Protestant majority could be prepared to consider Irish reunification as the better option. Others call that wishful thinking, but the fact that it's even conceivable is a seismic shift. Only time will tell.

ship of the Battle of Jutland (1916), permanently moored here, and the towering landmarks **Samson and Goliath**—two 140m (459-ft.) cranes that have come to symbolize the docks and Belfast's industrial heritage. Trams run every half-hour from either **Titanic Belfast** (p. 500) or **SS Nomadic** (p. 500). You buy tickets on board.

Departs from Titanic Belfast, 1 Olympic Way, Belfast, BT3 9DP; or SS Nomadic, Hamilton Dock, Queens Rd., Belfast, BT3 9DT. www.theweetram.com. No phone. Admission £5 adults; £4 seniors, students, and children 5–16; free for children under 5; £15 families. Tours every 30 min from Titanic Belfast and SS Nomadic daily June–Aug noon–5pm; weekends only Mar–May and Sept–Oct; noon–4:30pm.

Other Attractions

Belfast Castle ★ CASTLE Northwest of downtown and 120m (394 ft.) above sea level stands Belfast Castle, its 80-hectare (198-acre) estate spreading down the slopes of what is now **Cave Hill Country Park ★** (p. 504). Dating from 1870, this was the family residence of the third marquis of Donegall, and it was built in the style of Balmoral Castle, the Scottish residence of the British monarch. The outside is more interesting than the inside, which has been modernized and is now a popular wedding venue. The estate is a lovely place to visit, offering sweeping views of Belfast and the lough. Its cellars contain a Victorian arcade, a restaurant (open daily 11am–5pm and Tues until 9pm), and a shop selling antiques and crafts. According to legend, a white cat brought the castle residents luck, so look around for carvings featuring cats.

Signposted off Antrim Rd., 4km (2½ miles) N of city center, Belfast, BT15 5GR. www.belfastcastle.co.uk. © **028/9077-6925.** Free admission and parking. Tues–Thurs 9:30am–7pm; Fri–Sat 9:30am–9pm; Sun 9am–4:30pm; Mon 9:30am–4pm.

Belfast Cathedral (St. Anne's) ★ CATHEDRAL   Although the foundation stone on this monumental cathedral, also known as **St. Anne's,** was laid in 1899, it remained incomplete for more than a century; even now it still awaits a steeple. Blending architectural genres from Romanesque to Victorian to modern, the huge structure is more attractive inside than out. In the nave, the ceiling soars above black-and-white marble walls and stone floors, and stained-glass windows flood it with color. Carvings representing life in Belfast top the 10 pillars. The cathedral's most impressive features are the delicate mosaic ceilings of the tympanum, and a baptistery made of thousands of pieces of glass.

Donegall St., Belfast, BT1 2HB. www.belfastcathedral.org. © **028/9032-8332.** £5 adults; £4 seniors and students; £3 children 5–12; free for children 4 and under; £12 families. Wed–Sat 11am–3pm. Closed Mon. Sunday service 11am.

Cave Hill Country Park ★★ PARK   Atop a 360m (1,181-ft.) basalt cliff, this park offers panoramic views, walking trails, and archaeological and historical sights (including **Belfast Castle** ★, above). Its name derives from five small caves thought to have been Neolithic iron mines; several other ancient sites are scattered about the place, often unmarked. These include stone cairns, dolmens, and **McArt's Fort**—the remains of an ancient defensive hill fort in which Wolfe Tone and his fellow United Irishmen planned the 1798 rebellion. It's mostly gone now, but you can explore the ruins, which sit atop the park's most famous viewpoint. The **Cave Hill Visitor Centre,** on the second floor of Belfast Castle, contains information on the history of the park and the castle. You can also pick up maps of the park here. For a great walk around the entire park, check out **www.walkni.com**, a site promoting hiking in Northern Ireland. To explore the park's mountain-bike trails, rent a **Belfast Bikes** (p. 494) or hire a proper mountain bike at **Full Cycle,** 326 Crumlin Rd. (© **028/9074-1569**); make reservations at least 24 hours in advance, preferably a full week ahead.

Visitor Centre: Belfast Castle, off Antrim Rd., 6.5km (4 miles) N of city center, Belfast, BT15 5GR. www.belfastcity.gov.uk/cavehill. © **028/9077-6925.** Free admission. Park: 7:30am–dusk. Visitor Centre: Tues–Sat 9am–10pm, Sun 9am–5:30pm; Mon 9am–6pm.

Cultúrlann McAdam Ó Fiaich ★ CULTURAL CENTER   Located in a former church building on the notorious Falls Road (a Republican stronghold during the Troubles), this cultural and arts center is a friendly, inclusive place. It has a handy cafe, a tourist information point, and a well-stocked shop full of Irish interest books, traditional crafts, and music CDs. The **Dillon Gallery,** West Belfast's only public art gallery, showcases work by Irish artists and those from farther afield. The center's theater has a varied program of traditional music, plays, spoken word events, and films. Check website for listings.

216 Falls Rd., Belfast, BT12 6AH. www.culturlann.ie/en. ℭ **028/9096-4180.** Free admission. Mon–Fri 9am–5:30pm; Sat 9am–5pm; Sun 1–4pm.

Queen's University ★ UNIVERSITY   Founded in 1845 during the reign of Queen Victoria to provide nondenominational higher education, this is Northern Ireland's most prestigious university. The turreted main building, an imposing example of 19th-century Tudor Revival, may remind you of England's Oxford; its design was based on the Founder's Tower at Magdalen College. But there's much more to this university, which sprawls through 250 buildings and where 17,500 students are studying at any given time. The surrounding neighborhood is a quiet, attractive place to wander, and University Square on the north side of campus is simply beautiful. At one end of the square, Union Theological College, dating from 1853, housed Northern Ireland's Parliament after the partition of Ireland in 1921 until its abolition in 1972. Tours of the campus can be arranged on request; contact the university's welcome center for details. Access to parts of the campus may be restricted during exam times.

Queen's Welcome Centre, Queen's University, University Rd., Belfast, BT7 1NN. www.qub.ac.uk/home/welcome-centre. ℭ **028/9024-5133.** Free admission; tour £3.50. Mon–Fri 8:30am–5pm; also Sat–Sun 11am–4pm during summer vacation.

Especially for Kids

Belfast Zoo ★ ZOO   On the northern slopes of Cave Hill, near **Cave Hill Country Park** ★★ (p. 504), this zoo emphasizes conservation and education. Many rare species are bred here, including Hawaiian geese, lowland gorillas, red lechwe (a kind of antelope), sea bears, Barbary lions, and golden lion tamarins. The **Rainforest House** is a tropical environment

Queen's University, founded in 1845.

14

BELFAST | Exploring Belfast

filled with birds and jungle creatures. Most activity days are quite kid-oriented, although there are some more grown-up events too, such as all-day photography competitions. Special tours and events run all year. Check the website for up-to-date listings.

Antrim Rd., Belfast, BT36 7PN. www.belfastzoo.co.uk. ℂ **028/9077-6277.** Admission £13.50 adults; £6.75 seniors, students, and children 4–16; free for children 3 and under; £38 families. Apr–Sept daily 10am–6pm (last admission 4:30pm); Oct–Mar daily 10am–4pm (last admission 2:30pm).

W5 ★ SCIENCE CENTER   This great science play center for kids is part of the Odyssey Complex, a huge modern entertainment center in the Titanic District. Properly known as "Whowhatwhenwherewhy"—you can see why they abbreviate it to W5—this high-tech, interactive learning environment lets kids try out over 250 individual activities, all in the spirit of science-based fun. They can create animated cartoons, try to beat a lie detector test, and present the weather on TV. The Odyssey also contains a cinema, bowling alley, shops, restaurants, and a sports arena.

2 Queen's Quay, BT3 9QQ. www.w5online.co.uk. ℂ **028/9046-7700.** Admission £11 adults; £9 seniors, students, and children; children under 3 free; £34.50–£36.50 families. Mon–Sat 10am–8pm, Sun 10am–6pm. Last admission 1 hr. before closing.

Outlying Attractions: Belfast Lough

Belfast built up around the mouth of this coastal inlet; today the city's outer suburbs stretch along its north and south shores. There are a few worthwhile sights here. A dozen miles or so to the northeast, just off the M3 motorway, the castle town of **Carrickfergus** offers a nice break from the hustle and bustle of the city. Locals like to say that Carrickfergus was thriving when Belfast was a sandbank, and looking around its winding medieval streets, it's easy to believe. On the other side of the Lough, **Cultra** is home to the excellent **Ulster Folk & Transport Museum** ★★★ (see below).

Andrew Jackson Cottage and U.S. Rangers Centre ★ HISTORIC HOUSE   This re-created 18th-century dwelling is built in the style of cottages once lived in by Scotch-Irish settlers—including the ancestors of Andrew Jackson (1767–1845), the seventh president of the United States and the first president of Irish heritage. The cottage is decorated as it would have looked in the 1750s; also here is an exhibition devoted to the life of Jackson. Although it's a faithful reproduction, the house isn't the actual home of the Jacksons—that was demolished in the 19th century. Next door is a very small museum devoted to the U.S. Rangers, who were stationed in Carrickfergus during World War II.

2 Boneybefore, Carrickfergus, BT38 7EQ. ℂ **028/9335-8222.** Free admission. Wed–Sun 11am–3pm.

Carrickfergus Castle ★ CASTLE   Built in 1180 by John de Courcy, this massive Norman keep was Ireland's first real castle, designed to loom darkly over the entrance to Belfast Lough. Centuries later, its defensive location would prove prophetic, as William of Orange landed here on

Carrickfergus Castle guards the entrance to Belfast Lough.

Titanic exhibition at the Ulster Folk & Transport Museum.

June 14, 1690, en route to the Battle of the Boyne. The central part dates to the 12th century, the thick outer walls were completed 100 years later, and the gun ports are a comparatively new addition (only 400 years old). The outside is more impressive than the inside, which has been largely outfitted to trigger kids' interests, with waxwork figures riding horses, threatening to shoot people over the walls, et cetera. Sometimes actors in medieval costume add a touch of hammy fun. The castle has a visitor center and a small museum. In the summer, medieval banquets, a medieval fair, and a crafts market all add a touch of play and pageantry. *Note:* At this writing, a large part of the castle was closed for major repair work. This should be completed before 2021, but it may be wise to check ahead. Marine Hwy., Carrickfergus, BT38 7BG. ℗ **028/9335-8262.** Admission £5.25 adults; £3.95 seniors, £3.50 seniors, students, and children 5–17; free for children 4 and under; £15.75 families. Tues–Sun 9:30am–4:30pm. Closed Mon (except bank holidays). Last admission 30 min. before closing.

Ulster Folk & Transport Museum ★★★ MUSEUM/HERITAGE SITE

One of Northern Ireland's best living-history museums, the Ulster Folk & Transport Museum is made up of buildings rescued from demolition and reconstructed, piece by piece. Mostly dating from the 19th century, they include houses, schools, a chemist's shop, a pub, and even a working farm. The level of detail is impressive—the shops are fully decked out as they would have been in Victorian times, complete with shelves overflowing with authentic bottles, jars, and items of clothing. As you wander about, you may encounter a Victorian housewife engaged in day-to-day domestic drudgery or watch a village blacksmith working away in a forge using authentic period methods. The connected **Ulster Transport Museum** contains a wealth of historic vehicles, from old cars and small planes to buses and trams as well as a trove of rare Titanic artifacts.

Signposted off A2 (Bangor Rd.), Cultra, Hollywood, BT18 0EU. www.nmni.com/uftm. ℂ **028/9042-8428.** Folk or Transport Museum: £8.44 adults; £6.56 seniors and students; £5.16 children 5–17; free for children 4 and under; £17.80–£23.45 families. Mar–Sept Tues–Sun 10am–5pm; Oct–Feb Tues–Fri 10am–4pm, Sat–Sun 11am–4pm. Closed Mon except public holidays.

WHERE TO STAY IN BELFAST

Belfast's hotel scene increasingly rivals Dublin's, but at a significantly lower price. There are good hotels in every price range—the farther you go from the city center, the better the bargain. A good money-saving tip: Several hotels now offer packages that include entry to some of the city's biggest attractions. We've included some of the better offers below.

Expensive

Europa Hotel ★★ For some time this has been the lodging of choice for politicians, diplomats, and celebrities visiting Belfast. Perhaps that's why the IRA targeted it so heavily—the hotel was bombed 33 times between 1970 and 1994. You wouldn't know it to look at it now. The decor is subtly masculine; the lobby has marble floors and a modern gas fireplace. The large guest rooms are contemporary in style, with comfortable beds and sizeable bathrooms. Downstairs is a piano bar and the laidback—and slightly generic—**The Causerie** restaurant. Book yourself in for the afternoon tea, complete with sandwiches, scones, and cake. Check the website for deals such as dinner, bed-and-breakfast discounts or a package that includes entry to Titanic Belfast.

Great Victoria St., Belfast, BT2 7AP. www.europahotelbelfast.com ℂ **028/9027-1066.** 272 units. £95–£225 double, £479 suite. Parking £20 per day. Breakfast not included in lower rates. **Amenities:** Restaurant; 2 bars; gym; room service; Wi-Fi (free).

Grand Central ★★★ Opened in 2018, this hotel in the city center is the tallest in Belfast, offering panoramic views from the upper floors. Rooms are a good size, with sophisticated, neutral decor and orthopedic beds. Bathrooms are not huge, but they are big enough and feature rainfall showers. In the end, though, the views are the thing here—you get sweeping, bird's-eye views of the City Hall dome, the city center, and the hills beyond from all the upper-floor rooms. The restaurants and bars have high ceilings and enormous windows, letting in a flood of light. The ground-floor **Grand Café** is open in the morning for breakfast and coffee, and the **Seahorse Bar and Restaurant** offers upscale French-influenced cuisine and local craft gins. The trendy, 23rd-story **Observatory Bar** offers the best views in the house and pricey cocktails. Add exceptional service, and this is a great option.

9-15 Bedford St., Belfast, BT2 7FF. www.grandcentralhotelbelfast.com. ℂ **028/9023-1066.** 300 units. £165–£236 double. Lower rates do not include breakfast. Discount at nearby car park—£8 5pm–10am. **Amenities:** Restaurant; bar; cafe; gym; Wi-Fi (free).

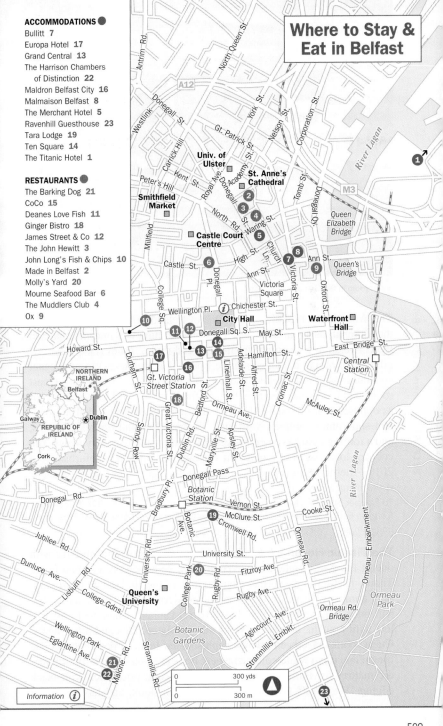

Where to Stay & Eat in Belfast

ACCOMMODATIONS ●
Bullitt **7**
Europa Hotel **17**
Grand Central **13**
The Harrison Chambers
 of Distinction **22**
Maldron Belfast City **16**
Malmaison Belfast **8**
The Merchant Hotel **5**
Ravenhill Guesthouse **23**
Tara Lodge **19**
Ten Square **14**
The Titanic Hotel **1**

RESTAURANTS ●
The Barking Dog **21**
CoCo **15**
Deanes Love Fish **11**
Ginger Bistro **18**
James Street & Co **12**
The John Hewitt **3**
John Long's Fish & Chips **10**
Made in Belfast **2**
Molly's Yard **20**
Mourne Seafood Bar **6**
The Muddlers Club **4**
Ox **9**

Information ⓘ

Guest room in the Grand Central Hotel.

The Merchant Hotel ★★★   One of Ireland's most luxurious hotels, the Merchant is a real treat. The Victorian building was once a bank, and the conversion is stunning, from the grand dining room (lacquered and gilded Corinthian columns, marble floors, ceiling friezes) to an elegant cocktail lounge (chandeliers and a gently curved, dark wood bar). Guest rooms are thoroughly modern, but ask for one with Art Deco–style decor as opposed to traditional—they're larger and better designed. The excellent **spa** comes complete with hydrotherapy pool and treatment rooms, and a rooftop gym has an eight-person hot tub with lovely city views. The cocktail lounge and **Great Room Restaurant** were fully refurbished in 2019. Afternoon tea is a bit of an event here, and popular, so book ahead if you want to indulge.

16 Skipper St., Belfast, BT1 2DZ. www.themerchanthotel.com. (℗) **028/9023-4888.** 62 units. £210–£330 double; £355–£720 suite. Valet parking. **Amenities:** Restaurant; bar; gym; spa; Wi-Fi (free).

The Titanic Hotel ★★★   This impressive hotel opened in 2017 with one of the best warehouse conversions we've ever seen. Located in the Titanic District in the former headquarters of the Harland & Wolff shipping company, it melds Victorian and modern decor spectacularly. The bar, once the drawing office, has a barrel-vaulted, windowed roof that lets light pour in, and the lobby is all soaring ceilings and artful decor. Guest rooms have been given a sophisticated look, in neutral chocolate brown and crisp white color schemes. Beds are king-size, with orthopedic mattresses. Bathrooms are nautical in white brick tiles with black edging. The **Wolff Grill** has a clean, elegant look, and has become a destination restaurant for local residents. Even if you're not staying here, consider booking a seat for dinner. It's a short taxi ride from the city center.

Queen's Rd., Titanic Quarter, Belfast, BT3 9DT. www.titanichotelbelfast.com. ℂ **028/9508-2000.** 119 units. £109–£239 double. Parking £10 5–10am or £15 for 24 hours. **Amenities:** Restaurant; bar; Wi-Fi (free).

Moderate

The Harrison Chambers of Distinction ★★   This bohemian Victorian residence in the Queens Quarter is jam-packed full of character and quirks. The heritage "chambers" (aka rooms) come with interesting features like bay windows, original fireplaces, freestanding baths, brass beds, and antiques collected by host Melanie over the years. Each room is unique—live out your literary fantasies in the CS Lewis Suite (the *Chronicles of Narnia* author was born in Belfast), complete with a mini library and an antique typewriter, or sink into a four-poster bed or freestanding bath accompanied by jazz records in the Ruby Murray suite, named for the popular Northern Irish singer.

45 Malone Rd., Belfast BT9 6RX. www.chambersofdistinction.com. ℂ **028/9460-0123.** 16 units. £119–£250 double. Free parking. **Amenities:** Wi-Fi (free)

Maldron Belfast City ★   This hotel earns rave reviews from visitors for its central location (just a few minutes' walk from City Hall), spacious rooms, and terrific views. The hotel is part of an Irish chain and the Maldron approach seems quite straightforward—the 237 rooms are good-sized with a clean, modern look, done in white and pale gray with bright yellow accents. The in-house restaurant has a healthy edge—breakfast options include lots of fruit, granola, yogurts, and fresh-baked breads alongside the usual eggs and sausages. The hotel has its own specialty coffee roast, **Red Bean Roastery,** that regulars swear by. The best views are from the 7th floor on up—some are quite spectacular. The hotel has no on-site parking, but the concierge can direct you to nearby parking garages. *Tip:* Check online for packages that include entry to **Titanic Belfast** (p. 500) and **SS** *Nomadic* (p. 500).

20 Brunswick St., Belfast, BT2 7GE. www.maldronhotelbelfastcity.com. ℂ **028/9600-1680.** 237 units. £113–£169 double. **Amenities:** Restaurant; bar; gym; Wi-Fi (free).

Malmaison Belfast ★★   This is the only Irish outpost of Malmaison, a British mini-chain that specializes in turning unusual historic buildings into hip boutique hotels. This four-story building used to be a seed warehouse, and it's gorgeous, with weathered stone walls and tall arched windows. Inside, the chic, playful design retains original industrial touches. Bedrooms are large, quiet, and comfortable, with low lighting, huge beds, and modern bathrooms—most have deep baths and walk-in showers. Breakfasts are large and varied—we love the

homemade granola. **Chez Mal** is the good in-house brasserie, and the **MalBar** is lively.

34-38 Victoria St., Belfast, BT1 3GH. www.malmaison.com/locations/belfast. © **028/9600-1405.** 62 units. £95–£188 double; £179–£328 suite. Discounted parking at nearby lot (£15/24 hr.). Breakfast not included in lower rates. **Amenities:** Restaurant; bar; gym; room service; Wi-Fi (free).

Ten Square ★★ Set in a historic building right behind City Hall, this boutique hotel aims to emulate five-star luxury hotels at a fraction of the cost. Its decor deliberately contrasts styles—exposed stone and tall arched windows in public areas; bedrooms treading the line between chic and kitsch, with polka-dotted carpet and blue velvet fabrics. The king-size beds, draped in pure white linens, are very firm. **Jospers** restaurant specializes in Irish meats, particularly steak, and the **Loft** bar has a great cocktail menu. The penthouse has a huge rooftop terrace with views across the city. Check the website for deals, including a *Titanic*-themed package.

Yorkshire House, 10 Donegall Sq., Belfast, BT1 5JD. www.tensquare.co.uk. © **028/9024-1001.** 131 units. £90–£180 double; £225–£765 suite. Breakfast not included in lower rates. Street parking only. **Amenities:** Restaurant; bar; Wi-Fi (free).

Inexpensive

Bullitt ★ This hip, modern hotel is positioned between the Titanic Quarter and the historic downtown. It has a chic, industrial design—the downstairs cafe has exposed metal beams, a polished concrete floor, and exposed support columns beneath moody lighting. Soundproofed bedrooms also have an industrial edge, with brightly painted metal racks for hanging clothes instead of closets. Beds are comfortable, and bathrooms are small but modern. A breakfast of granola and fruit is left outside your door every morning. You can pop downstairs for a latte from the espresso bar or seek out a hot breakfast in the restaurant. Very cheap deals are offered on the smallest hotel rooms.

40a Church Lane, Belfast, BT2 7GE. www.bullitthotel.com. © **028/9590-0600.** 74 units. £91–£138 double. **Amenities:** Restaurant; bar; Wi-Fi (free).

Ravenhill Guesthouse ★ A friendly welcome awaits from hosts Roger and Olive, whose handsome Victorian corner house has been converted into one of the best B&Bs in Belfast. The recently renovated rooms are simple but neat as a pin. You're in a residential area but not far from the action; the city center is about a 10-minute cab or bus ride away. Roger cooks delicious breakfasts, and guests can expect the full Ulster fry, in addition to options such as kippers with parsley butter and scrambled eggs. They bake their own traditional Irish wheaten bread from scratch, right down to milling their own flour.

690 Ravenhill Rd., Belfast, BT6 0BZ. www.ravenhillhouse.com. © **028/9020-7444.** 5 units. £75–£90 double. 2-night minimum at certain times. Free parking. Breakfast included. **Amenities:** Wi-Fi (free).

Tara Lodge ★★ This popular boutique hotel is well positioned for exploring the city—the **Botanic Gardens** ★ (p. 496) and **Ulster Museum** ★★★ (p. 502) are 10 minutes away on foot. The contemporary guest rooms are not big, but they're well designed and quiet, with large, comfortable beds. Instead of a closet, there's a metal rack for clothes in the corner—a U.K. hotel trend. The breakfast selection is excellent, and everything is made to order. The hotel has no in-house restaurant or bar, but staff can guide you to good eateries nearby. The hotel offers packages that includes the *Titanic Experience* (p. 266) or *Game of Thrones* location tours at discounted rates.

36 Cromwell Rd., Belfast, BT7 1JW. www.taralodge.com. © **028/9059-0900.** 34 units. £100–£135 double. Free parking. Breakfast included. **Amenities:** Wi-Fi (free).

WHERE TO EAT IN BELFAST

Belfast has an expansive foodie scene that is growing all the time. With a university and a booming business sector, there's demand for variety and affordability. In addition to the restaurants listed below, you can find plenty of options for light meals at places like **District** (www.district coffee.co.uk), which serves excellent coffee, sandwiches, salads, and breakfasts at three locations in town (82 Stranmillis Rd., 300 Ormeau Rd., 469 Lisburn Rd.). Another option is **Harlem** (34 Bedford St.; www. harlembelfast.com) in the Cathedral Quarter. Locals come to have breakfast or lunch in the trendy antiques-filled dining room. Harlem offers everything from porridge to scrambled eggs to red velvet pancakes with banana and Nutella, along with veggie options, tremendous lunches, and good coffee. If you're looking for a brunch or lunch to linger over, follow the locals to **Hadski's** (33 Donegal St.; www.hadskis.co.uk), an award-winning restaurant where the weekend brunch (eggs benedict with Parma ham; waffles with bacon and maple syrup) is legendary, and lunches are even better. It's a good idea to book your table online.

Expensive

Ginger Bistro ★★ MODERN IRISH The lively food and atmosphere keep the regulars coming back to this city-center favorite. This bistro wins rave reviews for dishes like roast hake with green cabbage, rosemary cream, ham shank and parmentier potatoes, or braised and glazed pork belly matched with garlic greens, coconut rice fritters, and pineapple. Staff are friendly yet professional, and the overall vibe is good food in a relaxed atmosphere. The restaurant is near both the Grand Opera House and the historic Crown Pub, so you could put together a great night out featuring all three.

68/72 Great Victoria St., Belfast BT2 7AF. www.gingerbistro.com. © **028/9024-4421.** Set menu £37 for 3 courses, £28–£29 for 2 courses. Wed 5–9:15pm; Thurs noon–9:15pm, Fri–Sat noon–9:30pm. Closed Sun–Tues.

The Muddlers Club ★★ MODERN IRISH It's named after a secret society that used to meet here 200 years ago, but there's nothing secret about the food in this gem in the Cathedral Quarter—the restaurant has won awards nearly every year since opening in 2015, including a Michelin star. But the atmosphere is more relaxed than formal fine dining. Chef Gareth McCaughey creates a seasonal tasting menu using the best local ingredients he can find—look for dishes like Strangford Lough hand-baked scallops served with local ham and baked Jerusalem artichokes and finished with Parmesan velouté foam, or North Atlantic cod served with chicken skin, chicken stock emulsion, salsify, and black trumpet mushrooms. The tasting menu is six courses, and the kitchen also does a vegetarian or vegan version. Book well in advance.

1 Warehouse Lane, Belfast BT1 2DX. www.themuddlersclubbelfast.com. Ⓒ **028/9031-3199.** Tasting menu £65 (£55 for vegetarian or vegan option). Tues–Thurs 5–9:30pm; Fri–Sat 12:30–1pm, 5–9:30pm. Closed Sun and Mon.

Ox ★★★ MODERN EUROPEAN Contemporary, seasonal, well-balanced flavors form the small but sumptuous menus at this Michelin-starred restaurant. The tasting menus change constantly, with local and seasonal availability a constant priority, but expect dishes such as celeriac velouté with chestnut and truffles, beef Châteaubriand with black garlic; or perhaps halibut served with burned lemon and curry. Paired wines are just £40 extra. The service strikes precisely the right balance between professionalism and friendliness—the waitstaff really know their stuff—and the modern dining room provides a sophisticated backdrop. Needless to say, reservations are essential. If, however, you can't quite stretch to dinner here, you can sample the restaurant's excellent wine list in the entirely informal **Ox Cave,** the adjacent wine bar, while enjoying cheese and light bites. The cellar hosts monthly wine tastings for £25 per person.

Dessert course at the Ox.

1 Oxford St., Belfast, BT1 3LA. www. oxbelfast.com. Ⓒ **028/9031-4121.** Tasting menu £65 six courses. Wed 6–9:30pm; Thurs–Sat noon–2:30pm and 6–9:30pm. Closed Sun, Mon, and Tues.

Moderate

The Barking Dog ★★ IRISH/INTERNATIONAL   There's some-thing quintessentially Belfast about this place: It's quirky, artsy, lively, but ultimately no-nonsense. The dining room has a funky pub feel, with exposed brick walls and old candelabras balanced on battered wood tables. If you sit in the front garden, you're separated from the street by a fence with paw prints all over it. Come for tapas or a full menu at lunchtime, or delicious pub and bistro-style favorites in the evening (steaks, pasta, fish, burgers, and the like). There are vegetar-ian, vegan, lactose-intolerant, and gluten-free menus too. Proving that connections to the show are pretty much everywhere here, the Barking Dog was allegedly one of the regular haunts for the *Game of Thrones* cast.

33-35 Malone Rd., Belfast, BT9 6RU. www.barkingdogbelfast.com. © **028/9066-1885.** Entrees £17–£32. Wed–Thurs noon–2:30pm and 5–9pm; Fri–Sat noon–2:30pm and 5–10pm; Sun noon–4pm and 5–9pm. No children after 9pm.

Coco ★★ MODERN EUROPEAN/INTERNATIONAL   Coco's styl-ishly whimsical dining room is plastered in modern art along with posters and photo-collages that set the tone. The contemporary menu is full of welcome surprises that innovate without overcrowding the more tradi-tional ingredients; saffron risotto is served with chili gremolata, for exam-ple, and roast monkfish comes with chanterelle mushrooms and squid ink sauce. For dessert, try the rich buttermilk panna cotta served with poached fruit. The three-course pre-theater menu (served until 7:30pm) is just £22, as is the "Date Night": three courses plus a bottle of wine for £65 per couple (available Mon–Thurs).

7-11 Linenhall St., Belfast, BT2 8AA. www.cocobelfast.com. © **028/9031-1150.** Entrees £17.50–£26. Wed–Fri noon–3pm 5:30–9:30pm; Sat 5:30–9:30pm; Sun 1–9pm. Closed Mon and Tues.

Deanes Love Fish (etc.) ★★ SEAFOOD   The mini-empire run by local celebrity chef Michael Deane has so far expanded to half a dozen restaurants. While each has its charms, **Deanes Love Fish** is our favorite. Adjacent to **Eipic** (© **028/9033-1134**), Deane's flagship formal restaurant on Howard Street (known for very good Irish-French cuisine), Love Fish is just as good but more casual. Here you'll find plates such as roast local salmon, cooked in olive oil and lemon with anchovy butter sauce; crab and chile linguine; beer-battered fish and chips; or maybe a buttery plaice *meunière.* The lunch at Love Fish is one of the city's best food bargains, where all main dishes cost £6.50. Also here is the excellent **Meat Locker** (© **028/9033-1134**), a laid-back grill where you can enjoy a pre-theater menu with main courses priced at around £10. Deane's other culinary out-posts include **Deanes Deli/Vin Cafe** (© **028/9024-8800**), at 44 Bedford St., and **Deane and Decano** (© **028/9066-3108**) on the Lisburn Road. In the University Quarter is the informal bistro **Deanes at Queens** (1 College Gardens; ✆ **028/9038-2111**).

36–40 Howard St., Belfast, BT1 6PF. www.michaeldeane.co.uk. ✆ **028/9033-1134.** Entrees £15.95–£26. Tues–Wed noon–3pm; Thurs–Fri noon–3pm and 5–9:30pm; Sat noon–10pm. Closed Sun and Mon.

James Street & Co ★★ MODERN IRISH   One of Belfast's most popular restaurants, James Street & Co (formerly James Street South) has built a great reputation on its creative modern Irish cuisine. With exposed brick walls and an industrial-chic vibe, the place may look unpretentious, but the food is reliably excellent—expect dishes like local pheasant with onion and creamed chestnuts, or a perfect rib-eye with blue cheese sauce. Kids are catered to with a surprisingly good menu that is a little more, well, grown-up than most places. There's an all-day menu at weekends.

19–21 James St. S, Belfast, BT2 7GA. www.jamesstandco.com. ✆ **028/9560-0700.** Entrees £18.50–£36. Mon and Thurs 5pm–9:30pm; Fri–Sun 1pm–9:30pm.

Molly's Yard ★ IRISH   Tucked away in the University Quarter in restored Victorian stables, this place is as justifiably popular for its relaxed atmosphere as for the delicious food. Appetizers such as fresh bread with tapenade go well with a glass of whatever you fancy. You could follow that up with some lamb with horseradish and potato gnocchi, cod with chili jam, or vegetable curry. The six-course tasting menu also comes as a vegetarian or vegan option, and the craft-beer selection is extensive.

1 College Green Mews, Belfast, BT1 1LW. www.mollysyard.co.uk. ✆ **028/9032-2600.** Entrees £16–£27. Tasting menu £25–£30 six courses. Mon–Sat noon–8pm. Closed Sun.

Mourne Seafood Bar ★★ SEAFOOD   This is one of the best places in Belfast for top-quality seafood. The dining room has a casual air—this is a seafood *bar* after all—but the food speaks for itself. Oysters are a specialty, served traditionally or Japanese-style with pickled ginger and soy dressing. Alternatively, you could go for some spicy piri-piri prawns with fresh focaccia bread to start, followed by one of the fresh daily specials like seared scallops with butternut squash risotto. The atmosphere is relaxed and convivial, and the prices are thoroughly reasonable for food this good. The restaurant doesn't take reservations at lunchtime, but evening booking is essential. A second branch is located on Main Street in Dundrum, just outside Newcastle, County Down (✆ **028/4375-1377;** p. 544).

36 Bank St., Belfast, BT1 1HL. www.mourneseafood.com. ✆ **028/9024-8544.** Entrees £9.50–£27.50. Tues–Thurs noon–9:30pm; Fri–Sat noon–10pm; Sun 1–9pm. Closed Mon.

Inexpensive

John Long's Fish & Chips ★ SEAFOOD   This casual, inexpensive eatery is widely acclaimed as the best fish and chips in Belfast. Its fans are legion and loyal. It's certainly been around a long time—the first John

Long's opened in 1914. It offers nothing fancy, just fresh fish in a light batter, quickly fried and served immediately, along with fries (called chips here) and mushy peas or, if you must, baked beans. "Good food and lots of it" is the motto. It also provides gluten-free alternative batter for those who need it, so everyone can have some fish. The menu is short and sweet; the fish is fresh and cheap. But get here early, it closes at 6:30pm (6pm Sat).
39 Athol St., Belfast, BT12 4GX. www.johnlongs.com. ✆ **028/9032-1848.** Entrees £4.50–£8. Tues–Fri noon–6:30pm. Sat noon–6pm. Closed Sun and Mon.

Made in Belfast: Cathedral Quarter ★★ MODERN   This trendy outlet for food and cocktails occupies some of the hip ground in Belfast's Cathedral Quarter with its highly designed dining room outfitted with vintage art, collectibles from the '60s, and a ceiling covered in magazine photographs. Cocktails are the main draw here—most are invented behind the bar—but there's also food to be had, including prawn and crab risotto served with homemade sourdough bread, or glazed pork belly with potato boxty (a delicious, savory Irish pancake; see box on p. 139). The owners take a sustainable/ethical approach—all meats are free-range; all vegetables are organic; and they support local farmers and producers. But mostly it's about the cool cocktails. Other outlets of Made in Belfast include the **Grill** (38 Hill St.; ✆ **028/9545-8120**), **City Hall** (4 Wellington St.; ✆ **028/9024-6712**), and **Made in South Belfast** (182A Lisburn Rd.; ✆ **028/906-7500**).
25 Talbot St., Belfast, BT1 2LD. www.mibni.co.uk. ✆ **028/9545-8120.** Entrees £14–£26. Thurs–Sun noon–9:30pm.

SHOPPING

Belfast is a surprisingly good place to shop. Start at Donegall Place, where the streets are lined with shops and the Victorian arcades are filled with gift and jewelry stores. Good buys are to be had on Belleek china, linen, and crystal from County Tyrone. Shops are typically open weekdays from 9 or 9:30am to 5 or 5:30pm, and open later on weekends.

The main shopping street is **Royal Avenue,** home of several well-known chain stores, while the **Westfield Castlecourt Shopping Centre** on Royal Avenue and the glass-domed **Victoria Square** shopping center are Belfast's main downtown multi-story shopping malls.

Antiques

Archive's Antiques Centre ★   Several dealers sell their wares at this sprawling center, with specialists in everything from silverware to pub memorabilia and militaria. 88 Donegall Pass, Belfast, BT7 1BX. www.archivesantiques-centre.co.uk. ✆ **028/9023-2383.**

Oakland Antiques ★★   This enormous antiques emporium specializes in furniture, glassware, and other household items from the 18th to early 20th centuries. 137 Donegall Pass, Belfast, BT7 1DS. www.oaklandantiques.co.uk. ✆ **028/9023-0176.**

Books & Stationery

No Alibis ★★ This excellent bookshop specializes in crime fiction from all over the world. It's a lovely place to linger. 83 Botanic Ave., Belfast, BT7 1JL. www.noalibis.com. ✆ **028/9031-9601.**

Fashion & Clothing

The Bureau ★★ One of the city's major men's fashion boutiques, selling a fantastic range of clothes and footwear from its airy, stylish shop on Newtownards Road, east of the Titanic Quarter. Portview, 310 Newtownards Rd., Belfast BT4 1HE. www.thebureaubelfast.com. ✆ **028/9046-0190.**

Food

Sawers ★★★ A treasure trove of all types of food, with more than 200 cheeses alone, this shop is so historic (it dates back to 1897) it even supplied nibbles to the *Titanic*. 5–6 College St., Belfast BT1 6ES. www.sawers belfast.com. ✆ **028/9032 2021.**

Jewelry

Steensons ★★★ Behind Belfast City Hall, this long-established jewelry shop is known for its beautiful pieces inspired by *Game of Thrones* (see box on p. 539); other popular lines include limited-edition pieces commemorating the *Titanic*. There's also a branch on Seaview Hall, New Road, in Glenarm, County Antrim (✆ **028/2884-1445**). Bedford St., Belfast, BT2 7FD. www.thesteensons.com. ✆ **028/9024-8269.**

BELFAST AFTER DARK

Belfast has a plethora of historic pubs serving friendly local crowds, along with a fast-growing scene of late-night bars for the young and trendy, mostly clustered in the University Quarter. If you're looking for a traditional pub, several of the best are tucked away in the pedestrian lanes off Donegall Place.

The **licensing laws** in Northern Ireland aren't as notoriously strict as they used to be. Pub hours are generally Monday to Saturday from 11:30am to 11pm and Sunday from 12:30 to 2:30pm and 7 to 10pm; bars stay open later. Nightclubs tend not to get busy until after the pubs close; admission ranges from a few pounds to about £15.

Bars & Clubs

Hell Cat Maggies ★ This fun bar is named for an infamous member of the Dead Rabbit gang who terrorized New York in the 19th century. A varied program of nightly live music keeps things lively, and the food is good. 2 Donegal Sq. W, Belfast, BT1 6JA. www.hellcat-maggies.com. ✆ **028/9099-4120.**

The Performing Arts

Belfast Empire ★   This former music hall is now one of the city's busiest live venues, with acts a few times a week and standup comedy every Tuesday. It's also a busy bar and nightclub, open until 1am every night except Sunday. 42 Botanic Ave., Belfast, BT1 1JQ. www.thebelfastempire. com. ℭ **028/9024-9276.**

Black Box ★★   This eclectic venue has a great program of theater, spoken word, cabaret, film, and other live events, as well as exhibition spaces featuring whatever's interesting in the worlds of photography and visual art. From Wednesday to Sunday nights, the Green Room bar offers pizza, beer, and free live music. 18–22 Hill St., Belfast, BT1 2LA. www.blackboxbelfast. com. ℭ **028/9024-4400.**

Grand Opera House ★★   One of the main landmarks of Belfast's Golden Mile, the Grand Opera House opened in 1895. The interior is full of late-Victorian detail, including an elaborately painted frieze on the high ceiling. Severely damaged twice by IRA bombs, it's a cornerstone of the Belfast live arts scene, hosting touring plays, ballet, and opera. Ticket prices vary, but expect to pay between £18 and £43. 2–4 Great Victoria St., Belfast, BT2 7HR. www.goh.co.uk. ℭ **028/9024-1919.**

Lyric Theatre ★★   The Lyric is a highly respected repertory theater producing original work and hosting touring plays. Ticket prices are generally between £12 and £25. 55 Ridgeway St., Belfast, BT9 5FP. www.lyric theatre.co.uk. ℭ **028/9038-1081.**

The Mac ★★   This cultural hub in the Cathedral Quarter has three art galleries, two theaters, a dance studio, and workshop rooms plus a bar and restaurant. Theater tickets cost from £14 to £25. 10 Exchange St. West, Belfast, BT1 2NJ. www.themaclive.com. ℭ **028/9023-5053.**

Pubs

Crown Liquor Saloon ★★★   There's a very real possibility that this impeccably restored Victorian gin palace is the handsomest pub in the world. See full review on p. 499. 46 Great Victoria St., Belfast, BT2 7BA. www. nicholsonspubs.co.uk/thecrownliquorsaloonbelfast. ℭ **028/9024-3187.**

Kelly's Cellars ★★   One of a couple pubs claiming to be Belfast's oldest, Kelly's Cellars certainly looks the part, with low doorways and a high-beamed ceiling. It's considered one of the best pubs in town for live traditional music; sessions are usually held on Tuesdays, Wednesdays, and Thursdays from 8:30pm on, and Saturdays from 4:30pm. 30–32 Bank St., Belfast, BT1 1HL. ℭ **028/9024-6058.**

The Morning Star ★   Another lovely traditional pub, the Morning Star has been in business since at least 1810. Originally it was next to a stagecoach terminus, providing sunrise pick-me-ups for overnight passengers—hence the name. The pub is famously hard to find: Pottinger's

Entry is a small, pedestrian-only alleyway off High Street, across from the post office; look for the iron arch over the entrance. 17–19 Pottinger's Entry, Belfast, BT1 4DT. www.themorningstarbar.com. © **028/9023-5986.**

White's Tavern ★★　White's Tavern has been serving liquor since 1630, which makes it even older than all of the above (though technically not the oldest pub; it began life as a wine shop). The decor is all old whiskey bottles and vintage photos around a fireplace. There's live music nightly. Upstairs, the **Oyster Room** serves up a small menu of hearty comfort food. Enter between Rosemary and High streets. 2–4 Winecellar Entry, Belfast, BT1 1QN. www.whitestavernbelfast.com. © **028/9031-2582.**

DAY TRIPS FROM BELFAST

15

M edieval castles, mountain ranges, coastal drives, and one of the most spectacular (and certainly unique) landscapes you'll find anywhere—all are within easy reach of Belfast. That is, if you don't mind driving down tiny, winding roads that take at least twice as long as they should to get anywhere. Though the destinations covered in this chapter are no more than about 60 miles in any direction from Northern Ireland's capital, it could take you up to 90 minutes to drive there—more if you take the scenic way. And frankly, why wouldn't you, when it's this beautiful?

As if that wasn't enough, the countryside these winding roads lead to is simply breathtaking—the verdant greens of the **Glens of Antrim,** the rugged **Mourne Mountains,** and the famously craggy coastline to the **Giant's Causeway,** surely one of the world's great natural wonders. Take the time to get out of your car and explore what this region has to offer. You may even leave thinking this was the highlight of your trip.

ESSENTIALS
Arriving

BY BUS **Ulsterbus** (www.translink.co.uk; ℰ **028/9066-6630**) runs buses from Belfast to Downpatrick, Carrickfergus, and Ballymena. While several other towns are reachable by bus, routes are long and circuitous— you're better off driving, or joining an organized tour.

BY CAR Most of the attractions listed in this chapter are easily accessible by car, with a journey time of between 1 and 2 hours (at most) from Belfast. Roads are good in the regions around the city, although traffic can be a problem, particularly during rush hour. In reasonable traffic, Comber is about a half-hour drive from the city; Strangford and Armagh, about an hour; Newcastle, 1¼ hours; Bushmills and the Giant's Causeway, 1½ hours.

BY TRAIN **Translink** (www.translink.co.uk; ℰ **028/9066-6630**) has train connections with several towns in the region, including Lisburn, Armagh, Bangor, and Portrush, although journey times can be long. The Translink/Ulsterbus website has a great journey planner.

PREVIOUS PAGE: **Giant's Causeway.**

THE CAUSEWAY COAST

The most extraordinary stretch of countryside in Northern Ireland, the glorious Causeway Coast stretches north and west from Belfast, curving around toward Donegal. This beautiful rocky shoreline includes the North's most striking sights: the awe-inspiring **Giant's Causeway** (p. 527) and the picturesque **Carrick-a-Rede Rope Bridge** (p. 523). The spectacular Causeway Coastal Route drive meanders along under bridges and stone arches, with the green Glens of Antrim on one side, and the crescent bays, sandy beaches, harbors, and huge rock formations on the other. The ocean gleams beside you as you curve along its craggy shores, and the light creates intense colors. In the spring and autumn, you often have the road all to yourself.

The drive is more or less equidistant from Belfast and Derry. It's possible to see all the sights in 1 day, staying in either city, although most travelers prefer to get a room on the coast and take their time.

Visitor Information

The principal tourist information centers in North Antrim are at Narrow Gauge Road, Larne (✆ **028/2826-2450**); Sheskburn House, 14 Bayview Rd., Ballycastle (✆ **028/2076-2024**); and the **Giant's Causeway Information Centre,** Main Street, Bushmills (✆ **028/2073-1855**). All offices are open daily year-round, though the Larne and Ballycastle offices are closed Sundays outside the midsummer season. The Giant's Causeway office stays open until 6pm in July and August.

Exploring the Antrim Coast

Carnlough ★ VILLAGE The first major stop along the Antrim Coast Drive is this quiet village, known for its glassy harbor bobbing with sailboats. It's a lovely place to wander around, sampling interesting little shops and restaurants. Just outside Carnlough is a peaceful yet little-known waterfall called **Cranny Falls.** To get there, look for a marked 1-mile walking trail beginning on the waterfront. After crossing the white-stone bridge, the route goes through idyllic countryside, following an abandoned railway bed, past a disused quarry, until it reaches the falls. Along the way, occasional markers tell you more about the history of the area.

Carnlough, Co. Antrim.

Carrick-a-Rede Rope Bridge ★★★ BRIDGE We'll start with some advice: *Don't look down.* This rope bridge stretches across a chasm 18m (59 ft.) wide and 24m (79 ft.) deep, swinging over the sea between the mainland and a small island. The bridge once had a practical purpose, allowing access to the island's salmon fishery, which has been here since 1755 (don't worry, they do regular maintenance). Now it also gives visitors a thrilling walk, but if you are afraid of heights, don't even think

THE causeway coastal ROUTE

One of the most memorable drives in Ireland, the 130km (80-mile) Causeway Coastal Route in County Antrim, from Belfast to the Giant's Causeway, offers sweeping views of midnight-blue seas against gray, unforgiving cliffs and deep green hillsides. The whole coastal route runs as far as Derry, but the most scenic section goes as far as the Giant's Causeway. You could do the whole journey in a few hours, but allow much longer if you can—it's the sort of drive you want to savor.

Once you leave Belfast and join the coast road (A2), about 26km (16 miles) north of Carrickfergus, the first town is **Glenarm,** decked out with castle walls and a barbican gate—you can tour the castle and gardens. In the picturesque seaside village of **Carnlough ★** (p. 523), you can take a pleasant hike to a waterfall. On up the coast, you'll find the National Trust village of **Cushendun ★** (p. 526), known for its tea shops and whitewashed cottages.

For the most spectacular views, detour off the main A2 road at Cushendun onto the **Torr Head Scenic Road ★★** (p. 529). Just note that this narrow, rugged, cliffside road can induce vertigo as it climbs in seemingly perilous fashion to the tops of hills that are bigger than you might think. On a clear day, you can see all the way to Scotland.

In the late spring and summer, you can take a ferry from the bustling town of **Ballycastle** to **Rathlin Island** (p. 528), where seals and nesting birds make their homes at the **Kebble National Reserve.** Or take a 15-minute detour south on the A22 from Ballycastle to see the picturesque **Dark Hedges,** a beautiful avenue of 200-year-old beech trees that intertwine overhead and were featured in an episode of *Game of Thrones.* (It's just past the Gracehill Golf Club on Bregah Rd.)

Farther west, the heart-stopping **Carrick-a-Rede Rope Bridge ★★★** (p. 523) allows the brave to cross on foot over to a small island just off the coast. Others may prefer to press straight on to the postcard-perfect little town of **Ballintoy,** filled with charming stone cottages and flowery gardens. Ballintoy is stretched out at the edge of **Whitepark Bay,** a wide, crystalline curve of sandy beach at the foot of rocky hills surrounded by green farms. On a sunny day, you might find it hard to go farther.

The last major stop is the eerily lunar **Giant's Causeway ★★★** (p. 527), one of the world's true natural wonders. And after all that adventure, don't you think you've earned yourself a tipple—to enjoy later, if you're the one driving—at the **Old Bushmills Distillery ★★** (p. 527)?

about it—like, seriously, what are you even doing here? And if you don't know whether you suffer from vertigo, this may not be the best place to find out. *Note:* A 19km (12-mile) coastal cliff path leads between the Giant's Causeway (p. 527) and the rope bridge. It is always open and worth the exhaustion.

8km (5 miles) W of Ballycastle off the A2 road. 119A Whitepark Rd., Ballintoy, Co. Antrim, BT54 6LS. www.nationaltrust.org.uk/carrick-a-rede. ✆ **028/2076-9839.** Admission £9 adults; £4.50 children; £22.50 families. July–Aug daily 9:30am–8pm; Mar–June and Sept–Oct daily 9:30am–6pm; Nov–Feb daily 9:30am–3:30pm. Check opening hours before visiting.

Day Trips from Belfast

NORTHERN IRELAND

Belfast

Map Area

Galway

Dublin

REPUBLIC OF IRELAND

Cork

Cushendun ★ VILLAGE   Back in the 1950s, the National Trust bought most of this charming seaside village to preserve it from over-development. Today, the seafront is lined with an elegant sweep of perfect white Cornish-style cottages, and the quaint teashops do a bustling trade. The Glendun River winds through the village, crossed by an old stone bridge, while down on the beach atmospheric sea caves line the shore. Just north of here, in a field overlooking the coast, stand the scant remains of **Curra Castle.** Cushendun is a good place to stop and take pictures before heading on down the main A2 road—or, if you want the most amazing views, the **Torr Head Scenic Road ★★** (p. 529).
Cushendun, Co. Antrim.

Dunluce Castle ★★ CASTLE   Between the Giant's Causeway and the busy harbor town of Portrush, the coastline is dominated by the hulking skeletal outline of what must have once been a glorious castle. This was the main fort of the Irish MacDonnells, chiefs of Antrim. From the 14th to the 17th century, it was the largest and most sophisticated castle in the North, with a series of fortifications built on rocky outcrops extending into the sea. In 1639, part of the castle fell into the sea, taking some of the servants with it; soon after that, it was allowed to fall into a beautiful ruin. The 17th-century courtyard survives, including a few buildings. The site

Sheep herder along the avenue of ancient beech trees known as Dark Hedges.

incorporates two of the original Norman towers dating from 1305. *An enticing footnote:* Recent archaeological digs here have uncovered the remains of a town thought to have been destroyed during a rebellion in 1641. Only a tiny fraction of what is now believed to exist has so far been excavated.

87 Dunluce Rd., Bushmills, Co. Antrim, BT57 8UY. © **028/2073-1938.** Admission £5.65 adults; £3.75 seniors, students, and children 5–17; free for children 4 and under; £17 families. Daily 10am–5pm (4pm Dec–Jan); last admission 30 min. before closing. Call to confirm times in winter.

Fishermen sell their daily catch in Carnlough's scenic harbor.

Giant's Causeway ★★★ NATURE SITE   A UNESCO World Heritage Site, this is an extraordinary sight indeed. Sitting at the foot of steep cliffs and stretching out into the sea, it is a natural formation of thousands of tightly packed basalt columns. The tops of the columns form flat stepping stones, all of which are perfectly hexagonal. They measure about 30cm (12 in.) in diameter; some are very short, others are as tall as 12m (39 ft.). Scientists believe they were formed 60 or 70 million years ago by volcanic eruptions and cooling lava. The ancients, on the other hand, believed the rock formation to be the work of giants. To reach the causeway, you walk from the parking area down a steep path for nearly 1.6km (1 mile), past amphitheaters of stone columns and formations with fanciful names like Honeycomb, Wishing Well, Giant's Granny, King and his Nobles, and Lover's Leap. If you wish, you can then climb up a wooden staircase to Benbane Head to take in the views, and then walk back along the cliff top. Regular shuttle service from the visitor center is available for those who can't face the hike. *Note:* The visitor center has a cafe, shop, interpretive center, and hugely expensive parking, justifying the fairly steep admission price. However, the Causeway itself is a free, open site, so if you can find safe and legal parking, there's nothing to stop you from walking down on your own.

44 Causeway Rd., Bushmills, Co. Antrim, BT57 8SU. www.nationaltrust.org.uk/giants-causeway. © **028/2073-1855.** Visitor center and parking: £13 adults; £6.50 children; £32.50 families. Visitor center June–Sept daily 9am–7pm; Mar–May Oct daily 9am–6pm; Nov–Feb daily 9am–5pm.

The Old Bushmills Distillery ★★ FACTORY TOUR   Licensed to distill spirits in 1608, but with historical references dating from as far back as 1276, this distillery is endlessly popular. Visitors can tour the working sections and watch the whiskey-making process. At the end of the tour, you can sample the wares in the **Potstill Bar.** Tours last about 25

GOING TO THE birds: A TRIP TO RATHLIN ISLAND

Want to get close to nature? Plan a trip to **Rathlin Island,** 10km (6 miles) off the coast north of Ballycastle. The tiny island is 6km (3¾ miles) long, less than 1.5km (1 mile) wide, and almost completely treeless, with rugged coastal cliffs, a small beach, and crowds of seals and seabirds in spring and summer. Once you get there, you'll realize that it's not quite as isolated as it seems—there's a resident population of about 100 people, plus a pub, a hostel, and a guesthouse, should you miss the last boat to shore.

Start with a visit to the **Rathlin Boat House Visitor Centre,** near the ferry landing at Church Bay (℘ **028/2076-2024**). The center contains an exhibit on the history of the islands, as well as plenty of handy visitor information. It's usually open from April to June, daily 10am to 4:30pm; July and August daily 10am to 5pm; and early September 10am to 4pm (check before visiting). Admission is free.

Rathlin is a favorite bird-watching spot, especially in spring and early summer when the birds are nesting. Given that there's little else to do here, it's no surprise that the island's biggest draw is bird-watching at the **Kebble National Nature Reserve** (℘ **028/7035-9963**) on the western side of the island, and the **RSPB Rathlin West Light Seabird Centre** (www.rspb.org.uk; ℘ **028/2076-0062**), located in Rathlin's unique "upside-down" lighthouse. Entry costs £5 adults, £3.50 students, and £2.50 children (first child and under 5s go free). From here you can watch colorful puffins, guillemots, kittiwakes, fulmars, razorbills,

and other birds. It's open mid-March to April and the first half of September daily from 11am to 4pm, and May to August daily from 10am to 5pm—but you should call ahead, as the warden may need to let you in.

Boat trips operate daily from Ballycastle pier; the crossing takes 50 minutes. Boat schedules vary and are always subject to weather conditions, but there are usually several crossings a day. (Do check for cancellations in bad weather, though.) To check times and book tickets, call **Rathlin Island Ferry** (www.rathlinballycastleferry.com; ℘ **028/2076-9299**). Round-trip tickets cost £12 adults, £6 children 5–15, free for children under 5, and £32 families; it's advisable to book in advance.

If you find yourself wanting to stay a little longer, **Coolnagrock B&B** (www.rathlin-island.co.uk; ℘ **028/2076-3983**), which has distant views of the Mull of Kintyre in Scotland, costs from £70 for a double. It's open April to October.

For more information about Rathlin, visit **www.rathlin-island.co.uk**.

minutes. The Bushmills coffee shop serves tea, coffee, snacks, and lunch. *Tip:* Although tours take place on weekends, the distillery itself is only in operation from Monday to Friday.

2 Distillery Rd., Co. Antrim, BT57 8XH. www.bushmills.com. ℘ **028/2073-3218.** Admission £9 adults; £8 seniors and students; £5 children 8–17; £25 families. No children under 8 on tour. Apr–Oct tours about every 20 min. Mar–Oct Mon–Sat 9:15am–4:45pm, Sun noon–4:45pm (last tours 4pm); Nov–Feb Mon–Sat 9:30am–4:45pm, Sun noon–4:45pm (last tours 3:30pm). Check opening times before visiting.

Torr Head Scenic Road ★★ SCENIC DRIVE   This diversion is spectacular, but it's not for those with a fear of heights or narrow dirt roads; nor is it a good idea to drive in bad weather. But on a sunny, dry day, the brave can follow signs from **Cushendun** ★ (p. 526) up a very steep hill at the edge of town onto the Torr Head Scenic Road. After a precipitous climb, the road narrows further and inches its way along the edge of the cliff overlooking the sea. Arguably the best views are to be had at Murlough Bay (follow the signs).

Torr Rd., heading N out of Cushendun, Co. Antrim.

Where to Stay in County Antrim

EXPENSIVE

The Bushmills Inn ★★   This very popular inn close to the Giant's Causeway makes a handy place to base yourself while exploring the area. It's been welcoming guests in one way or another since the 1600s, and it has centuries of charm. Lounges are warmed by wood fires, and there are little snugs and side rooms where you can settle down with a book. Rooms are modestly sized but have large, comfortable beds and modern baths. The **restaurant** (p. 532) is among the best in the region for locally sourced seafood and sturdy Irish cooking. There's casual dining in the bar, and high tea in the afternoon. Book early—this place fills up well in advance.

9 Dunluce Rd., Giant's Causeway, Bushmills, Co. Antrim, BT57 8QG. www.bushmills inn.com. ✆ **028/2073-3000.** 41 units. £170–£330 double. Free parking. Rates include breakfast. **Amenities:** Restaurant; bar; Wi-Fi (free).

15

DAY TRIPS FROM BELFAST

The Causeway Coast

An abandoned house at Ushet Point on south Rathlin Island.

Galgorm Resort ★★★ With its creamy-white buildings and vast green grounds, this riverside resort makes an impact from the moment you pull up outside. The reception rooms and lounges are in the original 19th-century house, where you'll find fires crackling at the hearth and polished oak paneling. Most guest rooms are in the well-designed modern extensions, which blend seamlessly with the old. Guest rooms have a masculine edge, with dark fabrics and tartan accessories. Some bathrooms are more modern than others—the newest rooms are the most up-to-date, but all are comfortable, spacious, and quiet, with rural views. The hotel has *four* restaurants, so you won't lack for food. The **River Room** offers formal dining, **Gillies Grill** serves brasserie fare, **Fratelli's** is a casual Italian in a vaulted space, and **Castle Kitchen** has a gastropub vibe. Plus, there's a formal tearoom, two bars . . . we genuinely lose count. Outside in the garden are heated seats and open fires. The friendly staff has thought of everything. The spa is simply huge, with pools, thermal suites, and hot tubs. You may never want to leave.

Fenaghy Rd., Ballymena, Co. Antrim, BT42 1EA. www.galgorm.com. © **028/2588-1001.** 125 units. £215–£450 double. Free parking. Rates include breakfast. **Amenities:** 4 restaurants; 2 bars; tearoom; championship golf course; pool; spa; Wi-Fi (free).

MODERATE

Whitepark House ★★ This lovely little place, just a couple of miles from the Carrick-a-Rede Rope Bridge (p. 523), was built in the mid-1700s and still retains a traditional feel. Beds are wrought-iron framed; one is a

Thermal Spa Village at the Galgorm Spa & Golf Resort.

THE GIANT'S CAUSEWAY: A poet's-eye VIEW

With what tremendous force, aerial powers,
Once did ye rage in subterraneous bowers.
When roused by torturing fires from all your cayes.
Ye swept the glowing lava's sulphurous wayes;
Ye then beheld the thundering waters pass
Through wide rent gulfs, and changed to instant gas;
Struggling for vent again they upward roll.
And burst their narrow bounds from pole to pole.
'Twas nature's throe, and from the labouring frame
The solid strata, midst encircling flame
Severed and torn, their serried peaks upreared
And o'er the foamy surge the new-formed land appeared.

—From "The Giant's Causeway"
by William Hamilton Drummond (1778–1865)

four-poster, while the others have canopies. Heavy silk fabrics lift the design of the rooms. Views of the well-tended garden are sweet, but ask for a room overlooking the sea if you want to wake up to a spectacular vista. Bob and Siobhan Isles are award-winning hosts and great cooks. Breakfasts are delicious—the full Ulster fry is the specialty, but Bob also takes care of his vegetarian guests (he is one himself).

150 Whitepark Rd., Ballintoy, Co. Antrim, BT54 6NH. www.whiteparkhouse.com. *028/2073-1482.* 3 units. £130 double. Free parking. Rates include breakfast. Children must occupy their own room (no discount). **Amenities:** Wi-Fi (free).

INEXPENSIVE

Ballylagan Organic Farm ★★★ Ballylagan is a working organic farm (the first in Northern Ireland), and at the center of it all is this welcoming little 1840s farmhouse. Owners Patricia and Tom Gilbert are passionate about what they do, and that passion shines through. All breakfast ingredients are completely organic, from the fresh-baked bread to the meat and eggs; home-cooked dinners can be provided if booked in advance. Guest rooms are in a separate building from the owners' home, giving everyone a bit of privacy. Painted in soothing colors, the rooms are large, with comfortable beds. Everything is thought of—tea and home-made cakes await your arrival in the guest lounge. For an extra charge of £10 you can use the wood-burning stove in your room.

12 Ballylagan Rd., Straid, Ballyclare, Co Antrim, BT39 9NF. www.ballylagan.com. *028/9332-2129.* 4 units. £75 double. 2-night minimum stay at certain times. Free parking. Breakfast included in guesthouse lodging. **Amenities:** Wi-Fi (free).

Londonderry Arms Hotel ★   A pleasant Georgian inn in Carnlough, the Londonderry Arms is a well-run, traditional kind of place. The building has its quirks—most of the inn is original, with a well-designed modern extension. Bedrooms are simple but comfortable, and a couple have views of the nearby sea. Triple and quad rooms can offer great savings for families or groups. (Check the website for special offers.) The old place could do with a facelift, in truth, but for this price most of us would accept the odd creak and frayed edge. An unexpected piece of historical trivia about this place: Winston Churchill was once (briefly) the landlord. He inherited it and sold it soon afterward.

20 Harbour Rd., Carnlough, Co. Antrim, BT44 0EU. www.londonderryarmshotel. com. ℓ **028/2888-5255.** 35 units. £115–£135 double. Limited free parking (on street). Breakfast not included in lower rates. **Amenities:** Restaurant; bar; room service; Wi-Fi (free).

Lurig View ★   The atmosphere at this sweet little B&B feels akin to a family home. The manager, Rose Ward, and her husband, Chris, are friendly as can be, and happy to help with planning sightseeing trips, making dinner reservations, and so on. Breakfast is served outside when the weather's good. Nearby, the pretty town of Glenariff is a popular coastal stop; and the beach is a short walk from the front door.

38 Glen Rd., Glenariff, Ballymena, Co. Antrim, BT44 0RF. www.lurigview.co.uk. ℓ **028/2177-1618.** 3 units. £75 double. Free parking. Rates include breakfast. **Amenities:** Wi-Fi (free).

Where to Eat on the Antrim Coast

In addition to the eateries listed here, the **Galgorm Resort and Spa** has four good restaurants (p. 530), open to non-guests as well as guests.

MODERATE

Bushmills Inn ★★ IRISH   This popular restaurant in the Bushmills Inn (p. 532) has all the ambience you'd expect in a 17th-century building. The tables are arranged around warming fireplaces, and the food is classic Irish—creamy seafood pie, slow-braised ham hock with cabbage, poached smoked haddock with sautéed potatoes. Sandwiches are on offer during the day. At night the menu becomes more elaborate. Light bites are available in the **Gas Bar,** and high tea can be taken in the afternoon. Booking is recommended.

9 Dunluce Rd., Giant's Causeway, Bushmills, Co. Antrim, BT57 8QG. www.bushmills inn.com. ℓ **028/2073-3000.** Entrees £14.50–£32. Food served daily noon–2:30pm and 4:30–9pm.

Harry's Shack ★★★ SEAFOOD   You don't get closer to the sea than this windswept restaurant right on Portstewart Strand beach. It's widely considered the best restaurant in the area, so don't let the casual vibe fool you. Inside is a sizeable dining room, with rustic wooden seating, and people book well in advance so they can dig into dishes like the garlicky

Harry's Shack, on Portstewart Strand Beach.

fresh mussels with homemade bread, pan-fried hake with chorizo and chickpeas, or cockles with capers and parsley. Desserts are fabulous here, so try to save room. Have a cocktail before dinner at the bar at the side of the shack. Breakfasts here are memorable.

118 Strand Rd., Portstewart, BT55 7PG. ℗ **028/7083-1783.** Entrees £13–£32. Food served Sun–Tues 10am–10pm; Wed–Sat 10am–11pm.

INEXPENSIVE

Red Door Tea Room ★ CAFE   This little cottage tearoom is cozy and welcoming inside, with a turf-burning stove and the day's menu chalked onto blackboards behind the counter. But if the weather allows you'll want to sit outside—the view from the garden over Ballintoy Harbour is nothing short of stunning. The Red Door serves tempting fresh cakes and desserts and light lunches.

Ballintoy Harbour, Ballintoy, Co. Antrim, BT54 6NA. ℗ **028/2076-9048.** Entrees £9–£14. Tues–Fri 11am–3pm; Sat–Sun 10am–4pm.

Thyme & Co. ★ MODERN IRISH   Another great little cafe on the Causeway Coast drive, Thyme & Co. serves tasty, healthful lunches. Ingredients are locally sourced, and the short menu is thoughtfully put together, featuring freshly baked pies, fishcakes made from salmon and smoked haddock, as well as gourmet sandwiches and wraps. In the summer, it stays open into the evenings on Fridays and Saturdays and serves thin-crust pizzas—a popular choice with locals.

5 Quay Rd., Ballycastle, Co. Antrim, BT54 6BJ. www.thymeandco.co.uk. ℗ **028/2076-9851.** Entrees £5–£9.95. Tues–Fri 10am–4pm; Sat 10am–4pm, 5:30–8pm.

Sports & Outdoor Pursuits

GOLF   North Antrim has several notable courses, including champion pro golfer Darren Clarke's home course, the **Royal Portrush Golf Club,**

The Red Hand of Ulster

Around Belfast and Northern Ireland, you'll frequently come across representations of a red hand. It's carved in door frames, painted on walls and ceilings, and even planted in red flowers in gardens. Known as the Red Hand of Ulster, it is one of the symbols of the region. According to one version of the old tale, the hand can trace its history from a battle between two men competing to be king of Ulster. They held a race (some say by boat; others say it took place on horseback) and agreed that the first man to touch Ulster soil would win. As one man fell behind, he pulled out his sword and cut off his right hand, then with his left, flung the bloody hand ahead of his competitor, winning the right to rule.

Dunluce Road, Portrush (www.royalportrushgolfclub.com; ✆ **028/7082-2311**). Royal Portrush has two links courses; its celebrated Dunluce Course has been ranked number 3 in the United Kingdom. Greens fees here range from £100 (Nov–Mar) to £255.

PONY TREKKING   **Watertop Farm Family Activity Centre,** 188 Cushendall Rd., Ballycastle (www.watertopfarm.co.uk; ✆ **028/2076-2576**), offers pony trekking and other outdoor activities. In the Portrush area, contact **Maddybenny Riding Centre,** Loguestown Road, Portrush (www.maddybenny.com; ✆ **028/7082-3394**); Maddybenny also has some self-catering cottages. For a trek in the hills or on the beach, try **Sheans Horse Farm** in Armoy, Ballymoney (www.sheanshorsefarm.com; ✆ **0775/9320-434**).

WALKING   **The Gobbins** is 3-hour guided cliff path walk with caves and sea views near Larne (www.thegobbinscliffpath.com; ✆ **028/9337-2318**). A section of the **Ulster Way,** 904km (560 miles) of marked trail, follows the North Antrim Coast from Glenarm to Portstewart. The **Moyle Way** offers a spectacular inland detour from Ballycastle south for 37km (26 miles) to Glenariff Forest Park. Last, but far from least, the **Causeway Coast Path** stretches for 47km (33 miles) from Ballintoy Harbour to Bushfoot Strand, near Bushmills. Short of sprouting wings, this is the best way to take in the full splendor of the North Antrim Coast. For a taster, **Away A Wee Walk** (www.awayaweewalk.com; ✆ **078-3770-3643**) will take you on a 5-mile tour of the Causeway cliffs. There are comprehensive guides to each route, including downloadable maps, on the excellent Northern Ireland walker's website www.walkni.com.

THE ARDS PENINSULA & MOURNE MOUNTAINS

The Ards Peninsula, beginning about 16km (10 miles) east of Belfast, curls around **Strangford Lough.** A wildlife reserve of great natural beauty, it's also lined with historic buildings and ancient sites, from the austere **Castle Ward** and the elegant **Mount Stewart House** to the mysterious, megalithic **Giant's Ring.** All are an easy drive from Belfast city center—you can reach most sights in half an hour, perfect for a day trip.

More outdoorsy types will want to press on to explore the Mourne Mountains, the highest mountains in Northern Ireland. The rocky landscape here is breathtaking—all gray granite, yellow gorse, purple heather, and white stone cottages. The ancestral home of the Brontës is here, in ruins. But the region is not desolate: You have forest parks, sandy beaches, lush gardens, and, of course, pubs to explore.

Visitor Information

The **Downpatrick Visitor Information Centre** at the St. Patrick Centre, Market Street (𝄞 **028/4461-9000**), is open daily. You can also get information at the **Newcastle Visitor Information Centre** at 10–14 Central Promenade, Newcastle (𝄞 **028/4372-2222**), and the **Kilkeel Visitor Information Centre** at the Nautilus Centre, The Harbour, Kilkeel (𝄞 **028/4176-2525**).

Exploring the Ards Peninsula

Two roads traverse the **Ards Peninsula:** the A20 (the Lough road) and the A2 (the coast road). The Lough road is the more scenic. At the southern tip of the peninsula in Portferry; you'll need to take a 10-minute car ferry ride (www.nidirect.gov.uk/articles/strangford-ferry-timetable; 𝄞 **030/0200-7898**) across The Narrows to the village of Strangford on the other side. Ferries run twice an hour weekdays more or less from 7:30am (8am Sat and 9:30am Sun) to 10:30pm (11pm on Sat).

Castle Espie Wetland Centre ★ NATURE SITE   This wildlife center, named for a castle that has long since ceased to be, is home to rare migratory geese, ducks, and swans. Some birds are so accustomed to visitors that they will eat grain from their hands. Guided trails are designed for children and families, and the center sponsors activities and events year-round. Every summer, the "duckery" becomes home to dozens of adorable, newly hatched goslings, ducklings, and cygnets. The restaurant serves good lunches (no duck on the menu . . .) and cakes.

78 Ballydrain Rd., Comber, Co. Down, BT23 6EA. www.wwt.org.uk/wetland-centres/castle-espie. 𝄞 **028/9187-4146.** Admission £8.54 adults; £7.27 seniors and students; £4.72 children 4–16; children 3 and under free; £22.59 families. Visitor center daily 10am–5pm (5:30pm on summer weekends). Reserve 10am–4:30apm. In winter, last admission 3:30pm.

Castle Ward ★★ HISTORIC HOUSE   About 2km (1¼ miles) west of Strangford village, this grand manor house dates from 1760. A hybrid of architectural styles melding Gothic with neoclassical, it sits on a 280-hectare (692-acre) country estate. Inside, kids can dress up in period clothes and play with period toys, while outside they can roam formal gardens, woodlands, lakes, and seashore, and even ride a tractor-trailer out to see the farm animals. A theater in the stable yard hosts operatic performances in summer. Castle Ward achieved a degree of latter-day fame as Winterfell, one of the key locations for HBO's *Game of Thrones* (see box on p. 539)—albeit heavily disguised.

Park Rd., Strangford, Co. Down, BT30 7LS. www.nationaltrust.org.uk/castle-ward. ℂ **028/4488-1204.** Admission £10 adults; £5 children; £25 families. Grounds: daily 9am–6pm. House: Mar–Oct daily 11am–4pm. House closed Nov–Feb.

Giant's Ring ★★ ANCIENT SITE   This massive and mysterious prehistoric earthwork, 180m (590 ft.) in diameter, has at its center a megalithic chamber with a single capstone. Ancient burial rings like this were thought to be protected by fairies and were left untouched, but this one is quite an exception. In the 19th century, it was used as a racetrack, and the high embankment around it served as grandstands. Today, its dignity has been restored, and it is a place of wonder for the few travelers who make the journey. It's 6km (3¾ miles) southwest of Belfast center, west off A24.

Near Shaw's Bridge, off Ballynahatty Rd., Ballynahatty, Co. Down, BT8 8LE. Free admission (open site).

Grey Abbey ★ RELIGIOUS SITE   On the eastern shore of Strangford Lough, the striking ruins of Grey Abbey sit amid a beautifully landscaped setting, perfect for a picnic. Founded in 1193 by the Cistercians, it

Medieval ruins on the grounds of Castle Ward.

contained one of the earliest Gothic churches in Ireland. Many Cistercian ruins were quite elaborate, but this one is surprisingly plain. Amid the ruined choirs is a fragmented stone effigy of a knight in armor, possibly a likeness of John de Courcy, husband of the abbey's founder, Affreca of Cumbria. There's a reconstructed medieval herb garden, and a small visitor center has exhibits on the abbey's history.

Main St., Greyabbey, Co. Down, BT22 2NQ. © **028/9181-1491.** Free admission. Abbey: Mon–Fri 8:30am–8pm; Sat–Sun 10am–8pm. Visitor center: Mon–Thurs 8am–4:30pm, Fri 8am–1pm; closed Sat–Sun.

Legananny Dolmen ★ ANCIENT SITE This mysterious granite *dolmen* (Neolithic tomb) on the southern slope of Slieve Croob is huge, and yet its massive capstone seems weightlessly poised on the uprights. Signposted halfway between Dromara and Castlewellan on the lower slopes of Slieve Croob Mountain, 40km (25 miles) south of Belfast.

Signposted off Legananny Rd. Leitrim, Co. Down, BT32 3QR. No phone. Free admission (open site).

Mount Stewart House, Garden, and Temple of the Winds ★★
HISTORIC HOUSE/GARDENS Once the home of Lord Castlereagh, this 18th-century house and lush gardens sits on the eastern shore of Strangford Lough. An impressive array of unusual plants flourishes here, thanks to a rare mild microclimate. Inside the house, the excellent art collection includes the *Hambletonian* by George Stubbs and portraits by Pompeo Batoni and Anton Raphael Mengs. The Temple of the Winds, a fine 18th-century banqueting house, is also on the estate, but it's only open Sunday afternoons (and not in winter). Admission to the house is by guided tour only.

Portaferry Rd., Newtownards, Co. Down, BT22 2AD. www.nationaltrust.org.uk/mount-stewart. © **028/4278-8387.** House & Lakeside Garden: £11 adults; £5.50 children; £27.50 families. House: Apr–Oct daily 11am–3:45pm; Nov–Mar Thurs–Sun 11am–3:15pm. Gardens: Mar–Oct daily 10am–4:30pm; Nov–Feb daily 10am–4pm. Temple: Mar–Oct Sun 2–4pm; closed Nov–Mar. Last admission 1 hr. before closing.

Nendrum Monastic Site ★ RELIGIOUS SITE Hidden away on an isolated island, this site dates from the 5th century. It's much older than Grey Abbey across the water, and the remains of the ancient community founded by St. Mochaoi (St. Mahee) are fascinating. Foundations show the outline of ancient churches, a round tower, and beehive cells. Other interesting details are concentric stone ramparts and a sundial, reconstructed from long-broken pieces. Its visitor center shows informative videos and has insightful exhibits. The road to Mahee Island crosses a causeway to Reagh Island and a bridge still protected by the 15th-century Mahee Castle.

Mahee Island, Ringneill Rd., Comber, Co. Down, BT23 6EP. © **028/9082-3207.** Free admission (open site). Visitor center: Apr–May Tues–Sun 10am–5pm; June to mid-Sept daily 10am–5pm; Mar and mid-Sept to Oct Tues–Sun noon–4pm; Nov–Feb Sun noon–4pm.

Portaferry Castle ★ CASTLE   Though it's little more than a small 16th-century tower house, at one time Portaferry Castle, together with another tower house in Strangford, controlled all the ship traffic through the Narrows. This piece of history stands right beside the harbor; it's worth popping your head in for a peek.

Castle St., Portaferry, Co. Down. Free admission. Easter–Aug Mon–Sat 10am–5pm, Sun 1–5pm.

Exploring the Mourne Mountains

Below the Ards Peninsula, the A2 continues south to the **Mourne Mountains** area, although if you're going there directly from Belfast, the A24 is a good shortcut. The drive from Belfast directly to Newcastle should take just under an hour. If you're driving up from Dublin, turn east off the Dublin-Belfast Road at Newry and take A2, following the north shore of Carlingford Lough, between the mountains and the sea. It's a drive you won't soon forget.

This outdoorsy region is dominated by the massive barren peak of **Slieve Donard** (839m/2,752 ft.). From the top, the view takes in the full length of Strangford Lough, Lough Neagh, the Isle of Man, and, on a crystalline day, the west coasts of Wales and Scotland. (The recommended ascent of Slieve Donard is from Donard Park on the south side of Newcastle.) If that's too high for you, head to the heart of the Mournes, to the exquisite **Silent Valley Reservoir** (p. 541). Recreational opportunities abound (p. 544), but it also has some intriguing old ruins to explore. **Newcastle,** a lively traditional seaside resort with a golden sand beach and one of the finest golf courses in Ireland, makes a good base for exploring the area; several small coastal towns strung along the A2 road—**Kilkeel, Rostrevor,** and **Warrenpoint**—offer their own low-key charms.

Castlewellan Forest Park ★★
NATURE SITE   Surrounding a fine trout lake and watched over by the stately mid-19th-century Castlewellan Castle (sadly, closed to the public), this forest park begs for picnics and outdoor activities. Woodland walks, a formal walled garden, and an interesting lakeside sculpture trail are among its attractions. Anglers can fish for trout (brown and rainbow) in the lake. You can get lost in the **Peace Maze,** an enormous hedge maze designed to represent the path to peace in Northern Ireland. The main draw is the **National Arboretum,** opened

Canoeing the lake at Castlewellan Forest Park.

khaleesi **DOES IT**

Unless you've been living beyond the Wall, you'll have heard of a little TV show called *Game of Thrones*. For nearly a decade, the HBO super-hit was the most popular show in the world—and much of it was filmed right here, in Northern Ireland.

Although *Game of Thrones* ended in 2019, it's still raking in big bucks for the local tourism industry. In many places you'll even find the kind of permanent information boards more usually associated with real-life history, instead describing what was filmed there. Major locations included **Castle Ward** ★★ (p. 535); **Cushendun** ★ (p. 526) and **Ballintoy** (p. 524) on the Antrim Coast Drive; and the **Tollymore Forest Park** ★★ in County Down (p. 541).

Many companies offer locations tours, but perhaps the best, and longest-running, come from **Brit Movie Tours.** The epic, 9-hour **Game of Thrones Tour from Belfast with Giant's Causeway** takes in many of the most scenic places used in the show. It really packs in a lot, in addition to various fan-related fun along the way, such as a quiz (dressing up is not unheard of). It includes a 90-minute visit to the Causeway (p. 523), which hasn't actually appeared in the show (but it would seem silly to pass and not stop). Tours depart daily at 9am from the Irish Tour Tickets Office at 10 Great Victoria Street, Belfast, and return roughly 9 hours later. In July and August, when the days are long, a second tour departs at noon. Tickets cost £39. Please note that due to the content, the tour is not suitable for children under 16. Private tours, in a people carrier, can be booked

for £480 to £700, depending on the number of people (maximum six).

The **Game of Thrones Winterfell Tour from Belfast,** another 9-hour event, takes in some locations to the south of Belfast, including Castle Ward. This option includes even more in the way of Westerosian hijinks, including photo ops with the prop Direwolf pups used in the show (important note: not actual puppies) and the chance to sit on an imitation Iron Throne. This tour departs at 9am from the tourism office on Donegall Square, Belfast. From March to September, there are tours on Friday, Saturday, and Sunday; from June to August, Monday, Tuesday, and Thursday to Saturday; from October to February, Saturdays at 9am. Tickets cost £65. Again, the tour is considered unsuitable for kids, although unlike the other tour, it does allow children from the age of 12 with written permission from a parent or guardian in advance (no price concession). The private version of this tour costs £650 to £1,100.

Disabled travelers should also note that, because of the historic and sometimes remote nature of the locations visited, neither tour is wheelchair-accessible.

Space on all tours is limited, so reservations are absolutely essential. For details and booking, call © **0844/247-1007** in Northern Ireland and Britain (© **44/207-118-1007** in the rest of the world) or visit **www.britmovietours.com**.

in 1740 and now 10 times its original size. The largest of its three greenhouses features aquatic plants and a collection of free-flying tropical birds. The town of Castlewellan, elegantly laid out around two squares, is a short distance away, as is the ancient fort of **Drumena Cashel** (see below).

Forest Office: The Grange, Castlewellan Forest Park, Castlewellan, Co. Down, BT31 9BU. © **028/4377-8664.** Admission and parking £5 per car. Daily 10am–sunset.

DOWNPATRICK: sainted TOWN

Legend has it that when St. Patrick came to Ireland in A.D. 432 to begin his missionary work, strong winds blew his boat to the ancient fortified town of Downpatrick, at the south end of Strangford Lough. He'd meant to sail up the coast to County Antrim, where as a young slave he had tended flocks on Slemish Mountain. Instead, as fate would have it, he settled here and converted the local chieftain Dichu and his followers to Christianity. Over the next 30 years, Patrick roamed through Ireland carrying out his work, but this is where he died. Some believe he is buried in the graveyard of Downpatrick Cathedral, although there's no proof. Because of all of this, the town tends to be crowded, largely with Catholic pilgrims, around St. Patrick's Day.

Stop in first at the **Down County Museum** (www.downcountymuseum. com; © **028/4461-5218**), The Mall, English St., BT30 6AH. Set in a converted jail, the museum tells the story of Down from the Stone Age to the present day. It also has a handy tearoom. The museum is open Wednesday to Saturday from 10am to 4pm. Entry is free.

Almost next door to the museum, at the end of the English Street cul-du-sac, is **Down Cathedral** (www.down cathedral.org; © **028/4461-4922**). Excavations show that Downpatrick was a *dún* (fort), perhaps from the Bronze Age, and its earliest structures were built on the site where this church now sits. Ancient fortifications ultimately gave way to a series of churches, each built atop the ruins of the previous incarnation,

Drumena Cashel ★ ANCIENT SITE   Ireland once had thousands of fortifications like this irregularly shaped stone-ring fort, a farmstead dating from the early Christian period. This is one of the better-preserved examples. During the age of the Viking invasions, it likely provided protection for the local population. Its walls, partially rebuilt in the mid-1920s, measure 2.7m (9 ft.) to 3.6m (12 ft.) thick. The *souterrain* (underground stone tunnel) is T-shaped and was likely used in ancient times for cold storage.

Signposted from A25, 3km (2 miles) SW of Castlewellan, Co. Down. Free (open site).

Dundrum Castle ★ CASTLE   The oldest visible portions of this castle's striking and extensive ruins date from the 12th century. This was once one of the mightiest of the Norman castles in Northern Ireland (second only to Carrickfergus), and it still commands the imagination. The enormous keep was built in the 13th century, as was the gatehouse. It was the home of the Maginnis family until the 17th century, when it was captured by Oliver Cromwell's army, who destroyed it in 1652. The hilltop setting is lovely, with panoramic views.

6.5km (4 miles) E of Newcastle, off A2, Dundrum, Co. Down, BT33 0NF. © **028/9082-3027.** Free admission. Castle: June–Aug daily 10am–5pm; Oct–Apr and Sept Tues–Sat 10am–4:30pm; Sun 1–4:30pm. Last admission 30 min. before closing. Grounds: Daily year-round.

over 1,800 years. The current cathedral is an 18th- and 19th-century reconstruction of its 13th- and 16th-century predecessors. Just south of the cathedral stands a relatively recent monolith inscribed with the name "patric." By some accounts, it roughly marks the grave of the saint, who is said to have died at Saul, 3km (2 miles) northeast. The tradition identifying this site as Patrick's grave seems to go back no further than the 12th century, though, when John de Courcy reputedly transferred the bones of saints Columba and Brigid to lie beside those of St. Patrick. The cathedral is open to visitors Monday to Saturday from 9:30am to 4pm and Sun 1–4pm. Entry is free.

A 5-minute walk away, the modern glass-and-steel **St. Patrick Centre,** 53A Market St., BT30 6LZ (www.

saintpatrickcentre.com; ✆ **028/4461-9000**), tells the story of Ireland's patron saint through high-tech displays and exhibits. It also has an exhibition devoted to the legacy of Irish missionaries who helped spread Christianity in Europe in the latter half of the first millennium. The center is open Monday to Saturday from 9am to 5pm (last admission 4pm); also Sunday 1 to 5pm in July and August. Entry costs £5.75 adults; £4.50 seniors and students; £3.50 children; and £14 families.

Downpatrick is about 34km (21 miles) southeast of Belfast. To get there from the city by car, take A24 then A7; the drive takes just under 40 minutes. You can also get there by bus (a 1-hr. trip) from the Europa Bus Station on Great Victoria Street.

Greencastle Royal Castle ★ CASTLE   The first castle on this site, built in 1261, faced its companion, Carlingford Castle, across the mouth of the lough. It was then a two-story rectangular tower surrounded by a curtain wall with corner towers. Very little of that survives; most of what you see is from the 14th century. It served as a royal garrison until it was destroyed by Cromwell's forces in 1652. Opening times are somewhat unpredictable, so call ahead before visiting.

6.5km (4 miles) SW of Kilkeel, Greencastle, Cranfield Point, Co. Down, BT34 4LR. ✆ **028/9082-3207.** Free admission.

Silent Valley Mountain Park ★★ NATURE SITE   This park surrounds the Silent Valley Reservoir, the major source of water for County Down. Easy, well-marked paths wind around the lake, and there's a coffee shop near the information center. A shuttle bus takes visitors from the center to the top of nearby Ben Crom; it runs on weekends in May, June, and September and daily in July and August.

Information Centre: Head Rd., Kilkeel, Newry, Co. Down, BT34 4HU www.niwater. com/silent-valley. ✆ **084/5744-0088.** Free admission. Parking £5 per car. Pedestrians £1.60 or 60p per child. Daily 9:30am–6pm.

Tollymore Forest Park ★★ NATURE SITE   All that's left of the once-glorious Tollymore House is this delightful 480-hectare (1,186-acre) wildlife and forest park. The park offers a number of walks up into the north slopes of the Mourne Mountains or along the Shimna River (known for its exceptionally fine salmon). The Shimna walk has several beguiling caves and grottos. The park is scattered with follies, such as faux-medieval castle gatehouses and other fanciful fakes. The forest is a nature preserve inhabited by a host of local wildlife like badgers, foxes, otters, and pine martens. And don't miss the trees for the forest—some exotic species here include the magnificent Himalayan cedars and a 30m (98-ft.) sequoia in the arboretum.

Off B180, 3.2km (2 miles) NW of Newcastle, Tullybrannigan Rd., Newcastle, County Down. ✆ **028/4372-2428.** Free admission. Parking £5 per car. Daily 10am–dusk.

Where to Stay in the Ards Peninsula & Mourne Mountains

Ards Peninsula sights are close enough to Belfast to allow you to get back to your Belfast hotel for the night, but if you're venturing out to the Mourne Mountains—particularly if you're engaging in the outdoor activities for which the area is justly famed—you'll need a place to lay your head overnight.

The Carriage House ★★ With a view of Dundrum Castle on one side, and a shimmering bay dotted with sailboats on the other, it's little wonder that this lovely little B&B inspires artistic sentiment. Owner Maureen Griffith is a collector of unique art, and her creative eye has furnished almost every corner of her terraced house with something wonderful to look at. She's also a great cook; breakfasts here are special, including produce picked fresh from the garden. She doesn't cook evening meals but will recommend places to eat within walking distance.

71 Main St., Dundrum, Co. Down, BT33 0LU. www.carriagehousedundrum.com. ✆ **028/4375-1635.** 3 units. £90 double. Breakfast included. Free parking (on street). **Amenities:** Garden; Wi-Fi (free).

Dunnanelly Country House

★★★ Just outside Downpatrick, this delightful country mansion is a truly idyllic retreat, set on beautiful grounds that stretch for miles. The decor inside mixes a feeling of history with a playful edge: traditional, Regency-style color schemes and furnishings offset by pieces of modern art, an interesting sculpture, or (memorably) an antique

Hiking the Mourne Mountains.

The Ards Peninsula & Mourne Mountains

DAY TRIPS FROM BELFAST

walk this way: THE MOURNE WALL TREK

Between 1904 and 1922, the 36km (22-mile) dry-stone Mourne Wall and dam was built to enclose Silent Valley. The **Mourne Wall Trek** follows the wall in a circuit that climbs over 15 of the Mourne Mountains' main peaks. The steep path is more than most hikers want to take on, and probably shouldn't be attempted in a single day (though some serious hikers have done it in a day). But it is a fine, long walk for experienced ramblers and offers wonderful views. You can join the pathway at several different places, and you can hike either clockwise or counter-clockwise. For more information about the route, including maps and a photo log of every stage, go to **www.mourne wall.co.uk**.

rocking horse, complete with mouth open in an oh-so-happy-to-see-you grin. The guest rooms are thoughtfully designed with large, modern bathrooms and have lovely views of the estate, tempting you to take a gentle stroll or invigorating hike. And you may need that exercise to help work off the hearty and delicious breakfasts. Guests have the use of a conservatory, a sitting room, and a separate game room. There's no dinner, but the owners can cheerfully point you in the direction of the best local pubs.

26 Rocks Chapel Rd., Downpatrick, Co. Down, BT30 9BA. www.dunnanelly countryhouse.com. © **077/1277-9085.** 6 units. £120 double. Free parking. Breakfast included. No children under 12 unless all 3 rooms booked by same group. **Amenities:** Wi-Fi (free).

The Slieve Donard Spa and Resort ★★   The spindly, neo-Gothic turret of this 1897 hotel stands like a beacon overlooking Dundrum Bay. The surroundings are certainly dramatic, but inside this is a relaxing, luxurious place. Bedrooms are good-sized and modern; many have views of the bay and Mourne Mountains. Executive bedrooms are bigger and have air-conditioning—a bonus if you're visiting during a rare heat wave. The excellent spa has a long list of treatments, from Ayurvedic regimens to hot stone massages and full-body salt scrubs. (Prices aren't cheap, however—expect to pay £85–£135 for a 1- to 2-hr. signature treatment.) The two restaurants are the formal **Oak Room** and the more relaxed **Percy French.** Dinner, bed-and-breakfast packages offer good savings.

Downs Rd., Newcastle, Co. Down, BT33 0AH. www.hastingshotels.com. © **028/4372-1066.** 180 units. £230–£400 double. Free parking. Breakfast included. **Amenities:** 2 restaurants; bar; gym; pool; room service; spa; Wi-Fi (£10 per day).

Where to Eat in the Ards Peninsula & Mourne Mountains

Brunel's ★★★ IRISH   Local flavors are prepared with imaginative flair at this excellent restaurant just a mile from the Slieve Donard Spa and Resort (see above). Mussels fresh from Strangford Lough are a simple but

15

DAY TRIPS FROM BELFAST

The Ards Peninsula & Mourne Mountains

delicious lead-in to a dish of coley (a fish similar to cod) cooked with smoked egg-yolk puree, or rigatoni with hay-baked celeriac. This is the kind of place where you'll witness a sea of cellphones taking photos of each course before demolition of the artful arrangements on the plate. The early-evening menu is a bargain—two courses for just £23, or three for £27—served until 9pm on Monday and Tuesday, and until 7pm Wednesday to Friday. *Another moneysaving tip:* Main dishes at lunch generally cost half, or even a third, of what you pay in the evening.

32 Downs Rd., Newcastle, Co. Down, BT33 0HJ. www.brunelsrestaurant.co.uk. ✆ **028/4372-3951.** Entrees £18–£34. Thurs noon–3pm, 5–9pm; Fri–Sat noon–3pm, 5pm–9:30pm; Sun 12:30pm–8pm.

The Daily Grind ★★ CAFE   A great place to know about for a quick lunch in Downpatrick, this funky cafe is a favorite of locals. It specializes in creative and tasty sandwiches, which go down nicely with a cup of fresh coffee if you can forgive the atrociously punning names ("Buy One Get One Brie," "Pitta Pocket or Two"—you get the idea). Try the Daily Grind Special, a delicious salad served with toast and chili jam. It also has vegan options, not to mention a host of tempting cakes. The cafe closes at 3:30pm.

St. Patrick's Ave., Downpatrick, BT30 6DW. ✆ **028/4461-7173.** Entrees £5.50–£9. Mon–Sat 10am–3:30pm.

Mourne Seafood Bar ★★ SEAFOOD   Situated just a street back from the quay in Dundrum, this seaside outpost of one of Belfast's best restaurants (p. 516) is worth traveling for if you're staying in the countryside—or worth a detour for a leisurely lunch. The menu is strictly oriented around whatever's good and fresh that day, but you may well be offered salt and pepper prawns with cucumber and soy, crispy whitebait (tiny, bite-sized fish, deep-fried), or a plate of oysters from Carlingford Lough. The only real snag is that it's hardly an undiscovered gem—you'll be lucky to get a table for dinner without a reservation on weekends, especially in summer.

10 Main St., Dundrum, Co. Down, BT33 0LU. www.mourneseafood.com. ✆ **028/4375-1377.** Entrees £8–£28. Wed–Fri 12:30–3pm, 5–10pm; Sat–Sun 12:30–10pm. Closed Mon–Wed.

Sports & Outdoor Pursuits

ADVENTURE SPORTS   For canoeing, rock climbing, bushcraft, watersports, and a variety of other intrepid activities in the Mourne Mountains, contact **One Great Adventure,** the Grange Yard, Castlewellan Forest Park, Castlewellan (www.onegreatadventure.com; ✆ **028/4377-0714**).

CYCLING   The foothills of the Mournes around Castlewellan are ideal for cycling, with panoramic vistas and very little traffic. In these parts, the perfect year-round outfitter is **Ross Cycles,** 44 Clarkhill Rd., Castlewellan (✆ **028/4377-8029**), signposted from the Clough-Castlewellan Road,

.8km (½ mile) out of Castlewellan. The shop carries mountain bikes for the whole family, including children's seats. You can park and ride or request local delivery. Daily rates start at around £10, with family and weekly rates available.

DIVING The Ards Peninsula's lakes and offshore waters are a diver's dream—remarkably clear and littered with wrecks. One of Europe's finest training centers, **DV Diving,** 138 Mount Stewart Rd., Newtownards, County Down (www.dvdiving.co.uk; ✆ **028/9186-1686**), offers diving courses.

GOLF **Royal County Down ★**, Newcastle, County Down (www.royal countydown.org; ✆ **028/4372-3314**), is nestled in huge sand dunes with the Mourne Mountains in the background. This 18-hole, par-71 championship course was created in 1889 and is still considered to be among the best. Greens fees are £290 to £300, depending on the day and time of year. Between November and April, prices drop to £90–£160. Not too far away, the **Kilkeel Golf Club,** Mourne Park, Ballyardle, Kilkeel (www.kilkeel golfclub.org; ✆ **028/4176-5095**), is a beautiful parkland course on the historic Kilmorey Estate. Greens fees are £40 weekdays and £50 on weekends and bank holidays.

COUNTY ARMAGH

A green, rolling stretch of gentle hills and small villages, County Armagh is also one of Northern Ireland's most rebellious Republican regions—you'll notice police watchtowers atop some hills, as well as the occasional barracks (mostly empty these days).

The handsome cathedral town of Armagh City makes a good touring base. A short distance outside the city, the small town of Bessbrook has historic cottages, the forests of Slieve Gullion, and ancient Navan Fort, the most important archaeological site in Ulster. The area's greatest natural attraction is a 40-minute drive north of Armagh City: Lough Neagh, Ireland's largest lake (see box on p. 546).

Visitor Information

The **Armagh Visitor Information Centre,** 40 Upper English St., Armagh (www.visitarmagh.com; ✆ **028/3752-1800**), is the main information point for the surrounding area. It's open all year, Monday to Friday from 9am to 5pm (and weekends in summer).

Exploring County Armagh

Armagh City's name, from the Irish *ard Mhacha* (Macha's height), refers to the pagan queen Macha, who is said to have built a fortress here. It's no coincidence that St. Patrick chose to base himself here—it was a bold challenge to the native paganism. The simple stone church that he built in the 5th century is now the stately St. Patrick's Church of Ireland Cathedral

LOUGH neagh

Now here's a great creation story: Irish lore maintains that Lough Neagh—the largest lake in Ireland—was created by the mighty giant Fionn MacCumhail (Finn McCool) when he dug up a chunk of earth to fling into the sea to create the Isle of Man. It must have been a sizeable chunk indeed to gouge out this 396 sq.-km (153 sq.-mile) lake.

The **Lough Neagh Discovery Centre,** Oxford Island, Craigavon, Co. Armagh (www.oxfordisland.com; ☏ **028/3832-2205**), is open Monday to Friday 9am to 5pm and Saturday and Sunday 10am to 5pm (6pm Apr–Sept). Admission is free. Part of the enormous, lush Oxford Island Nature Reserve, the center has an exhibition on the Lough and its history, plus information about the best walking trails. It also hosts occasional guided walks (or "rambles") through the reserve; prices and times of any upcoming tours are advertised on the website. There's also a cafe, craft shop, and tourist information center—where, handily, you can rent a pair of binoculars.

However, before you think about taking a dip in the cool, glassy waters, consider this: The lake's claim to fame is its massive population of eels. Yep, the waters are positively infested with the slimy creatures. Hundreds of tons of eels are taken from Lough Neagh and exported each year, mainly to Germany and Holland. The ages-old eel-extraction method involves "long lines" baited with up to 100 hooks. As many as 200 boats trailing these lines are on the lake each night (the best time to go fishing for eels). So maybe take a raincheck on that swim.

If you're not entirely creeped out by that, however, you can take a **boat trip** on the lovely lake. Boats depart regularly from the nearby **Kinnego Marina** (☏ **028/3832-7573**), signposted from the main road. The trip lasts about 45 minutes and costs about £10 for adults, £7 for children. It's advisable to call in advance to book. For a cultural tour of Lough Neagh with some history of the area and a trip with a local fisherman, take a 4-hour tour with **Lough Neagh Tours** (www.loughneaghtours.com; ☏ **028/7941-7941**). Tickets cost £45, and the tours leave from Cranfield Church at 36 Cranfield Rd., Randalstown BT41 3ND.

(p. 548). (Not to be outdone, Armagh City's Roman Catholic cathedral is also called St. Patrick's—see p. 548.) East of the town center, the city also boasts The Mall, a lush park lined with handsome Georgian town houses built of the colorful local limestone. To get to Armagh City from Belfast, take M1 and A3 southwest for 64km (40 miles); the journey takes a little less than an hour.

Armagh County Museum ★ MUSEUM   Intriguing Armagh-related artifacts going back to the Neolithic Age fill this history museum on the Mall. Highlights include a collection of 19th-century Irish bog oak jewelry; Irish police uniforms from the 1820s up to the mid–20th century; and a collection of elaborate fans from around the world, from as far back as the 1700s. Chillingly, the museum also has a genuine scold's bridle, an iron torture instrument and "correctional" device that was placed over a woman's head, with a spike inside her mouth to prevent her from talking.

St. Patrick's Cathedral in Armagh.

It's part of the same National Museums Northern Ireland collective that includes the excellent **Ulster Museum ★★★** (p. 502) and the **Folk & Transport Museum ★★★** (p. 507).

The Mall East, Armagh City, BT61 9BE. www.visitarmagh.com. ℭ **028/3752-3070.** Free admission. Mon–Sat 10am–4pm. Closed Sun.

Armagh Observatory and Planetarium ★★ PLANETARIUM

This state-of-the-art planetarium is a perfect place for kids with an interest in science and astronomy. The digital projection system, which has 3D elements, is impressive. During the summer there's usually a full program every day. Outside the planetarium, take a stroll around the **Astropark,** filled with scale models of planets. You'll pass the 200-year-old **Armagh Observatory** (still a working observatory and not open to the public).

College Hill, Armagh City, BT61 9DB. www.armaghplanet.com. ℭ **028/3752-3689.** Admission to show and exhibition area £8 adults; £5.75 children; £7 seniors and students; £25 families. Tues–Sun 10am–5pm. Closed Mon (except bank holidays).

Benburb Valley Park ★★ NATURE SITE

This sylvan park 11km (7 miles) northeast of Armagh on the River Blackwater contains the ruins of **Benburb Castle,** a squat fortresslike ruin dating from the Plantation of Ulster in the early 1600s. It occupies an impressive cliffside spot over-looking a gorge. In 1646, an Irish army defeated an Anglo-Scottish invasion force at Benburb, thus ending the brief Scottish bid to rule Ireland. The castle is on the grounds of a Servite priory; admission is free, but you have to arrange in advance if you want to do more than see it from the outside. Call the priory at ℭ **028/375-8241** for more information or contact the nearby **Benburb Valley Heritage Centre** (☎ **028/3754-9885**), which has exhibits on the area's history.

89 Milltown Rd., Benburb (take B128 off A29), Co. Armagh, BT71 7LY. ☎ **028/3754-8170.** Park: Free admission. Heritage Centre: £3. Park: Daily until dusk. Heritage Centre: Apr–Sept Mon–Sat 10am–5pm.

Navan Fort and Centre ★★ ANCIENT SITE   Believed to have been the royal and religious capital of Ulster from 1150 B.C. until the spread of Christianity, the Navan Fort is a mysterious place. Its central circular earthwork enclosure holds a smaller circular structure, and it all encloses an Iron Age burial mound. Even today, scientists do not really understand what it was used for, although they know that it was all set on fire around 95 B.C., possibly as part of a ritual.

On A28, signposted from Armagh center, 81 Killylea Rd., Co. Armagh, BT60 4LD. www.armagh.co.uk/navan-centre-fort. ☎ **028/3752-9644.** Admission £8 adults; £5 children; £6.50 seniors and students; £24 families. Tues–Sun 10am–5pm.

Peatlands Park ★ NATURE SITE   This park is a surprisingly lovely 240 hectares (593 acres) of lakes and peat bogs that effectively form one giant nature reserve. You wander through it on a well-designed system of walking paths, or (slightly more fun on rainy days) ride through it on a narrow-gauge railway. Nature walks and events are offered through the year. The park is southwest of Lough Neagh, just across the border into County Tyrone.

33 Derryhubbert Rd. 11km (6¾ miles) SE of Dungannon, at exit 13 off M1, Co Tyrone, BT71 6NW. ☎ **028/3839-9195.** Free admission to park. Rail ride: £2 adults; £1 seniors and children 2–16; £5 families. Vehicle access to park: June–Aug daily 9am–9pm; Mar–May and Sept–Oct daily 9am–7pm; Nov–Feb daily 9am–4:30pm. Railway: July–Aug Sat, Sun, and bank holiday Mon only 11am–4pm.

St. Patrick's Church of Ireland Cathedral ★ CATHEDRAL   Built on the site of St. Patrick's 5th-century church, Armagh's Anglican cathedral dates from the 13th century, although much of the current square-towered brown stone church was built in the 1830s. Inside the church are the remains of an 11th-century Celtic cross, and a strange granite carved figure known as the Tandragee Idol, which dates from the Iron Age. A stone slab on the exterior wall of the north transept marks the spot where Brian Boru, the high king of Ireland who died in the last great battle with the Vikings in 1014, is buried.

43 Abbey St., Armagh City, BT61 7DY. www.stpatricks-cathedral.org. ☎ **028/3752-3142.** Admission £3 adults; £2 seniors and students; free for children. Apr–Oct Wed–Sat 9am–5pm; Nov–Mar Wed–Sat 9am–4pm.

St. Patrick's Roman Catholic Cathedral ★ CATHEDRAL   Built in the mid-1800s, this Catholic cathedral is a grand Gothic Revival building on a hill, its slim twin spires dominating its portion of the town. Outside it's monochromatic gray, but inside is another story, as vividly painted mosaics bathe the interior in color. Unfortunately, a renovation in the

1980s added some modern touches that stand out starkly against its otherwise perfect 19th-century authenticity. The cathedral operates guided and self-guided tours (book in advance).

Cathedral Rd., Armagh City, BT61 7QX. www.armaghparish.net. ⓒ **028/3752-2813.** Free admission. Daily 8am–dusk. Tours Mon–Sat 10:30am–5:30pm; Sun noon–5pm. Guided tours £3; self-guided tours £2.

Where to Stay & Eat in County Armagh

Cross Square Hotel ★   This humble but pleasant inn sits on the main square in Crossmaglen, a little village about 20 miles south of Armagh town. Guest rooms are modern and fairly spacious; some overlook the square itself. Family rooms are enormous, with space enough for six people. A very good in-house restaurant has won awards locally. The restaurant also serves traditional afternoon tea (book ahead). The downstairs bar sometimes has live music sessions on weekends—these can go on late, so light sleepers beware. Crossmaglen is near the border with the Republic; it only takes slightly longer to drive here from Dublin than it does from Belfast (about 1 hr. 15 min.), so this could be a good stop if you're working your way up through Northern Ireland from the southern end.

O'Fiaich Sq., Crossmaglen, Co. Armagh, BT35 9AA. www.crosssquarehotel.co.uk. ⓒ **028/3086-0505.** 15 units. £97 double. Free parking. Breakfast included. **Amenities:** Wi-Fi (free).

Guest room at the Newforge House.

Embers ★★ CAFE/GRILL   For a reviving snack or meal in Armagh town, check out this casual spot, a 3-minute walk from St. Patrick's Church of Ireland Cathedral (see above). Embers serves great coffee and sandwiches, plus a full menu of crowd-pleasing bar-food favorites. It's very much "something for everyone" territory: fish and chips, fajitas, ribs, steaks, salads, and so on. Chase it all down with a comforting plate of deep-dish apple pie, served with a scoop of ice cream. The early-bird special—available every day except Sunday from 5 to 7pm—is a bargain at £14 for two courses, £17 for three.

7 Market St., Armagh City, BT61 7BW. www.embersrestaurant.co.uk. © **028/3751-8544.** Entrees £12.50–£25. Sun–Thurs 9am–9:15pm; Fri–Sat 9am–10:30pm.

Newforge House ★★★   What's not to love? Great food, warm hosts, and a restful night's sleep in a four-poster bed await you in this idyllic country mansion, only a half-hour's drive southwest of Belfast. Host John Mathers, whose family has owned this house since it was built in the early 18th century, is a trained chef, and his gourmet dinners are a real treat. (It's also open to non-guests, so be sure to make dinner reservations by noon on the day.) Seasonal menus, prepared with many ingredients from the house's own garden, feature local meats and seafood. Guest rooms are spacious and light-filled, with floor-to-ceiling windows; one room has a four-poster, while another has a king-size canopy bed. Check the website for special offers, including romantic weekend breaks.

58 Newforge Rd., Magheralin (halfway btw. Lisburn and Craigavon), Co. Armagh, BT67 0QL. www.newforgehouse.com. © **028/9261-1255.** 6 units. £155–£230 double. 2-night minimum on certain dates. Free parking. Breakfast included. Dinner £55. **Amenities:** Wi-Fi (free).

DERRY & THE LAKELANDS

Y
ou'd expect a city with two names to have some stories to tell. And sure enough, Northern Ireland's second city is full of surprises. Derry is *officially* called
Londonderry–but trust us when we tell you that this is
a somewhat thorny issue (see the box on p. 554 for
more on the fraught question of what to call Northern Ireland's second city). The 20th century was unkind to Derry, where some of the
very worst times of the so-called "Troubles" played out. But things
have changed dramatically in the past couple of decades, and now
an undeniable spirit of optimism and renewal reigns. There are still
problems here, and it's not as buzzing as Belfast, but the energy pro-
pelling Derry's cultural shift makes this a fascinating place to visit.

The Sperrin mountains (p. 564) are within an hour's drive of Derry, and
it's conveniently beside Donegal's picturesque Inishowen Peninsula (see
chapter 13), with the Giant's Causeway and the North Antrim coast
(p. 523) within day-trip distance.

ESSENTIALS
Arriving

BY BUS The fastest bus between Belfast and Derry, the no. 212, operated by **Ulsterbus** (www.translink.co.uk; ✆ **028/9066-6630**), takes just
under 2 hours. Ulsterbus also has service from Portrush and Portstewart.
From the Republic, **Bus Éireann** (www.buseireann.ie; ✆ **091/562000**)
offers a few buses a day from Galway (about 5½ hr.), Cork (7–9 hr.), and
Dublin (around 6 hr.). Most of the long-distance routes involve changes.

BY PLANE Service to **Derry Airport** (www.cityofderryairport.com;
✆ **028/7181-0784**) is provided by the budget airline **Ryanair** (www.
ryanair.com; ✆ **0818/303030** in Ireland, 0871/246-0000 in the U.K.) from
London Stansted, Liverpool, and Glasgow and Loganair from Edinburgh
and Liverpool (www.loganair.co.uk; ✆ **0344/800-2855**).

BY TRAIN Northern Ireland Railways (www.translink.co.uk;
✆ **028/9066-6630**) operates frequent trains from Belfast, which arrive at
the Londonderry/Derry Station—known by everyone as **Waterside Railway Station** (✆ **028/7134-2228**), on Duke Street, on the east side of the
Foyle River. The journey takes about 2 hours. A free Linkline bus brings
passengers from the train station to the city center.

PREVIOUS PAGE: **Mussenden Temple, near Castlerock in County Londonderry.**

DERRY CITY

Northern Ireland's second city is a vibrant place, surrounded by 17th-century walls that you can climb, walking the ramparts all the way around the town center. Although they were the focus of attacks and sieges for centuries, the 5-foot-thick fortifications are solid and unbroken to this day. Historians believe the city was modeled on the French Renaissance town of Vitry-Le-Francois, which in turn was based on a Roman military camp, with two main streets forming a central cross and ending in four city gates. It's made for walking, combining a medieval center with sprawling Georgian and Victorian neighborhoods.

Within Ireland, though, Derry is not known for its architecture, but for the fact that, in the 1960s and 1970s, the North's civil rights movement was born here, and baptized in blood on the streets. The "Bloody Sunday" massacre in 1972, in which British troops killed 14 peaceful civil rights protesters in Derry, shocked the world and led to years of violent unrest. In the **Bogside,** as the neighborhood at the bottom of the hill west of the walled section is known, the famed mural reading "you are now entering free derry" remains as a symbol of those times.

Happily, much of that sectarian strife seems to be behind Derry now, and it has begun to reinvent itself as a center of culture and commerce. Symbolic of the changes in Derry is the ***Hands Across the Divide*** sculpture that you pass as you cross the Craigavon Bridge into town. Erected

The sculpture *Hands Across the Divide* symbolizes an end to sectarian strife.

DERRY OR LONDONDERRY: what's in a name?

The short answer is: quite a lot.

Depending on which side of the border you're on, Northern Ireland's second city is called two different things. Road signs and maps in the Republic say **Derry**; in Northern Ireland they point to **Londonderry.**

This stubborn dispute dates to the Plantation of Ulster in the 1600s, when English settlers were given land in Ireland as an attempt to entrench Protestant rule. A new city was founded by the City of London trade guilds and named Londonderry in their honor. Nationalists have always objected to the term, preferring Derry, an Anglicization of *Daire Calgaich*, the name of the much older settlement that once stood on the same site.

During the Troubles, the dispute was a cause célèbre. Many attempts have been made to find a solution, including several unsuccessful court cases. Loyalists fiercely defend the name. But having a city with two names poses a knotty problem for residents and visitors alike— what to call it?

The best advice is just to be tactful. If you're drinking in a pub with a big Irish tricolor on the side, it's probably best to use Derry; but if they're flying the British flag, opt for Londonderry. Of the two, Derry is probably the more commonly used in town, and certainly throughout the Republic, so we've chosen to call it Derry in this book.

Fed up with having to make a political statement whenever they talk about their own city, residents have long since tried to find an acceptable solution to the Derry/Londonderry dilemma. In the 1990s, local radio DJ Gerry Anderson suggested the wry compromise "Stroke City." (American readers: Stroke is a slash in the U.K.) Quick-witted locals swiftly nicknamed the DJ "Gerry/Londongerry."

To see more evidence of how far back this titular dispute goes, look no further than a United States road atlas. Near Manchester, New Hampshire, is a small old town called Derry. In the early 19th century there was a dispute over its name, so a group of residents set up a new town just to the south called—you guessed it—Londonderry.

20 years after Bloody Sunday, it is a bronze sculpture of two men reaching out toward one another.

Also on an upbeat note, the comedy TV show "Derry Girls" has been a huge hit in recent years—the series is set during the Troubles in the 1990s but takes a light-hearted look at life through the eyes of five teens.

Visitor Information

The **Derry Tourist Information Centre** is at 1–3 Waterloo Place, Derry, B48 6BT (www.visitderry.com; © **028/7126-7284**). It's open daily year-round; from May to September, hours are Monday to Saturday 9am to 6pm (7pm June–Aug) and Sunday 10am to 5pm; in April and October the hours are weekdays 9am to 5:30pm and weekends 10am to 5pm; and from November to March the hours are Monday to Saturday 9:30am to 5pm and Sunday 10am to 4pm.

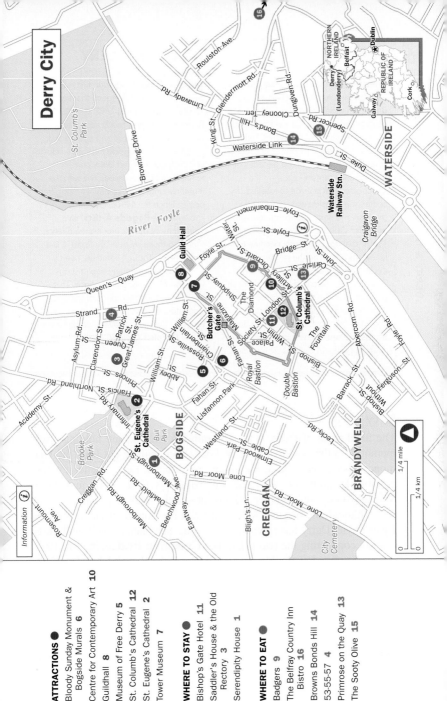

Derry City

ATTRACTIONS ●

Bloody Sunday Monument &
Bogside Murals **6**
Centre for Contemporary Art **10**
Guildhall **8**
Museum of Free Derry **5**
St. Columb's Cathedral **12**
St. Eugene's Cathedral **2**
Tower Museum **7**

WHERE TO STAY ●

Bishop's Gate Hotel **11**
Saddler's House & the Old
Rectory **3**
Serendipity House **1**

WHERE TO EAT ●

Badgers **9**
The Belfray Country Inn
Bistro **16**
Browns Bonds Hill **14**
53-55-57 **4**
Primrose on the Quay **13**
The Sooty Olive **15**

THE bogside: THE PEOPLE'S GALLERY

In many ways, the recent history of Derry is embodied in the district known as the Bogside. In the 1960s and 1970s, the neighborhood bore witness to violent scenes that shocked the world. Today, it's known as much for its powerful street art, chronicling those troubled decades of the late 20th century.

Located just outside the walled city center, the Bogside was developed in the 19th and early 20th centuries as a home for Catholic workers. In the late 1960s, civil rights protests became regular events here, and the residents declared their neighborhood as "Free Derry," independent of local and British government. The situation came to a head on January 30, 1972, later to be known as "Bloody Sunday," when British troops opened fire on a peaceful demonstration, killing 14 civilians. The soldiers said they'd been fired upon first; eventually, in 2010, after an inquiry that lasted 12 years and cost nearly £200 million, the British government finally accepted this was completely untrue and apologized.

Most of the Bogside has been redeveloped, but the Free Derry corner remains, near a house painted with the mural reading "you are now entering free derry." Since the 1990s, local artists known as the **Bogside Artists** have painted more murals around the district, similar to those on the Falls Road in Belfast (p. 497). Though some are overtly political in nature, many depict simple yet powerful messages of peace. This has effectively turned parts of the Bogside into a free art museum, and together the murals have become known as the **People's Gallery.**

City Layout

The focal point of Derry is the **Diamond,** a large square holding a war memorial in the center of the city. Four streets radiate out from the Diamond: Bishop, Ferryquay, Shipquay, and Butcher. Each extends for several blocks and ends at a gateway (Bishop's Gate, Ferryquay Gate, Shipquay Gate, and Butcher's Gate) cut into the thick city walls.

Although the original walled city was built on the west bank of the River Foyle, Derry has spread across to the east bank as well, with three bridges connecting the two sides. The **Craigavon Bridge,** built in 1933, is one of only a few double-decker bridges in the British Isles. The **Foyle Bridge,** Ireland's longest bridge, opened in 1984 and provides a dual-lane highway about 3.2km (2 miles) north of the Craigavon Bridge. The sleek, modern **Peace Bridge** links Ebrington Square with the rest of the city's central area. Its name refers to the fact that it joins two traditionally warring districts, the mostly Catholic **Cityside** and the largely Protestant **Waterside.**

West of the river are two major areas: the walled **inner city** and, outside the walls to the west, the area known as the **Bogside. Waterside** refers to streets near the waterfront, where most hotels and many restaurants are located. Also in Waterside is a small grassy viewing point called the **Top of the Hill,** where you can enjoy spectacular eagle's-eye views of the city. You'll never find your own way there, so take a taxi and bring your map. Short of a helicopter tour, this is the best way to get your initial bearings.

Exploring Derry City

Centre for Contemporary Art ★ ART MUSEUM   Drop in here to see new and touring works by contemporary artists from Ireland and farther afield. Themed seasons include visual art, film screenings, performances, and public debates. Recent seasons have included a fascinating but rather gruesome immersive installation centered around the concept of microbes and decay; and a performance-based project linking LGBT issues with climate change. It's all serious and fascinating stuff for grownup minds. With strong international links, the center often hosts residencies for artists from across the globe. Admission to most events is free, but there may be a charge for some; check website for up-to-date listings.

10–12 Artillery St., Derry, BT48 6RG. www.cca-derry-londonderry.org. © **028/7137-3538.** Free admission. Tues–Sat noon–6pm.

Guildhall ★ ARCHITECTURAL SITE   Just outside the city walls, between Shipquay Gate and the River Foyle, this Tudor Gothic–style building looks much like its counterpart in London. The site's original

Guildhall and the Peace Bridge.

structure was constructed in 1890, but it was rebuilt after a fire in 1908 and again after a series of sectarian bombings in 1972. The hall is distinguished by its huge, four-faced clock (designed to resemble Big Ben) and 23 stained-glass windows made by Ulster craftsmen, which illustrate almost every episode of note in the city's history. The hall is used as a civic center for concerts, plays, and exhibitions. *A nice bit of historical trivia:* The Guildhall clock is designed not to strike between midnight and sunrise. This is because at the time it was finished in 1890, the management of an expensive hotel nearby protested that a clock striking every hour through the night would disturb sleeping guests.

Shipquay Place, Derry, BT48 6DQ. (✆ **028/7137-6510.** Free admission. Daily 10am–5:30pm. Free guided tours July–Aug; inquire at reception.

Museum of Free Derry ★★ MUSEUM   Outside this small museum is an extraordinary piece of art, which may at first glance look like a long, rusty iron wall. But look again—it's a model of the actual sound waves from the 21 seconds in which the crowd on Bloody Sunday sang the civil rights anthem "We will overcome," shortly before 26 of them were shot, and 14 killed, by the British Army. Such a thought-provoking statement nicely frames the story told inside the museum, which reopened in a new location after a long refurbishment in 2017. Thousands of documents and artifacts related to the Irish Catholic civil rights movement of the mid– and late 20th century are housed here, while displays tell the story of Bloody Sunday and other key events in the "Troubles" of the 1960s to '90s. The timeline is clearly laid out and easy to understand; the calm, level tone makes the impact all the more powerful. The **Bogside** (p. 556) naturally becomes the focus for much of this history—so afterward, why not take one of the excellent **Free Derry Tours** of the district, which leave from the museum?

55 Glenfada Park, Derry, BT48 9DR. www.museumoffreederry.org. (✆ **028/7136-0880.** Admission £7 adults; £6 seniors, students, and children. Tues–Sat and bank holidays 10am–4pm. Closed Sun and Mon. Last admission 30 min. before closing.

St. Columb's Cathedral ★ CATHEDRAL   Within the city walls, near the Bishop's Gate, this Protestant cathedral was built by the Church of Ireland between 1628 and 1633 as a prime example of the so-called "Planters Gothic" style of architecture. It was the first cathedral built in Europe after the Reformation, although several sections were added afterward, including the impressive spire and stained-glass windows depicting scenes from the siege of 1688–1689. The chapter house contains a display of city relics such as four massive original padlocks for the city gates. On the porch, a small stone inscribed "in templo verus deus est vereo colendus" ("The true God is in His temple and is to be truly worshipped") is part of the original 1164 church. An old mortar shell on the porch was fired into the churchyard during the great siege of 1689; in its hollow core it held the proposed terms of surrender. Flags around the chancel window

One of the best ways to explore Derry is via its 17th-century stone walls, about 1.6km (1 mile) in circumference and more than 5m (16 ft.) thick. Climb the stairs to the top and you can circle the entire walled city in about 30 minutes. There are a number of stairways off of the parapets, so you'll never get stuck up there. If you start at the **Diamond,** as the square in the center of the walled section is called, walk down Butcher Street to climb the steps at **Butcher's Gate,** a security checkpoint between the Bogside and the city during the Troubles. Walk to the right across **Castle Gate,** built in 1865, and on to **Magazine Gate,** which was once near a powder magazine. Shortly after, you'll pass **O'Doherty's Tower,** which houses the worthwhile Tower Museum (p. 560). From there you can see the brick walls of the Guildhall (p. 557).

Farther along, you'll pass **Shipquay Gate,** once located very near the port, back when the waters passed closer to the town center. The walls turn uphill from there, past the Millennium Forum concert hall, and up to **Ferryquay Gate.** Here in 1688, local apprentice boys saved the town from attacking Catholic forces by locking the city gates—thus saving the town from attack, but launching the Great Siege of Derry, which lasted for months. (By the time it ended, nearly a quarter of the town's population was dead.)

Next you'll pass **Bishop's Gate,** where a tall brick tower just outside the gate is all that remains of the **Old Gaol.** The rebel Wolfe Tone was imprisoned here after the unsuccessful uprising in 1798. Farther along, the **Double Bastion** holds a military tower with elaborate equipment used to keep an eye on the Bogside—it's usually splashed with paint hurled at it by Republicans. From there you can easily access the serene churchyard of **St. Columb's Cathedral** (p. 558). From the next stretch of wall, you have a good view over the political murals of the Bogside down the hill.

A bit farther along the wall, an empty plinth stands where once there was a statue of Rev. George Walker, a governor of the city during the siege of 1689. It was blown up by the IRA in 1973. The small chapel nearby is the **Chapel of St. Augustine** (1872), and the building across the street from it with metal grates over the windows is the **Apprentice Boys' Memorial Hall,** commemorating the boys from the Great Siege of Derry. Walk but a short way farther, and you're back to Butcher's Gate.

Walk the 17th-century walls of Derry City for views and a history lesson.

were captured during the siege, a pivotal moment in William of Orange's war against James II. The war was ultimately decided at the Battle of the Boyne (p. 54), which is still commemorated annually in Northern Ireland by controversial parades, led by the Protestant Orange Order, on and around July 12.

17 London St., Derry, BT48 6RQ. www.stcolumbscathedral.org. ✆ **028/7126-7313.** Requested donation £2 adults; £2 seniors, students, and children. Mar–Oct Mon–Sat 9am–5pm; Nov–Feb Mon–Sat 10am–2pm; Sun for services only.

St. Eugene's Cathedral ★★ CATHEDRAL   Designed in the Gothic Revival style, Derry's Roman Catholic cathedral is appropriately located in the heart of the Bogside district, just beyond the city walls. The foundation was laid in 1851, but work continued until 1873. The spire was added in 1902. It's built of local sandstone and is known for its stained-glass windows depicting the Crucifixion, designed by famed stained-glass makers Meyer and Company of Munich.

Francis St., Derry, BT48 9AP. www.steugenescathedral.com. ✆ **028/7126-2894.** Free admission. Mon–Sat 7am–9pm, Sun 7am–6:30pm.

The Tower Museum ★★ MUSEUM   This engaging museum chronicles the history of Derry from the earliest times to the 21st century. It's located in **O'Doherty Tower,** a reconstructed medieval fortress originally built in the early 17th century (rather wonderfully to pay off a tax debt, rather than for any specific defensive purpose). The **Story of Derry** exhibition presents a chronology of life in the city from the first monastic settlers through the Plantation era, up to the turbulent 20th century, when the city was a focus of the civil rights movement. The main attraction, however, is the large, multi-floor exhibition **An Armada Shipwreck,** which tells the story of *La Trinidad Valencera,* part of the massive Spanish Armada that attempted to invade England in 1588. Separated from the main fleet, the ship sank during a storm. Four hundred years later the wreck was salvaged, together with an extraordinary hoard of treasure including clothes, shoes, pottery, cannons, goblets, and other items that reveal tantalizing glimpses of life on board.

Union Hall Place, Derry, BT48 6LU. www.derrystrabane.com/towermuseum. ✆ **028/7137-2411.** Admission £4 adults; £2.40 seniors and students; £2 children; £9 families. Daily 9am–5:30pm. Last admission 4pm.

Where to Stay in Derry

MODERATE

Bishop's Gate Hotel ★★   First opened in 1899, this sweet hotel is something of a local landmark. The Victorian-era decor is sympathetically preserved without being trapped in the past; guest rooms, for example, are chic and businesslike, with silver-gray and chocolate color schemes. A few rooms are fully accessible for those with limited mobility. **The Wig and Gown** restaurant is popular with locals for a special night out. There's also a champagne bar, and a library in which you can take afternoon tea.

The hotel recently added two self-catering apartments at **9 London Street,** in the building adjacent.

24 Bishop St., Derry, BT48 7DB. www.bishopsgatehotelderry.com. © **028/7114-0300.** 31 units. £109–£169 double; £189–£249 suite. Limited free parking (on street); otherwise, paid lot parking nearby. **Amenities:** Restaurant; bar; gym; Wi-Fi (free).

INEXPENSIVE

The Saddler's House & the Old Rectory ★★

Two charming buildings full of character with one pair of owners, these lovely B&Bs are among the best accommodations in Derry. Choose from the elegant **Merchant's House,** which was built in the mid–19th century (one of relatively few town houses from that period left in Derry), or **Saddler's House,** a slightly simpler, late-Victorian building. (Check-in for both is at the Saddler's House.) Each house has been beautifully maintained and renovated with design-magazine interiors and antiques scattered about. Breakfast is served in whichever house you choose. The same owners also have three self-catering places in Derry, including a small terraced cottage opposite the cathedral; an apartment in the old pump-house, within the walled part of the city; and a 1950s-style apartment. *Tip:* The Merchant's House family room sleeps up to five and has its own kitchen, for just £100 to £135 per night.

36 Great James St., Derry, BT48 7DB. www.thesaddlershouse.com. © **028/7126-9691.** 7 units. £75–£100 double. Limited free parking (on street); otherwise, paid street parking nearby. Rates include breakfast. **Amenities:** Wi-Fi (free).

Serendipity House ★

This popular black-and-white townhouse B&B is at the top of the hill overlooking Derry. Rooms are small but neat, with modern decor; most have lovely town views. Bathrooms are petite but clean. Most rooms have ensuite facilities, but a few have bathrooms a short distance away; if this matters to you, ask when you book. Breakfasts are of the carb-heavy, eggs-and-bacon variety, although fresh scones and pancakes are sometimes on offer. The old city is a pleasant 10-minute walk downhill—which means a pretty steep 10-minute walk uphill when you're coming back later. The same owners also have a second B&B, **Angel House,** located on Marlborough Street in the city center.

24–26 Marlborough St., Derry, BT48 9AY. https://cityofderryaccommodation.com/accommodation/serendipity-house/. © **028/7126-4229.** 9 units. £85–£120 double. Free parking. Rates include breakfast. **Amenities:** Wi-Fi (free).

Where to Eat in Derry

EXPENSIVE

Browns Bonds Hill ★★ BRASSERIE

One of Derry's best restaurants, Browns serves excellent Irish food with international influences. The menu uses plenty of local and regional ingredients, embracing traditional flavors with a touch of well-judged, modern innovation. Menus change frequently, but you're likely to encounter local seafood, steaks, wild wood pigeon, or honey-glazed duck. Vegetarians and vegans will be delighted to see a full menu of non-meaty options, including some tasty spiced carrot falafel. Browns also bakes its own bread, a delicious special recipe that includes Guinness—*and* you can buy the mix to take home. A more casual sister branch, **Browns in Town** (© **028/7136-2889**), is on Strand Road.

1 Bonds Hill, Derry, BT47 6DW. www.brownsrestaurant.com. © **028/7134-5180.** Tasting menu £60. Entrees £19–£28. Lunch Wed–Sat noon–2:30pm. Dinner Tues–Thurs 5–9pm; Fri–Sat 5–10pm.

MODERATE

The Belfray Country Inn Bistro ★ BISTRO   The dining room at this big hotel and restaurant, a short drive outside Derry, adds a rococo touch to the feel of a country pub. Imagine posh pub fare, and you've got it about right. The best dishes come from the grill—the truly hungry may like to tackle the "Cock and Bull," which features a half-chicken escalope and a 6-ounce filet mignon—but there are also several stir-fry and vegetarian options, as well as an extensive kids' menu. The inn also offers spacious rooms with big beds and neutral decor, but they're a bit pricey (around £115), given the location. The Belfray is on Glenshane Road (A6), about 5.5km (3½ miles) southwest of Derry city center.

171 Glenshane Rd., Derry, BT47 3EN. www.thebelfraycountryinn.co.uk. © **028/7130-1480.** Entrees £11–£22. Daily noon–3:30pm, 5–9:30pm.

The Sooty Olive ★ IRISH   Named after a kind of fishing lure, this trendy eatery in central Derry specializes in locally sourced food. The decor in the small dining room makes the most of the exposed brick walls, contrasting it with tasteful leather chairs and sofas. Similarly, the cooking makes the most of local ingredients in dishes like sea bream with black pudding and new potatoes, or duck breast with potato fondant. It also serves steak and skinny fries, as well as plenty of vegetarian options. Desserts are to die for. The wine list is small but well-chosen; try a bottle of the dark and spicy Basilisk Australian Shiraz (£30).

160–164 Spencer Rd., Derry, BT47 6AH. © **028/7134-6040.** Fixed-price menus £16–£18. Tues–Thurs noon–2:30pm, 5–9pm; Fri–Sat noon–2:30pm, 5–10pm; Sun 3–8pm.

INEXPENSIVE

Badgers Bar ★ IRISH   A friendly local pub right in the center of Derry, Badgers serves hearty traditional grub—stews, fish and chips, steak and Guinness pie, burgers, and the like—plus a few lighter options such as hot sandwiches and wraps. Plates are generous, and of course, you can wash it all down with a pint of the black stuff. The dining room is appealingly unreconstructed, with plenty of polished wood. No matter what the time of day, there always seem to be a few locals propping up the bar, which helps keep the atmosphere authentic.

16–18 Orchard St., Derry, BT48 6EG. © **028/7136-0763.** Entrees £6–£12. Food served Mon–Thurs noon–7pm; Fri–Sat noon–9pm; Sun noon–4pm. No children after 9pm.

53–55–57 ★★ INTERNATIONAL Once a hugely popular food truck, this place now has two permanent restaurants in Derry. 53–55–57 is the main outlet—near the River Foyle. The other, called **POD,** is nearby in a converted shipping container (124 Strand Rd.). Both have similar menus and the same ethos: fresh local food cooked incredibly well with no fuss. At both you can get burgers of all kinds, including tender, melting Wagyu beef burgers or chickpea and sweetcorn "vegenderry" burgers. A taco menu features fried squid tacos, Baja fish tacos, and sweet potato tacos with chipotle cashew salsa. It's casual, innovative, light, and affordable. 53-57 Strand Rd., Derry, BT48 7RT. www.pykenpommes.ie. ✆ **028/7167-2691.** Entrees £8–£15. Daily noon–9pm.

Primrose on the Quay ★★ CAFE This lovely cafe is old-fashioned without being at all stuffy. Drop in for a bowl of delicious soup, fresh sandwiches, or a tasty pie (served with a side of excellent chips—that's thick-cut fries around here). Or you could just have a plate of homemade scones and some tea. Service is cheery and prices are reasonable—just what you want for a casual lunch on the go. 2 Atlantic Quay, 110–114 Strand Rd., Derry, BT48 6JJ. https://primrose-ni.com. ✆ **028/7136-5511.** Lunch £4.50–£11.50. Mon–Tues 8am–5pm; Wed–Sat 8am–9pm; Sun 10am–6pm.

Derry After Dark

Derry pubs are an important part of the local fabric; hanging out in one is a good way to meet locals. Boozers are tied into the local music scene, so you'll frequently find bands playing. Pubs even host debating contests, in the midst of which you'll hear Irish eloquence at its well-lubricated best. Along **Waterloo Street,** just outside the city walls, a handful of Derry's most traditional and popular pubs are known for their live music. Walk from one end of Waterloo to the other—an act that will take you all of 2 minutes—and you'll likely find the bar for you.

Bennigans Bar ★★ A fairly new addition to the top tier of Derry's live music scene, Bennigans is known for its fantastic live jazz, which attracts performers from all over Ireland (and beyond). Sessions usually start at around 9pm. 13 John St., Derry, BT48 6JY. ✆ **028/7126-9127.**

Peadar O'Donnells ★★★ "Peadars" to the locals, this is one of the best places in Derry to hear traditional live music. Sessions are every night except Monday; generally they run from 10:30pm to about 1am weekdays, 7pm to 1am Saturdays, and 5pm to 1am Sundays—although spontaneous sessions have been known to start up pretty much anytime. The craic is lively, and the atmosphere is buzzing. 59–63 Waterloo St., Derry, BT48 6HD. www.peadars.com. ✆ **028/7126-7295.**

River Inn ★★ Allegedly Derry's oldest pub (the city walls form part of the building), the River Inn opened its doors in the 17th century. It also serves food, although people come for the atmosphere. 34–38 Shipquay St., Derry, BT48 6DW. www.riverinn1684.com. ✆ **028/7137-1965.**

DAY TRIPS TO THE SPERRIN MOUNTAINS

The beautiful Sperrin Mountains, a short drive southeast of Derry in County Tyrone, are filled with scenic walks, national parks, and extraordinary views, plus one really must-see site: the **Ulster American Folk Park** (p. 567). This is splendid, wide-open walking country, home to golden plover, red grouse, and thousands upon thousands of fluffy white sheep. There's no shortage of ancient sites, including standing stones (about 1,000 have been counted in these hills), high crosses, dolmens, and hill forts. Whether you're traveling on foot, wheels, or horseback, be sure to traverse the **Glenshane Pass** between Mullaghmore (545m/1,788 ft.) and Carntogher (455m/1,492 ft.), and the **Sawel Mountain Drive** along the east face of the mountain. The vistas along these routes through the Sperrins will remind you why you've gone out of your way to spend time in Tyrone.

Visitor Information

The **An Creagán Visitors Centre,** on the A505 road just outside Creggan (see below) is a good place to start, with tourist information and an interesting exhibition on the history of the area. Other area sites include the **Cookstown Tourist Information Centre,** Burn Road, Cookstown (*©* **028/8676-9949**); the **Dungannon Visitor Information Centre,** 26 Market Square, Dungannon (*©* **028/8772-8600**); the **Omagh Tourist Information Centre** at the Strule Arts Centre, Townhall Square, Omagh (*©* **028/8224-7831**); and the **Strabane Visitor Information Centre,** at the Alley Arts and Conference Centre, 1A Railway St., Strabane (*©* **028/7138-4444**). Generally they are open Monday to Saturday year-round from about 10am to 5pm; the Dungannon and Cookstown centers also open on Sundays in midsummer.

Exploring the Sperrins

An Creagán Visitors Centre ★ INTERPRETIVE CENTER   Beautifully designed to fit in with the craggy countryside around, this modern center is an excellent place to get your bearings when you first arrive in the Sperrins. A small gallery has an interactive exhibit about the mountains and the area; a few Bronze Age artifacts excavated from nearby sites are also on display. The helpful staff will give you all the information you need on walking and cycling routes, as well as maps and bicycle rentals (bikes can be rented for roughly £10 per day, £7 per half-day, or £35 per week). The center has a restaurant and craft shop, and even owns a few self-catering properties if you're interested in staying longer. (Prices start at £50 per night for a one-bedroom cottage in the low season.)

A505, Creggan (about 60km/37 miles SE of Derry), Omagh, Co. Tyrone. www. an-creagan.com. *©* **028/8076-1112.** Free admission. Daily 10am–9pm.

Beaghmore Stone Circles ★ ANCIENT SITE

In 1945, seven stone circles and a complex assembly of cairns and alignments were uncovered here, in remote moorland north of Evishbrack Mountain and near Davagh Forest Park on the southern edge of the Sperrins. Arranged inside the largest circle are around 800 small stones, christened the "Dragon's Teeth." No one knows what this intriguing bit of Bronze Age stonework was built for, but it may have involved astronomical observation and calculation. The layout has also led archaeologists to believe that the stones surround unexcavated megalithic tombs.

17km (11 miles) NW of Cookstown, signposted from A505, Co. Tyrone. No phone. Free admission (open site).

Drum Manor Forest Park ★ NATURE SITE   Once a private estate, this extensive park and woodland has numerous trails and three old walled gardens, one of them designed as a butterfly garden. Also on the grounds are a visitor center, a heronry, and a pond that attracts a variety of wildfowl.

4km (2½ miles) W of Cookstown on A505, Co. Tyrone. ⓒ **028/8675-9311** (forest ranger). Admission £3.50 per car; pedestrians £1 adults, 50p children. Daily 10am–dusk.

Gortin Glen Forest Park ★★ NATURE SITE   Nearly 400 hectares (988 acres) of conifers make up this serene nature park. The woodlands provide habitat for a variety of wildlife, including a herd of Japanese sika deer. A forest drive offers splendid views of the Sperrins. Here you'll also find a nature center, wildlife enclosures, trails, and a cafe. The park has three separate marked walking trails; details can be found at the visitor center on the B48 road just south of Gortin. The long-distance **Ulster Way** hiking trail also passes through the park; for more information on the Ulster Way, visit **www.walkni.com/ulsterway**.

Visitor center: On B48 (Glenpark Rd.), about 4km (2½ miles) S of Gortin, Co. Tyrone. ⓒ **028/8167-0666.** Free admission. Visitor center: Daily 10am–dusk.

Seamus Heaney Homeplace ★★ MUSEUM   East of the Sperrins, Nobel Prize–winning poet Seamus Heaney took inspiration for his work from the landscape and local people where he grew up in rural County Derry and went on to become the most widely published poet in the English language. The Seamus Heaney Homeplace in Bellaghy, near the family farm where he lived, tells the story of Heaney's life and work through an interactive exhibition plus books, archive material, and audio recordings with the voice of the poet himself. The exhibition is thoughtfully put together with lots of personal stories and photos. It's a lovely way to access Heaney's moving poetry whether you are a Heaney fan or a first-timer. There's also a library, digital archive, a cafe, and a fun creative zone for kids of all ages.

45 Main St., Bellaghy, Co Derry BT45 8HT.   www.seamusheaneyhome.com. ⓒ **028/7938-7444**. Admission £7 adults; £4.50 seniors, students, and children 8 and over; free for children 7 and under; £19 families. Free parking. Mon–Sat 11am–5pm; Sun 1pm–5pm.

The Ulster American Folk Park is a living-history museum.

Ulster American Folk Park ★★★ HERITAGE SITE   Another of the region's excellent "living history" outdoor museums, this one celebrates and commemorates the links between Ulster and the New World. It chronicles the story of those 18th- and 19th-century emigrants who left their homes in the north of Ireland to seek a new life overseas. The park contains authentic structures from the period—some of them actual dwellings reconstructed from elsewhere—to give an idea of the life they left behind. After looking around the humble thatched cottages, you can explore a period street with convincingly decked-out shops, manned by costumed actors. There's a full-size replica emigrant ship as well. The park has an active schedule of special events, including a respected bluegrass festival in the autumn. Check the website for listings.

2 Mellon Rd., Castletown, Co. Tyrone BT78 5QU. www.nmni.com. ✆ **028/8224-3292.** Admission £9 adults; £7 seniors and students; £5.50 children 5–17; £19–£25 families. Prices rise by a few pounds on major event days. Tues–Sun 10am–5pm. Last admission 3:30pm. Closed Mon except for NI Bank Holidays.

THE FERMANAGH LAKELANDS

In the extreme southwest corner of Northern Ireland, County Fermanagh is a lakeland area dominated by **Lough Erne,** a long, narrow lake with 154 islands and countless coves and inlets. The **Shannon-Erne Waterway** links the lake to the Shannon River system through the Republic of Ireland. Were you to cruise the whole length of the waterway between the village of Leitrim and Lough Erne, you'd travel 63km (39 miles), past 16 locks (gates), three lakes, and the Woodford River. At the south end of Lough Erne, **Enniskillen** is a good touring base for the region, with many overnight options if you intend to spend much time here.

In medieval times, a chain of island monasteries stretched across the waters of Lough Erne, establishing it as a haven for those seeking peace and contemplation. Traces of those monasteries can still be found on those unspoiled islands—and the Fermanagh Lakelands remains a peaceful place to get away from it all.

Visitor Information

The **Fermanagh Visitor Information Centre,** Enniskillen Castle, Enniskillen, Co. Fermanagh, BT74 7HL (✆ **028/6632-5000**), is open year-round Monday to Friday 9:30am to 5pm and Saturday 11am to 5pm; (also Sun 11am–5pm June–Sept). For an introduction to the Fermanagh Lakelands on the web, check out **www.fermanaghlakelands.com**.

Exploring the Lakelands

The hub of this lakeland paradise—wedged between Upper Lough Erne to the south and Lower Lough Erne to the north—is **Enniskillen,** a delightful town that was the medieval seat of the Maguire clan and a major crossroads between Ulster and Connaught. Both Oscar Wilde and Samuel

Beckett were once students here at the royal school. A handful of lovely historic homes are dotted around the midsection of the lake as well, including **Castle Coole ★** (see below), the **Crom Estate ★★** (see below), and **Florence Court ★★** (p. 570). At the northern tip of the lake, near the Republic of Ireland border, **Belleek** (see below) is known the world over for its trademark delicate bone chinaware.

Castle Coole ★ HISTORIC HOUSE   Not really a castle at all, Coole is in fact a lavish stately home on the east bank of Lower Lough Erne. This quintessential neoclassical mansion was designed by James Wyatt for the Earl of Belmore and completed in 1796. Its rooms include a state bedroom hung with crimson silk, said to have been prepared for George IV (1762–1830). A sprawling woodland estate surrounds the house. A classical music series runs from May to October. You can book a guided house tour when you arrive.

2.4km (1½ miles) SE of Enniskillen on A4, Co. Fermanagh, BT74 6JY. www.national trust.org.uk/castle-coole. ✆ **028/6632-2690.** Guided house tour: £5 adults; £2.50 children; £12.50 families. Grounds only: £5 adults; £2.50 children; £12.50 families. House May–Sept daily 11am–4pm. Grounds Mar–Oct daily 10am–6pm, Nov–Feb daily 10am–4pm. Last admission 30 min. before closing; last house tour 1 hr. before closing.

Crom Estate ★★ NATURE SITE   On the east bank of Upper Lough Erne, this nearly 800-hectare (1,976-acre) nature reserve is a splendid National Trust–owned estate, with forest, parks, wetlands, fen meadows, and an award-winning lakeshore visitor center. The numerous trails have concealed places for observing birds and wildlife. You can rent a rowboat and row out to the islands. A 19th-century castle is also located on the grounds, though it's not open to visitors. The estate is a great place to fish for bream and roach; permits and day tickets are available at the gate lodge. During the summer, weekends frequently feature special programs and guided nature walks. The estate also has several cottages available for rent by the week (about £300–£850). Call or check the National Trust website for more information.

34km (21 miles) S of Enniskillen via A4 and A34, then take signposted right turn. Upper Lough Erne, Newtownbutler, Co. Fermanagh, BT92 8AP. www.nationaltrust. org.uk/crom. ✆ **028/6773-8118.** Admission £5 adults; £2.50 children; £12.50 families. Grounds Mar–Oct daily 10am–6pm, Jan–Feb and Nov–Dec daily 10am–4pm. Visitor center Mar–May and Sept–Oct daily 11am–4pm, June–Aug 11am–5pm. Closed Nov to Mar. Last admission 1 hr. before closing.

Devenish Island ★★ NATURE SITE   The most extensive of the ancient Christian sites in Lough Erne, Devenish Island is a marvelous mélange of remnants and ruins, providing a glimpse into the lake's mystical past. In the 6th century, St. Molaise founded a monastic community here, to which the Augustinian Abbey of St. Mary was added in the 12th century. In other words, this is hallowed ground, even more so for the

Perhaps the most famous Irish homeware brand in the world after Waterford Crystal, Belleek Pottery has been making fine china since 1864. The **Belleek Pottery Visitor Centre,** 3 Main St., Belleek, County Fermanagh (www.belleek.com; *℃* **028/6865-9300**), is the world headquarters of the brand. You can visit their museum—which displays unique objects of Belleek pottery, such as the extraordinary International Centre Piece vase created for the 1900 Paris Expo—and also take factory tours. But of course, the reason most people come is to visit the enormous gift shop. It has a large selection of patterns from which to choose, in a wide price range. If you're not a china expert but still want to bring back some Belleek pieces from your trip, here are a few tips to ensure that your purchases become heirlooms

○ At the center, the china is displayed around the room. Look at all the pieces, and then note the item numbers of those pieces you like. Take the numbers to the central counter, and the boxed china pieces are brought to you.

○ Ask to see the pieces in the boxes to ensure they are what you wanted. Take the pieces from the sales assistant and look at them closely. This is delicate china, and it can have tiny imperfections that you can only see by getting up close and personal. We bought a lovely Belleek vase once that looked perfect but leaked through a nearly invisible crack.

○ The center will ship internationally if you don't want to risk taking your purchases on a plane.

○ If it looks good to you and you love it—buy it! You may not get the chance again.

The Belleek Centre is open from January to September Monday to Saturday 10am to 4pm (closed Sun); and from October to December Monday to Friday 10am to 3pm (closed Sat–Sun).

legend that the Old Testament prophet Jeremiah is buried somewhere nearby—if you can figure that one out. The jewel of Devenish is the perfectly intact 12th-century round tower, which was erected with Vikings in mind. A regular ferry to Devenish Island used to run in July and August from Trory Point, 6.5km (4 miles) from Enniskillen on A32, but at this writing it had stopped operating until further notice. Until it gets back up and running, the only way to get out there is to take the Lough Erne cruise offered by **Erne Tours** (p. 570) or a private water taxi tour with **Erne Water Taxi** (www.ernewatertaxi.com; *℃* **077/1977-0588**). To reach the jetty, take A32 north from Enniskillen toward nearby Irvinestown; after about 2 miles you will come to a roundabout. Almost immediately turn left (next to the gas station) down a small country road. After about ¾ mile you'll come to a fork in the road; turn left and look for the jetty on your right.

2.4km (1½ miles) downstream from Enniskillen, Co. Fermanagh, BT94 2FE. *℃* **028/9082-3207.** Admission to round tower £3 adults; £2 seniors and children.

CRUISING LOUGH ERNE by boat

One of the best ways to explore Lough Erne is by boat. **Erne Tours,** Enniskillen (www.ernetours.com; ℭ **028/6632-2882**), operates 2-hour cruises on Lower Lough Erne aboard the MV *Kestrel,* departing daily May through September from the delightfully named Round "O" Jetty, Brook Park, Enniskillen. Tours include a 45-minute stop on **Devenish Island** ★★ (p. 568). Erne Tours also runs dinner cruises. Upper Lough Erne cruises are operated on Sundays and Bank Holidays by **Share Holiday Village,** Smith's Strand, Lisnaskea (www.sharevillage.org; ℭ **028/6772-2122**). Fares for both cruises start at £10 adults, £9 seniors, £6 for children under 16, and £30 families. Call for reservations and to confirm times.

Independent boatmen offer ferry crossings to some of the many islands in Lough Erne, or you can book a bespoke tour with **Erne Water Taxi** (www.erne watertaxi.com; ℭ **077/1977-0588**). Besides Devenish Island, **White Island** and **Boa Island** are rich in archaeological and early Christian remains. On White Island, seven stone figures remain from a vanished 10th-century monastery inside a ruined 12th-century church. (The ferry to White Island runs from Castle Archdale Marina in Irvinestown; ℭ **028/6862-1892;** fare £5 round-trip.) Boa Island is connected to the shore by bridges; poke around the cemetery at the island's west end to find two ancient idols of the god Janus (with faces looking both ways), thought to date from the 1st century.

Enniskillen Castle ★★ CASTLE/MUSEUM   On the banks of Lower Lough Erne in Enniskillen, this impressive castle was built sometime around the first half of the 14th century but was significantly remodeled in the 17th. It's unusual in that the design owes more to the Scottish Baronial style of castle—note the small round turrets, redolent of Gothic motifs—than the fortresslike English-French style that predominates throughout Ireland. The castle is home to two museums, included in the ticket price, which were recently reopened after a major renovation. **Fermanagh County Museum** tells the story of the region's colorful history, with interesting sections on local crafts and the development of the castle from medieval times onward. The **Inniskillings Museum** houses the castle's large collection of militaria, historic weapons, uniforms, and other artifacts dating back to the 1600s.

Castle Barracks, Enniskillen, Co. Fermanagh, BT74 7HL. www.enniskillencastle.co.uk. ℭ **028/6632-5000.** Admission £5 adults; £3.50 seniors, students, and children; £13.50 families. Mon–Fri 9:30am–5pm, Sat–Sun 11am–5pm (Oct–May closed Sun).

Florence Court ★★ HISTORIC HOUSE   Set among dramatic hills, 13km (8 miles) southwest of Lower Lough Erne and Enniskillen, this 18th-century Palladian mansion was originally the seat of the earls of Enniskillen. Its interior is rich in rococo plasterwork and antique Irish furniture, while outside is a fine walled garden, an icehouse, and a water-wheel-driven sawmill. The forest park offers a number of trails, one leading to the top of Mount Cuilcagh (nearly 660m/2,165 ft.). Florence Court is the sister property to Castle Coole (p. 568).

Florence Court, off A32, Enniskillen, Co. Fermanagh, BT92 1DB. www.nationaltrust. org.uk/florence-court. © **028/6634-8249.** Admission gardens and forest park: £8 adults; £4 children; £20 families. House tour: £3 adults; £1.50 children; £8.50 families. House: May–Aug daily 11am–5pm, Mar–Apr and Sept–Oct Sat–Sun 11am–5pm. Gardens and park: Mar–Oct daily 10am–6pm, Nov–Feb daily 10am–4pm. Open public holidays. Last admission 1 hr. before closing.

Marble Arch Caves ★★ CAVES   Near the Florence Court estate (see above), these UNESCO-listed caves are among the finest in Europe for exploring underground rivers, winding passages, and hidden chambers. Electrically powered boat tours take visitors underground for a walking tour through the caves, and knowledgeable guides explain the origins of the amazing stalactites and stalagmites. Tours last 75 minutes and leave at 15-minute intervals. The caves are occasionally closed after heavy rains, so phone ahead before making the trip if there's been particularly bad weather recently.

Marlbank Rd., off A32, Co. Fermanagh, BT92 1EW. www.marblearchcaves.co.uk. © **028/6634-8855.** Admission £10 adults; £7.50 seniors and students; £5 children; £25–£28 families. Reservations recommended. July–Aug daily 10am–5pm (last tour); Mar–June and Sept daily 10am–4:30pm (last tour); Oct daily 10:30am–3pm.

Where to Stay in the Fermanagh Lakelands
EXPENSIVE

Castle Leslie ★★★   Actually just across the border in the Republic, this historic estate surrounded by lush grounds is one of the very best places to stay in the North, having welcomed a dazzling list of luminaries over the years (W. B. Yeats was a houseguest, Winston Churchill was a cousin of the Leslie family, and Paul McCartney and Heather Mills were married here in 2002). Strolling around the house you'll wander past Wordsworth's harp and the Bechstein grand piano on which Wagner composed *Tristan and Isolde.* Guest rooms are individually designed to varying degrees of grandeur; most are located in the converted hunting lodge. The outstanding in-house restaurant offers sophisticated dishes prepared with local ingredients, such as filet of sea bass with red pepper drops and baby carrots, or roast chicken with garlic and citrus dressing. You can also opt for a more casual meal at **Conor's Bar.** On the several hundred acres of grounds, horseback riding, clay pigeon shooting, and other outdoor activities can be arranged; there's also an elegant spa to smooth away the few cares you have left.

Glaslough, Co. Monaghan (Republic of Ireland). www.castleleslie.com. © **047/ 88100.** 121 units. £70–£250 double. 2-night minimum on summer weekends. Dinner, bed-and-breakfast packages available. Free parking. Rates include breakfast. **Amenities:** 2 restaurants; bar; room service; spa; Wi-Fi (free).

The historic estate of Castle Leslie is one of the North's top lodgings.

MODERATE

Finn Lough ★★   This surely qualifies as one of the most unusual places to stay in Ireland. The five-star lakeside compound at Finn Lough has a unique feature: so-called bubble domes, individual plastic dome cottages from which you can see the wide sky and verdant countryside all around you, all the time. If such an open environment isn't for you (although you're surrounded by foliage for privacy), more traditional cottages are tucked away around the compound. Most have three bedrooms, a kitchen, and a living room, as well as good Wi-Fi. You can dine in the on-site restaurant (inclusive packages are available), hire kayaks to paddle out on the pristine lake, or rent a mountain bike and explore the forests. On the other hand, you could just hide yourself away in your own cottage and enjoy the peace.

Letter Rd., Enniskillen, Co. Fermanagh, BT93 2BB. www.finnlough.com. ℂ **028/6638-0360.** 15 units. £155–£375 double; £295–£495 bubble dome; £295–£355 cottages and lodges. Free parking. No breakfast. **Amenities:** Wi-Fi (free).

Lough Erne Resort ★★★   With a glorious location overlooking Lough Erne, this hotel positively exudes old-school charm. It's one of Ireland's top golfing resorts, though you certainly don't have to be a golfer to enjoy what it has to offer. Guest rooms are comfortable and spacious; lake-facing rooms are definitely worth the extra cost to take in the view. The **Catalina Restaurant** (p. 573) is one of the best in the region. Book a treatment in the award-winning **Thai Spa,** then afterwards prepare to float away in the Lap Sabai ("deep sleep") relaxation room.

Belleek Rd., Enniskillen, Co. Fermanagh, BT93 7ED. www.lougherneresort.com. ℂ **028/6632-3230.** 120 units. £159–£359 double; £119–£369 suite. Check online for special offers. Free parking. **Amenities:** 2 restaurants; 2 bars; golf course; spa; Wi-Fi (free).

INEXPENSIVE

Belmore Court & Motel ★   The humble motel is so unknown in Europe that its few incarnations are considered quite exotic. At this quality budget option on the edge of Enniskillen, basic rooms are clean and modern, with compact kitchen areas and free Wi-Fi. Pay just a little more, however, and you get a lot of extra space, plus nice little touches like Nespresso machines, breakfast, and even (in the executive rooms) little balconies. Family rooms sleep four. The location isn't too far from the town center and nearby sights such as **Enniskillen Castle ★★** (p. 570) or **Castle Coole ★** (p. 568).

Tempo Rd., Enniskillen, Co. Fermanagh, BT74 6HX. www.motel.co.uk. ℂ **028/6632-6633.** 60 units. £65–£100 double; £160–£195 suite. Free parking. Rates include breakfast. **Amenities:** Wi-Fi (free).

Where to Eat in the Fermanagh Lakelands

The Catalina Restaurant ★★★ MODERN IRISH   The main restaurant at the excellent **Lough Erne Resort** (p. 572) has risen to become one of the most lauded in the region. Chef Noel McMeel makes elegant meals with plenty of locally sourced ingredients. Expect dishes like filet of halibut served with caramelized parsnip puree, or the chef's signature pork with apple and sage butter and maple jus. The vegetarian menu is

Bubble Dome room at Finn Lough.

small but good—try the mushroom and leek pithivier (round pastry pie) with whipped potato and toasted hazelnut.

At the Lough Erne Resort, Belleek Rd., Enniskillen, Co. Fermanagh, BT93 7ED. www. lougherneresort.com. ℭ **028/6632-2277.** Entrees £26–£35; fixed-price menus £60 (evenings) or £24.50–£29.50 (Sun lunch). Mon–Sat 6:30–10pm; Sun 1–2:30pm and 6:30–10pm.

The Jolly Sandwich ★ CAFE   This bright, light sandwich shop is a cheery place to grab a quick lunch or breakfast or create a picnic to go. As the name suggests, the specialty is freshly made sandwiches of all kinds, but there's more to this place than that. Towering stacks of American-style pancakes are often available, as well as homemade scones, elaborate cakes, gorgeous layered coffees, and steaming pots of tea.

3 Darling St., Enniskillen, Co. Fermanagh, BT74 7DP. ℭ **028/6632-2277.** All items £4–£8. Mon–Sat 9am–3pm. Closed Sun and Mon.

The Taphouse ★★ IRISH/INTERNATIONAL   Converted into a gas-tropub, this handsome old stone building is a good-looking place, with exposed stone walls, rugged wood floors, and leather furniture. The front bar is sleek and modern, contrasting beautifully with the aged setting. Dishes are smart reinterpretations of traditional pub food. You might start with some goat cheese fritters, or the soup with treacle bread. Main courses might include a creamy Thai curry or lamb chipotle mole. There's a separate menu for vegetarians and pescatarians.

46 Old Tempo Rd., Enniskillen, Co. Fermanagh BT74 4RR. www.thetaphouseennis killen.com. ℭ **028/6634-6800.** Entrees £10–£22. Daily 11am–11pm (food served until about 9pm).

Tully Mill ★★ IRISH   Relaxed and sophisticated, this bistro on the edge of the Florence Court estate (p. 570) is located inside an old water-mill. Plenty of local flavors find their way onto the three-course set menus, including some from the mill's own walled garden. Start with some wild mushrooms with bearnaise sauce, then go for the Silverhill duck with black cherry sauce, or some delicious curry crusted monkfish. A vegan menu has almost as much choice as the main offerings. Sunday lunches are popular here, with plenty of interesting fish and vegetarian options alongside traditional plates of roast meats. The quiet grounds also contain a few self-catering cottages; prices in summer start at around £260 for the weekend, £590 for the full week.

On the Florence Court estate, Co. Fermanagh BT92 1FN. www.tullymill.com. ℭ **028/6634-9879.** 3-course menu £35. Fri–Sat 5–10pm; Sun noon–5pm.

Sports & Outdoor Pursuits in the Lakelands

BOATING   Lough Erne is an explorer's dream, and you can take that dream all the way to the Atlantic if you want. The price range for fully equipped, four- to eight-berth cruisers is around £650 to £1,250 per week, including tax, depending on the season and the size of the boat. The many local cruiser-hire companies include **Erne Marine,** Bellanaleck (www. erne-marine.com; ✆ **077/0812-7700**), and **Carrickcraft,** Lurgan (www. cruise-ireland.com; ✆ **028/3834-4993** or 01/278-1666 from the Republic). On Lower Lough Erne, you can hire motorboats from **Manor House Marine,** Killadeas (www.manormarine.com; ✆ **028/6862-8100**). Charges average £65 to £90 for a half-day and £90 to £130 for a full day, depending on the size of the boat (maximum eight people). You'll have to pay a refundable deposit before heading out.

WALKING The southwestern branch of the **Ulster Way** follows the western shores of Lough Erne, between the lake and the border. The area is full of other great walks as well. One excellent 11km (6.75-mile; 3–7 hr.) hike leads from a starting point near Florence Court and the Marble Arch Caves (p. 571) along a boardwalk to the summit of **Mount Cuilcagh** (656m/2,152 ft.). For a detailed description of the route and downloadable map, visit **www.walkni.com/walks/585/cuilcagh-mountain**.

17

PLANNING YOUR TRIP TO IRELAND

C hances are you've been looking forward to your trip to Ireland for some time. You've probably set aside a significant amount of hard-earned cash, taken time off from work, school, or other commitments, and now want to make the most of your holiday. To accomplish that, you'll need to plan carefully. The aim of this chapter is to provide you with the information you need and answer any questions you might have, including: When to go? How to get there? Should you book a tour or travel independently? How much will it all cost? Here you'll find plenty of resources to help you make the most of your Irish adventure.

GETTING THERE
By Plane
The Republic of Ireland has three major international airports. They are, in order of size, **Dublin** (**DUB;** www.dublinairport.com; ℂ **1/814-1111**), **Cork** (**ORK;** www.cork-airport.com; ℂ **021/431-3131**), and **Shannon** (www.shannonairport.com; ℂ **061/712000**). Northern Ireland's main airport is **Belfast International Airport** (**BFS;** www.belfastairport.com; ℂ **028/9448-4848**).

The Republic of Ireland has several smaller regional airports. The airports at Donegal and Kerry offer service to Dublin; in addition, the airports at Donegal, Kerry, and Knock receive some (limited) European traffic. In Northern Ireland, the secondary airports are Belfast City Airport and Derry City Airport. Airline service to these smaller airports changes frequently, so be sure to consult your preferred airline or travel agent as soon as you begin to sketch out your itinerary.

By Ferry
If you're traveling to Ireland from Britain or the Continent, traveling by ferry is a good alternative to flying. Several car and passenger ferries offer reasonably comfortable furnishings, cabin berths (for longer crossings), restaurants, duty-free shopping, and lounges. You may be surprised, however, by how long it takes, even from super-near neighbor Britain; the quickest U.K.-to-Ireland ferry route is Holyhead to Dublin, which is a little over 3 hours; the sailing from Fishguard to Dublin takes well over 7 hours. From Cherbourg in France it's a surprisingly long 18 hours.

FACING PAGE: **Carrick-a-rede, a famous rope bridge on the north coast of Northern Ireland.**

TRAVEL disruptions IN IRELAND

From the very first wave of the SARS-CoV-2 virus, the Irish government introduced comprehensive measures to tackle infection rates, including compulsory mask-wearing, limited visitor numbers, stringent cleaning protocols, and contact tracing. Its most populous cities are those that saw the most pandemic disruptions. Currently, an **EU Digital COVID Certificate (COVID pass)** vaccine or recovery certificate (or national proof of vaccination for visitors from non-EU countries) is required for entry into hotel bars and restaurants, indoor events, cinemas and theaters, and gyms. Attendance is limited at theaters and sports arenas. You are required by law to wear face coverings in all public transport and in shops, libraries, theaters, museums, concert halls, banks, airports, and government buildings; exceptions include children under 9. You will find updated rules on Covid protocols and guidance on traveling to Ireland on the Ireland government website at **www.gov.ie**.

Our hotel and restaurant listings reflect what those establishments expect to offer when you arrive, but on-again off-again pandemic restrictions may impact that. Hotels may have reduced services, such as limited meal service or shuttered spas; if a certain amenity is important to you, check before booking. Many restaurants have cut back hours and/or the length of their seasons and have limited tables, so reserving ahead is essential. Keep in mind that the Irish government has intermittently issued curfews for evening activities, including meals. Your hotel desk staff can advise on specific local guidelines.

The worldwide staff shortage in the hospitality sector caused by the pandemic has also had an impact on the visitor experience in Ireland. As a result, you may find that overall service in Ireland is not up to its usual high standards.

At any time while traveling in Ireland, if you should develop Covid-19 symptoms, commercial testing facilities and most pharmacies offer PCR and antigen tests. The U.S. Embassy in Dublin has a dedicated webpage at **https://ie.usembassy.gov** with Dublin health alerts and the latest Covid-19 information for American citizens traveling to Ireland.

Prices fluctuate seasonally and depend on your route, time of travel, and whether you are on foot or in a car. Check with your travel agent for up-to-date details, but the lowest one-way adult fare in high season on the Holyhead to Dublin ferry starts at around £39, less if you book online in advance. A car usually costs from £119 including one adult passenger, plus £30 per extra adult, £15 extra child.

Irish Ferries (www.irishferries.ie; ℭ **0818/300-400** in the Republic of Ireland or 353/818-300-400 in Northern Ireland/U.K.) operates between Pembroke, Wales, and Rosslare, County Wexford. It also sails from Cherbourg and Roscoff in France.

Stena Line (www.stenaline.com; ℭ **01/204-7777**) sails from Fishguard, Wales, to Rosslare; and from Cairnryan, Scotland, and Liverpool, England, to Belfast, Northern Ireland.

P&O Irish Sea Ferries (www.poferries.com; ✆ **0871/664-2121** in Britain, 01/407-3434 in Ireland, or 352/3420-808-294 in the rest of the world) operates from Liverpool to Dublin and from Cairnryan, Scotland, to Larne, County Antrim, Northern Ireland.

TRIPS & TOURS
Package Tours

Package tours are simply a way to buy the airfare, accommodations, and other elements of your trip (such as car rentals, airport transfers, and even activities) at the same time and often at discounted prices.

One good source for package deals of all kinds is the airlines themselves. Most major airlines offer air/land packages, with surprisingly cheap hotel deals. Several big online travel agencies—such as **Expedia** (www.expedia.com), **Travelocity** (www.travelocity.com), **Orbitz** (www. orbitz.com), and **Lastminute** (www.lastminute.com)—also do a brisk business in packages.

Fully escorted tours mean a travel company takes care of absolutely everything, including airfare, hotels, meals, tours, admission costs, and local transportation. Although we hope this book will help you plan your trip independently and safely, many travelers still prefer the convenience and peace of mind that a fully escorted tour offers. They are particularly good for inexperienced travelers or people with limited mobility. They can also be a great way to make new friends. On the downside, you'll have little opportunity for serendipitous interactions with locals. The tours can be jam-packed with activities, leaving little room for individual sightseeing, whim, or adventure. They often focus on heavily trafficked sites, so you may miss out on many lesser-known gems.

Discover Ireland (www.discoverireland.com) can give advice on escorted tours and publishes up-to-the-minute deals on the front page of its website. **C.I.E. Tours** (www.cietours.com; ✆ **01/703-1888**) offers fully escorted tours, self-guided tours, and individual chauffeur-driven tours. **Hidden Ireland Tours** (www.hiddenirelandtours.com; ✆ **087/235-5293** or 125/1478-7519 outside Ireland) specializes in off-the-beaten-path tours of Kerry, Galway, and Donegal. **Authentic Ireland** (www.authentic ireland.com; ✆ **01/293-3088** or 188/8443-5259 outside Ireland) organizes escorted, self-guided, and private tours, as well as themed tours such as castle and golfing vacations. Those wanting to combine their trip with learning opportunities might be interested in the **International Summer School** program at the National University of Ireland, Galway (University Rd., Galway, Co. Galway; www.nuigalway.ie/international-summer-school), which includes courses on Irish language and history. Contact the course administrator at ✆ **091/495-442** for more information.

Special-Interest Tours
CYCLING

All-inclusive bicycle trips in Ireland can be booked from the United States with either **Backroads** (www.backroads.com; ☏ **800/462-2848**) or **VBT** (www.vbt.com; ☏ **800/245-3868**), both well-regarded companies. Tour packages include bikes, gear, luggage transportation via a support van, good food, and rooms in local inns and hotels of character—everything bundled into one price. In Ireland, **Irish Cycling Safaris,** Belfield Bike Shop, Belfield House, University College Dublin (www.cyclingsafaris.com; ☏ **01/260-0749**), offers cycling trips to practically every part of Ireland, including B&B stays and some meals.

GOLF

A host of U.S. companies offer package golf tours. Among them is **Premier Golf** (www.premiergolf.com; ☏ **866/260-4409**).

HIKING

For a full walking holiday package to County Kerry or County Clare and Connemara, the U.S.–based **Backroads** (www.backroads.com; ☏ **800/462-2848**) is one highly recommended operator. For guided walks in the southwest of Ireland, contact **Ireland Walk Hike Bike** (www.irelandwalkhikebike.com; ☏ **087/250-2434**). We've included walking-path suggestions in most chapters.

HORSEBACK RIDING

Hidden Trails (www.hiddentrails.com; ☏ **888/987-2457** from the U.S. or Canada) offers 7-day guided riding tours in several regions in Ireland, including the Wicklow Mountains, West Cork, and Connemara. We've included horseback-riding options in each chapter where we were able to find good providers.

GETTING AROUND

By Car

Although Ireland has a reasonably extensive network of public transportation, it will only be useful if you don't mind being confined to the major towns and cities or depending on organized tours for attractions that are farther afield. Trains tend not to go to charming small towns and villages, and great houses and castles are usually miles from any major town. Bus service to places off the beaten track can be infrequent.

Renting a car is not for everyone—particularly if you're not used to driving on small, winding European country roads (and on the *left* side of the road). But if you're intrepid enough to do it, this is by far the best way to get around. It will give you the most freedom and open up more choices to you than any other way of getting around. Put simply: Rent a car, and you'll see more of Ireland.

Hiking the Slieve League along the beautiful Atlantic coast in Donegal.

In the summer, weekly rental rates on a manual-transmission compact vehicle begin at around €350 and ascend steeply. Rates are much cheaper out of season. (Also bear in mind that in Europe, when a car is described as "compact," they really mean it.)

Unless your stay in Ireland extends beyond 6 months, your own valid driver's license (provided you've had it for at least 6 months) is all you need to drive in Ireland. Rules and restrictions for car rentals correspond roughly to those in other European nations and the U.S., with two important distinctions: Most rental-car agencies in the Republic won't rent to you (1) if you're under 25 or over age 74 (there's no upper age limit in the North) or (2) if your license has been valid for less than a year.

DRIVING LAWS, TIPS & WARNINGS

Highway safety has become a critical issue in Ireland during the past several years. The number of highway fatalities is high for such a small nation—Ireland regularly comes out near the bottom of European league tables for accident rates. In an effort to rein in Irish drivers, the Republic uses a penalty "points" system similar to that in the U.K. and the U.S. Although visitors won't have points added to their licenses, they may still be fined if they speed or commit driving infractions.

road rules **IN A NUTSHELL**

1. Drive on the **left** side of the road.

2. Road signs are in kilometers, except in Northern Ireland, where they are in miles.

3. On motorways, the left lane is the traveling lane. The right lane is for passing.

4. Everyone must wear a seat belt by law. Young children must be in age-appropriate child seats.

5. Children 11 and under are not allowed to sit in the front seat.

6. When entering a roundabout (traffic circle), give way to traffic coming from the right.

7. Another roundabout rule: Always go *left* (clockwise) around the circle.

8. Speed limits are 50 kmph (31 mph) in urban areas; 80 kmph (50 mph) on regional and local roads; 100 kmph (62 mph) on national roads, including divided highways (called dual carriageways); and 120 kmph (75 mph) on freeways (called motorways).

All distances and speed limits on road signs in the Republic of Ireland are in **kilometers,** while in Northern Ireland they are in **miles.** Take care if you're driving around the borderlands—the border is unmarked, so you can cross over from one side to the other without knowing it. It's easy to get confused and speed accidentally.

Getting used to left-side driving, left-handed stick shift, narrow roads, and a new landscape all present a challenge, especially if you're driving solo—it's helpful if you have somebody along to navigate. Some people even use tricks such as sticking a big arrow to the dashboard reminding you that the left is your default lane.

A GPS navigation device or a good mapping app on your phone (if you have service) can be invaluable in finding your way around, especially in the remote countryside. Nearly all rental firms offer them.

Roundabouts (what Americans call traffic circles or rotaries) are found on most major roads and take a little getting used to. Remember always to yield to traffic coming from the right as you approach a roundabout and follow the traffic to the left, signaling before you exit the circle.

One signal that could be misleading to U.S. drivers is a flashing amber light at a pedestrian traffic light. This almost always follows a red light, and it means yield to pedestrians but proceed when the crossing is clear.

The Republic has relatively few types of roads. **Motorways (M)** are major highways, the equivalent of interstates in the U.S. **National (N)** roads, which link major cities, are rarely more than two lanes in each direction (and are sometimes as small as one American-size lane). Most pass directly through towns, making cross-country trips longer than you'd expect. **Regional (R)** roads have one lane of traffic traveling in each direction and generally link smaller cities and towns. Last are the rural or unclassified roads, often the most scenic back roads. These can be poorly signposted, very narrow, and a bit rough, but they usually travel through beautiful countryside.

Both the Republic and Northern Ireland have severe laws against **drunk driving.** The legal limit is 35 micrograms of alcohol per 100 milliliters of breath. What that equates to varies by person, but even one pint of beer can be enough to put you over the limit. The general rule is: Do not drink and drive.

RENTING A CAR

Most rental companies offer their best prices to customers who reserve in advance from their home country. Ireland is a small country, and in high season it can virtually run out of rental cars—but long before it does, it runs out of *affordable* rental cars. Note that weekly rentals are almost always less expensive than day rentals, and keep in mind that the vast majority of available rental cars have **manual transmissions** (stick shifts). Automatics are available, but for a premium.

Prepare for a shock at the pump! Fuel is very expensive in Ireland. At first, those numbers may seem pleasantly small…until you realize that over here, fuel is sold in liters, not gallons. Expect to pay around €1.65 per liter (which works out to around €6 per gallon—roughly $6.80).

By law, you must be between the ages of 25 and 75 to rent a car in Ireland. The only documentation you should need is your driver's license and photo I.D., such as a passport, plus a printout of your reservation if you have one.

When you reserve a car, be sure to ask if the price includes: all taxes including value-added tax (VAT); breakdown assistance; unlimited mileage; personal accident or liability insurance (PAI); collision-damage waiver (CDW); theft waiver; and any other insurance options. If not, ask what these extras cost, because they can make a big dent in your bottom line. The CDW and other insurance might be covered by your credit card if you use the card to pay for the rental; check with your card issuer to be sure that there are no restrictions on that coverage in Ireland. (Not all cards do offer insurance protection for car rentals in Ireland.) Some travelers like to live dangerously and waive optional insurance. But when no CDW is purchased, many rental agencies will make you pay for any damages on the spot when you return the car—making even the smallest dent or scratch a potentially costly experience. To avoid any issues, take cellphone photos of your car with a time stamp, so that you have any dents and dings recorded and won't be charged for it.

If your credit card doesn't cover the CDW, consider buying Car Rental Collision Coverage from a third party. **Travel Guard** (www. travelguard.com; ✆ **1800/826-5248** in the U.S. and Canada) will insure you for around US$15 per day. In the U.K., **Insurance 4 Car Hire** (www. insurance4carhire.com; ✆ **0344/892-1770**) offers similar coverage.

By Train

Train travel is generally the fastest way to get around the country. **Iarnród Éireann** (**Irish Rail;** www.irishrail.ie; ℂ **1850/366222** or 01/836-6222) operates the train services in Ireland. Most lines radiate from Dublin to other principal cities and towns. From Dublin, the journey time to Cork is about 2½ hours; to Belfast, just over 2 hours; to Galway, just under 2½ hours; to Killarney, 3¼ hours; to Sligo, 3 hours; and to Waterford, about 2¼ hours.

In addition to Irish Rail service between Dublin and Belfast, **Translink** (www.translink.co.uk; ℂ **028/9066-6630**) operates routes from Belfast that include Coleraine, Derry, and 21 other localities in Northern Ireland.

One useful piece of lingo: When buying any sort of travel tickets—air, ferry, train, or bus—a "single" means one-way, a "return" is round-trip.

RAIL PASSES

The greatest value in European travel has traditionally been the **rail pass,** a single ticket allowing you unlimited travel (or travel on a certain number of days) within a set time period. The granddaddy of passes, the **Eurail Pass** (www.eurail.com) covers some 28 countries, including Ireland (thanks to recent changes, these passes now apply to both the Republic and Northern Ireland). Prices can be very reasonable for Ireland-only passes. However, if you're a citizen of the European Union (or a long-term resident), you'll need to purchase the equivalent **Interrail Pass** instead. See the box on p. 35 for details.

By Bus

Bus Éireann (www.buseireann.ie; ℂ **01/836-6111**) operates an extensive system of express bus services, as well as local service, to nearly every town in Ireland. The Bus Éireann website provides timetables and fares for bus service throughout the country. Similarly, **Translink** provides details on services within Northern Ireland (www.translink.co.uk; ℂ **028/9066-6630**). Bus travel in both countries is affordable, reliable, and comfortable—but also slow (see map on p. 587).

By Plane

Ireland is such a small country that there is very little point in flying from one end to the other. In any case, the options for internal flights seem to get more limited every year, partly because of improved roads and faster rail journey times. Daily flights on the Dublin–Kerry and Dublin–Donegal routes are operated by **Aer Lingus** (www.aerlingus.com) and **British Airways** (www.britishairways.com).

Irish Rail Routes

ATLANTIC OCEAN

North Channel

Portrush • Ballycastle
Coleraine
Larne Harbour
Derry   Ballymoney
Larne   Whitehead
Carrickfergus
Antrim   Bangor
Belfast York Road
Lurgan   BELFAST CENTRAL
Portadown   Lisburn
Enniskillen
Newry

Ballina   Sligo   Colloney
Foxford   Ballymote   Boyle   Carrick-on-Shannon
Castlebar   MANULLA JUNCTION   Dromod
Westport   Ballyhaunis   Longford
Claremorris   Castlerea
Tuam   Castlerea   Roscommon   Mostrim   Drogheda
Woodlawn   Mullingar   Mosney
Athenry   Athlone   Enfield   Balbriggan
Galway   Clara   Maynooth   Skerries
Ballinasloe   Kildare   Dublin Connolly
Attymon   Tullamore   DUBLIN
PORTARLINGTON   Dublin Heuston   Dublin Pearse
Portlaoise   Newbridge   Dun Laoghaire
Roscrea   Bray   Greystones
Cloughjordan   Athy   Wicklow
Ennistymon   Nenagh   Carlow   Rathdrum
Ennis   Birdhill   Temple-more   BALLYBROPHY   Arklow
Castle-connell   Kilkenny   Muine Bheag   Gorey
Limerick   Thurles   Thomastown   Enniscorthy
LIMERICK JUNCTION   Tipperary   Clonmel   Campile   Wexford
Charleville   Cahir   Rosslare Strand
Tralee   Rathmore   Carrick-on-Suir   WATERFORD   Rosslare Harbour
Farranfore   MALLOW   Ballycullane   Bridgetown
Killarney   Banteer   Fota   Wellington Bridge
Millstreet   Cork
Cobh

ATLANTIC OCEAN   Iris Sea   St. George's Channel   Mouth of the Shannon   ARAN ISLANDS

0   30 mi
0   30 km

By Bike

Cycling is an ideal way to explore the Irish landscape. Distances are quite manageable, and many hostels, B&Bs, and hotels offer bike storage and luggage transfers for touring cyclists. In this guide, we've listed bike-rental agencies in every county where we could find one.

As mentioned earlier, roads in Ireland are categorized as **M** (Motorway), **N** (National), or **R** (Regional). When it comes to bikes, it is illegal to cycle on motorways, but R roads are always suitable for cycling, as are the N roads in outlying areas with little traffic. Be prepared, however, for two inevitable obstacles: wind and hills. Outside the Midlands, hills are just about everywhere, and those on the back roads can have thigh-burning grades. (**Tip:** If you're biking in the west, plan your route from south to north—the same direction as the prevailing winds.) Note that you can bring your bike on all passenger ferries to Ireland's islands, often for no extra charge.

[FastFACTS] IRELAND

Area Codes   Area codes in Ireland range from one number (the Dublin area code is "1") to three. Area codes are included in all listings in this guide. Within Ireland, you dial 0 before the area code. Outside of Ireland, however, you do not dial 0 before the area code.

Business Hours   **Banks** are generally open 10am to 4pm Monday to Friday. **Post offices** (also known as An Post) are generally open from 9am to 5:30pm Monday to Friday and 9am to 1:30pm on Saturday. Some take an hour for lunch from 1 to 2pm, and small or rural branches may close on Saturday. **Museums and sights** are generally open 10am to 5pm Tuesday to Saturday and 2 to 5pm on Sunday. **Shops** generally open 9am to 6pm Monday

to Saturday with late opening on Thursday until 7 or 8pm. Most shops in larger towns and cities will also open on Sundays (typically from late morning to late afternoon). Major shops, such as department stores, often stay open much later than other businesses.

Cellphones   See "Mobile Phones," later in this section.

Disabled Travelers   For disabled travelers, Ireland is a mixed bag. Its modern buildings and cities are generally accessible, but many of its historic buildings often lack wheelchair access. Trains can be accessed by wheelchairs but only with assistance. If you plan to travel by train in Ireland, check out Iarnród Éireann's website (**www.irishrail.ie**), which includes

services for travelers with disabilities.

Finding accessible lodging can be tricky in Ireland. Many buildings here are hundreds of years old, and older hotels, small guesthouses, and landmark buildings still have steps outside and in. The rule of thumb should be: Never assume that a B&B, hotel, or restaurant has accessible facilities—ask about your requirements before booking. To research options prior to your trip, one excellent online resource is **www.accessibleireland. com**. For advice on travel to Northern Ireland, contact **Disability Action** (www. disabilityaction.org; ℂ **028/9029-7880**). The Northern Ireland Tourist Board also publishes a helpful annual "Information Guide to Accessible

Major Irish Bus Routes

ATLANTIC OCEAN

North Channel

ATLANTIC OCEAN

Portrush
Coleraine
Magherafelt
Letterkenny
DERRY
Larne
Ballybofey
Strabane
Donegal
Lough Derg
Omagh
Cookstown
BELFAST
Ballyshannon
Dungannon
Bundoran
Enniskillen
Monaghan
Portadown
Armagh
SLIGO
Ballinamore
Newry
BALLINA
Ballina
Clones
Blayney
Dooagh
Charlestown
Boyle
Carrick-on-Shannon
Cavan
Dundalk
Achill
Knock
Virginia
Carrickmacross
Castlebar
Mohill
Kells
Ardee
Westport
Strokestown
Drogheda
Claremorris
Ballyhaunis
LONGFORD
Navan
Leenane
Roscommon
Slane
Clifden
Tuam
Moylough
Mullingar
Kinnegad
DUBLIN
Roundstone
Oughterard
Ballinasloe
ATHLONE
Rhode
Bray
GALWAY
Loughrea
Moate
Edenderry
Portumna
Dr. Nua
Wicklow
Gort
Birr
Kildare
Naas
Lahinch
Ennis
ROSCREA
Portlaoise
Miltown Malbay
Nenagh
Durrow
Athy
Arklow
Shannon Airport
Thurles
Carlow
Tullow
Gorey
Kilkee
Cashel
Kilkenny
Enniscorthy
Kilrush
LIMERICK
Callan
Ballybunion
Adare
Tipperary
Clonmel
New Ross
WEXFORD
Listowel
Cahir
Callan
Rosslare Harbour
Rathluirc
Carrick-on-Suir
Dingle
Mitchelstown
WATERFORD
Tralee
Mallow
Fermoy
Cappoquin
Killarney
Dungarvan
St. George's Channel
Kenmare
Youghal
Bandon
CORK
Glengarriff
Bantry
Clonakilty
Skibbereen

Irish Sea

Mouth of the Shannon

0   30 mi
0   30 km

Accommodation," available from any of its offices worldwide.

Doctors
Healthcare in Ireland is comparable to that in other European nations. In the Irish system, private doctors and hospitals provide care and patients purchase healthcare insurance. See individual listings under "Fast Facts" in chapters 4 and 14.

Drinking Laws
The minimum legal age to buy alcohol in Ireland is 18. Children under 18 are allowed in pubs until 9pm, or 10pm from May to September, so long as they're with their parents or guardians. (In practice, pubs serving food often have separate dining areas, which can accommodate children later.) Pubs are allowed to stay open until 11:30pm during the week, and around 12:30am on weekends, though some have licenses that allow them to stay open later. Many pubs choose to close earlier on Sundays. These times are roughly comparable in Northern Ireland.

A restaurant can serve alcohol to diners if it has a liquor license (restaurants with no liquor license may allow you to bring your own alcoholic beverages—we state in our restaurant listings if this is the case). Alcohol is for sale at dedicated liquor stores (or "Off Licenses"), in addition to supermarkets and convenience stores. **Important note:** Drunk-driving laws in Ireland are very strict. Even

a single pint of beer could be enough to put you over the limit. If you're arrested for drunk driving, penalties range from a hefty fine to jail time. Rules in Northern Ireland are even more severe. The safest way is simply not to drink and drive.

Electricity
The Irish electric system operates on 220 volts with a large plug bearing three rectangular prongs. The Northern Irish system operates on 250 volts with a similar plug. To use standard American 110-volt appliances, you'll need both a transformer and a plug adapter. Most new laptops have built-in transformers, but some do not, so beware.

Embassies & Consulates
The **American Embassy** is at 42 Elgin Rd., Ballsbridge, Dublin 4 (dublin.usembassy.gov; ℰ **01/668-8777**); the **Canadian Embassy** is at 7–8 Wilton Terrace, 3rd floor, Dublin 2 (www.canada international.gc.ca/ireland-irlande; ℰ **01/234-4000**); the **British Embassy** is at 29 Merrion Rd., Dublin 2 (www.gov.uk/government/world/organisations/british-embassy-dublin; ℰ **01/205-3700**); and the **Australian Embassy** is at Fitzwilton House, 7 floor, Wilton Terrace, Dublin 2 (www.ireland.embassy.gov.au; ℰ **01/664-5300**). In Northern Ireland, there's an **American Consulate** at Danesfort House, 223 Stranmillis Rd., Belfast BT9 5GR (belfast.usconsulate.gov; ℰ **028/9038-6100**).

Emergencies
For the **Garda (police),** fire, ambulance, or other emergencies, dial ℰ **999.**

Family Travel
Recommended family travel websites include **Family Travel Forum** (www.myfamily travels.com), **Family Travel Network** (www.familytravel network.com), and **Family Travel Files** (www.thefamily travelfiles.com).

Internet & Wi-Fi
Wi-Fi is widespread in Irish hotels and B&Bs, even in rural areas. It's not universal, however. Most B&Bs and hotels provide it free.

Language
Ireland has two official languages: English and Irish (which is sometimes called Gaelic outside Ireland). All native Irish people can speak English. There is a strong national movement to preserve and expand the language, and the areas of the country where Irish is protected and promoted are known as **The Gaeltacht.** Irish is a complex and ancient language that you will not be able to figure out on your own; ask for help (in English) if you get lost. Also, everybody in the Gaeltacht regions speaks English.

LGBT Travelers
Homosexuality was legalized in Ireland in 1993 (1982 in the North), and same-sex marriages were ratified in the Republic in 2015. Nevertheless, gay and lesbian visitors should be aware that this is still a conservative country. Cities like Dublin and Galway are far more liberal in its attitudes (particularly

among the younger generation), but it's a good idea to proceed with caution when traveling in rural areas. Recommended websites for gay and lesbian travelers include **Gay Ireland** (www.gay-ireland.com) and **Outhouse** (www.outhouse.ie).

Lost Property   If your passport is lost or stolen, contact your country's embassy immediately. Be sure to tell all of your credit card companies the minute you discover that your wallet is gone and file a report at the nearest police station.

Mobile Phones   Before you leave your home country, check directly with your mobile phone provider to find out about using your phone overseas. You may have to ask for the "international roaming" capability to be switched on **before** you're overseas.

Unfortunately, using your own phone in Ireland can prove very expensive. Most mobile phone companies charge very large premiums on call charges made while abroad, but check before your travel if your provider offers a good roaming package. Be sure to turn off features such as location services and push notifications on your smartphone, or you could face **enormous** data roaming charges. Always use Wi-Fi if you need to download anything.

Some travelers prefer to **buy an Irish pre-paid SIM card** for their phone for their trip to Ireland. You can buy SIM cards in any phone shop, plus some grocery stores and at Dublin Airport and add it to your own phone—make sure your phone is "unlocked" before you travel.

Money   The Republic of Ireland uses the European currency known as the **euro (€).** Euro notes come in denominations of €5, €10, €20, €50, €100, €200, and €500. The euro is divided into 100 cents; coins come in denominations of €2, €1, 50¢, 20¢, 10¢, 5¢, 2¢, and 1¢, although the 1¢ and 2¢ coins are being phased out, so you might find a total is rounded to the nearest 5¢.

As part of the United Kingdom, Northern Ireland uses the **British pound sterling (£).** Notes come in denominations of £5, £10, £20, £50, and £100. Coins are issued in £2, £1, 50p, 20p, 10p, 5p, 2p, and 1p denominations.

The British pound is not accepted in the Republic, and the euro is not accepted in the North—if you're traveling in both parts of Ireland you'll need some of both currencies, although shops on the border tend to accept both. Note that pounds issued in Northern Ireland, while legal tender in Great Britain, actually **look** different. You may find that cabdrivers and small business owners in the North won't accept bills issued in Great Britain, and vice-versa. In that case, you can change the money into locally issued versions at any large central bank, free of charge.

Note for international travelers: Exchange rates can fluctuate wildly in the space of just a few weeks; before departing, consult a currency exchange website such as **www.xe.com** to check up-to-the-minute rates.

When it comes to obtaining foreign currency, please, **skip the currency exchange kiosks** in airports, train stations, and elsewhere. These give the poorest rates and charge exorbitant fees. Instead, order a small amount of foreign currency from your bank before leaving home, and then use your **debit card** for the duration of your trip. ATMs (in Ireland also called "cash machines" or "cash points") will give you a favorable rate, and you can withdraw however much cash you need for a day or so. Before you depart, be sure you know your personal identification number (PIN) and daily withdrawal limit. Confirm with your bank that your PIN will work in Europe and be sure to let them know the dates and destinations to which you're traveling— you don't want to find your card frozen while you're abroad!

Credit cards are accepted just about everywhere, save street markets, small independent retailers, street-food vendors, and occasional small or family-owned businesses. However, North American visitors should note that American Express is accepted far less widely than at home. To be sure of your credit line, bring a Visa or MasterCard as well.

In common with most of Europe, all shops and restaurants now use the "chip-and-pin" system for credit and debit card transactions, instead of having you sign. You just tap in your PIN code exactly like you would at an ATM. However, you will often find that those machines don't like foreign cards—in which case you will be asked to sign the old-fashioned way instead. (Still, carry some cash with you, just in case.)

Many places now allow you to pay for small amounts "contactless" simply by holding your card above the reader. Only certain cards have this capability, which is indicated with a logo similar to the Wi-Fi symbol. Paying this way is never obligatory, although it does make you feel like a magician, which is a bonus.

Pharmacies   Drugstores are called "chemists" and are found in every city, town, and most villages of any size. You'll find individual listings under "Fast Facts" in chapters 4 and 14.

Police   In the Republic of Ireland, a law enforcement officer is called a **Garda,** a member of the **Garda Síochána** ("Guardian of the Peace"); in the plural, it's **Gardaí** (pronounced **Gar-**dee) or simply "the Guards." Dial ℂ **999** to reach the Gardaí in an emergency. Except for special detachments, Irish police are unarmed and

wear dark blue uniforms, often with yellow hi-vis jackets or vests. In Northern Ireland you can also reach the police by dialing ℂ **999.**

Safety   By U.S. standards, Ireland is very safe, but, particularly in the cities, it's not safe enough to warrant carelessness. Be wary of the usual tourists' plagues: pickpockets, purse snatchers, and car thieves. Do not leave cars unlocked or cameras and other expensive equipment unattended, and by all means do not leave valuables visible in a car. Ask at your hotel which areas are safe and which are not. Take a taxi back to your hotel if you're out very late.

Senior Travel   In Ireland, seniors are referred to as "O.A.P.'s" (short for "Old Age Pensioners"). People over age 60 often qualify for reduced admission to museums and other attractions. Always ask about an O.A.P. discount if special rates aren't posted. **Discover Ireland** (p. 579) can offer advice on how to find the best discounts.

Smoking   Ireland and Northern Ireland both have broad antismoking laws that ban smoking in all public places, including bars, restaurants, and hotel lobbies. However, most restaurants and pubs have covered outdoor smoking areas.

Taxes   Sales tax (VAT, or value-added tax) is always included in the price shown on price tags. In the Republic, VAT rates vary—for

hotels, restaurants, and car rentals, it is 13.5%; for souvenirs and gifts, it is 23%. In Northern Ireland, the VAT is 20% across the board. VAT charged on services such as hotel stays, meals, car rentals, and entertainment cannot be refunded to visitors, but the VAT on products such as souvenirs is refundable. Save your receipts and present them at the Global Refund Desk when you get to the airport (they're located airside in the main terminals at Dublin and Shannon; in Dublin the desk is now an automated kiosk, located on the left just after you pass the Starbucks on the way to the departure gates). They can usually issue you a refund there and then. Some larger stores can issue you a Global Refund form and refund your VAT themselves, although you'll need to know your passport number, flight number, and departure time. In practice, this is usually much more fuss than it's worth.

Telephones   In the Republic, the telephone system is known as Eir; in Northern Ireland, it's BT (British Telecom). Every effort has been made to ensure that the numbers and information in this guide were accurate at the time of writing.

To call Ireland from home:
1. **Dial the international access code:** 011 from the U.S., 00 from the U.K., 0011 from Australia, or 0170 from New Zealand.

2. Dial the country code: 353 for the Republic, 44 for the North.

3. Dial the local number, remembering to omit the initial 0, which is for use only within Ireland (for example, to call the County Kerry number 066/12345 from the United States, you'd dial 011-353-66/12345).

To make international calls from Ireland: First dial 00, then the country code (U.S. or Canada 1, U.K. 44, Australia 61, New Zealand 64). Next you dial the area code and local number. For example, to call the U.S. number ✆ 212/000-0000 you'd dial ✆ 00-1-212/000-0000. The toll-free international access code for **AT&T** is ✆ **1-800-550-000;** for **Sprint** it's ✆ **1-800-552001;** and for **MCI** it's ✆ **1-800-551-001.**

To make local calls: To dial a local number within the same area code, drop the initial 0. To dial a number within Ireland but in a different area code, use the initial 0.

Time   Ireland follows Greenwich Mean Time from November to March, and British Summer Time from April to October. Ireland is 5 hours ahead of the eastern United States. Ireland's latitude makes for longer days and shorter nights in the summer and the reverse in the winter. In June, the sun doesn't fully set until around 11pm, but in December, it is dark by 4pm.

Tipping   For taxi drivers, hairdressers, and other providers of service, tip an average of 10 to 15%. For restaurants, a gratuity of 10 to 15% is usually customary; if a restaurant has an automatic service charge (for a group, for example), it will be specified on the menu. As a rule, bartenders do not expect a tip, except when table service is provided.

Toilets   Public toilets are usually simply called "toilets" or are marked with international symbols. In the Republic of Ireland, some of the older ones carry the Irish words FIR (men) and MNA (women). Free restrooms are usually available to customers at sightseeing attractions, museums, hotels, restaurants, pubs, shops, and theaters. Many gas stations (called "petrol stations" in Ireland) have public toilets, and a few even have baby-changing facilities.

Visas   Citizens of the United States, Canada, Australia, and New Zealand entering the Republic of Ireland or Northern Ireland for a stay of up to 3 months do not need a visa, but a valid **passport** is required.

Water   Tap water throughout the island of Ireland is safe to drink. However, the water treatment procedures may be different from those you're used to, and as such we recommend sticking to bottled drinking water where possible.

Wi-Fi   See "Internet & Wi-Fi," earlier in this section.

Women Travelers
Women should expect few problems traveling in Ireland. In small towns, you may attract a little attention if you eat alone in a restaurant at night, but you won't be hassled. If you drink in a pub on your own, though, expect all kinds of attention—even if you're reading a book, talking on your cellphone, or doing a crossword puzzle. (Irish men almost always respond well to polite rejection, though.) Take a cab home at night and follow all the usual caution you use when you travel anywhere. Essentially, don't do anything in Ireland that you wouldn't do at home.

PLANNING YOUR TRIP TO IRELAND

Women Travelers

Index

INDEX

Restaurants

PHOTO CREDITS

p. i: © Patryk Kosmider; p. iii: © Madrugada Verde; p. 1: © Steve Allen/Shutterstock.com; p. 3: Courtesy of Tourism Ireland/Bren Whelan; p. 4: Courtesy of Tourism Ireland/Chris Hill; p. 5: Courtesy of Fáilte Ireland; p. 6: © Owen J Fitzpatrick/Shutterstock.com; p. 8: Courtesy of Fáilte Ireland; p. 10: Courtesy of Galway Atlantaquaria; p. 13: Courtesy of The Europe; p. 14: Courtesy of Park Hotel Kenmare; p. 15: Courtesy of Aniar/Anita Murphy; p. 16: Courtesy of Inis Meain; p. 20: Courtesy of Tourism Ireland; p. 22: © Sonia Ricco/Shutterstock.com; p. 24: Courtesy of Tourism Ireland/Brian Morrison; p. 28: Courtesy of Fáilte Ireland/Rob Durston; p. 31: Courtesy of Fáilte Ireland/Martin Fleming; p. 36: © Stefano_Valeri; p. 38: © Sergio; p. 40: © gvictoria/Shutterstock.com; p. 44: © PJ photography; p. 46: © 4H4 Photography/Shutterstock.com; p. 48: © Maciek A; p. 50: Courtesy of Tourism Ireland/Caspar Diederik/@storytravelers; p. 51: © heikoneumannphotography; p. 55: Courtesy of Tourism Ireland/Tony Pleavin; p. 56: © John Farrell - sofarjohn/Shutterstock.com; p. 61: Courtesy of Fáilte Ireland/Ruth Medjber; p. 63: © glynnis2009; p. 65: Courtesy of Tourism Ireland/Brian Morrison; p. 69: Courtesy of Fáilte Ireland; p. 72: Courtesy of Fáilte Ireland/Rob Durston; p. 79: © Arcady/Shutterstock.com; p. 85: © Benoit Daoust/Shutterstock.com; p. 86: © Roy Harris/Shutterstock.com; p. 88: © James Horan; p. 96: Courtesy of Fáilte Ireland/Rob Durston; p. 97: © Sandra Mori/Shutterstock.com; p. 98: © James Horan; p. 103: © JordiCarrio/Shutterstock.com; p. 106: Courtesy of The Dub Web Fest Team; p. 109: © Anton_Ivanov/Shutterstock.com; p. 115: © William Murphy; p. 118: Courtesy of Tourism Ireland/James Fennell; p. 121: © travelevents/Shutterstock.com; p. 123: Courtesy of Butlers Chocolate; p. 128: Courtesy of The Radisson Blu; p. 145: Courtesy of San Lorenzo; p. 146: Courtesy of Chapter One; p. 147: Courtesy of Tourism Ireland; p. 149: Courtesy of The Greenhouse; p. 150: Courtesy of Lemon Crepe; p. 152: Courtesy of Aqua/Paul Sherwood; p. 153: Courtesy of Fáilte Ireland/Andrew Bradley; p. 156: Courtesy of Tourism Ireland; p. 161: Courtesy of Tourism Ireland/Jason Baxter; p. 166: Courtesy of Tourism Ireland; p. 169: © Chad and Steph; p. 173: Courtesy of Fáilte Ireland/Neal Houghton; p. 180: Courtesy of Tourism Ireland/Tony Pleavin; p. 181: © Bjoern Alberts; p. 189: © Irish National Stud/Fáilte Ireland;

PHOTO CREDITS

p. 191: Courtesy of Barberstown Castle; p. 196: Courtesy of Fáilte Ireland/Neal Houghton; p. 198: Courtesy of Tourism Ireland; p. 200: Courtesy of Tourism Ireland; p. 202: Courtesy of Tourism Ireland/ Chris Hill; p. 206: Courtesy of Tourism Ireland/James Fennell; p. 207: © Bob Grim/Shutterstock.com; p. 212: Courtesy of Fáilte Ireland/Leo Byrne; p. 215: Courtesy of Fáilte Ireland/Andrew Bradley; p. 217, left: Courtesy of Fáilte Ireland/Luke Myers; p. 217, right: Courtesy of Tourism Ireland/George Munday; p. 218: © Cait Eire; p. 220: © Osadchaya Olga; p. 228, top: Courtesy of Fáilte Ireland; p. 228, bottom: Courtesy of Fáilte Ireland; p. 230: Courtesy of Tourism Ireland/Brian Morrison; p. 232: Courtesy of Aldride Lodge; p. 236: © BOULENGER Xavier/Shutterstock.com; p. 238: Courtesy of Fáilte Ireland/Finn Richards; p. 239: © MNStudio; p. 241: © Ocskay Bence; p. 244: Courtesy of Tourism Ireland/Joshua McMichael; p. 248: Courtesy of Tourism Ireland/Brian Morrison; p. 249: Courtesy of Tourism Ireland/ Brian Morrison; p. 252: Courtesy of Tourism Ireland/Jed Niezgoda www.venividiphoto.net; p. 254: Courtesy of Tourism Ireland/Chris Hill; p. 259: Courtesy of Ichigo Ichie/Clare Keogh; p. 267: Courtesy of Fáilte Ireland/Liam Murphy; p. 268: Courtesy Ballyaloe Cookery School; p. 269: Courtesy of Tourism Ireland/Chris Hill; p. 270: Courtesy of Tourism Ireland/Tony Pleavin; p. 273: © Vaniljefeldt/Shutterstock. com; p. 276: Courtesy of The Spaniard; p. 281: © Lukasz Pajor; p. 289: Courtesy of Fáilte Ireland/Fennell Photography; p. 295: Courtesy of Tourism Ireland/Stephen Power; p. 296: © Reeks District; p. 301: Courtesy of Aghadoe Heights Hotel & Spa/Barry Murphy; p. 309: © mozzercork; p. 313: Courtesy of The Boathouse; p. 314: Courtesy of Maison Gourmet; p. 322: Courtesy of Ard na Sidhe Country House; p. 333: Courtesy of Greenmont House/Brid Ni Luasaigh; p. 336: © EyesTravelling; p. 337: Courtesy of Tourism Ireland/Chris Hill; p. 342: Courtesy of Tourism Ireland/Brian Morrison; p. 346: © Michael McLughlin; p. 350: Courtesy of Tourism Ireland/Stephen Power; p. 352: © Meghan Lamb; p. 358: Courtesy of Wild Honey; p. 360: Courtesy Lahinch Surf School; p. 361: © Photo Derek Cullen Fáilte Ireland; p. 364: Courtesy of Adare Manor/JACK HARDY; p. 370: Courtesy of Fáilte Ireland/Liam Murphy; p. 372: © Richard Melichar; p. 377: Courtesy of Tourism Ireland/Gareth McCormack; p. 387: Courtesy of Inis Meian; p. 388: Courtesy of Tourism Ireland/Chris Hill; p. 391: Courtesy of Tourism Ireland; p. 394: © Rihardzz; p. 395: Courtesy of Tourism Ireland; p. 396: Courtesy of Tourism Ireland; p. 403: Courtesy of Killary Fjord Boat Tours; p. 404: © Noradoa; p. 405: Courtesy of Tourism Ireland; p. 406: Courtesy of Ballynahinch Castle/Barry Murphy Photography; p. 407: Courtesy of Currarevagh House; p. 411: Courtesy of Delphi Adventure Resort/Elizabeth Toher Photography; p. 413: Courtesy of Failte Ireland/ Liam Murphy; p. 416: Courtesy of Tourism Ireland/Chris Hill; p. 418: Courtesy of Failte Ireland/Fennell Photography; p. 419: © Ian Murphy; p. 422: Courtesy of Failte Ireland/Simon Crowe; p. 425: Courtesy of Tourism Ireland/Gareth McCormack; p. 431: Courtesy of Tourism Ireland/Gardiner Mitchell; p. 436: © LunaseeStudios/Shutterstock.com; p. 437: © Paul Keeling/Shutterstock.com; p. 439: © Maria_Janus/ Shutterstock.com; p. 443: Courtesy of Ashford Castle/Kelvin Gillmor; p. 455: © Brendan Howard/ Shutterstock.com; p. 456: Courtesy of Tourism Ireland/Alison Crummy; p. 458: Courtesy of Temple House/STEVE ROGERS; p. 461: Courtesy of Eala Bhan; p. 464: © RonanmcLaughlin; p. 468: © Madrugada Verde; p. 472: © SannePhoto; p. 475: Courtesy of Harvey's Point Hotel/JULIA DUNIN; p. 478: Courtesy of Tourism Ireland/Gardiner Mitchell; p. 483: © Craig James Smith; p. 486: Courtesy of Fáilte Ireland/Adam Rory Porter; p. 487: Courtesy of Inishowen Gateway Hotel; p. 488: Courtesy of Fáilte Ireland; p. 490: Courtesy of Titanic Hotel Belfast; p. 496: © dvlcom/Shutterstock.com; p. 498: Courtesy of Tourism Ireland/Paul Lindsay; p. 499: Courtesy of Tourism Ireland/Paul Lindsay; p. 501: Courtesy of Tourism Ireland/Chris Hill; p. 505: Courtesy of Tourism Ireland/Tony Pleavin; p. 507, left: © SurangaSL; p. 507, right: Courtesy of Tourism Ireland; p. 510: Courtesy of Grand Central/JACK HARDY; p. 514: Courtesy of The OX/Elaine Hill Photography; p. 521: © S-F/Shutterstock.com; p. 526: Courtesy of Tourism Ireland; p. 527: Courtesy of Tourism Ireland/Brian Morrison; p. 529: Courtesy of Tourism Ireland/Bernie Brown; p. 530: Courtesy of Galgorm Spa & Golf Resort; p. 533: © Ballygally View Images; p. 536: © 4kclips; p. 538: © navorolphotography/Shutterstock.com; p. 542: © Paul Vance/ Shutterstock.com; p. 547: © Yossa Song/Shutterstock.com; p. 549: Courtesy of Newforge House/Geoff Telford Photography; p. 551: © silvester kalcik; p. 553: Courtesy of Tourism Ireland/Chris Hill; p. 557: © Susanne Pommer; p. 559: Courtesy of Tourism Ireland/Chris Hill; p. 566: Courtesy of Tourism Ireland/ Brian Morrison; p. 572: Courtesy of Castle Leslie; p. 573: Courtesy of Finn Lough; p. 576: © Sandra Mori/Shutterstock.com; p. 581: © Sander van der Werf